FIFTH CANADIAN EDITION

PASSPORT

An Introduction to the Tourism Industry

FIFTH CANADIAN EDITION

PASSPORT

An Introduction to the Tourism Industry

DAVID W. HOWELL

DAVID WRIGHT
Seneca College School of Tourism

NELSON REYNOLDS
*George Brown School of Hotel
and Tourism Management*

NELSON / EDUCATION

NELSON / EDUCATION

Passport: An Introduction to the Tourism Industry, Fifth Canadian Edition
by David W. Howell, David Wright, and Nelson Reynolds

Associate Vice President, Editorial Director:
Evelyn Veitch

Editor-in-Chief, Higher Education:
Anne Williams

Marketing Manager:
Kathaleen McCormick

Developmental Editor:
Theresa Fitzgerald

Photo Researcher:
Sheila Hall

Permissions Coordinator:
Sheila Hall

Production Service:
Macmillan Publishing Solutions

Copy Editor:
Wendy Yano

Proofreader:
Dianne Fowlie

Indexer:
Maura Brown

Senior Production Coordinator:
Ferial Suleman

Design Director:
Ken Phipps

Managing Designer:
Franca Amore

Interior Design:
ArtPlus Ltd.

Cover Design:
Jennifer Leung

Cover and Part Opener Image:
Andrew Penner/iStockphoto

Compositor:
Macmillan Publishing Solutions

Printer:
Webcom

Library and Archives Canada Cataloguing in Publication Data

Passport : an introduction to the tourism industry / [David W.] Howell ... [et al.].–5th ed.

Includes index.
First Canadian ed., 1995, written by David W. Howell and Robert A. Ellison.
ISBN: 978-0-17-610488-7

1. Travel agents–Vocational guidance–Canada–Textbooks.
2. Tourism–Vocational guidance–Canada–Textbooks.
I. Howell, David W., CTC
II. Wright, David, 1946-
III. Reynolds, Nelson

G155.5.P38 2009   338.4'79102371
C2009-900079-2

ISBN-13: 978-0-17-610488-7
ISBN-10: 0-17-610488-7

CONTENTS

PART 1   Welcome Aboard   1

Chapter 1   The Tourism Industry   2

Chapter 2   The Travellers   29

Chapter 3   The Business of Business Travel   53

Chapter 16   The Travel Agency   363

PART 7   Research, Training, and the Future   389

Chapter 17   Research, Training, and Future Ports of Call   390

PREFACE

Tourism is a dynamic and expanding industry that fosters economic and social development in Canada and other nations. It takes a combination of science, art, and good business practices to realize the economic and social benefits that tourism has the potential to produce. Nations need to pay attention to the major components of tourism, both as a product and as a process, and especially to human resource development through supporting the education and training of tourism professionals. As a contribution to that end and as an excellent way to foster a better understanding of the potential of tourism, the ever-changing nature of the tourism industry, and career opportunities in tourism, the fifth Canadian edition of *Passport: An Introduction to the Tourism Industry* has been revised and updated. As in the previous Canadian editions, *Passport* provides a comprehensive overview of the tourism industry: transportation; accommodation; food and beverage; events, meetings, and conferences; attractions; adventure tourism and recreation; travel trade; and tourism services. This overview clearly demonstrates how the industry is greater than the sum of its parts and, hopefully, will provide a solid introduction for anyone starting tourism studies.

Passport is the result of our commitment to advancing a conceptual framework as a foundation for tourism studies, while providing a Canadian perspective in a global context. The text moves from a general introduction of topics that are relevant across the tourism industry to topics that are specific to identifiable sectors of the industry. This fifth Canadian edition moves beyond preceding editions, but it still reflects the groundwork provided by David Howell before the book was Canadianized. It will probably continue to be known as "The Howell Book." We, the Canadian authors, are honoured to be associated with him and to have had the opportunity to build on his work.

Passport is a text designed to launch tomorrow's tourism professionals, no matter in which sectors they plan to work, specializations they pursue, or career paths they follow. It is an introduction to the industry and should serve both as a "passport" to understanding the supply and demand side of tourism as well as a source of information that will help them make better career decisions. Many topics are merely introduced because they will, most likely, be covered more fully in other courses. They are included in this text, however, so that students have a comprehensive overview of tourism on which to build. In addition to the topics that are presented, each chapter in *Passport* includes features on personalities and companies in the tourism industry and identifies career opportunities students may want to explore further.

Other unique characteristics of *Passport* include:

- Definitions related to tourism as a multisector, mixed enterprise system.

- A discussion of categories of travellers—why they travel and where they go.
- Examples of trends, issues, and challenges faced by the industry today.
- An overview of the structure of the channels of distribution in the tourism industry.
- Coverage of the impact of the Internet and e-commerce on suppliers, consumers, and travel trade intermediaries.
- An explanation of destination planning, development, and control in relation to communities, in addition to the tourism industry.
- Learning tools in each chapter that provide a real-world dimension to many of the topics presented.
- Concepts for the future; a call to consider the future from a multisector, global perspective, in addition to regional and Canadian ones.

ORGANIZATION OF THE BOOK

Passport is divided into seven parts and 17 chapters. Part 1 and Part 7 serve as bookends for the other five parts. They, however, do not need to be read in the order in which they have been presented. The rearrangement of material in this edition should make, we believe, additional logical modules, whatever sequence is followed.

Part 1: Welcome Aboard is an introduction to the whole tourism industry. Its four chapters cover the tourism industry, leisure travellers, business travellers, and destination development.

Part 2: Tourism Services Sector provides more information about the private and public supporters and promoters of tourism. Many of these are discussed in the examples presented throughout *Passport*, but in this part they are examined as part of the tourism services sector. They include retail enterprises, local industry associations, and organizations such as the United Nations World Tourism Organization.

Part 3: The Transportation Sector focuses on all modes of transportation—air, ground, and marine. The emphasis is on the role and significance of each mode in the current tourism industry, in addition to how they have evolved over time. The section on airline deregulation, and references to the U.S. air industry, has been reduced to make the material more relevant to Canadian students. Specific topics include conceptual framework for regulation, environmental considerations, security, development of motorcoach charters and tours, VIA Rail–Amtrak connections, and the growth of the cruise ship industry. Career opportunities that require various levels of education are identified.

Part 4: Hospitality Services yields insights on the hospitality services provided by the accommodation and food and beverage sectors of the tourism industry. Current venues and management systems are presented. Topics such as green management, accessibility, diversity, ethics, quality management, and information technology are addressed. Employment potential in each sector and an overview of employment options are presented in the sections on career opportunities.

Part 5: Tourism Generators introduces sectors of the tourism industry that make the tourism industry grow. Events, conferences, and even smaller meetings provide reasons for people to travel away from their home base. Attractions, festivals, and special events draw both leisure and business travellers to destinations. How these activities, as well as opportunities for adventure tourism and recreation, are catalysts in generating tourism business is considered. Products and services that are being developed to advance Canada as a premier four-season destination are presented in the three chapters in this section. Opportunities related to careers involved with generating tourism and providing tourism services are described.

Part 6: Travel Trade Sector features the sector of the tourism industry that links consumers with service providers. This part begins with an overview of channels of distribution, which involve tourism professionals who co-ordinate transportation, accommodations, food and beverage services, and attractions that are for sale to both individual leisure and business travellers directly, or through tour and charter packages. Trends and issues around the utilization of information technology, e-commerce, and business travel policies, in particular, are considered. Career opportunities in the tour industry are described, including opportunities in corporate travel management, commercial travel counselling, and travel agencies.

Part 7: Research, Training, and the Future is the last part of the book. It presents some concepts for the future and is a call to tourism professionals to consider challenges and opportunities that may appear in the future across the industry in Canada and globally. Hopefully, what is included will help people prepare for the future; develop sustainable destinations, products, and services that meet consumer expectations; and make positive social and economic contributions to society. An overview of the role played in the industry by research, education, and training is also provided. The benefits of research, occupational standards and certification, tourism as an academic discipline, and associations and councils that foster professional development in the tourism industry are some of the topics presented. Possible career opportunities across the tourism services sector are identified.

LEARNING TOOLS

Several tools are provided to help you better understand the scope of tourism and the content of this text.

Objectives Each chapter begins with a list of objectives. These highlight the main points in the chapter and the order in which they will be covered.

Glossary of Terms The tourism industry, like many others, has its own language, abbreviations, and acronyms. Words that may be unfamiliar to you are highlighted in bold type. They are listed under the Key Terms heading at the end of each chapter and are defined in the Glossary at the back of the book. Abbreviations and acronyms are spelled out the first time they appear in any chapter; thereafter, the abbreviated forms are used.

Check Your Product Knowledge Review questions are included throughout each chapter to help you check whether you understand what you have read. Or you may want to consider the questions before you begin to read the chapter as a way to help focus on what is presented.

Summary A summary in list format is provided at the end of each chapter. It will help you review content and identify the main ideas that were presented.

Key Terms A list of key terms, words that appear in bold type in the chapter, is found at the end of each chapter. Use it to check your knowledge of these terms. You will find any terms you can't define both in the chapter itself and listed alphabetically at the end of the book in the Glossary.

Websites A list of relevant websites is provided at the end of each chapter.

Special Features Each chapter includes two features designed to illustrate the scope and diversity of tourism enterprises and many aspects of people involved in the industry. A Profile feature is presented at the beginning of each chapter that you should find entertaining as well as informative. You will learn about the man behind the "Cook's tour," the Canadian hotel company that has been recognized as the leader in environmentally responsible hotel practices, the Canadian resort operator that has been successful in creating numerous four-season destination resorts and in diversifying into real estate operations, Canada's largest integrated food service operator, and other examples ranging from British Columbia to Newfoundland. The second feature, A Day in the Life of . . ., is presented at the end of each chapter; descriptions of events in the lives of service providers and tourists are given to help you understand what is involved in various activities. You will find examples that highlight many aspects of the industry, usually presented through the eyes of the individual involved. You will meet, for example, a family hotel operator, a woman traveller, a Canadian foreign sales representative, a food and beverage manager, a meeting planner, and a national park interpreter.

Worksheets Two worksheets are included at the end of each chapter. They are designed to reinforce what you have learned and to provide an opportunity for you to apply your knowledge to the tourism industry. Hopefully, the worksheets will encourage you to use the Internet to learn more about the industry and to solve hypothetical problems. Even if your instructor doesn't assign the worksheets, you can consider them independently and develop your ability to conduct research and solve problems. Some of the worksheets may be used for class discussion or your instructor may use others as tests to be graded.

Supplemental Resources A package of teaching and learning support materials accompanies this text:

- Instructor's Manual, including What Do You Think and Service Scenarios (which have been removed from the previous text and placed here).
- Test Bank/Computerized Test Bank
- PowerPoint Slides
- Website: www.passport5e.nelson.com

ACKNOWLEDGMENTS

Passport has evolved from the first Canadian edition as a result of the efforts of many individuals who have served as reviewers and authors of the Profile and A Day in the Life of . . . features. Feedback from educators across the country who have used it as a text in their programs has contributed greatly. The Canadian editions have built on author David Howell's earlier U.S. editions and we acknowledge the stage he set for the script we have been able to develop over five editions. We especially acknowledge the early developmental and organizational work undertaken by Dr. Margaret Bateman Ellison and Dr. Robert A. Ellison. We sincerely thank those who reviewed the earlier editions for their constructive comments: Julie Aumais, Mohawk College; Candace Blayney, Mount Saint Vincent University; Deborah Brannan, Seneca College; Janice Corkum, Nova Scotia Community College—Lunenberg; Patricia Cox, Saskatchewan Institute of Applied Science and Technology; Tom Delamere, Malaspina University-College; Allan Gray, New Brunswick Community College St. Andrews; Gary Hallam, George Brown College; Paul E. Hanna, University College of Cape Breton; Penelope Hull, Seneca College; Paula Laviolette, Mohawk College; Bob Lipsett, Northwest Community College; Nuala Mattson, Atlantic Business College; Cyndy Parker, New Brunswick Community College St. Andrews; Donna Pippy, College of the North Atlantic; Marie-Marthe Rennie, Niagara College; and Ron Spence, Okanagan University College. Special thanks go to the instructors who provided reviews for this fifth edition of the text: Dawn Aitken, Humber College; Edward Brooker, Niagara College; J. Michael Campbell, University of Manitoba; Debbie Cooper, Seneca College; Ruthanne Geddes, Cape Breton University; Annisa Mohammed, Centennial College; Bob Lipsett, Northwest Community College; Nuala Mattson, Atlantic Business College; Karyn Moore, Centennial College. Even if we did not respond to your suggestions, we assure you they were considered seriously.

Numerous individuals and organizations, cited throughout the book, provided background, data, and exhibits for this edition. Publications and website information from the Canadian Tourism Human Resource Council, the Canadian Tourism Commission, the Conference Board of Canada, Statistics Canada, and the United Nations World Tourism Organization, in particular, made it possible to reflect current issues and developments in Canada and globally. We thank them for being there and making information readily accessible.

Finally, we acknowledge the professional efforts of our Nelson Education staff. Completion of *Passport* required the attention, expertise, and patience of editorial, production, support, and marketing personnel. We thank each of them for their contribution to the making of a Canadian tourism textbook available for educators and students across Canada. Our sincere thanks go especially to Theresa Fitzgerald, Developmental Editor, and Anne Williams, Editor-in-Chief, for their encouragement and direction.

David Wright teaches in Markham, Ontario, at the Seneca College School of Tourism. He is currently curriculum coordinator and is working on developing partnerships with colleges and universities in India, Sri Lanka, and South Korea.

After university in Scotland and Canada, he began working in the travel industry in Europe, where he gained experience in both retail travel agency and tour operations. In the 35 years since, David has worked and travelled throughout Europe, Asia, Australia, New Zealand, and the Caribbean. He has developed curricula in Australia, Belize, El Salvador, Indonesia, Jamaica, and Malaysia, and has participated in tourism projects in Costa Rica, Cuba, Estonia, Latvia, Lithuania, St. Lucia, India, South Africa, South Korea, Sri Lanka, and Russia.

Prior to joining Seneca College in 1985, David was education coordinator and then executive director of the Canadian Institute of Travel Counsellors (CITC). He has developed several study guides and training videos, and is the author of CITC's text *Professional Travel Counselling*. David is a member of CITC, the International Society of Travel and Tourism Educators, and the Pacific Asia Travel Association Eastern Canada Chapter, of which he is a past chairman.

Nelson Reynolds has been a full-time faculty member at the George Brown School of Hotel and Tourism Management in Toronto since 1990. In 2004, Nelson also began teaching a variety of hospitality subjects, including Tourism, as a sessional faculty member for the School of Hospitality & Tourism Management at the University of Guelph.

On graduation from university, Nelson joined Deloitte Touche, Chartered Accountants, where his favourite audit client was Hilton Hotels. After training at the Geneva Intercontinental Hotel in Switzerland, Nelson joined the international travelling staff, where he performed accounting services or auditing inspections for Intercontinental Hotels in Jamaica, Iran, Afghanistan, Pakistan, Singapore, Thailand, Australia, New Zealand, Saipan, and the United States.

Next, Nelson served as financial controller at the Chateau Laurier in Ottawa; Loews Paradise Island Hotel, Nassau, Bahamas; and the Holiday Inn in Freeport, Bahamas. Desiring entrepreneurial experience, Nelson became a hospitality consultant; his clients included Princess Hotels and the Tides Inn. His most recent hotel positions were as financial and administrative director for the Treasure Cay Group of companies in Abaco, Bahamas, and general manager of the Peace & Plenty Club in Georgetown, Exuma.

When living in the Bahamas, Nelson taught for the College of the Bahamas School of Business in Freeport and for the University of West Indies Hotel Management degree program in Nassau. Accepting the position of chief training officer at the Bahamas Hotel Training College, Nelson initiated an extensive on-the-job training program for hotels located in the Family Islands of the Bahamas, bringing much needed training to numerous small resorts and tourism operators.

Nelson has conducted hospitality workshops in Estonia, Antigua, Trinidad, and the Bahamas. Passionate about travelling, Nelson has been privileged to work in 12 countries and has visited 56 additional countries, 45 U.S. states, and all 10 provinces. Presently, Nelson is working on two new textbooks: *Tourism: Introduction, Issues and Impacts* and *Accounting for the Hospitality and Tourism Industries*.

PART 1

Welcome Aboard

Objectives

When you have completed this chapter, you should be able to:

- Discuss the importance of the tourism industry to Canada and globally.
- Identify factors that influence the growth of the tourism industry.
- Explain the tourism industry's impact on economics and culture.
- Describe the building blocks of services.

- Discuss leisure as a concept that affects the tourism industry.
- Discuss how geography influences the tourism industry.
- Name areas of knowledge that are important to the tourism professional.

Welcome aboard! Bon voyage! With these traditional greetings, passengers on airplanes and cruise ships begin journeys to new destinations. This phrase also welcomes you—a future tourism professional—to the tourism industry.

You have chosen an exciting career. The tourism sector can be divided into eight areas: transportation; accommodation; food and beverage; attractions; meetings, events, and conferences; adventure tourism and recreation; travel trade; and tourism services. Any of these areas may provide career opportunities for you. A career in tourism could be your passport to the future.

Tourism spans the globe and provides employment and revenue in almost every nation. Furthermore, the tourism industry is a dynamic business and has become an important social and economic force in the world. According to the World Tourism Organization (UNWTO), world tourism has grown in the past 50 plus years and receipts from international tourism grew to US$733 billion in 2006—about $2 billion per day; international tourism arrivals expanded to 898 million international tourist arrivals; and tourism arrivals have increased 6.5 percent for the period 1950 to 2007 (see Table 1–1).

TABLE 1–1 International Tourism Arrivals*

	Arrivals (millions)		Growth Rate (%)	Market share (%)	
	2006	2007	2006/2007	2006/2007	2007
World	846.0	898.0	52.0	6.0	100
Africa	41.0	44.0	3.0	7.3	4.9
Americas	137.0	143.0	6.0	4.3	15.9
East Asia/Pacific	168.0	185.0	17.0	10.8	20.6
Europe	461.0	480.0	19.0	4.1	53.5
Middle East	41.0	46.0	5.0	12.2	5.1

*Data collected from tourism industry sources.
(Growth rate numbers have been rounded to the nearest million.)

SOURCE: Courtesy of the World Tourism Organization.

PROFILE

Pioneering the Age of Tourism

Thomas Cook, Founder of the World's First Travel Agency

Thanks to Thomas Cook, the age of the grand tour gave way to the age of tourism.

Thomas Cook, founder of the world's first travel agency (Thomas Cook) and entrepreneur extraordinaire, was born in England in 1808. In 1828, when he was 20, he became a Baptist missionary and an ardent supporter of the temperance movement.

One day in 1841, an idea occurred to Cook: Why not arrange for a special train between Loughborough and Leicester for those who planned to attend the upcoming quarterly temperance meeting in Leicester? Cook approached the Midland Counties Railway company, the company agreed to his proposal, and Cook advertised the arrangement. On July 5, the historic excursion took place—historic because it was the first publicly advertised excursion train to run in England.

Conditions were a bit rough. The 570 travellers were crammed into nine "tubs"—seatless third class carriages open to the elements. Already, however, Cook's planning skills were evident. He had negotiated a specially reduced fare of one shilling per person for the trip. He had also arranged for a picnic lunch to be served before the afternoon procession, and at the end of the line he set out tea for 1000 people. Despite the primitive conditions of the ride, the trip was a reasonable success. By 1844, the railway had agreed to run the excursion regularly if Cook would guarantee

the passengers. And he did, having by now left the ministry to start a travel agency.

In the next several years, Cook organized other temperance-related tours. These were especially popular with people of limited income who had never before had the opportunity to travel. As his agency grew, it began to serve all kinds of travellers, no longer limiting itself to the cause of temperance.

Cook's excursions did not venture outside the British Isles until he conducted excursions from Leicester to the French port of Calais for the 1855 Paris Exposition (a kind of world's fair). Foreseeing the business possibilities in European travel, the following year he organized "A Great Circular Tour of the Continent." Cook led the tour himself, but because he knew no foreign languages, also employed an interpreter. The tour left Harwich, England, and moved through Belgium, Germany, and France, finally ending back at the English port of Southampton. So many travellers had signed up for the tour that a repeat tour had to be scheduled six weeks later to take care of the overflow.

It took a few years for Cook's agency to institute regular service to Europe. Cook personally conducted another tour to Switzerland in July 1864, the same year his son, John Mason Cook, joined him in his firm (which became Thomas Cook & Son). John Mason Cook specialized in promoting the company's American tours. He did much to

make Thomas Cook & Son a worldwide travel agency.

Extremely energetic and a top organizer, Thomas Cook used his group purchasing power to gain concessions from railway companies and hotels. His agency was soon so dominant that he was able to impose on many hotels his system of accommodation cards. These were somewhat like vouchers. They entitled Cook's clients to reduced rates on rooms in hotels throughout the world.

Cook was not, however, without his critics. One writer compared his group tours to cattle drives. Yet business thrived. When Thomas Cook died in 1892, his business passed to his son. In June 2007, Thomas Cook AG merged with My Travel to form Thomas Cook Group plc. There are two Core brands—Thomas Cook and Airtours—and five additional principal brands—Neckermann, Condor, Ving, Direct Holidays, and Sunquest. The company operates in five main divisions: UK, Northern Europe, North America, Continental Europe, and German Airlines. Although Thomas Cook Canada was the largest retail travel operation in Canada, it was sold in 2006 to Transat A.T., which removed it from the North American market as its own retailer.

According to the corporate website, "Each year more than 19 million people choose to travel with Thomas Cook Group plc, buying holidays from their network of more than 3,000 owned or franchised travel stores, online or through their call centres.

Thomas Cook Group plc is a €12 billion revenue business, employing 33,000 people globally and operating a fleet of 97 aircraft ... and operating (either through direct control or via franchise arrangements) 46 hotels and other resort properties" ("Welcome," n.d.).

Cook's enterprising spirit changed the face of travel. It was he who coined the phrase "Cook's tour" to indicate a whirlwind tour that touches down in many places. In a larger sense, Cook was important because of the pioneering role he played in the field of organized mass travel.

Tourism is now the world's largest employer, accounting for one in every twelve workers. According to the Tourism Industry Association of Canada (TIAC) 2007 data, tourism directly employed 654 100 Canadians. In 2006, direct and indirect tourism employment totalled 1.8 million Canadians, or 11.0 percent of the work force (Statistics Canada, April 21, 2008).

But with a growing labour shortage and global recession, how will Canada's tourism economy fare? Immediately after the terrorist attacks of September 11, 2001, there was a decline in domestic air travel, reduced consumer confidence in air safety, and uncertainty about the future—and all of these problems were elevated by a weakening global economy. But there are lessons to learn from this. The UNWTO and the Canadian Tourism Commission (CTC) point out that after the terrorist attack in Luxor, Egypt, in 1997 and during the Gulf War of 1991, tourism declined globally as well as in those regions. However, within four years, tourism had climbed back to its pre-event levels (Glynn, 2001).

In 2007, tourism spending in Canada increased 4.3 percent to $70.6 billion: $54.4 billion by Canadians (77 percent) and $16.2 billion by foreigners (23 percent). Also in 2007, the tourism gross domestic product (GDP) in Canada increased to 3.7 percent of Canada's overall GDP (Statistics Canada, March 27, 2008). Canada's international travel deficit reached $10.3 billion in 2007, up $3.6

billion from 2006 (Statistics Canada, February 28, 2008) (see Table 1–2).

A DEFINITION OF TOURISM

The word "tourism" has been part of the English language since 1811, when it appeared in England's *Sporting Magazine*. However, the definitions of "tourist" and "tourism" varied widely until 1994, when the United Nations and the UNWTO arrived at definitions of tourism that are coming to be accepted internationally. Consider the following examples.

A traveller is any person on a trip anywhere, whatever that trip's length or purpose. A trip can be for pleasure, for visiting friends or relatives, for business or professional activities, or for health, religious, or other reasons. Travellers can be visitors who are engaged in tourism, and can be same-day visitors or tourists (overnight visitors). Visitors travel to places outside their usual environment for less than 12 months for a purpose other than the exercise of an activity remunerated from within the place visited (McIntosh et al., 1995).

In Canada, the usual definition of **domestic travel** is travel for any purpose and for any length of time, within 80 kilometres of home. Overnight travel of more than 80 kilometres, for any purpose other than remuneration, is considered *domestic tourism*. As no distance is specified for

TABLE 1–2 Canadian National Tourism Indicators, 2007/2006 (Current prices, seasonally adjusted)

Indicators	2007	2006
Total tourism expenditures	$70.6 billion	4.3%
Nonresident spending	$16.2 billion	–3.2%
Resident spending at home	$54.4 billion	6.7%

Note: Total tourism commodities includes total transportation, accommodation, food and beverage services and other tourism commodities (i.e. recreation and entertainment, travel agency).

SOURCE: Tourism Satellite Accounts, Canadian Tourism Commission/Statistics Canada.

inbound and outbound tourism, residents and nonresidents who cross an international border are engaged in tourism.

Tourism is the set of activities of a person travelling to a place outside his or her usual environment for at least one night and for less than 12 months and whose main purpose of travel is other than the exercise of an activity remunerated from within the place visited. These forms of tourism are summarized below:

- **Domestic tourism**—residents of a country visiting, at least overnight, places farther than 80 kilometres from their usual environment for purposes other than remuneration.
- **Inbound tourism**—nonresidents of a country visiting that country.
- **Outbound tourism**—residents of a country visiting places outside that country.
- **Internal tourism**—domestic and inbound tourism combined.
- **National tourism**—internal and outbound tourism combined.
- **International tourism**—inbound and outbound tourism combined (Meis and Naylor, 1996; Smith, 1995).

Eight categories of tourism based on types of experience at a destination are identified in Table 1–3.

Tourism has both a supply side (suppliers of products and services for tourism) and a demand side (overnight visitors and same-day visitors).

THE GROWTH OF TOURISM

According to National Tourism Indicators from Statistics Canada (March 27, 2008), nearly 30.2 million international travellers came to Canada in 2007 (down 18.9 million from 1999); over 25.6 million of these came from the United States (down 18.1 million from 1999). The recent decline in arrivals is due to an unfavourable exchange rate in 2007, the new stricter U.S. border regulations, higher fuel prices, and recession.

The World Tourism Organization (UNWTO) (January 29, 2008) reported international tourism arrivals reached 898 million in 2007. In its *Tourism 2020 Vision* (2001), the UNWTO forecast that international arrivals will reach 1.0 billion in 2010 and 1.56 billion by 2020.

Reasons for the Growth of the Tourism Industry

The modern tourism industry began in the late 1950s and early 1960s. Many companies that are now giants in the industry trace their origins to those days. There are several reasons for the growth of the tourism industry during that era. A relatively peaceful political climate encouraged travel. Stronger economies in the industrialized nations meant that people had more money to spend on travel. The introduction of passenger jet service made travelling faster, less expensive, and more comfortable. Television

---

TABLE 1–3 Categories of Tourism

1. **Ethnic** Travelling to observe the cultural expressions and lifestyles of peoples. *Typical activity*—taking a coastal steamer to the outports of Newfoundland.

2. **Cultural** Travelling to experience vanishing lifestyles that lie within human memory. Includes cultural ecotourism. *Typical activity*—lunching in the tavern at the Fortress of Louisbourg.

3. **Heritage** Travelling to view places and things from the past, either natural or built by humans. *Typical activities*—visiting Vimy Ridge, the Halifax Citadel; touring cathedrals and monuments or national parks.

4. **Environmental** Travelling to natural and environmental attractions to experience people–land relationships. Includes adventure/outdoor tourism and ecotourism. *Typical activities*—hiking in the Rockies, bird watching, viewing Niagara Falls.

5. **Recreational** Travelling to engage in sports and meet social contacts in a relaxed setting. *Typical activities*—golfing, gaming, attending performances, relaxing with family or friends, watching baseball.

6. **Sports** Participating in community-based sporting events as spectator, performer, or volunteer. *Typical activities*—Canadian Curling Association Brier, Vancouver 2010 Olympics.

7. **Business** Travelling to meetings, events, and conferences, perhaps combined with other types of tourism. *Typical activities*—attending annual professional conference, association meeting.

8. **Special interest** Travelling to participate in learning vacations, agritourism, festivals, and events. *Typical activities*—travelling to wine festivals, ranch holidays.

SOURCES: Valene Smith (1977), *Hosts and Guests* (PA: University of Pennsylvania Press), pp. 2–3; Todd Brandt (March 2001), "Sports Tourism and Social Benefit," *Communiqué*, p. 2; Canadian Tourism Commission (2001), "Canadian Tourism Industry: Vision & Mission," www.canadatourism.com/vision_mission, p. 3; "Sport & Tourism: Shaping Global Culture," *WTO Newsletter* (2001, 1st Quarter), p. 11.

ILLUSTRATION 1–1

A traditional winter sleigh ride is only one of the many leisure and recreation activities offered at the historic five-star Manoir Hovey, located in North Hatley, Cantons de l'est (the Eastern Townships) of Quebec.

SOURCE: Photo of guest sleigh ride activity courtesy of Manoir Hovey.

documentaries on subjects such as the wildlife of Africa, the mountains of Nepal, and the dancers of Bali inspired viewers to visit faraway peoples and lands.

Since 1970, the number of people travelling has grown even more, in both Canada and the United States. As Plog (1991) suggests, the North American psyche has changed; more people are now giving priority to leisure travel and de-emphasizing saving for a rainy day. Doing things now, not tomorrow, has become more important. This new psyche, coupled with the increased ownership of automobiles and improvements in the highway system, has enabled more people—especially families—to travel. More women are in the workforce, and because there are more two-income households, more families can afford to travel. Also, longer paid vacations from work have given people more time to travel. Front-end baby boomers have paid off their mortgages, are watching their kids leave the nest, and are at the peak of their earning power, so they have more income to spend on more extensive pleasure travel. The increase in the number of senior citizens has also been good for the tourism industry. Retired from jobs and freed from mortgage payments, many older Canadians now have the time and money to travel in any season. Finally, the operations of domestic and multinational businesses throughout North America and the world have done much to promote tourism products and services.

Impact of the Growth of Tourism

The tourism industry has had a huge impact on the world's national economies. International tourism receipts in 2007 amounted to US$856 billion (up over $123 billion from 2006), according to UNWTO's "Tourism Highlights," 2008 edition. The United States was the leader with US$96.7 billion, followed by Spain ($57.8 billion), France ($54.2 billion), Italy ($42.7 billion), and China ($41.9 billion). In addition, nations have recognized the potential of travel for improving relations among cultures. Because of the economic and cultural importance of the tourism industry, governments around the world are attaching more and more importance to tourism development and promotional planning.

Economic Impact Tourism has become a major contributor to Canada's economy. The number of employees in the tourism industries was 1.8 million in 2006, a 4.3 percent increase over 2005 (Statistics Canada, April 21, 2008). The food and beverage sector employs the greatest number of people (763 000 in 2006) and travel services employ the fewest (50 000 in 2006). Whatever these people do, it translates into billions of dollars in salaries and wages. In turn, workers in the tourism industry pour money back into the economy as they pay taxes and make purchases and investments. The Canadian Tourism Human Resource Council (CTHRC) estimates that the tourism sector will grow to employ 1.95 million people by 2015 (CTHRC, "Labour," n.d.). Furthermore, the tourism industry provides profits for hundreds of businesses and corporations.

The tourism industry has sometimes helped revive economically depressed areas. For example, waterfront restorations featuring shops, restaurants, and entertainment complexes are attracting tourists to the downtown areas of some major North American cities. Marketplace Square in Saint John, New Brunswick, and The Forks (La Fourche) in Winnipeg, Manitoba, are fine examples of successful restoration.

Cultural Impact "Understanding through travel is a passport to peace" was the slogan of the European Travel

ILLUSTRATION 1–2

The Rogers Centre (formerly SkyDome) and the CN Tower are two well-known Canadian constructed attractions in Toronto.

SOURCE: Corel.

Commission in the 1950s. Through travel, people of different cultures get to know one another, and this knowledge increases the possibility of peaceful coexistence among nations.

Environmental Impact A prosperous tourism industry can threaten or devalue the things that Canadians and visitors value. To encourage tourism and preserve the environment, the industry must foster values that support a nation's natural, social, and built environments. Too much tourism, poorly managed, can transform environments in ways that are unacceptable to the community. The right kinds of tourism, managed effectively, can enhance the environment and generate wealth for communities.

Canada's tourism industry realizes that sustainable development is crucial to its long-term success. Our system of national parks, historic sites, national conservation areas, heritage rivers, and world heritage sites attests to this country's commitment to conservation and sustainable practices. The industry's initiatives for sustainable development include:

- Fairmont Hotels & Resorts' environmental standards.
- The Tourism Industry Association of Canada (TIAC) Code of Ethics for Sustainable Tourism; the Tourism Industry Association of Nova Scotia (TIANS) Self-Audit Workbook for tourism operators.
- Controlled use of sensitive areas.
- Occupational standards for outdoor guides under the Canadian Tourism Human Resource Council (CTHRC) National Occupation Certification Program.
- Interpretive exhibits at major beach facilities in Prince Edward Island, designed to increase the public's environmental awareness.
- Comprehensive planning and management in tourism development in regions and communities (e.g., Lunenburg, Nova Scotia, a UNESCO World Heritage Site).

Canada enjoys a clean, safe, natural, and multicultural environment that it will be able to share with the world and future generations if its resources are not depleted. Tourists and tourism operators will need to work together to ensure that their impact on the environment is positive.

Employment Impact As the tourism industry grows, it generates new jobs. Between 1984 and 1990, employment in tourism industries grew faster (26 percent) than the total workforce (15 percent). However, when the recession began in 1990, employment in tourism dropped more sharply (by 3.4 percent compared to 1.8 percent). But there was a turnaround in demand in 1993, and tourism grew in Canada throughout the 1990s. By 2000, there was a growing labour shortage in tourism, especially in the food and beverage sector; as a result, operators began to address employee retention and human resource development. After September 11, 2001, there was a dip in demand. The overall growth in the labour force in Canada is supposed to decline from 1.4 to 0.4 percent by 2016. The Organisation for Economic Co-operation and Development (OECD) concurred—Europe will be facing a similar human resource challenge for the next few years. We will return to the projected growth of tourism employment in Chapter 17.

Check Your Product Knowledge

1. Who is a tourist? What is tourism?
2. How has the growth of tourism influenced the Canadian economy?

ILLUSTRATION 1–3

Tourist attractions, both natural and built by humans, draw travellers to an area.

SOURCE: Reprinted with permission of the Yukon Department of Tourism. Photograph: Richard Hartmier.

THE ORIGINAL EIGHT SECTORS OF THE CANADIAN TOURISM INDUSTRY

In 1997, economists from Canada, the United States, and Mexico created the North American Industry Classification (NAICS) to consolidate their tourism statistics. They divided tourism into five industries: transportation, food and beverage, accommodation, recreation and entertainment, and travel services (Emerit, 2008). To facilitate learning, we have divided tourism into its original eight sectors. These are identified in Figure 1–1 and covered extensively, starting with Part 2 of this textbook.

The Original Eight Sectors

Transportation This covers air transportation, ground (surface) transportation (e.g., trains, buses, taxis), and maritime or ocean-going transportation; more information is presented in Chapters 6, 7, and 8.

Accommodation This includes hotels, resorts, and many other forms of accommodations, which are discussed in Chapter 9.

Food and Beverage (F&B) This sector is the largest tourism-related employer; its many components are discussed in Chapter 10.

Meetings, Events, and Conferences This includes association meetings, corporate meetings; details are presented in Chapter 11.

Attractions This includes attractions (e.g., Niagara Falls), festivals (e.g., Stratford Festival), and special events (e.g., the Olympics in Vancouver 2010); this is discussed in Chapter 12 (with some information in Chapter 4).

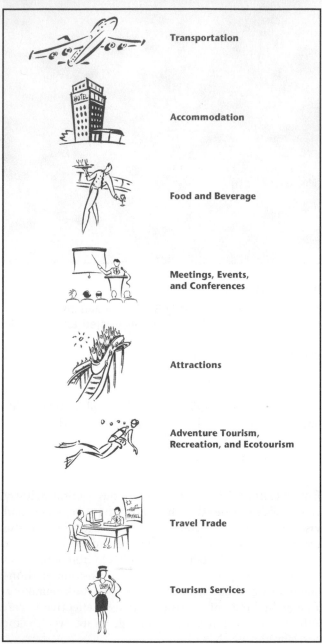

FIGURE 1–1 The Eight Sectors of the Tourism Industry

Adventure Tourism, Recreation, and Ecotourism
This includes "hard" adventure (whitewater rafting) and "soft" adventure (seeing the Northern Lights), recreation (skiing, sailing), and nature activities (birdwatching at Point Pelee, Ontario); more information is available in Chapter 13.

Travel Trade This includes wholesale companies (charter operators, tour operators, and inbound operators) and the travel mart (retail travel agencies, business travel departments, and travel clubs); more information is available in Chapters 14, 15, and 16.

Tourism Services This sector performs three functions: (1) provides support for tourism activities; (2) promotes other tourism sectors; and (3) directly serves the travelling public, such as reservation and information centres; further information is available in Chapters 5 and 17.

TOURISM AS A PRODUCT AND AS A SERVICE

Industries generate either products or services. Some authorities say the tourism industry provides products; others say it provides services. Actually, the tourism industry provides both.

Tourism as a Product

Almost all products are tangible; that is, they can be seen and touched, they have weight and occupy space. The tourism industry produces a few **tangible products**, such as food and beverages. However, most of its products are intangible—they cannot be seen or touched. **Intangible tourism products** include a flight on an airplane, a stay in a hotel room, a ride on a bus, relaxation on a warm beach, a reunion with family members, fun at a nightclub, a view of the ocean, and much more. None of these things can be weighed or measured or stored in a room. Tourism products exist as experiences, which create memories.

Tourism as a Service

A service industry has three special characteristics. First, it performs actions that benefit or serve customers. Second, the employees are professionals and they are expected to perform their duties with a high level of expertise and to be able to give their customers information and counsel. Third, a special attitude or relationship exists between the employee performing the service and the customer receiving it.

Tourism Professionals These people provide services that make up the travel experience by bringing the product to life. In the tourism industry, the relationship is *host–guest*. This relationship assumes that the host will

focus attention on the needs and welfare of the guest and strive to make the tourism experience happy and fulfilling. Hosts in the tourist industry must maintain a quality relationship with guests if they want them to return.

> ## Check Your Product Knowledge
>
> 1. What are the eight sectors of the tourism industry in Canada?
> 2. Why can the tourism industry be said to provide both products and services?

SERVICE: EVERYBODY'S BUSINESS

Services influence how people and organizations spend their time and money. A restaurant has more time to spend on its core menu if it buys its baked goods. A family on vacation may fly rather than drive to Ottawa to save time, stay at a bed-and-breakfast that is less expensive than a hotel, and walk to attractions instead of taking taxis so they can spend more money on meals.

Since the Industrial Revolution, the service sector has fuelled economic growth and allowed companies, institutions, and individuals to trade money for time. Increased disposable income and more leisure time have created a demand for personal services, especially in the spheres of entertainment, recreation, tourism, and education. The service sector now accounts for most of the world's economic production.

Human capital has replaced physical capital as the most important source of investment. The idea that goods alone constitute wealth is no longer valid. There is much evidence that services are real and make a positive contribution to economies.

An Explanation of Service

Berkowitz and his colleagues (2000) suggest there is a service continuum that ranges from intangible, service-dominated items to tangible, goods-dominated items. Tour guide services and festival performances are examples of service-dominated activities. Services are characterized by the "four Is"—intangibility, inconsistency, inseparability, and inventory—which are major concerns. In contrast, bottled water and souvenirs are at the tangible end of the continuum, and the four Is are not relevant in managing their production and marketing.

Intangibility Before purchasing a product, the buyer can hold, touch, and see it. A buyer can't do that with a service.

Inconsistency Inconsistency in services may be common due to different staff, weather conditions, etc., which vary from day to day. The tourism industry in Canada is working to address inconsistency in services by establishing industrywide standards and by promoting training for tourism occupations.

Inseparability Most consumers do not separate a service from the contact personnel who deliver it or from the servicescape—that is, the setting where the service occurs. So the service becomes the product.

Inventory In contrast to goods inventory, service inventory is a matter of idle production capacity—that is, having the capacity available to meet customer demand. Services not sold one day cannot be held in inventory; in contrast, goods inventory can be handled and stored, which involves costs.

THE BUILDING BLOCKS OF SERVICE

Success in marketing services depends on marketing managers understanding how consumers think while choosing, consuming, and evaluating services. Three stages are involved.

1. Pre-Purchase Stage

Consumers may not be considering all possible alternatives; rather they are choosing from a limited set of options or brands based on past experience, convenience, and knowledge.

2. Consumption Stage

Once consumers have selected a service such as a travel package, they engage in direct, interactive experiences with the benefits of the services in the package.

3. Post-Purchase Stage

Evaluation of the travel package occurs both during and after interaction with the services received. Consumers compare their perceptions of services—not the actual services—with their expectations. When perception outshines expectations, consumers are satisfied.

Guest Contact Personnel

Guest contact staff members are important. Customer service is a performing art that requires the right people cast in the right roles. Otherwise, customer satisfaction is not possible. The Walt Disney Company is well known for its superb customer service and offers three-day seminars on the Disney approach and delivery of customer service to executives from other enterprises who want to improve their services. Disney also offers internal training courses

ILLUSTRATION 1–4

Efficiency and effectiveness in communication are essential to excellent customer service in all sectors of tourism.
SOURCE: Keith Brofsky/Photodisc Green/Getty Images.

such as Disney Traditions (an introduction to the history and culture of Disney and the importance of culture to guest service), Operations, and Visions (of the Future).

In service operations, guest contact staff members are the product. They are also the source of product differentiation.

Staff Effectiveness

Schneider (1980) stresses that when measuring staff effectiveness, it is not enough to count the number of customers served or the number of errors made. More general factors, such as courtesy and style of performance, must also be considered. Managers have a role to play in creating a climate where good service is the norm. Then an environment will develop that encourages employees to give good service, and supports them when they do.

MANAGING THE SERVICE ENTERPRISE

Three out of four Canadians are employed in the service sector. Many economists believe the service sector holds the key to job creation in the future. Environmental changes such as changing workforce demographics, advances in technology, and massive changes in communications are fuelling the demand for services. Those services will need to be managed effectively to respond to that demand.

Human Resource Management

Human resources are the most important component of service operations. How they are managed influences employees' perceptions and, in turn, customers' perceptions. Two effective tools for bringing out employees' potential to deliver quality services are empowerment and enfranchisement.

Empowerment Contact personnel who are empowered have been freed from rigid controls—from instructions, policies, and orders—and are expected to take responsibility for their own ideas, decisions, and actions. Employees are most likely to develop a sense of empowerment in decentralized organizations that are less formal and have less specialized labour, wider spans of control, and short chains of command.

Enfranchisement Enfranchisement expands on the logic of empowerment, offering employees some control over what they earn and what they do to earn it. For example, front desk agents can be encouraged to up-sell services, and receive bonus points when they are successful.

Customer Loyalty Systems

Customer loyalty systems address three things: customer satisfaction, customer recovery, and customer retention. If the customer is satisfied, the other components are not needed. If the customer is not satisfied, all of the components will be needed. Service providers face the challenge of keeping customers from defecting if the service is not acceptable.

Customer Satisfaction A focus on customer satisfaction is necessary in today's marketplace. Some studies show that it can be three to five times more expensive to acquire a new customer than to hang on to an old one. A satisfied customer is a valuable asset. Jan Carlzon (1987), former CEO of SAS, emphasizes this point by suggesting that service firms must learn to manage "moments of truth—the sometimes fleeting, but always significant, contacts between the company and the customer." He believes that there is a moment of truth every time a customer interacts with contact personnel or a service system.

Customer Recovery Service errors happen. What matters is how contact personnel respond. When service is not provided as expected, customers perceive it as a service failure. Contact personnel need to be able to respond quickly and appropriately and provide an effective recovery. Research has shown that customer loyalty is increased when operations can correct an error or oversight with efficiency and effectiveness.

Customer Retention "Losing a customer isn't one lost sale—it can be a lifetime of them" (Lane and Dupre, 1997, p. 88). Being rude or inattentive once to a $2.50 take-out customer having only a coffee and doughnut can result in the loss of $312.50 a year from what otherwise would have been a loyal customer. A customer retention system is like a safety net. Four retention strategies are pricing, creating a customer franchise, managing defections, and guaranteeing service.

Service Quality

"Service quality is not a specific goal or program that can be achieved or completed but needs to be an ongoing part of all management and service production" (Bateson and Hoffman, 1999, p. 339). The concepts of service quality and customer satisfaction are intertwined.

Quality Culture To be successful in today's marketplace, service organizations must emphasize quality. Total quality management (TQM) is a strategy for developing quality services that satisfy customers' needs. If done properly, TQM results in a competitive advantage for the organization. To implement TQM, a service organization must develop a companywide commitment to quality at all levels and create a corporate quality culture that is committed to solving problems.

In Canada, the National Quality Institute (NQI) has been established to recognize business excellence. The NQI's first awards were presented in 1984; each fall, six awards are made at the Excellence Summit. In fall 2000, based on an NQI assessment of four of its properties, Delta Hotels, the largest first-class hotel company in Canada, was the first hotel company to be awarded the NQI's Canada Awards for Excellence.

Check Your Product Knowledge

1. Why are the four Is relevant to service management?
2. What are the three stages a consumer goes through in purchasing a service?

LEISURE AND RECREATION

In the previous section, we learned the significance of service in the tourism sectors and that services influence how people and organizations spend their time and money. Now we should study the concepts of leisure and recreation to understand what travellers do when away from home and why they do it. This knowledge will later prove useful when planning a marketing strategy to meet the motivations, needs, and expectations (MNEs) of an operation's target markets.

ILLUSTRATION 1–5

Recreation and tourism satisfy people's need for leisure and enhance life in the Far North, as well as in metropolitan areas.

SOURCE: Corel.

Leisure Is . . .

What is leisure?

MacLean, Peterson, and Martin, in *Recreation and Leisure: The Changing Scene* (1985, p. 7), suggest that leisure is "that portion of time not obligated by subsistence or existence demands. It represents discretionary or free time, time in which one may make voluntary choices of experience."

As society became industrialized, leisure grew in economic importance. Employers began providing time off from work as a fair reward for productivity. Paid vacations and a limited-hour workweek are normal practice today, but they weren't always.

Leisure services are provided by the public, not-for-profit, and commercial sectors and involve outdoor and indoor activities in all sectors of the tourism industry. Leisure services foster economic growth, increase public pride, promote national unity, and improve the quality of life. Leisure is now accepted as a necessity, not a frill. It has become vital to people's lives—everyone's, even if they don't have the money for exotic travel.

Anyone involved in providing leisure services should be mindful of how Canada's social demographics, and those of other countries, will unfold in the coming decades. Foote and Stoffman (1998) in *Boom, Bust and Echo 2000* stress that in the years ahead, *resting* will be one of Canada's most popular leisure activities. Participation and attendance at sporting events won't be as popular as reading, hobbies, and attending museums, the theatre, and other cultural events. They suggest that funds should be spent on walking trails, curling rinks, and swimming pools. Life expectancy is increasing and people are staying active longer. This raises the question, "Will healthier older people be more active than in previous generations?" What activities will the next generation pursue as they grow older? Will they be golfers, gardeners, or skiers? These questions and others need to be considered by leisure service providers.

Recreation Is . . .

"Recreation" comes from the Latin word *recreatio*, meaning recovery or restoration from something. Over the years the term has evolved to encompass activities that provide refreshment from the day's labours.

Recreation is also seen as having some purpose that benefits society. Because it is expected to be good for people in specific ways, recreation receives financial support and is organized to maximize its social and economic benefits. We can conclude, then, that recreation is a form of expression during leisure activity within a specific culture that generates enjoyment and has social and possibly political utility.

Check Your Product Knowledge

1. List examples of leisure services.
2. When did mass leisure first develop?
3. How does recreation benefit society?

LEISURE BEHAVIOUR

Why Do People Engage in Leisure Activities?

People's needs change over time as they strive to meet more than their basic requirements for survival. Leisure is a way to express one's personality, character, and interests.

ILLUSTRATION 1–6
High-risk leisure activities provide release from the humdrum of everyday living.
SOURCE: Corel.

People see it as something pleasant and beneficial that influences personal development. Bucher and his colleagues (1984) suggest that people engage in leisure activities for various reasons, including:

- **Relaxation** Time out from the daily grind allows people to reaffirm themselves.
- **Active enjoyment** Leisure allows people to apply their talents to positive, pleasurable activities.
- **Passive enjoyment** Spectator forms of entertainment provide stimulation without direct participation.
- **Release** Some people engage in high-risk leisure activities such as parachuting and whitewater rafting.
- **Recuperation** Some people renew and refresh their lives through leisure activities.

Leisure Participation

Some people participate less in leisure activities as they grow older, while others stop participating in some activities but replace them with others. Participation in leisure is influenced by education, income, marital status, gender, "leisure repertoire," preferences, motivation, attitude, and satisfaction, as well as age.

Leisure Repertoire The number of activities people engage in during leisure—that is, their leisure repertoire—depends on a number of things, including opportunity, age, health, and attitude.

Motivation People yearn to escape and also yearn to seek. Both yearnings affect people's leisure behaviour. People who do not participate in leisure activities may lack motivation or be bored. Boredom is often a result of negative leisure attitudes, a strong work ethic, low levels of leisure awareness, high levels of constraint, or low levels of self-motivation. When tourism professionals understand the factors that affect leisure motivation, they find it easier to tailor leisure services to individuals.

Leisure Attitudes The term "attitude" has been defined as *a learned predisposition to respond in a consistently favourable or unfavourable manner with respect to a given object* (Fishbein and Ajzen, 1975, p. 6). With respect to leisure, each individual possesses an overall attitude, as well as attitudes about specific activities. Once tourism professionals understand these leisure attitudes, they can (a) determine trends relating to leisure in society and to the relative importance of work and leisure, (b) improve leisure service delivery, and (c) help consumers clarify and improve their attitudes about leisure.

Leisure Satisfaction Satisfaction varies with the individual's level of need. According to McIntosh and his colleagues (1995), after individuals' basic needs (such as shelter, food, and safety) have been met, they tend to seek higher levels of leisure satisfaction (see Figure 2–2 in the next chapter). Leisure satisfaction ranges from a feeling of physical competence to knowing you are the best you can be in some form of leisure pursuit. The striving for leisure satisfaction presents a challenge to tourism service providers. They must be able to supply leisure services that will meet the demands of individuals and groups at various levels in the leisure satisfaction hierarchy.

Constraints on Leisure Behaviour The various constraints on leisure must also be considered. Lack of money, lack of transportation, lack of people to share an activity with, and limited access to an activity can all prevent people who want to engage in an activity from actually doing so. Also, a person may never have engaged in a specific activity before nor even know about it. Both inexperience and lack of knowledge can constrain people's leisure choices. There are also socioeconomic constraints: gender stereotypes or restrictions, marital status, stage in the life cycle, ageism, time available, and discretionary income.

It seems that leisure is becoming more and more central to people's lifestyles in Canada and elsewhere. Yet leisure is not yet fully understood and, until it is, tourism service providers will not be able to offer the leisure programs our diverse society needs. Furthermore, service providers must embrace the principle of sustainability in developing and managing their services; otherwise, the physical environment may be destroyed and leisure activities will be constrained. You will learn more about sustainability in later chapters.

Check Your Product Knowledge

1. Why do people engage in leisure activities?
2. What factors influence whether people participate in leisure activities?

LEISURE TOURISM IN CANADA

Leisure Tourism Products

All parts of Canada offer a wide variety of leisure products for domestic and international tourists. And new products are being created around CTC's vision (as at June 2008), "Compel the world to explore Canada" (CTC, "About," n.d.). The previous CTC vision statement was "Canada will be the premier four-season destination to connect with nature and to experience diverse cultures and communities." Other products based on aboriginal, culinary, adventure, ecotourism, and education themes have been earmarked for development under the leadership of the CTC and the destination marketing organizations (DMOs).

If the service providers deliver on their promises, the Canadian tourism industry will achieve its mission as stated by the CTC (as at June 2008): "Harness Canada's collective voice to grow tourism export revenues" (CTC, "About," n.d.). The CTC's previous mission statement was ". . . deliver world-class cultural and leisure experiences year-round while preserving and sharing Canada's clean, safe, and natural environments. The industry will be guided by the values of respect, integrity, and empathy."

Influencing Factors Natural, psychosocial, and technological factors will influence leisure tourism in the future and—more than likely—your role in the tourism industry. Remember the following:

1. There will be more people with more money and time to travel in Canada and abroad after they retire.
2. Today's careers tend to be 24/7/365, meaning that more and more workers will be able to engage in tourism leisure activities seven days a week.

ILLUSTRATION 1–7
Built in 1888, the Banff Springs Hotel is an early example of Canadian world-class leisure products.
SOURCE: Courtesy of Fairmont Hotels.

3. Leisure tourism will continue to be affected by energy costs, security policies, and the trends toward consolidation and globalization in the travel industry.
4. Economic trends and the "war on terrorism" will affect both domestic and international tourism.
5. Developments in communications and manufacturing will continue to increase the options available to consumers (e.g., online air ticket purchasing or "virtual" golf matches with Tiger Woods).
6. Environmental and recreational concerns will continue to grow in importance.
7. Demands for tourism leisure services will change as the "Boom, Bust, and Echo" generations mature and adjust the balance between leisure and work in their lives.
8. More single people will be seeking companionship through tourism leisure activities.
9. More people will be better informed and better educated, and will be emphasizing quality of life, self-development, physical and emotional health, and the "right to leisure."
10. More than likely, demand from domestic and international tourists for leisure services will increase;

opportunities for tourism destination and product development will expand.

11. Tourism leisure services will have to continue becoming more customized.

12. Leisure will continue to hold a variety of meanings for an ever-increasing multicultural tourism industry.

Check Your Product Knowledge

1. What is the vision for Canada as a destination?

2. Why is it important for leisure tourism service providers to understand the relationship between work and leisure?

THE TOURISM INDUSTRY IN THE MARKETPLACE

A marketplace can be anywhere buyers and sellers meet to exchange goods and services for money. In the tourism industry, the marketplace may be these places as well as an office in a travel agency, a trade show like Rendez-vous Canada, the front desk at a hotel, or a ticket reservation system for an event. The buyers are people acquiring the services they need for a tourism experience: transportation, accommodation, entertainment.

Free Enterprise or Mixed Enterprise?

The Canadian government owns Wood Buffalo National Park, the Fortress of Louisbourg, and the National Art Gallery, as well as many other parks, monuments, and historic attractions. In addition, federal, provincial, territorial, and municipal funds are used to build and operate the public infrastructure: transit systems, airports, docks, harbours, highways, and so on.

But these examples of government ownership of tourism enterprises and infrastructure are actually exceptions. Most tourism businesses in Canada are privately owned and operated. This is in contrast to many other countries, where governments own and operate most tourism enterprises.

Some people argue that Canada's tourism industry is part of the free enterprise system. In such a system, privately owned businesses are allowed to compete with one another in the marketplace with minimal government interference. Owners are free to make as much money as they can.

To the extent that it is part of the free enterprise system, the Canadian tourism industry is a business like

ILLUSTRATION 1–8

Rue de la Commune in Vieux (old) Montreal dates back to 1651 when it was a grazing area for animals (a public pasture); it is now part of walking tours and the beginning of most of the carriage rides (caleches) of Vieux Montreal and the Old Port.

SOURCE: © Stéphan Poulin.

any other. To stay in business, companies must produce good products and services, sell them at a fair price, and earn a profit. The possibility of making a profit constitutes an incentive for owners of companies to put forward their best efforts. Many economists believe that the free enterprise system is more efficient than a government-controlled system, better suited to change, and more conducive to growth. Others contend that the tourism industry in Canada functions within a mixed enterprise system, in that governments own and operate the parks, museums, and historic attractions, as well as the infrastructure.

For example, provincial governments have opened casinos in Gatineau (1996), Regina (1996), and Niagara Falls (2004), all to draw tourists. Also, governments are involved in promoting tourism and partnerships for other projects. Government ownership and funding coupled with privately owned businesses in the tourism industry yield a mixed enterprise system.

The Ps of Marketing

"Marketing" refers to those activities that direct the flow of goods and services from the producer to the consumer. The American Marketing Association states: "Marketing is the process of planning and executing the conception, pricing, promotion, and distribution of ideas, goods, and services to create exchanges that satisfy individual and organizational objectives" (Bennett, 1995, p. 166). To market products and services, tourism professionals must coordinate the four main Ps of marketing:

1. Product   3. Place
2. Price   4. Promotion

Marketing focuses on the consumer. These four Ps, together known as the "marketing mix," must satisfy the motivations, needs, and expectations (MNEs) of the target market. Thus, to satisfactorily blend the elements of the marketing mix, the professional must understand buyer behaviour. The successful tourism professional knows how to bring the right product or service to the right place at the right time at the right price.

1. Product This category includes all products and services provided by the sectors of the tourism industry. The three aspects of the good/service element of the services marketing mix to consider are exclusivity, brand name, and capacity management.

Products can be patented, but services can't. So services lack exclusivity. Branding can also be a problem because services are intangible. Creating brand identity is extremely important but difficult to do. Logos are often developed to differentiate one service from another, convey an image, and provide a point of reference when new services are introduced.

2. Price The price is based on the supplier's expenses in producing the product and the distributor's expenses in marketing it; the market price is established by supply and demand.

3. Place This category refers to any marketplace in the channel of distribution where the buyer and the provider are brought together by a seller (a retail travel agency, a business travel department, a travel club, a ticket counter, a front desk, a telephone line, or an e-business website).

4. Promotion This refers to the ways in which sellers create consumer interest. (television and radio, in newspapers and magazines, and on the Internet).

The Other Ps in Tourism Marketing Tourism professionals involved in marketing products and services may also be involved in coordinating five additional Ps (Tourism Canada, 1986; Getz, 1997):

- **Packaging** Products and services from one or more suppliers can be combined and offered to customers at a single price (e.g., ground transportation, theatre tickets, and hotel accommodations package).
- **Partnerships** Two or more companies or individuals may work together to satisfy tourists' needs. Airlines and hotel companies often form partnerships that grant air miles and discounted rates to frequent flyers.
- **Personnel** Trained, experienced, and skilled people with a positive attitude toward customers and

businesses are needed to guarantee that the products and services being marketed meet consumers' expectations when they are delivered.

- **Positioning** Positioning involves identifying and communicating the differences between a business and its competition.
- **Programming** Special events and activities can be planned as added incentives or value-added features for customers. Delta Hotel's Barrington Bear cookies and milk service for kids and special amenities for executive-class rooms are two examples of programming. One serves families and the other serves business travellers.

The Four Rs of Services Marketing

Many marketers of services now recognize that they are not ensuring their customers' satisfaction if they apply only the product, price, place, and promotion components of the marketing mix to their marketing strategies. Today's managers are also considering the four Rs—retention, referrals, relationships, and recovery (Sommers and Barnes, 2001).

Retention Ettorre (1997) reports there is evidence that the longer customers do business with a firm, the more profitable the firm becomes. These customers spend more and cost less to serve because they are generally more satisfied and are already convinced to buy.

ILLUSTRATION 1–9

The West Edmonton Mall has become a tourist attraction for visitors to Edmonton as well as a shopping mall for locals.

SOURCE: Image courtesy of West Edmonton Mall Property Inc.

Referrals Customers will refer their friends and associates to an operation that provides at least the level of service expected. Positive word-of-mouth can result in a lot of new business. Negative word-of-mouth spreads as well, and customers may never come back.

Relationships Firms use relationship-management programs to establish closer ties with customers. Using consumer databases, service providers can learn a great deal about their customers.

Recovery It is a given that no one—and no service organization—is 100 percent perfect. Many operations have procedures in place for when service problems arise. Often when recovery responses are rolled out, not only do consumers become satisfied, but they also become even more loyal.

Check Your Product Knowledge

1. In the tourism industry, where is the marketplace? Who are the buyers? Who are the sellers? What do they exchange?
2. What are the Ps of tourism marketing? Why are they all part of marketing tourism services?

THE UNITED NATIONS AND TOURISM

World Tourism Organization

The World Tourism Organization (UNWTO), a consultative agency to the United Nations, represents all the world's national and official tourist interests. The UNWTO has 160 member countries and territories and more than 350 affiliate members (UNWTO, n.d.). Its main objective is to promote tourism, not only as a source of revenue for tourist destinations, but also as a way to foster peace, understanding, health, and prosperity throughout the world.

Global Code of Ethics for Tourism

In April 1999, during a meeting of the United Nations Commission on Sustainable Development, the concept of a Code of Ethics for Tourism was ratified and the UNWTO was encouraged to pursue additional input from other sectors.

In October 1999, 10 principles forming the Global Code of Ethics for Tourism were approved by the UNWTO General Assembly meeting in Santiago, Chile. Upon approval of the code, the Secretary-General of the

UNWTO, Francesco Frangialli, issued the following message:

> The Global Code of Ethics for Tourism sets a frame of reference for the responsible and sustainable development of world tourism at the dawn of the new millennium. . . . With international tourism forecast to nearly triple over the next 20 years, members of the World Tourism Organization believe that the Global Code of Ethics for Tourism is needed to help minimize the negative impacts of tourism on the environment and on cultural heritage while maximizing the benefits for residents of tourism destinations. (UNWTO, "Global," 2001)

"Tourism Enriches" Campaign

In January 2004 in Madrid, Spain, at the First World Conference on Tourism Communications (TOURCOM), Frangialli launched the "Tourism Enriches" campaign, stating that "tourism enriches individuals, families,

ILLUSTRATION 1–10

The Global Code of Ethics for Tourism is one initiative in the World Tourism Organization's efforts to foster education and research for the tourism industry.

SOURCE: Courtesy of the World Tourism Organization.

communities and all the world." According to a February 16, 2004, UNWTO news release:

> The aims of the "Tourism Enriches" campaign are to promote tourism as a basic human right and way of life, to stimulate communication about the benefits of tourism as the most prospective economic activity for the local communities and countries, to enhance cooperation between destinations and the tourism industry with the local, regional and international media and to link individual tourism entities to the larger community of international tourism.

The UNWTO and the Millennium Development Goals

In February 2004, the World Tourism Organization was "converted" into a specializing agency of the United Nations. Referring to the UNWTO's new role, United Nations Secretary-General Kofi Annan wrote the following to UNWTO Secretary-General Frangialli:

> The UNWTO's activities, such as the Sustainable Tourism Eliminating Poverty programme, will contribute to strengthening collaboration within the United Nations system to promote socially, economically and ecologically sustainable tourism aimed at alleviating poverty and bringing jobs to people in developing countries. These objectives are fully consistent with the outcomes of the World Summit on Sustainable Development and the goals set out in the Millennium Declaration. (UNWTO, February 11, 2004)

The Millennium Declaration features eight goals that world leaders agreed to in 2000 to fight against poverty, hunger, disease, illiteracy, environmental degradation, and discrimination against women. The seventh of these Millennium Development Goals (MDGs) is to "Ensure Environmental Sustainability," which directly affects the tourism industry.

The Davos Declaration In October 2007, the Davos Declaration was formulated at the Second International Conference on Climate Change and Tourism in response to concerns of climate change. The conference's participants agreed that "there is a need to urgently adopt a range of policies which encourages truly sustainable tourism that reflects a 'quadruple bottom line' of environmental, social, economic and climate responsiveness" (Davos Declaration, 2007).

The UNWTO and Its "Climate Change and Tourism" Report

According to the UNWTO's report, "Climate Change and Tourism: Responding to Global Challenges" (2007), the tourism sector should respond to changing climate conditions if it is to evolve in a truly sustainable way—reducing its own greenhouse gas (GHG) emissions (mainly from the transportation and accommodation sectors) and responding to the impacts on its own operations (such as improving energy efficiency). The UNWTO, for example, has endorsed's the International Civil Aviation Organization's carbon emissions calculator, which determines CO_2 emissions from air travel. UNWTO Assistant Secretary-General Professor Geoffrey Lipman stated, "the time is now for the tourism community to advance its strategy to address what must be considered the greatest challenge to the sustainability of tourism in the 21st century."

Check Your Product Knowledge

1. How does the UNWTO view international tourism?
2. Why do the members of the UNWTO believe that the "Global Code of Ethics" is needed?
3. What are the aims of the "Tourism Enriches" campaign?
4. What actions did the UNWTO's 'Climate Change and Tourism' report recommend that the Tourism industry undertake?

GOVERNMENT AND THE TOURISM INDUSTRY

Although the majority of tourism enterprises in Canada are privately owned, they are not allowed to do absolutely anything they want. Local, provincial/territorial, and federal governments promote and regulate many enterprises, whatever their size and location. Knowing how the government affects the tourism industry is an important part of your product knowledge.

Government and Promotion

Recognizing the economic benefits, the three levels of government promote travel and tourism by providing facilities, publicity, concessions, and incentives.

Facilities The government spends tax dollars on building, maintaining, and operating facilities that enable people to travel. Funds for airports, highways, and river and harbour facilities are provided by various levels of government. The federal government, through Transport Canada, finances all air traffic control operations. Governments also finance facilities that attract visitors, such as convention centres and stadiums. Parks, monuments, historic sites, recreational areas, and scenic trails and waterways are also provided by government.

Publicity People living in Michigan have probably seen a television ad inviting them to visit Ontario. By calling a special toll-free number, potential visitors can order a travel package containing more tourist information. These activities are supported by the federal or provincial governments and are examples of how government tourism offices advertise attractions and events to stimulate tourism. As they look for ways to replace jobs lost in agriculture, fishing, forestry, and manufacturing, provincial governments in particular are acting to encourage visitors and expand the tourism industry.

Concessions and Incentives Governments also help the tourism industry grow by offering concessions and incentives. To attract a tourism company to an area, the local government may reduce or waive taxes for a certain time, thus enabling the company to use more of its financial resources in getting started.

Finally, national governments aid the tourism industry by providing travellers with incentives to spend more money. Tax-free shopping at duty-free shops in international airports is an example of this form of government support. Visitors to many countries can apply for tax rebates if they can prove through receipts that they paid the tax. In Canada, there was a GST (Goods and Services Tax) rebate until it was eliminated April 1, 2007; in the United Kingdom it is a VAT (Value-Added Tax) rebate.

Government Regulation

To ensure public safety and to maintain an orderly system, the government requires licences and certificates, imposes rules and regulations, levies taxes and fees, and controls international travel.

Licences and Certificates Provincial governments oversee the testing and licensing of automobile drivers, bus drivers, chauffeurs, and many other vehicle operators. Airline pilots and railway engineers are also tested and licensed, but by the federal government. All vehicles used in the tourism industry must be registered with the government. Also, vehicles used for public transportation are subject to periodic safety inspections, and transportation companies must be certified before they can do business.

Another type of licensing applies to the hospitality industry. Local governments issue food and liquor licences to restaurants and bars. These licences enable the government to control the number, location, and hours of such establishments. Accommodations must also be licensed; to keep operating, they must meet the terms set forth for health and safety.

Rules and Regulations To prevent monopolistic practices and unfair pricing, the government requires transportation companies to keep their tariffs (schedules of rates) on public file. It also approves or refuses to approve fares, routes, and hours of operation, and allows or disallows corporate mergers. Since 1988, however, the federal government has eased its regulation of the transportation industry. The Canadian Transportation Agency regulates the airlines and railways. The provincial governments oversee the motorcoach industry, which is still highly regulated in several provinces. Provincial governments also monitor working conditions in the tourism industry and enforce minimum wage laws. By federal law, employers are required to use the Workplace Hazardous Materials Information System (WHMIS) and train all employees in safe practices. National and provincial codes regulate building standards with respect to health and safety.

Taxes and Fees Tolls are one way a government can raise money. It can also levy taxes and charge fees for the use of other facilities; for example, there are airport landing fees and port and harbour charges. The revenue from sales taxes on tourism products—such as restaurant meals and hotel room stays—also goes to the government. In addition, areas or cities may levy taxes such as a hotel tax. Taxes and fees, if too high, can discourage companies and tourists from coming to a city, region, or country.

International Tourism The federal government encourages foreign travellers to visit Canada, but some visitors are definitely not welcome. These include terrorists, drug smugglers, illegal immigrants, and people with certain infectious diseases. By issuing visas and other documents, a government controls entry to its territory.

Through customs inspections and border checks, our federal government tries to control what products travellers bring into the country. For example, illegal drugs, explosives, and insect-infested fruit are dangerous to the health and welfare of Canadians and are not allowed.

Of course, before there can be any travel between Canada and another country, the two nations must have extended diplomatic recognition to each other. They must also have established embassies or consulates and negotiated agreements on commerce, navigation, visa issuance, and air transport rights. Since the attack on the United States in September 2001, all countries including Canada have been reviewing their current policies and practices with respect to international travel and trade.

New Border Rules between the US and Canada

WHTI In response to growing security concerns, the U.S. government has created the Western Hemisphere Travel Initiative (**WHTI**), which requires a valid passport or other WHTI-approved document (in lieu of a driver's licence and birth certificate) to enter the United States. WHTI has two phases:

Phase 1: Air travel—A passport or equivalent is required by all passengers travelling by air into the United States (already implemented as of January 23, 2007)

Phase 2: Land and sea travel—Effective June 2009, a passport or equivalent is required by all passengers travelling by land or sea into the United States.

NEXUS To enhance security and simplify border crossings for low-risk, pre-approved travellers, the United States Customs and Border Protection (CBP) has created a **NEXUS** card, which can be used to enter the United States and Canada. Ports of entry have designated NEXUS lanes to speed up border crossings for NEXUS cardholders.

CANPASS Similar to NEXUS, the Canada Border Services Agency (CBSA) has implemented the **CANPASS** Air program for pre-approved, low-risk travellers who will only need to have a camera recognize the iris of their eye as proof of identity to clear Canadian customs and immigration when arriving at participating Canadian international airports (Edmonton, Winnipeg, Calgary, Halifax, Ottawa, Montreal, Toronto, and Vancouver).

Check Your Product Knowledge

1. In what way do governments promote tourism?
2. Explain WHTI, NEXUS, and CANPASS.

GEOGRAPHY AND THE TOURISM INDUSTRY

By understanding geography, tourism professionals can know about specific physical and cultural conditions affecting tourism, and gain insight into the psychological and sociological factors affecting travel. Also, understanding how geography influences the tourism industry as a whole and how countries interrelate physically and socially is fundamental to advancing in the tourism industry.

Destination Geography

Many tourism professionals deal in destinations, or places, and need to be able to answer questions regarding three aspects of destinations: location, culture, and physical conditions.

Location A traveller's most basic question about his or her destination is "Where is it?" A travel counsellor must be able to locate the place on a map and show the client its position in relation to other cities, regions, or countries. The next question is "How do I get there?" Visitor information and travel counsellors must be able to provide **itinerary**, or routing, information. Along with this, they need to know how accessible a particular destination is, as well as the other services that are available or not available. When business and leisure travellers arrive at a destination, they expect to find guest contact personnel, from cabdrivers to guest service agents and room attendants, who can answer more specific questions.

Culture Culture refers to the political, historical, social, artistic, and religious characteristics of tourism destinations. Tourists seek answers to questions such as: What should I see and do? Will I be able to communicate with the people? What kind of food can I expect? How much money will I need? Is it safe to drink the water? Tourism professionals need to be able to respond accurately in relation to both the culture of the destination and the culture of the traveller.

Physical Conditions Physical conditions involve climate and landforms. Tourists will ask what the weather is like and what clothes to take, and need to be advised about any conditions that will seem unusual. This means that tourism professionals must be familiar enough with many destinations to be able to anticipate questions and respond appropriately.

System Geography

Besides knowing about specific destinations, tourism professionals need a broad overview of the influence of geography on travel. All tourism enterprises operate within a geographic system or area. Each system has its own climate, terrain, and political and cultural divisions that determine the level of tourist activity and the kinds of travel enterprises needed.

Physical Conditions Climate is a major influence on tourism. Warmer climates tend to draw more tourists than colder ones. In Europe, vacationers flock to the sunny Mediterranean. About 10 percent of Canadians go on a winter vacation in a southern location. In the United States, the warm states of Florida, California, and Texas account for more than one-quarter of tourism receipts. Seasonal variations affect transportation and accommodation rates. Rates are a factor in selling destinations. Therefore, travel counsellors need to be able to advise clients when rates are lower and when destinations may be crowded.

Terrain, too, has a strong influence on tourism. Some fortunate areas have a marvellous natural attraction that stimulates tourism. Tourism enterprises in a mountainous area can take advantage of the terrain by building ski resorts. An area with many lakes can build a resort industry offering swimming, water-skiing, and fishing. The climate and terrain of the Laurentian "playground," just north of Montreal, encouraged the development of a four-season resort industry.

The terrain determines how accessible an area is: Few people vacation in the Amazon Basin because the dense jungle makes travel difficult. Terrain also dictates transportation; if a large body of water lies between the starting point and the destination, the time, cost, and travel conditions of ferry transportation need to be considered.

Culture Geographic areas have political boundaries: city; province, state, or canton; and country. Governments influence how open or how closed an area is and place restrictions on travellers. For example, tourism components in Western Europe are more highly developed than in Eastern Europe because at one time, the governments of the Eastern European nations restricted travel. Travel to the Persian Gulf was severely restricted in the early 1990s after war broke out. In 2001, after the attack on New York City, travel in North America was monitored more rigorously and there were lineups at border crossings and airports. Some people elected to avoid travelling, especially by plane.

Tourism professionals should know about the requirements for passing from one political jurisdiction to another so that they can assist visitors. For international travel, this means helping clients obtain passports, visas, and other travel permits; informing them about necessary vaccinations; and explaining customs and currency regulations. For domestic travel between provinces, it requires being aware of certain information, such as differences in health coverage and costs.

Location Location influences travel and the type of tourism components, products, and services. Remote, underdeveloped locations may have a standard of living different from what a traveller is used to. Travellers need to be made aware of these differences and prepared for them.

Smaller countries with high standards of living and high population densities generate the most international travel. The countries of Western Europe are the best example: Travellers can cross several international boundaries in a short length of time. Canada and the United States do not generate as much international travel because of their large size and greater isolation. Australia and New Zealand are two good examples of geographic isolation hampering international tourism—although this is changing.

Learning about Destinations and Systems

Learning about geography is an ongoing process. Tourism professionals must keep up to date because destinations

and systems are constantly changing. Similarly, a political disturbance, terrorism, a natural disaster, or an unfavourable shift in the currency exchange rate could temporarily discourage travellers from going to a particular destination and influence prices set for the services provided. This was true immediately after the attack on the World Trade Center in New York City.

A destination may have peak times—that is, when there are too many people for the area to handle comfortably. In the summertime, London is extremely crowded with tourists. The number of tour buses visiting the Changing of the Guard ceremony at Buckingham Palace each day must now be limited. British tourism officials promote visits to the quaint villages outside London instead. Natural attractions may have a limited carrying capacity; if so, the number of people admitted is controlled on an hourly or daily basis.

If a destination has become polluted, travellers need to be informed. Some tourists will be very upset to see how acid rain is destroying many beautiful buildings and works of art in many European cities. They may be dismayed by the litter in many national parks in the United States. This presents an opportunity for federal and provincial tourism officials to position Canada in the minds of international tourists as a country with relatively unspoiled natural beauty and clean and well-kept cities.

Individuals working in the tourism industry can keep up with destinations and systems in several ways. One is through visits. They can take familiarization trips (**FAM trips**) to destinations, visit hotels and restaurants, sample attractions, and experience the local culture. FAM trips often are sponsored by airlines, resorts, and other travel and tourism suppliers to showcase established vacation spots and to help promote and sell new destinations. These trips enable service providers to determine whether these areas meet their clients' vacation needs. One can also learn about destinations through personal travel, or by talking to others about their travel experiences, reading travel and trade publications, viewing promotional videos, and visiting websites developed by destinations and service providers. A commitment to professional development through ongoing education and/or membership in professional associations will also advance one's knowledge about destinations and cultural diversity.

Check Your Product Knowledge

1. Why is a knowledge of geography important for tourism professionals?
2. What are three ways you would choose to learn more about destinations and their geographic systems?

TOURISM GROWTH AND THE TOURISM PROFESSIONAL

As the tourism industry grows, it will continue to recruit well-educated and highly motivated men and women for careers in the various sectors of the industry. These professionals include—to name only a few—information and travel counsellors, hotel and restaurant managers, airline pilots, recreation directors, tour operators, sales and marketing representatives, and event planners.

Realities of Tourism/Hospitality Positions

Students must realize that although there are many worthwhile rewards available to those who are interested in a long-term career in the hospitality and tourism field, the path upward may seem at times long and arduous. Entry-level positions in this field may not always be as glamorous as expected, but students should not become discouraged. Many operations are open 24/7 so employees, especially novice employees, are usually scheduled to work weekends, evening shifts, or even the midnight shift (midnight to 8 a.m.). Initially the pay rate may seem low, but it is usually higher than the minimum wage. The exception would be entry-level positions in most fast-food restaurants (also called quick-service restaurants, or QSRs) in the food sector where employees may start at the minimum wage, unless they are unionized and their collective agreement provides for higher wage rates. One must also realize that the skills, knowledge, and positive attitudes learned in any entry-level hospitality/tourism position are usually transferable to many other positions in either the tourism field or in other service industries.

Sometimes the pace of work may become quite hectic, or even chaotic, but part of the challenge and excitement is to see how one can cope with the stress in the workplace, such as the lunch-hour rush in any popular food and beverage outlet. Employees may find some of their tasks tedious, but all of one's duties are important to attain the overall goal of customer satisfaction, hopefully at a profit. The old saying "You must pay your dues" before you can climb the corporate ladder of success to the different levels of management often applies in many organizations, not just in the hospitality and tourism field. Most airline employees receive a limited number of discounted or free air tickets annually, many hotel employees receive a limited number of discounted or free hotel rooms annually, and most restaurant employees receive a free staff meal for each shift worked. More rewards and perks are received by those in supervisory and management positions—these depend on one's seniority, the type of operation, and the size and profitability of the organization.

Tourism Requires the Basics of Business You might be seeking a career in the tourism industry because of its glamorous image—exotic destinations, luxurious cruise ships, speedy jet travel, beautiful scenery, ancient castles, exciting activities, and entertainment. The tourism industry does, of course, have this attractive side. But it is also a business, and if you are going to be a successful tourism professional, you must understand the supply and demand sides of tourism, and tourism as a service industry, and you must practise the basics of business. These basics include communications, information management, accounting, financial management, human resource management, operations management, and marketing and sales. You must also understand the relationship between government and the tourism business and have a sincere desire to help people. Throughout this book you will find references to the motivations, needs, and expectations of tourists. These three forces shape people's travel plans, so successful tourism professionals make a point of understanding the MNEs of the people they serve.

Finally, as a tourism professional, you will need to be creative and flexible in keeping up with an industry that is constantly growing and changing. For those who are prepared to make the effort, the tourism industry offers many exciting and rewarding career opportunities. More career information will be presented in the following chapters.

Welcome aboard! Bon voyage! We trust you find each chapter an interesting and informative port of call.

A DAY IN THE LIFE OF A

Family Hotel Operator

You could say that I was quite literally born into my job. I own a hotel with 35 rooms in Niagara-on-the-Lake, Ontario. My grandfather bought the hotel in the 1940s, and when he retired 20 years later, my parents took over the business. I've lived in my parents' hotel all my life and began working here when I was about eight or nine.

My first jobs were to turn on the lights at night and put out the silverware in the dining room for lunch and dinner. Later I did all sorts of jobs around the hotel—cleaning rooms, cooking, waiting tables, fixing toilets, patching the roof, staffing the front desk. By the time I went to hotel management at Sir Sandford Fleming College of Applied Arts and Technology, I was already able to perform every job in my family's hotel.

After I graduated, I went to work for a large hotel chain as an assistant desk manager. It just wasn't the same as working for my own family, though. I soon quit and returned to Ontario to help my father manage our hotel. A couple of years later I met my wife. She had taken a summer job waitressing in our dining room. Today she is our bookkeeper and office manager.

My parents retired a few years ago and turned the entire hotel over to my wife and me. Now we have two children who are beginning to learn the business. Of course, I hope that when they grow up they will want to continue running the hotel.

During the summer tourist season, my day usually starts in the dining room and kitchen. I supervise the kitchen staff and help serve breakfast to our guests. Then I may hold a management meeting with my supervisory staff or spend a couple of hours in the office doing paperwork. In the afternoon, I visit the housekeeping and maintenance staff and check in with the front office to make sure everything is running smoothly. In the evenings, I again help out in the kitchen and dining room. I also spend a lot of time mingling with the guests, getting to know them and listening to their comments and complaints.

During the winter, I plan for the next season, order supplies, and oversee maintenance and repairs. I also attend trade shows and conventions to drum up business for my hotel among travel agents and tour operators. Sometimes I make recruiting trips to schools that offer hotel and restaurant courses to find new employees. Because ours is a seasonal business, we have to hire a new staff each year. Some years, many employees from the year before come back; in other years, most of our employees are new people.

Running a small family hotel like ours is very different from working for a large hotel chain. When you work for a chain, you are just a wage earner. When you run a family hotel, you are the owner of your own business. Chains employ large staffs. You may do only one job or learn only one part of the business. You can take a day off and someone else will be there to do your work. At a small family-owned hotel, you must be able to do every job because if someone takes a day off, there's no one else to step in. You have to roll up your sleeves and pitch in.

Running a family-owned hotel can be very difficult, but it also has special rewards. One of the great pleasures of running my hotel is that I have made a great many friends over the years. Some guests come back year after year. As a child, I played with the children of our guests. Now their children play with mine. I always look forward to a new tourist season because it means I will be able to renew many old friendships.

I love owning my own hotel because I like being my own boss. I really like working with the people—the employees and guests—who come to the hotel each year. Sometimes when the chef calls in sick or a toilet is overflowing, I might wish I were in another line of work, but not really. I love it even then.

Summary

- A calm political climate throughout most of the world, improvements in transportation, a rise in personal incomes, and increased leisure time have all stimulated the growth of travel and tourism, as well as a new North American psyche with regard to seizing opportunities now, not tomorrow.
- Tourism is an industry because it comprises companies that work as a profit-making system to provide travellers with products and services.
- Tourism products are mainly intangible, in that they include experiences such as a ride on a train, a visit to a national park, and a stay in a hotel.
- Tourism services provide benefits to travellers. They are performed by professionals within a host–guest relationship.
- The tourism industry in Canada functions in a mixed enterprise system—that is, privately owned businesses compete in the marketplace with government-owned parks, attractions, and infrastructure.
- To be successful in the marketplace, the tourism professional must bring the right product or service to the right marketplace at the right time and at the right price. The tourism professional, especially the travel counsellor, must also promote the product and determine whether it satisfies the consumer.
- Recognizing the tourism industry's potential to generate jobs, the government promotes tourism by providing facilities, publicity, concessions, and incentives.
- The government regulates tourism by requiring licences and certificates, imposing rules and regulations, levying taxes and fees, and controlling international travel. Government regulation seeks to protect the health, safety, and welfare of citizens.
- The climate, terrain, location, and politics of a geographic area affect the level and type of tourism activity.
- Tourism professionals should strive to give visitors a clear picture of any destination. Knowledge of the location, culture, and physical conditions of a destination enables tourism professionals—especially information and travel counsellors—to do this.
- Tourism professionals need to know about tourism, business, psychology, and geography. They must be able to adapt to a dynamic industry and understand various consumers' motivations, needs, and expectations (MNEs).

Key Terms

CANPASS   p. 20
domestic tourism   p. 5
domestic travel   p. 4
FAM trips   p. 21
inbound tourism   p. 5
intangible tourism product   p. 9
internal tourism   p. 5
international tourism   p. 5
itinerary   p. 20
national tourism   p. 5
NEXUS   p. 20
outbound tourism   p. 5
tangible tourism product   p. 9
tourism   p. 5
WHTI   p. 19

Internet Connections

Canada Border Services Agency (CBSA)
www.cbsa.org   p. 20

Canada Revenue Agency (CRA)
www.cra-arc.gc.ca

Canadian Tourism Commission (CTC)
www.corporate.canada.travel   p. 4

Canadian Tourism Human Resource Council (CTHRC)
www.cthrc.ca   p. 6

Cape Breton Whale Watching
www.cabottrail.com/whales

Culture (Canada)
Canada for Visitors
www.gocanada.about.com

Information for the Canadian Traveller
(Foreign Affairs Canada)
www.voyage.gc.ca

Delta Hotels
www.deltahotels.com   p. 11

Department of Homeland Security (USA)
www.dhs.gov

Fairmont Hotels & Resorts
www.fairmont.com   p. 14

National Quality Institute
www.nqi.ca   p. 11

Physical Conditions (p. 20)
Canadian Geographic Online
www.canadiangeographic.ca

Point Pelee
www.pelee.com   p. 9

Province/Territory Government Tourism Offices (p. 19)
Go to the government website of any of the provinces or territories and enter "tourism" in the Search window.

Statistics Canada
www.statcan.gc.ca   pp. 4, 5, 6

Thomas Cook
www.thomascook.ca   p. 3

Tourism Industry Association of Canada (TIAC)
www.tiac-aitc.ca   p. 4

Tourism Industry Association of Nova Scotia (TIANS)
www.tians.org   p. 7

Transport Canada
www.tc.gc.ca   p. 19

Travel Trade (pp. 2, 8, 9)
   The Great Canadian Adventure Company
   www.adventures.ca

United Nations (UN)
www.un.org   pp. 2, 4, 17, 18

United Nations World Tourism Organization (UNWTO)
www.unwto.org   pp. 2, 17, 18

United States Customs and Border Protection (CBP)
www.cbp.gov   p. 20

Walt Disney Company
disney.go.com   p. 10

WORKSHEET 1–1   Destination Geography

First, choose a destination—the more exotic and unfamiliar to you the better. Then do research on this destination, on the Internet if possible, so that you can draw up a geographic profile that would be useful to a tourist who is planning to travel to that destination.

Local Geography

1. Name of destination

2. Location of destination

3. How to get there

Cultural Geography

4. Language(s) spoken

5. General health conditions

6. Type of food

7. Type of clothing worn

8. Currency used and exchange rate in dollars

9. Cost of living

10. Availability of basic items

11. Unusual conditions or customs

Physical Geography

12. Climate, in winter and summer

13. On-season and off-season

14. Clothing needed

15. Terrain

16. Local transportation

WORKSHEET 1–2   The Ps of Marketing

In this chapter you learned about the Ps of marketing. Study the ad on this page and then answer the questions about the 9 Ps with respect to the ad.

1. Product

What are the tangible benefits of the product?

_____
_____
_____

What might be some of the intangible benefits of the product?

_____
_____
_____

2. Price

What is the cost of the product?

_____
_____

3. Place

Where can buyer and seller meet to transact business?

_____
_____
_____

4. Promotion

What has the seller done to create consumer interest in the product?

_____
_____
_____

5. Packaging

What does the "Great Escape Weekend" package include?

_____
_____
_____

6. Partnerships

Who are the partners involved in the "Great Escape Weekend"?

_____
_____

7. Personnel

If you participated in the "Great Escape Weekend," what opportunities would you have to assess the quality of the service?

_____
_____
_____

8. Positioning

(a) What market position is indicated by the ad?
(b) What features were presented to communicate the position?

_____
_____
_____

9. Programming

What events or activities could have been identified in the ad that would serve as incentives for a family with preschool children?

_____
_____
_____

GREAT ESCAPE WEEKEND

Starting Friday or Saturday
at the Granite Springs Resort

$682.00 per person
(double occupancy)

Includes the following:

- 4 nights' lodging
- 3 dinners
- buffet breakfast
- drink coupons
- nightly entertainment
- indoor pool & sauna
- cable TV

- free parking
- 3-day ski-lift pass at Silver Cloud Slopes
- kids' ski school at Silver Cloud Slopes
- airport transportation by Grayline Shuttle

Limited number of packages available.
Round-trip airfare additional.
Contact us for details.

Granite Springs Resort
P.O. Box 28
Snowton, QC J8X 4N2

1-800-333-3333

granitesprings@AOL.com

Objectives

When you have completed this chapter, you should be able to:

- Explain how the concept of travel has changed through the ages.
- Describe the three main groups of travellers and their motivations, needs, and expectations (MNEs).
- Explain why the tourism industry classifies travellers into groups or segments, and how tourism professionals obtain information about each segment.
- Explain why people travel for pleasure in terms of both Stanley Plog's theory of personality types and Abraham Maslow's theory of need satisfaction.

- Identify some of the reasons why Canadians might be interested in travelling within Canada.
- Describe the MNEs of inbound visitors to Canada.
- Discuss the special issues of international tourism, such as documentation, customs regulations and security, common health problems, and foreign currencies.

Passengers on the overnight Air Canada Flight 017 from Las Vegas are deplaning in Toronto. A couple who had been visiting family in Scottsdale, Arizona, pass through customs on their way to catch a flight to Halifax. A business executive glances at her watch and is worried the plane will have to be de-iced, thus delaying takeoff. University students, returning to Vancouver after their winter break, wait anxiously. They are flying on standby. An attendant driving a vehicle similar to a motorized golf course jitney takes a young, physically disabled male to his flight. As the Halifax-bound couple arrive at their gate, they see a group of tourists from Europe on their way to Prince Edward Island. The Europeans are on an ecotourism trip to Canada, a travel package that includes a helicopter flight to the pack ice in the Gulf of St. Lawrence to see newborn seal pups.

These are modern-day travellers, the guests who create demand for tourism services. "Travel" is often used synonymously with the term "tourism." In this chapter, as you consider "travellers," you will find it helpful to remember that "travel" includes the actions and activities of people taking trips to a place or places outside their home community for any purpose except daily commuting to and from work (McIntosh et al., 1995). The Canadian Travel Survey conducted annually by Statistics Canada defines a domestic "trip" as "travel to a Canadian destination at least 80 kilometres one-way from home for any reason" with some exceptions, including travel for more than one year.

In this chapter you will be introduced to the categories of travellers—why they travel and where they go.

A BRIEF HISTORY OF TRAVEL

There have always been travellers. The Old Testament describes the journey of the Israelites from Egypt to the Promised Land. The walls of a temple in Luxor, Egypt, chronicle the pleasure cruise of Queen Hatshepsut to the ancient land of Punt (possibly what is now Somalia). The Royal Ontario Museum in Toronto has a huge replica of these walls. History books provide accounts of famous travellers such as the Vikings, Marco Polo, and Christopher Columbus. Fossil remains of *Homo erectus* have been found in Africa, China, and Western Europe. So even prehistoric people were travellers.

Requirements for Travel

During the Industrial Revolution, which began in the mid-1700s in Europe, travel became more common. Around that time, a series of developments in transportation—the stagecoach, then the steamboat, and finally the railway—made travel easier in both North America and Europe. There were also social changes that contributed to the growth of travel. A middle-class society with money and leisure time was developing. Wishing to escape occasionally from bleak city life, these people travelled to seaside resorts for recreation.

PROFILE

A Man for All Seasons

Isadore Sharp, Chairman and CEO, Four Seasons Hotels and Resorts

Founded in 1960 by Isadore Sharp, Four Seasons traces its roots to a revolutionary idea at that time. It set about providing global business travellers with what they wanted: personalized service available round-the-clock. Thus, a new kind of luxury hotel experience evolved. The story of the Four Seasons under Sharp's more than 40 years of leadership is one of continuous innovation, remarkable expansion, and single-minded dedication to the highest standards. This Canadian-based company has combined North American friendliness and efficiency with the best international hotel-keeping traditions, and has redefined luxury for the modern traveller.

How did Four Seasons grow from one modest motel in downtown Toronto to being the world's leading operator of luxury hotels? In the 1960s and 1970s, international travel was an emerging trend. It led to demand for a new kind of luxury hotel service. Sharp recognized the opportunity the trend provided and capitalized on it.

Sharp grew up in Toronto and earned a degree in architecture from Ryerson Polytechnical Institute [now Ryerson University] in 1952. After graduating, he joined his father's small construction firm. Sharp founded the Four Seasons company when he built and opened his first motel in 1961 on Jarvis Street in downtown Toronto. It had 165 rooms. The venture was considered by some to be risky; it was, after all, in one of the least affluent neighbour-

hoods in the city and far from the business district.

But from the start, Sharp was an innovator, and his instincts have seldom failed him. As soon as his first motel was established, he built the Inn on the Park in Toronto's northern suburbs. This hotel was situated on a high point of land and had beautifully landscaped grounds. Despite initial scepticism about its location, the hotel flourished. In 1970, he decided to expand outside Toronto and built the five-star Inn on the Park (now called the Four Seasons London) in London, England. Once again, many thought he would fail. Why build a five-star hotel in a city that already offered several luxury hotels? The Four Seasons London, with its spacious rooms equipped for both business and relaxation, and with its friendly staff to make every traveller's wish a reality, was a success.

Sharp realized that the marketplace was lacking medium-sized hotels of exceptional quality, with exceptional levels of service. He set out to focus on this niche and embarked on a targeted course of expansion that has continued for more than 40 years. Today there are 76 Four Seasons Hotels and Resorts in 32 countries.

Sharp's company has changed over the years. In the 1970s, it concentrated on operating "medium-sized hotels of exceptional quality." Then, in the 1980s, it began to manage hotels instead of owning them. The company prospered by applying its sense

ILLUSTRATION 2–1

From its first hotel on Jarvis Street in Toronto, Four Seasons Hotels and Resorts has grown into one of the world's largest luxury hotel chains.

SOURCE: CP PHOTO/Steve White.

of quality and style to other companies' properties. As the Four Seasons expanded, the company became the first in North America to introduce items that are now accepted as industry standards: bath amenities, terrycloth robes, hairdryers, and multiple two-line telephones (i.e., in the guest room and bath). Four Seasons was the first to introduce the following and make them available at every property it operates: concierge service; 24/7 room service with innovative choices of cuisine; twice-daily housekeeping service; and round-the-clock one-hour pressing and four-hour laundry and dry-cleaning service.

"We have aspired to be the best hotel in every location where we operate," Sharp says. "Early in the company's history we decided to focus on defining luxury as service and that became our strategic edge. . . . They [the employees] are the standard bearers for the intuitive, highly personalized service we aspire to provide."

A new avenue of growth opened in the 1990s, when the company began extending its unique approach to leisure properties. By 2008, it had 29 resorts worldwide. Four Seasons innovations to serve the leisure traveller include strikingly designed rooms and amenities, extra-spacious baths, and intuitive, anticipatory service poolside and on the golf links. It makes available chilled towels and Evian spray, exceptional food and beverage options, and creative activities for all ages.

Following the success of Four Seasons Resorts, the company introduced Residence Clubs (a fractional ownership or timeshare concept) and Private Residences (apartments and condominiums that could be purchased outright) in several locations. The company was sold in 2007 to Bill Gates and Saudi Arabian interests.

One of the most important ingredients in the company's success is its commitment to a very high quality of service. It continues to find new responses to the changing lifestyles of global travellers and is willing to customize its services to meet their needs. The company's president of Worldwide Hotel Operations said: "Today, more than ever, time is our guests'

most precious commodity. What they value are services designed to help them use their time well, whether travelling for business or leisure. We see this with room service breakfast. No longer just for leisurely breakfasts in bed, it is used most by the business traveller to save valuable time. One can check e-mail, watch CNN, scan *The Wall Street Journal*, get dressed and have a full breakfast—all in the comfort of one's room and within a thirty-minute slot." Resort properties offer the Kids for All Seasons program, which provides supervised activities for children and lets parents have some vacation time too. By 2001, all Four Seasons resorts included on-site spa services. These various services are designed to make business travel more productive and efficient and leisure travel more enjoyable and comfortable.

This is the kind of service that has inspired loyalty among guests and made the company's name one of the most respected in the international hotel business. The hotel staff and managers pride themselves on their fast, friendly, and tactful service. Also, Four Seasons concierges are among the most highly skilled and dedicated in the world. They must be knowledgeable and helpful, must have a ready command of the geography and amenities of their city, must speak at least two languages, and, above all, must be able to maintain their professionalism and grace under fire. As Gander Lurer of the Four Seasons in Washington, D.C., says, "Our clientele expects the best. We never say no, never say can't."

Not surprisingly, the company has also been successful as an employer, and has one of the lowest turnover rates in the hotel industry. Four Seasons locker rooms and staff cafeterias are nearly as well appointed as the guest facilities. Employees are valued highly and are treated accordingly. Four Seasons employees were empowered—and practising it—before the term "empowerment" was coined.

Four Seasons is continuing to expand; around the world, it has more than 31 new properties under construction or in development. Some are business hotels in financial centres; others represent the next generation of exceptional destination resorts. The company was not immune to the global economic impact of September 11. It already had a strategy for responding to the tremendous acceleration in world travel, in both the leisure and the business markets; now it is faced with a new environment, at least in the immediate future.

Four Seasons has established a reputation for making business travel easier and leisure travel more rewarding through understated luxury and personalized, anticipatory service.

"We define the experience through the service we provide," says Isadore Sharp, "and we strive to offer the same high level of personalized service from visit to visit, and from hotel to hotel. It is this quality of service that is critically important to our guests, and the degree to which we can provide and evolve it, worldwide, is also the degree to which we can differentiate ourselves and stay ahead of the rest."

SOURCES: Peter Brierger, "Four Seasons to Double Properties," *Financial Post*, May 31, 2001, p. C3; *The Four Seasons Profile* (www.fourseasons.com).

In the twentieth century, the development of automobiles and motorcoaches created a demand for better roads, and people were soon driving all over Canada and the United States. Once transatlantic passenger jet service became available in the late 1950s, fast, comfortable, and economical international travel was possible.

In the past 50 years, the volume of travel has increased tremendously. This is partly the result of improvements in transportation, but economic prosperity and social change have also contributed. At one time, only wealthy people travelled for pleasure; in today's industrial societies, more people have enough income to spend some of it on travel. Many households are dual-income, and so have disposable income for travel. Paid annual vacations and holidays allow people more leisure time for travel. People are better educated today; in general, the more educated a person is, the more likely he or she is to travel. People are also living longer. Many senior citizens can afford to take trips any time of the year. For most Canadians, travel has become a normal part of the good life.

Reasons for Travel

At one time, people travelled out of necessity rather than for pleasure. They travelled to satisfy basic survival needs—searching for food and shelter or fleeing from enemies. Many people travelled in search of a better life. Perhaps they were looking for gold, silver, or other treasures. Or they were searching for fertile land to feed their families.

This is not to say that no one ever travelled just for fun. Even in ancient times, there was some pleasure travel. In a typical season, 700 000 tourists crowded into Ephesus, a city in Asia Minor, where they were entertained by acrobats, animal acts, jugglers, and magicians. Wealthy Romans made excursions to Greece to take in festivals, the theatre, and the Olympic Games.

Some people travelled just out of curiosity. They wanted to know what lay beyond the horizon or around the next bend in the road. In the Middle Ages, people went on pilgrimages to holy cities and shrines. During the Crusades (1095–1291), Christians tried to wrest control of the Holy Land from the Muslims; these were the most ambitious religious journeys of all. Passports date back to 1388, when Richard II (the Lion-Hearted) began requiring English pilgrims to obtain and carry permits before they could travel to France. There has been travel for the purposes of trade—in other words, business travel—for millennia. As long as 3100 years ago, Phoenician traders were sailing from port to port in the Mediterranean world. Early travel in China and India was based on trade.

Sites of historic and cultural significance have long attracted travellers. This reason for travel originated with the grand tour during the Renaissance and Elizabethan eras. As part of their education, the sons of the British aristocracy travelled extensively in Europe, often for up to

three years. Accompanied by tutors and servants, these young gentlemen visited cathedrals, castles, and galleries, especially those of France and Italy. They learned to speak several languages and were introduced to Europe's aristocracy.

Notions about medical cures have also influenced travel. In the 1800s, it was fashionable for members of the European aristocracy to visit various German spas (different spas claimed to treat different maladies). These people sipped mineral water by day and then entertained themselves at night with banquets, dancing, and gambling.

Check Your Product Knowledge

1. How is the modern concept of travel different from that of the Middle Ages?
2. In order for travel to occur on a wide scale, what conditions are necessary?
3. Why has travel increased in the past 50 years?

WHO TRAVELS TODAY?

At one time, wealthy travellers had similar expectations of travel. For example, in the 1920s anyone who was anybody took the grand tour of Europe. It was fairly easy for hotel managers, captains of ocean liners, and other travel professionals to anticipate the needs of these travellers and serve them satisfactorily.

Today's travellers are a much more diverse group. However, as a tourism professional, you can begin to understand today's travellers and their motivations, needs, and expectations (MNEs) by dividing them into three general categories: (1) the vacation and leisure traveller, (2) the business traveller, and (3) the traveller visiting friends and relatives (VFR). You will soon learn more about the differences within traveller market segments.

The Vacation and Leisure Traveller

People who exemplify the vacation and leisure travel segment include a family spending a week in Florida at Disney World, a college or university student spending the summer exploring Europe, and a retired couple taking a one-week cruise to Bermuda.

Discretionary Travel Vacation and leisure travel is often called **discretionary travel**. The word "discretion" refers to the ability to make a choice, judgment, or decision. Vacation and leisure travellers take trips because they want to—travel is voluntary for them. They choose whether to stay home, drive to the Laurentians, or fly to the Caribbean.

In the same vein, the money that vacation and leisure travellers spend is called **discretionary income**. Discretionary income is the money that's left over after life's necessities—shelter, food, clothing—have been purchased. People choose how they want to spend their discretionary income. Some choose to spend it on travel; others may choose to spend it on a boat or a second home. Since the competition is strong among many industries for consumers' discretionary income, the components of the travel industry must work together to persuade consumers to spend their money on travel.

The Pleasure Seekers In general, vacation and leisure travellers seek pleasure and relaxation. However, the concept of pleasure varies from individual to individual, so one person's idea of the perfect vacation is another person's idea of a total waste of time and money. Some travellers enjoy exploring ancient ruins; others prefer sunbathing by the ocean. More will be said about specific motivations for pleasure travel later in this chapter.

Another feature of vacation and leisure travel is that the pleasure comes not only during the trip but also before and after. Planning the itinerary, shopping for clothes to take, and researching the destination can be as enjoyable as the trip itself. Once back home, putting together a scrapbook of the trip or showing videos to friends and relatives sustains the pleasure.

The Family Travel Market Families are travelling more, but the trips are shorter. Families can choose from a number of options: adventure or outdoor travel, a cruise or theme park, a resort or ski centre are only some alternatives. Hotels are becoming more kid-friendly. Many include supervised activities for children of all ages.

A number of changes in family travel have occurred as the baby boomers move into the "empty nest stage" and toward retirement. The needs of both young people and seniors may need to be served simultaneously as intergenerational travel increases. More single-parent families are travelling. These families, which tend to stay longer in one place, represent a growth market. Until quite recently, most family packages were designed for two-parent families.

Globe-Trotting Seniors Statistics Canada reports that this country's senior population (65 and older) is the fastest growing in the world. By 2041, more than one in five Canadians will be over 65. Seniors usually go on longer trips, and their trips outside Canada generally last more than a month, including travel to the United States and overseas. For these people, Florida is the second most important American destination after the state of Washington, and almost 150 000 Canadian seniors travel to Nevada every year. Mature travellers also visit Mexico, where they can enjoy a warm, sunny climate and the chance to explore a rich culture and historical sites.

ILLUSTRATION 2–2
Intergenerational travel is a growing market segment.
SOURCE: © Bill Bachmann/Index Stock Imagery.

Senior travellers can take advantage of off-season rates and travel when it is less busy. They tend to travel in Canada in July to September but overseas in the nonpeak period. Seniors tend to drive more often than fly, and are more likely than other travellers to travel by bus. Two out of ten seniors' trips to the United States are by plane. Among seniors, more women than men travel, especially to the United States; for other age groups, the opposite is true. The tendency to travel increases with education, and in the future there will be more educated seniors than was the case in the past.

Nonfamily Travel The number of adults travelling to Canada without children has been increasing since 1990. The most typical American party travelling to Canada comprises two adults. However, solo travellers account for about one in five adult-only parties. Solo or not, adults are a different type of traveller. One-quarter of them arrive by plane. Also, they space their trips through the year, though the summer season is the most popular. Adults travel

ILLUSTRATION 2–3

Mature travellers enjoy active pursuits such as golf, walking, and hiking.

SOURCE: Photodisc Blue/Getty Images.

everywhere in the country; favoured destinations include Vancouver and Toronto. Couples especially favour Halifax and Victoria.

Mature travellers (51 and over) travel without children. Golf, walking, and hiking are among the activities that attract this group. They are contributing to the rise in demand for culture and heritage travel, which involves travelling farther and for longer time periods. Participants in cultural and heritage events tend to be women with postsecondary education. Because mature travellers often have higher incomes, they are a more upscale market segment. Mature business travellers take their spouses along 25 percent of the time. Over the next few years, combined business and pleasure travel with spouses may well be a growing market segment.

Adults travelling alone in Canada travel by plane twice as often, and by motorcoach four times as often, as adults travelling with children. They travel farther and commonly stay with friends and relatives. Their predominant activities include outdoor sports or activities, walking or hiking, swimming, and (less often) going to a bar or nightclub.

Purchasing Travel Products and Services When they purchase travel products and services, vacation and leisure travellers are essentially buying a pleasurable (they hope) experience. To satisfy their needs, vacation and leisure travellers select products and services from several of the tourism sectors.

Vacation and leisure travellers have time to shop around for the products that best suit their needs. Often they wait for discounted prices or a last-minute sale before choosing a trip. Their schedules are more flexible than those of business travellers, so they can take advantage of the travel restrictions that accompany discounted airfares. Vacation and leisure travellers are likely to purchase a package of travel products that includes transportation, accommodation, and sightseeing.

The Business Traveller

A sales representative who sells pharmaceutical products to physicians and pharmacists throughout New Brunswick, Nova Scotia, and Prince Edward Island; an efficiency expert who inspects operations at a company's branch locations; and the manager of a Manitoba farmers' co-op who must attend parliamentary hearings in Ottawa are all business travellers.

Business travel is **nondiscretionary travel**. Business travellers usually do not have a choice about whether to travel or where—travel is part of their job. They do it to get their work done.

The Frequent Business Traveller Most areas of the tourism industry define frequent business travellers as people who take 10 or more trips per year, with each trip averaging four nights. Because of the potential for repeat business, service providers can benefit by understanding and satisfying these travellers' motivations, needs, and expectations. Business travellers often stay in hotels and receive specialized services as preferred guests. These travellers typically enjoy instant check-in, special rates, and points for booking; service providers often call them by name and remember their preferences from their previous visits.

The Female Business Traveller Women are an important part of the business traveller market. In the early 1970s, when women began travelling for business in large numbers, the tourism industry wasn't quite sure how to treat them. Although service providers are learning to accommodate women's particular needs and are receiving sensitivity training, the question "What do women travellers want?" still hasn't been answered fully.

Many women treat business trips as a chance to escape from the detail-oriented responsibilities of family and office. Generally they travel alone, but some travel with children and combine business with pleasure, especially if they are single parents. Female business travellers should be offered the same respect that is afforded their male counterparts, and the same excellent service. However, they don't always get it.

The Professional Traveller A variation of business travel is professional travel. Professional travellers attend conventions and seminars related to their work. These meetings usually provide participants with information and skills to help them perform their jobs better. For example, a physician might attend a medical convention to obtain the latest information on the treatment of allergies. A sales representative might attend a seminar on how to improve selling skills.

Professional travel is discretionary in that attendance at conventions and seminars is often optional. At the same time, it is nondiscretionary in the sense that travellers do not decide the date or location of the convention or seminar. Some professional travellers are also business travellers, and vice versa. For example, a salesperson who often travels for business may also attend an annual sales convention.

Time as a Factor in Business Travel Time is very important for business travellers. They must arrive at meetings on time and they must get their work done on time. Since every minute away from their office costs money, they can't afford to waste time on delays and errors.

When they purchase travel products and services, business travellers are essentially buying time. Products that furnish speed, efficiency, and convenience of location provide them with time. Business travellers generally purchase air transportation to and from their destination, a rental car for on-demand local transportation, and accommodation in a major hotel near their meeting site. If they

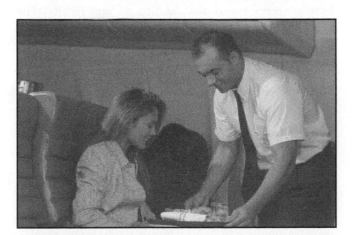

ILLUSTRATION 2–4

For business travellers, travel is part of a day's work.
SOURCE: Jack Hollingsworth/Photodisc Green/Getty Images.

have nonscheduled time, they may participate in leisure activities.

The schedules of business travellers are less flexible than those of vacation and leisure travellers. Often, because they can't plan their trips far in advance, they can't take advantage of discount airfares and other bargains. To obtain speed, efficiency, and convenience, business travellers must often pay higher prices for travel products and services. Quick, reliable service is a priority for most travellers, but especially for business travellers.

Other Motivations, Needs, and Expectations Male and female business travellers have the same MNEs. According to surveys, business travellers of both genders rank convenience of schedule as the number-one factor in choosing an airline, and convenience of location as the number-one factor in choosing a hotel. They often want to be able to do work while travelling to a business appointment. They want to be able to check in and out quickly at hotels and airports; they also want a hotel room that provides business support systems as well as the comforts and conveniences they need. They need quiet to think and relax. They appreciate a zone or floor designated especially for them. When travelling abroad, business travellers may have additional needs, especially in relation to communications. They may require translation services in order to conduct business.

Women travelling on business don't want to be treated rudely by flight attendants, called "honey" or "dear" by room attendants, or ogled by guest-service agents. Women appreciate the fact that nowadays most hotel rooms provide hair dryers, skirt hangers, and irons and ironing boards. When they dine alone in a restaurant, they don't want to be seated in a dark corner by the kitchen. Safety is always a concern for women, so they don't appreciate poorly lit parking areas, and it is unacceptable for the check-in agent to announce a female guest's room number in front of other people.

The Traveller Visiting Friends and Relatives

A father taking his children to Saskatchewan to visit their grandparents, alumni attending their college or university reunion, and a daughter returning home because her father is ill are travellers visiting friends and relatives. Some visiting friends and relatives (VFR) travel is discretionary; some is not. If the traveller is visiting high-school friends or spending some time with family members simply to enjoy their company, the travel is discretionary. If the traveller must take a trip because of an emergency, such as an illness in the family, the travel is nondiscretionary.

Travellers visiting friends and relatives for pleasure are like leisure travellers in their purchase of travel products. Travellers visiting friends and relatives because of an emergency are more like business travellers, with an added element of stress. In either case, they are likely to purchase only transportation, and perhaps some tourism products and services. The friends and relatives usually supply the meals and the accommodation.

Seniors are more likely to travel to visit friends and relatives (52 percent of their trips, versus 41 percent for all travellers). They are also more likely to travel alone by car when travelling in their home province. VFR travel is already a large component of overnight domestic travel, and is expected to expand in the next decade as more people retire and gain more leisure time. The VFR market is an important one, but it is a more self-reliant market and depends less on service providers in the tourism industry.

Check Your Product Knowledge

1. What are the three main groups of modern-day travellers?
2. What is the purpose of dividing travellers into these groups?
3. What are some of the characteristics of each group?

THE PLEASURE TRAVEL MARKET

Imagine that you're a travel counsellor in a retail travel agency. A woman who appears to be in her late thirties comes into your office. She introduces herself as Janet O'Neill and says she wants help planning a trip to Mexico. You ask if she would like to see brochures describing family vacations in Mexico, but O'Neill says she'll be travelling without her family. You then ask if she's seeking a sun vacation on the Mexican Riviera, but that's not it either. O'Neill tells you she's bored with the routine of everyday life. What she really wants is a vacation experience that will challenge her mind and imagination. After thinking for a moment, you suggest that she go to Mexico to study the architectural legacy of the Aztecs. She agrees that is a wonderful idea.

Discovering a vacation traveller's motives for travelling is very important. A travel counsellor needs this information in order to sell the client the right travel product for his or her needs. In O'Neill's case, a family vacation tour or a resort vacation would clearly have been the wrong product.

To define the product further, the travel counsellor needs to ask questions relating to the client's background and lifestyle. So, you would ask O'Neill questions such as: Do you want to travel alone or with a group? What kind of accommodation do you want? About how much money do you want to spend? How long do you want to stay? After discussing these questions, you and O'Neill may well agree

that she should join a study tour to Mexico that is being organized by the Museum of Civilization in Gatineau, Quebec.

Who Are the Market Targets?

Today's travellers are a diverse group with varying MNEs. Consequently, the tourism industry doesn't create one product and then try to sell it to everybody. For example, the industry recognizes that young, unmarried people form a market different from those for senior citizens and young families. The realization that the travel market is really many submarkets has fostered a concept known as **market segmentation**. At an early stage in tourism marketing, the present and potential market is divided into segments according to meaningful characteristics.

There are thousands of market segments, and there is no standard classification system. As you've already seen, a general classification system is that of vacation and leisure traveller, business traveller, and traveller visiting friends and relatives. But each of these can be further segmented according to travel habits and preferences, mode of transportation used, how travel arrangements are made, class of service purchased, and so on. Furthermore, each component of the tourism industry may have one or more ways of segmenting its own market. For example, airlines classify their customers into first class, business class, and economy class. But they also categorize them according to destinations and routes.

The tourism industry depends on two kinds of marketing research when identifying and describing each market segment. **Primary research** is carried out by the tourism industry itself. For instance, airlines, bus companies, and cruise ship lines—or marketing firms hired by them—conduct on-board surveys of passengers. Hotels leave questionnaires in guests' rooms and periodically review their guest ledgers to obtain feedback on their services and their clients' levels of satisfaction. Airlines and hotels interview travellers at airports and resorts. The other kind of research, called **secondary research**, is based on information from other sources, such as the regular census conducted by the federal government and studies conducted by the Canadian Tourism Research Institute of the Conference Board of Canada.

It is assumed that the travellers in a particular market segment have similar purchasing habits. With the information gathered through market research, the tourism industry can tailor specific products for that segment and plan specific marketing strategies. Target markets can be defined geographically, demographically (i.e., by age, income, education, race, nationality, family size, family life cycle, gender, religion, and occupation), and psychographically (according to values, motivations, interests, attitudes, and desires).

Geography Geography segments tourists in many ways. There are **destination visitors**, who come from a long distance; **regional visitors**, who live within four hours' drive of a destination; and **local residents**. The distance that tourists are from a destination, combined with what motivates them, dictates whether they will be attracted to tourism products and services. By understanding these variables, it is possible to develop the type of promotion needed to attract them.

Geography is also used to segment people by where they live. For example, people who live in cities often seek an escape to a quieter, rural environment to help them slow down and reduce the stress of urban living. Such a break is unlikely to appeal to those living in smaller, rural communities. These travellers, however, may well be interested in a weekend theatre and shopping package to Toronto. Similarly, during the months of November to March in northern latitudes, a Caribbean destination is likely to focus its marketing on attracting those seeking a break from the cold winter. Between May and September they may switch their marketing efforts to southern countries where the seasons are reversed or try to develop a new market, such as conferences or events.

Demographics **Demographics** refers to statistics and facts that describe market segments. Using demographic information, the tourism industry can describe vacation and leisure travellers with statements such as the following:

- More urban dwellers travel than rural dwellers.
- People with college or university degrees are more likely to travel than people without.
- Blue-collar workers tend to prefer group travel; executives and professionals tend to prefer more individualized travel.
- There is a strong relationship between travel and age. Seniors take longer trips and tend to travel by car or bus; 71 percent of the 18–24 age group travels, compared to 38 percent of the 65-plus age group.
- Well-educated people with high incomes tend to travel by air and stay in hotels; people with lower incomes and less education tend to travel by car or bus and stay with family and friends.
- Most overseas travellers have travelled abroad in the past.

Demographic information can uncover potentially lucrative markets for the tourism industry. For instance, Statistics Canada data reveal that there are several million people with disabilities in Canada. With the population aging, many seniors will join this segment of the tourism market. Many of these people would be willing to travel if the travel industry provided products and services to meet their needs. Travel enterprises are now reaching out to this market segment by modifying structures to allow for wheelchair access, allowing a helper to travel free or at a reduced price, and offering tours geared to people with disabilities. The Alberta Hotel & Lodging Association developed Access Canada, a training program for operators designed to improve accessibility for people with disabilities. The Hotel Association of Canada has since nationally promoted this manual to hotel management.

Psychographics Demographics limits itself to objective information, and so can't fully describe market segments. **Psychographics** furnishes more subjective information. Psychographic research asks travellers to reveal their activities, interests, and opinions. This information may suggest, for instance, that young people travel to experience excitement, independence, and new environments.

Psychographic information also relates an individual's life stage (i.e., position in the life cycle) to travel. Because they have more time and money, young singles and young childless couples tend to travel more for pleasure. Single parents and married couples with dependent children tend to travel less. When they do travel, they go by car or camper and stay with friends and relatives. Recently retired people and older married couples with no dependent children return to pleasure travel, buying air transportation and cruises.

Psychographic information is also useful for uncovering the attitudes of nontravellers. A great many people do not travel, even though they have the time and money. Barriers to travel may include fear of the unknown, fear of flying, security concerns, lack of interest, or even uneasiness about how to tip in a restaurant. Once these barriers are revealed, products and services can be designed to overcome them. For example, airlines introduced in-flight movies partly to keep nervous passengers from thinking about their fear of flying. Three- and four-day cruises let people sample cruising to decide whether they will like it. Nontravellers represent a vast, untapped resource for the tourism industry.

Psychographics show what travellers expect from their vacation experiences. The tourism industry markets its products and services based on these expectations. If a traveller is seeking glamour and romance, the product might be a trip to Paris, with accommodation in an elegant hotel. If a traveller is seeking outdoor adventure, then the product might be a whitewater rafting trip in Quebec.

There are many motivations for vacation and leisure travel, and travel experts have many ways of listing and organizing them. Several models have been developed to classify people according to psychographic types, including the following presented by McIntosh and his colleagues (1995):

1. Plog's venturer-dependable continuum.
2. The travel needs ladder, described by Pearce, which in turn is based on Maslow's hierarchy of needs.
3. The values, attitudes, and lifestyles (VALS) segmentation system.

All of these are tools that can be used for establishing tourism market segments.

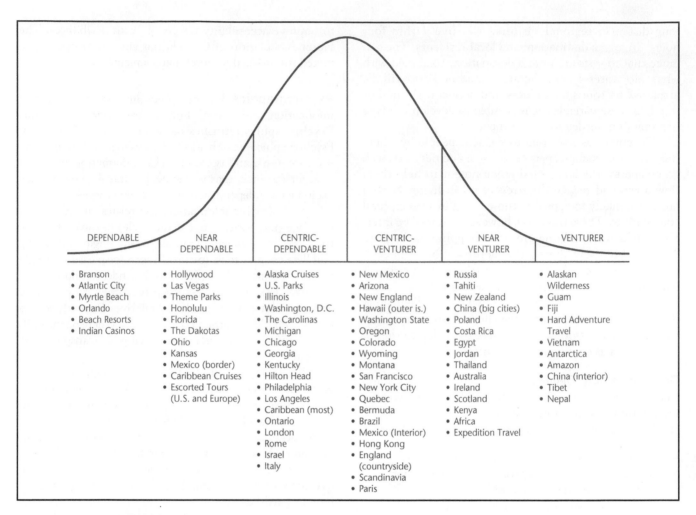

FIGURE 2–1 Plog's Continuum of Vacation and Leisure Travellers Showing the Psychographic Positions of Destinations (2003)

Tool 1 According to Stanley Plog (1991) an individual's personality determines his or her motivation for travel and choice of destination. Plog uses a continuum to describe vacation and leisure travellers (Figure 2–1 shows the continuum, along with possible destinations for each personality type). The continuum is in the form of a bell (or normal) curve, with small numbers at either extreme and the majority in the centre.

At one end of the continuum is the venturer personality. **Venturers** (formerly named Allocentrics) seek adventure, variety, and excitement. They want to experience totally different cultures and environments. They may choose to visit an isolated hill tribe in India, staying in native lodgings, eating native food, and participating in native dances and ceremonies. Venturers shun traditional destinations and modes of transportation. They may be seen driving a jeep across the Sahara or paddling a dugout canoe in the Amazon Basin. Venturers are trendsetters—they help establish new destinations. When those destinations become popular with other travellers, venturers move on to new territory.

At the opposite end of the continuum is the dependable personality. **Dependables** (formerly named Psychocentrics) tend to focus their thoughts on themselves and their families, and don't travel much. When they do go away, they don't venture too far from home. If they live in the Maritimes, they might travel to Saint John, Halifax, or Charlottetown. Dependables need consistency and reliability in their travel products. Often they return to the same place year after year. They don't want to experiment with accommodation, food, or entertainment. Nor do they want to experience personal stress or encounter unusual situations.

Falling between these two extremes are the centric personalities (Centric-Venturer and Centric-Dependable). Most vacation and leisure travellers fit into this category. Centric personalities travel for the sake of a break from their everyday routines. They want to strike a healthy balance between work and recreation. These people aren't afraid to try new travel experiences as long as these experiences are not too bizarre or challenging. The environment can't seem too foreign—a fast-food restaurant, like McDonald's, in the middle of a seventeenth-century building complex is reassuring to them. Centric personalities often go where their friends have gone. They tend to travel to familiar destinations, which will vary depending on whether they lean toward the venturer or the dependable end of the curve. For example, one could expect Centric-Dependables to travel to Canadian destinations such as Ontario whereas Centric-Venturers would tend to favour Quebec. Similarly, for foreign destinations, Centric-Dependables are more likely to choose the Caribbean, while Centric-Venturers would travel to Hawaii or England. As personalities move along the spectrum to the Venturer end (Near Venturers) they might

visit Hong Kong, Tokyo, and Singapore, but most places in Asia are too extreme for them. Again, those individuals tending toward the dependable end of the continuum (Near Dependables) will likely choose familiar destinations such as Florida, Las Vegas, Mexico and will only travel further afield on an escorted tour or cruise.

Tool 2 Douglas Pearce (1989) introduced the travel needs model, building on Abraham Maslow's theory that needs satisfaction motivates human behaviour. This travel needs model assumes that people's travel behaviour has a life cycle that reflects the hierarchy of their travel motives (see Figure 2–2). People start at different levels and over time move from one level to the next. They may

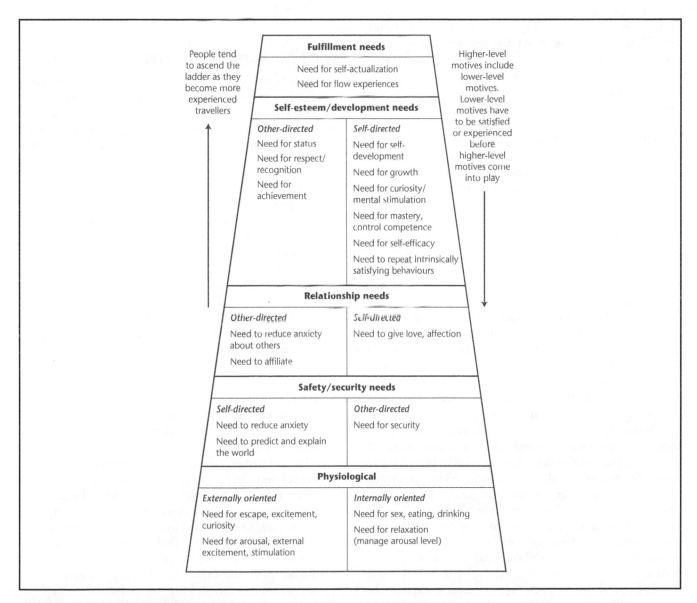

FIGURE 2–2 Travel Needs Ladder

SOURCE: From *TOURISM 7th edition* by McIntosh, Goeldner, and Ritchie, p. 446, 1995. This material is used by permission of John Wiley & Sons, Inc.

face barriers to their travel needs, caused by things such as money, health, and other people.

Maslow's theory suggests that vacation and leisure travellers are motivated by the desire to satisfy needs. The needs ladder retains Maslow's idea that lower-level needs must be met before upper-level needs. People who lack money for food, shelter, and clothing can't travel for pleasure. But after basic physical and emotional needs have been met, travel meets people's needs for esteem, respect, and self-actualization. ("Self-actualization" is Maslow's term for the highest level of personal fulfillment.)

Travellers who feel a need to be with other people may purchase an escorted group tour or a cruise with many planned activities. Travellers who feel a need for respect may purchase a travel product that will impress their friends and associates. This might be a trip to an exotic destination or a stay at a ritzy resort or hotel. Travellers who feel a need for self-actualization are beyond trying to impress their friends. Instead, they want a travel product that will help them develop physically, mentally, or spiritually. They might choose a bicycle tour through Ireland, a study tour of France's châteaux, or a trip to Mecca.

The travel needs ladder operates on different levels for different activities at different times. It also operates within a specific travel experience. For example, sudden terrorist activities at a destination will bring a vacationer's needs back down to the level of safety and security—at such times, the needs for esteem, respect, and self-actualization must be set aside. While on vacation in Europe, a traveller may receive news that a family member has become seriously ill. The sense of belonging to a family motivates the traveller to return home immediately.

Besides planning travel products and services to meet human needs, tourism professionals must recognize when needs change, and adapt their products and services accordingly. In the case of a traveller with a critically ill relative, a hotel manager might arrange for long-distance telephone calls and the tour escort might arrange for quick transportation back home to Canada.

Several levels of the needs ladder work together. The result is a complex understanding of travel motivation. It is assumed that motivation changes over time and across situations. In this model, destinations are seen as settings where holiday experiences may vary greatly. Destinations may or may not be able to provide what travellers are seeking from them. Travellers go to a destination and select activities and experiences from the available array in response to their psychological and motivational makeup.

The travel needs model can be used to explain the motives of different consumers in specific settings. Service providers can use the ladder's various sections to ask questions, the better to judge whether the product suits the

traveller. This model can also provide information to combine with the results of other tourism studies.

Tool 3 Lifestyle is how a person's activities, interests, and opinions are revealed through their way of life. Many researchers have studied lifestyle because it provides more information about market segments than demographics. The most widely accepted method is the values, attitudes, and lifestyles (VALS) system developed by research institute SRI International. This system divides a market's population into eight lifestyle types, and groups them under four categories: self-image, aspirations, values and beliefs, and products used. Since the introduction of VALS in the 1970s, many other ways have been developed to analyze and categorize lifestyle. However, VALS remains the best known and one of the most widely used.

What Are Barriers to Travel?

So far we have considered why people travel, and also who travels. It is relevant now to consider some of the many reasons why some people don't travel. Some barriers to business or pleasure travel are not easily overcome. Polovitz Nickerson and Kerr (2001) suggest the following reasons:

- **Cost** Discretionary income determines the distance we can travel and how long we travel. Two other dimensions of travel cost are the number of people travelling and what it costs to spend time at a destination.
- **Lack of time** Travelling takes time. Where we go is dictated by how much time we can use to get there and how we travel.
- **Accessibility or distance** Distance and time are intertwined. We are often limited as to the destinations we can reach in the time we have.
- **Age** Age affects our physical and mental abilities and dictates how we travel, how far, and whether we travel alone.
- **Health** Health, both physical and mental, determines not only our ability to travel but also whether we can arrange travel insurance. Without insurance, travellers have to personally cover unforeseen costs.
- **Fear** Fear is one of the most difficult barriers to overcome. Fear—of the unknown, or flying, or heights, or whatever—can be very real though not based on experience. Often, travel fears can be overcome with experience. Many people find planned tour packages just what they need to become travellers.
- **Travel tastes and experience** Personality, age, education, income, and experience influence our responses to this barrier. Dependables, if they travel at all, are apt to travel in their own area, where things are familiar. The more educated people are,

the more likely they are to seek new experiences; if experiences are positive, it encourages trying more of them.

Check Your Product Knowledge

1. Why is it important for a tourism professional to understand why people travel?
2. Why does the tourism industry divide the travel market into segments?
3. What is the difference between geographic, demographic, and psychographic information?
4. How can the characteristics of specific tourism market targets be identified?
5. Why is it important for tourism professionals to understand travel motivations?
6. What stops people from travelling?

DOMESTIC VACATION TRAVEL

Where do vacation and leisure travellers go? Canadians travel within their own country, to the United States, and to other countries. Travellers from the United States and other countries visit Canada.

See Canada

Domestic travel—that is, travel within one's own country—has always been popular among vacation and leisure travellers. About 80 percent of all travel is domestic.

Because of its vast size, Canada offers a diversity of travel experiences for all travellers, domestic as well as inbound. Travellers can enjoy the seashore of Prince Edward Island, the plains of Saskatchewan, the mountains of British Columbia, and the Badlands of Alberta. Lake Louise, Niagara Falls, and the tides on the Bay of Fundy are just a few of this nation's natural wonders. The climate also varies widely in Canada. The moderate climate of the lower mainland in British Columbia; the hot, dry summer weather on the Prairies; and the cold, snowy winters of Quebec have resulted in different and interesting lifestyles and activities. Descendants of Canada's early settlers have maintained their ethnic traditions in many regions. This diversity has been reinforced and modified by immigration since World War II, so travellers in Canada can sample cultures from all over the world.

Many Canadians, especially families with young children, find it less expensive to travel within Canada. Vacationers can usually save money travelling by passenger

ILLUSTRATION 2–5

Because Canada is so large, it offers a variety of sights, climates, and cultures to domestic and foreign travellers.
SOURCE: Corel.

car or recreational vehicle. A good system of roads, with restaurants and motels along the way, makes highway travel pleasant. In fact, highway travellers represent the largest segment of this country's tourists.

Many Canadians also find domestic travel more convenient. Travellers who stay in Canada rather than go overseas don't have to apply for passports, be inoculated against diseases, or exchange their currency.

World events influence vacationers' travel plans. After September 11, 2001, people felt fearful about flying or visiting New York City. This drastically affected many people's travel, both discretionary and nondiscretionary. Also, when the value of the Canadian dollar declines, as it did in the early 1990s, and again in 2001, Canadians tend to stay home. Conversely, when the Canadian dollar achieved parity with its U.S. counterpart in 2007, cross-border travel by Canadians increased while the number of inbound visitors from the United States slumped.

Where Do Travellers Go?

The following are just a few of Canada's many tourist attractions: Vancouver Island's Douglas firs, the Calgary Stampede, the Museum of Civilization in Gatineau, Parliament Hill in Ottawa, Upper Canada Village in Morrisburg, the Rogers Centre in Toronto, Peggy's Cove in Nova Scotia, Signal Hill in St. John's, the Laurentians north of Montreal.

According to Statistics Canada, Canadians took 206.4 million domestic trips in 2006. Canadian tourism recovered from a difficult year in 2003, as a series of adverse events (e.g., the war in Iraq, the outbreak of SARS, the power outage in Ontario, and the forest fires in British Columbia) affected international travel to Canada. All statistics fell but started to recover in 2006. Ninety percent of all domestic trips taken by Canadians were within their home province. Pleasure trips and VFR accounted for 88 percent of all domestic trips.

Overall, in 2006, Canadians took 182.6 million trips for pleasure or to visit friends and relatives and 24.8 million for business and other (12 percent). The number of pleasure and of VFR trips was about equal. These percentages were similar to the year before.

In 2004, average spending per trip was $170 for all domestic travellers. Trips averaged three nights, with travellers spending an average of $265 per overnight trip. After transportation, the restaurant sector reported the second-highest demand from travellers.

Table 2–1 shows the activities that Canadians enjoyed in Canada during 2004.

Check Your Product Knowledge

1. What is meant by "domestic tourism"?
2. What barriers to travelling are families likely to have to overcome?
3. What factors favour domestic tourism in Canada?
4. What are some of the characteristics of domestic trips in Canada?

TABLE 2–1 Participation Rate in Selected Activities in Canada, 2004

	Thousands
Visit friends	53 024
Visit relatives	77 192
Shopping	61 401
Sightseeing	35 170
Attend festival, fair, exhibition	7 775
Attend cultural event, play, concert	7 382
Attend aboriginal, native cultural event	1 384
Attend sports event	11 982
Visit museum, art gallery	8 176
Visit a zoo, aquarium, or botanical garden	5 284
Visit a theme or amusement park	5 285
Visit a national or provincial park	13 588
Visit historic site	9 256
Go to a bar or a nightclub	16 805
Go to a casino	5 570
Took a cruise or boat trip	3 694
Golfing	4 220
Swimming	12 240
Boating	8 234
Other water-based activities (excluding boating)	2 540
Fishing	6 416
Bird or wildlife viewing	3 526
Cross country skiing	1 018
Downhill skiing	3 794
Snowmobiling	1 179
Walking or hiking	21 818
Cycling	4 773
Other sport or outdoor activity	13 416

SOURCE: Adapted from Statistics Canada Canadian Travel Survey, CANSIM table 426-0006, Catalogue 87-212.

OUTBOUND VACATION TRAVEL

Canada has much to offer vacation and leisure travellers, but there are certain sights and experiences that are available only through travel to foreign countries. There is only one Eiffel Tower, and people must go to Paris to see it. Only India has the Taj Mahal. For many people, books and television documentaries about foreign countries can't replace the excitement of experiencing a different culture first-hand. Many Canadians dream about going to faraway places and consider their lives incomplete until they've travelled abroad or gone "south" to the United States, Mexico, or the Caribbean.

Travel to the United States

According to Statistics Canada, Canadians made 17.8 million overnight visits to the United States in 2007, a 11.1 percent increase from 2006 and the highest number since 1992. The most popular American destinations were New York, Florida, Washington, Michigan, and California. The longest vacations were spent in Florida, followed by California and Arizona. Many Canadians make extended shopping trips to outlet malls in the United States. Others travel to see plays on Broadway, visit Disneyland in California or Disney World in Florida, or try their luck in Las Vegas. Some Canadians from the Lakehead and the Prairies travel to Minneapolis, Milwaukee, or Chicago to watch the Toronto Blue Jays play. Popular winter destinations for Canadians—including "snowbirds" who winter for several months in the United States—are Florida, California, Arizona, and Hawaii. Canadians travel to the United States for camping and hiking in the summer, to admire the changing foliage in the autumn, to ski in winter, and to enjoy an earlier spring.

The portion of business travellers in 2006 was 14.6 percent, representing a decline from the traditional 19 percent; however, there was an increase in the number of Canadians travelling to the United States for pleasure

(56.2 percent). Most Canadians travelling to the United States drove there. Average spending per trip was CDN$640 in 2006. Although the number of people travelling to the United States declined immediately after September 11, 2001, the number of visitors has rebounded, especially as the Canadian dollar approached parity with the U.S. dollar.

Since September 11, 2001, immigration and customs checks have intensified at United States border crossings and at airports. As a result of increased security concerns, the U.S. Government introduced the Western Hemisphere Travel Initiative (WHTI), which requires all travellers entering the United States by air after June 1, 2009 to have a passport or other valid travel document. Travellers must also arrange for extra medical coverage.

Other Outbound Travel

Excluding the United States, Canadian travellers made a record 7.4 million trips to overseas destinations in 2007—up 9.9 percent from 2006. Business and VFR travel dropped, but pleasure travel increased. In 2007, the most popular overseas destinations for Canadians remained the United Kingdom and Mexico, followed by France, Cuba, and the Dominican Republic. The rise in the Canadian dollar, security concerns, and the slowdown in the U.S. economy all contributed to a total international travel deficit of about CDN$9.4 billion.

Travel to other countries usually requires far more preparation. Travellers must prepare various documents, obtain traveller's cheques or exchange currency, take health-related precautions, and inform themselves about customs regulations. Several publications are relevant to the concerns of foreign travellers. One of them, *I Declare*, is available free from the Canada Border Services Agency or on its website (www.cbsa-asfc.gc.ca). Travel counsellors often assist travellers with specific aspects of foreign travel so that they have a safe and pleasant trip.

INBOUND TOURISM

What do you know about the lifestyle of a British working-class person? Can you speak French? What type of food does a German prefer? How do Japanese customs differ from Canadian customs?

As a tourism professional, you will serve people from other countries as well as Canadians. Inbound tourism—that is, business, vacation, and leisure travel to Canada—is a rapidly growing segment of the travel market.

Table 2–2 shows inbound tourism to Canada in 2007. Overall, the number of overnight international travellers dropped to about 17.8 million. This was caused primarily by a drop in the number of American visitors. Visitors from countries other than the United States increased. Canada continued to fall in popularity worldwide as a

TABLE 2–2 Inbound Tourism Activity, 2007		
Tourists to Canada	Number (thousands)	% change from 2006
From the United States	13 371	−3.5
From overseas total	4 397	+2.9
United Kingdom	891	+5.9
France	379	+1.5
Japan	343	−14.4
Germany	318	+1.6
Mexico	251	+17.1
Korea (South)	213	+5.3
Australia	208	+16.7
China	156	+5.3
Hong Kong	116	+3.3
India	105	+16.9

SOURCE: Adapted from Statistics Canada, International Travel: Advance Information, 66-001-P, volume 23, issue 12, December 2007.

tourist destination, and by 2005 it had dropped out of the "Top 10" to twelfth. Clearly, tourism professionals must get to know inbound tourists' needs much better if they are to design appropriate products and services and reverse this trend.

Tourists from the United States

American travellers to Canada continue to be the largest group of foreign tourists, making up 75 percent of the foreign travel market in 2007. Almost half of all Americans coming to Canada visited Ontario, while about one-quarter headed for British Columbia, followed by Quebec and the Maritimes. Americans travelled to Canada for various reasons: About 60 percent were taking a holiday, 19 percent were visiting friends or relatives, and 12 percent had come on business.

Most Americans who came to Canada in 2007 came for a holiday. However, the overall total was down 3.5 percent from the previous year, caused by an increase in the Canadian dollar and the disruptions described earlier. Spending also declined to $7.1 billion.

Tourists from Overseas

After the disruptions of 2003, overnight travel to Canada by tourists from overseas fell for the first time since 1992. However, by 2007, the number of overseas visitors to Canada had begun to increase in most markets. In 2007,

ILLUSTRATION 2–6

Visitors to Quebec City can experience a little bit of Europe in North America.

SOURCE: Courtesy of Theresa Fitzgerald.

overnight visitors to Canada spent in excess of $5.9 billion. However, the rise in the Canadian dollar and the downturn in the world economy during 2008 has once again caused a decline in visitors to Canada.

In 2007, one-third of visitors from overseas chose Ontario as their destination. British Columbia was the second most popular destination, and Quebec was third. Compared with American tourists, travellers from overseas were more likely to come to Canada to visit friends and relatives.

Why Do Tourists Travel to Canada?

Just as Canadians often journey abroad to find their ancestral roots, foreign tourists often want to see the land to which their relatives immigrated. Family reunions are a common reason for visiting Canada. Canadians travel abroad to see old castles, cathedrals, and fortresses; foreign tourists are attracted by this country's youthfulness. In addition to the diverse landscape, they want to see Canada's architecture, technology, and pace of life. Canada is relatively young, and its more recent history of western expansion fascinates foreign tourists, as does the culture of Canada's aboriginal peoples.

Other Considerations

Receptive Operators A trip abroad represents a dream come true for Canadian travellers; in the same way, a trip to Canada represents a dream for foreign travellers. The **receptive operator**, a travel professional who specializes in arranging tours for visitors from other countries, is responsible for seeing that the dreams of international visitors don't become nightmares. In order for receptive operators to be effective, the marketability of Canadian products and services must be addressed continually to ensure they are of world-class quality. Two different examples are the websites of Jonview Canada (a major receptive operator) and Canada for Visitors (described as an online neighbourhood where expert "Guides" provide information, tips, reviews, blogs and other commentary on a host of subjects).

Receptive operators usually work in cooperation with overseas operators to plan and market tours. Besides handling the usual details of a tour—checking the itinerary; making arrangements with hotels, bus companies, restaurants, and tourist attractions; pricing the tour—they arrange for the special needs of the tour group, such as multilingual guides and interpreters. Foreign companies can set up their own receptive services in this country (Japan, for example, has operators on the West Coast), or Canadian travel agencies can specialize in another country's visitors. With the number of visitors increasing, receptive operators are growing in importance.

Today, international visitors are looking for new destinations in Canada. They want to go to the East Coast, the North, and farther inland to see how people in this country live. This interest in destinations other than major cities creates more opportunities for regional receptive operators, who know their region and its products and services better and can plan more efficient and interesting tours.

Increasing Marketability Inbound tourism can be an important source of jobs and revenue. To capture and maintain this lucrative market, the tourism industry and the Canadian public must overcome this country's shortcomings as a tourist destination.

Language is perhaps the largest barrier to overcome. When travelling to well-developed destinations overseas, most Canadians encounter English-speaking personnel in hotels and restaurants and at tourist attractions. However, international travellers to Canada cannot expect the same degree of service in their native language. Service providers should take this into account when creating printed materials and establishing multilingual guest services.

Check Your Product Knowledge

1. From what countries do most of our international visitors come?
2. What factors contribute to the fluctuation in the number of foreign travellers to Canada?
3. List four reasons why people from other countries want to visit Canada.
4. Why are regional receptive operators becoming more important?

THINGS TRAVELLERS NEED TO KNOW

No matter where they plan to visit, travellers need to know a variety of things about their destination. There are many decisions to make about a trip and a few basics to take care of first. The basics are especially important for the first-time traveller or a person who hasn't travelled recently. Being adequately prepared is important to the success of any trip. A person needs to know, in particular, about documentation, customs, health issues, and foreign currencies and languages.

Documentation Documentation refers to government-issued papers used to identify travellers. These documents include **passports**, visas, tourist cards, and vaccination certificates. When travellers enter or leave a country, immigration officials ask to see these papers. Documentation enables governments to regulate travel.

Customs and Immigration Governments regulate who may leave and who may enter a country, and what goods may be brought in and what goods may be taken out. Immigration (which involves people entering and leaving a country other than their own) and **customs** (which involves the regulation of goods entering and leaving a country) are usually handled as a single process, but may involve two or more government bureaux or agencies working together. In Canada, immigration procedures are handled by Canada Immigration Centres, which are part of Citizenship and Immigration Canada; customs matters are handled by the Canada Border Services Agency; and passports are issued to Canadian citizens by a special office of Foreign Affairs Canada.

ILLUSTRATION 2–7
Customs officers regulate what goods may be taken out of or brought into a country.
SOURCE: Canada Customs and Revenue Agency.

Outgoing customs checks are intended to prevent travellers from taking certain items out of a country. Some countries prohibit travellers from removing archaeological treasures, even if the traveller has paid for them. Incoming customs checks are to ensure that travellers pay the appropriate customs **duty** on foreign-bought items. These checks also seek to prevent the importation of items harmful to humans, animals, or plants.

Common Health Problems All travellers should consider immunization and medical care before leaving their own country. This is especially true for those who have a pre-existing medical condition that might flare up while they are away. Travellers can prepare for such an emergency by getting a directory of overseas doctors, which can be obtained from the International Association for Medical Assistance to Travellers (IAMAT; its Canadian headquarters are in Guelph, Ontario), or from the World Medical Association or the International Health Care Service. The World Health Organization (WHO) publishes *International Travel and Health*, which can be purchased from the Canadian Public Health Association on its website (www.who.int/ith).

Common health problems of people travelling abroad include diarrhea; jet lag—irregular sleeping habits and physical exhaustion—known medically as desynchronosis; and motion sickness while riding in a plane, car, train, or boat. Health Canada provides information for travellers through a network of public and private health and travel clinics across the country. Full details are available on the website (www.phac-aspc.gc.ca/tmp-pmv/).

Foreign Currency Travellers should be familiar with the currencies they will be using in the countries they plan to visit, and their values in Canadian dollars. A money conversion chart or a small programmable exchange calculator is a handy item for travellers to carry.

When exchanging dollars, travellers are actually buying a foreign currency. How much foreign currency one Canadian dollar will buy depends on the current rate of exchange, which changes daily. Political, social, and economic factors contribute to fluctuating exchange rates.

The rate of exchange often determines where travellers go. Canadian travellers tend to go to places where the dollar buys more and to stay away from places where it buys less. Mexico has been a travel bargain for Canadians because of the steady devaluation of the peso. Sometimes the exchange rate changes drastically while travellers are on vacation, so that they either run out of money or find themselves with more money to spend.

The Canadian dollar steadily lost value relative to the U.S. dollar for about thirty years and, at one point, fell to a value of U.S. 65 cents. In 2007, however, a number of factors (among them high global demand for oil and a slowdown in the U.S. economy) helped the Canadian dollar to again achieve parity with its U.S. counterpart. This was a boon to Canadian cross-border travellers, but it also contributed to a decline in U.S. visitors to Canada and to a large increase in Canada's travel deficit.

There are four ways to exchange money, and travellers will probably want to use a combination of these methods:

- Obtain foreign currency before departure.
- Use a credit card and be billed later in Canadian dollars.
- Buy traveller's cheques in U.S. dollars or other foreign currency before departure, and exchange them for cash as needed.
- Take a bank debit card that can be used at overseas ATMs, though it may not be usable in retail or hospitality operations.

Besides knowing *how* to exchange their money, travellers should know *where*. Banks offer the best exchange rates, but they also have limited hours and travellers often have to stand in line and go through a formal procedure. Banks may also charge a commission to exchange currency, so it may be preferable to use an ATM to avoid these charges. As an alternative, tourists can cash traveller's cheques at their hotel. This is convenient, but hotels charge a service fee.

Finally, travellers must know whether a country limits the amount of its own currency that may be brought in and out. Canadian travellers to the United States should also be aware of this. U.S. Customs requires travellers, on departure or arrival, to report if they are holding more than $10 000 in any monetary form (American or foreign currency bills or coins, traveller's cheques, money orders, investment securities, and so on). Some countries require travellers to purchase in advance set amounts of non-exportable currency.

Foreign Languages Some travellers worry about whether they will be able to communicate in a foreign country; others consider this part of the fun of travelling abroad. In the developed nations, where English is widely spoken, communication is generally not a major problem, especially if travellers are part of a tour group and hotels and attractions have been selected to cater to English-speaking tourists. Often, signs using pictographs guide travellers to restrooms, exits, subways, and other important destinations. As a country of immigrants, many Canadians are bilingual in either both official languages or in one official language and in the language of their heritage. This also helps in foreign travel.

However, tourists will find that they are well-received if they can speak at least a few words of the local language, such as "Good morning," "How are you?" and "Thank you." Being able to identify foreign words on menus and street signs makes travelling safer and more pleasant.

Travellers who intend to rent a car should learn the international road signs before leaving home—not while they're driving on the Autobahn (German expressway) for the first time! Canadians driving to the United States will have to adjust, or adjust back to, the use of miles for measuring distance. Some of the anxiety of driving in a foreign land has been reduced by the introduction of GPS (global positioning system) devices in rental cars. Travellers can also purchase portable units with maps and spoken directions for many countries either included or that can be purchased as an add-on.

Check Your Product Knowledge

1. Name four types of travel documentation. What is the purpose of each?
2. What are the two purposes of immigration and customs regulations for travellers entering Canada?
3. Name three health problems common among international travellers.
4. What are some ways in which money can be exchanged?

A DAY IN THE LIFE OF

Three Travellers

Female Business Traveller

I spend about 15 days out of each month travelling for business. Usually I know my travel plans well in advance, so my travel agent can get good flights and prices for me. Last week, for instance, I spent three days in Vancouver. I arranged that trip six weeks ago, and my agent got discount rates for me. Nowadays, there can be a penalty for cancellations, so I have to make sure I know exactly what I'll be doing. Sometimes, of course, I need to make last-minute plans or make changes during a trip. The agency's toll-free number helps when I have to make changes from far away.

My travel counsellor keeps a file on me. She knows that I prefer to fly business class and that I prefer certain airlines because I have some frequent flier bonuses to build on. She even knows I prefer an aisle seat. When she books a flight for me, she gets a seat assignment and boarding pass in advance so that I don't have to stand in line when I arrive at the airport.

My travel counsellor also knows my hotel needs and makes the necessary reservations. She knows that my first requirement is that the hotel be near my meeting location. But I insist on certain standards. I don't like eating alone in hotel restaurants, so room service is important, especially since I often have to spend the evening before a meeting reading papers and preparing. When I know I will have to meet with clients in my hotel room, I ask my agent to book a suite for me. I also like to exercise while I'm away, so I want a hotel with a swimming pool and an exercise room.

The primary thing I look to my travel counsellor for, though, is a trouble-free trip: direct flights or good connections, a comfortable hotel, and no surprises.

Emergency Traveller

Recently, my husband and I had to make an unexpected trip to Winnipeg to attend my uncle's funeral. Since I was appointed executrix of his will, we also had to spend some time there sorting matters out. We had only two days' notice before the trip, but our travel counsellor was able to make good arrangements.

In our case, we had little flexibility—we had to get from Saint John to Winnipeg as quickly as possible. We also needed a rental car. I was pleased that the travel counsellor saved us money by arranging a compassionate airfare for our flight and by getting us a subcompact rental car. We had only two suitcases, and all we needed the car for was to get us around town. It certainly wasn't a pleasure trip, and we didn't expect to do any sightseeing.

Our counsellor was also helpful in suggesting that we not book a round-trip flight. Sure enough, the settlements didn't go quite as smoothly as we had hoped, and we had to stay two days longer than we'd anticipated. Waiting to book the return flight until we knew our departure date was a good idea.

An experienced travel counsellor made an unpleasant trip a lot easier. The counsellor's understanding of the purpose of our trip and our travelling needs really helped us out. The next time we take a vacation, I know where we'll go to make our travel arrangements.

Family Vacation Traveller

Finally, our family was able to take the vacation we'd been planning for some time—a trip to Disney World. It was a package tour suggested by our travel counsellor, with the flight to Tampa, the bus trip to Kissimmee, and the accommodation all included in one price.

It was a good choice. It gave us enough structure to have something to do when we wanted it, and enough freedom to explore other attractions if we wished.

The flight was our kids' first, and the airline we were booked on seemed to take a special interest in children. The hotel we stayed in was fantastic—two well-guarded swimming pools, several game rooms, shuttle service to Disney World, and state-certified child care for a nominal fee—a great help for our one "parents' night out." We would never have found such a perfect place on our own.

I really have to hand it to our travel counsellor, in fact, for sizing up our family and its needs after only a short conversation. We've never had a better time on a vacation. Of course, there's always next year.

Summary

- People have travelled throughout history for a variety of reasons. For most of history, travel was difficult and dangerous.
- For travel to flourish, there must be an efficient system of transportation and protection for travellers. Pleasure travel also requires that people have leisure time and money to spend.
- Largely because of economic prosperity, more people in industrialized societies are travelling than ever before. For them, travel has become a symbol of the good life.
- Modern-day travellers are a diverse group. Travel professionals must match appropriate products and services to each traveller's motivations, needs, and expectations (MNEs).
- There are three main groups of travellers. For vacation and leisure travellers, travel is discretionary, or voluntary. For business travellers, it is nondiscretionary. For travellers visiting friends and relatives (VFR), travel may be one or the other.
- Many types of experiences, such as learning about other cultures, participating in sports, and being with other people, give vacation and leisure travellers pleasure.
- The tourism industry designs products and services to meet the needs of particular market segments. Demographics (statistical information) and psychographics (information on interests and attitudes) help the industry understand the marketplace.
- According to Stanley Plog, an individual's personality (venturer [allocentric], dependable [psychocentric], or centric [midcentric]) determines travel motivation and choice of destination.
- Based on Abraham Maslow's theory of needs satisfaction, Pearce suggests that people's travel behaviour has a life cycle and that they move from one level of need to another, possibly facing barriers to their travel needs caused by things such as money, health, and other people.
- Market research can be better informed through establishing lifestyle variables than through demographics.
- Most Canadian vacation and leisure travellers take trips within Canada or to the United States. Destinations offering beautiful scenery, sunshine, and culture attract the most visitors.
- Inbound tourism has been increasing. To maintain this market segment, travel professionals must also become familiar with the MNEs of international visitors.
- Vacation and leisure travel abroad offers unique experiences. International travel, however, requires more preparation, such as obtaining documentation, learning customs regulations, taking measures to safeguard health, exchanging currency, and learning some basic phrases in a foreign language. Travel professionals must be able to assist travellers with these preparations.

Key Terms

customs p. 45
demographics p. 37
dependable p. 38
destination visitors p. 36
discretionary income p. 33
discretionary travel p. 32
documentation p. 45
duty p. 45
local residents p. 37
market segmentation p. 36
nondiscretionary travel p. 34
passport p. 45
primary research p. 36
psychographics p. 37
receptive operator p. 44
regional visitors p. 37
secondary research p. 36
venturer p. 38

Internet Connections

American Travellers to Canada (p. 43)
An American's Guide to Canada
http://americansguide.ca

Canada for Visitors
www.gocanada.about.com

Canada (p. 41)
Canada Border Services Agency (CBSA)
www.cbsa-asfc.gc.ca

Canada Cool
www.canadacool.com

Canada for Visitors
www.gocanada.about.com

Canada Live Webcams and Travel Information
www.leonardsworlds.com/country/canada.htm

Destinations Canada
www.destinationscanada.com

Free Travel Guides
www.free-travelguides.com

Jonview Canada
www.jonview.com/production/ p. 44

Canadian Tourism Research Institute (CTRI)
(The Conference Board of Canada)
www.conferenceboard.ca/ctri p. 36

Canadian Travellers (p. 42)
Consular Affairs Bureau
(Foreign Affairs Canada; free travel publications)
www.voyage.gc.ca
For further information, click on Travel Reports.

Customs and Immigration Requirements
for Canadians
www.beaware.gc.ca

Passports: Passport Office (Canada)
www.ppt.gc.ca

Travel Medicine Program: Health Canada
www.phac-aspc.gc.ca/tmp-pmv/

Western Hemisphere Travel Initiative (WHTI)
www.travel.state.gov/travel/cbpmc/cbpmc_2223.html

Culture (Canada) (p. 44)
Canada for Visitors
www.gocanada.about.com

Four Seasons Hotels and Resorts
www.fourseasons.com   p. 30

Hotel Association of Canada (HAC)
www.hotelassociation.ca   p. 37

Information for the Canadian Traveller
www.voyage.gc.ca

Province/Territory Government Tourism Offices:
Go to the government website of any of the provinces
or territories and enter "tourism" in the Search
window.   p. 43

Statistics Canada
www.statcan.gc.ca   pp. 41, 29, 33, 37

Tourism Services (p. 29)
Canadian Tourism Commission (CTC)
www.corporate.canada.travel

Canadian Tourism Human Resource Council (CTHRC)
www.cthrc.ca

World Travel Directory
www.theworldtraveldirectory.net

WORKSHEET 2–1   Foreign Travel: FAM Trip

Imagine that your travel agency has sent you on a FAM trip to Warsaw, Poland. Search the Internet, and use the space below to record your findings.

1. How to get there from Yourtown

   _____

   _____

2. How to obtain a visa

   _____

   _____

3. Currency used and exchange rate in dollars

   _____

   _____

4. Customs rules

   _____

   _____

5. What clothes to pack

   _____

   _____

6. Where to stay

   _____

   _____

7. Recommended restaurants

   _____

   _____

8. Things to see and do at your destination

   _____

   _____

9. How to get around at your destination

   _____

   _____

10. What to do in case of a medical emergency

   _____

   _____

11. Additional tourist information

   _____

   _____

WORKSHEET 2–2   Inbound Tourism

Travellers to Canada have different MNEs. Based on the information given below and on information available on destination websites, draw up a suitable itinerary for each of the following examples of travellers.

1. Inge Edberg and Katerina Petersen, university students from Sweden, want to go hiking, visit a friend in Calgary, and meet Canadian students—all on a low budget. Projected trip length: one month.

_____

_____

_____

_____

_____

2. Dr. Mario Alvarez, a doctor from Venezuela, is attending a summer convention in Quebec City. His wife and daughter are accompanying him. After the convention, his wife wants to do some shopping and see a musical, and his daughter wants to visit Cavendish, Prince Edward Island. Projected trip length: one week.

_____

_____

_____

_____

_____

3. Twelve French tourists travelling as a group want to see Canada from coast to coast. Projected trip length: three weeks.

_____

_____

_____

_____

_____

4. James Chang, an architect from Hong Kong, wants to see the monuments of modern Canadian architecture and visit family in Vancouver. Projected trip length: two weeks.

_____

_____

_____

_____

_____

Objectives

When you have completed this chapter, you should be able to:

- List reasons for business travel.
- Classify Canadian business travel.
- Explain the main differences between business travel and vacation travel.
- Describe the motivations, needs, and expectations (MNEs) of business travellers.
- Explain the difference between pure incentives and sales incentives.
- Tell how airlines compete for the business of the business traveller.

- Describe the efforts of car rental chains and railways to meet the needs of the business traveller.
- List the special services and facilities that the accommodation industry offers business travellers.
- Describe the work of business travel departments (BTDs) and corporate travel agencies.
- Discuss careers related to business travel.

Air Canada Flight 820 from Toronto to Ottawa is nearly full. Occupying window seat 6A is Jill Rosendahl. Jill works for a company that produces training materials for Financial Post 500 companies. Part of Jill's job is to interview clients to find out what information and skills they want their sales representatives to learn. On this trip, Jill plans to meet with the marketing staff of a software company.

Sitting in seat 6C, on the aisle, is John Wu. Wu is a field engineer for a laboratory equipment manufacturer. He spends 80 percent of his time on the road, helping customers install equipment and troubleshooting when problems develop.

Across the aisle from Wu, in seat 6D, is Maria Tremblay, who is a microbiologist for the Saskatchewan Department of Health. While in Ottawa, she'll attend the annual meeting of the Canadian Society of Microbiologists. When she returns to work, she'll report to her colleagues on what she learned at the meeting.

Frank Delgado has seat 6F. Just a few months ago, he started his own small-tool manufacturing company. At present, Delgado employs 10 people. He's going to the Ottawa area to visit manufacturing plants that might be

able to use his company's tools in their production processes.

What do these four people have in common? You probably recognize that they are all **business travellers**. Unlike tourists, who travel for fun and pleasure, business travellers must travel to do their work. Travel is part of their job description.

Business travellers may work for a private company, a government agency, or a nonprofit organization, or they may be self-employed. They travel to buy and sell goods and services, visit branch offices, attend company meetings, or seek new business opportunities. They may also travel to attend conferences and seminars related to their field, although sometimes this type of travel is referred to as professional rather than business travel.

TRAVEL FOR BUSINESS

Canada is a trading nation. Canadians can purchase products from all over the world because businesspeople have negotiated agreements with one another. Often, they have had to travel in order to accomplish this.

PROFILE

No Substitute for Business Travel

Denise LeBlanc, Travel and Meeting Manager, Tempra Atlantic Gaz Inc.*

No one has yet invented a substitute for business travel, and Denise LeBlanc, travel and meeting manager for Tempra Atlantic Gaz Inc., is confident no one ever will.

"Technology like teleconferencing is fine," she said in an interview, "but when you're talking about a multimillion-dollar deal, some things just don't get done on a teleconference screen. Sooner or later, you're going to want to shake hands face to face with the person you've just handed that kind of money to."

LeBlanc, a native of Quebec, started out 20 years ago with Tempra Atlantic Gaz Inc., first as a dispatcher and later in the offshore department. Over the years, she progressed up the corporate ladder to her current position, where one of her responsibilities is managing travel services for Tempra.

As a travel manager, her duties involve scheduling travel for all company employees, overseeing the scheduling and maintenance of the company's corporate aircraft, setting corporate travel policy and procedures, and negotiating rates and services with airlines, hotels, and other travel suppliers. Her travel department arranges about 1000 trips a year for some 200 travellers.

When LeBlanc started out, the idea of a corporate travel department was still relatively new. Today these travel departments perform a very necessary service for many corporations—keeping business travel costs as low as possible. LeBlanc has witnessed two major innovations that she says have revolutionized business travel and spurred the growth of corporate travel departments: airline deregulation and information technology.

When the House of Commons was considering airline regulatory reform in the late 1980s, LeBlanc was serving on the board of directors of the Canadian Business Travel Association (CBTA), the professional organization for corporate travel managers. She and her colleagues lobbied hard for reform. They believed that regulatory reform would spur competition and lower airfares for business travellers.

In the 1990s, LeBlanc went on to become treasurer, president, and chairman of the board of the CBTA. The organization's main purpose is to educate and assist its members in carrying out their jobs as corporate travel managers.

Another important function of the CBTA, according to LeBlanc, is to enable members to "network with one another." For example, if a travel manager needs to arrange for an employee's trip to an unfamiliar city, he or she can call a counterpart in that city to get directions to the employee's meeting place and to find out where the best hotels and restaurants are located.

LeBlanc believes that advances in information technology have been nearly as important, if not more important, than regulatory reform in helping corporate travel managers save money. In the early days, corporate travel departments had to depend on airlines and travel agents to seek out the lowest fares and rates. Now, well-equipped departments have their own computer reservation systems (CRSs) and hotel reservation systems and book directly.

One of the continuing problems of business travel is that it is often spur of the moment, so business travellers often cannot take advantage of discount rates that other airline passengers can get by making reservations weeks or months in advance. But, LeBlanc said, CRSs do help corporate travel departments plan ahead as much as possible and seek out the lowest fares and rates even at the last minute.

LeBlanc believes that automation will continue to propel dramatic changes in business travel and travel in general: "More travellers will be self-booking and obtaining e-tickets via the Internet. Then, when they check in at Departures they'll run a card through an electronic reader before advancing through Security. There will be less contact with people when boarding a plane."

LeBlanc believes that, if anything, business travel will continue increasing in years to come. The opening of the former Soviet Union and Eastern Europe to Western companies, the forging of the European Union into one big market, and the expansion of business in Asia have resulted in business executives and other personnel travelling more than ever.

"It's just human nature to be curious, to want to see your counterpart face to face, to cultivate acquaintances, and seek out new customers," she said. "Travel is still a major tool to enhance business opportunities, no matter what kind of business you have."

*The company name is fictitious.

A Brief Business Travel History

Travel for the purpose of developing new business opportunities has been going on for some time. The early explorers were actually business travellers, in that they were interested in enriching themselves and in expanding the trade of the country that sponsored them. In the seventeenth century, for example, Henry Hudson was commissioned by the Dutch East India Company to find a northwest sea passage to Asia. He didn't find it, but his explorations helped develop the fur trade in North America.

In the nineteenth century, people began to travel to international trade expositions, where they could display new products. The first of these was the Great Exhibition of 1851, held in the Crystal Palace in London. Inventors and entrepreneurs from the United States and Europe displayed new products such as reapers and dental instruments. When visitors to the exposition became interested in obtaining these products, businesses were encouraged to manufacture and distribute them on a wide scale.

After World War II, major corporations expanded their facilities all over Canada, the United States, and the world. They did this to be closer to local markets or to take advantage of lower tax rates or cheaper labour. The need for on-site visits was another stimulus for business travel. At the same time, worldwide trade expanded. Today, Canadians can purchase clothing manufactured in Mexico, television sets made in Japan, and cars assembled in Germany. Likewise, some products made in Canada fill the shelves of stores in other countries.

Canadian Business Travel

For Canadian purposes, there are five basic classifications of business travel: domestic business travel within Canada, both intraprovincial and interprovincial; Canadian businesspeople travelling to the United States; Canadian businesspeople travelling overseas; businesspeople from the United States travelling to Canada; and businesspeople from overseas travelling to Canada.

Domestic Business Travel According to Statistics Canada, of the 206.4 million domestic trips taken by Canadians in 2006, about 25 million, or 12 percent, were for business and convention purposes. Note that in Canada, cars are used for same-day travel and overnight nonbusiness travel, whereas airplanes are used roughly six times more for overnight business travel than for overnight nonbusiness travel.

Travel agencies and tour operators play a significant role in business travel. About 40 percent of travel agencies' gross revenues comes from sales to businesspeople or government employees engaged in work-related travel; tour operators derive just over 5 percent of their revenue from the same two groups of business travellers.

Expenditures for overnight business travel account for about one-third of the total for overnight travel. Most business travellers are between 35 and 54. On average they spend at least twice as much per trip as pleasure travellers. According to American Express surveys of business travel in Canada between 1987 and 2000, spending on travel and entertainment more than doubled, then dropped by over $1.5 billion in 2001 to just under $11 billion. This was the result of a slow economy and the events of September 11, 2001. However, business travel in Canada continued to be troubled by a sluggish economy and events such as the SARS crisis and BSE (or "mad cow disease") scare in 2003. These factors, together with a decline in airline fares and hotel rates, and a rise in the value of the Canadian dollar contributed to a drop in business travel spending.

Business Travel between the United States and Canada Business travel to the United States from Canada increased throughout the 1990s. This is mainly because the North American economy grew, for many reasons: the Canada–U.S. Free Trade Agreement of 1988, the North American Free Trade Agreement (NAFTA) of 1994, the globalization of the economy, and the Open Skies Agreements of 1995 and 2005, which place fewer restrictions on air travel between the two countries.

In the 1990s, business air travel by Canadians to the United States rose 5.3 percent per year; for Americans coming to do business in Canada, the growth rate was 3.9 percent per year. Most business travel starts or ends in Ontario, followed by Quebec, British Columbia, and Alberta.

According to Beyrouti (2001), spending by American business travellers in Canada breaks down as follows: 41 percent on accommodation, 20 percent on food and beverage, 12 percent on transportation, 5 percent on recreation, 7 percent on other things, and 15 percent not stated. Canadians travelling in Canada spend as much on food and beverage but half as much on accommodation.

Since 2001, American companies have been holding back on business travel because of a slowdown in the American economy and higher travel costs. The travel industry has responded with aggressive pricing, especially by hotels (*Communiqué*, "Corporate?" October 2001). The rapid rise of the Canadian dollar against the U.S. dollar in 2007 has also had a negative effect. Travel is seen as an essential part of doing business, and business travel to Canada is expected to continue, if at a slower rate.

Canadian Business Travel to Overseas Countries Travel by Canadians to countries other than the United States increased in 2007 by 9.9 percent.

Overseas business travel became more important in the mid-1990s as Canadian firms emerged from the recession. There was a recognized need to diversify export markets so as to rely less on the American market. Several government-led trade missions travelled to Asia and Europe, and overseas business travel began to increase, with particular emphasis on Asian markets. Overseas business travel is generally of longer duration and more expensive than domestic and transborder business travel.

Overseas Business Travel to Canada It is estimated that total spending by overseas business travellers is about half that of American business travellers, and the volume is growing.

BUSINESS TRAVEL AND THE TRAVEL INDUSTRY

A study by American Express in 1999 suggested that mid-sized companies would drive the growth in the Canadian travel market in the three following years. Companies that spend less than $1 million were expected to be 50 percent of the market by 2002. Not only would the companies be travelling more, but also more employees would be taking

ILLUSTRATION 3–1

Hotels and motels provide accommodations and often the sites for business meetings.

SOURCE: Image courtesy of Fairmont Hotels and Resorts.

business trips. However, the events of September 11, 2001, followed by the Iraq war and the SARS crisis in 2003, meant that there has been little, if any, growth in business travel.

Senior managers are more interested in travel's impact on the bottom line, and are overseeing travel budgets and travel policies more closely. Companies are controlling costs by using the Internet and booking no-frills airlines rather than full-service flights. Many are consolidating travel arrangements with preferred travel agencies. However, fewer than half of all mid-sized companies have designated someone to manage travel and expenses. This presents opportunities for travel agencies to develop services such as the following geared to mid-sized companies:

- Access to corporate rates for airfare, hotel, and car rentals.
- Personalized services delivered by small teams of travel counsellors.
- The option of outsourcing expense management administration.
- Access to interactive booking facilities.

The American Express 2005 International Business Traveller poll of 1040 corporate travellers from Europe, Africa, North America, Latin America, Australia, and Asia East found the following:

- 80 percent of Canadian business travellers participate in frequent flyer programs.
- 44 percent of Canadian business travellers are price sensitive.
- 26 percent of Canadian business travellers highlighted flat-bed seats as the most important feature.
- 52 percent reported trip delays as the most irritating factor.
- 41–50 percent reported that in-room Internet access was the most important service sought in a hotel.

The tourism industry supplies products and services that make business travel possible. Travel agencies help travellers arrange their trips by securing airline tickets and making hotel reservations. Airlines and railways provide transportation to the destination. Car rental agencies furnish local transportation. Hotels and motels provide accommodations and sites for business meetings. For relaxation, business travellers can take part in many events provided by the public and private sectors, such as shopping, attending a concert, or seeing a ball game.

The Business Travel Bonanza For the tourism industry, business travellers are a gold mine. Canadian and American firms spend billions a year on business travel. Business travellers fill about half of all nonresort hotel rooms and domestic airline flights.

Firms in the tourism industry compete strongly for their share of business travel revenues. Airlines compete with other airlines, car rental agencies compete with other car rental agencies, and hotels compete with other hotels. The goal is always to woo business travellers by providing the best products and services at the best prices.

Characteristics of Business Travel Business travel has other features that make it attractive to the tourism industry. Vacation travel tends to be heaviest in summer and to taper off in winter; in contrast, business travel happens year-round and so provides a steadier source of income.

Business travellers tend to spend more freely than other travellers. Business-related travel and entertainment expenses are often tax-deductible because they are viewed as costs of doing business. Many business travellers are on expense accounts.

Business travel tends to be inelastic. When a meeting is scheduled out of town or an emergency arises in an out-of-town plant, businesspeople have to be there—they can't wait for bargains. Unlike vacation travellers, business travellers often have no choice but to book flights at the last minute; consequently they are ineligible for advance-purchase discounts. This usually translates into higher revenues for the tourism industry. However, the demand for simplified fares has allowed low-cost carriers to attract the business market. The result is that the proportion of business travel booked on discount airlines increased from less than 10 percent in 2001 to about 40 percent on WestJet in 2008.

In times of recession, travel costs go up and vacation travellers tend to stay home. Business travellers have to keep travelling at whatever the going rate happens to be. In fact, recessions can actually encourage business travel, because businesspeople feel that they must get out and try even harder to develop their accounts and expand their businesses.

Business travel can stimulate vacation travel. If business travellers are favourably impressed with a destination, they may return to it for a vacation, this time bringing their families along, and tourism companies benefit twice.

For travel agencies, business travel can require less work than vacation travel. Many business travellers visit the same destinations over and over, so once the account has been established and client profiles created, arrangements usually become straightforward and routine. However, many business travellers are notorious for making last-minute changes in their itineraries. This results in extra work under pressure for the travel counsellor.

The Cost Factor

With business travel, the company, not the traveller, usually foots the bill. Although expense may not seem to be as much of a concern for the business traveller as it is for the vacation traveller, business travellers cannot be wildly extravagant. After convenience, the cost of the ticket or room is the business traveller's next consideration.

The circumstances of the business traveller also determine how much money he or she spends. The expectations of a corporate executive with an unlimited expense account are different from those of a struggling entrepreneur. A government employee may be travelling on a **per diem** allowance (the amount of money a business traveller is permitted to spend each day for expenses).

With changing federal tax laws and with competition in the airline industry shrinking as a result of mergers and bankruptcies, travel costs are expected to rise even more. As a result, many companies are striving to control their travel expenditures. Mulroney (2000) reports that some experts make the following suggestions for trimming costs:

- **Make the suppliers come to you—online** For instance, at www.priceline.com, users can post date, price, and destination; suppliers then bid on the request according to what they have available.
- **Appoint a travel manager** Having a knowledgeable travel manager can help reduce costs.
- **Develop a written travel policy** A written **travel policy** that sets limits and oversees travel spending prevents overspending.
- **Shop around for a travel agent** Some do not charge service fees.
- **Use your corporate credit card wisely** Some suppliers offer cash back, and points can be used to upgrade without added expense.
- **Book as far in advance as possible** Best fares come from booking 14 to 21 days ahead.
- **Red-eye flights can be worth the aggravation** These can cut costs by 40 to 50 percent.
- **Book farther to save money** It may cost less to book farther, Halifax–Vancouver, and get off and back on at a city in between, such as Calgary.
- **Mix business and pleasure** Stay over a Saturday to cut costs and have time to take in the sights.
- **Plan ahead** Combine business at several destinations into one trip.
- **Weigh economy against business class** If there isn't time to do work, economy class could be fine.
- **Take advantage of linked airlines** Destinations can be added cost-efficiently, and points are gained for the whole trip.

Many companies also try to save money by negotiating discounts directly with hotels, airlines, and car rental agencies. In such cases, employees stay only in certain hotels (e.g., in suburban or airport locations rather than downtown); schedule meetings for nights when hotels are less busy; use specified airlines and car rental firms; and ask employees to make sure to gas up before returning cars.

Travel and entertainment costs have more than doubled since 1987, and have sometimes been identified as the second-largest controllable cost for both small and large corporations. According to an American Express survey of business travel management, Canadian businesses could save $1 billion a year by implementing better travel and entertainment policies.

Check Your Product Knowledge

1. What is the main difference between a vacation traveller and a business traveller?
2. Why does the tourism industry actively seek the business of business travellers?
3. Explain how business travel tends to be inelastic, and what this means to the tourism industry.
4. What is the purpose of a company travel and entertainment policy?
5. What can business firms do to cut travel costs?

INCENTIVE TRAVEL PROGRAMS

Incentive travel programs have become an important segment of the corporate travel market. Major corporations began to use travel as an incentive in the 1950s, and since then incentive travel programs have been introduced by thousands of small and medium-sized companies. Incentive travel accounts for about US$9 billion a year in North America; the Canadian market generated 10 percent of this total (Wintrob, 2000).

Incentive Travel Defined

There is some disagreement within the industry as to how incentive travel should be defined. Purists maintain that the term should be used only to describe incentive trips that are strictly for pleasure. Others say that it should include trips that combine business and pleasure. It is, however, universally accepted that incentive travel is a reward for achievers.

James E. Jones, former president of Meeting Planners International, defines incentive travel as "the application of travel as a motivational award for the accomplishment of a business objective." The objective is typically a sales target. A company sets specific quotas for its sales staff. Salespeople who meet their quotas qualify for a trip. The theory is that the increases in sales more than cover the costs of the trips awarded. According to Shaw (2000), a successful campaign can generate a 15 percent increase in annual sales. Companies run incentive travel programs not only to reward sales performance and achieve new sales goals, but also to improve morale and reduce employee turnover. Whatever the reasons for incentive travel programs, all involve travel as a motivational tool.

Salespeople, dealers, and distributors are the most popular targets for incentive programs. "That's because there are hard numbers by which to measure their achievements and calculate the trip's return on investment" (Seaforth, 2000). In recent years, travel has also been used to motivate other types of employees, such as engineers, production personnel, support staff, and managers, as well as to acknowledge teamwork. It is anticipated that these will be the prime growth areas for incentive programs in the future.

Characteristics of Incentive Travel Programs

The Canadian chapter of the Society of Incentive and Travel Executives said that incentive packages range in cost from $1500 to $10 000 a head. Most are under $2000. How much they cost tends to be linked to how well the economy is doing. These programs can be "pure incentives" or "sales incentives."

Pure incentives, as the name implies, are strictly for pleasure. No business meetings or sales calls are scheduled during the vacation. Having reached the required performance objective, the employee is rewarded with the prize of a luxury vacation for a job well done. Destination is the key motivator. Workers are more likely to increase production if the reward is a trip to a glamorous location. It might be a big city, a foreign capital, a resort, or a natural attraction. The incentive can also be a cruise. Pure incentives represent about one-third of incentive travel programs.

Sales incentives are combination vacation/business trips; most of them include mandatory meetings. The amount of time spent on business-related activities varies with the objectives of the sponsoring company. There may be a single visit to a company factory or a series of meetings at which participants are introduced to new product lines, shown new sales techniques, and so on. Usually, more time is allotted to pleasure than to business. An attractive destination is still the most important factor, but the availability of suitable meeting facilities must also be considered. Sales incentives represent two-thirds of incentive travel programs.

According to Seaforth (2000), things have changed considerably since the early days of incentive travel. Sun and sand are still big draws, but today's travellers want more leisure time and less structure. New Zealand and Costa Rica are attractive to the more adventurous types, and Europe is a popular cultural destination. Group travel is the most common, but some companies are introducing individual incentive packages. The weeklong experience has been reduced to four or five days, and attention is being given to making it an "experience" as opposed to a "trip." Weekend programs are growing in popularity.

Whether the package is a pure incentive or a sales incentive, it is always of the highest quality. Winners expect a better class of service than do most other travel clients, so accommodations are deluxe and all-inclusive. Their spouses, whose vacation expenses are also paid for by the company, often accompany employees.

Most programs involve groups rather than individuals. Incentive programs have been organized for groups as large as 10 000, but between 50 and 100 is a more common size. The greatest growth in recent years has been in the small-group market, with an average of 10 participants per trip.

Incentive Travel Planners

Large corporations and businesses that sponsor incentive travel programs sometimes have their own in-house incentive planners. These company employees rarely spend all their time on incentive travel. They can also be involved in public relations, advertising, and planning meetings and trade shows. Incentive travel planning is often the responsibility of the corporate meeting planner.

A handful of companies do nothing but arrange incentive travel programs. Much like tour operators, they negotiate with suppliers and create attractive packages. Incentive companies are usually both wholesalers and retailers. Incentive planning typically involves more promotion than meeting planning. Professional planners are involved with the travel aspects of the incentive program; they also help set the program's objectives.

Not every company can afford to use an incentive travel firm. Companies that can't may turn instead to travel agencies that specialize in incentive travel. Incentive travel planning is similar to group travel planning, although it typically means more work, since the agency is also involved in marketing the incentive program. Sometimes the travel agency works with the sponsoring company to set the program's objectives.

The Society of Incentive and Travel Executives (SITE), which has over 2000 members in 87 countries and a chapter in Canada, is the most important organization for incentive travel planners. SITE holds many trade shows and seminars throughout the year for its members. Well-known incentive travel houses in Canada include Meridican Incentive Consultants, Carlson Marketing Group, Maritz, and the Wynford Group.

Check Your Product Knowledge

1. What purposes do incentive travel programs serve in an organization?
2. What is the difference between a pure incentive and a sales incentive?
3. What are the three different types of incentive travel planners?

TRANSPORTATION SYSTEMS AND BUSINESS TRAVELLERS

For a business trip, travellers can choose to fly, drive, or take a train. The average distance of a domestic Canadian overnight business trip is 636 kilometres. Driving to the destination can cost less money, but is often more expensive in terms of time lost for business. So, business travellers are more likely to choose to fly and generally pick the airline with the most convenient schedule.

Sometimes a train is the best choice, especially for trips between major cities in densely populated areas, such as the Washington–Boston corridor, or the Windsor–Quebec City corridor, or parts of Europe and Japan.

Once at their destination, travellers need transportation from the airport or train or bus station to their hotel. They may also need transportation to meeting sites or for making scattered sales calls. For local transportation, travellers can choose among taxis, limousines, subways, buses, or rental cars. Since rental cars and taxis provide on-demand transportation (that is, transportation whenever the traveller needs it), business travellers are more likely to choose these means of travel. On-demand transportation is generally more expensive than buses or rapid transit, but for the time-conscious business traveller, the flexibility is well worth the extra cost.

Airline Service

When John Wu arrived at Ottawa's airport, the airline's manager of special services was there to help him and other frequent business travellers make their connecting flights. If there had been time, Wu could have relaxed for a while in a VIP lounge.

After regulatory reform of the airlines, competition for passengers became intense. Airlines have tried to attract *vacation* travellers mainly through discounts; they have tried to attract *business* travellers mainly through special services. A wide array of products and services has been developed to cater to the needs of business travellers. However, when there is a downturn in the economy and a freeze on travel budgets, business travellers are not as willing to pay for those services. After the terrorist attacks in New York and Washington in 2001, security measures dictated which services would be allowed.

Business-Class Service Some airlines have business-class sections on their planes, especially those used for international flights. **Business class** falls between coach class and first class in terms of price and amenities. It aims to satisfy the business traveller's need for comfort, quiet, and special attention. Passengers receive complimentary drinks and headsets, better meal options, and increased service. Since business travellers generally prefer to keep their briefcases and suitcases with them, they are offered more room for carry-on luggage. The seats are larger and farther apart so there is more legroom. AA has lie-flat seats specifically designed for frequent business travellers. These seats also feature additional legroom and lumbar support.

Many airlines are now providing amenities even after the flight is over. The most notable service is free transfers between local airports or from the airport to downtown. For example, Japan Air Lines offers free minibus transfers between LaGuardia Airport and Kennedy Airport in New York City.

Frequent flyer programs were originally designed to pull travellers away from the multitude of low-fare carriers that sprang up after deregulation in the United States in 1978. The hope was to encourage brand loyalty by awarding bonuses to faithful travellers. It was believed that if travellers had to choose among airlines for a particular flight, they would choose the one with which they had already accumulated distance points.

Since 1981, when American Airlines introduced them, frequent flyer programs have become very popular. Every major airline now has its own program, with millions of travellers participating. Program members earn distance points every time they fly on a partner airline. Air Canada's Aeroplan points are earned at one point per mile (about 1.6 kilometres) for full-fare travel in economy class or business class, where available. Domestic travel on discounted economy fares earns half a point per mile. Points can be redeemed for travel on Air Canada or any of its Aeroplan partners, including airlines, hotels, and car rental companies.

Most frequent flyer programs have tie-ins with hotels, car rental chains, other airlines, and even cruise lines. A visit to the Aeroplan website (www.aeroplan.com) will provide the latest information on tie-ins as well as the details of the program. For example, Aeroplan members can also earn distance points by flying on United Airlines, staying in a Delta Hotel, or renting a car from Avis. Companies participating in the tie-in program benefit from increased patronage; for that reason, they pay the airline for the right to participate in its club.

A question that commonly arises is: Who should be able to benefit from the business traveller's bonus points? Some companies feel that since they pay for their employees' tickets, the coupons should be turned in to them. Companies can then reduce their travel costs by applying the coupons to trips by other employees. Other companies regard frequent flyer points as compensation for having to travel, and allow employees to keep these benefits for their personal use.

Keeping track of points can become quite confusing, especially if the traveller belongs to more than one program. Books, newsletters, and computer software are available to help travellers with record keeping and to inform them about changes in the programs. A company's business travel department or travel agency may keep track of a traveller's points.

Although frequent flyer programs have been very successful, there have been some problems. One problem has been overcrowding on flights to popular vacation destinations, such as Hawaii, when travellers are using their bonus vouchers or coupons. On any given flight, it's entirely possible that not one passenger in first class has paid for his or her ticket! Awarding free seats to frequent flyers, of course, prevents the airlines from selling those seats to "paying" customers and making a profit on them. Attempts on the part of airlines to raise distance requirements for popular destinations have angered program members, who feel that this is the equivalent of changing the rules in the middle of the game.

Another problem has been with coupon brokers in some countries. These people buy bonus points from frequent flyers. They redeem the points and then turn around and sell the tickets to the public at a discount. Say, for example, a traveller in the United States has earned enough points for two coach tickets to Europe that would ordinarily cost about $1200. The traveller may instead sell his points to a coupon broker for $500. The broker then obtains the tickets and sells them to a couple from Regina for $750. Everyone except the airline makes money on such deals.

Although coupon brokering is legal, airlines have been battling this practice on the grounds that it deprives them of ticket sales (the couple should have bought the tickets from the airline for $1200). Besides filing lawsuits, airlines have been formulating new rules to curb abuses, such as the requirement that bonus tickets be transferred only to travellers with the same last name.

Because of the problems, some airlines would like to do away with frequent flyer programs altogether, but no company wants to be the first to end them. Certainly, the programs have been highly effective marketing tools, and it seems likely that the airlines will continue to use them. Besides encouraging product loyalty, club memberships provide airlines with convenient databases. Instead of paying for expensive advertising time on national television, airlines can market their products and services through direct mailings, including e-mail, to frequent flyers—the group most likely to purchase them anyway.

Airport Comforts Many airlines provide private lounges where their frequent flyers can relax or work between flights or before an appointment. Members of Aeroplan can purchase a membership for an annual fee. Airports, too, provide special facilities geared to business travellers, and more retail opportunities and hospitality services are being added as many airports are being privatized.

At many airports, travellers can take advantage of full-service **business centres**. These centres provide foreign money exchange as well as postal and notary services and photocopying and fax machines. Also, travellers who find themselves short of cash can obtain emergency funds.

ILLUSTRATION 3–2
Many airlines provide private lounges where frequent flyers can relax or work between flights.
SOURCE: Image courtesy of Kaiser Air.

Most major airports have conference rooms—or rooms at an adjoining hotel—that they rent to corporations. Executives from all over the country can fly in, attend a meeting, and fly out again without ever having to leave the airport.

Corporate Discounts Canadian consumers are accustomed to seeing advertisements proclaiming 10 percent off the price of a refrigerator or 25 percent off the price of a sweater. Discounting—selling merchandise at less than the standard price—is a standard practice in marketing.

Airlines offer corporate discounts directly to companies in order to gain their business. By designating an airline as its preferred carrier and promising a certain volume of travellers, the corporation gets dollars off each airfare it purchases.

Airlines offer various types of discounts. A systemwide discount, offered by major carriers with extensive routes, applies to any combination of cities to which the company's employees normally travel. A city-pair discount is offered where there is intense airline competition between two points, such as Toronto to Montreal. A group discount—different from a discount offered to groups for a one-time trip—may be offered when a corporation has many employees frequently travelling to the same place. For example, a California movie studio periodically sends production crew members from Los Angeles to Vancouver for filming. These employees fly at discounted rates each time they make the trip.

Although discounting is common, the airlines don't advertise that they give corporate discounts. Deals are made behind closed doors and are not discussed publicly.

Airlines don't want to reveal the specifics of particular deals for fear that they would have to make the same deal with every other corporation.

Airlines don't particularly like giving discounts. For one thing, there is no assurance that corporations will remain loyal, so time and effort spent in negotiations may be wasted. Airlines also worry about fighting discounting wars with other airlines, which could drain them financially. Revenues lost to discounting must be recovered either through higher costs to vacation travellers or through reduced services. But these solutions can backfire on an airline if it ends up turning customers away.

Corporate Rebates Another popular sales tool is the **corporate rebate**. A discount is money off the listed price; in contrast, a rebate is cash back after the purchase has been made. For example, after a corporation has purchased products and services totalling $25 000, an airline might give the corporation a rebate of 4 percent.

In a typical rebate offer, a consumer purchases (for example) three packages of light bulbs and sends proof of purchase to the manufacturer. The manufacturer then sends the consumer a cheque for $1. Offers of cash rebates are commonly used in advertising for new cars and appliances.

Car Rental Service

To compete for the business of business travellers, car rental chains employ tactics similar to those of the airlines. These tactics include corporate discounts and rebates, club memberships with tie-ins to frequent flyer and frequent stay programs, and special incentives.

To get a standard discount, corporations contract to do a certain amount of business (say, $10 000 a year) with the car rental agency. Each time an employee rents a car from that agency for business travel, the corporation gets from 10 to 30 percent off the regular price. The type of car (i.e., luxury or economy) and distance restrictions (if any) are specified in the contract.

The major car rental chains—including Avis, Budget, Enterprise, Hertz, and National—have fairly well saturated the corporate market. They are now competing with second-tier rental companies for small-business customers. By requiring lower volumes and offering attractive incentives, newer companies such as Alamo, Dollar, and Payless are doing well against the industry giants.

Because of the tie-in with Air Canada's Aeroplan, John Wu usually rents from Avis. As a member of Avis' Preferred Service, Wu is entitled to express rental service at airports. By calling ahead and reserving a car, he can bypass the rental counter and go directly to the rental lot. When returning the car, all he has to do is leave it in the lot—his company is billed by mail. Enterprise Plus and Budget Rapid Action provide similar services for business travellers in a hurry.

ILLUSTRATION 3–3

Travellers can take advantage of car rental kiosks found at airports.

SOURCE: Courtesy Tilden Rent-a-Car System Ltd.

Many agencies now offer cellphones in some cars. This is ideal for businesspeople who must be in constant communication with their home office or with clients. Even when trapped in a traffic jam, they can conduct business by phone.

Car rental agencies are constantly introducing other incentives as well. These include computerized driving directions, 24-hour emergency road service, and destination travel guides.

Rail Service

It costs up to about $750 and takes about three hours to fly from Montreal to Toronto in economy class. This includes the cost of a taxi, preboarding, and the time it takes to drive from the airport to downtown. (The actual flight time is usually about one hour.) By rail, it costs about $200 and takes about five hours to travel from Montreal to Toronto. With advance purchase, an economy seat is around $125. The traveller goes from city centre to city centre without having to deal with traffic. Most trains are equipped with on-board telephones so that passengers can communicate with clients and colleagues en route.

For some trips, the train is easier and cheaper than the plane. This is especially true where the distances are not great. In Canada, most rail business travel is along the Windsor–Quebec City corridor. In the United States, trips between cities in the northeast corridor (New York City–Washington, D.C., New York City–Boston, Washington, D.C.–Philadelphia, and so on) lend themselves well to train travel. Los Angeles–San Diego and Milwaukee–Chicago are also convenient train trips. Furthermore, Amtrak has plane/train packages that enable passengers to travel one way on one mode and return on

the other. In Europe, where many major cities are only 200 or 300 kilometres apart, travel by train is the rule rather than the exception.

Domestic Rail Service In Canada, VIA Rail's VIA 1 service is available in the Windsor–Quebec City corridor on certain trains. It is attractive for many business travellers because it provides advance reservations, seat selection service, preboarding privileges, complimentary meals, newspapers, magazines, beverages, spacious seats and conference tables, 110-volt plugs for computers at the passenger seats, and room to stretch and walk around. Business travellers can park and board trains in convenient suburban locations such as Dorval, on the Montreal lakeshore, and Guildwood, 21 kilometres east of Toronto's Union Station.

Canadian trains are also being used for meetings and incentive travel programs. VIA Rail has introduced Priva service with a range of customized services aboard both VIA 1 and economy cars running between Windsor and Quebec City. Also, the Comfort Plus economy service allows planners to upgrade and accommodate groups up to 600. Other options for programs on trains can be arranged through Ontario's Agawa Canyon Tour train and British Columbia's Rocky Mountaineer. Inbound tour operators

ILLUSTRATION 3–4

Trains give business travellers the facilities they need to be productive en route.

SOURCE: Courtesy of VIA Rail Canada.

such as Toronto-based Jonview Canada Inc. say these trains have unique appeal. They have booked train incentives for various European companies (Saltzman, 2000).

American Rail Service Amtrak's Acela service between Boston and Washington, D.C., is designed for business travellers and has a reputation for speed and efficiency. There are frequent arrivals and departures. Travellers can make reservations by telephone, e-mail, or the Internet, any hour of the day or night. They can pick up their tickets at a special express window shortly before their train leaves.

Once on board, business travellers have room to relax. The club cars have tables so that they can spread out their paperwork. They are offered free continental breakfasts and hors d'oeuvres. All of these extras are meant to lure business travellers away from airlines.

Foreign Rail Service In Europe, a network of high-speed trains is designed for business travel. These modern, clean, and comfortable trains even provide stenographic and photocopying services for their business passengers. Canadian travellers who travel often in Europe can purchase various types of passes that allow unlimited travel for a specific time period. Some passes, such as the France Vacances Pass, are good for one country only; others, such as the famous Eurailpass, are good for many countries.

In Japan, where few cities are far apart, train service has been developed to a high level. Japan, in fact, has some of the fastest, safest, and most punctual trains in the world. A business traveller who needs to get from Tokyo to Osaka (around 320 kilometres) in a hurry can take the Shinkansen, a train that travels over 400 kilometres an hour. Japanese National Railways also boasts the world's most tightly scheduled train service. Canadian travellers to Japan can purchase rail passes through Japan Airlines.

Check Your Product Knowledge

1. How does the business-class section of an airplane meet the needs of the business traveller?
2. What is the purpose of frequent flyer programs?
3. What are some services provided for business travellers at airports?
4. Name two services provided by car rental agencies that are especially appealing to business travellers.
5. In what types of geographic areas can rail service compete effectively with air service?

ACCOMMODATION SERVICES AND BUSINESS TRAVELLERS

The accommodation industry provides two categories of facilities geared to business travellers—hotels and motels, and conference and convention centres. Many communities strongly promote the construction of convention centres because they attract business travellers. Convention and conference centres are described in more detail later in this chapter and in Chapter 11.

Hotels and Motels

At 6 a.m., John Wu hears a knock on the door of his hotel room. As he had expected, it's the executive-floor concierge with his morning wake-up call. When Wu opens the door, the concierge greets him with a cheery "Good morning" and hands him a cup of coffee and the morning newspaper.

At a roadside motel, a wake-up call might be a phone call from the desk clerk. At a hotel catering to frequent business travellers, services are provided with much more style and flair. Although convenience of location is the main reason for selecting a certain hotel, business travellers look for other features as well. Increased competition for the business traveller's dollar has brought about a host of special facilities, amenities, and services.

Business-Class Accommodations In response to business travellers' demands for accommodations separate from those for tourists, hotels mainly for business travellers have been developed (see Chapter 9). These hotels, which include luxurious **all-suite hotels** and more practical budget hotels, offer a more sedate atmosphere.

Major hotels may scatter business suites among their regular hotel rooms, or they may offer executive floors for business travellers. Executive floors are often the top floors of the hotel. For still more privacy, guests can often enter the hotel through a separate entrance and take a separate elevator to their floors. There may also be a special hotel desk that allows express check-in for business travellers. The rooms in the executive section generally cost from 5 to 25 percent more than a regular double room or the regular corporate rate. The decor is more elegant, and there are other amenities in addition to ironing boards, bathrobes, hair dryers, and coffeemakers.

A popular feature found on many executive floors is the executive lounge, where business travellers can relax after a long day of meetings. There, travellers find snacks, a wet bar, and books and magazines provided by the hotel. The hotel may also employ a **concierge,** whose job it is to pamper business travellers. (See "A Day in the Life of a Hotel Concierge" on page 69.) The concierge may search for missing luggage, arrange sightseeing tours, repair clothing, send flowers, and call for taxis.

Business Facilities Most hotels that cater to business travellers set aside an area for working. In the past, this area typically provided photocopying machines, fax machines, personal computers, and other business equipment. Today, more hotels are providing in-room high-speed Internet hookups and workstations with ergonomic lighting and seating to accommodate guests' personal laptop computers. As necessary, most hotels can provide assistance for business travellers who need help preparing documents for presentation at meetings or taking care of correspondence.

Other Amenities Hotels can provide other amenities that appeal to business travellers. Health and fitness centres are becoming *de rigueur*. The better ones offer an exercise room, a jogging track, a swimming pool, and tennis and racquetball courts; more facilities are providing fully equipped spas. These amenities allow guests to release the stress of working and travelling, and to continue their usual exercise regimen. For guests who prefer to exercise in privacy, the hotel may furnish in-room aerobics programs on a closed-circuit TV channel.

For guests who prefer not to dine alone in a restaurant, hotel room service is available. The quality of room service in most hotels is improving, as management sees another source of profit. Guests can now order gourmet meals even late at night. The meals are prepared quickly and served elegantly. Or deluxe continental breakfast and dinner can be eaten in a private lounge, as in Sheraton properties and many Delta Hotels.

Facilities for Women Jill Rosendahl appreciates the full-length mirrors, skirt hangers, and other amenities that hotels provide to please their female guests. The increasing number of business travellers who are women has led to improved hotel service in two important ways: More attention is paid to providing better security and to other details appreciated by women. These improvements have benefited all travellers, not just women. For example, hotels have installed better lighting in their bathrooms so that women can see better to put on their makeup. Men also appreciate good lighting when they're shaving, as well as the convenience of in-room hair dryers. Irons and ironing boards have also become standard equipment. Feedback, however, shows that women bring their own bathroom amenities so that they can continue their personal grooming regimes. Having such amenities supplied is not really a required service.

Hotels are starting to do better at providing healthier dining options. Many women do not like eating in dining rooms but find the options on room service menus are poor. They would prefer a lighter, leaner cuisine, with breakfast items available even at night; they would also prefer that meals be delivered by female room service personnel.

Improvements in security decrease the chances that hotel guests will be robbed or attacked. Largely because

ILLUSTRATION 3–5

Hotels seek to attract fitness-conscious business travellers by offering a pool and exercise facilities.

SOURCE: Image courtesy of Fairmont Hotels and Resorts.

there are more female business travellers, many hotels now provide adequate lighting in halls and parking ramp areas, keyless or deadbolt locks, viewers on guest room doors, and closed-circuit surveillance in elevators and hallways. On request, hotels also provide security escorts to and from parking areas. Yet safety remains a concern, and hotel staff members still discriminate against women travellers, even after they have received sensitivity training. When picking a hotel, women are known to consider safety before comfort, location, and cleanliness.

Crowne Plaza and InterContinental brought a panel of businesswomen together to act as an advisory council to answer the question: "What do women business travellers really want?" They determined that progress has been made since the 1980s in some countries. According to McArthur (2001), in Canada and the United States women are usually given rooms near the elevator, while in Europe they are placed at the end of long, dark corridors. Asia's hotels lead the world in catering to female guests. The Ritz-Carlton Hong Kong even offers a number of baths featuring aromatherapy, bubbles, or flower petals. The Crowne Plaza has also reviewed its promotional materials and now is making an effort to depict women business travellers more appropriately—brochures no longer show women with bulging shopping bags.

Frequent Stay Programs Similar to frequent flyer programs, **frequent stay programs** are offered by many hotels. To encourage repeat business, hotel chains offer incentives such as room discounts, complimentary cocktails, and express check-in and check-out. After staying a certain number of nights, guests are entitled to bonuses, such as free travel, free rental cars, or free accommodations.

Because of the tie-in with Air Canada, travellers might choose a Delta Hotel. They would also earn bonus points that can be redeemed for food and beverage awards at Delta Hotels, and for travel awards. After a certain number of stays, the traveller receives a free upgrade to a more deluxe room.

Wu also patronizes Sheraton Hotels, where he can earn bonus points for a variety of free travel awards. Since he is always in a hurry, he appreciates Sheraton's in-room video check-out system. When he presses a code on a box near the television, his bill appears on the screen. He can quickly review it and authorize it for payment, completing the check-out process. On his way out of the hotel, he can pick up a printed copy at the desk or arrange to have it mailed to his office.

Conference Centres

When Jill Rosendahl's company reorganized, the management needed to explain the new structure to the employees and help them establish new working relationships. Instead of trying to do this in an office setting—where there are too many distractions—management decided to conduct a two-day retreat at the Taboo Resort, Golf and Conference Centre in Gravenhurst, Ontario, an all-season resort, conference centre, and hotel with an international reputation.

A **conference centre** is a special facility designed to enhance various types of corporate learning. A company might rent space at a conference centre for sales meetings, brainstorming sessions, or employee training. Such a centre is like a resort, with sleeping accommodations, dining rooms, and recreational opportunities. But there are also excellent facilities for meetings. Conference centres are often located away from the hustle and bustle of an urban setting. They provide a peaceful, quiet place where employees can concentrate and gain a fresh outlook. Le Château Montebello, halfway between Ottawa and Montreal, and said to be the "largest log cabin in the world," opened in 1930 as an executive resort. It later became an exclusive club; then, in the early 1970s, it was opened to the public. Since then many local, national, and international groups have benefited by meeting there.

Convention Centres

Every year, millions of North Americans travel to conventions, conferences, seminars, and workshops. Annual revenues from meetings and conventions in Canada and the United States reach billions of dollars. Because of the economic benefits that conventions bring to a community, cities compete with one another to attract them. Any city with a **convention centre**—a huge facility providing exhibition areas and a variety of meeting spaces—has an edge in this competition. Consequently, almost every city with

ILLUSTRATION 3–6

Many cities build convention centres and hotels to increase the number of business travellers who visit the city.

SOURCE: Photo by Indu Ghuman.

a population of 50 000 or more has already built one or is in the process of doing so. Convention centres range from the World Trade and Convention Centre in Halifax, Nova Scotia, where the G-7 Economic Summit was held in 1995, to Canada's largest convention facility, the Metro Toronto Convention Centre at the foot of the CN Tower and adjacent to the Rogers Centre, and the Telus Convention Centre in Calgary, formerly the Calgary Convention Centre.

Check Your Product Knowledge

1. What are the types of accommodation designed to meet the needs of the business traveller?
2. How do hotels meet the business traveller's need to get work done?
3. What changes have hotels made to accommodate female business travellers?
4. How do travellers become members of frequent stay programs? What are the benefits of belonging?
5. What distinguishes a conference centre from a convention centre?

CHANNELS OF DISTRIBUTION

In the days before airline deregulation, making arrangements for a business trip was fairly easy. Only two or three airlines flew between major cities, and each one offered about the same services and charged about the same fares. Most business travellers made their own arrangements or had their secretaries make them.

After deregulation of the airline industry—1978 in the United States; 1984 and 1988 in Canada—making travel arrangements became more complicated. Both countries saw an influx of new airlines, followed by a period of consolidation and contraction. Innumerable products have flooded the marketplace, and prices of products and services are constantly changing. Following airline deregulation came deregulation of the channels of distribution; businesses other than travel agencies could now sell airline tickets, and this further complicated the marketplace.

Business travellers depend on several main channels of distribution to help them through the travel maze. They use the services of internal business travel departments, or corporate travel agencies, or they book direct via the Internet. The typical corporate travel agency is a regular travel agency with a specialty service for corporate clients. The corporation usually funnels all its travel business through this agency. Corporate and agency travel managers may choose to belong to the Canadian Business Travel Association, a professional organization that seeks to educate and inform both its members and the business community in general about trends and issues in business travel.

Self-booking technology is the most important of the new technologies. In response to an American Express survey conducted in 2001, eight out of ten people indicated they were looking forward to using such tools in their travel planning. Others said they welcomed the speed and 24-hour access. Improving the option to self-book will have a noticeable impact on travel departments and corporate travel agencies. By 2004, more than half of Air Canada's bookings within Canada were made online, and half of this number was generated through the airline's dedicated travel agency website.

Business Travel Departments

A **business travel department (BTD)** is a separate department within a corporation that handles the travel arrangements of the corporation's employees. Sometimes the BTD's staff works with a selected commercial travel agency. In other companies the staff is organized to function like a commercial travel agency, with its own agency supplies and direct access to a sponsoring airline through a GDS. The Internet is used to look up flights, contact airlines, make reservations, and issue tickets. BTD staff members also make reservations for accommodations and arrange for car rentals and other services.

Clearly, companies with in-house BTDs have a large volume of travel, which they feel they can handle more efficiently themselves. Some also feel that they can negotiate better discounts and rebates by dealing directly with the airlines.

BTDs can also provide travellers with detailed information about their destinations. For example, an executive planning a trip to Beijing can ask the BTD to do research and provide information on the culture and business practices of that country. Travel agencies cannot be expected to conduct thorough political and economic research on every country in the world. BTDs, on the other hand, can gather detailed information on the countries with which their company deals.

In some companies, BTDs also handle personnel relocation and plans for meetings and conventions. If the company has a fleet of cars, the BTD will often be in charge of scheduling and maintenance. If the company operates corporate aircraft, the BTD will coordinate scheduling with the corporate flight department. More companies are operating their own aircraft or chartering aircraft to do business.

Corporate Travel Agencies

Aisle seat, low-calorie meals, compact car. These are some of the details in John Wu's computerized client profile. His travel counsellor keeps this information on file so that he can make arrangements for John's trips quickly and accurately. This is just one of the ways counsellors at travel agencies seek to please their corporate clients.

Travel agencies are still the main channel of distribution for corporations. However, they face a great deal of competition, mainly from business travel departments. Since BTDs can negotiate discounts and rebates with suppliers, to stay competitive, some travel agencies feel compelled to offer their corporate clients similar rebates, which come out of the commissions the agencies receive from their suppliers.

A great deal of competition exists among travel agencies themselves as they bid against one another for corporate contracts. A handful of agencies are **mega-agencies**—travel agency chains such as Carlson Wagonlit Travel and American Express. Mega-agencies bring millions of dollars of business to travel service suppliers and often receive higher-than-average commissions. As a result, they are willing and able to provide rebates and other services demanded by major corporate buyers. Smaller agencies could not offer the same rebates and stay in business.

Travel Management Services Because of airline regulatory reform, travel agencies no longer provide just basic ticketing and reservations services. To win commercial accounts, travel agencies must offer complete **travel management services**. They cannot expect to gain a company's business by mailing out a simple brochure. Now they

ILLUSTRATION 3–7

Corporate travel agencies face competition from BTDs.
SOURCE: Ken Usami/Photodisc Green/Getty Images.

must present a well-prepared proposal in which they demonstrate an understanding of the client's needs and show how the client will save time and money. The following are some of the travel management services that clients expect from a corporate travel agency:

- Help in developing and monitoring a travel policy.
- Quarterly and monthly travel management reports.
- Delivery of documents to the corporate office or to a drop box at the airport.
- A website and e-mail line so that clients' employees can change arrangements easily while travelling.
- Extended office hours.
- A frequent traveller monitoring program.
- Group meeting planning.
- Up-to-date information on changes in the tourism industry.

Of course, to provide these services the agency must be fully automated—especially because business travellers tend to make frequent itinerary changes at the last minute.

Computer software has been developed to help travel agencies audit a corporation's total travel budget. This software can, for example, track employees' travel and entertainment spending, and review trips to ensure they meet travel policy requirements.

It's becoming commonplace for corporations to deal directly with service suppliers, especially with the airlines. Industry analysts believe, however, that most corporations will continue to rely on the expert services of travel agencies to help them sort out a complicated market. Although suppliers may wish to reduce their reliance on travel agencies, they realize that travel agencies can provide a much wider distribution network.

Government Accounts Another result of regulatory reform in Canada has been that federal and provincial governments now use commercial travel agencies as well as BTDs to make travel arrangements for their employees. With the trend toward privatization, governments are utilizing the services of travel agencies to a greater extent.

Check Your Product Knowledge

1. What are three reasons why a corporation would establish its own business travel department?
2. What advantages does a mega-agency have over a small travel agency?
3. What are some examples of travel management services that are designed to meet the needs of the business traveller?
4. What impact has self-booking technology had on business travellers and travel agencies?

CAREER OPPORTUNITIES

As a future tourism professional, you may want to choose a career related to business travel. Two challenging and rewarding careers are corporate travel manager and commercial travel counsellor. The main requirement for each of these careers is flexibility—you must be able to adapt to changes that occur in travellers' itineraries and in available products and services. These changes occur weekly, daily, and sometimes even by the minute!

Corporate Travel Manager

Corporate travel managers establish and monitor a company's travel budget and travel policy. They may serve as a liaison between the company and an outside travel agency, or they may manage a company's in-house travel department. Travel managers are responsible for choosing the agency that will handle the company's account.

Managers of a BTD are responsible for the travel arrangements for executives, salespeople, and other employees who are authorized to travel. Depending on the size of the company, they may make these arrangements themselves or supervise a staff. If the company is very large, a corporate travel manager may also supervise the travel of other divisions of the company.

A BTD manager must also find new and innovative ways to provide business travel services that benefit the company and its employees. The BTD manager arranges corporate discounts with suppliers and must therefore possess excellent negotiating skills.

As business travel increases and as companies seek to control their travel costs, more companies are employing corporate travel managers. In fact, people who at one time worked in their company's purchasing or accounting department created many current positions. They saw a need for travel to be handled as a separate function and convinced company executives to let them set up a program. Other corporations outsource their travel management instead of having a person in-house who handles travel.

Because of the need to prepare financial reports, corporate travel managers should have a business background in marketing and accounting. They should also be thoroughly familiar with GDSs. Many corporate travel managers have had experience as reservationists with an airline or as travel counsellors with a travel agency.

At present, about 70 percent of corporate travel managers are women. Corporate travel managers can advance by assuming the same position in a larger company.

Commercial Travel Counsellor

Commercial travel counsellors work for agencies specializing in making travel arrangements for corporations. Besides being able to look up schedules and rates and make reservations, commercial travel counsellors must be well acquainted with products and services geared to business travellers. They must be able to relate the following information:

- Special business services and amenities offered by hotels.
- How to qualify for lower airfare.
- The most convenient hotel.
- The best way from the airport to downtown.
- Changes in frequent traveller programs.

Counsellors at travel agencies keep up-to-date files on their business clients. These files state the client's travel preferences so that arrangements can be made quickly and accurately. A greater degree of relationship management is expected as part of the travel service provided.

Commercial travel counsellors with more experience may become involved in writing and presenting proposals to gain corporate accounts, and in managing corporate accounts. They need strong negotiating skills for these tasks. They may also be asked to analyze the profitability of accounts. For example, some accounts offer high volumes but result in little profit for the agency because of low-yield tickets and delays in payment.

Postsecondary training is becoming more important for travel counsellors. Courses in computers, business administration, and accounting are essential for counsellors working on commercial accounts. If business travellers will be going abroad, counsellors must know about foreign fares and transportation. They must also know about the culture and customs of an area and about health and visa requirements. Of course, personal travel experience is invaluable. More information on professional certification is presented in Chapter 17.

Commercial travel counsellors can advance by becoming agency managers or directors. They can even go into business for themselves. As with hotels, there are more opportunities for advancement in an agency with many branch offices. Because of agency mergers and competition, the employment outlook for commercial travel counsellors is uncertain, but there is a role to play in the travel management services that agencies are starting to provide.

A DAY IN THE LIFE OF A

Hotel Concierge

As a hotel concierge, my job is to solve problems for the guests in my hotel, who are predominately business travellers. I sit at a desk in the lobby where guests can come to ask for information, complain, or seek help. Usually their most pressing problem is where to find a good restaurant or how to get theatre tickets. Sometimes their needs are more difficult to meet, but I take great pride in trying my best to solve every problem.

To many Canadians, a concierge is a doorkeeper at a European hotel or apartment house. Concierge is French for "guardian" or "doorkeeper" and comes from the French *cierge* (candle). It can also mean a janitor or building superintendent. In fact, at European hotels, a concierge is more like a private secretary for guests, especially business travellers. The concierge makes the arrangements and performs the tasks that a private secretary might perform, such as making restaurant reservations, booking airplane flights, reserving rental cars, and hiring limousines.

Concierges are very common in European hotels, and they are gaining popularity in North American hotels as well. In some hotels, the concierge is called the assistant manager for guest relations. Some hotels consider having a concierge an unaffordable luxury. Others have learned that concierges are very useful because they free the front desk staff to concentrate on making reservations, renting rooms, and preparing bills. In addition, concierges generate much goodwill for the hotel, thus ensuring return visits.

I am a member of Les Clefs d'Or, which means "the Golden Keys." This is an international association of concierges, which has about 3000 members worldwide. Many concierges wear the concierge's symbol of crossed gold keys on their lapels. Many years ago, the crossed keys meant that the concierge was the person in charge of the hotel's keys. Now, of course, we don't literally keep the keys; still, I like to think we are the key to making sure our guests have a pleasant stay.

Concierges are sometimes asked to do very difficult, if not impossible, tasks. One of my colleagues was once asked to stock a guest's private zoo with 20 pairs of animals. Another arranged a facelift for a client, and still another colleague once organized the purchase of a townhouse for a guest. More often, however, the problems we solve are less difficult. We find lost luggage and passports, make reservations for guests at nearby restaurants or at hotels in other cities, arrange for baby-sitters, and help foreign guests with language problems.

As a concierge, I must be very resourceful and discreet. Concierges have to know a lot of people, because we have to be able to tap many different sources to obtain hard-to-get items, like tickets for sold-out shows and sporting events. In addition, concierges enjoy the confidence of their clients, even up to the point of helping them out of embarrassing situations. Our clients count on us to keep our mouths shut about their business, and we do.

At the best hotels, the concierge is a high-level employee, sometimes even a member of management rather than of the service staff. Some concierges at large hotels head their own staff of five or six assistant concierges. Concierges usually have to work their way up to their position by serving in other positions, such as desk clerk. It usually takes several years on the job for a person to acquire the training and experience necessary to be a first-class concierge.

I am one member of a four-person team that provides concierge services at my hotel. Some people learn to be concierges at the International Concierge Institute in Paris, a training school for concierges. I was promoted to concierge after graduating from a university program in hotel and restaurant management and working at the front desk for five years. In addition to my formal training, I speak French and Spanish as well as English. Knowing at least one foreign language is a must for concierges. Some of the best concierges know several languages.

Two years ago, a **Virtual Concierge** service was introduced at my hotel. It is accessed through the hotel's high-speed Internet system in guest rooms and a terminal in the hotel lobby and is used to track VIP guests' history and special requirements, follow up on guest requests and daily concierge tasks, access currency rates, provide information on various local events, attractions, and other necessary information. As well as providing the traditional concierge services, concierges also keep the Virtual Concierge up to date by working with the online service provider. After all, we know from our contacts and guest requests what information needs to be provided.

We also use the Internet to seek out information for guests. DineAid.com, with its online restaurant directory, makes booking reservations for dinner in the area really easy and provides guests with information to help them make a decision. They don't just have to take my advice, but if they don't, I don't get rewarded as frequently by establishments for making referrals.

I love my job because it is so interesting and challenging. Many of our business guests stay with us frequently. I enjoy helping them, and I especially enjoy being confronted with a difficult problem that takes all my ingenuity to solve. That is when I function at my best. I think being a concierge is the perfect job for me.

Summary

- Business trips are taken for the purpose of buying and selling goods and services, developing business opportunities, visiting branch offices, and attending business-related meetings.
- Business travellers provide the tourism industry with a great deal of income. The tourism industry appreciates business travel because it tends to be nonseasonal and less variable.
- The various components of the tourism industry compete with one another for the business of the business traveller. They especially attempt to meet the needs and expectations of frequent business travellers.
- Business travellers expect speed, efficiency, and comfort from travel products and services. They are willing to pay higher prices to have their needs met, but cost is still a factor in selecting an airline or a hotel.
- Incentive travel programs form part of recognition programs and are used as motivational tools for employees by corporations and businesses.
- Airlines attempt to meet business travellers' needs by scheduling frequent flights to major destinations and by providing business-class services and special airport lounges. They also reward frequent flyers with bonus points, which can be redeemed for free travel and other rewards. Airlines also negotiate discounts and rebates with corporations.
- Car rental chains compete for the business traveller's dollar by offering discounts, special privileges for club members (such as speedy rental procedures), and other incentives (such as free upgrades and phones).
- Hotels help business travellers relax and get work done by providing all-business-class accommodations and office space. Hotels also offer frequent stay programs to encourage repeat business.
- In densely populated regions, and anywhere the distance between major cities is not great, rail service is often less costly and more efficient than air service for business travellers.
- Business travel departments and corporate travel agencies help business travellers make arrangements for their trips. To win corporate accounts, travel agencies must propose a program of travel management and offer a wide array of services.

Key Terms

all-suite hotel   p. 63
business centres   p. 60
business class   p. 59
business travel department (BTD)   p. 66
business travellers   p. 53
concierge   p. 63
conference centre   p. 65
convention centre   p. 65
corporate rebate   p. 61
frequent flyer program   p. 60
frequent stay program   p. 64
incentive travel   p. 58
mega-agency   p. 66
per diem   p. 57
pure incentive   p. 58
sales incentive   p. 58
travel management services   p. 66
travel policy   p. 57
Virtual Concierge   p. 69

Internet Connections

Aeroplan
www.aeroplan.com   p. 60

American Express
(Business Survey of Canadian Business Travel)
www.vdr-service.de/portal/cms/obj/_offen/
kompetenzzentrum/literatur/amex_global-business-
travel-forecast2008_20071022.pdf   p. 55

Business Meeting Resources
   Canadian Society of Professional Event Planners
   (CanSPEP)
   www.cspep.ca

   International Society of Meeting Planners
   www.ismp-assoc.org

   Meeting Professionals International (MPI) Canadian
   Council
   www.mpiweb.org/CMS/mpiweb/mpicontent.aspx?
   id=159

Carlson Marketing Group
www.carlsonmarketing.com   p. 59

Carlson Wagonlit Travel
www.carlsonwagonlit.com   p. 59

Hogg Robinson Group
www.hrgworldwide.com

Incentive Groups (p. 58)
   Society of Incentive and Travel Executives
   (Canadian Chapter)
   www.sitecanada.org

   Maritz Travel Company
   www.maritz.com

   Meridican Incentive Consultants
   www.meridican.com

Travel Resources (p. 54)
   Canadian Business Travel Association (CBTA)
   www.cbta.ca

   National Business Travel Association Canada
   www.nbtacanada.org

   Statistics Canada
   www.statcan.gc.ca

Wynford Group
www.wynfordgroup.com   p. 59

WORKSHEET 3–1   Meeting the Motivations, Needs, and Expectations of Business Travellers

Contact an airline, a hotel, a car rental agency, and a travel agency in your area directly or through the Internet. Find out what services and amenities that each one offers to meet the MNEs of business travellers. Record your findings below.

Airline _____	Yes	No
Business-class section		
Airport lounge		
Free transfers		
Frequent flyer program		
Other:		

Hotel _____	Yes	No
Business-class area		
Office facilities		
Recreational facilities		
Frequent stay program		
In-room Internet access		
Other:		

Car Rental Agency _____	Yes	No
Express service		
Mobile phones		
Tie-ins		
Emergency road service		
Other:		

Travel Agency _____	Yes	No
Client profiles		
Ticket delivery		
Frequent flyer monitoring		
Website		
E-mail		
Computer reservation system		
Other:		

WORKSHEET 3–2 Incentive Travel Trip

Canada is a popular incentive travel destination. Suppose you were employed by an incentive program planning firm and were approached by Mary Kay Cosmetics to organize a one-week program, somewhere in Canada, for 25 incentive winners, 10 from Canada and 15 from the United States.

The goal of the program is to network and to have fun, as well as to provide educational and inspirational aspects. Keeping this in mind, use the Internet to check out what VIA Rail, Rocky Mountaineer, Silversea Cruises, and Regent Seven Seas Cruises have to offer. Then outline a program for Mary Kay that involves either a cruise or train component. Remember that many of the participants will have attended other outstanding incentive travel events.

Objectives

When you have completed this chapter, you should be able to:

- Determine what attracts tourists to different destinations.
- List and describe each of the steps involved in the planning and development stages of a destination.
- Identify the four stages of the product life cycle and apply them to a specific case in destination development.

- Distinguish between the multiplier effect and revenue leakage.
- Discuss the physical, economic, and social impacts of tourism.
- Explain how tourism can help preserve a local culture.
- Identify the possible negative effects of destination development on a local environment.

Travellers use channels of distribution—that is, information services in the tourism services sector—to purchase goods and services from the tourism providers in the accommodation and transportation industries. People usually travel to destinations to participate in at least one of three sectors of the tourism industry:

1. Adventure tourism and recreation (e.g., whitewater rafting, hunting, fishing, skiing, golfing).
2. Attractions (e.g., galleries, historical sites, museums, theme parks) and natural wonders.
3. Meetings, events, and conferences (e.g., conventions, training sessions, festivals).

These three sectors are covered in Part 5 of the text. In this chapter, we focus on the destinations themselves—especially on destination development.

Some destinations have existed for hundreds, even thousands, of years. They were not created as tourist destinations, but over the years they have become important tourism centres. Obvious examples include cities such as Montreal, New York, London, and Paris, and natural attractions such as Niagara Falls and the Grand Canyon. Other destinations have been developed specifically to attract visitors. These include Caribbean resorts and theme parks such as Disney World and Canada's Wonderland, just north of Toronto.

DESTINATIONS DEFINED

Every decision to travel is a response to one of two questions: "Where do I want to go?" or "Where do I have to be?" Tourists and vacationers ask the first question; business travellers and those visiting friends or relatives ask the second. Whatever the traveller's motivations, needs, and expectations (MNEs), the destination is always a location.

Components of Tourism Destinations

Whatever the destination, adequate facilities and services must be in place there to attract visitors and satisfy their needs. Otherwise the destination will not be viable. There are five necessary **tourism destination components** (Polovitz Nickerson and Kerr, 2001):

1. **Natural resources** A tourism destination must have the climate, terrain, water, and vegetation to support activities for visitors, and must be beautiful enough to attract them. Important tourist areas in Canada include our extensive wilderness (for outdoor adventure and ecotourism); beaches and provincial and national parks (for vacations); forests, lakes, and rivers (for hunting and fishing); and mountains and countryside (for winter sports and other outdoor recreation) (Davidoff et al., 1995).

A Commitment to Create Memories for Guests and Staff

Intrawest Corporation

Intrawest ULC is a world leader in the development and management of experiential destination resorts. Their resort network ranges from the tops of towering mountains to championship golf courses and pristine beaches around the world. Intrawest offers the allure and beauty of nature with the promise of creating the best memories, again and again.

Intrawest has captured the hearts of a loyal and growing customer base with more than eight million annual skier visits on eleven mountains, thousands of golfers on a network of championship golf courses, and thousands more visiting lakeside and ocean beaches. In addition, they offer the world's best heli-skiing and heli-hiking adventures. (Intrawest, "About Us," n.d.)

Intrawest Corporation, based in Vancouver, was a successful real estate company for 20 years. In 1994, it began to concentrate on developing and managing four-season mountain resorts. The following are the properties established or acquired by Intrawest:

Intrawest Resort Club, Whistler, B.C.

Panorama Mountain, B.C.

Mont Tremblant, Quebec

Mont St. Marie, Quebec (sold in 2002)

Stratton, Vermont

Snowshoe Mountain, West Virginia

Mammoth & June Mountain ski operations, California (1/3 interest)

Blue Mountain Resort, Collingwood, Ontario (50 percent interest in 1999)

Steamboat Ski & Resort Corporation (2007)

In 1996, Intrawest signed an agreement with Disney Vacation Club that allows members of both clubs to exchange privileges. In 2000, Intrawest announced village developments at Lake Las Vegas Resort in Nevada and at Les Arcs in France. In 2001, Intrawest opened its first Club Intrawest urban property in Vancouver. In 2002, Intrawest launched a new community concept called Storied Places, "small, exclusive private residences with limited commitment and personalized service." In July 2003, it was announced that Whistler Blackcomb will host the alpine events at the 2010, Winter Olympics. With its new and planned developments in the United States, Intrawest has positioned itself as the industry leader in North America.

Due to its acquisition by Fortress Investment Group LLC, Intrawest is no longer a publicly traded company. On October 26, 2006, Intrawest's shares were delisted from both the New York Stock Exchange (NYSE) and the Toronto Stock Exchange (TSX) (Intrawest, "Investor," n.d.).

In November 2006, Intrawest announced the retirement of Joe Houssian, after 30 years with the corporation.

Intrawest Resorts has an eight-stage approach to "make mountains move." It has implemented a **pedestrian village** strategy that provides facilities and activities for guests 24 hours a day, 365 days a year. The point is to offer a year-round high season. The eight stages are as follows:

1. Start with a mountain and enhance skiing.
2. Build a place for people to stay longer.
3. Attract more skiers with new facilities.
4. Add more real estate to attract yet more people.
5. Expand year-round facilities to respond to increased demand and to maximize use of new facilities such as shops, hotels, and restaurants.
6. Respond to the increased demand for resort real estate that follows increased occupancy and room rates.
7. Continue to provide a total resort experience for year-round destination visitors. This generates critical mass.
8. Shift the drive train into higher gear by adding more mountain resorts and increasing opportunities for network synergy.

Intrawest's approach is logical and is designed to achieve three goals: (1) increased number of visits, (2) increased revenue per visit, and (3) increased real estate values. Intrawest has a clear vision for itself. It believes in the logic and magic of mountain resorts. It strives to create magic—places that offer enriching, enlightening, and exciting experiences. Places that bring friends and families together and create indelible memories. This magic is built on a rock-solid understanding of the market—an understanding that mitigates risk and generates profit. Without the logic, there is no magic. Without the magic, there is no profit. Therein lies the *real* magic.

Both *SKIING* magazine (1997 to 2007—11 consecutive years) and *Transworld Snowboarding* magazine (2006 and 2007) have named Whistler Blackcomb the number-one ski resort in North America, and *SKI* magazine has ranked Mont Tremblant the number 1 ski centre in Eastern North America. The Stratton resort in Vermont has received a Silver Eagle Award for environmental excellence in fish and wildlife habitat protection, and the Governor's Award for Environmental Excellence and Pollution Prevention. The Quality Council of British Columbia awarded Intrawest its Award of Distinction for Customer Focus.

ILLUSTRATION 4–1

Whistler Blackcomb Mountain Resort is one of many Intrawest resort developments in Canada and the U.S. Whistler stats include over 8100 skiable acres, one vertical mile, more than 200 trails, three glaciers, 38 lifts, and 12 alpine bowls.

SOURCE: © Matt Ragen/Shutterstock.

Intrawest can also be applauded for implementing a corporate strategy for destination development that works. It has demonstrated that it can take underperforming resorts and use a "warm bed" approach (i.e., increase accommodation capacity) to transform them into four-season villages. These villages stimulate tourism and employment and real estate investments; they also expand a region's tax base. Intrawest has done a great deal to develop the ski industry, *and* Canada, as a destination. Its success is expected to continue in the foreseeable future.

SOURCES: Intrawest website (www.intrawest.com); Intrawest Corporation Annual Reports; Danielle Rouleau, "Blue Skies," *Hotelier* Special Report (May–June 1999), p. 17; "Expanding the Experience," *Communiqué* (Summer 2000), p. 6; "Intrawest Corp." Case Study, *National Post* Business, January 2004, pp. 22–25; Roberta Avery, "Muskoka: Four-season living takes shape in cottage country," *Toronto Star* (August 7, 2004), p. N1. "Mont Tremblant Resort delighted to welcome Casino Mont-Tremblant (April 13, 2008) www.tremblant.ca/media/press; "Intrawest Announces Leadership Change" (www.newswire.ca).

2. **Infrastructure** Once a destination has been identified for development, an **infrastructure** must be built to support visitors. Infrastructure includes utilities (heat, electricity, water, etc.), transportation and communication facilities, and community services. All of these are necessary to support hotels, restaurants, shops, attractions, sports complexes, and so on.

3. **Superstructure** Once the infrastructure is in place, a **superstructure** can be built. Sometimes the features of destinations built by humans become part of the attraction. Montreal's Notre-Dame Basilica is the second-

largest church in North America and the CN Tower in Toronto is one of the world's tallest structures.

4. **Transportation systems** Once the infrastructure is in place, transportation systems follow. These systems rely on the infrastructure and superstructure that have been developed. For example, cruise ships need to dock, and cruise passengers need facilities on shore after they disembark. Airlines need runways, control towers, and terminal gates, and airline passengers need transportation systems to get from the airport to the hotel (and back, later on).

5. **Hospitality of the hosts** A destination will not flourish if tourists do not feel welcome. So an important component of destination development is making sure the destination gains a reputation for hospitality. Factors affecting hospitality include the social and political climate, the local culture and laws, and attitudes toward outsiders. Those who come in contact with tourists must be helped to understand that tourism is everyone's business and that they are hosts. Welcoming attitudes and quality service are necessary to complement the destination's superstructure. Surveys have shown that friendliness ranks high on the list of what tourists consider important in a destination. They are more likely to return to destinations where they have been made to feel welcome.

Other factors affect the choice of destination. These include ease of access, price, and suitability of accommodations. However attractive a destination may seem, many people won't go there if it is too hard to reach or too expensive.

Nontourism business practices can affect tourism. For example, in regions where the forest industry practises clearcutting, tourists may be shocked at the sight of denuded mountains and decide not to return. Other tourists will boycott the area and never visit it. Government and business need to work together to ensure sustainable development.

What Attracts Travellers to Different Destinations?

People choose a particular destination according to their motives for travelling. A vacationer who simply wants to lie in the sun for a week will probably choose a warm seaside resort. A traveller who wants to learn about Italian art might decide to visit museums in Rome, Florence, and Venice. Figure 4–1 identifies nine travel motivators that can influence a traveller's choice of destination.

Recreation People who travel for recreation might choose to relax on the beach at Cavendish, Prince Edward Island, or play golf in Banff National Park, or go skiing in the Laurentians. They are attracted to the destination by the climate, the natural amenities, and the recreational facilities. Recreational travel can also be for the purpose of shopping (in Hong Kong) or gaming (in Montreal, Windsor, or Las Vegas). And, of course, a vacationer might be attracted to a destination because it offers a wide range of activities. At Club Med resorts in the Caribbean, vacationers can sunbathe, play tennis, water ski, socialize, shop, and amuse themselves in countless other ways.

Culture Museums, art galleries, theatres, and historic sites are all cultural attractions. Some people travel to experience an earlier way of life—for example, in Upper Canada Village in Morrisburg, Ontario, or in Colonial

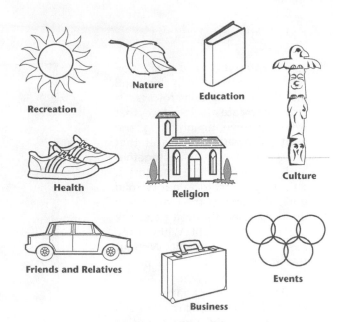

FIGURE 4–1 Motivators for Travel

Williamsburg in Virginia. Others want to learn about twentieth-century art and culture at the Louvre in Paris, or to enjoy live theatre in London's West End or at the Charlottetown Festival. For many travellers, the local people themselves are a cultural attraction. Some cultural destinations can be exotic—for example, Inuit villages on Baffin Island, Maya ruins in Honduras, or the Polynesian Culture Center in Hawaii. The common denominator is that people travel to these destinations to enrich their cultural perspectives.

Nature Many people travel to experience the great outdoors. They are attracted to natural wonders such as the Grand Canyon, Death Valley, the Canadian Rockies, and the tides of the Bay of Fundy. The desire to "get back to nature" often encourages vacationers to forgo the conveniences that hotels offer. Instead, they stay at campsites, lodges, and trailer parks.

The Trans Canada Trail, currently under development, will be the longest trail in the world, at more than 18 000 kilometres. It will pass through every province and two territories. It is being designed to satisfy the needs of walkers, cyclists, horseback riders, cross-country skiers, and snowmobilers (where possible). Ecotourists travel to unusual places to observe ecological systems and endangered species in their natural habitats. Some people travel great distances to Grand Manan Island in the Bay of Fundy to watch whales, and visit nearby Machias Seal Island to observe the puffins.

Education Some tourists choose a destination for its educational value. A retired person may register for an Elderhostel program and participate in a four-week learning program overseas that provides insights into a host country's history, language, arts and literature, customs, and so on.

Events Many people plan a vacation around a special event. It can be a sporting event (the Olympics, the Grey Cup, the Kentucky Derby), a celebration (Edmonton's Capital Ex or Capital City Exhibition), the Carnival in Rio de Janeiro, a concert or play (the Shaw Festival at Niagara-on-the-Lake), or a spectacle (the running of the bulls in Pamplona, Spain). The event itself is the attraction, not so much the city where it is held. Most people who attend the Montreal Jazz Festival do so because they want to hear the music, not necessarily because they want to spend time in Montreal. If the festival was held in Winnipeg, they might be just as likely to go there.

Health Many people are motivated by a desire to improve their health and physical fitness. Some travel great distances for an extended stay at a health spa or weight loss camp. Such destinations are popular not only because of the facilities available but also because they usually have an attractive setting, typically in the mountains or by the ocean.

Religion Modern-day pilgrims travel to religious sites such as Vatican City, Fatima in Portugal, Jerusalem in Israel, the Ganges River in India, Mecca in Saudi Arabia, and Sainte-Anne-de-Beaupré in Quebec.

Friends and Relatives Many people travel to a destination because friends or relatives live there. As with event-oriented travel, the destination is of less importance than the motivation for travelling. (Some vacationers visit friends or relatives in a destination that they would want to visit anyway; perhaps they have in-laws in Hawaii.)

ILLUSTRATION 4–3

The Royal Tyrell Musuem of Paleontology is located near Drumheller, in southeastern Alberta and has been open since 1985. It has been estimated that the museum and related tourism activities may be contributing around $15 million into the local economy.

SOURCE: Image courtesy of Royal Tyrell Museum.

Business Business travellers travel to make sales calls, consult, or attend conventions, conferences, and the like. The destination is somewhere they have to be. Meeting planners do, however, try to schedule meetings at appealing destinations so that those attending can combine business with pleasure. A conference could be held at Monterrey, California, where there are facilities for golf, tennis, swimming, and so on. Business travellers often turn a business trip into a minivacation by tacking on a few nonwork days at the beginning or end. (For a more detailed discussion of business travel, please refer to Chapter 3.)

Clearly, the categories outlined above are not mutually exclusive. A traveller need not visit a destination solely for its recreational attractions or its educational value. He or she may want to lie in the sun, learn how to windsurf, lose weight, participate in an educational seminar, and experience the local culture, all at a single destination. Such a person is attracted to the destination that can best satisfy all of these motivations.

ILLUSTRATION 4–2

Charlottetown, capital of Prince Edward Island, is home to a very popular cultural attraction—the Charlottetown Festival.

SOURCE: The Confederation CentreYoung Company in performance during the 2004 Charlottetown Festival in Charlottetown, P.E.I. Photo: Louise Vessey.

Check Your Product Knowledge

1. What kinds of facilities are needed at almost all destinations?
2. What are six reasons that tourists are attracted to destinations?

DESTINATION DEVELOPMENT

Destination development begins with an idea and with the selection of a site. The idea can come from the government of a developing nation that sees tourism as a way to increase its foreign currency reserves. Or it can come from an entrepreneur who sees an opportunity to make a profit, perhaps by converting an unspoiled island into a vacation resort.

Whoever has the idea for development, the next stage is planning. Tourism has a tremendous impact on an area's natural, social, and technological environments. This is especially true in developing countries, but needs to be remembered in developed countries as well. With careful planning, the negatives can be minimized and the positives maximized. Developers must take into account both the needs of the potential visitors and the effects of development on the host community. Benefits must be weighed against costs in terms of economic, physical, and social carrying capacity.

The Planning Stage

The first stage of destination planning can be broken down into five main components: market analysis, site assessment, financial studies, environmental impact studies, and social impact studies. The second stage then establishes the vision, mission, and goals for a destination and determines the strengths and weaknesses of several development alternatives. Then an alternative is selected and developed (see Figure 4–2).

Market Analysis Market analysis involves studying travel trends and tourists' preferences. This makes it possible to forecast the demand and compare it to the existing supply and thus determine the feasibility of a new development. Unless there is clearly a demand for the development—that is, enough potential visitors to create demand for new services—there is little point in going ahead with the development.

Market analysis can also suggest what type of development might be most successful. Surveys may reveal that travel for cultural reasons is on the increase. Or they may identify a trend toward more luxurious accommodations, or a trend toward combining business trips with vacations. Such findings ought to influence decisions on which types of facilities and amenities should be provided.

Site Assessment Site assessments answer two main questions: "What do we have?" and "What else do we need?" If existing attractions include a long sandy beach, clear blue water, and plenty of sunshine, developers may well conclude that they need a golf course and marina to attract more visitors.

Infrastructure assessments determine whether the area can physically handle an influx of tourists. Will new roads

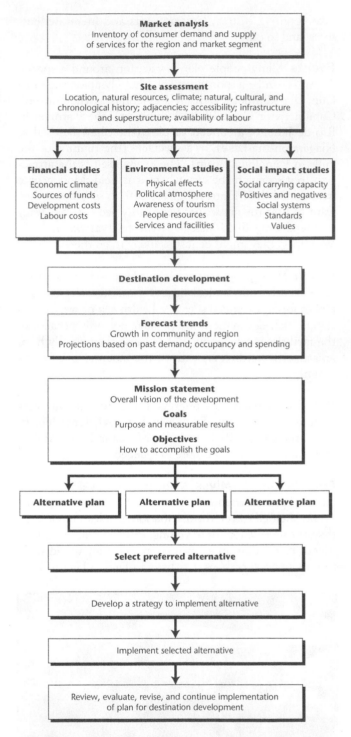

FIGURE 4–2 How a Destination Is Developed

be needed, or will it be enough to improve the old ones? Is there adequate drinking water? How will garbage be disposed of?

Site assessment also considers superstructure needs. In many developing regions, the superstructure will need to be built from scratch. Hotels, restaurants, convention centres, recreation facilities, shops, and other visitor amenities need to be in place to provide services. A destination developed around an attraction without support services will encounter problems. Intrawest has demonstrated how underperforming resorts can be transformed into four-season pedestrian villages that pay off in year-round demand (see this chapter's Profile feature).

Present and future transportation needs must be considered to determine whether the destination will be accessible to major markets. New roads and railways may have to be built. Airports and port facilities may have to be expanded.

Finally, the site assessment must consider the local labour supply. If the local population isn't large enough to supply the necessary labour, workers will need to be brought in from outside to build and staff hotels, restaurants, and other visitor facilities. This will create demand for staff housing. Tourist destinations like Banff, Alberta, have had to create superstructure to accommodate both guests and employees.

Financial Studies Early in the planning process, developers must estimate the project's cost. They also need to determine where and how they are going to arrange financing for the development. Capital can come from private investors, real estate investment trusts (REITS, refer to Chapter 9), or, in the case of developing nations, from international agencies such as the United Nations Development Programme and the World Bank Group.

A good financial study must determine the project costs for each stage of development, and consider where the money for each stage will come from. Developers, of course, want to make a profit. But they must also consider the economic impact of the development on the host community so, for example, the financial study ought to project the effect of the development on local property values and on local employment patterns. A successful development will minimize the negative economic impact and maximize the positive.

Environmental Impact Studies At some point in the planning process, decision makers must consider the physical effects that a sudden influx of visitors will have on the local natural and built environments. An environmental impact study asks questions such as: How many visitors can the beaches handle and still remain clean? How many high-rise hotels can be built before the destination loses its appeal? What is the destination's carrying capacity?

Carrying capacity refers to the maximum number of people who can visit the destination without causing an unacceptable deterioration in the physical environment and without an unacceptable decline in the quality of the experience. Carrying capacity is a concern for Canada's national parks, especially the four mountain national parks: Banff, Jasper, Kootenay, and Yoho.

In April 1997, after public consultation and a study of the local ecology, a new management plan for Banff

National Park was tabled in the House of Commons. It was designed to guide the park's overall direction for the following 10 to 15 years, and to serve as the framework for all decision making within the park. This plan is a decisive step toward a sustainable future for the park.

Social Impact Studies Equally important are studies of tourists' likely impact on the host community. Local people may well resent the arrival of large numbers of affluent tourists. In developing countries, the introduction of foreign cultures with different social standards has the potential to compromise local customs and value systems. Social impact studies aim to minimize this negative impact and to create a healthy relationship between local residents and tourists. With careful planning, the positive social effects on the host community can outweigh the negative ones.

ILLUSTRATION 4–4

The shrine of Sainte-Anne-de-Beaupré, near Quebec City, is a very popular religious site in Canada.

SOURCE: Image courtesy of Canadian Tourism Commission.

Involvement in Tourism Development

The Development Process Pearce (1989) suggests that there are three types of development: integrated, catalytic, and coattail. Disney World was an integrated development because it involved the following:

- One developer
- Balanced development
- Rapid development
- Functional form
- Isolation
- High priced

With catalytic developments like Whistler, British Columbia, and Banff, Alberta, one development project follows another. Initially there is a centralized development that establishes the infrastructure and superstructure. Then secondary developers, often local companies and individuals, are encouraged to add facilities that require less capital investment. This creates interdependency. If the initial development is successful, other entrepreneurs will become involved. Often the principal developer establishes compatibility requirements to ensure success, and the local government determines the pace of growth.

Coattail development is commonly found near existing natural or cultural attractions like national parks and historic sites. Cavendish, Prince Edward Island, with its boardwalk, Rainbow Valley, Anne of Green Gables attraction, and golf course, has developed around a national park. There may be duplication and redundancy if similar businesses are established, leading to competition among service providers and a healthy business environment. Coattail development usually evolves without a plan; so that tourists will continue to be attracted to the area, community involvement may be necessary to regulate the quality of old and new businesses.

The Role of Government Tourism can be an important source of revenue for governments at all levels, which is why governments often play an active role in destination development. Public sector tourist organizations focus mainly on promoting and regulating tourism, but sometimes they also become involved in destination planning.

The federal government and the province of Quebec have provided financial assistance to Intrawest in the form of interest-free loans and grants. Intrawest has used the loans and grants to build year-round tourist facilities at Mont Tremblant, Quebec.

World Tourism Organization Two United Nations World Tourism Organization (UNWTO) objectives are to improve people's access to education and culture through travel and to raise standards of living in developing countries by promoting tourism in these areas. The UNWTO also provides a forum for addressing problems that affect tourists everywhere, such as the problem of international terrorism. And it tries to increase tourism worldwide by encouraging governments to ease restrictions on international travel.

The UNWTO studies international tourism trends and devises standards, measurements, forecasts, and marketing strategies. Thus, it can provide valuable information to tourism promotion agencies in individual countries. (More information about the UNWTO can be found in Chapter 1.)

National Tourism Organizations National tourism organizations (NTOs) promote their countries as tourist destinations. NTOs vary widely in structure and organization. Some are independent government ministries. Others are government agencies or bureaux within larger departments. Still others are quasi-public tourism authorities. However they are organized, most have these functions:

- Promote inbound tourism through publicity and advertising campaigns.
- Conduct research into tourism.
- Draft tourism development plans, both national and regional.
- License and regulate hotels, travel agencies, tour guides, interpreters, and the like.
- Train hotel staff, tour guides, interpreters, and other tourism service personnel.
- Operate resort facilities.

An NTO's goals and policies can range from simply attracting as many visitors as possible to protecting a nation's cultural heritage. Egypt's National Tourist Board vetoed a resort proposed by a Saudi financier because of concerns about possible damage to the Pyramids. In Canada, the NTO is the Canadian Tourism Commission (CTC), established in 1994 and made a Crown corporation in 2001. The CTC is discussed in more depth in Chapter 5 as a component of the tourism services sector.

Many NTOs have moved beyond promotional and marketing activities to assume greater responsibility in the planning process. This is especially true in countries such as Mexico, Thailand, and South Korea, where destination areas are being planned and developed. Governments often develop destinations in cooperation with domestic and foreign private companies; for example, Mexico's government helped develop and fund the resort area of Cancun.

For decades, government involvement in tourism was most pronounced in the Eastern European countries. An NTO such as Intourist (renowned as the official state travel agency of the former Soviet Union) used to have complete control over tourism in that country. Intourist even functioned as a tour operator, selling travel arrangements to foreign visitors. Intourist was privatized in 1992 and is now 66 percent owned by Moscow-based holding company Sistema.

Provincial and Local Tourism Organizations
Provinces and cities promote tourism for the same reasons

that national governments do: to obtain tourist revenues and to encourage economic development. Tourism is among the largest retail industries in Canada. It is an important source of revenue across Canada. Every province and territory has an official agency responsible for travel promotion and development. Tourist offices (TOs) develop and distribute promotional literature, entertain travel writers, and even try to lure film crews in the hope that the resulting movies will generate favourable publicity. Following the lead of major cities that have convention and visitors' bureaux to promote their cities, most provinces have also begun to promote themselves as destinations for convention sites.

Tourist promotion is just one aspect of the work done by provincial and local TOs. Many also do long-range planning and monitor existing tourist facilities on a regular basis. Many provincial and local TOs are helping draft policies on land use and infrastructure and performing environmental impact studies. They are also examining and trying to improve attitudes toward tourists and tourism. TOs have graduated from doing "Visit scenic . . ." promotions to examining the long-term impact of tourism. Finally, they are conducting studies relating to issues such as sustainability, seasonality, financial benefits, and the quality of visitor experiences.

The Need for Greater Government Involvement

The trend toward greater government involvement at all levels in tourism development is a positive one. In underdeveloped countries in particular, governments need to formulate policies to ensure that destination development suits the country and its residents. Developing nations cannot afford to rush headlong into destination development without considering the possible negative effects. If they do, they may be sacrificing their future in exchange for today's tourist dollars.

With a carefully planned and well-managed program of tourism development, governments can reap positive benefits, both economic and intangible. The latter often include an improvement in the country's image both at home and abroad, a widening of educational and cultural horizons, and a general improvement in the quality of life.

Before we move on to examine the positives and negatives of destination development, let's take a look at a specific example of development.

An Evolving Destination: Walt Disney World

Walt Disney World near Orlando in central Florida is a good example of how to develop a destination for tourism.

The seeds for Disney World were planted almost 5000 kilometres to the west, in California's Orange County. There, in the mid-1950s, Walt Disney built a family-oriented amusement park called Disneyland. Based on characters and events from Disney's popular movies, its 98 hectares offered everything from a ride in the Mad Hatter's giant teacups to a fairy-tale castle.

ILLUSTRATION 4–5
Walt Disney World is a good example of how to develop a destination for tourism.
SOURCE: Corel.

The only "mistake" Disney and his staff made was in underestimating just how popular Disneyland would become. Millions of people flocked there. They spent money inside the amusement park, of course. But right outside the park, they gave their money for food, lodging, and recreation to independent businesses whose only reason for existence and success was their proximity to Disneyland. Every business in Anaheim, where the park is located, rode Disneyland's coattails to prosperity. WED Enterprises, the corporation that developed the second Disney park, learned from what happened at Disneyland.

Disney World is an integrated development. In the 30-plus years since it opened, WED has turned a central Florida swamp into a self-contained development covering roughly 4000 hectares (of the 12 000 the company owns). A number of different enterprises have been created at Disney World over the years. The first to open was the Magic Kingdom (1971), a Disneyland-like theme park and resort. Epcot Center (Experimental Prototype Community of Tomorrow) and World Showcase followed in 1982. The MGM Studios Theme Park, a tribute to Hollywood, opened in 1989. Between then and 1995, The Boardwalk, Pleasure Island, Typhoon Lagoon, and Blizzard Island were developed. In 1996, the Disney Club Resort was added as well as a vacation community called the Disney Institute, which provides both enrichment and enjoyment. A convention resort, the Coronado Springs Resort, and the Wide World of Sports community opened in 1997. The Animal Kingdom (1998), a live-action adventure park that celebrates animals, is five times the size of the Magic Kingdom and has been developed to feature the real, the mythical, and the extinct.

Disney Cruise Line vacations, which blend a three- or four-day stay at Disney World with a three- or four-day cruise on one of Disney's two ships, the *Disney Wonder* and the *Disney Magic*, began in 1999. The cruise line pushes the boundaries of Disney World and the philosophical boundaries of Disney entertainment.

Florida offers a number of natural advantages as the site for Disney World. Its climate allows year-round operation and construction. Its east coast location means that Disney World does not compete with Disneyland, and draws people from Canada and Europe. The Florida government, aware of the potential revenue, passed statutes that gave Disney World virtual independence. Disney's staff has had complete control over the entire development. Every phase since the first has been financed by profits from existing operations.

Disney World will likely keep enlarging and expanding; favourite attractions will be revised, updated, and added to—as Walt Disney once said—"as long as there is imagination left in the world" (Kurtti, 1996).

The Life Cycle of Destinations

Disney World has been in operation for more than three decades (since 1970) and has been recognized globally as a world-class attraction. But not all tourist destinations are as fortunate as Disney World. Some rise from obscurity to the height of popularity and then fall back into obscurity in a short space of time. Others go in and out of fashion cyclically. The Côte d'Azur in southern France has gone through several phases of popularity and decline since it was first developed as a health spa for the wealthy at the end of the nineteenth century.

To understand how destinations rise and fall in popularity, we can look at the **product life cycle theory**, a basic marketing concept (see Figure 4–3). The theory identifies four stages in the life cycle of a product: inception, growth, maturity, and decline.

During the **inception stage**, the destination is discovered, usually by a few Venturer travellers who don't like to go where everyone else goes. The host community usually welcomes this first wave of tourists—as well as investors—and there is considerable personal contact between visitors and residents. As word spreads, this "unknown" spot increases in popularity and enters the **growth stage**. Hotels, restaurants, and other tourist-oriented facilities are built by the local residents, though typically not to any well-thought-out plan. Toward the end of the growth stage, relations between tourists and residents tend to become more personal.

As advertising campaigns attract more and more visitors, the destination reaches the **maturity stage**. At this point, local residents begin to lose control over the development of tourism. Big hotels and restaurant chains move into the area, and facilities and services become standardized. A significant part of the local population comes to depend on tourism for its living. Employment patterns and social standards are altered. By the end of the maturity stage, the local people have begun to resent the growing number of tourists and the loss of their own cultural identity.

The final stage—**decline**—is reached when the destination becomes oversaturated with tourists. The site has exceeded its carrying capacity. For the local population, the negative effects of tourism now outweigh the benefits. For the visitors, the destination's attractions have lost their appeal. The beaches have become overcrowded, the site has been commercialized, and the natives are no longer friendly.

Carrying capacity can be measured in three different ways. If local residents are squeezed out of local activities, a destination's economic carrying capacity has been

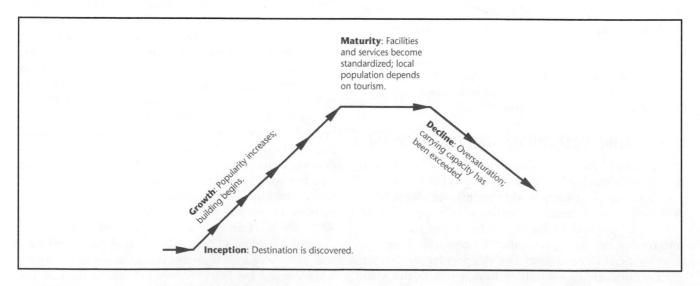

FIGURE 4–3 Life Cycle of a Destination

reached. If the beaches become contaminated, historic buildings are damaged, or traffic becomes congested, the physical carrying capacity has been exceeded. If local residents' tolerance of tourists has reached its limits, then the destination has surpassed its social carrying capacity.

Since carrying capacity is based on two intangibles—the characteristics of the tourists and the characteristics of the destination and its population—it is difficult to determine a destination's carrying capacity. Destination planning should, however, always include a reasonable estimate of carrying capacity. Doing so can help ensure that the destination remains in the maturity stage of its life cycle for as long as possible and forestalls advancing into decline.

Not all destinations pass through every stage outlined here. A few never progress beyond the inception stage. This is especially true for remote destinations. Others go straight from discovery to maturity, bypassing the growth stage. The Fiji Islands and Guam are good examples of this. And some, such as Disney World and the resort area of Cancun in Mexico, moved directly to maturity without passing through either of the two early stages.

Some destinations lose their appeal as tourist attractions without ever reaching their carrying capacity. This can be the result of unpredictable factors. Political events, for example, have often changed tourists' minds on the desirability of a destination. Cuba was once a very popular vacation spot, especially for residents of the eastern United States and Canada. It was inexpensive and warm, and it had legalized gambling and magnificent ocean fishing. When Fidel Castro overthrew the Batista dictatorship in 1959 and declared Cuba a communist country, North American tourists stopped going to the island. Cuba has once again become a destination for Canadian tourists, however, and the Cuban government supports the development of facilities and services to meet tourists' expectations. Civil unrest has had similar effects on tourism in the Middle East and Northern Ireland. In the past few years, however, Ireland has regained some of its appeal, and tourism is making a positive contribution to its economy. Politics in the Middle East are still unpredictable, and this has had a negative impact on tourism.

Unfavourable changes in currency rates can also discourage tourists from visiting a foreign country. The reverse is also true, of course: Mexico became a very popular destination for Canadians and Americans after the peso plummeted against the dollar; from the 1980s to 2007, the higher U.S. dollar gave U.S. tourists to Canada an advantage, but in 2007 the Canadian dollar increased and the number of American visitors has been declining.

A tourist destination can decline in popularity through the loss of the natural resources that made it

ILLUSTRATION 4–6
Whistler Village is an example of a development that was carefully thought out to create a year-round tourist destination.
SOURCE: Courtesy of Rebecca Hull.

attractive in the first place. A lake or river may run dry; a beach may be polluted by an oil spill. Finally, the growth of rival destinations can have a negative effect on existing destinations. Each new theme park, for example, draws travellers away from the others. It can be a challenge for older parks to maintain a competitive advantage.

Sometimes an unpredictable factor can cause a destination to become more popular. The popularity of the thrilling 2004 bestseller *The Da Vinci Code* inspired tourists to follow the "Grail trail" and visit London, Paris, Rome, and Scotland to see the artwork and architecture described in the novel (CBS News, 2004). After the 2004 vineyard movie *Sideways*, some of the Santa Barbara County's (California) wineries experienced a 300 percent increase in visitors (Yoshino, 2004). Similarly, the *Anne of Green Gables* television series has increased tourism in Prince Edward Island. Japanese girls have been reading the *Anne of Green Gables* books, on which the series was based, for several decades. Prince Edward Island has become such a popular destination for Japanese tourists visiting North America that some tourist publications there are trilingual: English, French, and Japanese.

Check Your Product Knowledge

1. What is involved in the planning stages of destination development?
2. How do the four stages of the product life cycle apply to understanding destinations and their development?

THE ECONOMIC IMPACT OF DESTINATION DEVELOPMENT

When a destination is developed for tourism, the influx of tourists has a tremendous impact on the local and national economy. Regardless of their reasons for travelling, all tourists spend money during their stay at a destination. Visitor spending provides income and profits for businesses as diverse as hotels, campgrounds and RV parks, restaurants, gas stations, golf courses, grocery stores, and souvenir shops. Local, provincial, and national governments receive revenues from sales taxes, occupancy taxes, and alcohol and gasoline taxes, and from user fees for campgrounds, parks, ski slopes, highways, and other amenities. Perhaps most important of all, tourist dollars generate employment for local residents.

A few figures illustrate just how large a contribution tourism can make to the economy. According to Statistics Canada (March 27, 2008), tourism spending by Canadians and visitors in 2007 was $70.6 billion ($3.7 billion more

than in 2006). The World Travel & Tourism Council (WTTC) (n.d.) reported in 2007 one job in twelve worldwide was a tourism-related position. And the Canadian Tourism Human Resource Council (n.d.) stated that in 2006, 1.66 million Canadians were employed in the tourism industry, representing 10.1 percent of Canadian workers.

According to the UNWTO website, Canada has not placed in the top 10 in International tourism arrivals since 2003, when Canada fell from 7th position (2002) in the World's Top Tourist Destinations to its current 12th.

Tourism is the world's largest growth industry, and international tourism has been increasing at an average of 9 percent annually for many years. According to the Tourism Satellite Accounting (TSA) research of the WTTC and its strategic partner Accenture, "the long-term forecasts point to a mature but steady phase of growth for world Travel & Tourism between 2009 and 2018, averaging a growth rate of 4.4% per annum." It is also "expected to generate close to US$8 trillion in 2008, rising to approximately US$15 trillion over the next ten years" (WTTC, March 6, 2008).

In the United States, tourism creates millions of jobs and generates taxes for all three levels of government. Figures for other nations are not as high as in the United States, but that does not mean that the economic impact of tourism is any smaller. In fact, in many developing countries it is considerably greater. Tourism is almost the only source of export income for some countries, such as the Cayman Islands (CIA, 2004).

Tourism Dollars and the Multiplier Effect

The flow of tourism dollars into a local economy is a complicated process. Let's look at an example to see how the money spent by a single tourist at a resort is distributed.

Liz Clare spends $3000 during her vacation at Montego Bay, Jamaica. We can break her expenditures down like this: $1200 for a hotel room, $600 for restaurant meals, $375 for a rental car, $525 for recreation and entertainment, and $300 for souvenirs and miscellaneous items. These expenditures represent direct spending—that is, money that goes directly from the traveller into the economy. It would seem simple to deduce that the local economy has $3000 more than it would have had if Clare had decided to vacation elsewhere. In fact, that $3000 means considerably more to the economy, because of what economists call the multiplier effect (see Figure 4–4).

Clare's $3000 does not stop working once it has reached the hotel operator and the owners of the other tourist facilities. The money is respent several times, generating more income and further employment. The Montego Bay restaurants, for example, must buy food and beverages from local suppliers, who in turn must make purchases from local farmers. Part of Clare's $3000 also goes to pay wages to the employees of the hotel, the restaurants,

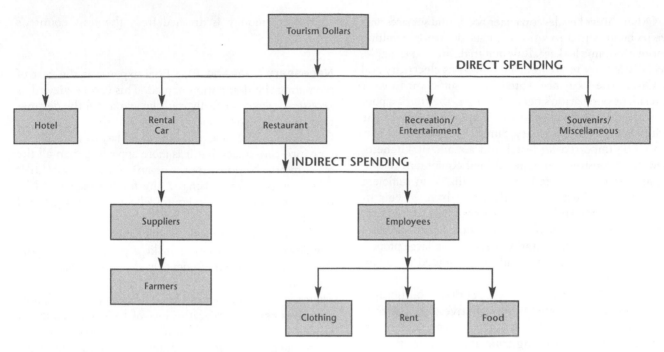

FIGURE 4–4 Tourism Dollars and the Multiplier Effect

and other tourist businesses. The workers in turn pay rent, buy groceries, and so on. These successive rounds of spending generated by Clare's initial spending are known as **indirect spending**.

The Tourism Multiplier Clearly, the total of all income is far greater than the initial $3000 spent by Clare. The actual amount by which the country's income will increase can be worked out using a formula called the **tourism multiplier**. Direct and indirect tourist expenditures affect more than income; multipliers can also be estimated for sales, output, employment, and payroll.

The Concept of Leakage In the example of Clare, we assumed that the whole of her $3000 flowed into the Montego Bay economy. Actually, not all of that money stays in the local economy. Many of the goods and services that are needed to satisfy tourist desires have to be imported. Clare, for example, enjoys a glass of wine with her evening meal. Wine is not produced locally, so it has to be imported. Part of her $3000 leaves the local economy as payments to overseas wine growers.

Leakage is the economic term for money that flows out of the economy to purchase outside resources. More imports mean greater leakage and less money circulating in the local economy—a lower tourism multiplier. Many Caribbean resorts have to import most of the goods that tourists buy. As a result, they have a relatively low multiplier. Clare's $3000 may in fact contribute only $1500 to the local economy. If an area has sufficient resources to produce all the necessary goods and services, tourist expenditures remain in the area in their full amount and the

multiplier is high. Clearly, the more developed the local economy, the higher the multiplier.

Tourism and the Balance of Payments

Countries develop tourist destinations in order to earn foreign currency and to reduce their balance of payments deficits. A country's balance of payments is the difference between payments for imports and receipts from exports. (Remember that tourism is an export industry.) Unfortunately, the developing nations that have the most to gain from tourism very often are the ones that suffer from the highest leakages. Foreign exchange receipts are substantially reduced because a large proportion of tourist expenditures and profits flow out of the country to foreign investors and foreign suppliers. As a result, tourism rarely eliminates large balance of payments deficits.

Canada traditionally runs a negative balance in its tourism account. According to Statscan, Canada's international travel account deficit reached $10.3 billion in 2007, up $3.6 billion from 2006 (Statistics Canada, February 28, 2008). The challenge for Canada is to attract more visitors from other countries, and to encourage more Canadians to travel within Canada and spend more dollars here.

Where the Money Goes Some destinations have to import meat, vegetables, and even water to cater to tourists. Tourism can also increase local residents' demand for imported goods. With the influx of affluent foreign tourists, residents of developing countries are exposed to new consumer goods and develop a taste for them. And with higher incomes as a result of tourism development, they can now afford to buy them.

Other things besides consumer goods and services may have to be imported to satisfy tourists' demands, resulting in more economic leakage. Raw materials are one example, especially as they relate to utilities such as electricity and gas. Often, the local raw materials are sufficient to meet the resident population's needs, but then the tourists pour in, and suddenly coal has to be imported to meet the soaring demand for electricity. Similarly, propane gas may have to be imported for hotel and restaurant kitchens. Likewise, if construction materials and equipment (elevators, air conditioners, etc.) are not available in sufficient quantity in the host country, they will have to be purchased elsewhere. And a country without a domestic automobile industry is going to have to import cars and buses to satisfy tourists' transportation needs. So a large proportion of tourist revenues may end up being used to pay for imported materials and equipment.

Another factor that reduces a country's tourism revenues is the income earned by foreign investors. The early stages of destination development require a massive investment of capital. Developing countries cannot afford to finance large-scale infrastructural and superstructural projects, so they are forced to seek financial assistance abroad. Without foreign investment, the destinations could not be developed for tourism. But developing countries must then spend years repaying loans and paying interest on the investments.

Multinational corporations are also affecting tourism revenues in host countries. International hotel and restaurant chains have opened properties in resort destinations throughout the world. Because they are foreign-owned, most of their revenues are transferred out of the host country. Countries also lose out on tourist revenues when airfares are paid to foreign-owned airlines. Few developing nations can afford to operate their own airlines.

The following example illustrates how large amounts of money can leak out of the host economy. A couple from Saskatchewan decides to vacation in the Bahamas. They make air and hotel reservations through a travel agency in Regina. They are booked on a Canadian air carrier, Air Canada, flying through Toronto to Nassau. They stay in a hotel that is part of an American chain and they eat at an American-owned restaurant. They hire a Hertz rental car for a couple of days; they drink beverages bottled in the United States and elsewhere. The only money that remains in the host country is a few dollars for souvenirs and the wages paid to local employees.

Then there are management fees. Many local hotels that are not part of a chain are managed by foreign corporations, which are paid a fee for their services. If the local labour force is not big enough, foreign workers may have to be imported to fill jobs in hotels, restaurants, and other tourist-oriented businesses. Salaries may have to be paid to foreign entertainers who perform in the local nightclubs, to visiting sports professionals who give golf and tennis lessons, and to other nonlocal employees. In all these ways,

even more money is drained from the host country's economy.

Necessary Leakage One final expense is the cost of promoting the destination abroad. This can be viewed as *necessary leakage*—it really can't be avoided if the destination is going to attract tourists. In the competitive Caribbean market, each island resort has to advertise to convince consumers that it is more appealing than all the other resorts. National tourist organizations promote their destinations by advertising in the foreign media and by offering FAM trips to foreign travel counsellors and travel writers.

This discussion of leakage may make you wonder how any destination manages to make a profit from tourism. But many do, not only in developed nations (where leakages tend to be lower) but also in developing countries. Planning is the key to success. For example, developing countries can minimize the loss of tourist revenues by implementing plans aimed at reducing imports of tourism-related items. One way is by supporting local industries. Another is by offering incentives to local hoteliers, thereby reducing foreign control of the hospitality industry. The number of foreign employees in managerial and professional positions can be reduced if local residents are educated and trained in the relevant disciplines.

All of these measures help ensure that a greater percentage of tourism revenues stays in the host country and that the economic benefits of destination development—employment, income, and tax revenue—outweigh possible negative effects.

Check Your Product Knowledge

1. What is the multiplier effect?
2. What is leakage, in the context of tourism?

THE SOCIAL IMPACT OF TOURISM

The success of destination development is most commonly measured in economic terms. However, we should not overlook the social, cultural, and physical impacts of tourism. The residents of Canmore, Alberta, fear that their town may lose its "rustic charm" if the pace of development quickens. There is concern in many quarters that Canmore could become another Banff. The thrust of Canmore's strategy is to get the economy and the environment to work together.

It is now widely recognized that destination development causes social change, both positive and negative.

The social effects of destination development tend to be less significant in developed countries. Less-developed nations are more likely to experience the negative social effects of tourism. When tourism replaces other economic activities, or when a destination is developed too rapidly or too intensively, the social impact can be especially damaging. Here again, intelligent planning is extremely important. With conservative scheduling, good management, and an understanding of local needs, the negative social impact of destination development can be minimized.

Socioeconomic Impact

The economic impact of destination development can have social implications. The most obvious socioeconomic effects relate to population growth, changing employment patterns, increased incomes, and rising property values. In the early stages of destination development, labourers must be hired to build hotels, restaurants, and recreation and entertainment facilities and to upgrade the local infrastructure. Once the destination has opened to tourists, people are needed to staff the facilities. In developing countries, the local population is rarely large enough to provide the necessary labour. Workers must therefore be brought in from outside. The migrant workers will require housing, perhaps schools for their children, and other amenities.

A rapid influx of workers from away can cause serious social problems. The new workers may find it difficult to fit into the community. The local residents may resent their presence and actively discriminate against the newcomers.

Another problem revolves around what to do with the construction workers when the development boom is over. Some of the migrant workers will return home; others will stay on to work in the tourist facilities. People who worked steadily during the construction phase may be faced with unemployment. A related problem arises when tourism is strictly seasonal. What happens to the local workers during the off-season? Some may return to traditional economic activities, such as farming or fishing, but this in itself can lead to other types of social strain.

Changing Employment Patterns Many local residents find their social status in the community altered after they take tourism-related employment. This can have positive or negative results, or both, in Canada and other destinations.

Many women enter the job market for the first time when tourism development occurs. This can raise family incomes, improve women's self-esteem, and expand their awareness of the outside world. But it can also disrupt the existing social structure, especially in countries where men have traditionally been the only wage earners. A husband may have difficulty accepting the fact that his wife can earn more money working in a tourist hotel than he can from fishing or farming. Demand for daycare increases, and

rates of divorce and juvenile delinquency may rise. Also, women working in tourist-oriented jobs may decide to postpone marriage and childbearing.

Traditional relationships between the young and the old may shift as young people find work in tourism. Established local industries such as agriculture and fishing may suffer as workers are drawn toward tourism. A farmer may decide there's a better living to be made as a hotel cook's assistant than by scratching out a crop of corn from a rocky field. A young man whose father and grandfather both fished for a living may decide that instead of following the family tradition, he would rather wait tables at a dockside restaurant. The pay is often better.

Increased Incomes The higher incomes that tourism employment brings can radically change local lifestyles. Suddenly the local residents can afford consumer goods (many of them imported) that were once beyond their purchasing power. This can lead to demands for better housing and schools, and to changes in dress and eating habits. People who once worked the land or the sea for their living may come to appreciate a steady paycheque. But if tourists stop coming to the destination, local residents will have to either return to their traditional occupations—and former lifestyles—or leave the community. In either case, the social consequences can be serious.

Rising Property Values If demand increases for land for tourist facilities, property values can soar. Local buyers may be priced out of the market. Local renters may discover they have no place to live if low-priced rental properties are demolished to make way for luxury hotels. Small businesses may be forced to close if they can no longer afford to pay the increased rents.

These effects can be especially devastating in communities that have large numbers of fixed-income senior citizens or low-income families. When gaming was legalized in Atlantic City, working-class residents were faced with the choice of paying high rents or moving out of the area.

Resentment Resentment tends to be most pronounced in destinations where tourism is the community's main source of income. Tourists are most often welcomed in the early stages of development, but eventually—usually late in the maturity stage—all the community's activities become geared to accommodating tourist demands, and by then the limits of local tolerance have usually been reached. By this stage, the mere physical presence of large numbers of tourists may create resentment. Congestion may have become a problem, and local residents may now be tired of sharing overcrowded facilities and overtaxed services with visitors. Perhaps they see vacationers living in luxury while their basic needs are going unmet. An extreme example of this clash between affluence and poverty arose in Ivory Coast in West Africa. There, a resort hotel was using 570 litres of water per room per day, while

ILLUSTRATION 4–7

Atlantic City casino hotels overlook the Atlantic Ocean and are located along the world-famous 6-kilometre-long Boardwalk (opened in 1870).

SOURCE: Image courtesy of Atlantic City Convention & Visitors Authority.

local villagers did not yet have running water in their homes.

Foreign ownership and employment can be another cause of resentment, especially when foreign employees manage resorts and earn high salaries while the menial work is left to local residents. Anger can also grow from the perception that tourists are causing a decline in moral standards. Crime, gaming, and prostitution have all been known to increase in areas that become tourist destinations.

Cultural Effects

An influx of tourists from other cultures can profoundly affect the local culture. One of the most common results of tourism is the demonstration effect: The host community adopts the social and cultural values of the visiting tourists. Most people who can afford to travel abroad are from Canada, the United States, and Western Europe, so it is mainly Western values that are spread throughout the world in this way. Critics argue that as a result, many local

cultures are in danger of disappearing. Others contend that the adoption process works both ways: Local residents may adopt tourist values, but at the same time, tourists adopt the values of the countries they visit (this is known as "cross-adoption"). For example, the North American interest in foreign cuisine has grown in part because so many Canadian and American tourists enjoyed eating local foods while abroad.

There is also disagreement about the effects that tourism development has on local traditions. Some people say that local artistic standards suffer when cheap reproductions of native crafts are mass-produced for tourist consumption. They also claim that commercialization has a negative impact on local religious and social customs. In some places, for example, ceremonial dances that were once performed for religious purposes are now being staged to entertain tourists.

On the positive side, tourism has been credited with helping traditional arts and crafts survive. There is ample evidence to support this claim. In the southwestern United States, the interest that tourists have shown in native

ILLUSTRATION 4–8

The Fortress of Louisbourg National Historic Park on Cape Breton Island, Nova Scotia, is an eighteenth-century reconstructed French town, complete with costumed staff re-creating life in 1744.

SOURCE: Image courtesy of Canadian Tourism Commission.

cultures has greatly increased the demand for local pottery, jewellery, weaving, and so on. The native people of the American southwest have resisted the temptation to turn out mass-produced imitations, so the quality of their products has remained high. The same holds true in parts of Canada. The demand for souvenirs has kept alive the Inuit craft of soapstone carving and East Coast cottage crafts such as knitting and quilting.

Tourism can even contribute to ethnic preservation. By the 1950s, the Cajuns of Louisiana had been almost totally assimilated, and their unique identity had almost vanished. When Cajun Louisiana was developed as a tourist destination in the 1950s, local residents began taking pride in their cultural origins. Tourists from all over the United States expressed their appreciation for the hot, spicy Cajun food and the distinctive Cajun music, and took an interest in the Creole language. Tourism thus helped the Cajuns preserve their cultural heritage and retain a separate identity. (Incidentally, the Cajuns present a good example of the cross-adoption discussed earlier: Local residents adopt the values of visitors from other parts

of North America, and in turn the tourists adopt certain Cajun habits, such as their food and their music.)

Similarly, Acadian culture in the Maritimes (from which the Louisiana Cajuns were expelled in the 1700s) has been strengthened through destination development. Examples include the Fortress of Louisbourg, the largest ongoing restoration project in Canada, which showcases about 50 buildings as they appeared in 1744; Port-Royal in Nova Scotia, a reconstruction of the habitation established by Champlain in 1605; and the historic village of Caraquet, New Brunswick. Thousands of Acadian descendants flocked to Nova Scotia in August 2004 for the third World Acadian Congress to celebrate Acadian culture. Events such as the Congress should stimulate tourism in the Maritime provinces (Aitken, 2004).

Unfortunately, an influx of tourists from different cultures can have less desirable consequences. The Pennsylvania Amish lived in quiet obscurity for hundreds of years until they were "discovered" as a tourist attraction. The Amish had no desire to make a profit from tourism; they just wanted to be left in peace. Others, however, had different ideas. They built motels, restaurants, golf courses, souvenir shops, and gas stations to cater to the growing demands of tourists. Today, the Amish are subjected to prying stares from busloads of visitors. They are photographed like freaks in a sideshow. Tourism has disrupted their way of life.

On a positive note, destination development often pays cultural dividends to the residents of the host community. Entertainment and recreational facilities developed for incoming tourists—including cinemas and theatres, cultural centres, sports stadiums, golf courses, and ski slopes—can also be used by the local residents. Cultural events such as the Charlottetown Festival and the Toronto Film Festival are not merely tourist attractions—they also enhance the cultural lives of the local population.

The Physical Impact of Destination Development

Finally, destination development affects the physical environment. Measurements can be taken of air, water, and soil quality. The local plants and animals can be studied, and protected as necessary. Property values can be assessed. Traffic patterns can be charted.

In both developed and underdeveloped countries, the emphasis must be on a controlled rate of development that minimizes harm to the natural environment. Farsighted planning can reduce conflicts over land use between local residents and developers. If a destination is developed too rapidly, irreparable damage may be done. In developed countries, destination development can strain the existing infrastructure, causing pollution and overcrowding. Even natural resources may be threatened. In certain national parks, for example, traffic congestion and littering are constant problems. If a site's natural beauty is ruined by commercialization and the local lake is teeming with tourists and drink bottles and cans, the residents naturally resent the tourist intrusion. However attractive tourism development may seem, developers must always bear in mind the needs and feelings of the local people.

Destination development can also help preserve and even restore the physical environment. In an underdeveloped area, it can upgrade an inadequate infrastructure. If done properly, development leads to improved water supplies, better sewage facilities, and better roads. In Africa, some wildlife species have been saved from extinction by conservation efforts. Governments realized that if they allowed native animals to die out, they would lose a natural resource that attracted thousands of tourists. In Canada, the mountain sheep have been saved in the Canadian Rockies as well as the piping plover on Prince Edward Island. Clearcutting is being addressed in British Columbia and beach access issues in Nova Scotia. Developers in other countries have enhanced the natural beauty of certain destinations by devoting part of their investment capital to conservation projects. Clearly, planning is vital to the proper development of any tourist destination.

Synergy in Destination Development

Synergy is what exists when the sum of the parts is greater than the whole of the parts, as in "two plus two equals five." Potential examples in tourism development are evident when a business capitalizes on the tourism that already exists in its home city.

If the city or region is already a tourist destination, there are probably opportunities to develop new businesses, such as a bakeshop, a bookstore, or a rental shop for bikes or camping gear. Other examples of opportunity are restaurants, bars, bed-and-breakfasts and hotels, and attractions such as heritage sites and recreation facilities.

The slogans "Tourism Is Everybody's Business" and "Be Kind to Our Tourists—They're Good for Us" are familiar. Yet many sales are lost through indifference and ignorance at the counters of many small businesses in tourist towns in Canada. Training in service and sales techniques is needed. The Superhost Program has been initiated across Canada through our Tourism Education Councils for just that purpose. In addition, customer contact personnel need knowledge of the other activities available to tourists. A salesperson who directs tourists to other events in the community is encouraging additional spending in that community, and perhaps a longer stay by the tourist.

Deterrents to Destination Development

There are many deterrents that may affect the continuation of the successful development of a destination, such as tourist overcrowding, pollution and environmental degradation, political instability, and fluctuating currency rates. The two most powerful destination deterrents would be a disease epidemic and terrorism (safety and security).

In 2003, the SARS epidemic devastated the tourist economies of Hong Kong and the Toronto area, and severely damaged tourism in several other Asian countries. Terrorist incidents include the May 2003 car bombings in Casablanca, Morocco (20 died); the October 2002 car bombing that destroyed a nightclub in Kuta, Bali, Indonesia (190 died); the 1997 shooting massacre in Luxor, Egypt (58 tourists died); the 700 injured in London bombings in July 2005; and the nearly 200 people killed by 10 train bombings in Madrid in March 2004.

In January 2008, Forbes magazine, printed an article "World's Most Dangerous Destinations" and listed the following destinations: Somalia, Iraq, Afghanistan, Haiti, Pakistan, Sudan, Congo, Lebanon, Zimbabwe, and Palestine (Ruiz, 2008).

Rok Klancik of the UNWTO believes that most destinations recover, since the perception of risk will change over time and "tourism is resilient."

New Trends in Destinations

Nostalgia Tourists Nostalgia has become a significant factor in destination choice for some travellers. Travel agents have pointed to "**nostalgia tourists**" who want to return to memorable places, such as a honeymoon location (Eturbonews, January 2, 2008).

Favourite Destinations According to a recent survey, the top four favourite travellers' destinations (and their scores) are India (94.55), Italy (93.95), Thailand (93.55), and Australia (93.0). India's best features being culture (97.17), value for money (94.78), and variety of attractions (96.30) (Conté Nast Traveller, n.d.).

Emerging Destinations Many of the classic or traditional destinations (Paris, Rome, London) have become too crowded and expensive. Instead, Pamela Lassers of Abercrombie & Kent recommends cities like Bucharest (Romania), Sofia (Bulgaria), Warsaw and Krakow (both in Poland). Other travel experts recommend Pula (on the Istrian peninsula of Croatia), Ljubljana (Slovenia), Namibia (southwest Africa), the Maldives (an archipelago south of Sri Lanka), Huatulco (southeast of Acapulco in Mexico), and Panama (Weiss, 2006).

Check Your Product Knowledge

1. How do employment patterns change as a result of destination development?
2. What is the demonstration effect?

CAREER OPPORTUNITIES

Most destination development positions carry a great deal of responsibility and require a high level of education. Many workers in this field are hired on a consulting basis.

Representative careers include developer, financial adviser, market researcher, planner, architect, interior designer, landscape architect, anthropologist, and sociologist, some of which are discussed in more detail below.

Representative Careers

Market Researcher Market researchers help a developer decide if there is a market for the planned destination. Most provincial tourist organizations have research staff members who help them spot market trends and plan developments.

Planner Planners work with developers at each stage of development. They take information from market researchers, land-use specialists, architects, and others, and try to draw conclusions from it. A planner develops a master plan for a development and looks for ways to finance all its stages.

Architect/Interior Designer/Landscape Architect Once the decision has been made to build, and once funding has been found, architects, interior designers, and landscape architects begin to design the destination. If the destination is a resort, all of the buildings in the complex are designed by architects around a common theme that blends with the natural environment. An interior designer plans the interior of individual buildings, develops space plans, and specifies furnishings and other fixtures. A landscape architect designs the grounds around the facilities— lawns, gardens, walkways, access roads, etc.

Sociologist and Anthropologist A tourist destination can have huge social and cultural impacts, so sociologists and anthropologists must be consulted to assess those impacts and to suggest how negative outcomes can be minimized. Sociologists usually focus on the effects of tourism on developed areas; in contrast, anthropologists usually study tourism's impact on undeveloped areas.

A DAY IN THE LIFE OF A

Member of the CTC's Global Sales Force

The Canadian Tourism Commission (CTC) employs 50 people around the world to sell Canada as a destination. These people are located in more than a dozen cities in Europe, the United States, and Asia, including Seattle, Dallas, Chicago, Boston, London, Paris, Düsseldorf, Milan, Tokyo, and Taipei.

The representatives' agendas are packed with meetings, sales calls, seminars, and negotiations, as well as workshop presentations that promote Canadian destinations. In the course of a month, they disseminate information about Canada to thousands of people. It isn't a nine-to-five job; weekends can be as busy as weekdays. These reps form a team working on behalf of a first-class destination—Canada.

Sales reps' days are packed; The agenda of one of them is summarized below. The other 49 members of the CTC's global sales force are just as busy and contribute just as much to the project of creating year-round demand for Canadian destinations.

Representative in Seattle

8:00 a.m. On the phone at home, recruiting Canadians for a travel show at the Vancouver Aquarium to promote Vancouver Island. Eighty tour operators, agents, and representatives are expected to attend.

9:00 a.m. Met with the new Horizon Airlines sales manager. Filled him in on details of April's familiarization trip to the Rockies' new Kicking Horse ski resort. Wants to see more Canadian packages.

11:00 a.m. Met with J.G. from Whistler Resort to discuss website. Had met earlier in the week with Expedia. Whistler hopes to work out a deal with Expedia, and there may be potential for ski slopes in eastern Canada to join in.

2:30 p.m. Met with representatives of a large German operator. In 2000, they brought 150 000 Germans to the United States and 6000 to Canada. Want to see number for Canada increase to 15 000. Worked out details for a site inspection trip to Ottawa in April, based on earlier site visits to Montreal and Quebec City.

3:30 p.m. Met with J.B. of Tourism Nanaimo and the Canadian Consul General. Helped prepare for discussions with Horizon Airlines about new flights to Nanaimo.

7:30 p.m. Attended monthly meeting of the Boeing Travel Club with local travel agent. Program was an illustrated talk about eastern Canada, cross-country VIA Rail trip to Jasper, and the Rocky Mountaineer train tours. Went very well, and 36 members signed up for trips at US$3600 per trip.

SOURCES: Based on "Showcase Canada," *Communiqué*, Vol. 3, Issue 10:18, and Susan Iris (March 2001); "Moving Forward CTC–U.S. Sales Force," *Communiqué*, Vol. 5, Issue 2: 5–6.

Summary

- People choose destinations according to their motivations for travel. Motivators include recreation, culture, health, friends and relatives, and business.
- Early steps in destination planning include market analysis, site assessment, financial studies, environmental impact studies, and social impact studies.
- After the analysis stages, trends are forecast. If these are acceptable, a mission statement for the development can be finalized, alternatives can be considered and selected, and an implementation strategy can be developed and executed (and later evaluated).
- National, regional, and local tourism organizations promote travel to individual countries, regions, and cities. They are also involved in the planning process.
- Destinations rise and fall in popularity. The product life cycle theory identifies four stages of destination development: inception, growth, maturity, and decline.
- Political changes, the loss of natural resources, and the success of rival destinations can contribute to a destination's decline in popularity.
- Economic benefits of destination development include increased employment, tax revenues, and personal incomes.
- Tourist dollars are respent several times within the local community (the multiplier effect).
- Tourist dollars flow out of the local economy when imported goods and services are purchased (leakage).
- Destination development results in social change. It leads to population growth, changing employment patterns, and increased incomes.
- The presence of affluent tourists can cause resentment in the host community.
- Destination development can revitalize local cultures, but it can also place stresses on those cultures.
- The negative environmental impact of destination development can be minimized with careful planning.
- There are many deterrents that may affect the continuation of a successful development of a destination; the two most powerful would be a disease epidemic and terrorism (safety and security).

Key Terms

Internet Connections

WORKSHEET 4–1 Provincial Travel Organizations

What does your province do to promote itself as a tourist destination? Obtain promotional information from your province's travel organization website and print materials, or look through newspapers and magazines. For each of the motivations for travel listed below, briefly describe the attractions your province offers.

Recreation

_____

_____

_____

_____

Culture

_____

_____

_____

_____

Nature

_____

_____

_____

_____

Education

_____

_____

_____

_____

Health

_____

_____

_____

_____

Religion

_____

_____

_____

_____

Friends and Family

_____

_____

_____

_____

Events

_____

_____

_____

_____

Business

_____

_____

_____

_____

List any attractions in your province or territory that are not promoted but should be.

WORKSHEET 4–2   Carrying Capacity

"Carrying capacity" refers to the amount of tourism a destination can handle without negative effects. In each of the situations described below, identify which kinds of carrying capacity (economic, physical, social) are being exceeded. Explore regional websites for more information. Then suggest how the problems can be alleviated.

1.   The sandhills surrounding a small town in Alberta have become a popular place to ride off-road vehicles and dirt bikes. The traffic is destroying plants and animals, disrupting breeding cycles, and scaring wildlife out of the area. Conservation groups and local residents are concerned about the irreparable damage being done, but businesspeople do not want to lose the income generated by the riders.

_____

_____

_____

2.   A beautiful lake in Quebec has been a summer vacation spot for more than 200 years. It once consisted of small, individually owned cottages, but in the past decade, several time-sharing condominiums and a large high-rise luxury hotel have been built. Chic boutiques and upscale interior design stores are driving the older, smaller businesses out of town. Business and residential rents and property taxes have skyrocketed. The newer, larger businesses generally bring their own employees, so local employment has not risen. The locals bitterly resent what is happening.

_____

_____

_____

3.   A fishing village on the Digby Shore in Nova Scotia has become a popular tourist destination. Pleasure craft are crowding out the fishing boats that have traditionally used the public landing and harbour facilities. Waterfront property is so valuable for tourism-related purposes that some fish buyers and commercial marinas are selling out. The fishers, the businesses that support them (marine supply, boat repair, and so on), and the businesses that depend on them (such as the fish processors and retailers) are furious and are becoming desperate.

_____

_____

_____

4.   A small town on Lake Winnipeg has become a favourite weekend and summer retreat for Manitoba residents. They are now buying second homes there or renting properties for the summer. From Friday night to Sunday night, the town is crowded and noisy. Year-round residents have to wait in line at local stores, service stations, and restaurants. New bars and a dance club have opened to entertain the visitors from Winnipeg. Drinking and drug use have increased among area teenagers, and the locals blame the visitors for this. Even some of the visitors are beginning to criticize the new honky-tonk atmosphere.

_____

_____

_____

PART 2

Tourism Services Sector

Chapter 5

Objectives

When you have completed this chapter, you should be able to:

- Identify and explain the three major categories of travel and tourism organizations that promote and support tourism.

- Give examples of promotional campaigns in the public and private sectors.

- Discuss how retail sales support and promote the tourism industry.

- Understand the scope and importance of selling as the follow-up to promotion in the marketing process.

- Describe the role of governments in promoting tourism nationally and globally through organiza-

tions such as the Organisation for Economic Co-operation and Development, the World Travel and Tourism Council, and the World Tourism Organization.

- Understand the background development of the Canadian Tourism Commission, its hybrid public/private nature, and its role in tourism promotion and tourism research.

- Explain the roles and activities of provincial and territorial tourism offices.

- Distinguish between the two main types of convention and visitors' bureaux, and their functions.

Betty and Bob Wojowcowski live in the southeastern United States. They have always wanted to experience a true winter holiday. They are unsure where they should go for a two-week holiday. As money is not an issue, they are thinking of Colorado, New England, Canada, Switzerland, or the Scandinavian countries.

Ralph Miner is president of his provincial heating and plumbing association. He is responsible for advising the association on the location of its annual convention for the next three years. Some 400 suppliers attend each year. There are many mid-sized cities where they would like to meet; the major problem is finding a site with enough display space for the equipment that all the suppliers would like to bring and display. He wonders where he can find information on suitable locations.

Jennifer Farley is in her last year of high school. She has spent the past two summers working as a waitress at a summer resort. This has been an enjoyable experience, and she is thinking of pursuing a career in tourism and hospitality management. While at the resort, she interacted with students from various colleges and universities who were studying in a variety of tourism programs. She wonders where she should go and what program to follow.

Sally O'Reilly is a potter in one of the Newfoundland outports. Most of her sales are made to visiting tourists during the short summers and during the spring and fall, the shoulder seasons. She cannot afford to advertise extensively, but wishes she could reach two market targets. Her first market target would be to have additional tourists travelling to her studio while they are visiting her province; the second would be to reach potential buyers in the off-season, from around Thanksgiving in mid-October to Victoria Day in May.

Jacques des Ormeaux is retiring from the navy next year. His goal is to return to his childhood Acadian home and open a bed-and-breakfast. Having travelled throughout the world in his 25 years with the navy, he would like to attract an international clientele, especially from Europe, South Africa, Australia, New Zealand, Hong Kong, Singapore, and Japan. He wonders how to reach such a diverse market.

What do Betty and Bob, Ralph, Jennifer, Sally, and Jacques have in common? They all need information. They all need to communicate with someone or some organization that promotes or supports tourism: the **tourism services** sector. This chapter discusses components of the tourism services sector such as private and public promotion, the selling of tourism, and retail sales that support tourism.

PROFILE

The Canadian Tourism Commission Is Crowned

"CTC vision: Compel the world to explore Canada."

—CTC *Annual Report*, 2007.

In 1995, the Canadian government established the Canadian Tourism Commission (CTC) to promote Canada's tourism industry. The CTC officially became a Crown corporation in January 2001. From its rather humble beginnings as a branch of a government department, it has evolved into a powerhouse that has kick-started Canada's flagging tourist industry. It now operates more like a private sector firm. It is still accountable to Parliament through the Industry Canada minister, but as a Crown corporation it has more autonomy to achieve its goals. It is a unique public/private partnership that is industry-led, market-driven, and research-based.

Its status as a Crown corporation allows it to keep pace with a dynamic and ever-changing industry. Its staff members work closely with private sector partners to increase Canada's visibility as a tourist destination.

In the beginning, government support was $15 million. In 1999 the federal government contributed $66 million; monies from public and private sector partners amounted to $90 million. By 2007, the federal government allocation to the CTC was $76.5 million, and its private sector partners more than matched this figure with a contribution of $89.6 million.

Partnerships

The CTC believes in industry participation and has formed partnerships that are integral to its work. Through these partnerships, the CTC helps the Canadian tourism industry to market Canada as a desirable travel destination. The commission also helps the industry make decisions based on timely and accurate information. Partnerships with provincial, territorial, regional, and local government agencies, and with hoteliers, tour operators, attractions, and transportation companies—operations both large and small—have yielded real and remarkable results socially as well as economically.

Goal, Vision, Mission and Mandate

The CTC markets Canada as a premier four-season tourism destination. Its approach concentrates on global markets or consumer market segments where there is the highest potential for return on investment. The CTC is working to encourage tourism operators to set their priorities according to the organization's goal, vision, mission, and mandate:

Goal: Grow tourism export revenues for Canada.

Vision: Compel the world to explore Canada.

Mission: Harness Canada's collective voice to grow tourism export revenues.

Legislated Mandate:

- Sustain a vibrant and profitable Canadian tourism industry;
- Market Canada as a desirable tourism destination;
- Support a cooperative relationship between the private sector and the governments of Canada, the provinces and the territories with respect to Canadian tourism; and
- Provide information about Canadian tourism to the private sector and to the governments of Canada, the provinces and the territories.

The CTC Organization

The CTC has a 26-person board with members from the private and public sectors of the tourism industry. The board sets the direction for the commission. There are four standing committees established by the Canadian Tourism Act. These are the Executive Committee; Governance and Nominating Committee; Audit Committee; and Human Resources Committee. Currently, there are also seven working committees that focus on sectoral areas and seven in-market advisory committees that focus on geographic markets:

Working Committees
1. Europe/Latin America Marketing
2. Asia/Pacific Marketing
3. Product Innovation
   and Enhancement
4. Meetings, Conventions &
   Incentive Travel Marketing
5. Research
6. U.S. Marketing
7. Canada Marketing

The board selects the committee chairs from the private sector. The committee chairs develop programs in consultation with industry representatives, drawing on CTC staff as needed, and present their programs to the CTC board for approval.

Once a program has been approved by the CTC board and the program strategy and resource allocations are in place, negotiations begin on tactics and implementation. Detailed operational plans are brought back to the CTC board to ensure they are in line with the program as it has been approved. Committee chairs are responsible for the program's implementation, and CTC staff members are accountable to them.

The CTC's staff supports the board's activities and carries out the programs developed by the committees and approved by the board, working with both private and public sector partners. A five-year strategy for cultural and heritage tourism was established. Adventure travel and ecotourism gained ground, and support for small and medium-sized enterprises was addressed through partnership opportunities. In 2007, the CTC's top priorities were:

1. Consumer relevancy;
2. Align market allocations to achieve highest return on investment;
3. Differentiate Canada;

In-Market Advisory Committees
1. United Kingdom
2. France
3. Germany
4. Mexico
5. Japan
6. Australia
7. South Korea

4. Leverage media exposure of the Vancouver 2010 Olympic & Paralympic Winter Games; and
5. Organizational excellence.

Thanks to the efforts of the CTC's research committee, Canada is leading the way in having the United Nations World Tourism Organization, the tourism committee of the Organisation for Economic Co-operation and Development, and the United Nations Statistics Commission endorse the Tourism Satellite Account, a global standard for reporting tourism statistics.

The CTC is continuing to develop its advertising and sales program for the American conventions and meetings market in conjunction with visitors' bureaux, hotels, airlines, and destination marketing organizations (DMOs). The CTC believes that in this information-based economy, image ads in trade publications, relationship-building, and greater use of the Internet are necessary to move Canada up the list of locations that American meeting planners will consider. American organizations often seek "foreign yet familiar" experiences, and the CTC's advertising and promotions are geared to highlighting Canada's strength in this regard.

In 2007, the CTC introduced a new look and brand, *"Canada. Keep Exploring."* Canada's stunning scenery, uncrowded landscapes, and pristine environment

are magnets for European tourists, and the CTC is capitalizing on these. However, it has been difficult to market new regions in Canada because of the dominance of Canada's traditional gateway destinations, Toronto and Vancouver. Media coverage in the Asia/Pacific region is increasing, but Canada is still an expensive destination, and Canada's key competitors, such as Australia and New Zealand, are aggressive marketers. The CTC has implemented a multiyear research plan for the Asia/Pacific market. It considers Latin America to be an emerging market: Between 1995 and 2007, the Mexico market grew more quickly than any other international market. Tourists are coming from major markets where CTC staff members are working to build Canada's appeal. Statistics indicate that Canadians themselves are keen on exploring this country's attractions. This is thanks in no small part to the CTC's efforts and partnerships.

Future Challenges

Canada has moved from twelfth to eleventh place in world international receipts from tourism, but it faces several challenges in the next few years if it is to move higher:

- Canada's share of outbound travel is declining in some major markets—the United Kingdom, Japan, France, and Germany.
- Marketing investment by the CTC and the Canadian tourism industry is falling behind that of our international competitors.
- The deficit in Canada's balance of trade in tourism is expected to increase over the next five years.

As a Crown corporation, the CTC is in a position to form partnerships and lead the Canadian tourism industry in addressing the challenges it faces. The key will be for it to think globally but act regionally.

SOURCES: *CTC Annual Report* 1999–2007 (www.canadatourism.com/annual report/generalactivities/vision&mission), July 2001, November 2007; Helena Katz, "CTC 'Puts on the Crown,'" *Communiqué*, January–February 2001, p. 1; Katz, "New Structure at the Top for the CTC," *Communiqué*, January–February 2001, p. 19; Katz, "Tobin Launches Travel Canada Marketing Campaign," *Tourism*, December 2001, p. 4.

TOURISM PROMOTION

Reference is made throughout this textbook to the various organizations that promote travel and tourism. In this section we look more closely at private and public promoters. Travel and tourism organizations involved with promoting and supporting tourism fall into three main categories:

1. **Private:** Airlines, railways, and other transportation suppliers; hotels and other accommodation suppliers; attractions; tour operators; and travel agencies.
2. **Public:** International, national, provincial, territorial, state, and municipal government tourism offices.
3. **Quasi-public:** Private promotional organizations that receive government funding, such as regional tourism organizations and convention and visitors' bureaux (CVBs).

Government tourism offices and private sector suppliers differ in many ways. One of these differences is fundamental: Government tourist offices encourage tourism development and promote tourism but do not actually sell it; suppliers do both. For example, the Italian Government Travel Office promotes travel to Italy, but the organizations that actually sell the travel arrangements are the airlines, railways, tour operators, and so on. There are a few exceptions; for example, even now, some Eastern European government tourism offices both promote and sell travel products. In Canada, as in Italy, private sector organizations sell travel arrangements.

Private Promoters

All private travel and tourism associations use **promotion** as an aid to sales. At one end of the scale there are the airlines, such as Air Canada, that spend millions of dollars a year on advertising. At the opposite extreme are the mom-and-pop motels, minor sightseeing attractions, and local motorcoach companies, which can afford only a few hundred dollars a year for promotional activities. Regardless of the size of the organization, all depend to some extent on promotions to motivate consumers to buy their products and services.

In this section we present an overview of the ways private suppliers promote themselves and their products. **Advertising** is by far the most common form of promotional activity. Generally, the major tourism companies advertise in the national media, while smaller companies with limited geographic markets use the local media.

There are variations both within and among the various sectors of the tourism industry. Below, we examine each sector in turn. This overview is not designed to be comprehensive, but rather to highlight various facets of promotion in each sector.

Key Industry Groups

Until 2003, tourism in Canada was described as an industry with eight sectors. This categorization was changed to create a North American Industry Classification System under NAFTA. This change allows Canada, the United States, and Mexico to gather consistent statistics to build their Tourism Satellite Accounts.

The new classification system recognizes five key industry groups within the tourism sector. These groups are Accommodations; Food and Beverage Services; Recreation and Entertainment; Transportation; and Travel Services. The Tourism Industry Association of Canada (TIAC, discussed later) also represents tourism businesses in five additional categories important to its membership: Travel Services (visitor reception centres, call centres); Travel Trade (tour operators, travel agents); Travel Media; Attractions; and Festivals and Events.

Although the new system standardizes definitions and how statistics are collected, and is recognized by the CTC, Canadian Tourism Human Resource Council (CTHRC) and TIAC, it does not necessarily clarify the discussion in this text, which is based on the original eight sectors of the tourism industry. For this reason, the original classification has been retained for the following discussion.

Accommodation Sector Providers in this sector range from the large international chains such as Holiday Inn ("On the Way") to small local operators such as the Do Drop Inn ("Stay for only $59"), to B&B properties.

The chains promote themselves through corporate websites as well as in generic ads on network television and in the large-circulation newspapers and magazines. Ramada ("You're Somebody Special at Ramada") and Hyatt ("the Hyatt Touch") are two major advertisers.

Individual properties, whether independent or part of a chain, are creating websites with links to related travel topics. B&Bs are also going online, besides listing themselves in regional and provincial travel directories. Many also use local media in the shoulder seasons and off-season to influence local people to come stay.

Adventure Tourism and Recreation Sector At one time, the category of adventure tourism and the subcategory of ecotourism were heavily promoted by public promoters. Today, through the CTC's efforts, various product clubs are being created to develop and promote private sector initiatives across Canada. These range from watching the Northern Lights in the Northwest Territories to whale watching off the coasts of British Columbia and the Atlantic provinces. In 1997, New Brunswick used the theme "the New Tide of Adventure" to emphasize adventure tourism. This slogan capitalized on the tides in the Bay of Fundy, which are the highest in the world. Private operators then joined together as the Fundy Product Club to develop and promote their products and services.

Many operations in the adventure tourism sector, and related operations in the accommodation sector, are on a small scale, typically owned by individuals or families. Many rely on word-of-mouth for promotion; today, many also have websites. Most depend on listings in provincial

ILLUSTRATION 5–1
Many operators that offer adventure products piggyback their promotions with public promotions and gain visibility by collaborating with other businesses.
SOURCE: Reprinted with permission of the Yukon Department of Tourism. Photograph: Richard Hartmier.

tourism directories; some place ads in newspapers or specialty magazines. Medium-sized operations do more advertising in the print media. Some Canadian operators advertise in certain markets in the United States. The key is to tie in and piggyback on public promotions and collaborate with other businesses, especially on the Web.

The recreation category includes both individual and team sports, and both commercial and spectator sports. Ski resorts advertise in newspapers and magazines aimed at skiers, with themes such as "Ski Mont Tremblant." On television, the airlines advertise flights from eastern Canada to skiing destinations in western Canada. Resorts that feature recreational activities such as golf, tennis, horseback riding, and skiing usually establish websites, in addition to preparing brochures. They also advertise in newspapers and specialty magazines, and pay to be listed in provincial or territorial tourism office directories.

Spectator sports advertise to obtain immediate action, perhaps even on the day of the event. Visitors to the community purchase the local newspaper to find out information about the activity. The sports section of a Vancouver paper on a Saturday in July might have ads for the BC Lions football team, playing that evening, and horse racing at Hastings Park on Sunday, as well as advance-notice ads for the Greater Vancouver Open golf tournament and the Molson Indy at Concord Pacific Place, both in August. Many spectator sports have corporate sponsors. Nowadays, information about events is also available online, and tickets can be reserved and paid for through Web transactions.

Attractions Sector Attractions can be natural, such as the Reversing Falls at Saint John, New Brunswick, or human-built, such as the Aviation Museum in Ottawa. The private and public sectors promote both types of attractions. For example, British Columbia and Alberta promote the Rocky Mountains in their tourism brochures. At the same time, operators in various sectors outside these regions promote the Rockies as a destination. Advertisers in these sectors use most types of media to reach various market segments. Many have websites, and many of these offer virtual tours.

The promotion of human-built attractions varies with the type and size of the attraction. Promotions for the West Edmonton Mall tend to be broad (i.e., they try to reach everybody); promotions for the Canadian Railway Museum at Delson/Saint-Constant, Quebec, are much narrower (e.g., through magazines for railway enthusiasts).

Many managers of attractions built by humans are developing websites; some promote retail sales of their associated merchandise through catalogues aimed at past visitors or likely visitors. The latter can be gleaned from lists of subscribers to particular magazines or lists of people attending conventions in the city where the attraction is located.

Meetings, Events, and Conferences Sector Events are usually short-lived compared with attractions. They may even be held only once in a community. Most advertising is in local newspapers, perhaps supported by some radio and TV promotion. An event at the Rogers Centre, especially if it is the only Canadian performance, attracts visitors from other provinces and neighbouring states. Yearly events such as the Calgary Stampede and the Charlottetown Festival are promoted in provincial tourism brochures. Electronic box offices and online program information are commonplace for both live entertainment and sporting events.

Yearly conferences and conventions tend to rotate between cities and even between countries. Those businesses in other tourism sectors (e.g., accommodation, food and beverage, events and attractions) need to get their information into the advance promotional packets sent to potential conference delegates, and into the registration kits provided to delegates on arrival and registration. Promoters in the private sector work with public promoters, such as convention and visitors' bureaux.

Attendees can often register for an event on the conference's website. After viewing choices of accommodation online, they can then reserve a room electronically.

Food and Beverage Sector Large firms, especially franchises such as McDonald's, Swiss Chalet, and Red Lobster, do extensive national advertising on television and in the local print media, and distribute flyers or coupons offering specials. Smaller local firms advertise on radio and in the print media. Upscale establishments typically advertise in local city magazines such as *Toronto Life*, and selectively on radio and TV; mostly, however, they rely on satisfied clientele to refer visitors, friends, and relatives.

The beverage sector can be divided into two categories: alcoholic and nonalcoholic. Both do extensive national, provincial, regional, and local advertising. The former category may face restrictions, depending on the jurisdiction. Local wineries can advertise plant tours to promote their wines. The nonalcoholic category comprises mainly soft drinks and various types of bottled water. Soft drink manufacturers usually have large advertising budgets and use most media.

Many tourists want to sample local and regional cuisines. People in the tourism industry must be aware of this need and either provide local fare or be knowledgeable about where to find it. Programs such as "A Taste of Nova Scotia" can be implemented and promoted. Websites such as DineAid.com allow travellers to learn about dining options in an area and make reservations before they leave home or while travelling.

Transportation Sector All six components in this sector—airlines, car rental companies, railways, motorcoach companies, cruise lines, and ferry lines—promote themselves extensively. Like most businesses, transportation companies have gone online, offering information and possibly reservations services through their websites or via links with partners in the transportation sector or other sectors of the tourism industry.

Airlines The airline industry spends more on advertising than any other segment of the tourism industry. Newspaper advertising accounts for almost half of airlines' total advertising expenditures. One of the most successful advertising campaigns of all time was United Airlines' "Come Fly the Friendly Skies." Delta's "We Love to Fly and It Shows" and American's "Something Special in the Air" are two slogans that have been used effectively in the airline war of words. Air Canada has used themes such as "You're Always a Winner with Air Canada" and "The Choice of Frequent Flyers" in conjunction with its partner airlines.

Foreign airlines, such as British Airways and Lufthansa, also advertise in Canada. For years, Delta used "One Ticket, One Airline, All of America" in Canada to emphasize that it serves 220 cities in the United States from five cities in Canada.

ILLUSTRATION 5–2

Advertisers target various market segments, as this ad does.

SOURCE: Courtesy of VIA Rail.

Car rental companies Like the airlines, car rental companies spend most of their advertising dollars on magazine and newspaper ads and television spots. Because business travellers are the major rental car users, the companies place many ads in business publications such as *Canadian Business*, *The Wall Street Journal*, and *Business Week*. Car rental companies often share advertising costs with individual airlines to promote fly/drive packages.

In Canada, Budget has used "The Smart Money Is on Budget." Thrifty has used Wayne Gretzky as a celebrity spokesperson. Hertz and Avis are two big promoters, battling each other with slogans such as "Hertz. Exactly." and "We Try Harder," respectively.

Railways VIA Rail and Amtrak are in a unique position in that neither has a direct competitor; each is the only passenger railway in its own country. However, each has to compete with other transportation suppliers and with private automobiles.

VIA Rail divides its advertising expenditures between the print and broadcast media. It has used the theme "Take a Look at the Train Today." More recently, it emphasized "Silver & Blue Class" to promote its refurbished transcontinental passenger equipment, and "EnVIAble" to publicize the quality of its service. VIA has promoted the Canrailpass for travelling across Canada and the Corridorpass for travelling between Windsor and Quebec City. It also joined Amtrak in offering the North American Rail Pass under the slogan "North American Free Train Agreement." British Rail and European railway companies also advertise in Canada and the United States, in particular to promote BritRail passes and Eurailpasses.

Motorcoach companies Because most motorcoach companies are small, they tend to advertise exclusively in local media. The exceptions are the big names such as Greyhound, Trailways, and Gray Line, which run nationwide ad campaigns. Many motorcoach companies have used "Take the Bus and Leave the Driving to Us."

Cruise lines Cruises, being so glamorous, would seem to cry out for television promotion. Until recently, however, surprisingly few cruise lines used TV as their main advertising medium. With the success of Carnival Cruise Lines' "Fun Ships" campaign, other cruise lines realized the importance of TV advertising. Royal Caribbean, Norwegian Cruise Line, Holland America, Princess Cruises, and Disney, with its character cloud formations, are now also big TV advertisers. Most cruise lines advertise heavily in the print media as well, and make extensive use of brochures. The Internet has become almost a required form of promotion for the cruise industry.

Ferry lines Marine Atlantic, which connects Newfoundland with Nova Scotia, has used the theme "Great Connections." Bay Ferries encourages people to sail

ILLUSTRATION 5–3

Carnival's "Fun Ships" campaign has been one of the industry's most successful.

SOURCE: Image courtesy of Carnival.

between New Brunswick and Nova Scotia through its "Take the Quickest Way across the Bay" promotions.

Travel Trade Sector Tour operators promote their products mainly through print advertising, brochures, and travel catalogues, and now also offer Internet options. They also resort to specialty magazines and direct mail.

Generally, travel agencies have always served small geographical areas, so they spend most of their advertising dollars in the local media and on direct-mail campaigns. Now, with the trend toward larger agencies and franchise operations, they are resorting more to national advertising. Both tour operators and travel agencies promote their services on the Internet.

Tourism Services Sector This sector has both private and public promoters. Besides travel suppliers and travel agencies, retail establishments are the main private operators. As they promote their services, they promote destinations as well. National media support highway gas stations. Local shops in tourist zones may be limited to local tourist directories and word-of-mouth advertising. Merchants in other areas or in malls may band together to promote their shops and services to potential visitors in other cities ("Come Shop With Us," "Enjoy Our Night Life"). Selected television and radio spots are targeted at specific audiences. Private promotions of goods and services usually benefit by following through on public sector promotions.

Another category of private tourism promotion is the promotion done by tourism industry associations (TIAs) in each province, territory, and state. TIAs work with regional and sector partners and all levels of government; provide opportunities for networking, education, and research; and inform the public and members of the private and public sectors of the industry about issues and trends that are affecting tourism. Canada's national TIA is the Tourism Industry Association of Canada; in the United States, it is the Travel Industry Association of America.

Private Promotion Partnerships

Interrelationship of Sectors Sometimes a promotion features several tourism sectors. For example, a Vancouver travel agency (travel trade sector) may run a newspaper ad featuring a golf summer-weekend package at Whistler. The trip to Whistler is made in a rented car (transportation sector), lodging is at the Marriott Residence Inn Whistler (accommodation sector), the golf game is at the Big Sky Golf and Country Club (recreation sector), and featured dining is at the Bearfoot Bistro (food and beverage sector). Short-term and ongoing promotion partnerships benefit both the partners and the destination.

Future Sponsorship of Certain Events and Sports In the past, some events, festivals, and spectator sports had alcohol and tobacco companies as **sponsors**. Governments, however, have placed various restrictions on the promotions these firms may do. For example, the 2003 Montreal F1 Grand Prix was cancelled when the government enforced its ban on tobacco advertising. This adversely affected destination travel and tourism receipts. Similar action could affect the future of certain sponsored cultural events and spectator sports.

In-House Departments versus Outside Agencies Most of the major travel suppliers do their own promotions through their public relations or advertising departments. Smaller organizations tend to hire the services of professional agencies. Typically, an agency is hired to:

- Plan the promotion campaign and think up a campaign theme.
- Conduct market research so the campaign can be targeted at the best prospects.
- Write the ad copy and prepare the layout.
- Buy media time and space for the client.

The agency may also plan and carry out public relations for the client (writing press releases, arranging press conferences and interviews, and so on). Some organizations prefer to hire a separate public relations agency.

Other Private Promoters

There are a number of national and international travel associations that promote travel and tourism. Some of these, such as the Association of Canadian Travel Agencies, represent a single segment of the travel industry. Other associations include the American Society of Travel Agents, the International Association of Tour Managers, and the Caribbean Hotel Association, which focus on marketing, advocacy, and lobbying activities. In Canada, there are several nationally recognized private advocacy groups:

- Association of Canadian Travel Agencies (ACTA)
- Association of Tourism Professionals (ATP)
- Canadian Federation of Chefs and Cooks (CFCC)
- Canadian Restaurant and Foodservices Association (CRFA)
- Hotel Association of Canada (HAC)
- Meeting Professionals International (MPI)
- Tourism Industry Association of Canada (TIAC)

The Tourism Industry Association of Canada is a good example of an organization that promotes tourism through lobbying. It was founded in 1930 to encourage the development of tourism in Canada. It has formed partnerships with provincial and territorial tourism organizations as well as the American-based National Tour Association. In its lobbying, TIAC focuses on removing legislative and regulatory barriers to growth and development in the Canadian tourism industry. TIAC also manages Rendez-vous Canada, the nation's premier annual tourism industry marketplace.

Other organizations that bring together a wide range of private sector travel interests are the World Travel and Tourism Council, the Pacific Asia Travel Association, the Africa Travel Association, and the Caribbean Tourism Organization.

The World Travel and Tourism Council (WTTC), based in London, England, and founded in 1990, is a global forum for travel and tourism. Members of the council are drawn from all sectors of the tourism industry. It has regional offices in North and South America, Asia/Pacific, and Europe. As of 2008, the only Canadian representative on the 18-member executive committee was the president and CEO of Rocky Mountaineer Vacations. The WTTC's current policy platform includes the following:

- Envision the future for travel and tourism and make it "everybody's future."
- Measure and communicate travel and tourism's strategic and sustainable contribution.
- Promote the positive image of travel and tourism as a provider of jobs and opportunities.
- Encourage free access, open markets, open skies, and the removal of barriers to growth.

- Match customer and infrastructure demand.
- Develop access to capital resources and technological advancement.
- Promote responsibility in natural, social, and cultural environments.

Pacific Asia Travel Association (PATA) Founded in 1951, PATA is one of the most highly regarded travel associations and is the recognized authority on Asia/Pacific travel and tourism. In 2008, more than 2000 firms belonged to PATA—airlines, cruise lines, hotels, tour operators, and travel agencies. The association leads the collective efforts of nearly 100 government, state, and local tourism bodies, more than 55 airlines and cruise lines, and hundreds of travel companies. It has a global network of more than 70 local chapters, with a total membership of 17 000 travel professionals. PATA's mission is to enhance the growth, value, and quality of Asia/Pacific travel and tourism. It conducts travel marts that bring together buyers and sellers, offers seminars and familiarization tours (FAM trips) for travel agents, and produces sales support literature.

Check Your Product Knowledge

1. What are the differences between large firms and small ones in the accommodation, attraction, adventure tourism, and food and beverage sectors, in relation to how they promote themselves?

2. How are private sector tourism industry associations involved in promoting tourism?

3. Why are marketing and advocacy groups necessary in the tourism industry?

4. What are some of the differences between the PATA and the WTTC?

5. Why would a promotion feature more than one sector of the tourism industry?

6. What do you think will happen to certain events and spectator sports if further restrictions for sponsors are placed on alcohol and tobacco firms? Should restrictions be increased or reduced? Explain.

SELLING TOURISM

Advertising and other forms of promotion stimulate interest in travel products and services, but the final step in the marketing process is up to suppliers and travel agencies. After products and services have been promoted through private, public, and quasi-public activities, suppliers and travel agencies have to sell them.

HAVANA
Sol y Son
May, June, September & October

Price for these weekend fams is $199 net, per person, double occupancy and departures are on Fridays.

Price includes: roundtrip airfare with Cubana from Toronto; roundtrip transfers; two nights accommodation in Havana (Fri–Sun); a city tour of Havana with hotel site inspections; applicable taxes and Cuba tourist card.

ILLUSTRATION 5–4
Suppliers use FAM trips to promote their products to travel intermediaries.
SOURCE: http://www.travelweek.ca.

How Suppliers Sell

Airlines, car rental companies, hotels, and other travel suppliers typically target their sales efforts at travel intermediaries rather than individual clients. Sales representatives work both outside the employer's office, making personal calls on prospective accounts (**outside sales**), and inside the office, selling either face to face or over the telephone or on the Internet (**inside sales**) to clients.

Outside Sales The size of a supplier's outside (or field) sales force depends on the size of the company. With smaller suppliers such as B&Bs, trailer parks, and local sightseeing companies, a single person—usually the owner—assumes all sales responsibilities. At the opposite end of the continuum, a major supplier such as an international airline will have a highly complex outside sales organization, typically structured as follows:

- An international sales force, with a vice-president for each international region.
- A national vice-president of marketing and sales.
- Regional sales forces under regional sales managers.
- District sales forces under district sales managers.

Sales representatives call on travel agents, tour operators, and business travel intermediaries such as business travel department (BTD) managers, corporate and association meeting planners, and incentive travel planners.

Besides making initial sales, sales reps must service existing accounts. This usually involves arranging seminars and FAM trips and negotiating deals.

Inside Sales The major airlines, car rental companies, and hotel chains all maintain central reservations offices. Sales reps in these offices handle incoming e-mail, faxes, and telephone calls from travel counsellors, tour operators, and other travel intermediaries.

Suppliers sell directly to the public through sales outlets in major urban areas, and also in airports, hotels, convention centres, and so on. Sales outlets are used mainly by airlines and car rental companies. Sales representatives respond to inquiries from potential clients who either contact them by telephone or e-mail or visit the office.

The main difference between inside sales and outside sales is that with the former, the prospect approaches the seller, whereas with the latter, the seller approaches the prospect. Inside salespeople are not, however, mere order takers. If the salesperson can identify the customer's needs, he or she may be able to generate more sales than were initially requested. For example, a client who calls to make a flight reservation may be persuaded to buy a fly/drive package or to make hotel reservations.

How Travel Agencies Sell

Travel agents sell products on behalf of suppliers. The emphasis is on inside sales to individual clients. This can be done face to face or online.

Inside Sales Travel counsellors sell to the public over the telephone, online, or in person. Clients who visit travel agencies tend to have a less clear idea of the travel products and services they want to buy than do clients who go directly to suppliers. To make the sale, the travel counsellor has to turn these half-formed plans into firm travel arrangements.

Outside Sales Most outside selling involves selling to groups and to corporate accounts. However, more and more outside sales reps also sell to individuals.

Sales reps selling to groups must identify the needs of the group as a whole. The initial contact is made through a decision maker representing the group; this is followed by a sales presentation before the entire group.

Sales reps selling to corporate accounts are usually selling the services of the travel agency rather than a one-time travel product. Their aim is to secure commercial accounts over a long period of time, by persuading corporate decision makers to use the agency for all its travel arrangements. In many medium-sized and smaller agencies, the owner or manager assumes responsibility for outside sales. With smaller agencies, part-time employees also do outside sales work.

Check Your Product Knowledge

1. Why is selling an important part of the tourism marketing process?
2. What is the difference between inside and outside sales?
3. How do travel agencies promote and support tourism?

RETAIL SUPPORTERS

This section discusses retail sales in support of tourism. But even here, there is overlap between tourism sector sales and retail support sales, and between retail support sales to tourists and those to nontourists. **Retail sales to tourists** refer to goods and services generally available and bought by travellers; retail sales to nontourists are the same goods and services, but bought by locals.

Retail supporters of tourism have existed since the early days of travel. Initially, hotels were built in central business districts to accommodate rail travellers. These hotels often incorporated a store in or near the lobby where newspapers, cigarettes, soft drinks, and sundries, including souvenirs, could be purchased. After World War II, retail sales in support of tourism increased. Vacation time, on average, increased from two weeks in the 1940s to four weeks in the 1960s. Automobile ownership skyrocketed and divided four-lane highways were built. There was a need for services to support automobile-based tourism. An example was the development of Highway 401 from Windsor to the Quebec border. At one time, travellers had to leave Highway 401 to find support services. Today, motels, fast-food franchises, and full-service gas stations on North America's highways provide gas, food, showers, sundries, clothing, and souvenirs for tourists and truck drivers. Whether travel is by car, plane, or train, retail is an integral part of a trip.

Adventure Tourism and Recreation Tourists participating in adventure tourism and recreation usually have a choice of where to buy the equipment and supplies necessary for the activity—at home or at the destination. Ski shops have opened at ski hills, gasoline stations to service boats are found at lakesides, hunting supplies can be purchased from guides and outfitters, golf and tennis pro shops are available on site, and clothing stores abound to satisfy tourists. Mountain Equipment Co-op and Tilley Endurables have stores and publish catalogues for people preparing for recreation and adventure. Other retail outlets specialize in cruisewear and travel items such as suitcases and travel accessories.

Attractions Retail shops abound near attractions and other tourism sectors. Some argue that natural attractions such as Niagara Falls are overcommercialized. The area around Magnetic Hill outside Moncton, New Brunswick, has been developed to such an extent that the "magnetic" phenomenon of the hill has been lost. Banff is another natural attraction where there is concern about overcommercialization; yet another is Cavendish Beach, Prince Edward Island, where the boardwalk shops attract heavy vehicle and pedestrian traffic within sight of the beach and sand dunes. The need for a balanced approach to developing retail establishments around natural attractions is a concern in destination planning and development.

ILLUSTRATION 5–5

Retail shops develop to serve tourists in unique areas such as Piccadilly Circus in London, England.

SOURCE: Corel.

There are also support retail services for attractions built by humans, such as museums, art galleries, sport stadiums, and observation towers. Most of these have shops associated with them; some also publish catalogues from which merchandise can be ordered. Profits from these services are typically used to support the gallery or museum. Sometimes a specific area of a city or region becomes a destination attraction. Examples include Old Montreal, the Fortress of Louisbourg, Niagara-on-the-Lake, the Forks in Winnipeg, and Gastown in Vancouver. Tourist shops in these areas are integral to the destination's attraction. Some retail shops capitalize on this by "piggybacking." One example is COWS on Prince Edward Island, which began as an ice cream parlour but now also sells clothing and other "fun products," advertising in its 12 stores across Canada (plus one in the United States), as well as through a catalogue and its website (www.cows.ca).

Meetings, Events, and Conferences By definition, meetings, events, and conferences are of limited duration; even so, they spawn considerable retail sales. Besides whatever accommodation and food and beverage sales are made while these activities occur, there are spin-off sales. Attendees and delegates purchase souvenirs and mementos, even if just a T-shirt, to take home.

Transportation The automobile resulted in more tourism, which led to the development of service stations, motels, and fast-food outlets. Public transportation also generates retail sales. When rail passenger service predominated, the major railway stations housed a limited number of shops. Contrast this with Canada's major airports; in the past decade, they have been redeveloped to include retail outlets. For example, Pearson International Airport in Toronto has a mini-shopping mall. Some European airports and railway stations have food supermarkets and specialty food stores such as bakeries, vegetable markets, and fish stalls. They have become destinations in themselves. On many major airlines, travellers can shop while airborne through in-flight catalogues.

Travel Trade Travel agents sell not only **primary items**, such as transportation and accommodation, but also **secondary items**, such as medical insurance and trip cancellation insurance. Many tours and charter trips have a component that includes visiting retail stores. A European tour may feature visits to makers of cheese and wooden shoes in the Netherlands, or clocks and chocolate in Switzerland.

Tourism Services Vast numbers of guidebooks and travel videos are available for sale in the private sector. Many provinces and states have also entered retail sales. British Columbia has published *British Columbia Magazine* for many years; it now has a catalogue section for purchasing books, prints, and other items. The Canadian Tourism Commission (CTC) has a partnership with Roots Canada that allows Roots to use the CTC Maple Leaf logo.

Check Your Product Knowledge

1. What is the difference between retail sales to a tourist and those to a nontourist?
2. How do retailers support tourism?
3. What examples can you identify of retail sales in support of tourism in each of the tourism sectors?
4. Why would the CTC partner with Roots Canada?

PUBLIC PROMOTERS

This section provides information about the World Tourism Organization (UNWTO) and the Organisation for Economic Co-operation and Development (OECD), and examines the role of national tourism offices (NTOs) for countries in general and for Canada and the United States in particular. A public tourism organization can be global (UNWTO), regional international (OECD), national (NTO), or state, provincial, or territorial. This section also examines quasi-public promoters, such as regional tourism organizations and convention and visitors' bureaux.

ILLUSTRATION 5–6

The World Tourism Organization has helped standardize tourism signs.

SOURCE: Microsoft Clipart.

World Tourism Organization

The World Tourism Organization (UNWTO), the only intergovernmental organization of its kind, is an official consultative organization to the United Nations. Its mission is to promote and develop tourism as a significant means of fostering international peace and understanding, economic development, and international trade. The UNWTO works to harmonize tourist policies among nations and stimulates cooperation among countries in technical matters. This includes such things as standardizing equipment, signs, terms, and phrases. For example, in the past 20 years the UNWTO has approved over 60 international symbols for tourism and recreation signage. In 2001, it approved a set of recommendations for a new standardized signage system for water sports.

The UNWTO also contributes to tourism development and marketing by supporting research and by serving as an international clearinghouse for information. It works to devise methods for forecasting, developing, and marketing tourism that can be used by other tourist organizations. Since 1990, the UNWTO has worked with the CTC and the UN to develop a system for generating comparable tourism statistics across nations (Tourism Satellite Accounts).

Organisation for Economic Co-operation and Development

The Organisation for Economic Co-operation and Development (OECD) was established in 1961 and is headquartered in Paris, France. Thirty countries are now members.

The OECD promotes international investment, cooperation in the movement of capital, and trade in services. The OECD's Tourism Committee fosters the development of tourism by studying problems. For this, it utilizes OECD research and analysis. It also consults with representatives of member and nonmember economies and with labour, business, and other groups. Like other committees, the Tourism Committee benefits from the OECD's analyses of investment trends and policies in relation to labour relations, trade, the environment, taxation, and competition policies.

National Tourism Organizations

National tourism organizations (NTOs) represent the highest level of government involvement in tourism promotion. Many nations around the world have NTOs, although their roles vary considerably. Some NTOs are autonomous ministries within the government and play a major promotional role; an example is the Bermuda Department of Tourism. Other NTOs are agencies within government departments and play a lesser role.

The Atlantic and Caribbean nations actively promote tourism. Jamaica launched a major promotional campaign in the late 1970s to reverse the decline in tourism brought about by unstable political conditions on the island. The campaign was very effective, and Jamaica is now one of the most popular destinations in the Caribbean. A later campaign, "Come to Jamaica and Feel All Right," was also successful. To capture a larger share of the tourist market, Barbados launched its "Play the Bajan Way" campaign.

Australia, another big foreign advertiser in Canada and the United States, has used two catchy slogans: "Australia—The Wonder Down Under," and "Come and Say G'day." More recently, Australia used the controversial phrase, "Where the bloody hell are you?" Aggressive marketing has certainly helped bring more tourists to Australia, but so too have two unforeseen factors. One was the renewed outbreak of terrorism in Europe in 1986, which encouraged many North American tourists to seek safer vacation destinations. The other was the phenomenal success of the Australian films *Crocodile Dundee* and *Crocodile Dundee II*. No doubt, there was also a positive spin-off from the 2000 Summer Olympics.

European NTOs promote their countries both individually and as a group within the European Travel Commission (ETC). In the wake of a terrorism outbreak in 1986, the ETC held a series of tourism supermarts throughout Canada and the United States in an attempt to revitalize interest in Europe as a destination for Canadians and Americans. The marts were targeted at travel counsellors, but the ETC also took the campaign directly to consumers with "Invitation to Europe" advertising supplements in major North American dailies.

NTOs use a variety of promotional techniques but emphasize tourism industry shows and travel marts, international tourism conferences, FAM trips, and, above all, advertising.

Canada's National Tourism Organizations

Until the mid-1990s, Tourism Canada, a branch of Industry Canada, was the Canadian agency responsible for encouraging and supporting the growth, excellence, and

ILLUSTRATION 5–7

Nations around the world recognize the importance of tourism to a country's economy.

SOURCE: Photo by Indu Ghuman.

competitiveness of Canada's tourism industry. Tourism Canada had one of the best tourism promotion campaigns in the world. It aimed its efforts at various market targets: Canada (to encourage Canadians to travel within their home country), the United States, the European market, the Asia/Pacific market, and the business travel market. Canada spent more money than any other country on advertising in the American media. You may remember the ads that promoted Canada as "The World Next Door."

However, Canada presented a fragmented image, as each supplier, operator or destination conducted its own promotion. With a single tourism authority, industry resources could be combined with government funding for marketing to create a more consistent image.

The Canadian Tourism Commission (CTC) was established in 1994 to promote Canada as a tourist destination. The Commission became operational in 1995, with a board of directors representing federal and provincial governments as well as private businesses involved in tourism. Its goal was to create a $100 million marketing fund, with matching funds from the provinces and industry, and to re-establish Canada as a global force in the global tourism industry. In 2001, after five years of promoting Canada and establishing public/private partnerships, the CTC became a Crown corporation (see this chapter's Profile).

The United States' Tourism Organizations

The U.S. government has traditionally left the job of tourism promotion to private industry. However, individual states have been quite active in promoting themselves to potential tourists in other states, Canada, and overseas countries.

In the United States, formal recognition of the importance of international tourism came with the signing into law of the National Tourism Policy Act of 1981. However, the U.S. government's efforts in travel and tourism promotion still did not equal those of other countries. The

USTTA, the only federal agency dealing with tourism, was buried in the Department of Commerce and was underfunded. In 1996, the USTTA was replaced by a nonprofit organization called the National Tourism Organization, whose mandate is to promote inbound tourism in conjunction with private industry.

Why is the U.S. federal government reluctant to promote tourism? To begin with, many policymakers are uncertain about the government's role in the tourism industry. In the spirit of capitalism, these people think that government should not interfere in private enterprise. Government involvement in tourism would establish a precedent for the government to subsidize other industries. However, in 2008, the Travel Industry Association of America and the United States Department of Commerce teamed up in a public/private partnership to create a comprehensive online source of travel information designed specifically for international travellers. The website (DiscoverAmerica.com) is available in five languages and contains many interactive features, including an interactive map, activity finder, traveller stories, and booking options.

In contrast, most American states are quite active in tourism promotion. Their activities range from running traditional state tourism offices to funding convention centres and stadiums. In some states, the funding of facilities has been controversial. Many people see it as necessary to attract visitors; others feel they are being forced to do it to remain competitive with other states for convention and tourism business.

Several states promote themselves in Canada, especially just before and during the winter season. TV watchers in eastern Canada see many ads from Alabama, Florida, and Texas. To Canadian viewers on a dreary Canadian winter day, these ads have impact and appeal.

Canada's Provincial and Territorial Tourism Organizations

In Canada, **provincial and territorial tourism organizations (PTTOs)** play important roles in public sector promotion. PTTOs promote travel and tourism within the province or territory, in Canada as a whole, and overseas. Every province and territory has an official tourism agency. The CTC has formed partnerships with the provincial and territorial offices (and with the private sector as appropriate). Also, representatives from PTTOs sit on the CTC's board of directors.

PTTOs rely heavily on television ads, but also use websites and magazine, newspaper, and radio advertising. Most PTTOs work closely with the private sector to develop advertising campaigns. In Nova Scotia, the private sector and the PTTO have formed a Partnership Council to create and direct the province's marketing strategy.

PTTOs also promote tourism by:

- Producing and distributing travel guides and travel videos.
- Staging travel conferences.
- Participating in travel trade shows.
- Conducting FAM tours for travel writers, tour operators, and travel counsellors.
- Operating highway information centres.

Every province and territory tries to come up with a catchy slogan to lend continuity to its promotional campaign. Often these are used on licence plates as travelling billboards and include the following slogans:

- "Super Natural British Columbia" (British Columbia)
- "Canada's Ocean Playground" (Nova Scotia)
- "Look What's Tucked Away in Our Little Corner of the World" (Newfoundland and Labrador)
- "It Feels So Different" (Quebec)
- "Yours to Discover" (Ontario)
- "Land of Living Skies" (Saskatchewan)
- "Purely Spectacular" (Northwest Territories)
- "Alberta, in All Her Majesty" and "Explore and Experience" (Alberta)
- "The Gentle Island" (Prince Edward Island)
- "Maritime Magnifique" (New Brunswick)
- "Canada's Arctic—Undiscovered" (Nunavut)

Both the Yukon and Manitoba have used the word "friendly" in their slogans, as in "Friendly Yukon" and "Friendly Manitoba." The use of slogans in Canada and the United States was influenced by the successful "I Love New York" campaign. That one was dreamed up in 1977 when New York City was on the verge of bankruptcy. Although initially conceived as a way of promoting just the city, it has since been extended to encourage inbound tourism to all parts of the state. The slogan, because it was still appealing, was used effectively after the terrorist attacks on New York City in 2001.

Sometimes provinces link up to promote an area of the country, quite often with assistance from the federal government. An example would be the 1991 campaign "A Coast of Difference," which was sponsored by the four Atlantic provinces and the Atlantic Canada Opportunities Agency. It was aimed at New Englanders and central Canadians.

Quasi-Public Promoters

Quasi-public promoters of travel and tourism are private promotional organizations that receive government funding. They include regional tourism organizations and convention and visitors' bureaus.

Regional Tourism Organizations Many provinces promote tourism through regional or area associations. Examples include the South Shore Regional Tourism Association in Nova Scotia and the Southern Ontario Tourism Organization, both of which promote wine regions in their areas. Public sector participation in these organizations is through the various local governments— the counties, cities, villages, and townships. Tourism services suppliers represent the private sector.

Convention and Visitors' Bureaux Most big cities in Canada and the United States promote local tourism through **convention and visitors' bureaux (CVBs)**. CVBs are usually either:

- Attached to the local government, either as a department within the Chamber of Commerce or within the municipal government.
- Independent nonprofit organizations backed by the private sector and funded in part by local government.

All CVBs promote their cities as venues for meetings, conventions, and seminars. Several CVBs own the convention centres in the cities they represent. To this end, they aim their promotional efforts at corporate and association meeting planners. CVBs also promote pleasure travel through campaigns directed at tour operators, motorcoach companies, travel counsellors, and the general public. The Calgary Convention and Visitors' Bureau is an example of a CVB in a large city.

CVBs act as liaisons between potential visitors and the businesses that will host them if they come. In both business and pleasure travel promotion, the key word is cooperation. CVBs work to encourage local businesses to work together to promote the entire city as an attractive destination.

Check Your Product Knowledge

1. What is the UNWTO's mission? How is it being accomplished?
2. What is the OECD's mandate? Why does it have a Tourism Committee?
3. Name three national tourism offices that play a major role in tourism promotion.
4. What is the European Travel Commission?
5. List five ways that provincial and territorial tourism offices promote tourism.
6. CTC board members are representatives of what groups or organizations? What is the CTC's role? What are its responsibilities?
7. List the committees of the CTC.
8. Why are some organizations considered quasi-public promoters of tourism?
9. What are the two main types of convention and visitors' bureaux?

A DAY IN THE LIFE OF A

Provincial Tourism Bureau Worker

What I like best about my job as a tourism training specialist is that there is always something different to do every day. I work for a provincial tourism bureau. My main assignment is to organize conferences and workshops for the travel and tourism industry. I am also involved in helping the colleges and universities in my province develop courses for people training for careers in the tourism industry.

Yesterday I conducted a workshop for several dozen employees of a city convention and visitors' bureau to help them develop their communication skills so they can deal more effectively with the public. I had to give a short lecture, show a 20-minute film developed by my office, then lead the participants in role-playing exercises. In one such exercise, some of the participants pretend to be angry tourists whose hotel reservations have been cancelled, and others pretend to be hotel managers who try to find ways to help the travellers.

I give dozens of similar workshops each year to employees of hotels, restaurants, tourist attractions, and tour boats. My aim is to train tourism workers to be helpful and attentive to their customers so that visitors form a good impression of our province and want to come back. Besides leading these workshops, it is my job to organize them, invite the participants, and solve any problems that arise. One minor problem at yesterday's workshop, for example, was that there was no outlet to plug in the film projector, so I had to find an extension cord.

I also serve on a committee sponsored by the Ministry of Education to develop a grade 8 career course. The course is intended to provide an overview of the many different kinds of careers students can choose after they graduate from high school, college, or university. My role is to make certain that travel and tourism careers are included in the course, because tourism is the second-largest industry in our province.

Besides serving on several similar education committees, I send hundreds of information packets each year to high-school and community college guidance counsellors throughout the province so that they can advise students about travel careers. I have also developed a speakers' bureau so that those schools and colleges can invite people in the industry to come and talk to the students about travel and tourism careers.

Another part of my job is to field complaints from tourists and pass them on to the hotels, restaurants, and attractions that are the subjects of the complaints. Most complaints have to do with cancelled reservations, sold-out shows, long waits in line, and similar problems. As a provincial employee, I can't do anything about the complaints, but I try to impress on the restaurant, theatre, or hotel how important it is to make guests feel wanted and appreciated. I try to convince them that it is worth their while to send a letter of apology.

I had to pass a very difficult interview to qualify for this job. At one point, I had to give a mock marketing presentation for a panel of judges. Since the main part of my job involves making presentations to groups of people, I had to show the interviewers I was able to do that. Fortunately, I have worked as a teacher, a travel agent, and an in-charge flight attendant, so I have had a lot of experience talking to groups of people.

I was hired for a very specific job, but there are other jobs in tourism bureaux that require other training and experience. For example, several people in my office answer calls on our provincial tourism hotline. These operators send out information packets, take complaints, and answer questions about such things as highway routes, attractions, ski conditions, and the weather. The main requirement for their job is the ability to be fast, accurate, and courteous. Hotline operators who can speak a foreign language are especially useful, because more and more foreign visitors come to our province every year.

Our office is small, like most provincial tourism offices. We employ only about 30 people. The advantage is that we are friendlier and more like a family than a big, impersonal office. The drawback is that because our office is so small, there is little room for advancement or promotion. Still, I enjoy my job so much that I can't imagine doing anything else.

CAREER OPPORTUNITIES

Private Sector

Most of the larger services suppliers have their own promotional and sales departments. Airlines, cruise lines, car rental companies, and hotels are the major employees. VIA Rail and Amtrak also have marketing staffs.

Careers are available in advertising, public relations, market research, and sales. Sales forces can be inside or outside (i.e., home office or in the field).

Advertising and Public Relations Agencies A few advertising and public relations agencies specialize in tourism promotion, both for travel suppliers and for government tourist offices. Ad agency employees, who must have strong creative skills, may eventually rise to become art directors or senior media planners. Public relations professionals write press releases, handle press inquiries, and arrange interviews and press conferences.

Travel Writing and Travel Photography Travel writers and photographers are employed by the travel trade press (*The Canadian Travel Press*, *Travelweek Bulletin*, *Travel Weekly*, and others) and by the consumer press. The consumer press includes travel publications such as *Travel and Leisure*, general-interest magazines that feature occasional travel articles, and the major newspapers that have weekly travel sections. Travel writers and photographers are employed both full-time and as freelancers. Competition is intense, especially for travel photographers.

Tourism Industry Associations TIAs require people to market the industry, arrange education and networking events, conduct research, and inform members and the public about issues and trends. They also need lobbyists and advocates to ensure the industry is treated fairly.

Public Sector

Governments hire many tourism professionals to do research and marketing, and to work with the public (e.g., in information centres). There are numerous opportunities in public sector management.

At the national level, the CTC involves people in advertising and marketing, research, and policy proposals for the tourism industry. The provincial tourism offices require the same skills. On the world stage, career opportunities for economists, statisticians, researchers, and policy analysts are found in organizations such as the OECD, the WTTC, and the UNWTO.

Summary

- Travel and tourism organizations involved in promoting and supporting tourism fall into three main categories: private, public, and quasi-public.
- Advertising, the promotional tool used most widely in the tourism industry, is the use of paid media space or time to attract customers.
- Co-op advertising is the sponsoring of advertisements by two or more companies.
- The tourism sector is divided into five key industries to facilitate the collection of statistics for the Tourism Satellite Account.
- The tourism services sector supports the other sectors through promotion and development.
- Public relations activities, targeted at the media, are staged to create a positive image of a company and its products. Press releases and press conferences are common public relations tools.
- In the private sector, tourism is promoted and sold by airlines, hotels and other suppliers, and tour operators and travel agencies.
- Sales support, an extension of the advertising effort, uses brochures, travel videos, and point-of-purchase displays.
- Most supplier sales reps sell to travel intermediaries, not to the general public.
- Sales promotional activities are targeted at prospective clients and travel intermediaries. They include special offers, travel shows, FAM trips, and sales contests.
- Outside sales reps work outside the employer's office. Inside sales reps make sales by telephone, or in person with prospective clients who visit the office.
- Travel agencies sell products on behalf of the suppliers to individual clients, groups, and corporations.
- Tourism has contributed to the development of accommodations (especially motels and campgrounds), highway service stations, and fast-food outlets. These in turn support the tourism development.
- In the public sector, tourism is promoted by national and provincial tourism offices. These offices promote destinations but do not sell travel products.
- The Canadian Tourism Commission (CTC), a private/public partnership, is Canada's NTO. The CTC replaced Tourism Canada, a department of Industry Canada, in 1995 and became a Crown corporation in 2001.
- Most major cities promote tourism through convention and visitors' bureaux.

Key Terms

advertising   p. 103
convention and visitors' bureaux (CVBs)   p. 113
inside sales   p. 108
national tourism organizations (NTOs)   p. 111
outside sales   p. 108
primary items   p. 110
promotion   p. 103
provincial and territorial tourism organizations
    (PTTOs)   p. 112
quasi-public promoters   p. 113
retail sales to tourists   p. 109
secondary items   p. 110
sponsor   p. 107
tourism services   p. 100

Internet Connections

American Society of Travel Agents (ASTA)
www.asta.org   p. 107

Association of Canadian Travel Agencies (ACTA)
www.acta.ca   p. 107

Canada (p. 112)
    Canada Cool
    www.canadacool.com

    Canada Live Webcams and Travel Information
    www.leonardsworlds.com/country/canada.htm

    Destinations Canada
    www.destinationscanada.com

Canadian Tourism Commission (CTC)
www.corporate.canada.travel/en/ca/index.html   p. 112

Destination Marketing Association International
www.iacvb.org

Discover America
www.DiscoverAmerica.com   p. 112

European Travel Commission
www.visiteurope.com   p. 111

Organisation for Economic Co-operation and
Development (OECD)
www.oecd.org/department/0,3355,en_2649_34389_1_1_
1_1_1,00.html   p. 111

Pacific Asia Travel Association (PATA)
www.pata.org   p. 108

Province/Territory Government Tourism Offices (p. 112)
    Go to the government website of any of the
    provinces or territories and enter "tourism" in the
    Search window.

Rendez-vous Canada
www.rendezvouscanada.travel   p. 107

Tourism Industry Association of Canada (TIAC)
www.tiac-aitc.ca   p. 103

Travel Industry Association of America (TIA)
www.tia.org   p. 107

World Tourism Organization (UNWTO)
www.world-tourism.org   p. 111

World Travel and Tourism Council (WTTC)
www.wttc.org   p. 107

WORKSHEET 5–1   **Promoting the Tourism Product in the Private Sector**

Tell how you would promote each of the tourism products shown below. Choose one advertising technique, one promotion technique, and one sales technique. Write your suggestions in the table below. Be as specific as possible.

	Product	Advertising	Support and promotion	Selling
1. A tour of Ottawa for grandparents and their grandchildren.				
2. A wine tour of France and Germany, hosted by a local radio personality.				
3. A 24-day Alaskan cruise.				
4. The opening of a couples-only resort in Mexico.				
5. A wilderness camping trip for physically disabled adults.				
6. New air service to Eastern Europe and Russia.				
7. A university alumni tour to China.				
8. A budget motel near the Trans-Canada Highway.				
9. Travel insurance.				
10. Vacation travel arranged by a small neighbourhood travel agency.				

WORKSHEET 5–2 Public Tourism Promotion

Select three of the five key industry groups in the tourism sector and suggest public promotion activities appropriate for each.

1. Industry Group _____

Description of Promotion _____

_____

_____

_____

_____

2. Industry Group _____

Description of Promotion _____

_____

_____

_____

_____

3. Industry Group _____

Description of Promotion _____

_____

_____

_____

_____

PART 3

The Transportation Sector

6

THE AIRLINE INDUSTRY

Objectives

When you have completed this chapter, you should be able to:

- Understand the size, scope, and importance of the transportation sector.
- Compare the different types of regulatory environments.
- Discuss the concerns about the natural and built environments.
- Name aircraft and events significant in the development of the airline industry.
- Distinguish among types of aircraft in service today.
- Compare air carrier aviation and general aviation.
- Discuss charter aviation in Canada.
- Identify the parts of an airport.
- Describe types of air routes.
- Compare multilateral agreements with bilateral agreements, and explain how they make the international air system work.

- Discuss the role of the International Air Transport Association (IATA).
- Discuss the effects of the 1978 Airline Deregulation Act in the United States, and of airline regulatory reform in the 1980s in Canada.
- List factors that influence airfares.
- Explain how IATA calculates international airfares.
- Discuss the impact of the 1995 and 2005 Open Skies agreements between Canada and the United States.
- Discuss the restructuring of the airline industry, including the emergence of new entrants and strategic alliances between and among airlines in different countries.
- Compare the structure of the Canadian airline industry in the 2000s with earlier decades.

THE TRANSPORTATION SECTOR

The transportation sector includes three industries: the airline industry (Chapter 6), the surface travel industries (Chapter 7), and the cruise and marine industry (Chapter 8). In the following section we provide a brief introduction to the transportation sector in tourism, the regulatory environment of transportation, and the impact of transportation on the natural and built environments.

Transportation in Tourism

The size of Canada's transportation sector was discussed in Chapter 1. In Canada, public transportation accounts for almost half of the total spending on tourism commodities. Note that this does not include spending on private transportation—mainly the private automobile (see the next chapter). Air travel accounts for about half the spending in

Canada on public transportation; one-quarter of this spending is by non-Canadians (in that sense, it is an export).

The transportation industry is different from many others in that it operates in a regulated environment.

The Regulation–Deregulation Continuum

Some industries are "affected with the public interest," wrote Lord Chief Justice Hale in the seventeenth century, in reference to the rates that innkeepers of the day should be able to charge. This still holds true today. All provinces have some sort of Accommodations Act, which requires that rates be posted on the inside of each guest room door. Similar conditions are present in the transportation industry. This sort of government activity is known as "regulation." Every country has its own regulatory environment.

PROFILE

Going Above and Beyond

WestJet

The concept and business plan for WestJet was conceived in 1994. Calgary entrepreneur Clive Beddoe (president of the Hanover Group of Companies) found it more cost-effective to buy an aircraft for his weekly business travel between Calgary and Vancouver. When he was not using this airplane, he made it available on a charter basis to other business travellers through Morgan Air, owned and operated by Tim Morgan. The successful response to this initiative made it apparent to Morgan and two others—Donald Bell and Mark Hill, both businessmen—that there was an opportunity to start a low-fare airline that would satisfy the needs of western Canadians.

Over the next several months, the four-man team of Beddoe, Bell, Hill, and Morgan worked on the concept that became WestJet. They examined other low-cost carriers in North America, especially Southwest Airlines and Morris Air. They planned to start up as a low-cost, low-fare, short-haul airline with three aircraft. Financing was obtained, staff was hired and moved into a Calgary office, and aircraft were purchased in late 1995 and early 1996. Operations commenced on February 29, 1996, with service connecting five cities: Vancouver, Kelowna, Calgary, Edmonton, and Winnipeg.

Expansion, both in additional aircraft and cities served, occurred rapidly. Victoria, Regina, and Saskatoon were added in 1996, Abbotsford/Fraser Valley in 1997, and Thunder Bay and Prince George in 1999. An initial public offering of 2.5 million shares was made in July 1999. The capital raised was used to purchase more aircraft and to build a new head office and hangar facilities in Calgary. The year 1999 presented WestJet with an opportunity to expand its services; that was a year of great change and restructuring in the Canadian airline industry. WestJet announced it would extend its low-fare strategy across Canada. In 2000, it added service to Moncton, Ottawa, and Hamilton. As expansion continued, in 2004, WestJet added U.S. destinations and made Toronto its eastern hub. WestJet Vacations was launched in 2006, and by 2008 the airline had added Hawaii, Mexico, and the Caribbean to its routes.

WestJet is proud of its customer service and believes in providing exceptional value "going above and beyond." It is committed to being the very best choice for customers' travel plans, and it believes in posting comparative information on its website. Guests that call a friendly "Super Sales Agent" wait an average of 90 seconds on hold. In 2006, the national ombudsman received 476 complaints about the airline industry; only 18 of these related to WestJet. In 2008, its on-time performance was about 83 percent, compared to the U.S. industry average of 78 percent.

Customer service continues to be a priority. Aircraft had leather seats installed in 2002, and the following year WestJet expanded its participation in the Air Miles reward program. In 2004, legroom was increased and live TV was offered on board. In 2007, WestJet was the first North American airline to launch an electronic boarding pass.

Summer 2001 saw the finalization of an agreement between WestJet and Sabre, the global distribution system used by around 50 000 travel agencies worldwide. This system will expand the availability of WestJet flights to a worldwide market. The original concept has succeeded. WestJet is a vibrant airline that in 2008 served 47 cities across Canada, the United States, Mexico, and the Caribbean with a fleet of next-generation Boeing 737-series aircraft.

WestJet is publicly traded on the Toronto Stock Exchange, with Clive Beddoe as president, CEO, and chairman. In 2003, the company placed second overall in "Canada's Most Respected Corporations Survey" sponsored by KPMG and conducted by Ipsos-Reid, and first in customer service in the same poll. This overall ranking continued the improvement from the 7th place achieved in 2002, and the 147th place attained in the 2001 survey. From 2005 to 2008, the company was voted Canada's most admired corporate culture in the Waterstone Human Capital annual study.

SOURCES: WestJet *Annual Report, 1999–2007,* www.westjet.com, www.bts.gov/programs/airline_information/.

What is regulated? In any regulatory market there are certain conditions, often referred to as "freedoms." Some of the main ones are discussed below.

Entry Think of a particular route—say, Toronto to Ottawa. Under regulation, the right to serve that route is restricted. An aspiring new entrant has to apply to a regulatory board and prove there is a demand among the public for additional service. The existing carriers will of course oppose such an application.

Exit An existing carrier—which may be the only carrier—may wish to abandon a certain service, and apply to the regulatory board to that end. That carrier may have trouble succeeding, as communities and passengers will oppose the application.

Rate/Fare Setting A transportation firm may wish to change its prices, or adjust them to reflect the type of travel (e.g., business or pleasure) or the time of day, week, or year. Regulators often have a great deal to say about prices, often establishing a zone between minimum and maximum allowable fares. This is to ensure that the industry isn't damaged by destructive competition.

Freedom to Manage In a regulated environment, managers may not have all the freedom they want to manage—that is, to innovate and make changes. The terms of operation may be quite strict. For example, a regulation may require that only propeller aircraft serve the Montreal-to-Fredericton air route. If an airline wants to use a jet aircraft on Fridays and Sundays when demand is much higher than through the week, it won't be permitted to because of the terms under which it was granted the route.

Mergers and Acquisitions In the transportation industry, regulation also involves the approval of mergers and acquisitions. Will the regulatory board permit competitors to combine to reduce duplication and achieve cost reductions, and thereby increase profits? This can result in reduced or eliminated services. After deregulation in the United States and regulatory reform in Canada, there were many new entrants in the transportation sector. Some of these new firms grew, but most did not and either left the industry or were taken over by other firms.

The Continuum

Economic regulation encompasses five major environments. Each is briefly examined below.

Open Market In this environment there are no barriers to entry, exit, the setting of rates, or mergers and acquisitions, and management is free to determine services. Very few jurisdictions have an entirely open market, though some approach it in some aspects.

Monopoly This is the opposite of open markets. One operator is awarded the exclusive right to serve a particular route or a particular region—sometimes even an entire country—as a designated carrier. This operator may be state-owned or privately owned. Most motorcoach companies are privately owned but have sole operating authority on their routes. VIA Rail is a Crown corporation with a monopoly. Of course, both the motorcoach companies and VIA Rail face competition from the airlines and from private cars.

Regulation There is little difference between a regulated environment and a monopolistic one. The main difference relates to the number of carriers permitted to have operating authority. In both the United States and Canada, air travel was more or less a monopoly until 1978 and 1984, respectively. Canada had the equivalent of three national carriers; the United States had 12 trunk-line carriers earning more than $1 billion per year. In a regulated environment it was difficult for existing carriers to set fares (seat sales were unknown), start or drop routes, merge, or manage in an innovative manner. Also, there were never any new entrants. Eventually, both countries reduced the amount of regulation. Canada reformed its airline regulations while the United States went even further, to deregulation.

Deregulation The United States made this "revolutionary" move in 1978 for a variety of reasons. Most growth was occurring in the Sunbelt states and, in a regulated environment, most transportation firms could not get new or additional operating authority to serve cities in those states. Also, regulation was blamed for a weak transportation system in the United States.

After deregulation, entry and exit became easier. Any airline could serve any route provided it could obtain a "slot" at the terminal. Freedom also came to pricing and, as a result, many budget airlines entered the industry. Management could manage. The Civil Aeronautics Board, the industry's regulatory agency, was disbanded under deregulation legislation.

Regulatory Reform Canada adopted a more "evolutionary" approach to deregulation for two reasons: The recession of the early 1980s weakened existing carriers and the dominant Canadian airline, Air Canada, was government-owned. Entry, exit, and fare setting became easier as airline managers were given greater freedom to manage. However, Canada did retain a national regulatory agency, now called the Canadian Transportation Agency. Greater freedom for management means, among other things, that rates and fares have only to be filed with the regulatory body; they don't have to be approved by it. This in turn means that seat sales can be announced quickly.

Transportation in Canada is currently governed by the Canada Transportation Act 1996, which was amended in 2007. The government has implemented an "Open Skies" policy toward air transportation negotiations that encourages airline competition and provides opportunities for Canadian airlines and airports to develop. The government's goal is to negotiate several individual "Open Skies" agreements similar to the 2005 agreement with the United States. Such agreements provide more access for airlines and fewer restrictions on how they provide service.

Impact of Transportation on the Natural and Built Environments

All transportation modes affect the environment. Four of these modes carry passengers. The biggest environmental concerns are pollution (of the air and water, but also visual and noise pollution), congestion, and urban sprawl. These concerns are intertwined.

Urban sprawl has resulted in longer commutes, the building of more roads, and more congestion and pollution around major cities. Nowadays the Macdonald–Cartier Freeway (Highway 401) around Toronto is busy all the time, not just during rush hour.

Transportation affects more than our environment; it also affects our physical and mental health. The planet's ozone layer is breaking down, as evidenced by the increase in ultraviolet radiation reaching the earth's surface (hence, the UV index you hear reported in the weather forecasts). People with respiratory problems are affected by air pollution. Beaches are closed by water pollution. Those living near airports and highways have difficulty sleeping. The night sky is now barely visible in urban centres. At one time, most Canadians could be proud of this country's pristine environment. Not anymore.

The "malling of America" has occurred. Shopping centres now look the same everywhere from St. John's, Newfoundland, to San Diego, California, and from Prince George, British Columbia, to Pascagoula, Mississippi. What are tourists looking for? Something different! Historic sites need to be protected, preserved, and rejuvenated. They are part of the built environment.

Each chapter in this book about the transportation sector will have a section on the environment.

Check Your Product Knowledge

1. Why is the transportation sector a big component of total tourism expenditures?
2. Compare various methods of regulating transportation. Which do you prefer? Explain.
3. Name the different impacts of transportation on the natural environment.

THE AIRLINE INDUSTRY

The Canadian airline industry has changed considerably since the 1950s, when Air Canada (then Trans-Canada Airlines) had a transcontinental monopoly. This monopoly was broken at the end of the 1950s, when Canadian Pacific Airlines was allowed one flight a day across Canada. By the end of the 1960s, regional air carriers were allowed to compete with the national carriers in selected geographical areas. By the end of the 1970s, the equivalent of three national airlines were competing on transcontinental routes. By the late 1980s, Canada had a duopoly— Air Canada and Canadian Airlines with their associated regional and commuter airlines. The early 1990s saw the restructuring of these two airlines. The mid- to late 1990s saw the growth of charter carriers such as Air Transat, and the development of new, low-cost entrants such as western Canada's WestJet. In the late 1990s, **strategic alliances** were created among several carriers based in different countries, so that seamless worldwide travel could be provided for travellers; for example, Air Canada, United Airlines, Thai Airways International, Lufthansa, and SAS (Scandinavian Airlines System) formed the Star Alliance. Since 2001, Canada has had one large near-monopoly carrier, Air Canada (which had swallowed Canadian Airlines), smaller carriers such as WestJet, and commuter lines such as Bearskin Airlines.

The word "turbulence" best describes the environment of the airline industry in the first years of the twenty-first century. Air Canada has had to deal with the aftermath of its takeover of Canadian Airlines; it introduced two

ILLUSTRATION 6–1

Improved airplane design, trained pilots, and an increase in public confidence in air travel all contributed to the growth of commercial aviation in the years after World War II.

SOURCE: Photodisc/Getty Images.

discount brands called Tango and Zip, both of which were dissolved in 2004, and a regional carrier called Jazz. Canada 3000 took over Royal and Canjet and then went bankrupt following the terrorist attack on September 11, 2001. Jetsgo, launched in 2002, suddenly ceased operations in 2005 stranding passengers just before March break. In the United States there have been mergers and takeovers (American and Trans World) and planned mergers and takeovers (United Airlines and USAir). Rapidly rising fuel costs in 2008 led to the closure of several airlines and to massive losses for the airline industry, which had just begun to recover from earlier troubles.

Overseas, the situation is similar. Ryanair has become a leading European discount carrier. British Airways and American Airlines had their proposed joint transatlantic venture turned down again by regulators. Air France and KLM merged in 2004 then in 2009 purchased a 25 percent share in Alitalia after a takeover bid was rejected. Delta and Northwest also merged in 2008 to create the world's largest airline. In 2000–01, the airline industry was affected adversely by a slowing economy, with less business and leisure travel. Then on Tuesday, September 11, 2001, four commercial planes were hijacked in the eastern United States. Two of them flew into the towers of the World Trade Center in New York City. This event affected trade, travel, and tourism.

A BRIEF HISTORY OF AVIATION

Canada and Canadians participated in the development of the aviation industry almost from its inception. John McCurdy, who flew a Silver Dart over Baddeck Bay, Cape Breton, in 1909, made the first piloted flight in Canada. The first commercial cargo flight in Canada was in 1913, when newspapers were carried from Montreal to Ottawa.

International aviation—involving planes that leave the airspace of one country and enter the airspace of another—has grown at the same time as domestic aviation. Almost every part of the world is now accessible by aircraft. Most countries—the United States is the biggest exception—developed state-owned airlines. The growth in air travel has been the single most important factor in the development of modern tourism. It is the central ingredient on which much else depends, including the hospitality industry, the tour industry, the cruise industry, and the car rental industry.

Types of Aircraft

We will describe aircraft in two ways: by type of engine and by purpose.

Engine Type Modern airplanes either have jet engines or are propeller-driven. Both types are in service worldwide.

Jet aircraft, powered by turbine engines producing tremendous thrust, can cruise at speeds up to 1000 kilometres an hour. Cabins are pressurized so that the aircraft can fly at high altitudes (10 000 metres and above). **Pressurization** involves artificially increasing the cabin air pressure so that it is almost the same as at ground level. Because jets are fast and comfortable, they are used for long-distance and medium-range domestic and international flights. The turbojet was the first successful jet engine. Although it is still used on some planes, it has been superseded by the turbofan engine, which operates more efficiently and quietly at low speeds.

Propeller-driven airplanes, or props, fly more slowly and at lower altitude than jets. There are two types of props: those with piston-powered engines plus one or more propellers (small airplanes) and those with turbine engines plus propellers, known as turboprops (medium-sized planes). Most turboprops and some piston-powered aircraft are pressurized. However, several models are not pressurized and so must fly below 4000 metres, often in the weather rather than above it.

For the first 50 years of modern aviation, all airplanes were piston-powered. Airplanes powered by turboprop engines entered commercial service in the 1950s. Jet aircraft replaced turboprops for long-distance flights in the 1960s, but many turboprops are still in use over shorter distances (650 kilometres or less). The introduction of long-distance jets doomed scheduled ocean-going service between continents; it also provided the impetus for the modern cruise industry. New propeller-driven aircraft are being designed for the growing regional and commuter airlines. Manufacturers, such as Bombardier, are earning a large share of this market.

ILLUSTRATION 6–2

Small propeller-driven aircraft continue to play an important role in the adventure and outdoor recreation tourism sector.
SOURCE: Dallas Peloquin.

Purpose Aircraft can also be classified according to the particular markets they are designed to serve.

- **Short-haul flights** The regional/commuter market is served by a variety of single- and twin-engine planes carrying between 19 and 60 passengers on short-haul flights of 160 kilometres or less. The Bombardier Dash-8 Q Series (Q for Quiet), manufactured in Toronto, carry 35 to 80 passengers depending on the model.
- **Short- to medium-range flights** Twin-jets, such as the Boeing 737 series, operate in the short to medium range (1600 kilometres or less) and usually carry between 100 and 190 passengers. There are more 737s flying today than any other type of commercial aircraft. The Bombardier BRJX is a twin-jet 110-seat airplane with a range of 2600 kilometres.
- **Long-haul flights** The long-haul transcontinental and intercontinental market is served by the largest jets of all—the twin-jets (the Boeing 767 and the 777, and Airbus A-300 series), and four-engine jets (the Boeing 747 and Airbus A380). These planes vary in capacity from 180 to 850 passengers and fly within the range of 5000 to 15 200 kilometres. The two major manufacturers (Boeing and Airbus) have taken a different approach to aircraft development. Boeing will introduce the twin-engine 787 Dreamliner in 2009, which is designed to carry 200–330 passengers. Airbus introduced the massive A380 in 2008. This aircraft is a four-engine, double-decker that can accommodate 525–850 passengers. While the Boeing 787 will be the centrepiece of a linear route network, the Airbus A380 will focus on major centres in a hub-and-spoke system.
- **Special-purpose flights** This category includes flights by helicopters, seaplanes, and amphibious vehicles. There are all-helicopter and all-seaplane airlines in several countries.

ILLUSTRATION 6–3

Air Canada's Boeing 777 was designed for fuel efficiency.

SOURCE: Brian Losito/Air Canada.

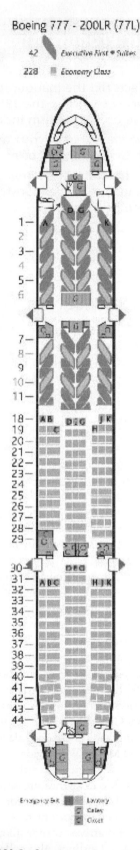

Boeing 777 - 200LR (77L)

42 Executive First ● Suites

228 Economy Class

Emergency Exit | Lavatory

Galley

Closet

ILLUSTRATION 6–4

Typical aircraft configuration.

SOURCE: Reprinted with permission of Air Canada.

Check Your Product Knowledge

1. What effects did the inauguration of passenger jet service in the 1950s and 1960s have on the tourism industry?
2. Name two ways that aircraft may be classified. Give examples of each.
3. What was the state (structure/composition) of the Canadian airline industry at the turn of the new century?

TYPES OF AIR SERVICE

In Canada and the United States, aircraft provide services in two broad areas—civilian and military. Civilian services can be further divided into air carrier aviation and general aviation.

Air Carrier Aviation

Air carrier aviation refers to privately owned companies that offer for-hire public transportation of passengers, cargo, and mail. An air carrier, also known as a **common carrier**, can be a small company with 100 employees and a dozen aircraft, or it can be a huge conglomerate with 40 000 employees and hundreds of aircraft. Air Canada, Delta Airlines, and United belong in the category of air carrier aviation.

Some airplanes are designed to transport passengers only. Others have removable seats, extra-wide doors, and machinery for loading and unloading so that they can transport either passengers or cargo. Still others are designed solely to transport cargo. These airplanes look like passenger airplanes except they have no windows. The largest cargo planes, such as the Boeing 747F, can carry 100 tonnes 8000 kilometres nonstop. In recent years, small-package carriers that guarantee overnight delivery to major cities across Canada and the United States have found a lucrative market. These include Federal Express, UPS, Purolator, and Menlo Worldwide.

Air carriers provide services on either a scheduled or a nonscheduled basis. Most airlines are scheduled airlines, which set arrival and departure times for all their flights. Timetables are extremely important to scheduled carriers; most flights depart and arrive on time about 90 percent of the time. Nonscheduled airlines, also called **supplemental airlines** or **charter airlines**, provide air travel at lower rates than regular fares on **scheduled airlines**. Planes can be chartered from supplemental airlines or from airlines operating scheduled flights.

Classification Systems in the United States

Since the Airline Deregulation Act of 1978, air carriers in the United States have been classified on the basis of revenue or annual earning:

- Major air carriers earn $1 billion or more yearly.
- National air carriers earn $75 million to $1 billion yearly.
- Large regional/commuter carriers earn $10 million to $75 million yearly.
- Medium-sized regional/commuter carriers earn less than $10 million yearly.

A classification system based on revenue is realistic and flexible, and accurately describes what is happening in the industry. If business is brisk, a regional carrier could be a national carrier next year. Conversely, a major carrier could drop to a national carrier if sales fall. Every major carrier in the United States is also an international carrier, operating scheduled services to foreign nations. Some national carriers even have international flights.

Classification Systems in Canada

Airlines in Canada were at one time classified in much the same way as those in the United States. The Canada Transportation Act 1996 now governs air carrier regulations in Canada. This Act replaced the National Transportation Act of 1987, which set different rules for southern and northern Canada. The Canadian Transportation Agency (CTA) grants an applicant a licence to operate in southern Canada if the applicant is a Canadian company and can prove it is "fit, willing, and able." That means it must have an operating certificate from Transport Canada and sufficient liability insurance. However, existing carriers in northern Canada can block a new applicant if they can prove that the new licence would lead to a significant reduction in the level of service or create instability.

Currently, the CTA classifies air services in Canada in the following way:

- Domestic
- Scheduled international
- Non-scheduled international

The CTA also issues permits for charter flights within the above categories.

International Air Carriers No nation has as many airlines as the United States, and very few have as many as Canada; indeed, most have only one. Even the leading industrial nations rarely have more than three carriers. Typically, these nations have one long-haul/international, one regional/commuter, and one all-charter operator.

Domestic Charter Air Service At one time a charter passenger had to belong to a specific group that would charter a plane for the trip. Charter service was provided by both regularly scheduled airlines and those classified as charter carriers. For example, the major Canadian carriers would offer charter service to the southern United States and the Caribbean. The scheduled carriers did not have regular route operating authority, but could fly on a charter basis.

The tight restrictions on charter service have relaxed over the decades. Through the early 1990s, the clearest distinctions between the traditional major scheduled carriers and the traditional charter carriers were the number of communities served and the frequency of service. Since the late 1990s, however, the traditional charter air carriers have expanded their regular intercity services.

By 2004, Air Transat (with its tour subsidiaries) and Skyservice (serving ALBA Tours, Conquest Vacations, Sunquest Vacations, and Signature Vacations) were the main charter carriers in Canada. However, new charter carriers such as Sunwing Airlines continue to enter the market.

International Charter Air Service International charter passengers are carried by both Canadian and foreign air carriers. In 2000, the former 1978 policy for international charter air services was heavily revised. The need for advance booking was removed, minimum stay requirements were done away with, and restrictions on one-way travel were lifted. According to Transport Canada, the new policy maintains a distinction between international charter services and scheduled air services to preserve the integrity of the international scheduled air services covered by Canada's bilateral air agreements.

Air Canada reduced its charter services in the 1990s because of new scheduled routes to the United States under the Open Skies agreement and the advent of strategic alliances with other airlines. In Canada about 2.5 million passengers travelled on charter services in 2005 compared with about 91 million on scheduled services. Major charter destinations include Europe in summer and the United States and the southern regions (the Caribbean, Mexico and Latin America) in winter.

General Aviation

General aviation refers to all civilian aircraft except those used by the commercial airlines. In terms of revenue, general aviation is far less important than air carrier aviation. In terms of number of aircraft, however, it is of far greater significance. Few general aviation aircraft fly the jet routes, which begin at an altitude of 6000 metres. General aviation in Canada accounts for about 50 percent of all aircraft movements at airports with air navigational services. The majority of activity takes place at noncontrolled airports. Recreational flying accounts for most general aviation, representing 75 percent of all registered aircraft and 66 percent of Canada's pilots.

Check Your Product Knowledge

1. What is the difference between air carrier aviation and general aviation?
2. How important is charter air service in Canada?
3. How does the classification system for airlines in the U.S. differ from that in Canada?

AIRPORTS: TRANSPORTATION TERMINALS FOR THE SKIES

The world's major airports are international crossroads, handling thousands of passengers and hundreds of flights each day to and from every corner of the globe. Atlanta's Hartsfield Airport (89.4 million passengers in 2007) has replaced Chicago's O'Hare International Airport (76.2 million passengers in 2007) as the world's busiest. Every minute at Hartsfield during the 6 a.m. to midnight period, two or three planes take off or land. Some international airports resemble cities. The airport at Frankfurt am Main, Germany, features 24 restaurants and bars, a variety of boutiques, medical and dental offices, banks, a supermarket, a disco, four movie theatres, and two railway stations.

Canadian Airport Passenger Data

Data on passengers at Canadian airports are classified by three types of services: Canadian and foreign carriers' major scheduled services, regional and local scheduled services, and major charter services. Thirty-six airports not operated by Transport Canada are members of the Canadian Airports Council (CAC). These 36 are classified into Level I airports (8), which handle more than one million passengers a year, and Level II airports (28), which have regularly scheduled passenger service but handle fewer than one million passengers a year (see Table 6–1).

Canadian City Pair Passenger Data

In Canada, nearly half the domestic air travel takes place along 11 routes involving nine large Canadian cities: Victoria, Vancouver, Calgary, Edmonton, Winnipeg, Toronto, Ottawa, Montreal, and Halifax. Air Canada dominates with about 75 percent of available capacity. At the opposite extreme are small private airfields with limited facilities, little daily activity, and no scheduled flights.

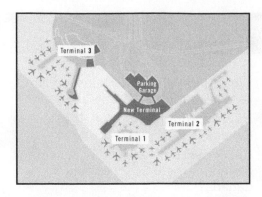

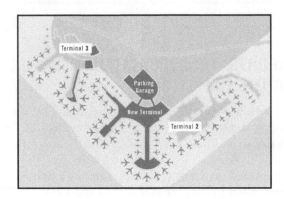

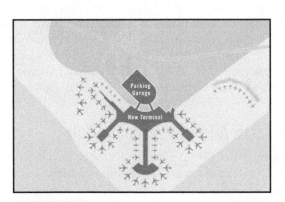

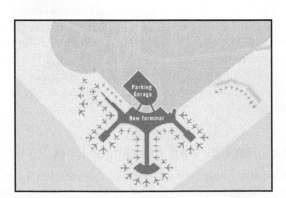

ILLUSTRATION 6–5

Pearson International Airport in Toronto is expanding through several phases until 2015.

SOURCE: Courtesy of Greater Toronto Airports Authority.

TABLE 6–1 Top Eight Canadian Airports Ranked by Passengers, 2007

Rank	Airport	Passengers (millions)
1	Toronto-Pearson	31.5
2	Vancouver	17.5
3	Montreal-Pierre Elliott Trudeau	12.4
4	Calgary	12.2
5	Edmonton	6.0
6	Ottawa	4.1
7	Winnipeg	3.6
8	Halifax	3.5

SOURCE: Airport websites.

Passengers by Sector: Domestic, Transborder, and International

The number of domestic air passengers peaked in the late 1980s, then declined, was flat at about 20 million through the early to mid-1990s (no doubt reflecting recessionary conditions), and then grew in the late 1990s. Overall growth was about 20 percent. Transborder traffic grew steadily, except during 1990–91 (recession), reflecting the opportunities and threats of freer trade and the Open Skies agreement of 1995. Overall growth was about 70 percent. International traffic also grew steadily, essentially doubling. This upward trend has continued. In 2006, there were over 63 million domestic passengers, compared with about 21 million transborder and 17 million international passengers.

Check Your Product Knowledge

1. Why do you think domestic passenger traffic was lower for the period 1991–95 than in the late 1980s and late 1990s?

2. What factors do you think account for the steady growth in transborder and international air passenger traffic?

3. Which airports do you think have benefited from the growth in transborder and international traffic?

Types of Airports

Civilian airports can be classified into two types: air carrier airports and general aviation airports. Air carrier airports, of which there are about 450 in Canada and 570 in the United States, are used by scheduled airlines—the majors, nationals, and regionals. They can also serve general aviation aircraft, especially corporate airplanes. General aviation airports—often unpaved and unlit—serve all types of aircraft except scheduled airline planes.

Airport Ownership

In Canada and the United States, a railway company owns not only the trains it operates but also the tracks and stations used by its trains. Bus companies generally own the stations out of which their buses operate. The same is not true for airports; very few airlines own and operate the airports they serve. Instead, they rent space.

In Canada, the Aeronautics Act governs ground and air services and facilities. Transport Canada used to own and manage airports. At one time it was responsible for the air navigation system, which has since been privatized and is now operated by NAV CANADA. It is also responsible for the airspace over the western part of the Atlantic Ocean; on September 11, 2001, it was instrumental in tracking and guiding the "ordered" landing of hundreds of planes.

In 1987, the federal Transport minister announced an initiative to lease airports to local airport authorities. Vancouver International Airport was the first to be leased. The National Airports Policy of 1994 declared that the federal government would retain ownership of 28 airports, but local airport authorities would operate and maintain them. This transfer, on a 60-year lease basis, took place during the mid- to late 1990s. In 2002, the federal government proposed substantial increases in lease payments. Variations in rents were quite apparent: Pearson International (Toronto) paid more than 10 times the combined totals for Montreal (Pierre Elliott Trudeau International and Mirabel International—$125 million against $11 million). Therefore, in 2005, the federal government introduced a new, more equitable rent formula based on a percentage of gross revenues. Although the new formula reduced airport rents, it still placed a disproportionate burden on Pearson, whose landing fees are among the world's highest.

In the United States, most airports are small, privately owned facilities. Their owners mainly serve recreational flyers. There are, however, more than 5000 publicly owned and operated airports in the United States. These include all large airports serving metropolitan areas. State, county, or city governments administer publicly owned airports. Airports often enter into a contract with a **fixed-base operator (FBO)**. The FBO sells fuel, rents hangar space to aircraft owners, provides maintenance and repairs, and gives flying lessons. The FBO pays rent, and usually a percentage of gross revenue, to the airport.

Air carriers pay for use of airports through landing fees, rents on counter and office space, and fuel and registration taxes. As landlord, the governing authority also charges rent to car rental companies, coffee shops and stores, and other concessions in and around the terminal building.

Airport Location

Because of the space required by runways, even the smallest airport needs 2 hectares of land. Medium-sized airports require 200 to 600 hectares, while large airports require 6000 hectares. Dallas–Fort Worth Airport, the largest airport in the United States, covers 7000 hectares of land—more than 70 square kilometres. Mirabel Airport, near Montreal, would have been larger than Dallas–Fort Worth if it had been fully developed; however, it was closed to passenger traffic in 2004.

The large amount of land required by airports makes them difficult to site and construct. The rapid growth of airline traffic and the increase in the size of airplanes have together created a constant demand for more space. In the 1940s and 1950s, airports were constructed on what were then the outskirts of metropolitan areas. In the 1960s and 1970s, airports remained on these sites while suburbs sprang up around them. As a result, many communities today must contend with the noise and congestion caused by nearby airports.

The Layout of an Airport

Airports vary in layout depending on their size and when they were built. Early airports were far simpler in design than those being built today.

The Terminal Building The **terminal building** is the heart of the airport complex. It is where passengers purchase or present their tickets, check in or retrieve baggage, and board or leave an airplane. Besides ticket counters and waiting areas, the terminal building has a weather station, a briefing room for pilots, a dispatch office for communicating with ticket counters and planes, and the office of the airport manager. Car rental agencies, shops, restaurants, cocktail lounges, and banks are also found in the terminal buildings at major airports.

Other Parts of an Airport Major airports have the following areas:

- The **cargo terminal**—one or more separate buildings where mail or freight is processed.
- The **control tower**—the nerve centre of the airport, usually adjacent to the passenger terminal. From the glass-enclosed top level, or cab, air traffic controllers use radar, radio, and signal lights to direct traffic in the air and on the ground.

- **Hangars**—the buildings where planes are stored and repaired. The hangars must be far enough from the runways to avoid interference.
- **Runways**—the strips of land on which airplanes land and from which they take off. Runways must be long enough and wide enough to accommodate the airplanes using them. Transport Canada sets size specifications. There must also be a clear zone at either end of the runway. To accommodate a jumbo jet, a runway, including its clear zone, might be 6.5 kilometres long.
- The **loading apron**—the parking area at the terminal gate where the airplane is refuelled, loaded, and boarded.
- **Taxiways**—lanes for the airplane to use when going from the apron to the runway or from the runway to the hangar.

Airports and Route Structures

An airline route is the path an airplane takes in delivering its services. Airports are the delivery points along the path. To make the most efficient use of their airplanes, airline managers plan routes carefully, using three main patterns or structures.

When an airplane flies to a destination in one direction and then turns around and repeats the flight in the opposite direction, it has completed a **linear route**. A linear route may have intermediate stops, which generate additional revenue at little cost. An example is Calgary–Edmonton–Yellowknife–Norman Wells–Inuvik.

On a **hub-and-spoke route**, a major airport becomes the centre point for arrivals from and departures to many other airports. This airport is like the hub of a wagon wheel: The smaller airports that surround it form the rim, and the flights that connect it to the rim are the spokes. These route structures in turn overlap to create an ever-widening air route system. For example, the airport at Calgary, Alberta, is the hub for flights to the smaller cities around it. In turn, Toronto is a hub city with Calgary on its rim, and London, England, is a hub city with Toronto on its rim. In this last case, the airport at Toronto functions as a **gateway airport** in that it services scheduled international flights.

With the increase in international tourism, many cities have had to expand their airport facilities, and some now have more than one airport.

A third type of route structure combines the linear and the hub-and-spoke models. As many flights as possible are scheduled to arrive in a particular city (the hub) at the same time. The same planes depart one hour later on linear routes to their originating cities after picking up passengers from connecting flights. For example, Passenger 1 arrives in Toronto on plane A from Calgary. She immediately boards plane B, which is returning to Halifax, while Passenger 2, who just got off plane C from London, Ontario, catches plane A, which is returning to Calgary.

Check Your Product Knowledge

1. What are the classifications for civilian airports?
2. Who owns the airports in the United States? In Canada?
3. List the main parts of an airport.
4. What are three types of airline route structures?

SECURITY AT AIRPORTS

International airports have become global crossroads; they have also become killing grounds for disputes half a world away. Bombings, shootings, and hijackings have prompted governments and airport officials to tighten security at international airports.

In June 1985, after terrorists hijacked a TWA jet shortly after takeoff from Athens, Greece, strict security measures were imposed. These focused on inspecting passenger baggage and ensuring that all passengers passed through metal detectors before boarding. After September 11, 2001, security measures were tightened and enhanced. Particular measures for those flying to the United States include the requirement that passengers supply the following in advance of travel: date of birth, gender, nationality, and passport number; also, for those with another form of national documentation, the numbers of those papers. Since 2004, the U.S. Government has been phasing in the Western Hemisphere Travel Initiative (WHTI), which was introduced to strengthen U.S. border security after the terrorist attacks of September 11, 2001. The legislation requires all persons entering the United States after June 1, 2009 to have a valid passport or other acceptable travel documents. These documents include the NEXUS card, government-issued security enhanced photo ID cards, and "smart" cards that contain encoded information. These smart cards will include personal information that can be read by a scanner: address, driver's licence number, telephone number, credit rating, and so on. This will provide a profile of the person's "stability." The idea is that the more stable a person's life, the less likely he or she is a terrorist. Future measures are likely also to include the use of smart biometric markers linked to the ID card—computerized scans of fingerprints, palms, faces, even the insides of eyeballs.

In 2002, the Canadian Government created the Canadian Air Transport Security Authority (CATSA) to protect the public by securing critical elements of the air transportation system. Among its activities, CATSA is responsible for pre-board screening at major airports, hold

ILLUSTRATION 6–6

Security procedures at airports have been tightened since September 11, 2001.

SOURCE: Richard Sheinwald/Bloomberg News/Landov.

baggage screening, non-passenger screening, implementation of a restricted area identity card, and airport policing funding agreements. CATSA uses these mechanisms to help secure Canada's air transportation system.

The airlines, the travel industry, and regulators are looking for solutions to speed up the long lines at airports and reduce the advance waiting time and passenger frustration, yet increase security.

Check Your Product Knowledge

1. What are the advantages and disadvantages of using smart ID cards and biometrics?
2. What is the WHTI and how has it affected travel to the U.S.?
3. What is the role of CATSA?

AIRLINE INDUSTRY REGULATION

Governments are involved in the airline industry at three different levels of regulation: Commercial flights between countries are regulated by international agreements, individual governments enforce economic and air safety regulations within each country, and governments regulate international travellers by requiring them to carry documentation and observe health and customs regulations.

How the International System Works

Governments realize that rules are necessary to ensure that airlines operate smoothly between countries. A system for conducting international aviation has evolved through three channels:

1. Multilateral agreements reached at worldwide conferences.
2. The negotiation of bilateral agreements.
3. Membership in international organizations.

At the present time, the international system is a compromise between total government control and totally independent decision making by the airlines.

Worldwide Conferences Every nation claims ownership of the soil within its boundaries and the sea close to its shores; in the same way, it claims ownership of its skies. The fundamental principle of sovereign skies was first affirmed at the Paris Convention on the Regulation of Aerial Navigation in 1919, and reaffirmed at subsequent conventions. It requires countries to negotiate the mutual use of airspace. Accordingly, a country must receive permission before its aircraft can fly through another's airspace.

Another important principle established at the Paris Convention was that every aircraft must have a nationality; that is, an aircraft must be validly registered in a specific nation and must be accountable to that nation for its operations. This principle is especially important in the event of an infraction of international air law.

The Havana Convention of 1928 resulted in the standardization of operating procedures, such as issuing tickets and checking baggage. This agreement enabled international airlines to work together more easily.

The 1929 Warsaw Convention on International Carriage by Air established limits to liability in the event that a passenger was injured or killed, or baggage or cargo was lost or damaged. This agreement was amended in 1955 by the Hague Protocol and again in 1971 by the Guatemala City Protocol.

The agreements reached at these conventions are multilateral; that is, they involve more than two nations and are equally binding on all nations that sign them. More recent conventions have established procedures for dealing with hijackings and other crimes committed aboard international flights.

The Freedoms of the Air Toward the end of World War II, representatives of all but one of the member countries of the United Nations (i.e., the Soviet Union) gathered in Chicago to renew the principles of international air law. Among other accomplishments, the Chicago Convention of 1944 formulated the Five Freedoms, which have greatly affected international aviation. Also called the Flying Freedoms, these statements categorized the ways in which a carrier of one nation can pass through, land in, and depart from another nation. They provide a basis for international negotiations. Over the years, three unofficial freedoms have been added to the list.

Figure 6–1 summarizes the eight freedoms and offers an example of each. The first two freedoms are called "transit rights" and have been widely accepted on a multilateral basis. Freedoms three, four, five, and six are called "traffic rights" and have not been completely accepted. The seventh and eighth freedoms are allowed only in special circumstances.

Bilateral Agreements In 1946, the United States and the United Kingdom negotiated a bilateral agreement that became a model for subsequent agreements. Signed in Bermuda and referred to as the Bermuda System, this agreement incorporates the spirit of the Flying Freedoms.

During negotiations, governments decide on the routes to be served, the airports to be used, the frequency and capacity of flights, restrictions for taking off and landing, and procedures for approving fares and tariffs. Usually the airlines are asked to consult about fares with the International Air Transport Association.

Canada and the United States negotiated a bilateral agreement in 1966, amended it in 1974, and negotiated an Open Skies agreement (discussed below) in 1995 and in 2005.

International Air Transport Association (IATA)
IATA is an airline service organization headquartered in Montreal and Geneva. It was founded in 1919 by a group of European airlines and reorganized in 1945. Today around 230 of the world's airlines belong to IATA as either full or associate members. This represents about 93 percent of scheduled international air traffic. IATA carries out several important functions for members, including:

- Provides a forum for airlines to meet and discuss mutual concerns.
- Recommends fares and tariffs for government approval.
- Represents the airlines in travel agency affairs.
- Promotes air safety and environmental protection.
- Encourages worldwide air travel.

Another important organization is the International Civil Aviation Organization (ICAO), also based in Montreal. Founded by the Chicago Convention, the ICAO is now an agency of the United Nations. The ICAO concerns itself mainly with setting standards for aviation equipment and operations. It also organizes world conferences and mediates disputes between members. Its current focus is to enhance the safety and security of civil aviation, minimize its effect on the environment, promote the efficiency and continuity of aviation operations, and strengthen the rule of law.

Traffic Conferences To make air travel easier to describe and organize, the IATA has divided the global airline community into three areas (see Figure 6–2).

The United States has often disagreed with the airfares established by the IATA and has negotiated bilateral pacts to bypass them.

Most of IATA's members are **flag carriers,** or national airlines representing individual nations. For example, El Al is the flag carrier for Israel, and Japan Airlines (JAL) is the flag carrier for Japan. All carriers registered in other nations are known in Canada as **foreign flags.** Many flag carriers are owned or subsidized by governments. Because they receive funding from their governments, flag carriers can offer lower fares and survive despite financial losses. Therefore, some countries, such as the United States, reserve the right to disallow airfares to and from that country if they are unrealistically low.

First Freedom. The right of an airline to overfly one country to get to another.

Second Freedom. The right of an airline to land in another country for a technical stopover (fuel, maintenance) but not to pick up or drop off traffic.

Third Freedom. The right of an airline, registered in country X, to drop off traffic from country X into country Y.

Fourth Freedom. The right of an airline, registered in country X, to carry traffic back to country X from country Y.

Fifth Freedom. The right of an airline, registered in country X, to collect traffic in country Y and fly on to country Z, as long as the flight either originates or terminates in country X.

Sixth Freedom. The right of an airline, registered in country X, to carry traffic to a gateway—a point in country X—and then abroad. The traffic has neither its origin nor ultimate destination in country X.

Seventh Freedom. The right of an airline, registered in country X, to operate entirely outside of country X in carrying traffic between two other countries.

Eighth Freedom. The right of an airline, registered in country X, to carry traffic between any two points in the same foreign country.

Examples of Freedoms of the Air
First Freedom. Delta Airlines departs from Atlanta and overflies Canada en route to London.

Second Freedom. Japan Airlines departs from Copenhagen, Denmark, and lands in Anchorage, Alaska, en route to Tokyo. The stop in Alaska is for fuel and a crew change. Japan Airlines is not allowed to carry passengers or cargo to or from Anchorage.

Third Freedom. Delta Airlines departs from Atlanta and carries American citizens to London.

Fourth Freedom. Delta Airlines departs from London and carries British subjects to the United States.

Fifth Freedom. Delta Airlines departs from Atlanta, stops en route in London, and boards passengers there for its continuation to Frankfurt, Germany.

Sixth Freedom. Northwest Airlines, carrying Norwegian passengers from Oslo bound for Tokyo, may stop over in Minneapolis-St. Paul, Minnesota, a gateway city.

Seventh Freedom. British Airways flies nonstop from Frankfurt, Germany, to Washington, D.C., without stopping in Great Britain.

Eighth Freedom. Air France, a French carrier, carries traffic between Frankfurt and Berlin—all within Germany.

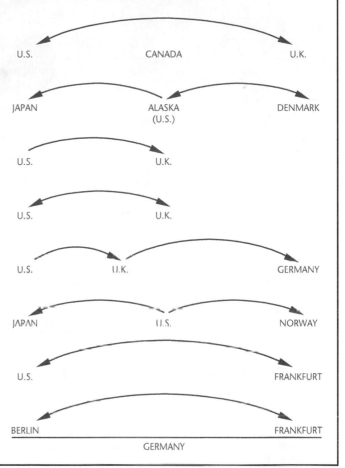

FIGURE 6–1 The Eight Freedoms of the Air

Check Your Product Knowledge

1. What are the three main channels for regulating the international air system?
2. Why are the Flying Freedoms important?
3. Name two organizations that help regulate the international airline industry.

REGULATING DOMESTIC SERVICE— CANADA AND THE UNITED STATES

This section examines the regulation of domestic service in Canada and the United States. The airline industries of these two countries have long been different from those of most other countries because of the emphasis on private ownership.

Domestic Service—Canada

The Aeronautics Act of 1919 extended federal government regulation to the aviation industry. This act created an air board to hear requests from applicants wishing to start air services.

The Canadian government was concerned about the developing trunk-line system in the United States, which threatened to divert Canadian east–west airline traffic into the United States through feeder services drawing on Canadian cities. A government-owned carrier, Trans-Canada Airlines (TCA), now Air Canada, was established as a subsidiary of Canadian National Railway. TCA was given a Canadian monopoly on transcontinental and international routes.

TCA's monopoly was broken after World War II, when Canadian Pacific Airlines (CP) was awarded international routes to Asia, Australia, and South America. However, it

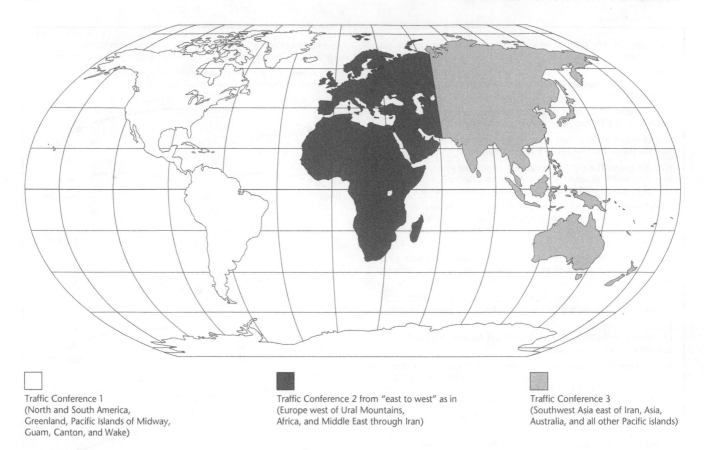

☐ Traffic Conference 1
(North and South America,
Greenland, Pacific Islands of Midway,
Guam, Canton, and Wake)

■ Traffic Conference 2 from "east to west" as in
(Europe west of Ural Mountains,
Africa, and Middle East through Iran)

▨ Traffic Conference 3
(Southwest Asia east of Iran, Asia,
Australia, and all other Pacific islands)

FIGURE 6–2 The World Traffic Conferences

was not allowed to compete on the transcontinental route until 1958. The Canadian government had finally recognized that CP needed a domestic system that would link Canadian travellers to its international routes. Canadian Pacific Airlines later became CP Air, then Canadian Airlines until it was taken over by Air Canada in 1999.

Canada and the United States reached a bilateral air agreement in 1966. Air Canada was awarded the majority of new routes to cities in the United States as the Canadian carrier.

The Period of Regulated Competition The Canadian Transportation Act of 1967 established the Canadian Transport Commission (CTC). After the mid-1970s, the CTC began encouraging regulated competition. More liberal charter regulations were introduced gradually after 1974. However, the scheduled carriers insisted that the new lower-fare services not threaten the profitability of scheduled services. The charter carriers helped expand the tourism market for Canadians by providing inexpensive flights to foreign destinations not served by regular carriers. The scheduled carriers also began operating charters themselves, especially to southern resort destinations in the winter, when east–west traffic was in its low period.

By 1980, the equivalent of three airlines were competing on transcontinental routes. It had taken more than 40 years since the founding of a Canadian airline system, and 22 years since the breaking of the TCA transcontinental monopoly, for Canada's airline industry to achieve this level of competition and consumer choice. The United States had deregulated its airline industry in 1978.

Regulatory Reform While the Canadian airline industry was retrenching, the American airline industry was seeing new entrants, new routes, new services, and lower airfares under **deregulation**. Some Canadians were travelling to American border cities to take advantage of the lower fares. Realizing that changes were needed, the Canadian government in 1984 introduced a new framework for regulatory reform in transportation that minimized economic regulation. This legislation provided consumers with a wider range of price and service options and invigorated the airline industry.

The mid-1980s saw the emergence of new low-cost regional and commuter airlines operating mainly propeller aircraft. Most of the new entrants were or became affiliates of the major carriers, who reduced or vacated the shorter routes that had been served by jet aircraft. The regional affiliates took over these shorter routes, typically on a hub-and-spoke basis. Some communities were upset about losing direct jet service to major centres. However, most communities now had more flights per day to the hub, and usually service provided by more than one airline.

The National Transportation Act of 1987

The new National Transportation Act (NTA) of 1987, effective January 1, 1988, recognized that a safe, economic, efficient, and adequate network of transportation was essential to serve the needs of shippers and travellers, and to maintain the economic well-being and growth of Canada and its regions. A new regulatory body, the National Transportation Agency, replaced the Canadian Transport Commission. The National Transportation Act of 1967 had emphasized competition between modes. The stated objective of the new NTA was to increase competition within modes as well.

The major problem—what to do with federally owned Air Canada—was recognized in air regulatory reform. Air Canada, with more than a 50 percent share domestically, most of the transborder routes to cities in the United States, and many of the international routes to other countries, was the dominant airline in the Canadian airline industry. With access to the public purse, Air Canada was able to engage in uneconomic practices.

Air Canada was privatized in 1988, which placed it on the same footing as the other private carriers. This ensured fairer competition, even though Air Canada was still dominant. The other major carriers decided to compete with Air Canada by making mergers, which resulted in the formation of Canadian Airlines.

The Canadian Airline Industry in the Early 1990s

The net effect of the air regulatory reform in Canada in the 1980s was less competition instead of more. Now, the airline industry essentially consisted of two major carriers, Air Canada and Canadian Airlines, with their associated regional and commuter airlines. Both airlines experienced financial difficulty in the early 1990s, reflecting the prolonged recession and the inevitable pain of restructuring. The operating statistics, including passenger kilometres flown, load factors, and employment, were down from the late 1980s. Also, there was increased competition from charter operations.

Two major policy issues unfolded in the mid-1990s: airline restructuring and the Open Skies agreement between Canada and the United States.

Airline Restructuring

The two major airlines continued restructuring in the mid-1990s in their efforts to survive domestically and position themselves internationally. Domestically, both airlines reduced their payrolls, modified their routes, and changed the number and type of aircraft used. Both Air Canada and Canadian Airlines entered into cooperative arrangements with several carriers, and Canadian negotiated to sell 25 percent of its equity to American Airlines.

Open Skies

In February 1995, Canada and the United States signed a trade agreement to liberalize airline service on transborder routes. The agreement, commonly referred to as **Open Skies**, granted any Canadian carrier the right to serve any destination in the United States. American carriers were also given the third and fourth freedoms of the air, subject to a three-year phase-in period for flying to Montreal, Toronto, and Vancouver.

The implications of Open Skies for free trade and tourism were considerable. Free trade between Canada and the United States (and later Mexico under the North American Free Trade Agreement of 1994, or NAFTA) was creating business opportunities, but this was not clear from looking at airline schedules. Nonstop or one-stop service between major cities was limited, and even fewer cities had a choice of service between competing carriers. A major reason for this was the shift in economic activity to the growing cities in the American Sunbelt. It was difficult for business and tourist travellers to fly between Canada and the Sunbelt without stopping, and possibly changing planes, along the way.

The lack of transborder air service was a major concern for tourism in Canada. More tourists were taking shorter three- and four-day trips. They did not want to spend half their time waiting in air terminals for a connecting flight. A successful Open Skies agreement that opened up more transborder routes was imperative if this problem was to be solved.

Note that Open Skies 1995 did not grant Fifth Freedom rights. An American carrier could fly from New York to Toronto but it could not then fly directly to another Canadian city such as Winnipeg or Vancouver. A new Open Skies agreement was negotiated in 2005 that expanded access for the airlines of both countries, and that liberalized fifth freedom rights to third country markets.

The travelling public, not just the airline industry, has gained under Open Skies. There are now more direct flights to more destinations, which has reduced waiting and travel times.

Air Canada and Canadian Airlines were quick to take advantage of Open Skies, but their approaches differed substantially. Canadian Airlines emphasized a traditional hub-and-spoke pattern. It focused on shuttling passengers from the major Canadian hubs of Vancouver, Calgary, and Toronto to the American hubs of Los Angeles, Dallas/Fort Worth, and New York. Its partner, American Airlines, provided the connecting service from the hubs to destinations within the United States. Also, Vancouver became a gateway to the Pacific Rim for American passengers.

The purchase of Canadair jets, with 50-seat capacity and lower operating costs, made it feasible for Air Canada to apply a **hub buster strategy**. This involves bypassing hub cities and instead providing direct service to destinations in the United States. Air Canada now provides more nonstop transborder services than any other carrier or alliance of carriers.

New Entrants The mid-1990s saw new discount airlines entering the Canadian market: Some were short-lived but WestJet has thrived (see this chapter's Profile). It offered fares that were about 50 percent lower than those prevailing before startup. Costs were low for several reasons: The company carried almost no debt, its labour costs were lower (although it did offer employees a profit-sharing scheme), it used a ticketless reservation system, it served no meals during flights, and it didn't provide baggage retrieval service on connecting flights (connecting passengers had to retrieve and carry their own luggage).

Strategic Alliances In 1997, both Air Canada and Canadian Airlines forged alliances with other major carriers to form global networks. Air Canada joined the Star Alliance; Canadian Airlines joined One World (see Table 6–2).

The advantages of alliances relate to purchasing, operating, and marketing. Air Canada achieved cost savings

through the joint purchasing of fuel, in-flight meals, and the airplanes themselves. Also, the alliance gives it access to more than 210 000 employees around the world. The airlines involved have moved their airport facilities closer together so that they can use one another's staff, counters, and baggage equipment. The alliance has also simplified marketing: It has become easier to book reservations for international travel; travellers now have access to better connections and more services.

Many passengers have a favourite airline and do not appreciate finding themselves booked on another. So airlines in an alliance must set minimum service standards and make it clear to customers which airline operates the service for which they bought the ticket.

The Canadian Airline Industry in the New Millennium The Canadian airline industry in the 2000s is vastly different than it was even five years earlier. Canadian Airlines lasted slightly longer than a decade before being taken over by Air Canada in 1999. Other changes include the growth of WestJet, the quick collapse of several new entrants, the move by charter carriers into scheduled intercity service, and the subsequent bankruptcy of Canada 3000 in November 2001. Also, today all airlines are active on the Web and working hard at marketing themselves directly to consumers. This has alienated the traditional channel of distribution—the travel agencies.

Today, the Canada Transportation Act 1996, which is administered by the Canadian Transportation Agency (CTA), governs air carrier regulations in Canada. The Act was amended in 2007. The CTA administers transportation legislation and government policies, including essential regulation, to promote an efficient transportation system. Part of the CTA's mandate is to license air carriers, resolve complaints, and participate in international bilateral negotiations.

The Middle Years of the First Decade of the 2000s What will the Canadian airline industry be like in the next few years? There will be more turbulence in the short run. Air Canada, with its affiliate Air Canada Jazz, will continue as the dominant carrier. WestJet continues to grow. Other regional carriers, such as Bearskin, will probably expand more slowly. There have been new entrants, such as Porter Airlines, and there may be more.

Domestic Service—United States

Airlines in the United States are privately owned, but they are subject to regulation by the federal government. The justification for this control is that airlines use federal airways and engage in interstate commerce.

Deregulation The U.S. Civil Aeronautics Board (CAB) was established in 1938 to regulate the airline industry. As part of its mandate, the CAB established a system of trunk lines and feeders, which lasted until 1978. Proponents of deregulation argued that the CAB had become too powerful and that airlines should have the right to choose new

TABLE 6–2 Global Airline Alliances, 2008

Star Alliance	One World	Sky Team
Air Canada	American Airlines	Aeroflot
Air China	British Airways	AeroMexico
Air New Zealand	Cathay Pacific	Air France-KLM
ANA (All Nippon Airways)	Finnair	Alitalia
Asiana Airlines	Iberia	China Southern
Austrian Airlines	JAL Japan Airlines	Continental
bmi (British Midland)	LAN	CSA Czech Airlines
Egyptair	Malév	Delta Airlines
LOT PolishAirlines	Qantas	Korean
Lufthansa	Royal Jordanian	Northwest
SAA (South African Airways)		**Associates**
SAS (ScandinavianAir System)		Air Europa
Shanghai Airlines		Copa Airlines
Singapore Airlines		Kenya Airways
Spanair		
SWISS		
TAP Air Portugal		
TAM Airlines		
Thai Airlines International		
Turkish Airlines		
United Airlines		
US Airways		
Regional Members		
Adria		
Blue 1		
Croatia Airlines		

SOURCE: Alliance websites.

markets and abandon unprofitable ones. A free market-place would promote lower airfares, better air service, and a wider selection of flights through an expanded route system. Most economic regulation ended with the passage of the Airline Deregulation Act in 1978, which permits air carriers to enter and leave the marketplace as desired. By virtue of a "sunset clause," the CAB ceased operations at midnight on December 31, 1984.

The New-Entrant Carriers After deregulation, more than 150 carriers chose to compete with the established scheduled airlines. **New-entrant carriers** are of four types:

- **Interstate carriers** Airlines that once operated within a state, such as Air California, became interstate carriers when they expanded their routes across state lines.
- **Supplemental carriers** Companies such as Transamerica Airlines, which had been offering domestic all-charter flights, began providing scheduled services.
- **Commuter carriers** Deregulation, and new rules allowing commuter carriers to fly larger airplanes, brought about enormous growth in this sector. Many nonscheduled air taxi operators left general aviation and began competing as scheduled commuter carriers.
- **Brand-new entrants** These airlines did not exist in any form before 1978. By offering cut-rate prices, they have greatly affected the tourism industry. They can charge less because they fly used aircraft, employ nonunion workers, and offer "no-frills" flights.

Effects of Deregulation With the new-entrant carriers, competition became even fiercer, with price wars a common result. In their efforts to get ahead of the competition, airlines have been looking for new places to sell tickets, new ways to advertise them, and new ways to package them.

Supporters of deregulation contend that the public has benefited through greater choice, lower fares, and expanded routes. Critics say the growth has resulted in congested airports, the potential for more accidents, and the loss of service to smaller communities. Many well-known airlines (Braniff, Eastern, Pan Am) have gone out of business; several new entrants have already merged with other carriers, thus reducing choice.

Some airlines have entered into code-sharing partnerships. In a **code-sharing agreement**, a small regional or commuter airline flies under the code of a major airline. That way, the major airline can serve the smaller cities that generate too little traffic to fill its own larger planes. Continental Airlines has a code-sharing agreement with Rocky Mountain Air. Travellers who book a Continental flight to Aspen, Colorado, may find that they have to transfer to Rocky Mountain Air for the last part of the journey. This often involves a transfer from a large jet to a small turboprop.

Safety Regulation Economic regulation has largely ceased; federal regulation of aircraft safety continues. The biggest responsibility of the Federal Aviation Administration (FAA), part of the U.S. Department of Transportation, is to direct air traffic in the federal airways so that accidents don't happen. The federal airway system covers 560 000 kilometres. From ground level, the airways extend almost 23 000 metres above the earth's surface. All aircraft flying between 5500 and 23 000 metres are monitored constantly by ground-based radar control. With the exception of certain controlled airspace restrictions introduced after the events of September 11, 2001, aircraft flying below 5500 metres usually fly by a system of visual rules and are not necessarily monitored by the FAA.

Other responsibilities of the FAA include:

- Establishing and enforcing safety standards.
- Certifying and monitoring the skills and health of pilots.
- Certifying the safety of aircraft.
- Investigating accidents (along with the National Transportation Safety Board).
- Setting standards for design and construction of new aircraft and equipment.

Industry Regulation The scheduled air carriers of the United States are represented by the Air Transport Association (ATA), which lobbies the federal and local governments on behalf of the scheduled airlines and actively promotes airline travel. In a similar way, the Regional Airline Association (RAA) represents the nation's regional and commuter air carriers.

The Airlines Reporting Corporation (ARC) was established by the ATA in 1984. ARC serves as a link between the American airlines that belong to the ATA and the 25 000 retail travel agencies that are accredited to sell the airlines' tickets. ARC's role, and that of the International Airline Travel Agency Network (IATAN), which is the international counterpart of ARC, will be discussed in Chapter 16.

Check Your Product Knowledge

1. Why was the American airline industry deregulated in 1978? What were the results?
2. Why did the Canadian airline industry undergo regulatory reform in the 1980s? What were the results?
3. What is Open Skies? What are its major features?
4. Why did the Canadian airline industry undergo restructuring? How successful have new-entrant carriers been?
5. Why do international air carriers form strategic alliances? Do customers always like alliances?

THE AIRLINE INDUSTRY PRODUCT

Every industry has a product. The airline industry's product is a flight on an airplane. A travel professional must determine the motivations, needs, and expectations (MNEs) of travellers and then sell them the right products.

Factors Affecting the Price

Matching each traveller with the right product at the right price is not always easy, especially since deregulation. In the deregulated marketplace there may be several different types of airfares for a trip from Toronto to Vancouver. Sometimes it is less expensive to fly from coast to coast than to a city 2000 kilometres away. The price of a ticket is no longer based on distance. Nowadays it is also based on the type of journey, the type of flight, the type of service, and whether or not the flight is restricted.

Type of Journey Journeys are of four types. A **one-way trip** begins in an originating city and ends in a destination city (e.g., Winnipeg to Vancouver). A one-way journey can be made on more than one flight (e.g., Winnipeg via Edmonton to Vancouver).

A **round trip** begins in an originating city, goes to a destination city, and returns to the originating city. The routing must be the same in both directions. Example: Halifax to Toronto to Halifax. Buying a round-trip ticket is sometimes cheaper than buying two one-way tickets.

A **circle trip** is similar to a round trip, with an important difference: The outbound journey differs from the return journey in terms of either the routing or the class of service. For example, a traveller can go from Montreal to Vancouver via Toronto and then return from Vancouver to Montreal nonstop. Or that traveller can fly first class from Montreal to Vancouver, and economy class on the return.

An **open-jaw trip** is interrupted by surface travel. For example, a traveller may proceed from Toronto to Vancouver by air, then from Vancouver to Winnipeg by rail, then from Winnipeg to Toronto by air. An open-jaw trip can also be a journey with a return destination other than the originating city. Such a trip may take a traveller from Edmonton to Vancouver, then from Vancouver to Calgary.

Type of Flight Flights are of four types. One type is nonstop service, with no scheduled stopovers en route. A second type is **direct or through service**. Here, there can be one or more intermediate stops en route, but the passenger remains aboard the same plane.

A third type is a connecting flight. With an *online connection*, the passenger changes planes but remains with the same airline. Air Canada, for example, can offer a flight from Vancouver to Toronto connecting with another Air Canada flight from Toronto to Halifax. An airline can change planes for any number of reasons, including mechanical difficulties and seating considerations. With an **interline connection**, the passenger changes both airplanes and airlines. A passenger can fly on Air Canada

ILLUSTRATION 6–7

Flight attendants provide for the comfort and safety of travellers in all service classes.

SOURCE: Image courtesy of David Wright.

from Halifax to Boston, then on United Airlines from Boston to Washington.

Agreements among airlines to honour the tickets of other carriers make interline connections possible through interlining. **Interlining** permits the use of one standard ticket instead of separate tickets for each flight. The same system also makes it possible to check baggage through to its final destination. Interlining is an international as well as a domestic practice. Some new entrants and regional commuters do not participate in interlining agreements.

Intermodal ticketing, which makes it easier to coordinate different modes of travel, has become another popular travel product. In a system similar to interlining, the passenger buys one ticket for through travel using, for example, an airplane and a bus, or an airplane and a cruise ship, or an airplane and a rental car.

A fourth type of flight is the **stopover**. With a stopover, the passenger requests that the trip be interrupted at some intermediate point for 12 or more hours. A passenger can thus fly from Toronto to Saskatoon on Monday, remain in Saskatoon until Wednesday evening, and then fly on to Vancouver.

Type of Service Forty years ago, in-flight service on a domestic airliner consisted of a cold box lunch and a pack of chewing gum to relieve eardrum pressure. Today, passengers eat hot meals, drink cocktails, listen to music, and watch movies.

The type of service passengers receive depends on where they sit in the cabin, and they often pay accordingly. The most common **configuration**, or seating arrangement, consists of a first-class (F class) cabin and a coach or economy-class cabin, but an airplane can have all coach seats or, less often, all first-class seats. Larger jets may have several coach cabins. Aircraft cabins are further classified as narrow body (one aisle) and wide body (two aisles).

Some airlines offer business class or executive class (C or J class). Halfway between first class and coach in amenities, business class serves people who want a quiet place to work and who expect better service than passengers flying with discounted tickets. Air Canada created a new, stylish, custom-designed environment as a standard feature for all its business-class service.

Passengers in first class are provided with elaborate meals served on fine china, complimentary alcoholic beverages and movies, and individualized service. First-class seats are at the front of the plane, farther away from the engine noise. They are also wider and have greater pitch (that is, more room between the knees and the seatback). On many airlines today, first class and some business class seats convert to a bed, which provides even more comfort. Coach seats are closer together and narrower, and vary in comfort depending on their location in the cabin. Coach passengers often receive complimentary meals on flights longer than four hours, but they may have to pay extra for alcoholic beverages and for headsets for listening to music and watching in-flight movies.

Airlines usually provide in-flight services for passengers with special needs. For example, they assist challenged travellers, take care of children travelling alone, and cater to passengers with special dietary needs.

Unrestricted and Restricted Airfares With an **unrestricted airfare**, also called a **nondiscounted airfare** or **normal airfare**, a passenger can board any plane going to his or her destination that has an available seat. People must pay extra for the convenience of an unrestricted airfare.

A **restricted airfare**—also called a **promotional, discounted,** or **excursion airfare**—is the airlines' version of a sale or a bargain. The less expensive the airfare, the more restrictions there are, which can include some or all of the following:

- Advance-purchase requirement (up to a month prior to departure).
- Minimum/maximum length of stay at the destination.
- Fixed itinerary and departure times (no last-minute changes).
- Limited departure dates (good only on certain days of the week).
- Nonrefundable cancellation penalty.
- Capacity control (only a limited number of seats available on any given flight at the discounted fare).
- Nontransferable ticket (i.e., one airline may not honour certain excursion-fare tickets from another airline).

Because they generally have more flexible schedules, vacation travellers or those visiting friends and relatives (except in emergency situations) are more likely to purchase restricted airfares than are business travellers.

Since deregulation, airlines have found themselves promoting discounted tickets in order to fill seats that would otherwise remain empty. The philosophy is that half a fare is better than none. The result is that passengers in the coach cabin on any flight will have spent varying amounts of money for the same type of seat and service, depending on whether they purchased a restricted ticket. In effect, restricted airfares have done away with two-tier pricing and replaced it with a three-tier system: first-class, economy, and excursion fares.

In an effort to combat no-shows, a number of airlines have introduced financial penalties for cancellations. **No-shows** are people who make reservations but fail to use them. Another way airlines protect themselves against no-shows is to **overbook**, or sell more seats than they actually have. However, when an airline overbooks and no one cancels, the airline is liable and must compensate the passengers who are denied boarding. This compensation is often a cash settlement plus transportation on the next available flight, or a free upgrade in class of service.

International Airfares IATA members hold conferences to discuss international airfares. On the basis of rules and principles developed by the organization, it decides on rates for city pair combinations throughout the world. To reduce the complexity of calculating airfares in different currencies, it expresses all international airfares in **neutral units of construction** (NUCs). A formula converts NUCs into specific currencies for actual transactions.

IATA, like domestic carriers in Canada and the United States, calculates the price of a ticket on the basis of distance flown, type of service, and whether the fare is restricted or unrestricted. Many IATA airfares are based on distance flown. The actual distance flown between destinations is measured and then compared with a maximum allowable number of kilometres, which is usually about 20 percent greater than the actual number. The "bonus" distance enables passengers to make stopovers at intermediate cities along the route. This process of computing international airfares is called "fare construction."

Using this method of computing fares, the cost of an international airline ticket is usually directly related to the number of kilometres flown. This means that a trip from Washington, D.C., to Paris (6100 kilometres) should cost more than a trip from Washington, D.C., to Caracas (3300 kilometres). However, market factors such as greater competition and promotional fares can actually make a longer trip less expensive.

Marketing in the Jet Age

Prior to the Airline Deregulation Act of 1978 in the United States, and airline regulatory reform in Canada in 1984 and 1988, airline marketing focused on service. To lure passengers, airlines promoted in-flight amenities and friendly skies. After deregulation, marketing focused on pricing. Discounted advance-purchase airfares made people realize they could travel farther at reasonable prices. In recent years, however, there have been some signs of a return to service-oriented marketing. Business-class service and all-first-class service are examples of this trend.

In the 1990s, the airlines became quite adept at **yield management**. The development of sophisticated databases capable of predicting types of trips (e.g., short-notice business trips versus advance-purchase VFR trips) and the timing of trips (i.e., by time of day, day of week, time of year) have enabled airlines to optimize fare revenues (i.e., the yield, hence the term "yield management") on particular flights.

However, airlines may not always optimize their expected yields. A competitor may slash prices on certain city pairs. Some potential clients may remain loyal to a higher-cost airline because of a frequent flyer program. Conversely, some customers may feel that the service did not warrant the airfare, no matter how cheap.

Check Your Product Knowledge

1. Describe the four types of journeys.
2. How does seat location influence the airfare?
3. List five typical restrictions on a discounted airfare.
4. How do airlines protect themselves against no-shows?

AIRLINE INDUSTRY CONCERNS

Present-day concerns in the airline industry include the environment, air rage and airport rage, consumer complaints, and rising costs.

Concern for the Environment

As stated at the beginning of this chapter, transportation and the environment strongly influence each other.

As Air Canada is this country's dominant carrier, an overview of its commitment to the environment is appropriate. Air Canada's statement of environmental policy (see its website: www.aircanada.com/en/about/environment/index.html) lists several commitments:

- Compliance with applicable environmental legislation and regulation, and any other requirements to which Air Canada subscribes.
- Identify, prioritize, and address environmental risks.
- Maintain corporate environmental policies and standards to operate the airline in an environmentally responsible manner.
- Set and review strategies, objectives, and targets to ensure continuous improvement of environmental performance year after year.

- Make environment a component of business decisions, ensuring the environment is considered in planning of new, and changes to existing, materials, processes, equipment, and facilities.
- Prevent pollution at source.
- Use resources efficiently and minimize waste and emissions.
- Communicate with stakeholders such as governments, non-governmental organizations, industry peers, suppliers, employees, unions, customers and communities to resolve problems, engender cooperation, facilitate mutual understanding, and contribute to the development of responsible and cost-effective environmental standards and legislation.
- Conduct ongoing audits, take corrective action, and monitor progress.
- Hold management accountable for providing leadership on environmental matters, for achieving the specific targets and objectives the corporation has developed, and for providing training and resources.
- Ensure employees comply with Air Canada's environmental policies and procedures.

Roles and responsibilities for the environment are indicated on a flow chart that extends from the president and CEO down through a corporate safety and environmental board to an environmental affairs department and then to branch and department managers and employees. Activities under the company's environmental management system include communicating with various stakeholders, conducting environmental audits, and ensuring that employees comply with policies and procedures. Air Canada has further strengthened its commitment to the environment by creating a link on its website that lets passengers purchase offsets to reduce their carbon footprint. Also, the airline cooperates with the Air Transport Association of Canada, ATA, and IATA committees and other Star Alliance members on environmental safeguards.

Aviation is one of the most rapidly growing sources of greenhouse gases. For this reason, some airlines have introduced carbon offset programs to encourage their passengers to help reduce their impact on the environment. This means that passengers pay for someone else to cut emissions on their behalf. The ICAO in 2008 introduced a standard way to calculate how much air passengers should pay to offset their carbon emissions.

The European Union (EU) has also demanded that U.S. airlines pay for their carbon dioxide emissions and join the EU emissions trading scheme (or an equivalent system in the U.S.), or face restrictions on flights to the EU. This issue will be part of future negotiations on the transatlantic airline market.

Concern about Air Rage and Airport Rage

Why does it appear that more travellers are becoming upset on airplanes and in air terminals? Years ago, air rage (or sky rage) was rare and usually involved an unruly passenger who had to be ejected from a flight, which sometimes required a nonscheduled stop at the nearest airport. Anxiety caused by delays, cramped conditions, and restrictions on smoking are the main causes of this behaviour. Only about 25 percent of incidents are caused by excessive alcohol consumption. Other causes are seen to be flight delays and airport renovations and expansions. More travellers who get upset vent themselves, sometimes physically, on air crews and terminal personnel. Air rage and airport rage in fact are no worse than 20 years ago. However, terrorism is among the factors that have caused increased awareness of the problem, and incidents are more likely to be reported today.

Consumer Complaints

In 2000, the Canadian Transportation Agency established the Air Travel Complaints Commissioner. A consumer with a complaint against an air carrier should first try to resolve it directly with the carrier; if that person does not achieve satisfaction, the commissioner will attempt to resolve the situation through mediation. The commission documents its work at six-month intervals. The reports include the number and nature of filed complaints, the airlines involved, how the complaints were dealt with, and any problems of a systemic nature.

Consumers cannot make complaints about customer service issues, such as the quality of meals or the attitude of airline staff. These are the responsibility of the airline. Similarly, the Canadian Transportation Agency cannot assess damages for such things as lost income, pain and suffering, mental anguish or loss of enjoyment.

One of the biggest grievances for consumers is the way airlines advertise their prices. Generally, airlines advertise a price that does not include taxes, fuel surcharges, or other fees. This means that a trip advertised at $99 one way, may end up costing the consumer as much as $750 for a round trip. Consumers find this type of pricing confusing and irritating. It has also upset the travel trade in Ontario and Quebec, where provincial legislation demands that registered retailers and wholesalers show the total amount that a consumer will pay in the advertised price for all travel products. (However, PST and GST need not be included in the advertised price.) This legislation does not apply to airlines, which are regulated by the federal government. Although the Canada Transportation Act gives the federal government power to control air price advertising, it has not done so as yet.

Rising Costs

All airlines are concerned with rising costs, but this is even more of an issue for the **legacy carriers**. Legacy carriers are those that existed prior to deregulation in Canada and the U.S. These airlines tend to be unionized, have a large bureaucratic structure, and often have a large number of older, less fuel-efficient aircraft in their fleet. Together, these factors have made it more difficult for legacy carriers

than for new entrants to adapt to changing conditions. New entrants are usually not unionized, which lowers their payroll costs and allows for more flexible staff scheduling and assignments, their debt loads are frequently lower, and they often fly newer, more fuel efficient aircraft.

The situation was exacerbated by the rapid increase in oil prices during 2007–08. Many airlines (not just legacy carriers) went out of business during this period, and even more drastically cut their routes, fleets, and workforce. In addition, large and fluctuating fuel surcharges became commonplace, which increased consumer dissatisfaction. Another result was that airlines began to charge for services that were once included in the price of a ticket. Meal and beverage charges are commonplace, and many airlines now charge for seat selection, or blankets, pillows, and headphones in flight. Fees for overweight luggage and checking a second bag are now charged by many airlines, and some have begun to charge for all checked luggage. One airline has even replaced all its cockpit manuals with information on disc in an effort to reduce weight and therefore costs. In general, airlines are moving to à la carte pricing where passengers choose the services they wish and pay accordingly.

Check Your Product Knowledge

1. What are airlines doing to help reduce their environmental impact?
2. What are some of the causes of air rage?
3. How can a consumer lodge a complaint against an airline?
4. What are airlines doing to combat rising fuel costs?

CAREER OPPORTUNITIES

The air carrier industry employs thousands of people in a wide variety of jobs requiring different levels of education, training, and experience. Airline pilots and flight attendants are the most visible employees, but there are many others behind the scenes.

Employees in the international airline industry can work at a gateway airport in Canada or the United States or at an airport station in a foreign country. (Note: Canadian citizens often find it extremely difficult to obtain employment as pilots or flight attendants with foreign airlines because of visa restrictions.) International airline employees—especially those in direct contact with the public—may need to be bilingual or multilingual. Those working for an international airline should be well informed about, and accepting of, different cultures.

Jobs in the airline industry can be placed in two main categories: flight crew and ground crew.

Flight Crew

The flight crew includes the pilots who fly the airplane (the flight deck crew, or cockpit crew) and the attendants who provide in-flight and passenger safety services (the cabin crew).

Flight Deck Crew There are usually either two or three pilots, the exact number depending on the type of aircraft. In larger aircraft that use three pilots, the cockpit crew generally includes a captain, or senior pilot, who makes the flight plans, operates the airplane, and supervises the other crew; the first officer, or co-pilot, who assists the captain, charts the airplane's route, and computes flying time; and the second officer, or flight engineer, who inspects the airplane before it takes off and after it lands, monitors all instruments and gauges during the flight, and calculates the amount of fuel needed. The latest models of aircraft are designed for two-person crews, with the second officer no longer required.

Nearly all airlines are unionized, so a pilot's career is influenced by the seniority system, which determines promotions. New pilots for large airlines begin as second officers; in 5 to 10 years they might become first officers. It sometimes takes 20 years to reach the rank of captain. With the new-entrant carriers, promotions tend to come faster, since most of these companies aren't unionized.

Cabin Crew There can be as many as 30 in-flight attendants, the actual number depending on the size of the airplane and the proportion of first-class to coach passengers. Flight attendants provide for the passengers' comfort and safety. Among other duties, they serve in-flight meals and beverages, demonstrate safety equipment, check seat belts, and cope with medical emergencies. Flight attendants personally represent the airline; in a very real sense, they personify it.

Cross-Training In some nonunion airlines, members of the flight crew also perform the duties of the ground crew. For example, flight attendants work in customer service, and flight officers have scheduling and dispatching duties. Cross-training is more common among the new entrants.

Ground Crew or Staff

A commercial airplane flight would not be possible without the work of the hundreds of people in the ground crew. Jobs on the ground are found in the following areas: reservations, passenger services, aircraft and building maintenance, safety regulation and airline security, in-flight and freight services, and management and sales.

Reservations An airline reservations agent is usually the first contact a prospective passenger has with the airline. Reservations agents answer customers' questions about flight schedules, check the availability of flights, and book passengers.

ILLUSTRATION 6–8
The airline reservations agent is the first contact a potential passenger has with an airline.
SOURCE: Brian Losito/Air Canada.

Passenger Services These employees work mainly in the terminal building. Airline ticket agents sell tickets and keep records, tag luggage, assign seats, announce flight arrivals and departures, and board passengers. Customer service agents deal with passengers with special needs, such as challenged travellers and children travelling alone. Ramp agents see that the passengers' baggage is loaded on the correct flight.

Maintenance Maintenance employees work either for a specific airline or for the local airport authority. Plumbers, carpenters, electricians, and painters maintain airport buildings. Other maintenance workers plough snow and clear debris from the runways. Probably the most important maintenance workers are the mechanics and engine specialists who service and repair the airplanes.

Other Personnel Airline dispatchers schedule airline flights and ensure that Transport Canada regulations are enforced. Airports that allow general aviation aircraft to use their facilities may employ a fixed-base operator, who provides small-aircraft operators with flight information, fuel, and hangar space.

Security officials inspect baggage and electronically search passengers. Private security companies hired by the airport authority employ most uniformed security personnel.

Flight kitchen or catering personnel prepare passenger meals. Aircraft cleaners supply the airplane with items such as clean towels, fresh water, and magazines. Freight handlers process cargo and air freight and load and unload it.

A DAY IN THE LIFE OF A

Flight Attendant

People think of my job—a flight attendant for an international airline—as glamorous and exciting. And it is. I get to travel to other countries and to meet interesting people. But it's a lot of hard work, too. Flight attendants are the airline employees that passengers see the most. This means they are often the employees that passengers remember most clearly. I think of myself as an ambassador of goodwill for the airline. If I do my job well, people will travel with our airline again.

Most of what I do falls into one of two categories: safety or service. I think the most ignored speech in the world is the one I give at the beginning of each flight when I point out the emergency exits, explain the use of the oxygen masks, and tell people where the life jackets are found. Flying is so safe today that most people take an uneventful flight for granted. In fact, I've never been in an accident myself. Still, simulators train us for emergencies. We learn how to evacuate passengers quickly, safely, and calmly. A flight attendant has to stay calm—especially when passengers are panicking.

I'm also trained in first-aid procedures. I have a friend who actually attended at a birth on a flight. Fortunately, there happened to be a doctor on board who did the actual delivery. One time, a passenger on my flight had a heart attack—and there was no physician aboard. I was able to help

that person until we could make an emergency landing.

Service is the other major part of a flight attendant's job. Service involves everything from serving meals and drinks to calming nervous flyers to coping with belligerent passengers. Basically, I have to be "people-conscious"—often I can sense a passenger's need before he or she voices it.

Some of the neediest passengers are children who are alone on a flight. Frequently, parents will see a child onto the plane and arrange for someone—say, a grandparent—to meet the flight at the destination. The airline I work for treats these small passengers with extra care. They get a special badge, and the flight attendants keep an eye on them during the whole trip. Sometimes a child is frightened or lonely, and I'm sort of a friend, nurse, and parent all rolled into one. I especially feel like a parent when someone asks me for the twentieth time, "Are we there yet?" But part of my job is to answer the question politely and with a smile—every time.

As I said earlier, the airline I work for flies international as well as domestic flights. I speak French fluently—a real advantage for me on overseas flights. Most of the other attendants speak either French, Spanish, or German in addition to English. On a flight several weeks ago, a French businessman broke his only pair of reading glasses during the flight. He was so upset that even though

he spoke English well, he wasn't able to communicate in it at the time. In French, I assured him that on landing we could guide him to an optometrist who would replace his glasses.

A second language also helps during layovers—the nights and days I spend away from my home base in Montreal. On international flights, layovers are at least 12 hours, sometimes as long as 36 hours. I may be away from home for a week or so at a time when we lay over in several European cities in a row. During a layover, my food, lodging, and transportation are paid for by the airline. Layovers are forced R&R—rest and relaxation. I sightsee, visit friends I've made on previous flights, or just relax.

On my last flight we had a two-day layover in Paris. I'd already seen the Eiffel Tower, Notre Dame, and all the other Paris sights. This time I rented a car and visited the château region along the Loire. It's an easy day's drive from Paris. The two days left me refreshed and ready to give "service with a smile" on the way back to Canada.

Of course, during my real vacation time, I can take advantage of the low-cost flights offered by my airline or by others we have reciprocal agreements with. Then I sit back and enjoy being the passenger. Believe it or not, I even listen to the flight attendant's speech about oxygen masks and life jackets—you can never know too much in an emergency!

NAV CANADA Employees Air traffic controllers coordinate the flights of airplanes to prevent accidents and minimize delays. They work in accordance with Transport Canada rules and regulations. Some controllers give pilots permission to take off and land (airport traffic controllers); others instruct pilots en route between airports (air route traffic controllers).

Station Manager Every airline operating a scheduled service has a station at the airport, which is run by a station manager. It is his or her responsibility to see that flights are coordinated and that the weight, balance, and load of each departing flight is calculated. The station manager is employed by the airline.

Airport Manager Every airport has a manager who deals with the airlines, oversees maintenance of the buildings and runways, monitors businesses operating in the airport, handles public relations, and makes sure that Transport Canada regulations are enforced. The airport authority employs the airport manager. There may be assistant managers in charge of specific areas, such as cargo services.

General Office Every major airline maintains a corporate headquarters. Air Canada's is in Montreal. A general office (GO) is the centre for administrative and technical departments, major maintenance, and training. Most public relations and advertising work is also carried out by the GO.

Sales Offices Most airlines operate sales offices, which are not to be confused with city ticket offices or airport ticket counters. The sales reps that work out of these offices work to obtain more business for the airline by calling on the intermediaries and decision makers, such as travel agencies and business travel departments.

Summary

- Firms in the transportation industry operate in a regulated environment.
- Domestic and international airline industries began to grow rapidly after World War II. The development of bigger, faster, and more comfortable planes increased the popularity of air travel.
- Modern aircraft either have jet engines or are propeller-driven.
- Civilian air services are divided into air carrier aviation and general aviation. Air carrier aviation specializes in carrying passengers and/or cargo on a large scale.
- Major airports are federally owned and leased to local airport authorities and require large amounts of land. General aviation airports are privately owned.
- Airlines plan their routes for maximum efficiency, by either the linear concept or the hub-and-spoke concept.
- International aviation is more complex than domestic aviation because governments must negotiate the use of sovereign airspace.
- Multilateral agreements reached at worldwide conferences have helped define the use of airspace.
- Bilateral agreements are used to work out the specific details of traffic rights between two nations.
- The International Air Transport Association (IATA) helps regulate the international air system.
- The Canadian airline industry has seen several distinct stages:
  1. The establishment of a Crown corporation, Trans-Canada Airlines (now Air Canada), which operated as a sanctioned monopoly on transcontinental routes from 1937 to 1958.
  2. The emergence of stronger regional carriers under the 1966 Regional Air Policy.
  3. A period of regulated competition as a result of the National Transportation Act of 1967.
  4. The regulatory reform period of the 1980s, which resulted in a duopoly of Air Canada and Canadian Airlines, with affiliated carriers.
  5. A period of uncertainty in the 1990s, characterized by operating losses, international alliances, negotiations between carriers in Canada and the United States, and Open Skies negotiations.
  6. A stage of optimism in the mid- to late 1990s, which included implementation of Open Skies, new entrants, restructuring of Canadian Airlines, worldwide airplane sales by Bombardier, and strategic alliances by carriers globally to form seamless air travel around the world.
  7. A stage of consolidation in the early 2000s, around which time Canadian Airlines was taken over by Air Canada.
  8. The growth of discount carriers and brands, including WestJet.
- In the United States, the government controlled the routes, schedules, and rates of domestic carriers until 1978. Economic regulation ended with the Airline Deregulation Act. Safety regulation continues under the Federal Aviation Administration (FAA).
- Air travellers can buy reduced-price tickets if they are willing to accept various restrictions.
- Factors influencing the price of an airline ticket include the distance flown, the type of journey, the type of flight, and the level of service.
- Thousands of airline employees, both flight crews and ground crews, are involved in the transportation of passengers and cargo.

Key Terms

cargo terminal   p. 129
charter airlines   p. 126
circle trip   p. 138
code-sharing agreement   p. 137
common carrier   p. 126

Internet Connections

Airbus
www.airbus.com/en/   p. 125

Air Canada
www.aircanada.ca   p. 122

Airlines Reporting Corporation (ARC)
www.arccorp.com   p. 137

AirSafe
www.airsafe.com

Air Transport Association (ATA)
www.air-transport.org   p. 137

Air Transport Association of Canada (ATAC)
www.atac.ca   p. 140

Bearskin Airlines
www.bearskinairlines.com   p. 123

Billing and Settlement Plan (BSP)
www.iata.org/ps/financial_services/bsp/

Blue Sky: Canada's New International Air Policy
www.tc.gc.ca/pol/en/ace/consultations/
blueSkyPolicy.htm

Boeing
www.boeing.com/commercial/   p. 125

Canadian Airports Council (CAC)
www.cacairports.ca   p. 127

Canadian Air Transport Security Authority (CATSA)
www.catsa-acsta.gc.ca/english/index.shtml   p. 130

Canada Transportation Act
www.tc.gc.ca/acts-regulations/GENERAL/C/ct/act/
ct_a.htm   p. 122

Canadian Transportation Agency (CTA)
www.cta-otc.gc.ca   p. 122

Federal Aviation Administration (FAA)
www.faa.gov   p. 137

International Airline Travel Agency Network (IATAN)
www.iatan.org   p. 137

International Air Transport Association (IATA)
www.iata.org   p. 132

International Civil Aviation Organization (ICAO)
www.icao.int   p. 132

NAV CANADA
www.navcanada.ca   p. 129

Regional Airline Association
www.raa.org   p. 137

Transport Canada
www.tc.gc.ca   p. 126

Western Hemisphere Travel Initiative (WHTI)
travel.state.gov/travel/cbpmc/cbpmc_2223.html   p. 130

WestJet
www.westjet.com   p. 121

WORKSHEET 6–1   Airline Industry Update

Go to the Transport Canada *Annual Report* by following the links on its website (www.tc.gc.ca) and update the following:

- Size of airlines currently based in Canada:

_____

_____

- Competition in domestic city pairs:

_____

_____

_____

- Passengers by sectors: domestic, transborder, and international:

_____

_____

_____

_____

_____

- Are there any trends? Are there any changes in global alliances?

_____

_____

_____

_____

_____

_____

_____

_____

_____

_____

_____

_____

_____

WORKSHEET 6–2   Travel Arrangements

What travel arrangements and airfares can you offer the following customers?

1. A university professor in Kingston, Ontario, wants to attend an international conference in Sydney, Australia. The conference will be held in six months. The university will pay for the professor's trip, but funds are limited.

_____

_____

_____

_____

2. A couple is planning their honeymoon, which is three months away. They want to fly from Winnipeg, Manitoba, to Miami. They want to stay for a few days, then board a ship to cruise the Caribbean for 10 days. They will fly from Miami to Winnipeg the same day the ship returns. The trip is a wedding present from the bride's wealthy father, so money is not a major factor.

_____

_____

_____

_____

3. A 60-member high-school marching band from Red Deer, Alberta, wants to tour several cities in Germany this summer. The group wants to begin and end its tour in Frankfurt. Although the band members have been working for months to raise money for the trip, they must travel as inexpensively as possible.

_____

_____

_____

_____

4. A businessman must fly out of Toronto tomorrow morning to arrive as early as possible in Ottawa. He wants to return to Toronto as soon as possible after 8 p.m.

_____

_____

_____

_____

5. Two Ottawa parents and their two preschool children want to visit family in St. John's for Christmas. It is now mid-October. They are flexible about when they fly. They plan to stay about two weeks and want to fly back to Ottawa from St. John's. They would prefer not to change planes, but flying as cheaply as possible is their priority.

_____

_____

_____

_____

6. An 80-year-old woman wants to go from Halifax to Vancouver two weeks from now. It is difficult for her to walk, so she does not want to change planes. She wants to travel first class.

_____

_____

_____

_____

Objectives

When you have completed this chapter, you should be able to:

- Trace the rise and decline of the railway passenger industry in Canada and the United States.
- Describe the government's role in revitalizing passenger rail service through VIA Rail Canada and Amtrak.
- Describe the different types of accommodations and services offered by VIA Rail Canada and Amtrak.
- Compare the importance of passenger trains in Canada and the United States with that of trains in other countries.

- Explain the growth of the charter and tour businesses in the motorcoach industry.
- Discuss the effects of deregulation on the motorcoach industry.
- List and describe the types of motorcoach tours now available.
- Describe the close connection between the car rental and airline industries.
- Describe the various urban public transportation systems, the needs they fulfill, and the problems they alleviate.

The surface transportation industry is at a turning point. Amtrak and VIA Rail have purchased new equipment, and both are seeking additional funding. After years of decline (as measured in passenger kilometres), the motorcoach industry's intercity services are enjoying a comeback. Bus lines and car rental companies continue to restructure and consolidate in an effort to be more efficient and to compete more effectively with airlines. For similar reasons, the surface transport industry is positioning itself as more efficient and less polluting on a per passenger basis than the airline industry. In some cities, mass transit systems are expanding as a response to traffic congestion and energy concerns; in other cities, these systems are struggling. The Canada Transportation Act was revised in 2007. Clearly, the present environment is a dynamic one.

Air transportation has been popular for decades, but travel by land is still the way most people go from one place to another. The various sectors of the surface travel industry—the railways, the motorcoach and car rental industries, and mass transit systems—all play a vital role in modern transportation in Canada, the United States, and overseas. But except for the car rental industry, all of these sectors have suffered periods of decline in Canada and the United States in the post-World War II period. They have lost passengers to the airlines and especially to the private automobile. (In Canada and the United States,

cars now account for more than 90 percent of all intercity passenger kilometres.) The Canadian and American passenger rail services have been able to stay alive by reorganizing themselves, and the motorcoach industry has turned to the charter and tour business to offset the decline in scheduled services. Clearly, both railway and motorcoach companies are adjusting to the changing needs of travellers.

THE RAILWAY INDUSTRY

For many people in Canada and the United States, trains are an important mode of transportation. Some people use them every day to get to work. Businesspeople take high-speed trains (HSTs), such as the Acela Express between Boston and Washington, because they are a fast, comfortable, and easy way to travel from one city centre to another. Canada has studied the feasibility of high-speed trains in the Windsor–Quebec City corridor. Families travel on special family-excursion fares to visit relatives. College and university students take the train to go home during school break. Retirees planning to spend the worst of the winter in Florida travel south in Auto Trains, which transport passengers and their cars. Trains, then, can satisfy the motivations, needs, and expectations (MNEs) of many kinds of travellers.

PROFILE

Improving Service Levels, Reducing Expenses

VIA Rail

VIA Rail Canada Inc. is an independent Crown corporation. Its mission is to provide and manage safe, efficient, and environmentally responsible rail passenger services. VIA owns railway rolling stock (such as diesel engines and passenger cars), as well as stations and other buildings. However, it uses the tracks of other railways; 97 percent of its trains run on Canadian National Railway (CNR) tracks. VIA serves more than 450 communities and carried almost 4.2 million passengers in 2007.

VIA Rail was established in 1978. Like other transportation firms, it transformed itself in the early to mid-1990s. After 1992, it accomplished what many thought was impossible: It improved service levels even while drastically reducing overall expenses. Between 1990 and 2007, it reduced its reliance on government operating funding by 51 percent, increased revenues by 100 percent, and increased passenger miles by 14 percent.

VIA offers four types of services: corridor, western, eastern, and remote. The corridor, between Quebec City and Windsor, provides two-thirds of its passenger revenues, with several trips per day between cities. Business travellers account for 30 percent of VIA's corridor passengers. VIA competes with other modes between downtown Toronto and downtown Montreal by providing an under-four-hour express service. The train has the advantage of space, comfort, and service. To increase its market share in the corridor, VIA is focusing on responsive service and on increasing the frequency of its trains.

The western and eastern services appeal to cost-conscious intercity travellers, and also to domestic and international tourists who want to see Canada up close. Capacity has been added to the *Canadian* (Toronto to Vancouver), and an all-inclusive meal plan for "Silver & Blue" first-class passengers

has been introduced. The eastern service is as casual and cozy as a bed-and-breakfast in the country.

VIA provides essential service to a number of remote Canadian communities. Improvements are being made to service, and these communities are being marketed as tourist destinations.

In 1997, VIA introduced a new, state-of-the-art, customer-focused reservations system, RESERVIA, which was updated in 2003. It costs less to operate and is able to respond rapidly to changing market conditions. Travellers and travel agents can access information and book travel on VIA through major global distribution systems such as Sabre, Galileo, Worldspan, and Apollo.

In 2007, VIA Rail announced an investment of $516 million in capital projects over five years to revitalize rail passenger service in Canada. Key data for VIA Rail for selected years are shown below.

Financial indicators (millions)	1988	1992	1996	2000	2004	2007
Operating expenses	790.1	487.1	389.8	404.7	443.8	486.2
Operating revenue	220.3	155.8	184.5	240.7	258.7	285.6
Operating loss	569.8	331.3	205.3	164.0	185.1	200.6
Government funding (capital and expense)	NA	388.9	245.2	170.0	197.6	213.0
Operating statistics (000s except for ratios and last two statistics)						
Revenue/expense ratio (%)	27.9	32.0	47.3	59.5	58.8	58.9
Total passengers carried	6 415	3 601	3 666	3 795	3 887	4 181
Total passenger miles	1 428	817	892	904	851	874
Government operating funding passenger mile (cents)	35.7	42.1	25.2	18.2	20.8	23.0
Train miles operated	12 496	6 483	6 472	6 621	6 771	6 658
Car miles operated	72 045	35 993	40 491	45 121	48 396	46 362
Passenger load factor (%)	52	57	59	56	53	55
Average number of passenger miles per train mile	114	126	138	137	126	131
On-time performance (%)	NA	90	84	83	70	77
Number of employees	6 873	4 478	3 000	2 958	3 027	3 017

SOURCE: VIA Rail, Annual Report, 1988–2007; Transport Action 22(5/6), 2000, p. 7.

Air travel is fast, but there is little to see along the way. Rail travel offers passengers time to sit back and enjoy the passing scenery. For many, a train journey is more than a matter of reaching a destination promptly; "getting there" is part of the experience.

In this section you will learn something about railways past and present—their proud history and their current problems. You will also learn about railways in other countries and about the great trains of the world.

A Brief History of the Railways

The period from 1900 to the 1920s was the "Golden Age of Railways." By then, railway passenger services offered all the amenities of modern living, including electric lighting and steam heat, sleeping cars, dining cars, and washrooms. Train travel was no longer a matter of getting from point A to point B—it had become a distinctly pleasurable experience.

Next came a period of competition. The growth in car ownership and the development of intercity bus services cut into the railways' passenger business. Few could afford to travel during the Great Depression. World War II brought a temporary upturn, but by the 1950s and 1960s, intercity passenger services were declining in both Canada and the United States. By 1980, the railways' share of passenger kilometres (including kilometres travelled by car) had fallen below 5 percent. Over the same period, the number of operating passenger trains plummeted. Two other factors besides the automobile contributed to the decline in rail passenger service:

1. **The airline industry** After long-distance air routes came into service, it was much quicker and sometimes less expensive to travel by plane. Train travel could remain competitive only in the heavily travelled Windsor–Quebec City corridor in Canada, in the northeast corridor between Boston and Washington, D.C., and on a few other medium-distance routes.
2. **The railway industry's financial structure** The fixed costs of railways are much higher than for other forms of surface transportation. For example, railways have to spend large sums on equipment, maintenance, and labour. In tandem with this, there were political conflicts over the roles that government and private enterprise should play in the industry.

Faced with heavy annual losses, many railway companies dropped their more unprofitable services, which usually meant passenger routes. Pessimists predicted that all passenger service would end by the 1970s. Clearly, something had to be done to save the passenger train. Some people believed that the government should **nationalize** the railway industry—that is, take over control of it. Opponents of this idea pointed out that nationalized railways in other countries had suffered heavy losses. In the end, a compromise was reached.

Canadian Passenger Railway Service

In 1976, the Canadian government issued a report on the future of the rail passenger service in Canada. That report recommended the creation of VIA Rail Canada to take over passenger service from the CNR and Canadian Pacific Railway (CPR). An analysis of VIA Rail reveals six distinct periods: transition (1976–78), retrenchment (1979–84), steady state (1985–89), amputation (1990), emphasis on the corridor (the 1990s), and renewal (the 2000s).

Transition (1976–78) This period saw the establishment of VIA Rail. The name and colours of VIA Rail were introduced in 1976, along with a combined CNR/CPR timetable. In 1977, VIA Rail was established as a Crown corporation by order-in-council and began marketing passenger services for CNR and CPR. In 1978, VIA Rail took over equipment from CNR and CPR and began managing and operating trains directly. Note that VIA Rail was not directly controlled by Parliament; rather, it was a Crown corporation operating trains on contract with the Department of Transport. Government subsidies were provided for VIA Rail operations.

Retrenchment (1979–84) When the railways themselves operated passenger trains, no route could be abandoned without a hearing before the regulatory authority, the Canadian Transport Commission (now the Canadian Transportation Agency). After VIA Rail was established, the

ILLUSTRATION 7–1

VIA Rail passenger service offers a comfortable way to travel from one city centre to another.

SOURCE: Image courtesy of VIA Rail Canada Inc.

Transport minister could shut down routes without such hearings. Some restructuring was done in 1979, mainly in the Maritime provinces, but the biggest cutbacks happened in 1981, when 20 percent of the VIA system was terminated.

Steady State (1985–89) Some abandoned routes were restored, including the *Atlantic* (Montreal to Halifax) and the *Super Continental* (through Jasper, Alberta). The steady-state period also saw regulatory and funding changes. The government wanted to reduce the deficit and expected VIA Rail to find new ways to attract customers, operate more efficiently, and reduce its government subsidy. The Royal Commission on National Passenger Transportation was announced in 1989, with the mandate to consider the viability of a national, integrated, intercity passenger system.

Amputation (January 1990) On January 15, 1990, Canada's rail passenger system was basically cut in half, from 810 trains weekly to 396, from 33 routes to 14, and from 6700 employees to 4600. Also, it was announced that federal subsidies, around $550 million in 1989, were to be cut to $350 million by 1992. The effect of all this was to reduce passenger services on CP tracks. The biggest cut was the route of the *Canadian* (Toronto to Vancouver via Calgary and Banff). The *Super Continental* (through Jasper) survived, but on a reduced basis.

Emphasis on the Corridor (the 1990s) The focus of VIA Rail shifted to the Quebec City–Windsor/Sarnia corridor (where it stays). Eighty-five percent of VIA's passengers travel along the corridor. Some corridor routes that were cut in 1990 were restored in 1992. The corridor services provide an integrated network of intercity trains offering LRC (light, rapid, comfortable) equipment, convenient schedules, VIA 1 first-class service, and a limited number of stops. VIA 1 is promoted as the most comprehensive concept in first-class travel ever offered in the corridor. The types of marketing that had been used for decades in the airline industry were now being applied to first-class rail travel in the central corridor.

Western and eastern transcontinental services were rather sparse after the 1990 cutbacks. The major routes were the *Canadian* (Toronto–Vancouver), the *Skeena* (Jasper–Prince Rupert), the *Ocean* (Montreal–Halifax), and the *Chaleur* (Montreal–Gaspé). Stainless-steel passenger cars, originally purchased in 1955 for the *Canadian* and the *Dominion*, were restored to transcontinental service in 1993 after an investment of $200 million. Five main types of cars are part of this restored fleet: coach cars, Skyline dome lounge cars, sleeping cars (with showers), dining cars with white linen service, and Park cars with "bullet" observation lounges.

There were other developments in the 1990s. The **Canrailpass** was introduced. The Vancouver–Seattle Amtrak service was reintroduced in 1995. A new reserva-

If you have dreams of an exciting yet affordable Canadian discovery tour, why not look at a CanRailPass? It's the winning way to see Canada come alive as it entitles you to either 12, 13, 14 or 15 days unlimited rail travel within a 30-day consecutive period. Economy seats for CanRailPass holders are limited; please reserve early. Upgrades to sleeping accommodation are permitted, however during high season reservations for Silver & Blue class aboard "The Canadian" between Toronto and Vancouver can only be made within 21 days of departure. Up to 3 additional days can be purchased in advance before commencement of travel.

VIA CANRAILPASS

Maximum of 3 additional days permitted.

12 days of unlimited travel in a 30-day period CAN$	Low Season 01 Jan-31 May 2004; 16 Oct-31 Dec 2004	High Season 01 Jun-15 Oct 2004
Adult	461	741
Additional Days (per day, max. 3 days)	40	63
Youth (2-24 years inclusive/ Student)*	415	667
Senior (60 years and over)**	415	667
Additional Days (per day, max. 3 days)	36	57

*Proof of age required 2-17 years, proof of age and ISIC card required 18-24 years.
**Proof of age required. All rates above are exclusive of Canadian GST (7%).

ILLUSTRATION 7–2

A Canrailpass allows unlimited travel on VIA Rail trains in designated areas.

SOURCE: Image courtesy of VIA Rail Canada Inc.

tions system came online in 1997. An Amtrak–VIA Rail North American Rail Pass was introduced in 1998. For an overview of the financial and operating performance of VIA Rail, see this chapter's Profile.

Renewal (2000 to date) Between 2000 and 2003, Transport Canada invested about $1 billion in capital projects to revitalize rail passenger service in Canada. In 2007, the government committed a further $516 million over five years to upgrade equipment, infrastructure, and stations. In addition, some other improvements announced included:

- Rebuilding passenger locomotives and the LRC fleet, allowing more high-speed trains.
- New waste-management procedures were developed to end the disposal of human waste on tracks.
- New European-style passenger equipment was introduced. The total passenger fleet is slated to grow by more than one-third in the next 20 years.
- Consumer choice along the corridor routes was enhanced by increasing the frequency of service, adding new departure times, and modernizing equipment to enable faster trip times.
- Overnight sleeper service in the corridor was expanded to appeal to business travellers.

ILLUSTRATION 7–3

Dome cars provide spectacular views for travellers.

SOURCE: Image courtesy of VIA Rail Canada Inc.

The new equipment enabled VIA Rail to improve service levels throughout the network, thus increasing ridership, revenues, and profitability. VIA feels that the new equipment is an important step toward ensuring the long-run financial health and stability of rail passenger services across Canada.

Current VIA Rail Service VIA Rail operates up to 503 trains each week over a 12 500-kilometre network linking 450 locations in Canada. It carries around 4.2 million passengers a year in five regions. A visit to the company's website (www.viarail.ca) provides detailed information on cities served, fares, types of service, discounts, and rail passes such as the Commuter pass, Corridorpass, Canrailpass, and North American Rail Pass.

The routes of VIA Rail and Amtrak connect at various points, providing north–south rail service between Canada and the United States. The 30-day North American Rail Pass, good for travel on both VIA Rail and Amtrak, allows travel on approximately 45 000 kilometres of track. A train trip on this pass must include travel in both Canada and the United States. Anyone can purchase the pass.

Other Regularly Scheduled Rail Services Other rail passenger services are available in Canada. BC Rail offers the year-round *Cariboo Prospector* between North Vancouver and Prince George. In summer, the *Whistler Explorer* travels from Whistler to Kelly Lake. Algoma Central provides service between Sault Ste. Marie and Hearst, Ontario, on selected days of the week. The *Northlander*, operated by Ontario Northland, connects Toronto with Cochrane, Ontario.

Rail Tours/Land Cruises Rail tours were pioneered by Rocky Mountaineer Vacations. A Rocky Mountaineer tour is like a land cruise, with GoldLeaf or RedLeaf Service in a bilevel dome car. The train operates three routes during daylight hours between Vancouver and Jasper, Calgary, or Banff, stopping overnight at a hotel en route. Meals and transfers are included in the package. Rocky Mountaineer offers a unique way to see the scenery of the Canadian Rockies.

Several other rail tours now operate in Canada, including Royal Canadian Pacific, *Whistler Northwind*, and the *Bras d'Or* (VIA Rail). Canadian Pacific aims at the high-end market (prices start at $6600–$7400 per person) with a four-day, three-night offering. Its Royal Canadian Pacific travels a loop west from Calgary to Golden, then south to the Crowsnest Pass, then back to Calgary.

BC Rail's *Whistler Northwind* makes a weekly round trip from Vancouver to Prince George. Guests spend a night at a Whistler resort and another at 100 Mile House.

VIA Rail's *Bras d'Or*, between Halifax and Sydney, provides an excellent opportunity once a week to observe the flora (trees leafing out in the spring, the lakes and highlands in summer, and autumn leaves) and fauna (eagles and gulls, deer and foxes) at a reasonable price. Add-on tour packages featuring stays at Cape Breton resorts are available.

Federal Regulation The Canada Transportation Act of 1996 created the Canadian Transportation Agency (CTA) to regulate this country's railways and railway services, including VIA Rail. The Act was revised in 2007. All passenger fares and conditions are regulated by the CTA.

United States Passenger Railway Service

Rail passenger service in the United States is provided mainly by Amtrak, commuter rail lines (some operated by Amtrak), certain state operations, and rail tourism lines. Amtrak is in a very similar position to that of VIA Rail. It introduced new equipment, particularly the Acela Express trains (built by Bombardier) in the northeast (Boston–Washington) corridor, a new paint scheme, and logo. It has a National Growth Strategy but has received inadequate

TABLE 7–1 Selected Comparison of Amtrak and VIA Rail for 2007

	Amtrak	VIA Rail	Ratio
Revenue	CDN$2.5 billion	$285.6 million	8.8:1
Passengers carried	25.8 million	4.2 million	6.1:1

SOURCE: Amtrak and VIA websites (www.amtrak.com and www.viarail.ca).

capital funding and had a brush with insolvency in 2002. A brief comparison of Amtrak and VIA Rail for 2007 is shown in Table 7–1. Given that the population in the United States is about 10 times that of Canada, the lower ratio indicates that rail service is more important in Canada. It should be noted that Amtrak also carries an additional 200 million people per year in commuter service.

The U.S. government created the semipublic, federally subsidized National Railroad Passenger Corporation, better known as Amtrak, in 1970. It was to be financed jointly by payments from participating railways and by federal subsidies. Amtrak took over almost all of the American intercity passenger networks in 1971. As a first step, routes and services were cut in half. Service was concentrated along high-density corridors such as Boston–New York–Washington, Los Angeles–San Diego, and Miami–Orlando–Tampa.

Amtrak still depends on federal subsidies for operating expenses and capital expenditures for plant and equipment. Amtrak differentiates between long-distance (Superliner, Viewliner, Amfleet II, and Auto Train) and short-distance (Amfleet I, Amtrak Cascades, Horizon, and Acela) trains. Detailed information is on the Amtrak website (www.amtrak.com).

Amtrak serves more than 500 stations in 46 states (Alaska, Hawaii, South Dakota, and Wyoming are the exceptions), D.C., and three Canadian provinces. A recent extension of service in the northeast corridor from Boston to Portland, Maine, allows tourists to take the ferry to Yarmouth, Nova Scotia. Amtrak operates more than 33 000 route kilometres; it owns about 1000 route kilometres, between Boston and Washington, and elsewhere in the

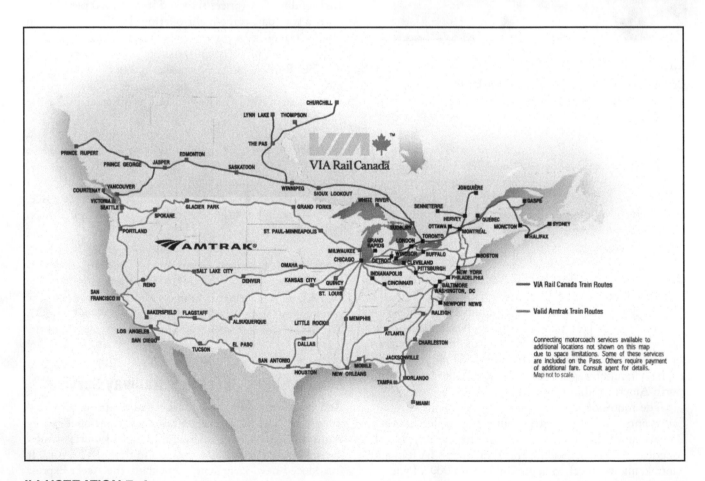

ILLUSTRATION 7–4

The 30-day North American Rail Pass allows travel on both Amtrak and VIA Rail if a trip includes both Canada and the United States.

SOURCE: Courtesy of VIA Rail Canada.

northeast. It mainly uses the tracks owned by the freight railways. On weekdays, Amtrak operates up to 315 trains per day, excluding commuter trains; these include 100 trains in the intercity business unit and 48 trains in the Amtrak West business unit (Washington, Oregon, and California).

The Future of Amtrak In 2007, Amtrak received government funding of US$1.3 billion, including US$521 million in operating funds and US$495 million for capital investment. Amtrak has implemented significant financial reforms and is now focusing on repairing its equipment and infrastructure and improving the reliability of existing operations.

The Amtrak Reform and Accountability Act of 1997 mandated that Amtrak reach operational self-sufficiency by December 2002 or face liquidation, but this had not happened as of 2008. There are several factors in favour of continued funding to Amtrak, both capital and operating: an aging population, urban congestion and pollution, the cost of building airports and highways, the desire of freight railways to make money on some routes, and volatile energy prices. The impact of September 11, 2001, may be a factor.

Other U.S. Rail Passenger Service Other U.S. rail passenger service includes commuter, state-supported, and rail tourist lines including service to parks. Many major cities have commuter rail service. Several states support rail passenger service, mainly by subsidization of Amtrak-operated service in the state. For example, Vermont supports the Vermonter. There are numerous rail tourist lines operating steam locomotive excursions; other organizations operate sightseeing dinner trips. A new type of rail service is that to national parks. The major example is the Grand Canyon Railway line in Arizona. In season it operates several trains per day, many powered by steam engines, from parking lots located about 30 kilometres from the canyon. This is an attempt by the U.S. Park Service to reduce park congestion and pollution from automobiles.

High-Speed Rail Service There is a growing realization that the demand for intercity travel in certain states and regions may be best served by rail, rather than building additional roadways and airports. The High Speed Rail Investment Act (HSRIA) was reintroduced into the U.S. Senate in 2001. Proposed funding of CDN$18 billion would be used only for new high-speed rail corridor development, and not for maintaining Amtrak's existing services.

Federal Regulation In 1887, the U.S. Congress established the Interstate Commerce Commission (ICC) to regulate competition between railways and to ensure reasonable passenger and freight rates. The Surface Transportation Board replaced the ICC in 1995. The Department of Transportation (DOT) is also involved in the railway regulatory process. The Federal Railroad Administration, a division of the DOT, sets safety standards for the industry and inspects rolling stock (locomotives and cars), tracks, and signal systems.

Foreign Railway Passenger Service

In many countries outside North America, railways are still a major form of transportation. Most of these railways are owned and operated by governments.

Europe Passenger trains are still vitally important in Europe. Most European railways are government-owned and -operated. Few make a profit, but European governments consider efficient and extensive passenger railways an essential service.

Other factors besides government subsidies account for the survival of passenger trains in Europe:

- **Private car ownership** More Europeans are buying cars, but car ownership is still below the levels in Canada and the United States.
- **Price of gasoline** Gasoline is much more expensive in Europe than in Canada.
- **Proximity of major cities in Europe** Few Western European capitals are as far apart as the major population centres in Canada and the United States. It takes about the same amount of time to travel from Geneva to Paris by train as it does to fly. Train travel in Europe is more comfortable than air travel, less expensive, and less subject to traffic and weather delays. It is also more convenient, in that it goes from one city centre to another.
- **Reliability of rail services** Trains almost always depart and arrive on schedule.
- **Price of air travel** It is almost always much less expensive to take a train than a plane.
- **Sustainable mobility** High-speed trains emit considerably less CO_2 than a comparable journey by air.

The cooperation and coordination among European railways is extensive. The national systems of each country are integrated into the International Inter City network, which provides first-class rail travel through nine Western European nations. The Channel Tunnel, the Chunnel, opened in 1994, enables people to travel by rail between England and France in just over two hours. In 2007, the high-speed train operators in seven European countries formed Railteam to offer travellers seamless travel across international borders in Western Europe. This network is expected to triple in size by 2020.

Another example of cooperation among Europe's railways is the series of **Eurailpasses** available. The Eurail Global Pass is good for unlimited first-class travel throughout the 21 participating countries. Select Passes (valid in three, four, or five bordering countries), Regional Passes, Single Country Passes, and Eurail Youthpasses (for people under age 26) also are available. These passes are sold only outside Europe; people living in Europe are not eligible to use them. Great Britain does not participate in Eurailpass; it offers a separate series of **BritRail passes** (Consecutive, Flexible, and Single Country) for rail travel in the British Isles. BritRail also offers the London Plus Pass, which permits travellers to take day trips on a flexible basis.

European trains differ from North American trains in several ways. To begin with, most European trains have first- and second-class sections. The differences between the two classes involve price and comfort—there is more room in first class, and there are generally fewer passengers. Another distinctive feature of European trains is that many railway cars are divided into compartments with six or eight places in each. On overnight trips, passengers can sleep in the regular seats, or they can reserve (by paying a supplement) a **couchette**, which is a bunk in a second-class compartment. Wagons-lits are coaches containing private sleeping compartments for one or two people.

Overnight train travel offers a number of advantages. For example, Canadian tourists in France can enjoy dinner in Paris and then board an overnight train to the Riviera. They can sleep in a couchette, wake up in Nice in time for breakfast, and then spend the day at the beach or exploring the countryside. They will have saved money by travelling by train instead of plane and by spending the night in a couchette instead of a hotel. And instead of wasting the better part of a vacation day travelling, they can enjoy the sights at their destination.

Most long-distance trains in Europe are considerably faster than their North American counterparts. The French **TGV (train à grande vitesse)**, the fastest, cruises at speeds up to 260 kilometres an hour. The TGV makes the trip from Paris to Lyons, a distance of 420 kilometres, in a mere 160 minutes. The regular TGV travels at about the same speed as the Amtrak Acela service between Boston and Washington—250 kilometres an hour. France is building several new high-speed lines from Paris to the east and the southeast.

European governments continue to invest in high-speed rail. Germany, Spain, and Italy have expanded their routes

ILLUSTRATION 7–5

High-speed trains offer comfort and efficiency throughout Europe.

SOURCE: Gareth Fuller/EPA/Landov.

and a Trans-European Rail Network system is progressing. The extensive development of a European high-speed rail system is a significant competitive threat to the airlines, particularly on routes between 400 and 700 kilometres.

Other Foreign Railways Railways are an important form of passenger transportation in Latin America, Asia, Africa, and Australia. As in Europe, most of the railways are government-owned and -operated. Few, however, are as advanced as the European system.

Government-owned Japanese National Railways operates most passenger services in Japan, but Japan also has some private railway companies. Experts consider the Japanese passenger train system the finest in the world. Service is so fast, comfortable, and reliable that domestic airlines have made little headway. The Shinkansen bullet trains cross that densely populated nation at speeds in excess of 200 kilometres an hour. Japanese engineers are currently working on a new type of high-speed train called the Maglev (magnetic levitation).

Great Trains of the World Here are some glamorous trains:

- Today's passengers on the Orient Express can start their journey in London or Paris. After crossing France, the train winds through the Swiss and Austrian Alps, cuts through the Brenner Pass to Italy, and arrives in Venice in time for cocktails and dinner.
- The Trans-Siberian Special makes a leisurely 19-day journey from Moscow to Mongolia.
- The Blue Train provides a 24-hour luxury trip from Cape Town to Pretoria, South Africa.
- The Royal Scotsman meanders through the Scottish Highlands pulling renovated Victorian and Edwardian railway cars. Staff members, of course, wear kilts.
- The Ghan makes a weekly journey through outback Australia between Darwin and Adelaide.

Channels of Distribution

In their Golden Age, the railways did not have to worry much about selling themselves. Today, VIA Rail and Amtrak have to work hard to promote themselves against stiff competition from the airlines. With catchy slogans such as "All Aboard Amtrak," "America's Getting into Training," and "Discover the Magic—Amtrak," Amtrak is trying to convince the public that trains are once again a good way to get around the country. In the early 2000s, Amtrak promoted the North American Rail Pass, presenting it as "One little pass as BIG as your travel dreams." VIA Rail has used the slogan "Taking the Train with VIA—It's the Ideal Way to Travel."

The Reservations System Both Amtrak and VIA Rail have modernized their reservations and ticketing systems, so reserving rail tickets has never been easier. Both companies inherited antiquated reservations systems when they took over the passenger services in the 1970s. Since then, they have entirely computerized themselves and now have nationwide reservations and information networks, as well as websites where passengers can book seats directly.

Types of Fare Both VIA Rail and Amtrak have tried to lure passengers back to trains by offering competitive fares. They also offer group and family discount fares, short-term promotional fares, and passes that allow unlimited travel for specific lengths of time. Amtrak has entered the tour market as well, and developed rail/fly packages in conjunction with United Airlines.

Publications Detailed information on railways fares, schedules, and services in Canada, the United States, and the rest of the world can be found in a number of publications. For information about Canadian and American trains, the materials published by VIA Rail and Amtrak are invaluable. Check their respective websites for further information. A number of publications provide information about international rail services, including the *Thomas Cook Continental Timetable* and *Thomas Cook Overseas Timetable*; *Eurail Guide: How to Travel Europe and All the World*; and Fodor's *Railways of the World*. The VIA Rail, Amtrak, Railteam, and Eurail websites can be readily accessed.

ILLUSTRATION 7–6
The domestic motorcoach tour is a vacation alternative.
SOURCE: Courtesy of Brewster Transportation and Tours.

Check Your Product Knowledge

1. What effect has increased car ownership had on the North American railway industry?
2. How did the federal governments act to save rail passenger service in Canada and the United States in the 1970s?
3. Why has the rail passenger industry been able to survive in Europe?
4. Describe how VIA Rail and Amtrak are trying to encourage more people to ride trains.
5. How do you think the development of high-speed rail in Europe over the next ten years will affect the airlines?

THE MOTORCOACH INDUSTRY

The motorcoach, more commonly known as the bus, has played a major role in the surface travel industry throughout the world. It is the most widespread and the least expensive form of public transportation. Travellers use motorcoach services for a variety of reasons, depending on their MNEs:

leisure, business, or VFR. Motorcoaches cover a vast network of intercity and urban routes, and carry more people and serve more communities than trains. Because buses travel over almost every highway and many secondary roads in this country, the bus industry is well equipped to serve the needs of travellers heading for remote areas or small towns. It is also the most fuel-efficient form of intercity travel.

The Origin of Motorcoaches

The motorcoach, invented in the 1890s, is really a descendant of the horse-drawn stagecoach. The name "stagecoach" evolved because the coaches travelled in stages, stopping at scheduled places along the route to change horses. By the early 1900s, there were urban bus services in London and New York. Self-propelled bus service in Canada began in 1892 in Hamilton, Ontario. The first intercity service in the United States was started in Oregon. The Greyhound bus company began in Minnesota in 1914. Many small bus lines started around the same time—perhaps more than 5000—but through consolidations and mergers, Greyhound became the largest carrier.

Canadian Greyhound Coaches started its first service in 1929, from Calgary to Lethbridge. In 1935, Greyhound Canada and Greyhound U.S. developed interline agreements that lasted until 1987, when Greyhound U.S. was sold.

The intercity network expanded rapidly with improvements in road conditions and bus design. Transcontinental bus service began in the United States in 1928. By the 1930s, the bus industry was challenging the railways' monopoly of public passenger transportation in the United States. This did not happen in Canada until the 1950s, because of the slower development of the road system.

The Motorcoach Industry Today

The motorcoach is still the most accessible form of transportation in Canada and the United States. Intercity buses carry more passengers than trains, and serve far more communities than do airplanes and trains combined. For thousands of communities, buses are the only form of public transportation. In Canada, buses serve around 3000 communities; rail and air each serve around 500. Since the end of World War II, there have been two major trends in the motorcoach industry: Regularly scheduled passenger services have declined, and the bus charter and tour business has expanded.

Scheduled Services In 1994, Canada had 46 intercity bus companies. Twenty-seven of these generated revenues of at least $500 000, and 19 others generated between $200 000 and $499 999. Today there are about 28 principal operators. This is a sharp decline in the number of bus companies, reflecting consolidation, route transfers, and termination of operations.

Between 1975 and 1993, ridership (defined as provided by intercity carriers, charter carriers, and school bus operators) declined from 34 million passengers to 10.8 million. By 2005, intercity traffic had rebounded to 16.5 million annually. There were around 100 main terminals and an additional 1600 agencies (local businesses that sell bus tickets).

Regulation in Canada

Until 1954, the federal government left the regulation of the bus industry to the provinces. That year, Parliament passed the Motor Vehicle Transport Act, which gave the

ILLUSTRATION 7–7
Modern motorcoaches provide comfort and facilities that match those of trains or planes.
SOURCE: Image courtesy of Great Canadian Coaches Inc.

provinces the authority to regulate the following areas of the intercity bus industry: market entry and exit, fares and route regulations, licensing of drivers, registration of buses, and bus safety. In 1987, the federal government passed a revised version of the Motor Vehicle Transport Act. In March 1999, it introduced amendments to that act to phase in economic deregulation of the bus industry over a two-year period. It became apparent that this transitional approach was not acceptable to some provinces and to some segments of the industry. Revised amendments were reintroduced in the Senate (Bill S-3) in 2001.

Most bus companies have a monopoly on their routes. A provincial utility board or commission grants these monopolies.

The American Motorcoach Industry

The scheduled intercity bus industry in the United States has declined severely from its peak in the 1940s. By the early 1970s, the number of operating intercity bus companies had plummeted to around 1000, and although the gas crisis of 1973–74 provided a temporary reprieve for the industry, many people returned to private transportation when gas prices fell. In the five years up to 1977, scheduled route service declined 54 percent. As with rail travel, the boom in automobile ownership in the post-World War II years contributed to this decrease. So did increasing competition from the airline industry, especially on long-distance routes.

The American Bus Association industry profile for 2008 indicates that around 3800 private motorcoach companies were operating in the United States, with 39 000 buses in use for regular route service, tours and charters, and special operations. The same year, 631 million passengers were carried by bus.

One-third of bus kilometres are logged for charters; 8 percent are logged for tours and sightseeing. The 10 most popular cities to visit by bus were (in alphabetical order) Atlantic City, Branson (Missouri), Chicago, Las Vegas, Los Angeles, Nashville, New York, Orlando, Toronto, and Washington (D.C.). Motor Coach Canada reports that a fully loaded bus (average 46 passengers) on a charter or tour making an overnight stay contributes between $7000 and $14 000 to the local economy in expenditures, including meals, lodging, shopping, admission fees, souvenirs, and local taxes.

Deregulation in the United States Government regulation of the bus industry was introduced in the United States with the Motor Carrier Act of 1935, which gave the ICC control over all motor carriers. Regulation was relaxed somewhat in later years, and then eliminated completely by the Bus Regulatory Reform Act in 1982.

Since deregulation, bus companies have had much greater freedom. They can set their own fares and decide which routes they want to operate. These changes have generally reduced bus fares. Deregulation has also made it easier for new companies to enter the bus market and for existing companies to extend their operating authority. Hundreds of new charter and tour companies have come into existence since 1982.

Many new companies have adopted aggressive marketing and advertising programs to sell their charters and tours. Some older companies have been unable to adjust to the new conditions of the highly competitive market and have gone out of business.

Motorcoach Charters and Tours

The one bright spot for the motorcoach industry has been the dramatic growth in the charter and tour business. In the past two decades, many new bus companies have been formed (especially in the United States), and the vast majority of these have entered the charter and tour field. This increase is due mainly to deregulation and to a change in people's vacation patterns. Statistics Canada data show that charter revenues were $200 million in 1990, increased gradually to around $210 million in 1994, and then rose substantially to over $400 million in 2006. Scheduled intercity service revenues have also increased from around $280 million in 1990 to around $589 million in 2006. However, in 2000, Statistics Canada changed the way it collected data and this may partially explain the figures.

Major North American Bus Companies

The major bus companies in Canada and the United States have a complex and intertwined history. Until the mid-1980s, the two giants were Greyhound Lines and Continental Trailways. However, bus deregulation in 1982, as well as inflation and the recession of the early 1980s, brought about the need for strategic change. First, the parent of Greyhound Corporation sold its American operations, although the Canadian operations were still controlled by the American parent company. Greyhound U.S. then purchased Trailways Bus, the largest member of Continental Trailways. The remaining Trailways—formerly Continental Trailways—could no longer compete equally with Greyhound.

Greyhound Lines of Canada underwent restructuring in 1996, and in 1997 was taken over by Laidlaw Inc. (now part of FirstGroup America). Laidlaw, based in Hamilton, Ontario, purchased Greyhound U.S. in 1999. After 12 years apart, the two companies were together under the same ownership. Integration of the two networks began.

Greyhound Canada Greyhound Canada carries more than 6.5 million passengers a year on a route system linking 1100 communities. In the 1990s, its bus operations were aligned with Canadian travel patterns; some routes were discontinued because they were not economically feasible. The average one-way trip is 400 kilometres. Greyhound operates mainly in Ontario and the western provinces. Through interline agreements with other bus companies, Greyhound offers coast-to-coast service in Canada. It also offers service to the United States through Greyhound U.S., and to Mexico through Greyhound Mexico. Tour services are offered through corporate partners such as Gray Line Tours (based in major Canadian cities). Greyhound Canada is a unit of FirstGroup America, the leading provider of public bus transportation services in North America: ambulance, intercity bus, municipal, and school bus.

Trailways Trailways Transportation System is a franchise organization composed of independent transportation companies and other tour and travel-related firms. There are 80 franchise companies in 31 states, as well as in Ontario and British Columbia. Today, most of Trailways' intercity division members have regional interline agreements with Greyhound to provide long-haul service. Trailways' strategy is to become a fully expanded and highly integrated transportation and travel service organization.

Coach Coach USA, founded in 1995, is now the largest provider of motorcoach, tour, and sightseeing services in the United States, with operations in over 120 cities. Its affiliate, Coach Canada, operates in Ontario and Quebec.

In addition to Greyhound, Trailways, and Coach, there are thousands of smaller companies that provide local scheduled intercity service, or charter and tour service, or both. Figure 7–1 shows the route of a motorcoach tour within North America.

Sightseeing Companies Gray Line, the world's largest sightseeing company, offers about 1500 North American

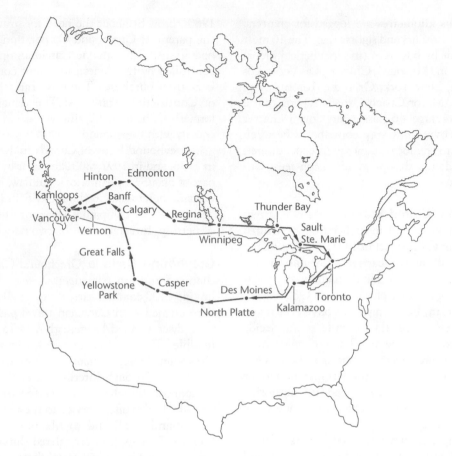

FIGURE 7–1 A Typical Motorcoach Tour of Western Canada and the United States (23 Days)

excursions daily. It is an association of about 150 independently owned and operated companies, with offices throughout the United States and Canada and in major cities overseas. In Canada, Gray Line is associated with Greyhound. American Sightseeing International is another large sightseeing company, with representation in about 50 cities in the United States and another 50 cities in other countries. Both companies have expanded their services to include charters, limousine services, and transfer transportation. There are also regional sightseeing companies in Canada, such as Brewster.

Bus Services in Other Countries Both government-owned bus lines and independent companies provide inter-city services in most foreign countries. Government-run buses often operate in conjunction with the national railways.

Motorcoach Travel as a Product

The motorcoach industry in Canada and the United States earns billions of dollars each year carrying travellers to out-of-the-way places and over short distances. For many people, bus service is the only available form of public transportation. For some, it is indispensable.

In recent years, the motorcoach industry has focused on the development of tour programs.

Types of Tours To attract more passengers, many bus companies offer package tours and chartered motorcoach services. Several types of tours are available:

- **Charter tours** are taken by clubs, organizations, school parties, and other pre-formed groups. Any group can charter (i.e., hire) a bus from a charter operator for a day trip to, for example, a sports event, museum, shopping centre, or casino. Holiday packages lasting a week or more are also available; usually these include accommodations, meals, and sightseeing trips in addition to the bus ride. On a charter trip, a tour escort does not accompany the group.
- **Escorted tours** are accompanied by trained tour escorts, and are scheduled group tours that travel from major cities in the United States and Canada to tourist destinations throughout North America. Popular destinations include national parks, the Rocky Mountains, New England, the Gaspé Peninsula, and the California and Nova Scotia coast-lines. Many companies also offer escorted tours in Europe. Escorted tours can last anywhere from five

days to four weeks; they include hotel accommodations and most meals, and the tour escort travels with the group for the entire trip.

- **Independent package tours** visit several cities or places of interest on regular scheduled buses. Hotel accommodations and sightseeing are included.
- **City package tours** are similar to independent package tours, but visit only one city.
- **Intermodal tours,** tours that include more than one form of transportation, are a fairly recent trend in the industry. The idea for intermodal tours began in 1974 with a ticketing agreement between Greyhound and Amtrak to connect nine of Greyhound's routes with Amtrak services. A fly/motorcoach tour in Canada might combine air travel from Toronto to Calgary with a one-week tour by bus of national parks that ends in Vancouver.

Buses as Transfer Transportation The term **transfer** refers to any change in transportation in the course of a journey. Buses are used extensively to transfer passengers between airports and hotels or city centres. Many hotels and motels offer their own complimentary bus service to and from the airport.

The Motorcoach versus Other Modes of Travel
The big attraction of the motorcoach has long been its low cost relative to other forms of public transportation. However, in recent years the airlines have reduced their fares sufficiently to compete with bus companies, especially on trips of more than 800 kilometres. Instead of trying to keep competing for passengers with the airlines, several bus companies have decided to join them by offering intermodal tickets. Thus, an airline might offer a ticket that combines air passage to a major airport with bus service for passengers travelling from the airport to a more remote destination.

Many people are reluctant to travel any significant distance by bus because they believe that buses are uncomfortable. In fact, modern long-distance buses are much more luxurious than earlier models. Air conditioning and restroom facilities are standard features.

In an attempt to lure travellers away from airplanes, many bus companies have stepped up their promotion efforts. Some bus lines offer passes that enable a passenger to tour the country at a discount price. Many of these tours are only promoted overseas to attract inbound tourism; others have been advertised in Canada and the United States to attract domestic tourism. Further, the industry promotes bus travel as more environmentally friendly than other forms of transportation.

Channels of Distribution

Bus tickets can be obtained through several channels of distribution, including the Internet. Many short-distance passengers buy their tickets at the bus station just before

boarding, or from the bus driver. Many bus companies subscribe to a computer reservations system and can accept reservations and issue tickets before the departure date. Travellers can also purchase tickets for bus trips, escorted tours, charter tours, package tours, and intermodal tours from travel counsellors. Tours can be booked through a tour broker as well.

Motorcoach tour information can be found on websites and in tour brochures, travel guides, and the like. Detailed information on fares, schedules, and other aspects of motorcoach tours is provided in *Russell's Official National Motor Coach Guide* and *Russell's Official Canada Bus Guide*.

Motorcoach Associations

In Canada, Motor Coach Canada represents the motorcoach industry; in the United States, there is the American Bus Association. There are also regional and provincial associations such as the Quebec Bus Owners Association (l'Association des proprietaires d'autobus de Québec) and the Ontario Motor Coach Association. Motor Coach Canada was established in 1996 to fill an advocacy void at the federal level. It examines tourism and transportation issues, including infrastructure needs, marketing, multimodalism, and safety standards.

Check Your Product Knowledge

1. How have the patterns of bus use changed in recent decades?
2. In what way is the intercity bus a more essential form of transportation than either the train or the airplane?
3. What have been the main results of deregulation of the bus industry? Why was Greyhound Canada separate from Greyhound U.S. for 12 years?
4. What are the five main types of tours offered by bus companies?

THE CAR RENTAL INDUSTRY

A business traveller flies from Edmonton to Toronto for a four-day sales trip. He rents a car to make numerous sales calls at companies in the area. A family flies from Vancouver to Halifax for a two-week vacation. They rent a car and drive up the coast to Cape Breton, stopping to admire the scenery and visit the tourist attractions along the way. A retired couple flies from Victoria to Montreal to see their grandchildren, who live just outside the city. They rent a car to explore the Montreal area and visit the Eastern Townships.

ILLUSTRATION 7–8

Many travellers choose to rent a car once they arrive at their destination because of the freedom it offers them.

SOURCE: © Anton Vengo/SuperStock.

These travellers illustrate how the car rental industry meets the MNEs of all types of travellers. The car rental industry is different from other transportation industries in that it allows travellers complete control over their schedules and itineraries. Travellers are free to venture to a remote destination that can't be reached by public transportation, to find a quaint, out-of-the-way country inn, or to make a spontaneous change in travel plans.

A Brief History of the Car Rental Industry

Hertz—today's largest car rental firm—started in 1918. Avis began in 1946, and National in 1947. Discount opened its first Ontario location in Hamilton in 1980 and then expanded into the Maritimes in the mid-1980s.

The car rental industry really began to prosper when the first commercial jet airliners came into service in 1958. A car provides business travellers with the mobility they need to conduct business, and ensures that they don't have to rely on taxis and other forms of public transportation. The idea of having car rental desks at airports was pioneered by Warren E. Avis.

The Car Rental Industry Today

The car rental industry has expanded impressively in terms of both revenues and the number of rental cars on the road. The top firms in the United States are Cendant (now the Avis Budget Group), Hertz, Enterprise, and Vanguard (Alamo and National). Currently, National has about 300 locations in Canada, Avis about 214, Hertz about 167, and Budget about 415. There are over 5000 companies operating in Canada and the United States today, and this number is growing every year. Aggressive companies, such as National in Canada and Dollar, Thrifty, and Alamo in the United States (the first two are part of the Dollar Thrifty Automotive Group), have won a greater share of the market in recent years.

The car rental industry is still heavily tilted toward business travellers, but the leisure market is expanding rapidly, from 10 percent of rentals in 1971 to about 35 percent in the 1990s. The growing popularity of **fly/drive packages**, which are vacation packages that include both airfare and a rental car, has been a major factor in this growth. The popularity of these packages has been stimulated by lower airfares and cut-rate car rental prices. It is predicted that the leisure market will continue to be the major growth area in the car rental industry.

Competitive Industry The car rental industry has always been highly competitive. With the arrival of new companies in the 1980s, this competition intensified. The larger companies were forced to reduce prices and offer promotional inducements in an attempt to hold their share of the market.

Types of Companies Car rental companies have two main types of operations: corporate and licensee. Most of the larger firms, including Hertz, Avis, and National, are mainly corporate operations. They purchase the cars and rent them to consumers. After the cars have been driven 30 000 to 40 000 kilometres, these companies resell them at used-car prices.

Location The larger car rental firms have both in-town and suburban locations, but most business is still conducted at airports. A car rental company's location affects its rental rates and the convenience with which renters can pick up their car. Thrifty does about two-thirds of its business in the airport market and one-third in the local market. Many smaller car rental companies keep their costs down by not having airport counters; their cars are at off-airport locations. Some firms provide free transportation from the airport to the car rental location.

Advertising Advertising has had a remarkable effect on the car rental market. Back in the 1960s, Avis launched its "We try harder" campaign to challenge Hertz's domination of the industry. Hertz responded with its "We're #1" slogan, and now most companies spend heavily on national advertising. Enterprise, the largest car rental company in North America, used "Pick Enterprise, we'll pick you up"; Discount, "Proudly Canadian"; and Hertz, "Great cars, great rates, great service." A few years ago, Hertz used golf legend Arnold Palmer in its "Superstar in rental car" campaign. Thrifty has used Wayne Gretzky in its advertising.

Car Rental Clubs Many car rental companies offer free club memberships to car renters in an attempt to promote customer loyalty. Clubs such as the Hertz #1 Club, the Avis

Wizard Program, and National's Emerald Club have computerized information systems that help car rental companies keep track of the names and preferences of frequent renters. Club members enjoy faster, more efficient service. Some clubs provide express service, which allows members to avoid the rental counter and go directly to the courtesy bus for the short trip to the rental car. Most car rental firms are also associated with an airline frequent flyer program, so that clients can earn airline reward points when renting a vehicle.

The Car Rental Process

Travellers should know they must meet certain qualifications before renting a car. They should also know about the various rental rates, the makes and models of cars available, and the extra charges they may incur.

Qualifications Usually, to qualify to rent a car, a client must:

- Have a valid driver's licence. Some foreign countries require an international driver's licence, which can be obtained from an automobile club.
- Be of a certain age. In Canada, the minimum age depends on the car rental firm and its insurance policy. Usually it is 21; it may be as high as 25. In some countries there is a minimum and maximum age; the minimum is usually 25, the maximum may be 65.
- Have a major credit card. A traveller without a credit card must be cash-qualified. A cash deposit equal to the expected rental amount plus a specified percentage is required.
- Be personally responsible. A traveller who does not have a major credit card must be able to offer an employer's name and address.

Rates Several years ago, companies charged a flat-rate daily fee with an additional charge for the number of kilometres driven. As competition increased, many firms began to offer **unlimited-kilometre plans** that allowed clients to travel as far as they wanted for a flat fee within the allotted rental period. With a **kilometre cap**, clients are allowed a certain number of free kilometres each day and are then charged from 20 to 30 cents extra for each additional kilometre driven. Most of the smaller companies continued to offer unlimited-kilometre plans so that they could compete with the larger firms. Some leading companies have returned to offering unlimited-kilometre plans in an effort to grab a larger portion of the leisure market.

Rates vary according to the size of the car and do not include gasoline, taxes, or charges for extra services. Many companies offer the following types of rates:

- **Regular rate** A standard charge for the day, usually with an added amount for kilometres driven.
- **Special rate** A discount rate for weekly, weekends, or holidays. A special rate can also include an unlimited-kilometre plan.

- **Corporate rate** A discount rate for employees of companies with a high rental volume.

Makes and Models Thirty-five years ago, each rental company concentrated on cars from just one North American manufacturer, such as General Motors or Ford. Usually, only three or four models were offered to customers. Today, many different models are available, as are vans, trucks, and even chauffeur-driven limousines. Travellers with special requirements can also be accommodated, such as physically disabled drivers who need cars with hand controls or other special equipment, and those who need wagons or recreational vehicles.

Many rental firms provide charts showing which cars are available within each class. There are four basic classes of rental cars:

- **Subcompact**—a small car.
- **Compact**—an average-sized car.
- **Standard**—a full-sized car.
- **Deluxe**—a large luxury car that usually comes equipped with many extras.

If a customer has a reservation but no car in the requested class is available, most companies upgrade to the next higher class at no extra charge.

In the late 1990s and early 2000s, several car rental companies added other categories, such as minivan, sport, sport utility, and convertible, to satisfy the MNEs of customers. Hertz has a Prestige category (Audi, Volvo, Lincoln, Lexus, etc.).

Some tourists like taking their accommodation with them by renting a recreational vehicle (RV) or a trailer. Some rent for a trip or two, then make a purchase decision based on the experience. Others continue to rent instead of tying up their capital on a major purchase. Some Canadians go "RVing" in Canada during the summer and shoulder seasons and then venture south to warmer weather in the winter. Some rental websites give a guided tour of the vehicle to be rented.

Charges Most rental companies charge for extra services such as the following:

- **Drop-off** The renter does not always find it convenient to drop off the car where it was rented. Many companies allow clients to drop off the car at any location owned by the same company. This may be free within a state or province but there is often a **drop-off charge** for this service.
- **Gas** Car rental firms usually charge clients for gasoline when cars are returned with less than a full tank. Prices are much higher than those charged at most gas stations, so clients usually save money by filling the tank before returning the car.
- **Extras** For a supplementary fee, many companies offer additional options, such as a GPS system, booster, child or infant seats, and hand controls.

- **Insurance** Clients are liable for a specified initial amount of damage to the car. Car rental firms offer clients a **loss/damage waiver (LDW)** for a fee of about $25–30 per day. An LDW is not insurance, but it relieves clients of their liability for this initial amount of damage. It also provides coverage for loss of the use of the rental car should an accident occur. For an additional fee of about $10, car rental firms also offer **personal accident insurance (PAI)**, which provides coverage in case of bodily injury to the client.
- **Lost keys** A fee is charged if the client loses the keys to the rental car.

Car Rental Companies Abroad

The 1950s was a period of rapid growth in the car rental industry throughout the world. American companies began to enter the overseas market in the 1960s and are now represented almost everywhere. Hertz, with offices in more than 147 countries, dominates the world market. Many other large North American companies also have offices abroad. Even so, the American car rental market is still larger than that of the rest of the world combined.

Besides the American companies operating abroad, there are foreign car rental firms that serve travellers overseas, including Europcar, Auto Europe, and Europa Rent-a-Car. Some firms offer both American and foreign cars.

Driving Abroad Travellers who rent cars abroad should be aware of the different driving conditions and practices in some countries. For instance, in Great Britain, Australia, the Bahamas, and some other countries, driving on the left side of the road is standard. The steering wheel is on the right side of the car, and shifting gears must be done with the left hand instead of the right. In most foreign countries, cars tend to be smaller than in Canada and the United States. In Europe, most rental cars have manual transmissions and many companies have switched to diesel-powered cars, which are less expensive to run and maintain (although the price of diesel is now generally higher than for regular gasoline).

Speed limits abroad are usually posted in kilometres, which is convenient for Canadians. Canadians travelling in the United States will have to become used to (or remember) the imperial system, which uses miles. Speed limits vary from country to country but tend to be higher in foreign countries than in Canada and the United States. For example, the speed limit on many roads in France is 110 kilometres an hour. The expressways (autobahns) in Germany have no real speed limit, and some cars race along at speeds of 120 to 160 kilometres an hour. Canadians and Americans should be aware that many rental car firms do not allow their cars to enter Mexico. One firm, on its website, warns that Canadian import laws prohibit Canadian citizens from taking American-owned cars into Canada.

Channels of Distribution

Several channels of distribution are used in the car rental industry, including online travel sites, travel agencies, business travel departments (BTDs), and car rental central reservations offices and websites. Rentals through travel counsellors were negligible in 1975; by 1997, they accounted for about 50 percent of the car rental business. Then online booking came into practice, and the percentage decreased. Reservations for employees of large companies are often made through BTDs; these clients usually receive the car rental firm's corporate rate.

Because most travel counsellors depend on airline global distributions systems (GDSs) for information on car rental availability, smaller car rental companies that are not part of a GDS may suffer by not being as accessible. Counsellors often make car rental reservations on a GDS as part of a package that includes an airline ticket and a hotel room. They can also make reservations by calling the toll-free number of the car rental company's central reservations office. Counsellors earn commissions from car rental firms, just as they do from other travel and tourism suppliers.

Check Your Product Knowledge

1. What has been the major factor in the success and growth of the car rental industry?
2. How have Hertz and Avis responded to competition from smaller, highly aggressive car rental companies?
3. How does the location of a car rental firm affect the rate charged for the rental car?
4. What qualifications are required of a person who wants to rent a car?
5. Why would a tourist want to rent a recreational vehicle?

MASS TRANSIT SYSTEMS

The term **public transportation** refers to any organized passenger service available to the general public within a small geographic area. Commuter buses and trains are the most important components of public transportation. These carry millions of people back and forth to work each day, either within a city or between a city and its suburbs. For people living in urban areas, public transportation systems are an essential service. In some combination, local, provincial or state, and federal governments heavily subsidize most

ILLUSTRATION 7–9
The Montreal subway system is quiet, clean, and efficient.
SOURCE: Corel.

systems. The term **mass transit** refers more specifically to the movement of people within large metropolitan areas. The most important forms of mass transit are urban buses, subways, and taxis.

As a tourism professional, you may be called on to provide information on mass transit in Canada, the United States, and foreign cities. You may be asked the best way to get from the Brussels airport to the central railway station in downtown Brussels, or how to travel on the Métro in Montreal, or how to reserve a limousine in Dallas.

In this section you will learn about urban mass transit, about getting around in cities in Canada and the United States, and about the transportation systems in some key world cities.

Urban Buses and Trolleys

Buses are the main form of urban mass transit. Urban buses operate over short distances within a city. Most cities in Canada and the United States have bus service only. Several cities have reserved special traffic lanes for buses in downtown areas. These were developed to speed up bus service and so encourage drivers to leave their cars at home.

In many metropolitan areas, privately operated buses or vans or extended cars, often called airport limousines, provide passenger service between the airport and the city centre. Airport limousine service usually operates at fixed intervals and is regulated by the airport. In many cities, large hotels have their own cars or vans to take guests to and from the airport. Some local city buses also provide this service.

Many cities are bringing back **trolleys**, formally known today as **light rail transit (LRT)** vehicles. LRTs carry some 500 000 passengers a day in cities like Boston, Buffalo, Philadelphia, New Orleans, Los Angeles, and San Francisco. Edmonton opened the first new LRT system in North America in 1978. Calgary followed in 1981, Vancouver in 1986, and Ottawa in 2001. Toronto has had trolleys for

almost a century (it calls them streetcars or, more affectionately, the Red Rockets). Toronto now plans a series of LRT lines across the city. Trolleys are more reliable than buses. Also, since they run on their own tracks, they can bypass a lot of city traffic. Furthermore, they are nonpolluting.

The famous cable cars of San Francisco were overhauled and once again carry passengers up and down the city's steep streets. To cope with traffic congestion in downtown areas, a few cities have tried **monorail** systems. These are elevated urban transit systems that run on one rail. In Canada, the number of passengers using urban transit has remained somewhat constant since 1994, at around 1.6 billion trips a year.

Commuter Rail Systems

Canada has a few traditional, heavy-rail commuter systems. Montreal has the oldest system in Canada. It is operated by the Montreal Urban Community and has two main lines: the former Canadian Pacific Lakeshore service, and the former Canadian National service through the Mount Royal tunnel. GO Transit—"GO" standing for "Government of Ontario"—was established in 1968 to link Toronto to its extensive suburbs. This service is coordinated with bus and subway services. The West Coast Express runs from Mission City into Vancouver.

Subways

A **subway** is a passenger transportation system that operates either wholly or partly underground. All subways run on rails. Montreal, Toronto, New York, Boston, Baltimore, Philadelphia, Chicago, Atlanta, Los Angeles, San Francisco, and Washington, D.C., all have them. Toronto has three main lines. A fourth line, more properly an LRT, runs above ground.

Subways can move large numbers of people quickly, cheaply, cleanly, and quietly. Many travellers find subways the fastest and easiest way to get around a city, once they overcome their reluctance to learn the system.

A few cities in the United States have developed rail links from the airport to the city centre—for example, New York, Philadelphia, and Cleveland. A similar link has been announced for Toronto.

Taxis and Limousines

Taxis and (to a lesser extent) limousines play an important role in public transportation. This kind of service, known as **on-demand public transportation**, does not keep regular schedules. Rather, passengers arrange individually for service. In most areas you can get a taxi by hailing it on the street or at a taxi stand. In other areas, the taxi must be summoned by phone. Limousines are privately owned and operated chauffeur-driven cars, often hired for special occasions or for business purposes. Usually, limousines are reserved by phone. Fees can be calculated on a per-hour basis or by distance travelled.

In most cities, taxi fares are indicated on a meter and calculated according to distance travelled. However, fares can also be calculated by zone. For tourists and business travellers unfamiliar with a city, taxis are an extremely convenient way to get around. They also provide an easy link between the railway station or airport and the traveller's destination in the city.

Taxis and limousines are integral to the service systems at airports and railway stations. For a traveller who has just disembarked from a plane, a taxi often provides the transfer to the city centre. The plane–taxi combination is yet another example of intermodal transportation.

Mass Transit in Foreign Cities

One of the first things a traveller arriving in a foreign city has to learn is how to get around that city. Will a taxi be the fastest and easiest way to go from the hotel to the trade show on the outskirts of town? Or is there a subway line that makes the trip without too much bother and avoids the rush-hour traffic? Transportation facilities, conditions, customs, and relative costs vary widely among cities. Following are some highlights of urban transit systems around the world:

- **London, England** The legendary cabbies of London have to pass a very stringent test to demonstrate their knowledge of the city's streets. Most London cabbies still drive traditional black taxis that offer old-fashioned comfort and lots of headroom. The London Underground, known locally as "the Tube," has a reputation for dependability, cleanliness, and civility. The Green Line runs directly to Heathrow Airport. The famous red double-decker buses make bus travel in London a tourist's delight.
- **Paris, France** The Paris Métro, built in 1900, is considered by many to be the finest subway system in the world. It is certainly the fastest, with trains averaging over

ILLUSTRATION 7–10

The double-decker bus is a familiar sight on London streets and is a great favourite among tourists.

SOURCE: Corel.

100 kilometres an hour on its newest line. The main stations have Métro maps, which light up when you push a button to show the best route to your destination.
- **Moscow, Russia** Moscow takes the prize for the world's grandest subway. Marble columns, glittering chandeliers, and paintings adorn the subway's stations.
- **Tokyo, Japan** Tokyo's subway is the most heavily used in the world. To pack as many riders as possible into each car during rush hour, the subway employs white-gloved "pushers."

Ferry Commuter Systems

Ferries are of minor importance to most urban environments, but are important in a few cities: North Vancouver to Vancouver, Dartmouth to Halifax, Lévis to Quebec City. In Toronto, ferries run from the Toronto Islands. In the United States, ferry systems are of vital importance in New York City and Seattle. In 2001, Sydney, Australia, launched a solar-powered harbour ferry. In many places, ferries are popular for sightseeing. In Halifax, Atlantic Tours Gray Line and Ambassatours had a military landing craft-type vehicle modified as "Seymour the Seal," and use it to offer a combined city–harbour tour. A competitor has two vehicles, known as "Harbour Hoppers." Evening "sunset–starlight" cruises are available, which are quite delightful, especially when there is no fog!

Channels of Distribution

Tickets or tokens for mass transit are usually sold directly at bus or subway stations. Information about a city's mass transit system is usually available from the local tourist office or Chamber of Commerce, or at the token booths in subway stations. Subway maps, information on bus routes, and tips on using taxis are often found in guidebooks for the particular destination, be it Paris, Mexico City, or Washington, D.C. Many foreign destinations offer visitors local transportation passes that can be purchased prior to arrival. One example is the London Pass.

Check Your Product Knowledge

1. What forms of mass transit carry travellers between an airport and its city's centre?
2. Explain why many cities are building LRTs today.
3. Which Canadian and American cities have subway systems? What advantages does a subway system offer?
4. Why would a city want a high-speed rail connection between downtown and its airport?

CONCERN FOR THE ENVIRONMENT

The various transportation modes have societal impacts. They generate air, noise, and water pollution; they also relieve or exacerbate congestion, and affect patterns of land use and the development of infrastructure. Transportation is a big contributor to air pollution. About 50 percent of carbon monoxide, 33 percent of ozone hydrocarbons, 50 percent of nitrogen oxides, and 21 percent of suspended particles are linked directly to transportation activities. Current motor vehicle emissions standards need to be improved. Acid rain is another concern.

Noise pollution is a fact of everyday city life. Many cities have bylaws restricting the hours of operation of their airports. Major access roads are now being built with barriers to minimize the impact of vehicle noise; older roads are being retrofitted with noise-reducing panels to protect neighbourhoods.

Water quality is another concern. Water pollution can result from chemical spills and from the dumping of garbage along roadsides. Urban development, including the building of roads and parking lots, reduces the amount of land available to absorb rainwater and runoff. As a result, many urban environments are seeing increased flooding during rainstorms.

Land-use planning is becoming more important. New airports and roads take a great deal of land, and prevent that land from being used for anything else.

An important issue is global climate change, which has been linked to an increase in greenhouse gases and damage to the ozone layer. Public transportation has a role to play in slowing climate change. But are commuters and travellers, including tourists, going to be willing to drive less?

The Ontario Motor Coach Association reports that a 55-passenger bus can take 27 cars off the highways, thus reducing congestion and the need to build or expand highways. From a fuel-efficiency perspective, intercity buses are twice as efficient as trains, three times more efficient than cars or mass transit, and four times more efficient than airplanes.

Check Your Product Knowledge

1. What are the main ways that surface transportation contributes to pollution?
2. Are urban commuters and intercity travellers willing to stop using their cars, or stop using them as much?

CAREER OPPORTUNITIES

Career opportunities in the surface transportation industries are varied. Many require mechanical expertise or driving skills. Others involve a knack for sales and promotion.

The Railway Industry

Probably the best-known jobs in the railway sector are engineer and conductor. Engineers are responsible for the safe operation of trains; conductors oversee the safety of passengers. Some careers in the railway sector involve public contact, or sales and service, or both (e.g., reservations clerk, sales representative).

Railway employment declined steeply throughout the twentieth century. This sharp decrease can be attributed to automation and to a general decline in the industry. At the present time, career opportunities in the railway industry are limited.

The Motorcoach Industry

Bus operators include intercity drivers, local transit drivers (within cities), and special-service drivers (charters, tours, and sightseeing). Dispatchers assign drivers to buses and coordinate the movement of buses in and out of the bus terminal. Careers involving public contact and sales and service include ticket agent, tour manager, tour representative, and sales representative. Clerical and general office positions are also available. Employment prospects in the charter, tour, and sightseeing areas of this sector have improved in recent years.

The Car Rental Industry

Preparing the car for the customer is an important part of the car rental service. Maintenance and service workers and mechanics make sure each car is clean and in good working order. Other positions, such as reservations agent and customer service representative, involve contact with the public. Station managers run rental offices and supervise rental representatives; sales representatives sell the services of their company to airlines, travel agents, and businesses. The number of car rental companies increases each year, so career opportunities in this industry are expected to remain good.

The Mass Transit Industry

Many careers in mass transit involve driving taxis, limousines, urban buses, or subways. Subway operators open and close subway doors and announce the stops. Dispatchers regulate the flow of bus and subway traffic. Attendants in subway stations sell tokens or tickets to the public.

A DAY IN THE LIFE OF A

Car Rental Agent

Some people think my job as a car rental agent is routine and easy. In some ways, I guess it is, but I help provide a very important service to many travellers and I am proud of my work. The car rental agency I work for has a desk in the baggage claim area of a large airport. When people know they are coming to my city and will need to rent a car, they usually reserve one over the telephone. I also receive many calls from travel counsellors who want to reserve cars for their clients. When customers arrive at the airport, they pick up their luggage and then simply walk over to my counter to get the car they have reserved.

It is my job to process the necessary forms for people who are renting cars from my agency. I explain the rental terms to the customers and have them sign a rental agreement. I also tell them about the types of insurance that are offered. Customers must either leave a cash deposit or provide a credit card so I can bill the rental to their credit card account. Most customers use credit cards rather than cash.

I must make sure the car the customer has ordered is clean, filled with gas, and available for use. Some car rental agencies charge just a flat daily fee for the use of their automobiles. Other companies, like mine, charge a flat fee plus an additional amount per kilometre. When a customer rents a car, part of my job is to verify the kilometres driven so that the agency will know exactly how much to charge when the car is returned.

I also check in cars when they are returned. This involves checking the distance driven and the condition of the car and then computing the customer's bill. Since most people pay by credit card, I process the credit card charge and provide the customer with a receipt. Many customers rent automobiles while on business trips, and they need the receipts to get reimbursement from their companies.

My job is an entry-level job, the kind that is the first many people take in a particular business or industry. I have been a car rental clerk for a year. I hope to be promoted to station manager in another year or two. A station manager directs all operations at a car rental office or at a rental station in an airport, bus depot, or train station. The station manager is in charge of supervising the employees, running the desk or building, and managing the cars assigned to his or her station. I could also be promoted to customer service representative. In that position, I would handle customers' problems or complaints.

In order to get this job, I had to be a high-school graduate. After I was hired, I took a four-week training course. I learned how to fill out forms, process credit cards, take reservations, greet the public, and so on. Car rental agencies strive to be very professional. The company I work for provides its employees with attractive, businesslike uniforms and makes sure all employees treat customers with great courtesy and respect.

You may not think my job requires many skills, but there are several things that I need to do well. I need a good command of English, of course, since I work at a Canadian airport. Sometimes I wish I could speak a second language, since many of our foreign visitors aren't fluent in English. Some of my co-workers can speak French, Spanish, or German. They are very handy to have around when I have difficulty communicating with a foreign customer.

I need to be able to operate a computer so that I can take reservations and fill out forms. I must also be able to write legibly and spell accurately, since other people will be following my handwritten work orders. Most of all, I must have excellent math skills and be able to use a calculator, because I spend a good deal of time working with figures. Much of my work involves adding up bills and calculating distance charges.

I got my job by answering an advertisement in my local newspaper. Some of my co-workers applied directly to the agency, some through a school placement office. Many new car rental agencies have started up in recent years, so there are a lot of new jobs in the field. Also, jobs as rental agents open up all the time as people are promoted or change jobs. A car rental agent doesn't earn a big salary, but there are plenty of opportunities for advancement to better-paying jobs.

Summary

- Private automobiles, intercity buses, and airlines began to challenge the railways in the 1920s. After World War II, the railway industry declined rapidly.
- VIA Rail, a Crown corporation, took over the intercity railway passenger network in Canada in stages between 1976 and 1978. Amtrak, a semipublic railway corporation, took over and revamped the intercity railway passenger network in the United States in 1971.
- VIA Rail and Amtrak are both receiving new equipment and some new funding. Both need additional funding.
- Railway systems in Europe and throughout the world continue to provide extensive service.
- The first motorbuses appeared at the start of the twentieth century. By the 1930s in the United States and by the 1950s in Canada, buses were a common sight on highways.
- Scheduled motorcoach passenger service declined after World War II as car ownership and air travel increased.
- In Canada, the provinces are responsible for regulating the motorcoach industry. The deregulation of the American motorcoach industry in 1982 resulted in the entry of many new companies in the growing charter and tour business.
- Greyhound Canada restructured itself in 1996 and was purchased by Laidlaw (now FirstGroup America) in 1997. Laidlaw purchased Greyhound U.S. in 1999.
- Charters and tours have become as important as intercity ridership to motorcoach companies.
- The car rental industry began to grow rapidly in the late 1950s, a boom that continues today.
- The success of the car rental industry is closely related to the growth of air travel—especially business air travel.
- Mass transit systems are essential to urban life, helping to ease traffic congestion and air pollution.

Key Terms

Internet Connections

WORKSHEET 7-1 Individual Bus or Rail Tour

Pick a region of Canada or the United States to visit for a ten-day or two-week tour. Decide where you want to go, where to stop over, for how long, and what you will see and do. Obtain brochures or visit the websites of bus companies, rail companies, and local sightseeing companies (bus, rail, boat, helicopter, or other local transportation). Compare the advantages and disadvantages of both rail and bus for the long-distance and intercity travel portions of your tour. Estimate travel time and cost. Which mode, or combination of modes, would you prefer? Explain your choices.

Motorcoach Travel

Region _____

_____

_____

Bus or rail line(s) _____

_____

_____

Route/itinerary _____

_____

_____

Kilometres travelled (each part) _____

_____

_____

Cost of ticket (each part) _____

_____

_____

Other expenses _____

_____

_____

Stopovers (where and how long) _____

_____

_____

Kind of accommodations (each stopover) ____

_____

_____

Expenses (each stopover) _____

_____

_____

Attractions or activities (each stopover) ____

_____

_____

Railway Travel

Region _____

_____

_____

Bus or rail line(s) _____

_____

_____

Route/itinerary _____

_____

_____

Kilometres travelled (each part) _____

_____

_____

Cost of ticket (each part) _____

_____

_____

Other expenses _____

_____

_____

Stopovers (where and how long) _____

_____

_____

Kind of accommodations (each stopover) ____

_____

_____

Expenses (each stopover) _____

_____

_____

Attractions or activities (each stopover) ____

_____

_____

WORKSHEET 7–2   Renting a Car

You are a travel agent. You have just finished arranging a round-trip flight from Yourtown to San Francisco for Rosalind Burton. While in California, Burton plans to rent a car and tour the redwood forests in the northern part of the state. She would like to drive a compact car with automatic transmission. She has never rented a car before and is somewhat apprehensive about the rental process.

Reserve a rental car for Burton. Choose a car rental company and find out the rates and charges for the type of car she wants. Also, find out the company's procedures for renting a car. Record your findings on the form below.

Name of car rental company _____

_____

Information needed before renting a car _____

_____

Rates _____

_____

Makes and models available in compact size _____

_____

Charges _____

_____

Options available _____

_____

Insurance price and information _____

_____

Where to pick up car _____

What to do in case of mechanical failure or accident _____

_____

What to do before dropping off car _____

_____

Where and how to drop off car _____

_____

Objectives

When you have completed this chapter, you should be able to:

- List the highlights in the history of sailing ships and steamships.
- Give reasons for the decline of point-to-point passenger service and the rise of the cruise industry.
- Give examples of theme cruises.
- Explain the differences between freighter cruises and standard liner cruises.
- Describe some key marketing techniques used by contemporary cruise companies.
- Evaluate fly/cruise and land/cruise packages.

- Discuss the concept of the cruise ship as a floating hotel.
- Interpret a cruise ship deck plan.
- Identify the factors that affect the price of a cruise.
- Outline the regulations affecting cruises.
- Understand safety and security concerns.
- Understand the increasing concern for the environment.
- Compare promotion by various entities: the Cruise Lines International Association, individual cruise lines, and geographical regions.

The words "choppy waters" and "rough seas" describe the cruise industry's environment in the early 2000s. Many large ships have been launched, creating temporary overcapacity and some bargain prices for travellers, and higher fuel prices have squeezed cruise lines' profit margins. At the same time, the oldest baby boomers started turning 55 in 2001 and this bodes well for cruising's growth. Canada's ports, both east and west, anticipate continued growth, and this will require expansion of terminal facilities. There has been some industry consolidation; for example, in 2003 P&O Princess Cruises and Carnival Cruises merged to create the world's largest cruise group, Carnival Corporation, although each group member operates under its own name.

The cruise is widely regarded as the most glamorous of all travel products. Words like "romance," "excitement," and "adventure" spring to mind when we think about cruising. The romance of the seas is nothing new, but the cruise industry is. The rich and famous have been taking cruises since the 1920s, but mass-market cruises have been available only since the early 1960s. Shipping companies developed the concept of the contemporary cruise in response to the decline in cruise passenger traffic following the advent of the jet age. Cruises are now offered on oceans and waterways throughout the world, on ships ranging in size from luxury liners carrying more than 3000 passengers to small yachts carrying just a dozen. The contemporary cruise is a remarkable marketing achievement. The ship is no longer simply a means of transportation—it is a destination in itself. Cruising has become a total vacation experience.

The cruise industry's success has been phenomenal and it is among the fastest-growing segments in tourism. Between 1980 and 2007, the number of people taking cruises each year in the North American market increased from 1.4 million to over 12 million. The number of cruise ship passengers passing through Vancouver increased from about 400 000 to over 1.3 million in 2007. More than 25 new cruise ships, valued at more than $10 billion, were delivered in the late 1990s. They included three ships in excess of 100 000 gross registered tons (GRT), as well as the *Disney Magic* and *Disney Wonder* for the new Disney Cruise Line. Forty new ships were delivered between 2002 and 2004, ranging from small ships for coastal cruising to the Cunard Line's huge *Queen Mary 2*, at that time the largest, longest, and tallest liner ever built (150 000 GRT). By 2009, Royal Caribbean plans to launch a cruise ship of 220 000 GRT that carries 5400 passengers. A further 26 ships are planned for the North American fleet between 2006 and 2010, which numbered 143 vessels in 2005.

PROFILE

Two Canadian Port Cities: Halifax and Vancouver

About one in five Canadians can trace their family origins back to Pier 21, the immigration shed in Canada's east coast port at Halifax, and today most cruise ship passengers in Canada pass through the modern Canada Place terminal in Vancouver.

Halifax, founded in 1749 as a garrison town, has long been a port of entry to Canada. Between 1928 and 1971, Pier 21 welcomed 1.5 million immigrants. During World War II, about 370 000 troops bound for the war in Europe boarded troop ships at Pier 21. Inbound came over 100 000 refugees, 3000 evacuee children, and 50 000 war brides and their 22 000 children. As air travel replaced transatlantic ship crossings, immigrants began flying to Montreal and Toronto instead, and Pier 21 stopped receiving new Canadians. Pier 21 was reopened in 1999, and today cruise ships bring tourists to its terminal area.

In 1995, the federal government provided $4.5 million to help restore Pier 21 as a monument to the immigrants who entered Canada through Halifax. Visitors to Pier 21 can see exhibits, read experiential stories, consult a roster of ships that an ancestor and/or relative might have disembarked from, conduct a genealogical study, and tour a railway car. The site, which in 2007 was voted one of Canada's Seven Wonders, is recognized as a National Historic site and hopes to be designated as a National Museum of Immigration.

The number of cruise ships and passengers arriving at Halifax has increased in recent years. Tourists can travel to the downtown area by various means, including the "Harbour Hopper," which travels on both water and

ILLUSTRATION 8–1

Pier 21: Innovative interpretative centre in Canada's last remaining immigration shed. Today, cruise ships dock here.
SOURCE: Courtesy of David Tonen.

land. Places of interest include the Citadel, the Halifax town clock, the public gardens, the historic properties, the casino, many churches (including St. Paul's on the Grand Parade), Point Pleasant Park, and Theodore Tugboat for the children.

While dining in one of Halifax's many superb waterfront restaurants, you can watch the harbour traffic: ferries, cruise and container ships, yachts and other pleasure craft, and perhaps even the *Bluenose II*. The setting sun and the lights of the city are quite romantic.

In contrast to Pier 21, Canada Place in downtown Vancouver is a modern facility with a 10-peaked roof resembling a cluster of unfurled sails. It was built as the Canadian Pavilion for Expo '86. In 1987, it was converted into the Vancouver Trade and Convention Centre and turned over to the province of British Columbia. The complex, which dominates the waterfront, has a mixture of private and public sector components. Among these are a cruise ship terminal, an IMAX theatre, the World Trade Centre, the Convention and Exhibition Centre (which accommodates groups from 10 to 10 000), the Pan Pacific Hotel (500 rooms), and a parkade. Passenger services within two blocks of the complex include bus services, the Skytrain and Westcoast Express rail services, Sea Bus and Seaplane terminals, and a heliport.

Vancouver generates more Canadian cruise ship traffic than all other major Canadian ports combined. In the 1990s, passenger traffic grew from less than 400 000 to about 1 million in 2007. In the early 2000s, a third cruise berth was built to meet demand.

What could be more romantic than an evening meal at the Salmon House on the Hill, watching a cruise ship glide under the Lion's Gate Bridge at dusk as the city lights twinkle?

Halifax and Vancouver: two great cities, two great ports.

In this chapter, you will learn about the development of the cruise industry and about the different types of cruises that are available. You will read about cruise programs and about the physical layout of cruise ships. You will also learn how cruise companies have successfully broadened the appeal of cruises through aggressive marketing techniques.

THE ORIGINS OF THE CRUISE INDUSTRY

The passenger ship industry went through several different eras between the 1700s and the present (see Figure 8–1). First was the age of the sailing ship. Many of these ships were built in the Maritimes for transatlantic cargo service with a few passengers. They were followed by the legendary clipper ships, which carried both passengers and freight. The age of steam, of which Samuel Cunard of Halifax was a pioneer, began around 1840. A Cunard ship might carry 50 cabin passengers but 10 times that number in **steerage** class. This was followed by the great age of the luxury liners, from the late 1800s to the mid-twentieth century. A **liner** is an ocean-going passenger vessel that follows a fixed route on a fixed schedule.

By the 1920s, 80 percent of all steamship passengers were American. There were three classes of service: cabin class, steerage (which most immigrants took), and tourist class. The number of passengers crossing the Atlantic rose sharply between 1902 and 1929, from 200 000 to more than 1 million. Many of the ocean liners had all the comforts of a five-star resort hotel: private baths, sumptuous meals, and lavish public rooms. The Great Depression and World War II set the industry back; however, new large liners were still being built, including the Cunard Line's *Queen Mary*, which could carry more than 2000 passengers. The fourth age, called the modern age, thrived for 13 years after World War II, largely because of a boom in tourism. By 1958, there were 25 companies and 70 ships operating on transatlantic routes. Most passengers were American and Canadian, but most shipping lines were European.

The first nonstop flight of a commercial jet airliner across the Atlantic was made in 1958. That event marked the beginning of the end for the passenger ship industry. By 1958, 50 percent of all transatlantic passengers were flying; by 1959, this had risen to 63 percent. Airplanes overtook passenger liners because they could better satisfy the MNEs of all types of travellers, most of whom wanted to spend more time at their destinations and less aboard ship. The Cunard Line ended its Canadian service in 1967; Canadian Pacific ended its Montreal–Liverpool service in 1971, with 24 000 passengers compared to 90 000 in 1960.

The Birth of the Cruise Ship

The development of the modern cruise is a classic example of necessity being the mother of invention. If the shipping companies could not compete with the airlines, they would compete with the resort hotels by offering the cruise as a complete vacation. "Getting there is half the fun" gave way to "Being here is all the fun."

Early cruises catered to a small, rich elite. The "contemporary" cruise that was developed in the early

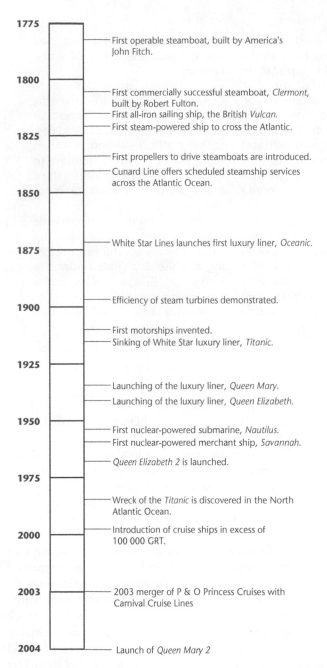

1775	First operable steamboat, built by America's John Fitch.
1800	First commercially successful steamboat, *Clermont*, built by Robert Fulton.
	First all-iron sailing ship, the British *Vulcan*.
	First steam-powered ship to cross the Atlantic.
1825	First propellers to drive steamboats are introduced.
	Cunard Line offers scheduled steamship services across the Atlantic Ocean.
1850	
1875	White Star Lines launches first luxury liner, *Oceanic*.
1900	Efficiency of steam turbines demonstrated.
	First motorships invented.
	Sinking of White Star luxury liner, *Titanic*.
1925	Launching of the luxury liner, *Queen Mary*.
	Launching of the luxury liner, *Queen Elizabeth*.
1950	First nuclear-powered submarine, *Nautilus*.
	First nuclear-powered merchant ship, *Savannah*.
	Queen Elizabeth 2 is launched.
1975	Wreck of the *Titanic* is discovered in the North Atlantic Ocean.
2000	Introduction of cruise ships in excess of 100 000 GRT.
2003	2003 merger of P & O Princess Cruises with Carnival Cruise Lines
2004	Launch of *Queen Mary 2*

FIGURE 8–1 Milestones in Maritime History

1960s was targeted at a much broader segment of society—the tourist market. To widen the appeal of the cruise, the traditional three-class division (first, cabin, and tourist) was abandoned in favour of a single, high-class accommodation.

Shipping companies began converting their passenger liners into tropical cruise ships in the early 1960s. Some could be transferred to the cruise trade with comparative ease. The *France*, for example, became the *Norway*, flagship of Norwegian Cruise Line. Others, such as the *Queen Elizabeth*, proved uneconomical to operate and were withdrawn from service by 1970.

The established companies kept building luxury superliners throughout the 1960s, but these were intended to serve a dual purpose. In summer they served as **point-to-point** liners—that is, they took passengers from one destination to another. In winter they served as warm-water cruise ships. Cunard's *Queen Elizabeth 2* (launched in 1967 and withdrawn from service in 2008) reflected the demands of the new cruise market. Its on-board facilities included bars, lounges, shops, four swimming pools, a nightclub, and a children's playroom. All cabins were fitted with air conditioning and a private bath or shower. The *QE2* had a passenger capacity of 1700 and a crew of 900. This 2:1 **passenger-to-crew ratio** was to become standard on most cruise ships.

The next development was the year-round cruise. In this, Norwegian Cruise Line was a pioneer, packaging the first mass-market, year-round cruises from Miami to the Bahamas in 1966. With the Caribbean becoming the most important cruising area, Miami was rapidly replacing New York as the number-one port in the United States. New companies such as Royal Caribbean Cruise Lines introduced fleets of ships designed specifically for Caribbean cruising.

When Bob Dickinson joined Carnival Cruise Lines in 1973, the company owned only one ship and was on the verge of bankruptcy. Dickinson was hired to direct the foundering company's sales and marketing division. His sales and marketing ideas have transformed the cruise industry and helped make Carnival the largest and "most popular cruise line in the world."

Dickinson practically reinvented the cruise industry. When he started out with Carnival, the modern cruise industry was in its infancy; the people who took cruises were mainly older, wealthy people who saw cruising as a quiet, elegant way to travel to a vacation destination.

One of Dickinson's first innovations was to develop the "Fun Ship" concept—the idea that a cruise was not just a way to get from port to port but rather an entire vacation in itself. The Fun Ship concept was also a way to let people know that cruises were not just for older travellers but also for families, young couples, and singles looking for romance. Dickinson also sought to change the image of cruises as being too expensive for the average vacationer. His idea was to promote the cruise as an entire vacation package at a price that was competitive with any other type of vacation or tour package. Dickinson's strategies worked so brilliantly that within three years, Carnival had earned enough profit to purchase a second ship, the *Empress of Britain*, which was renamed the *Carnivale*. In 1978, Carnival added a third ship to its fleet—the *Festivale*. These three ships made week-long round-trip cruises from Miami to various Caribbean ports. In the mid-1980s, the company began building new cruise ships.

Coupled with an extensive TV advertising campaign to attract consumers, Dickinson's marketing strategies have paid off handsomely. Carnival's bookings and profits have grown steadily every year.

The focus of technological improvements for cruise ships shifted to fuel efficiency, reduced operating costs, and continued improvements in passenger comfort. The use of aluminum for a ship's superstructure (the part of the ship above the main hull) meant that the new cruise ships were much lighter than the earlier liners. As a result, they consumed less fuel. Passenger comfort was greatly increased by the introduction of **stabilizers**, which minimize side-to-side roll. The development of radar meant that ships could steer clear of the worst storms. As more vessels were built for cruising, on-board amenities greatly improved. Cabins were standardized, with private bathrooms and air conditioning throughout. More space was given over to public rooms and outdoor open decks. Dining rooms were located higher in the ship so that passengers could view the sea while dining.

Check Your Product Knowledge

1. What new type of passenger appeared during the 1920s? How did these passengers differ from earlier types of ocean travellers?
2. What effect did transatlantic jet travel have on the passenger ship industry?
3. How do modern cruise ships differ from the luxury ocean liners?

CRUISES OF TODAY

A new round of cruise ship building started in the late 1990s and has continued into the 2000s, spurred by the withdrawal of many older ships that could not satisfy new safety standards set by the **Safety of Life at Sea (SOLAS) Convention**. The new vessels offer a variety of choices regarding size, itineraries, amenities, comfort, and safety. A new vessel with 2000 passengers does not require much more crew than an old vessel with 1000 passengers. As cruise ships become larger and begin competing harder for clients, marketing approaches have changed. Mainly, direct marketing is being used more heavily, and Internet sales are becoming more important.

The number of passengers taking cruises has risen spectacularly—from 1.4 million in 1980 to 12.6 million in 2007 in the North American cruise market. About 78 percent of all passengers are North American. In just 20 years, Carnival, a leader in the Caribbean with 22 "Fun Ships" and 85 ships under all brands in 2008, has seen its business increase from 100 000 to over 1 million passengers a year. Carnival Corporation, the parent of Carnival Cruise Lines, also owns Cunard Line, Holland America, Seabourn, and Costa Cruises, and in 2003 merged with P&O Princess Cruises.

The number of cruise lines rose rapidly for two decades, but recently there has been a consolidation. Today, there are about 50 companies offering a wide variety of cruises on about 200 passenger vessels. In 2008, 24 lines belonged to the Cruise Lines International Association (CLIA), a regulatory and promotional organization founded in 1975. (CLIA is discussed in detail later in this chapter.)

Some of the new lines are owned and operated by American companies, but most are in European hands. Greek, Italian, Norwegian, Dutch, and British lines dominate the industry.

The Walt Disney Corporation entered the cruise industry in 1998 with the *Disney Magic* and *Disney Wonder*. These two vessels have Victorian-styled lobbies similar to those of the grand passenger ships of the 1920s, and a replica of a pirate ship on the deck designed for children. New passenger terminals have been built at Port Canaveral, Florida, and at an island in the Bahamas. A sample week-long package tour includes three or four days at Walt Disney World, a three- or four-day cruise, and one day in the Bahamas.

Cruising is growing rapidly in all parts of the world. The European Cruise Council (ECC) reported that in 2006 there were 44 cruise lines in Europe operating 118 ships. Another 47 vessels sailed for non-European lines.

A number of cruise ships fly what is known as a **flag of convenience**. This flag signifies that a ship of one nation is registered under the flag of another. For example, Carnival's ships, although American-owned, sail under the Liberian flag. Foreign registry enables shipping lines to cut labour costs and to avoid the strict controls and high taxes imposed in their country of origin.

A Wide Array of Cruises

The cruise industry has responded to the varying MNEs of travellers by offering a wide variety of cruise types and cruise destinations. Cruise lines sail to every conceivable maritime location, from the spectacular coast of Alaska to the icy waters of Antarctica. There are cruises to fit every need and pocketbook, and of almost any time length, from short (3 to 4 days), to popular (7 to 10 days), to world (up to 90 days). Table 8–1 shows the growth of the North American cruise market from 1980 to 2007, which reflects the increasing popularity of cruises.

World Cruises A world cruise is the ultimate journey, the vacation of a lifetime for those who can afford the time and the expense. For three months, passengers are pampered with first-rate personal service, superb cuisine, international entertainment, and shore excursions to exotic ports of call. The cost can be staggering and it's hardly surprising that the market for world cruises is relatively limited.

TABLE 8–1 Growth of the North American Cruise Market since 1980

	Actual (millions)	Yearly % growth
1980	1.4	
1985	2.2	+11.4%
1990	3.3	+10.0
1995	5.0	+10.3
2000	7.0	+8.0
2003	9.5	+10.2
2007	12.6	+7.2

SOURCE: CLIA Cruise Finder, www.cruising.org.

World cruises usually begin in the first week of January and end in early April. Some call at as many as 30 ports on the way. All ships travel in an east–west direction, generally entering the Pacific through the Panama Canal, then continuing on to Asia and the Indian Ocean, then entering the Mediterranean through the Suez Canal before returning to the North Atlantic. A few take a more southerly route, sailing around the tip of South America and South Africa.

Cruise lines sell not only the complete world cruise but also segments of it. In this way, they cater to travellers who want to savour the luxury and excitement of a world cruise but cannot afford the whole trip. Once again, the supplier identifies a customer need and markets a product to satisfy that need. Typical segments include New York to Los Angeles, Los Angeles to Singapore, Hong Kong to Singapore, Singapore to Rio de Janeiro, and Southampton to Barbados. To encourage travellers to sign up for portions of world cruises, cruise lines offer generous credits for air travel to the port of **embarkation** (the boarding of passengers onto a ship) and back from the port of disembarkation.

Short Cruises At the bottom of the pyramid are cruise ships that offer short cruises of only three to five days. These ships give passengers a chance to visit an offshore destination and see if they like the cruise experience.

ILLUSTRATION 8–2

Short-term cruises let passengers experience destinations and sample the cruise experience.
SOURCE: © Richard Cummins/SuperStock.

Carnival Cruise Lines has made this the cornerstone of its business and has been very successful. Passengers can take a three- or four-day cruise, or take a seven-day cruise around the Caribbean or to Alaska. Many other cruise lines offer these short-term cruises. Some cruise lines even offer "Cruises to Nowhere." These are ships that head out past the American 5-kilometre limit for parties and casinos. These trips are usually only overnight or for a weekend. According to CLIA, about 28 percent of all cruises in 2006 were 3–5 days in length.

Popular Cruises The next step up are the 6- to 8-day cruises. These cruises sell the most. About 57 percent of all cruises were of this duration in 2006. Most people can take a week off work during the summer or winter, and the cruise market has adapted to this opportunity. Depending on the season, you can find ships in most waters of the world, particularly in North American waters—the Caribbean, Mexico, and Alaska—or in the Mediterranean. In the Caribbean market, we have seen the development of **megaships** to meet clients' MNEs. These ships serve 2500 passengers or more at a time.

Most people, when they think of cruising, think of older people enjoying the ambiance of the cruising life. This can still be true of cruises that last longer than seven days, because most older travellers have the time and money for longer cruises. Many cruise lines that offer seven-day cruises also offer longer trips that include more ports of call and more diverse destinations.

The top of the pyramid is occupied by the all-suite cruise ships and by the suites on ships with longer itineraries. Here, intimate service is the key. A single sitting for meals, personal cabin stewards, and all-inclusive packaging set these ships apart from others. The itineraries are longer, many lasting nine days or more. The destinations may be the same as for other cruise ships, but more time may be spent at each, or additional ports may be added to offer more diversity. Seabourn and Crystal Cruise Lines are two companies that offer all-suite cruise ships. These cruises cost $800 to $2000 a day per person.

Canadian Cruise Ship Traffic

Cruise ship traffic at major Canadian ports from 1990 to 2007 is shown in Table 8–2. Transport Canada's 2007 *Annual Report* noted that the number of cruise passengers at all ports except Montreal showed an increase after some years of declining numbers.

Cruises by Geographical Area

Short sea cruises are the mainstay of the cruise industry, accounting for by far the largest number of passengers. Warm-water cruises that emphasize "fun and sun" are the most popular. However, the Alaskan cruise routes are becoming more heavily travelled.

The Caribbean The Caribbean was the first area developed, in the 1960s, for modern cruising and it has remained the most popular region for Canadian and American tourists. It offers a wealth of tropical islands within a small geographic area. As many as five or six islands can be visited during a one-week cruise. A typical Caribbean cruise is shown in Figure 8–2.

The Caribbean cruise appeals mainly to travellers who want to relax in the sun en route and then experience a little local culture at the destination. The Caribbean offers exotic attractions, but it is still familiar and "safe" for travellers who don't want to experience a completely foreign culture.

The islands of the western Caribbean are within a day or two's sailing of Florida ports such as Miami, Port Everglades/Fort Lauderdale, and Tampa. Nassau in the Bahamas is one of the most common destinations. San Juan, Puerto Rico, serves as a base for cruises to the Virgin Islands, Guadeloupe, Martinique, Barbados, and other eastern Caribbean islands.

Another popular cruise destination is Bermuda. One-week cruises to Bermuda, with three days of sailing and four days in port, leave from New York City. Bermuda cruises are so popular that Bermuda's government has

	Passengers				
Year	**Vancouver**	**Montreal**	**Quebec City**	**Halifax**	**Saint John**
1990	388 000	31 000	35 000	24 500	1 800
1994	591 400	33 900	36 400	37 700	23 600
1998	873 100	32 600	43 850	47 990	28 400
2002	1 125 252	38 000	66 365	157 036	71 168
2006	837 823	40 565	64 720	169 824	87 759
2007	960 000	34 809	66 152	176 895	133 676

TABLE 8–2 Cruise Ship Traffic at Major Canadian Ports, 1990–2007

SOURCE: Adapted from Transport Canada annual reports.

SEVEN-DAY CRUISE

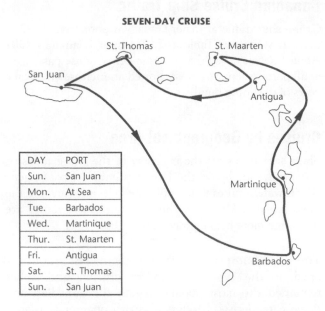

DAY	PORT
Sun.	San Juan
Mon.	At Sea
Tue.	Barbados
Wed.	Martinique
Thur.	St. Maarten
Fri.	Antigua
Sat.	St. Thomas
Sun.	San Juan

FIGURE 8–2 A Typical Caribbean Cruise Route

placed strict limits on the number of ships allowed to visit the island. The purpose is to minimize the negative effects of tourism on the environment.

In the early days, cruise ships sailed to the Caribbean only in winter, generally on seven-day voyages. The winter season is still the busiest, but many Caribbean lines now operate year-round, offering cruises between 2 and 14 days. Three- and four-day trips have become more popular in recent years.

More than 30 cruise lines operate in the Caribbean. Carnival maintains a casual atmosphere and action-filled on-board program on its "Fun Ships." The *Grand Princess* of Princess Cruises—the world's first 100000-GRT cruise ship—entered Caribbean service in 1998. It carries 2600 passengers and features a virtual-reality theatre, three show lounges, three main dining rooms, 750 cabins with verandas, and five pools.

The Mexican Riviera The Mexican Riviera is the most popular destination for cruises from west coast American ports, and in recent years has been one of the fastest-growing areas in the cruise trade. More than a dozen lines now run there regularly, offering fun in the sun with the added attraction of ports such as Mazatlan, Puerto Vallarta, and Acapulco. Most cruises last seven days or longer and depart from Los Angeles in winter and spring.

Trans-Canal A number of cruise lines offer the Mexican Riviera and the Caribbean on the same cruise. Passengers pass through the Panama Canal on 19-day cruises between Los Angeles or Acapulco and Fort Lauderdale. Longer cruises begin or end at Vancouver.

Alaska Ships that sail south from Los Angeles during the winter season often head north to Alaska in summer. Alaska is currently the fastest-growing destination in the cruise market and the third-largest cruise region in the world. Alaska cruises are targeted at a different market from the "fun in the sun" cruises. The passenger list may include naturalists, whale watchers, and other adventurers, for whom natural wonders are more important than sun.

Seven-day cruises from Vancouver sail up the protected waters of the Inside Passage to the spectacular Glacier Bay National Monument, calling at far northern ports such as Ketchikan, Skagway, Juneau, and Sitka. Fourteen-day Alaska cruises depart from Los Angeles and San Francisco. The cruise ship terminal in Vancouver is Canada Place (see this chapter's Profile).

Growth in the Alaskan cruise market has created both opportunities and concerns. Some cruise lines, such as Princess Cruises, have invested in rail cars and wilderness lodges for a "land cruise" in Alaska (see the section on land/cruise packages). Such tours have been aggressively marketed by Holland America as well as Princess Cruises. The state of Alaska is quite concerned about environmental protection (see the section on concern about the environment later in this chapter).

The Hawaiian Islands Holland America offers periodic 15-day round-trip cruises from San Diego to the Islands. Honolulu is often a port of call on long South Pacific trips departing from Los Angeles or San Francisco. American Hawaii Cruises operates year-round seven-day cruises of the Hawaiian Islands, calling at all the major ports. The line offers air/cruise packages to encourage people to fly to Honolulu, the port of departure and return.

The Eastern United States and Canada The coastal waters of New England and the Atlantic provinces have attracted many people, especially senior citizens. Originally, cruise ships operating in this area were small, with a maximum capacity of 1000. Their size enabled them to get in and out of ports that were too small for larger vessels. Nowadays, small ships still serve this region, but the larger ports also see larger ships. Coastal cruise ships are generally quieter than the luxury liners that cruise the Caribbean and the Mexican Riviera. They have a larger proportion of elderly passengers on board, and there is less demand for lively entertainment such as discotheques. As always, different travellers have different MNEs.

Seasonal cruises operate along the eastern seaboard from Newfoundland to Florida. An east coast cruise may last three weeks, with a focus on scenery and historic coastal towns. Shorter cruises of the Atlantic provinces, New England, Chesapeake Bay, the Intracoastal Waterway between Baltimore and Savannah, and the Florida coast are available. Many vessels serving the east coast in summer go south to the Caribbean in winter.

ILLUSTRATION 8–3

Spectacular scenery such as this makes Alaska cruises the fastest-growing sector of the cruise market.
SOURCE: Patrick Lam.

The Mediterranean The Mediterranean is the main cruising area in Europe and the most popular destination after the Caribbean. Cruise lines usually concentrate on either the eastern or the western Mediterranean. A few lines operate cruises throughout the region. The eastern Mediterranean offers attractions similar to those of the Caribbean: plenty of sun and a rich diversity of islands grouped closely together. The area is steeped in history. For travellers on Mediterranean cruises, culture can be as strong a motivator as lying in the sun.

Piraeus, the port for Athens, is the major point of departure for the Greek cruise lines, which dominate the eastern Mediterranean. As in the Caribbean, cruise companies have begun offering more three- and four-day sailings in an attempt to attract first-time cruise passengers. Western Mediterranean cruises usually depart from Genoa and call at Barcelona, Majorca, Minorca, Gibraltar, and ports on the North African coast.

Northern Europe Norway's North Cape is to Europe what Alaska is to the United States. As in Alaska, the main attraction is the scenery—in this case, the spectacular fjords of Norway's coast. Cruises lasting 7, 10, or 14 days leave from ports such as Copenhagen and Hamburg during the short June–August season. Ships sail up the Norwegian coast as far north as Tromsø and Hammerfest. Some cruises continue even farther north into the Barents Sea.

Copenhagen and Hamburg are also departure points for cruises into the Baltic Sea. Here the emphasis is less on scenery and more on the ports visited, which include St. Petersberg, Helsinki, Stockholm, and Tallinn.

Repositioning Cruises A final type of sea cruise worth noting is the **repositioning cruise**. Many cruise lines transfer ships from one cruising area to another between seasons. A line may have a ship that cruises in the Caribbean in winter and in the Mediterranean or northern Europe in summer. Cruise lines, instead of running empty ships across the Atlantic at the end of winter, market these repositioning voyages as special short cruises. Repositioning cruises are also common between the Mexican Riviera and Alaska. You can check the websites of various cruise lines to determine which ships will be repositioned, and when.

Theme Cruises and Special-Interest Cruises

Many of the larger cruise companies try to vary their cruise programs by occasionally offering cruises structured around particular themes. French-owned Croisières Paquet pioneered the theme cruise in 1968 with the first of its many classical music festivals at sea. Other lines were quick to see the value of theme cruises as a marketing tool and began to develop cruises to fit a wide range of special interests. Theme cruises can be broken down into several categories, each reflecting the different motivations of different travellers:

- Recreation (sports, backgammon, bridge).
- Culture (classical music, opera, big band music, film, theatre).
- Education (history lectures, professional study programs, financial planning).
- Health (diet and exercise).
- Hobbies (stamp collecting, photography, gourmet cuisine, wine tasting, murder mysteries).

Most of the lines try to hire top-name celebrities to lecture and perform on theme cruises. For example, on its thirty-fifth music festival cruise, Paquet featured renowned international performers such as violinist Isaac Stern and flautist Jean-Pierre Rampal.

Some smaller companies run nothing but adventure and academic cruises. The emphasis is on exploration, or study, or both. Guest scholars lecture on history, zoology, botany, archaeology, anthropology, and related topics. Instructors can even require their student-passengers to complete homework assignments. This is quite a contrast to "fun in the sun"! Clearly, these highly specialized cruises are targeted at a completely different market than are the warm-water cruises.

Ships for adventure and academic cruises usually accommodate fewer than 150 passengers and are designed to reach out-of-the-way areas not served by the larger cruise liners. A number of American companies have stepped into the market and are operating a variety of cruises to exotic locations. These companies include Society Expeditions and Special Expeditions.

Ecotourism Cruises

Some cruise lines, especially the smaller specialized ones, have started to emphasize ecotourism. Selected advertisements promote whale watching, ecoadventure, and cruises to the Galapagos Islands and into the Amazon Basin. A Canadian firm, Ecomertours, features both discovery and thematic ecotours along the lower St. Lawrence aboard the *Echo des Mers*, a 44-passenger ship with a crew of 18. The five- to seven-day Discovery ecotours explore flora and fauna such as whales near the Saguenay River, birds and Virginia deer on Anticosti Island, and the Minganie, an archipelago with impressive limestone monoliths carved by the motion of the sea. The thematic ecotours, usually two to four days, focus on islands and fjords, bird watching and whale watching, and national parks.

Freighter Cruises

The world cruise fleet is supplemented by about 80 freighters that provide accommodation for a limited number of passengers on worldwide itineraries. Freighter cruises are an alternative for travellers who prefer to avoid the crowds on large cruise liners. They carry a maximum of 12 passengers; if they carry more, they are required to have a doctor on board. These cruises last anywhere from one to four months. Travellers who cannot spare that much time can purchase segments of longer cruises. A big attraction of freighter cruises is that they often put in at ports not usually visited by the scheduled cruise lines.

Freighter cabins are as large and as comfortable as those found on cruise ships and are often more moderately priced. On the negative side, on-board entertainment and amenities are extremely limited. Also, schedules and itineraries are subject to change at short notice. Every effort is made to make the cruise as enjoyable as possible, but the ship's major business is carrying freight, not pampering guests. So freighters are for more adventurous travellers, those with different MNEs than, for example, Caribbean cruise passengers. Marine Link Tours conducts freight boat tours of the British Columbia coast.

River Cruises

River cruises have much in common with coastal cruises. On both types, the vessel never leaves sight of shore. There is always something for passengers to see, so on-board distractions don't have to be as numerous as on ocean-going cruises. A river cruise, like a coastal cruise, tends to appeal more to mature travellers.

In North America, the Mississippi is the most popular river for cruising. At the height of the steamboat age, thousands of paddle wheelers plied the Mississippi. Today the two best-known riverboats in service are the *Delta Queen*, last of the old-time steamboats, and its modern sister ship, the *Mississippi Queen*. Both are operated by the Delta Queen Steamboat Company, which offers year-round (excluding January) 3- to 12-night cruises of the Mississippi and Ohio rivers. Shorter cruises depart from New Orleans and call at antebellum mansions and at the historic riverboat towns of the lower Mississippi, including Baton Rouge, Natchez, and Vicksburg. Longer cruises may include stops at other cities, such as Memphis, St. Louis, and St. Paul on the Mississippi, and Cincinnati and Pittsburgh on the Ohio.

Seasonal cruises are also offered on the Hudson River, St. Lawrence River, and the rivers of the Pacific Northwest. The *Canadian Empress* of St. Lawrence Cruise Lines offers four-, five-, or six-night cruises of the calm inland waters of the historic St. Lawrence and Ottawa rivers. Ontario Waterway Cruises of Orillia offers Rideau Canal/Trent–Severn waterway cruises. In 1994, the *Norweta*, a small Mackenzie River passenger vessel, began cruising Great Slave Lake in the Northwest Territories. The week-long expedition offers day trips for hiking and for observing the summer nesting grounds of over 200 species of birds and waterfowl, as well as a visit to the Dene community of Snowdrift.

The waterways of Europe are well travelled by cruise vessels between April and October. Luxury liners carrying up to 200 passengers cruise the Rhine, Rhone, Moselle, and Danube. Tiny barges chug along the smaller rivers and canals of England and France. Trips on the Volga River between Moscow and St. Petersburg are also available. More adventurous travellers can cruise the Dnieper River and Black Sea coast.

More exotic riverboat cruises are available in Asia, Egypt, and South America. These trips appeal to the same type of traveller who takes ocean-going adventure cruises. Several vessels cruise the Yangtze River in China, an especially popular cruise with the Three Gorges Dam set to change the landscape when the dam is fully operational in 2011. Several other Asian countries, such as India and Cambodia, have entered the luxury river cruise market. Hilton International has year-round sailings up the Nile, where the tombs and temples of the pharaohs are the major attractions. The Sun Line's *Stella Solaris* sails to one of the most exotic of all cruise destinations—the Amazon. In Australia, the Murray River and Don River in Tasmania are also popular.

Great Lakes Cruises

The five Great Lakes make up a vast inland sea system. The area around these lakes is home to many millions of people, and more potential tourists and cruise travellers are within driving or flying range. There would seem to be a huge potential for Great Lakes cruise travel. Among the cruise lines currently operating there are Heritage Cruise Lines, with Georgian Bay/Lake Huron cruises, and Great Lakes Cruise Company.

Yacht Charters

Yachts can be chartered with or without a crew. In the first category, the people chartering the yacht decide the itinerary but leave the actual task of sailing to a professional crew. However, passengers are sometimes given sailing lessons. In the second category, the yacht is chartered by a group of experienced sailors who operate the vessel themselves.

The Caribbean is the main area for charters. Yachts can also be chartered in the Greek Islands and off the New

ILLUSTRATION 8–4
River cruises are a popular and relaxing way to see a destination.
SOURCE: Image courtesy of Canadian Tourism Commission.

England coast. The Charter Yacht Brokers Association represents yacht owners in the United States and abroad and acts as a wholesaler of charters.

Tall Ships

Visits of an armada of "tall ships"—classic sailing ships and training vessels for naval cadets—from various nations to cities such as Halifax and other east coast ports, Quebec City, and New York—created a new interest in travelling on them. Tourists can now sail on a variety of tall ships. On some of them, they can help crew.

Point-to-Point Crossings

The cruise trade has been the main area of growth for the shipping industry in the past 30 years. But point-to-point liner crossings have not disappeared entirely. In 2004, Cunard's *Queen Mary 2* replaced the *QE2* on regular six-day crossings between Southampton, England, and New York from April to December. Passengers have the option of flying British Airways one way.

Air travel is much faster than sea travel. Even so, point-to-point crossings still offer a number of distinct advantages. At the simplest level, they are the only alternative on transoceanic routes for people who don't like to fly. Also, passengers are free to take much more baggage by sea than by air—an important consideration for those planning an extended stay at their destination. And for those who have the time, the crossing is a minivacation in itself. The cost of a transatlantic crossing is not much more than first-class airfare, which is quite a bargain when you bear in mind that all meals and accommodations are included.

Ferries Ferry service is the one form of point-to-point water transportation that has been largely unaffected by the increase in air traffic. Ferry routes tend to be short and comparatively inexpensive. Ferries often operate on routes poorly served by air, and a number of them serve some destinations that are accessible only by ferry. Not all ferry routes are short. Some ferries steam for several hours and offer cabins, restaurants, and recreation rooms. In spite of these creature comforts, ferry companies do not pretend to be in the cruise business; their priority is transportation from point A to point B.

Some ferries are intermodal. Besides passengers, they carry cars, trucks, and even railway cars. Intermodal ferries can be as large as cruise ships.

There are ferries operating throughout the world. For example, they connect islands to one another in Japan, Indonesia, and the Philippines. Currently, the English Channel is one of the busiest ferry crossings in the world. Each year a staggering 50 million passengers cross between southern England and northern Europe. Of course, the opening of the English Channel tunnel (the Chunnel) in

1994 reduced the number of ferry passengers. Even so, the ferry business is an extremely important part of the passenger shipping industry.

Canada's coasts have extensive ferry services. Most routes in British Columbia are between the lower mainland and Vancouver Island, such as the Tsawwassen–Swartz Bay route. Other routes include Vancouver–Nanaimo and Horseshoe Bay–Nanaimo.

Ferry services on the east coast operate between the different provinces and between Nova Scotia and New England. The Confederation Bridge fixed link replaced the Marine Atlantic route between Prince Edward Island and New Brunswick, in 1997. The Marine Atlantic routes across the Bay of Fundy between New Brunswick and Nova Scotia, and between Nova Scotia and Maine, were privatized in 1997. This leaves the route between Nova Scotia and Newfoundland, as the major Marine Atlantic route. Other routes, now served by Bay Ferries in the summer only, are Nova Scotia to Prince Edward Island, and Nova Scotia to Maine. The "Cat," a high-speed car ferry, jets at 90 kilometres per hour twice a day between Nova Scotia and Bar Harbor, Maine. The international routes have casinos on board, which operate while ferries are in international waters.

Check Your Product Knowledge

1. Why are the Caribbean and Mediterranean such popular cruise areas?
2. Name three cold-water cruise areas.
3. Give two advantages and two disadvantages of cruising by freighter.
4. What are some of the attractions of a point-to-point crossing?
5. Why has cruise passenger traffic at the port of Vancouver increased so dramatically?
6. Do you see growth potential for cruises on the Great Lakes/St. Lawrence system?

CRUISE MARKETING

Only about 7 percent of Canadians and Americans have taken a cruise. There are almost 250 million people in those two countries ready to become first-time cruisers! Repeat business accounts for about 60 percent of cruise passenger traffic. In this section you will learn how the cruise industry is trying to tap this vast potential market.

Broadening the Appeal of Cruises

There are two main reasons why the cruise industry has not been able to capture a larger share of the travel market:

1. Lack of public awareness about the range of cruise products available.
2. Misconceptions about cruising.

Individual cruise companies and the Cruise Lines International Association have addressed the first problem by aiming major advertising campaigns and other promotional efforts at potential cruisers.

Far too many people still think of cruises in terms of traditional cruises—that they are only for the rich and the elderly, that they last for several weeks, and that they are expensive, upscale, and formal. In fact, most contemporary cruises are short, inexpensive, and organized to appeal to a much broader market. A key marketing tool used by today's cruise companies is the three- or four-day cruise. Cruise lines have used these shorter cruises to attract many first-time passengers. About 80 percent of all passengers on three- and four-day cruises are first-timers. Having experienced and enjoyed a shorter cruise, they are more likely to take longer cruises with the same company in the future.

The three- and four-day cruises have been especially popular with people under 40. Families with young children can take advantage of baby-sitting services, and many lines now offer programs for young children and teenagers. Another incentive is greatly reduced rates for children sharing their parents' accommodation. Today, there are more passengers between 25 and 40 (30 percent) than there are over 60 (22 percent). More than 40 percent of all first-time passengers are under 40.

Many cruise companies are also pursuing commercial business. Several ships are now equipped with facilities to handle meetings and conventions, and cruises are being used increasingly as incentives. (Incentive travel is discussed in Chapters 3 and 11.)

Cruise/"Other" Packages

Cruise lines are also marketing cruises over a wider geographic area. **Fly/cruise packages,** sometimes referred to as air/sea packages, are now readily available. Cruise passengers are flown to and from their port of embarkation, wherever they live in North America. The airfare is often included in the package price and can be greatly reduced. Cruise lines arrange air transportation on scheduled or chartered airlines. As an alternative, they may issue passengers an air travel credit; passengers then make their own travel arrangements. The credit is deducted from the cruise fare.

Fly/cruise packages now account for almost 75 percent of all cruise bookings. They have been very successful at attracting first-time passengers, especially those who live far from the major cruising ports. Fly/cruise packages are most often used to transport passengers to warm-water ports such as Miami, Fort Lauderdale, and Los Angeles.

The advantage for passengers is that they spend their entire vacation at sea in warm weather. On a practical level, it means they can bring one wardrobe instead of two.

A variation is the "fly one way, cruise the other" package. This type of package was first introduced on transatlantic routes in the early 1960s. Cunard and British Airways have maintained the tradition with an outward journey from New York on the *Queen Mary 2* and a return from Europe by a regular jet flight. This type of package reduces point-to-point travel time, which allows passengers to custom-tailor their vacations.

Land/Cruise Packages Many of today's cruise lines have developed **land/cruise packages**. Typically, the land section of the package involves a short stay in a hotel at or near the port of embarkation. It can be taken either immediately before the cruise or after it is over. American Hawaii Cruises offers passengers booking their seven-day Hawaiian Islands cruise the option of a three-day/two-night vacation at an island hotel. In Canada, Atlas Tours has an Alaska–Yukon–Canadian Rockies tour that combines travel by cruise ship, motorcoach, rail, and air. Globus' "Heart of the Canadian Rockies" tour combines travel by motorcoach and snowmobile (on the Columbia Icefields) with a cruise through the Gulf Islands.

A stroke of marketing genius packaged a four-night Bahamas cruise with a three-day Disney World vacation. Premier Cruise Lines pioneered this concept, which became one of the most popular of all land/cruise options. The Disney World segment typically includes accommodation at an Orlando hotel; admission to the Magic Kingdom, Epcot Center, and Disney–MGM Studios; a tour of the Kennedy Space Center; and the use of a rental car.

Cruise/Rail Packages For years, many passengers on Alaska and Canadian west coast cruises combined rail and ship travel. Examples are Vancouver to Prince Rupert by ship, and then by rail on VIA Rail. Or to Alaska by ship, then the Alaska Railroad to Fairbanks, and perhaps fly home from there. Recently, cruise lines have invested in providing **cruise/rail packages** and have added railway equipment so they can provide, for example, the land portion of tours to Alaska. Princess Cruises and Cruisetours now feature travel by ship to Alaska on the *Grand Princess* followed by a rail journey on the Midnight Sun Express, with Princess's own open-air observation platform and ultra-dome rail cars. Along the route Princess has developed a system of lodges for its guests.

Two-level dome/diner/lounge cars have been built for the Royal Celebrity Tours/Royal Caribbean Alaska tour. Passengers travel for seven days by ship from Vancouver to Alaska; there, they can travel by train on new rail cars for another two to seven days, all the way to Fairbanks. Lunch and dinner are served on the dome car's lower level. Guests stay overnight in new luxury hotels, where breakfast is served. The new rail cars operate on the Wilderness Express of the Alaska Railroad.

THE CRUISE AS A PRODUCT

The cruise is a unique travel product, one that combines both transportation and a destination. This section focuses on the cruise ship as a destination. You will read how ships function as "floating hotels" and how cruise programs are structured. You will also look at the physical layout of a cruise ship and at the factors that affect the price of a cruise.

The Ship as a Hotel

Almost every cruise ship calls at one or more ports during its journey. This represents the transportation element of the cruise product. Yet, on most cruises, the ship itself is the main attraction. A cruise ship is definitely a floating hotel. For vacation travellers, the ship must combine all the services of a resort hotel with the amenities of a vacation on dry land. For business travellers, the cruise ship must be able to offer all the facilities of a convention hotel or convention/conference centre.

Meeting Passengers' MNEs Because passengers cannot leave the ship while it is at sea, the cruise line must ensure that everything they might need or want is on board. A passenger's most basic needs, of course, are for food and a place to sleep. Many require the services of a laundry and a hairstylist. Others may expect a gym or health centre on board. Some will want to attend religious services. Business executives may need to keep in touch with the shore by phone, fax or email, and may also need access to a computer while on board. Clearly, the ship must provide a wide array of services, especially on longer voyages.

Then there is the question of how to amuse the passengers while they are on board. A few are content to laze in the sun all day. But most expect a variety of on-board activities and nightly entertainment. It is hardly surprising, then, that most ships are so heavily staffed. There is a division between the ship's crew, or ship's company, and the hotel crew, or staff.

The ship's crew includes the captain, first, second, and third officers (or "mates"), engineering officers, radio officers, medical officers, pursers, and ordinary and able crew. The ship's crew is responsible for the safe operation of the vessel.

The hotel crew is responsible for passenger services and entertainment on board the ship. It includes the hotel manager, the cruise (or social) director, stewards (including cabin stewards, dining room stewards, wine stewards, night stewards, and deck stewards), the kitchen and galley staff, bartenders, service workers (e.g., barbers, hairstylists, launderers, librarians, masseurs, photographers, printers, and shop assistants), and entertainers, instructors, and lecturers.

Cruise guides and manuals often indicate the ratio of passengers to hotel crew members. Many cruise ships have one crew member for every two passengers. Generally, the higher the crew ratio, the better the level of passenger service.

Physically Disabled Passengers Physically disabled cruise passengers have special needs that may require individualized attention and supervision, as well as special facilities. Some cruise ships are fitted with ramps, elevators, and other devices for circumventing obstacles. There may be cabins on board that have been modified for passengers in wheelchairs. However, not all cruise lines have the facilities to accommodate physically disabled travellers.

The Cruise as a Vacation at Sea

A cruise program typically has four main elements: meals, activities, entertainment, and time on shore. The balance among these will vary with the type of cruise. A warm-water cruise is likely to emphasize on-board activities and entertainment; an adventure cruise is more likely to emphasize time ashore. Even on a theme cruise, where everyone shares a common interest, the elements must be flexible enough to suit the needs and expectations of different kinds of passengers. The following are the typical elements of a modern mass-market cruise.

Meals On most cruises, eating ranks as one of the most popular activities. All cruise lines excel in the quality and quantity of their food. The cuisine can be international or feature ethnic dishes. Many of the foreign-owned lines offer a taste of their home country or port of registry. The Norwegian Cruise Line features exotic specialties such as reindeer pâté. Most cruise passengers eat at the same table every day, where they are served by the same waiter. Some cruise lines are experimenting with a "freestyle" concept (e.g., different times, tables, waiters, and perhaps dress codes).

Activities Cruise directors schedule a full program of daytime activities while the ship is at sea. Exercise classes are popular with many passengers. Instructors may be on hand to give lessons in golf, tennis, dancing, photography, painting, flower arranging, and foreign languages. Guest lecturers often give talks on the history and local culture of

DAWN PRINCESS
THIS IS YOUR QUICK REFERENCE FOR DINING HOURS

VENETIAN DINING ROOM - *Emerald Deck 6*		
Breakfast	Open Sitting	7:00am - 9:00am
Luncheon	Open Sitting	Noon - 2:00pm
VENETIAN DINING ROOM - *Emerald Deck 6*		
Traditional Dining	Dinner First Sitting	6:00pm
	Dinner Second Sitting	8:15pm
FLORENTINE DINING ROOM - *Plaza Deck 5*		
Personal Choice Dining		5:30pm - 10:00pm
(For reservation please call 3463)		
HORIZON COURT - *Lido Deck 14* - Open 24 Hours		
Breakfast Pastries and Beverages		4:00am - 6:00am
Buffet Breakfast		6:00am - 11:30am
Luncheon Buffet		11:30am - 4:00pm
Snack Buffet & Hot Sandwiches		4:00pm - 5:30pm
Dinner Buffet		5:30pm - 10:30pm
Bistro		10:30pm - 4:00am
THE STERLING STEAK HOUSE - *Horizon Court* - *Lido Deck 14*		
($8.00 per person cover charge)		6:30pm - 10:00pm
(For reservation please call 14302)		
SUNDAE'S ICE CREAM BAR - *Deck 12*		11:00am - 5:00pm
AFTERNOON TEA - *Venetian Dining Room, Deck 6*		
		3:30pm - 4:30pm
LA SCALA PIZZERIA - *Dolphin Deck 8*		11:00am - 4:00pm
		6:00pm - Midnight
ROOM SERVICE — 24 HOURS DIAL 9000		

ANY CHANGES IN DINING HOURS WILL BE ADVISED IN THE PRINCESS PATTER
PLEASE NOTE, ALL INDOOR DINING AREAS ARE DESIGNATED AS NON-SMOKING

ILLUSTRATION 8–5

Cruise ship passengers have many dining and snack options.

SOURCE: Image courtesy of Devinder Ghuman.

A cruise ship can't always tie up to a pier when it reaches a port; the ship may be too big to use the normal docking facilities. In such cases, the ship rides at anchor in the harbour, and passengers are taken ashore in small boats called **tenders** or **lighters**.

On three- and four-day cruises, the stay in port is limited to a few hours—just enough time for passengers to do some sightseeing and shopping, and maybe take in some local entertainment. A few cruise lines have purchased islands or stretches of beach in the Caribbean for the exclusive use of their passengers during shore excursions. On longer cruises, passengers can spend as long as two or three days at a destination.

What Is and Is Not Included One of the greatest attractions of a cruise is that it is essentially an all-inclusive vacation. In this respect, it has much in common with a tour package. Most major expenses are prepaid, so

ILLUSTRATION 8–6

Royal Caribbean Cruise Line passengers enjoy an early morning workout on the sports deck, one of the 13 exercise activities offered in the line's Shipshape program.

SOURCE: Courtesy of Royal Caribbean Cruise Lines.

the islands to be visited. Other events include swimming pool games and deck activities, a daily bingo session, and tournaments.

Entertainment Many passengers head to the main lounge for the nightly musical variety show. Cabaret singers and piano players perform in the lounges and bars, which are more intimate. Many cruises hold a masquerade party and talent night for the passengers. Most liners have at least one ballroom, where passengers can dance to an orchestra. Discos and nightclubs are now almost standard; so are casinos. First-run movies and classic favourites are shown in the ship's movie theatre.

Shore Excursions Shore excursions are an important part of almost every cruise. They can sometimes be the main attraction, especially on adventure or academic cruises. When booking a cruise, passengers do not have to commit themselves to shore excursions; these can be purchased individually or as a package from the shore excursion desk on board.

ILLUSTRATION 8–7

There is always something for passengers to do on board a cruise ship.

SOURCE: Image courtesy of Devinder Ghuman.

passengers don't have to carry large sums of money. Included in the cruise price are:

- Ocean or river transportation.
- Shipboard accommodations.
- All meals.
- On-board entertainment and activities.
- Most services.
- Transfers from ship to shore when in port.

Transportation to the port of embarkation may also be included.

Costs *not* included in the price are those that reflect personal choice:

- Shore excursions.
- Port taxes.
- Medical expenses.
- Laundry (or valet), spa treatments, and other personal services.
- Computer time.
- Expenditures in shops on board.
- Gambling chips in the casino.
- Beer, wine, and spirits.
- Tips.

All passengers must pay **port taxes** on disembarkation at any port during the cruise. These taxes vary greatly but are usually in the region of $15 to $20 per person at each port.

Tipping can be a cause of considerable confusion, since passengers are not always sure who or how much they should tip. Individual cruise lines usually issue recommendations for tipping hotel and dining room personnel.

Cruise Pricing

Cruise ships have the highest overheads in the travel industry. To cover operating costs, cruise lines must achieve 80 to 90 percent occupancy rates. (In contrast, airlines can break even at 60 to 65 percent, and hotels at 55 to 60 percent.) Pricing is the key to making sure a cruise ship leaves port as full as possible. All cruise lines offer tiered pricing to attract passengers across a wide range of income levels. On a single cruise there can be more than a dozen price categories. The most expensive category (deluxe) can cost twice as much as the least expensive (economy). For the extra money, the cruise passenger gets a better cabin.

Cruise lines also offer discount fares. Many lines have off-season rates, as well as reduced rates for clients who book well in advance. Others offer discounts for repeat cruisers. Another promotional pricing technique involves accommodating the third or fourth person in a cabin at a reduced rate.

Four main factors determine the cruise price: duration, season, cabin location and size, and ship profile.

Duration of Cruise Duration as a factor should be fairly obvious: A two-week cruise is likely to cost more than a seven-day cruise. Costs are usually calculated on a per diem (daily) basis. Per diems make it easier to compare costs for different cabins or for different cruises. Table 8–3 presents an example of cruise pricing for two cruise lines.

Season Cruise prices can vary considerably with the time of year the ship sails. Prices are highest during the peak or high season (winter in the Caribbean, summer in Alaska), and lowest during the off-season or low season.

TABLE 8–3 The Per Diem Cost of Cruising (CDN$)		
	Cruise Line (Cost of a suite)	
Length of Cruise	**Holland America**	**Carnival**
7 days	$200–600	$115
4–5 days	$300–400	$120
3–4 days	$250–350	$120

Cabin Location and Size Cabin location is the biggest factor influencing price. As a general rule, the higher above the water, the more expensive the cabin will be, because higher cabins afford passengers a better view and are usually closer to public areas. Also, cabins located amidships cost more than cabins either forward or aft, because any side-to-side movement (roll) or up-and-down movement (pitch) is less pronounced amidships. Furthermore, outside cabins are more expensive than inside cabins. In fact, an outside cabin on even the lowest deck costs more than an inside cabin on the highest.

Cabin size is another cost determinant, as is the number of passengers in the cabin. In shared cabins, the third and fourth occupants usually travel at a reduced rate. At the other extreme, single occupants have to pay a single supplement. Even though there are many different cabin price categories, all passengers are entitled to the same level of service. The passenger travelling in the least expensive inside cabin enjoys the same menu, the same entertainment, the same activities, and the same choice of shore excursions as does the passenger in the most deluxe suite.

Ship Profile The final factor affecting the price of the cruise is the ship profile, or type of ship. The space ratio for a ship is calculated by dividing the **gross registered tonnage (GRT)** by the number of passengers carried. The GRT represents the amount of enclosed space on the ship. For example, the GRT of the *Disney Magic* at 85 000, divided by 1760 passengers, yields a space ratio of 48.3. Ships with a high space ratio feel (and are) more spacious for passengers.

The Physical Layout of a Ship Often, the cruise line shows the physical layout of its ships on its website. Some liners have as many as 10 decks. Passenger accommodations are usually concentrated in the lower decks; the upper decks are reserved for public rooms, swimming pools, and activity areas. Typically, meeting rooms are located away from the noisiest parts of the ship. Liners designed for warm-water cruising have larger areas of open sun deck on board than ships sailing to Alaska or northern Europe. Some ships are fitted with all-weather sliding roofs, called **magrodomes**, which can be closed in bad weather.

Cabins (or staterooms) are either **outside cabins** or **inside cabins**. Outside cabins have portholes or windows and a view of the ocean. Most cabins are designed to accommodate two passengers, usually in twin beds **(berths)** but sometimes in a double. Smaller cabins are designed for singles or two economy-minded passengers and have an upper and a lower berth. Larger cabins can accommodate up to four passengers and are suitable for families or for young people who want to save money by sharing. The largest and most comfortable cabins are the suites and mini-suites, which usually feature fixed double beds, separate dressing and sitting areas, and a bath as well as a shower.

Check Your Product Knowledge

1. What is the difference between the ship's crew and the hotel crew?
2. What are the four components of the cruise program?
3. What pricing techniques do cruise lines use to achieve high occupancy rates?
4. What costs are not usually included in the price of a cruise?
5. List four factors that affect the price of a cruise.
6. Why would a cruise line show the physical layout of its ships on its website?

CHANNELS OF DISTRIBUTION

Until recently, 95 percent of passengers booked their cruises through travel agents; this meant that the cruise industry was more dependent on travel counsellors than other segments of the tourism industry. This is changing as a result of direct marketing and the Internet. CLIA reported that by 2006 the proportion of cruisers booking through a travel agency had steadily declined to 78 percent.

Until recently, most cruise line websites were for information and entertainment purposes only, and did not offer online booking. This has changed. Today, almost every cruise line offers online booking. One company offers Web surfers four easy options: "1. Use our travel agent finder. 2. Have our personal vacation planner contact you. 3. Speak to one of our cruise specialists (toll-free number). 4. Online booking."

The following information is typically found on cruise line websites: activities, accessibility, amenities, booking assistance, deck plans, e-mail notification of specials, gifts and video orders, online booking, prices, request for brochures, ship tracking, and streaming video.

Selecting the Cruise

Selecting and selling a cruise is one of the quickest and least complicated of all travel agency transactions. It is also one of the most lucrative. Agency commissions on cruises are considerably higher than on other travel products. The travel agency gets a commission on every component of the cruise product—transportation, accommodation, meals, entertainment, and sightseeing—and all from a single supplier.

Probably the hardest task for the travel professional is matching the MNEs of different travellers to different cruises. Few clients who come into a travel agency know which specific ship they want to cruise on. Some may not even know

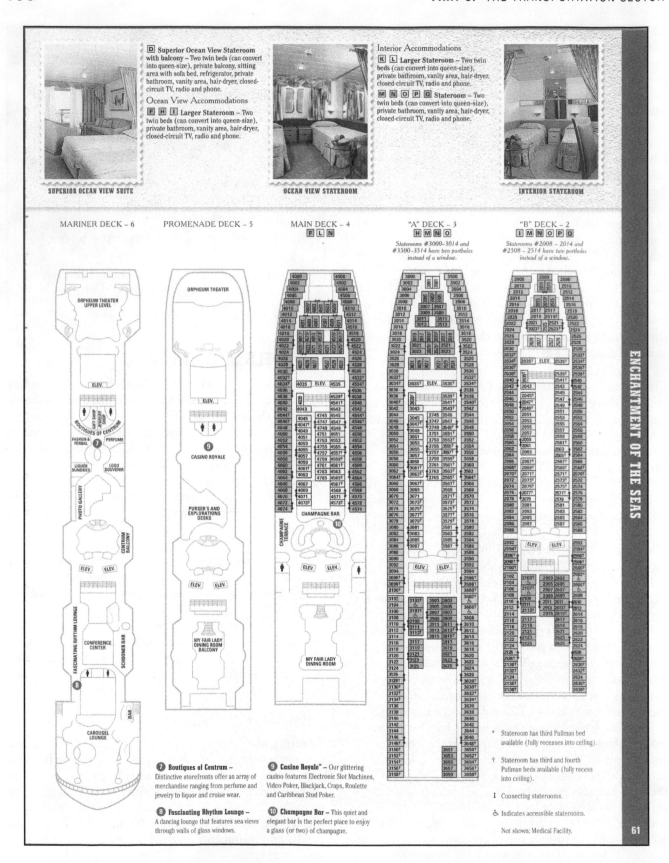

ILLUSTRATION 8–8

On large liners, passenger accommodations are usually concentrated on the lower decks. The cabins are either outside or inside cabins.

SOURCE: Courtesy of Royal Caribbean Cruise Lines.

which geographic area they want to visit. It is the travel counsellor's job to find the right ship for each potential passenger. The counsellor must first establish the MNEs of the client. Is this man looking for a ship with lots of entertainment and opportunities to socialize? Does this woman prefer a quiet atmosphere, formal dining, and older passengers?

After gaining some idea of the client's MNEs, the travel counsellor can start to narrow down the choice of ships and itineraries. There are a number of helpful reference works:

- The *Official Steamship Guide International (OSGI)* provides up-to-date listings of cruise schedules throughout the world, as well as information on cruise lines and featured ports of call.
- The *OAG Worldwide Cruise and Shipline Guide* offers much the same information as the *OSGI*, as well as information on port taxes, staff/passenger ratios, and maps.
- The *OHG Cruise Directory* is similar to the *OSGI* but includes deck plans and ship profiles.
- *Ford's International Cruise Guide* provides extensive information about individual cruise ships.
- *Ford's Freighter Travel Guide* lists freighter cruises, river cruises, and yacht charters.
- The *CLIA Cruise Manual* has profiles of ships and CLIA cruise lines, maps of ports, detailed descriptions of on-board cruise programs, and information on reservations procedures.
- *Garth's Profile of Ships* contains descriptions of more than 200 vessels.
- Websites of individual cruise line companies.

The counsellor also shows the client some cruise brochures. Once a particular ship has been chosen, the next stage is to analyze deck plans and decide on a cabin category and a specific cabin.

The Reservation Process

Some cruise reservations are still made manually—that is, the travel counsellor calls a toll-free number to reach the cruise company. Computer availability is, however, widespread. The airline reservations systems used by travel agencies offer cruise information and bookings. A number of cruise lines have set up links with CruiseMatch, a reservations system owned by Royal Caribbean Cruise Lines.

Generally, a cruise line requires the passengers' name(s), address, e-mail address, phone number, date of birth, gender, nationality, and credit card details to make a reservation.

Reservations for cruises are required well in advance, especially for longer cruises. A deposit must be made to confirm the reservation. Final payment is usually required between 30 and 60 days before the cruise begins. The cruise line issues tickets about 30 days before departure.

A client who cancels a reservation is usually charged a cancellation penalty, which becomes progressively higher the closer to departure the client cancels. Cruise lines guarantee to provide a full refund if a sailing is cancelled. They also reserve the right to change the itinerary or substitute another ship.

Check Your Product Knowledge

1. Through which distribution channel are cruises usually sold?
2. What is the normal procedure for paying for a cruise?
3. How are websites changing the channels of distribution?

THE REGULATION AND PROMOTION OF CRUISES

The cruise industry is one of the least regulated sectors of the tourism industry. Although not entirely free of government intervention, cruise lines are largely free to choose their own itineraries, change their schedules, and set their own prices. The industry also benefits from government promotion.

Government Promotion and Regulation

Governments promote the cruise industry mainly by building and maintaining ports, port facilities, and harbours. In Canada, most seaports are owned and operated by Transport Canada; in the United States, seaports are owned and operated by local governments. Harbour and port authorities regulate the industry by charging port taxes.

In Canada, the Canadian Coast Guard is responsible for maritime safety. In the United States, the U.S. Coast Guard acts as harbour master and enforcer of government safety requirements, and must approve construction plans for each new ship. Once in active service, all vessels are regularly checked to make sure they meet current safety regulations. Canadian and American maritime safety standards are among the strictest in the world. This is a benefit, in that Canadian and American ships are exceptionally safe. At the same time, these standards also mean that Canadian and American ships are much more costly to build and operate than foreign ships.

All cruise ships that call at North American ports, regardless of their country of registry, must meet not only Canadian and American standards but also international safety standards set by the Safety of Life at Sea (SOLAS) Convention. October 1, 1997, was the date by which the world's cruise fleet had to adhere to new, stricter SOLAS standards. As a consequence, several well-known ocean liners built in the 1950s and 1960s were taken out of service.

Federal restrictions in the United States were greatly reduced in 1985. This means that any foreign vessel can now call at any number of American ports during a cruise, provided that it also visits at least one foreign port. Another federal regulatory agency in the United States is the U.S. Public Health Service. Agents regularly inspect the galleys and dining rooms of all ships calling at American ports. They set standards of hygiene and overall sanitation. In Canada, this function is carried out by Health Canada through its Cruise Ship Inspection Program.

Safety and Security Concerns

Cruise travellers need to be aware of what can go wrong regarding personal safety, health matters, ship safety, and the unscheduled termination of a voyage. Although rare, theft, physical assault, and sexual assault may occur. Cruise passengers may feel carefree and let their guard down after they have put to sea. Common sense and vigilance should prevail, both on board ship and at ports of call. Illness and medical emergencies can occur. Travellers, especially those with pre-existing conditions, should note which facilities and trained medical personnel are available. Also, distance from shore may be a factor. Most North American cruises are within range of the coastline, so helicopters are available in case of a major emergency.

Ships do encounter problems. In recent years there have been some fires at sea and some engine breakdowns. The failure of an air-conditioning system can be quite unpleasant in a warm climate. Every year there are problems with overcrowded ferries. Tragedy can strike fast. In May 2001, a Norwegian Cruise Line ship had trouble with its autopilot off Vancouver Island. When the autopilot was turned off, the ship listed and several people were injured. In November 2007, a small cruise ship named the *Explorer* and operated by GAP Adventures sank in the Antarctic after striking an iceberg. All 154 passengers and crew were successfully evacuated.

Unexpected terminations of cruises also occur. This may happen if the cruise line is not financially solvent. One example was the seizure in September 2000 in Halifax of the *SeaBreeze* by creditors of Premier Cruises. Passengers from New York were stranded, and those wishing to start their voyage by embarking in Halifax could not. This vessel finally left Halifax in December 2000, with only a small crew, but it sank off Virginia. The U.S. Coast Guard rescued the crew.

Concern for the Environment

Environmental issues are becoming more important for the cruise industry. These issues include harbour bottom stir-up (by the ship's propellers); erosion of harbour and riverbanks (by large waves from ships travelling too quickly); wastewater discharge, both grey water (from sinks, showers, laundries, and kitchens) and black water (from effluent); discharges (oil, wastewater, and toxic and hazardous substances); air pollution (stack gases); and garbage.

Some cruise regions have been quite active with agreements and legislation. The Florida–Caribbean Cruise Association signed a Memorandum of Understanding with the Florida Department of Environmental Protection, which promotes maximum reuse and recycling. In addition, the memorandum encourages education, training, and management of waste streams using new technology. Alaska has proposed a cruise ship pollution bill, which has the support of the North West Cruiseship Association.

Some ports of call have had to limit the number of cruise ships that may enter, because of carrying capacity limitations. Some cruise lines have designated certain ships as nonsmoking.

Cruise Lines International Association

The Cruise Lines International Association (CLIA) is a trade association of cruise lines that promotes cruises in North America. Since it was founded in 1975, it has devoted itself to promoting cruises as desirable vacation experiences and to improving the industry's public profile. It has become the most important external marketing organization for its member cruise lines. In 2006, CLIA merged with a sister organization, the International Council of Cruise Lines (ICCL). As of 2008, 24 cruise lines, accounting for 97 percent of the cruise business marketed from North America, were members of CLIA. A recent CLIA program promoted February as National Cruise Vacation Month.

The CLIA is also a regulatory body that sets rules and standards for travel counsellors who sell CLIA cruises. Counsellor training is an important priority for the association, which trains counsellors through its Agency Training Program and a video training course. The CLIA promotes agency cruise sales by encouraging vacationers to see member travel agents for cruise counselling. About 16 500 travel agencies are affiliated with CLIA. The organization introduced an individual membership category in 2007 for agents who work in CLIA member agencies. Its website is very popular; one component features profiles of member cruise lines and over 140 ships.

Cruise Line Company Promotion

Each cruise line also promotes itself individually. Some corporations own more than one line. For example, Princess Cruises and P&O Cruises are sister companies within P&O Princess Cruises, which also owns Swan Hellenic in the United Kingdom and AIDA in Germany. This enables the parent company to target individual cruise lines to different market targets and/or regions. Sometimes vessels are transferred from one sister company to another. The *Ocean Princess* was transferred to P&O in 2002 and renamed the *Oceana*.

Carnival Corporation promotes the "World's Leading Cruise Lines": an alliance of several cruise lines. Carnival merged with Princess Cruises and P&O Cruises in 2003. Holland America Line, Cunard, Yachts of Seabourn, Costa

Cruises, and the Carnival "Fun Ships" are among the many brands that Carnival promotes separately. It promotes these member lines as sharing a commitment to quality and value, and as offering cruise vacations that appeal to a range of lifestyles and budgets and that sail to the world's most exciting destinations.

Regional Promotion

Table 8–2 showed the increase in cruise traffic to Halifax, Nova Scotia. This increase can be explained by the marketing efforts of the Atlantic Canada Cruise Association, formed in 1998, and the New Atlantic Frontier, a group of about 30 ports along the eastern seaboard from New York to Montreal. These ports have combined their marketing resources to promote cruise travel to their destinations.

The North West CruiseShip Association represents nine member companies that bring 97 percent of cruise ship visitors to Alaska. Part of its mission is to develop strong partnerships with communities and businesses in Canada, Alaska, and the Pacific Northwest. The Florida–Caribbean Cruise Association has 15 member companies, and represents and promotes its members' cruises in that region.

Check Your Product Knowledge

1. In what ways do governments promote and regulate the cruise industry?
2. What is the role of CLIA?
3. Why do cruise lines do promotion both individually and collectively?
4. In what areas should passengers be concerned about security and safety?
5. Why is there an increasing concern for the physical environment within which the cruise industry operates?

CAREER OPPORTUNITIES

The cruise industry employs about 10 000 North Americans, most of them American because of the number of departures from ports in the United States. This makes it one of the smallest employers in the travel business. Most cruise ships are of foreign registry and usually hire their crews overseas. The few exceptions to this are the positions of purser, social director, entertainer, lecturer, and, occasionally, medical officer. However, there are a number of cruise-related jobs and CLIA reports that almost 154 000 people were employed in such positions in 2006.

On Board

The two basic categories of employment on board a cruise ship are ship's crew and hotel crew (or staff). Ship's crew members are responsible for the mechanical operation of the ship. Hotel crew members perform duties similar to those of a resort hotel's staff.

Ship's Crew The captain is the most important person on board. He or she is in charge of the entire ship and is responsible for its operations and for the safety of its passengers and crew. First, second, and third officers, who direct the navigation of the ship and the maintenance of the deck and hull, assist the captain. Engineers operate and maintain the engines and other mechanical equipment. The purser is in charge of the ship's paperwork and handles monetary transactions. Able crew members are responsible for much of the deck equipment.

Hotel Crew The hotel crew heavily outnumber the ship's crew on most cruise ships, especially on those that offer a wide array of services and activities. A cruise ship often has a hotel manager who is responsible for the smooth running of all hotel services on board. The cruise director and his or her staff arrange and supervise social and recreational activities for the passengers; this is very similar to what a tour escort does on land.

On most cruise ships, the steward department has more employees than either the deck crew or the engine department. Cabin stewards have the same duties as hotel room housekeepers: They clean cabins, change beds, and so on. Dining room stewards act as servers under the watchful eye of the captain of the dining room. Wine stewards serve wine at tables; night stewards provide room service; and deck stewards hand out deck chairs, serve drinks on deck, and otherwise see to the passengers' comfort. There is always, of course, a large kitchen staff, including a number of chefs. Food and beverage managers arrange and cater private parties on board. Butchers and bakers are present on all but the shortest cruises.

The increase in family cruising and educational cruises has created seasonal demand for daycare workers and teachers. Many other service jobs must also be filled; for example, launderer, hairstylist, shop assistant, bartender, athletic instructor, photographer, entertainer, lecturer, librarian. Any ship that carries more than 12 passengers is required to have a doctor on board. The larger ships will have more than one, as well as a staff of nurses.

Ashore

A cruise line's general office ashore is divided into several departments:

- Sales and marketing.
- Individual reservations.
- Group reservations and sales.
- Fly/cruise sales.
- Ticketing.
- Accounting.
- Management information.
- Data processing.
- Systems analysis.

A DAY IN THE LIFE OF A

Purser

I am a purser for a large cruise ship. My ship takes people on seven-day cruises of the Caribbean. It sails each Sunday from Miami and returns the following Saturday. I have many duties aboard ship, but my main job is to look after the passengers in much the same way that a hotel desk clerk helps hotel guests.

We are beginning a new cruise today so I will go to the airport and greet our cruise passengers. Our vans pick up the passengers and their belongings and drive them to the ship. On the ship, I will collect the passengers' return air tickets and lock the tickets in our office for safekeeping until the end of the cruise.

My fellow pursers and I will help the passengers find their cabins, check their valuables, and cash their traveller's cheques. On the first day, passengers always have lots of questions, and it is part of our job to answer them. Most people ask first about where and when they will be eating their meals and about where various shops and recreation facilities are located.

Including me, there are eight pursers on the cruise ship. Since we staff the purser's office 24 hours a day, we work different shifts. We also have different duties. I work mainly with the passengers. Other pursers are in charge of the financial aspects of operating a cruise ship. They collect and count the revenues from the ship's shops and services. These include our shore excursions, casino, diving expeditions, hair salon, restaurants, and bars.

My boss is the chief purser. He supervises all of the pursers and several of the other cruise personnel. The chief purser is personally responsible for all of the ship's revenues and the passengers' valuables. He must also make sure that the ship and its passengers obey all laws and regulations in foreign ports.

My boss always says that to be a good purser you have to like people—and I do. Cruise passengers are on vacation, and they expect to be pampered. One of my main tasks is to make sure they enjoy themselves as much as possible. I must also be able to get along with my fellow crew members. I have to share a cabin with another person, and I have to work closely with others for a week at a time.

A purser has to be able to react calmly and capably if there is a crisis. A passenger may become seriously ill or have to leave the ship suddenly because of a personal emergency. I am the one who arranges for an ambulance or emergency transportation in those instances. Pursers must also enjoy being problem solvers. If passengers have complaints, they often come to me first, and it is my job to try to resolve their problems.

My job as a purser was not an easy one to get, nor are other cruise ship jobs. Hundreds of people apply for each position. The best way to prepare yourself for a purser's job is to learn a foreign language and some office skills such as typing, accounting, and computer operations. Many cruise lines will not hire a purser who cannot speak at least one foreign language. Most pursers have business training or have already worked as travel counsellors or hotel desk clerks.

I started out as a reservations clerk at a resort hotel. Then I applied for jobs with small cruise lines that took people on lake and river cruises. My first shipboard job was as a cook on a Mississippi paddle boat. Then I just kept applying to all of the Caribbean cruise lines until I finally landed this job. If you want a job on a cruise ship, you have to be very persistent.

Most people think a job like mine is very glamorous. For the most part, it is. I get to live on a beautiful ship and travel around the Caribbean from November to April, when the weather is very cold in the north. On the other hand, I have to be away from my family for five months at a time, and I am often too busy to really enjoy the ports we visit. Still, the pay is good, and the work is very enjoyable. I will probably look for a job on land in another three or four years. Meanwhile, I plan to keep on cruising.

Entry-level positions ashore are mainly in reservations and telephone sales. The reservations and group sales departments of many cruise lines are almost identical to those at airline and tour companies. Cruise lines also have professional, regionally based sales forces. Sales reps target travel agencies, group and tour organizers, and other intermediaries. They do not sell directly to the public. From entry-level positions, employees can move to supervisory positions in the sales, groups, or fly/cruise departments, or to the marketing department.

Summary

- Scheduled passenger service by ship was introduced in the early nineteenth century.
- A major steamship line was founded by Sir Samuel Cunard of Halifax.
- Mechanical improvements paved the way for the first superliners at the beginning of the twentieth century.
- The first half of the twentieth century was the great age for ocean liners. The comfort of passengers became a vital consideration for shipping lines, which competed with one another by providing ever-more-luxurious accommodations.
- The advent of the jet age in 1958 signalled the decline of point-to-point passenger services.
- With the birth of the modern cruise industry in the early 1960s, the ship itself became the destination. Cruise lines, most of which are European-owned and -operated, began to offer a wider variety of cruises.
- A new generation of larger cruise vessels began entering service in the late 1990s.
- The availability of shorter cruises, special-interest cruises, fly/cruise packages, and land/cruise packages has broadened the industry's appeal, attracting younger passengers and more first-time clients.
- Large luxury liners serve the popular Caribbean, Mediterranean, and Mexican Riviera cruising areas. Other popular areas are Alaska, the Hawaiian Islands, the eastern United States and Atlantic provinces, and northern Europe. Smaller vessels cruise along inland waterways and to more exotic locations. Ferries provide point-to-point transportation over short distances.
- A cruise ship functions as a floating hotel, offering passengers a wealth of services, activities, and entertainment. Often there is a crew member for every two passengers.
- The price of a cruise is determined by voyage duration, season, cabin location and size, and type of ship.
- The most desirable accommodations are outside cabins located amidships, high above the water, where the view is at a maximum and the motion of the ship is at a minimum.
- The majority of cruises is booked by travel counsellors. This is changing: Online travel services and cruise line websites have made online booking possible.
- Federal governments regulate the cruise industry by setting health and safety requirements. International safety standards are set by the Safety of Life at Sea (SOLAS) Convention. Governments also promote cruising, as does the Cruise Lines International Association (CLIA).
- Environmental awareness is increasing in the cruise ship industry.

Key Terms

berth   p. 189
cruise/rail package   p. 185
embarkation   p. 178
flag of convenience   p. 177
fly/cruise package   p. 185
gross registered tonnage (GRT)   p. 189
inside cabin   p. 189
land/cruise package   p. 185
lighter   p. 187
liner   p. 175
magrodome   p. 189
megaships   p. 179
outside cabin   p. 189
passenger-to-crew ratio   p. 176
point-to-point service   p. 176
port tax   p. 188
repositioning cruise   p. 181
Safety of Life at Sea (SOLAS) Convention   p. 177
stabilizers   p. 177
steerage   p. 175
tender   p. 187

Internet Connections

Bay Ferries
www.nfl-bay.com   p. 184

Canada Place
www.canadaplace.ca   p. 175

Carnival Corporation
http://phx.corporate-ir.net/phoenix.zhtml?
c=140690&p= irol-index   p. 173

Carnival Cruise Lines
www.carnival.com   p. 176

Cruise Lines International Association (CLIA)
www.cruising.org   p. 177

Cunard Line
www.cunard.com   p. 173

Disney Cruise Line
http://disneycruise.disney.go.com/disneycruiseline/
index   p. 173

European Cruise Council (ECC)
www.europeancruisecouncil.com   p. 177

Halifax, Nova Scotia
www.region.halifax.ns.ca   p. 174

Holland America
www.hollandamerica.ca   p. 177

Marine Link Tours
www.marinelinktours.com   p. 182

North West CruiseShip Association
http://nwcruiseship.org   p. 192

Norwegian Cruise Line
www.ncl.com   p. 176

P&O Cruises
www.pocruises.com   p. 173

Pier 21
www.pier21.ns.ca   p. 174

Princess Cruises
www.princess.com   p. 180

Royal Caribbean Cruise Lines
www.royalcarib.com   p. 173

Safety of Life at Sea (SOLAS)
www.imo.org/Conventions/contents.asp?
topic_id=257&doc_id=647   p. 177

Sample Cruise Ship Menus
www.vacationstogo.com/cruise_dining.cfm   p. 186

Sample Shipboard Activities
www.quickticketfinder.com/
cruise-ship-activity.htm   p. 186

Seabourn Cruise Line
www.seabourn.com   p. 177

Transport Canada
www.tc.gc.ca   p. 179

WORKSHEET 8–1   Cruise Marketing

You are a travel counsellor specializing in cruises. Many people who have never experienced a modern cruise still have misconceptions about cruises. Explain how you would answer each of the following questions asked by potential cruise vacationers.

1. Isn't a cruise vacation expensive? _____

_____

2. Are there different classes of service on cruise ships? _____

_____

3. What's there to do on a cruise? I'd be bored sitting in a deck chair all day. _____

_____

4. Don't mostly older people take cruises? _____

_____

5. Would I need a tuxedo? Would my wife need an evening gown? _____

_____

6. What does "different sittings" for meals mean? _____

_____

7. What if I don't like the people I'm seated with for dinner? _____

_____

8. What do I do about tipping? _____

_____

9. I think I'd feel isolated out there in the middle of the ocean. Is there any communication with the rest of the world? _____

_____

10. I'm afraid of getting seasick. Isn't this a common problem? _____

_____

WORKSHEET 8–2 Website or Brochure Information

Visit the websites or obtain the brochures of two different cruise lines and compare them.

Cruise line   _____   _____

General Cruise Line Information   _____   _____

Number of ships in line   _____   _____

Registry   _____   _____

Geographic areas offered   _____   _____

Deposit and payment schedule   _____   _____

Cancellation policy   _____   _____

Special features   _____   _____

Activities   _____   _____

Amenities   _____   _____

Booking assistance   _____   _____

Deck plans   _____   _____

E-mail notification of specials   _____   _____

Gifts and video orders   _____   _____

Online booking   _____   _____

Prices   _____   _____

Request for brochures   _____   _____

Ship tracking   _____   _____

Streaming video   _____   _____

Other   _____   _____

Specific Cruise Information

Name and type of cruise   _____   _____

Destination and duration   _____   _____

Accommodation you would choose   _____   _____

Cost   _____   _____

Ports of call   _____   _____

Airfare tie-in (e.g., fly/cruise)   _____   _____

Special features (e.g., dining, lounges)   _____   _____

PART 4

Hospitality Services

Objectives

When you have completed this chapter, you should be able to:

- Describe the early history of hospitality and the business of innkeeping.
- Give reasons for the growth of the hotel industry after the nineteenth century.
- Explain what is meant by market segmentation in the accommodation sector.
- Classify accommodation options available to consumers with respect to price, location, configuration, and category.

- Describe the functional and organizational structure of an accommodation facility.
- Discuss the environmental/accessibility factors that influence accommodation products and services.
- Describe the impact of the Internet on distribution channels for branded and independent lodging properties.

Ever since the first lodging houses accommodated travellers in ancient lands, people have been making a living providing accommodation for travellers. Today, of course, lodging properties offer more than just a room for the night. Many provide meeting rooms, restaurants, bars, and other facilities to attract and serve a variety of guests. Some cater to a particular segment of the travel market, such as business travellers, convention delegates, or leisure tourists. Others offer basic, no-frills service to all guests.

According to the Hotel Association of Canada fact sheet, there were more than 440 000 rooms in more than 8300 hotels, motels, inns, and resorts in Canada in 2006. Lodging places range in size from inns with just a few rooms to huge hotels that can accommodate up to several thousand guests. With about 199 000 workers in 2006 (up from 172 300 in 1997), the accommodation sector accounts for 12 percent of all tourism-related jobs in Canada. That makes it one of the larger employers in the tourism industry.

ORIGINS OF THE ACCOMMODATION SECTOR

The term "hospitality" evolved from the old French word *hospice*, meaning to provide care and shelter for travellers (Walker, 2001).

Innkeepers

The first innkeeping laws were encoded in Babylon (now Iraq) in the eighteenth century B.C.E. in the Code of Hammurabi. During the Greek and Roman eras, religion played an important role in the development of hospitality: Many priests, pilgrims, and missionaries journeyed to temples and other holy places in the eastern Mediterranean. The demand for lodging places increased significantly after the Romans built an extensive highway system. Inns were segmented into *posting houses* and *inns*. The former were part of the government postal service and lodged Roman officials. The latter provided accommodation for the general public, and could be primitive or luxurious.

In the Middle Ages, hospitality was considered a Christian duty. Many monasteries and other religious institutions served as inns, offering free accommodation and food for pilgrims and other travellers. Innkeepers, first in Rome and then in Britain, began using trademarks such as vines or family coats of arms to publicize their establishments. This early form of "branding" helped wayfarers find houses devoted to providing safe lodging. Thus, the English inn emerged. By common law, innkeepers were duty bound to serve the public without discriminating (Skerry, 1972). In the fourteenth century, innkeepers throughout Italy belonged to a guild that allowed them to sell wine, and licensed inns were common. Many of those inns have been passed down from generation to generation up to today.

A Long History of Service

Fairmont Hotels & Resorts

Fairmont Hotels & Resorts emerged in October 1999, when the Toronto-based Canadian Pacific (CP) Hotels acquired the U.S. luxury Fairmont Hotels chain. Fairmont is now claiming to be "the largest luxury hotel management company in North America."

Canadian Pacific Hotels began in 1886 with the opening of the Mount Stephen House, high in the Canadian Rockies. CP Hotels then began opening its famous chateau-style hotels: Banff Springs (1888), Chateau Lake Louise (1890), and Le Château Frontenac (1893). Fairmont Hotels was established in 1907 with the opening of the Fairmont San Francisco.

In 1998, CP purchased both the Canadian National hotel chain (which included the famous Château Laurier hotel in Ottawa and the popular Jasper Park Lodge in Alberta) and the Delta hotel chain (which included the 1590-room Delta Chelsea hotel in Toronto—the largest hotel in Canada). CP continued its expansion by acquisition with the purchase of the Princess Hotel chain, which operated hotels in Bermuda, Barbados, and Mexico. In October 2007, Fairmont sold Delta Hotels to the British Columbia Investment Management Corporation ("bcIMC") (Delta Hotels, 2007).

Fairmont's Mission Statement

"Turning moments into memories for our guests."

Engaging Service

"Within a Fairmont experience, every guest is offered a warm welcome and is made to feel special, valued and appreciated."

Unrivalled Presence

"We transport our guests to extraordinary places steeped in unique architecture, expressive décor and magnificent artistry."

Authentically Local

"Fairmont's guests should experience an authentic reflection of each destination's energy, culture and history" (Fairmont, "Our Philosophy," n.d.).

Striving for excellence usually has its rewards. Fairmont has been the recipient of numerous prestigious industry awards, including the following:

- Worldwide Hospitality Award, 2006 (Best Corporate Social Responsibility Program)
- Canada's Top 100 Employers, 2008—as featured in *Maclean's* magazine
- Cause + Action Awards, 2007 (Top Eco Hospitality Program)— *Strategy Magazine*
- World Travel Awards, 2006 (World's Leading Hotel Brand Internet Site)
- Global Tourism Business Award, 2006—from World Travel & Tourism Council
- World's Best Business Hotels, 2007—Travel + Leisure
  Le Château Frontenac; Fairmont Olympic Hotel, Seattle; Vancouver Airport Hotel
- Four and Five Diamond CAA–AAA Awards, 2007
  Five Diamond Hotels: Scottsdale Princess, Fairmont Olympic Hotel, Seattle Five Diamond Restaurants: The Banffshire Club

ILLUSTRATION 9–1

Fairmont Hotels & Resorts is the largest luxury hotel company in North America. Three of its most famous hotels are the Fairmont Château Laurier in Ottawa, the Fairmont Royal York in Toronto, and the Fairmont Le Château Frontenac in Quebec City.

SOURCE: www.fairmontimagegallery.com.

at The Fairmont Banff Springs; the Newport Room at The Fairmont Southampton.
- Forbes Traveler 400 List, 2007 Chateau Whistler, Banff Springs, Chateau Lake Louise

In 1990, years before environmental issues became a popular concern, the Fairmont's Green Partnership Program addressed challenges in waste and water management, energy conservation, and purchasing. In Phase I, the focus was on recycling and reducing packaging; later, wet waste was targeted. A big goal was to reduce food waste and handle leftover food in the best way possible. Under the Green Partnership Program, Le Château Montebello in Quebec has a composting program and uses the resulting material as fertilizer, and the Royal York in Toronto channels leftover food to relief agencies.

Phase II has focused on diverting waste from landfills to composting. By 1999, employees could elect to participate in 150 different environmental initiatives. Fairmont's Community Outreach program is part of Phase II and includes the following initiatives:

1. Adopt-a-Shelter
2. Endangered species protection
3. Golf courses accredited by Audubon
4. Eco-Meet
5. Food redistribution

National Geographic Traveler magazine considers the Fairmont Hotels & Resorts Green Partnership Program to be the most comprehensive environmental program in the North American hotel industry.

According to *Hotelier* magazine, in 2006, Fairmont Hotels & Resorts had the second largest hotel revenue in Canada ($2.9 billion).

SOURCES: Lou Cook, "Profitability and Environmentalism Go Hand in Hand," *Lodging*, October 1999, pp. 67–70; Ann Layton, "Environmentally Responsible Hotel Practices," speech sponsored by the Sheraton Centre Toronto at the International Council on Hotel, Restaurant & Institutional Education Conference, July 2001; Allan Lynch, "Greening the Bottom Line," *Hotelier*, May–June 1999, p. 7; "Our Philosophy," and "Awards and Accolades," Fairmont Hotels & Resorts website (www.fairmont.com/philosophy, accessed February 2008).

Accommodations didn't improve much after this until the advent of long-distance stagecoach travel in the seventeenth century. English inns and taverns gained a reputation for cleanliness and comfort and set the standard for accommodations in other parts of Europe. The first inns in North America were established in seaport towns rather than along stagecoach routes. As the population moved inland, inns and taverns began to appear along rivers, canals, and post roads (roads used for carrying the mail).

Two early Ontario inns, Willard's Hotel (1795) and Cook's Tavern (1822), are preserved at Upper Canada Village in Morrisburg, Ontario. Food at New World inns was plentiful, but accommodations offered little privacy, and travellers shared beds when it was crowded.

The atmosphere in a typical North American inn of this period was much more informal than in a European lodging place. Meals were served family-style at a communal table, and guests from all walks of life mingled freely with one another. In Europe, in contrast, only the wealthy could afford to travel and stay at inns; once they had arrived, travellers tended to keep to themselves.

The more democratic spirit of North American inns was reflected in the special status conferred on innkeepers. In Europe, innkeepers were regarded as servants; in colonial North America, innkeeping was an honourable profession. An innkeeper could be entrusted with information, and his opinions were respected.

Hoteliers

The early nineteenth century was a time of transition for the accommodation sector in North America. The new trend was away from inns and taverns toward hotels, which were based on a French concept and considered more elegant. Thus, small roadside inns gradually gave way to larger, more elegant city hotels along rail lines and in port cities that offered a much broader range of amenities. With the invention of the elevator in 1853, hotels began to expand upward. A typical city hotel of the second half of the nineteenth century was five or six storeys high and had as many as 200 guest rooms. Public rooms, such as dining and reading rooms, were now a feature of most hotels. Both men and women were welcome at all hotels, but it was not appropriate for the sexes to mingle in public areas. Women were provided with separate entrances and sitting rooms, and they dined apart from the men.

The CPR became a major hotel owner. Its hotel system came into existence because Sir William Van Horne did not want to have trains hauling heavy dining cars up mountain grades. Consequently, meal stops were substituted at strategic locations in the western mountains. Van Horne felt it essential that the new terminal city of Vancouver, as an entry point from Asia, have a first-class hotel. The original Hotel Vancouver was opened in 1887 shortly before the CPR opened the Banff Springs Hotel in Rocky Mountain

Park (now Banff); these prestigious, one-of-a-kind hotels across Canada now operate under the Fairmont flag.

At the opposite extreme of the luxury city hotels were the smaller hotels built close to railway stations. These were inexpensive but often lacking in cleanliness, comfort, and service. Few commercial travellers at the beginning of the twentieth century could afford to stay in the luxury hotels, yet many found the smaller hotels near the stations unsatisfactory. The Great Depression of the 1930s had a devastating effect on all sectors of the tourism industry, including the hotel business. Because fewer people could afford to travel, demand for accommodations declined until after World War II.

Check Your Product Knowledge

1. What were significant happenings in the early history of innkeeping?
2. What effect has transportation had on the accommodation business?

THE MODERN ACCOMMODATION SECTOR

The hotel industry rebounded during and immediately after World War II as the volume of travel increased. It also changed drastically. The automobile and the jet plane had a profound effect on travel patterns and led to the development of different types of hotels. Motels, motor hotels, resort hotels, and convention hotels, as well as no-frills and all-suite hotels, evolved to cater to the varied needs of specific market segments. After 40 years, the American Hotel & Motel Association (AHMA) acknowledged the range of lodging options by changing its name to the American Hotel & Lodging Association (AHLA).

By the 1990s, through franchising and management contracts, hotel chains had established themselves as the dominant force in the industry, in North America and abroad.

Many alliances have emerged in recent years to strengthen the accommodation product offered in North America and overseas. For example, Canada's Delta Hotel chain merged with Canadian Pacific Hotels (but Delta Hotels was sold in 2007), which has a controlling interest in Fairmont Hotels & Resorts. CP now operates its chateau properties under the Fairmont flag as a means of gaining recognition internationally. Since many international guests recognize the "Fairmont" brand name but may not be familiar with the brand name "Canadian Pacific," the CP Hotels chain renamed all of its upscale hotels with the Fairmont brand name after the merger. A **brand** is a word or a device (design, sound, shape, or logo) that is used to distinguish one seller's goods from those of competitors.

Types of Lodging

Lodging properties can be classified in a number of ways: by size of the property, by price, by location, by the facilities offered, by the amenities, by physical layout, by the market(s) served, by the accommodation product provided, by affiliation, and by ownership.

Table 9–1 lists terms commonly used in the accommodation sector, along with their definitions.

Hotels

Hotels comprise the largest category of lodging and the category with the most subcategories. Some hotels fit more than one subcategory. Four of the ten classification criteria for hotels—price, location, physical layout, and markets—are discussed below.

1. Price There are luxury hotels, boutique hotels, upscale commercial hotels, midscale commercial hotels, and budget/economy hotels within the price tiers of hotels.

Luxury hotels vary in size, but all offer full services, extensive facilities, and amenities such as health clubs, gourmet restaurants, room and valet service, salons, limousine services, and concierge services. These hotels have two or three staff per guest. Guests may be travelling for business or pleasure, and may be paying as much as several thousand dollars per night. Luxury hotels are found at resorts and in major cities, and can be very large—400 rooms or more. Four Seasons Hotels & Resorts serves this market internationally. The Park Hyatt in Toronto, the Ottawa Westin, and the Hotel Omni in Montreal are some of the luxury hotels in Canada.

The typical *boutique hotel* has a unique design and caters to a limited target market. The rates are high but not as high as those of luxury hotels. Guests are attracted by the hotel's appeal and service. Most of these hotels have fewer than 150 rooms and are located in "trendy" urban areas. The Hotel Place d'Armes in Montreal is a 48-room nineteenth-century building in Old Montreal.

An *upscale commercial hotel* serves business travellers, convention guests, and tourists. These hotels are expensive, but the rates cover a variety of high-quality services. For example, they provide business facilities and support services, and often health clubs. These hotels tend to be located within easy reach of the city's downtown and financial district. They are also large—up to 2000 rooms. The Delta Chelsea (1590 rooms) and the Fairmont Royal York (1365 rooms), both in downtown Toronto, are examples of large Canadian hotels.

Midscale commercial hotels are moderately to expensively priced and provide accommodation for more price-sensitive guests. They target business travellers during the week and families and sports groups on weekends. They can be as large as upscale commercial hotels, but their amenities are more limited. The Fort Garry Hotel in Winnipeg, Manitoba, and the Lord Nelson Hotel in Halifax, Nova Scotia, are examples.

TABLE 9–1 Accommodation Terminology

Single	Room with one bed.
Twin	Room with two beds.
Double	Room with one double bed.
Double-double	Room with two double beds.
Suite	Room with one or more bedrooms and a living room.
Penthouse suite	Suite with access to the roof, maybe has a swimming pool, and with access to a tennis court.
Confirmed reservation	The hotel promises to hold a room up to a designated time.
Guaranteed reservation	The hotel promises to hold a room unless the guest cancels by a specified time, such as 4 p.m. or 6 p.m.
Weekly rate	Discount rate charged for a stay of a week or more.
Rack rate	Standard daily rate.
Weekend rate	Discount rate charged for weekend stay.
Run-of-the-house rate	Discount rate for block bookings, or group rate.
Corporate rate	Discount rate for members of organizations or employees of corporations; usually negotiated ahead of time based on anticipated volume of business.
Continental breakfast	Light breakfast usually including coffee, juice, and a roll or pastry.
Full breakfast	Cooked breakfast, often including eggs, bacon, and toast (often referred to as "American breakfast").
EP	European Plan: A rate that includes the room only and no meals.
CP	Continental Plan: A rate that includes continental breakfast.
BP	Breakfast Plan: A rate that includes full breakfast.
AP	American Plan: A rate that includes three full meals.
MAP	Modified American Plan: A rate that includes continental or full breakfast and dinner.
Family plan	Special family rate that allows children to share their parents' room at no additional charge.
Limited service	Basic lodging services, possibly without food and beverage.
Full service	More than lodging services, for example, food and beverage, business support services, and recreation facilities.
ADR	Average daily room rate.
Occupancy rate	Number of rooms sold as a percentage of the number of rooms available.
RevPAR	Revenue per available room: Calculated as ADR (average daily rate) multiplied by occupancy rate.

SOURCE: Canadian Travel Human Resources Council (www.cthrc.ca). Reprinted with permission.

Budget/economy properties are less expensive and are also smaller—50 to 150 rooms. They target short-stay automobile travellers. Special market niches include seniors and economy-minded corporate travellers. They are usually located in the suburbs, near major highways and one or more chain restaurants. If a budget property serves food, it will be only a complimentary continental buffet. These properties can charge lower prices because they offer fewer staff per guest and limited facilities and amenities, and because they are cheaper to design and build. In North America, a number of chains provide this level of service. Most of them are franchise operations. Independently owned properties tend to be older and usually are drive-up-to-unit motels.

Motel 6 was the first budget motel chain (1963). Today such chains are classified as economy/limited-service hotels/motels. Days Inn, with 1800 locations supported by its parent company, Cendant Corporation, is the world's largest franchisor of upper economy lodging. The Holiday Inn Express format was introduced by Holiday Inn as its answer to market demand for budget accommodation.

2. Location A hotel's location often suggests what kind of property it is. For example, airport hotels cater mainly to business travellers, whether the services provided are economy, midscale, or full service. Services at these hotels—restaurants, transportation, business support services, and the like—are coordinated with the airport's hours and operations. Prices vary with the level of service provided. These properties can be independents or they can be part of a chain. For example, in Vancouver, the Delta Airport Hotel is part of a chain; in Halifax, the Airport Hotel is an independent.

Motor hotel/motel properties tend to be located off highway interchanges, near attractions or shopping malls, or in suburban areas. Many are independently owned and market themselves through a **referral group** rather than through affiliation with a brand name. Before internationally recognized brand names came into vogue, Keddy, Wandlyn, and Rodd were well-known signs for independently owned motor inns along highways in the Maritimes.

Downtown hotels are, obviously, located downtown in urban settings, near attractions and the business district, in the city's heart. Guests tend to be business travellers and tourists. The hotels can be luxury or basic, and prices and services vary accordingly. In Toronto there are more than 20 such hotels, including the Sheraton Centre, Novotel, and the Hilton.

Suburban properties are located in city suburbs, sometimes in industrial parks. Most of them are moderately priced and offer limited services—perhaps food and beverage services, meeting rooms, and exercise facilities. They are geared to corporate travellers. Low weekend occupancy can be a problem.

Boatels are permanently docked floating hotels. They can be found where land is scarce or very expensive. Boatels offer alternative accommodation when destinations require lodging for a major event such as the Olympics. The same services are provided as in land facilities; rates are based on the level of service provided.

3. Physical Layout *Room configurations* in lodging properties are designed to provide guest units and public areas to meet a variety of consumer needs and demands. These configurations are affected by where the property is located; in turn, they affect the prices charged.

In *all-suite hotels*, each suite includes a living area, a separate sleeping area, a bathroom, and a food preparation area. Corporate travellers (weekdays) and families (weekends) began demanding these hotels in the 1980s and 1990s. Prices range from economy to luxury. Most guests stay three to six days. Halifax, Toronto, and Ottawa all have a Cambridge Suites Hotel.

Extended stay/residential accommodations serve long-term guests. Most business travellers stay 8 to 14 days. Besides a sleeping area and kitchen facilities, these properties provide living and dining facilities, on-site convenience stores, and common areas for socializing. They tend to be moderately priced. Minto Place Suite Hotel in Ottawa offers weekly and monthly as well as daily rates. The Pacific Palisades Hotel in Vancouver is developing a reputation for accommodating movie industry types for extended periods.

Bed-and-breakfasts (B&Bs) are small properties found in Europe and North America. In Newfoundland, they have been known as "hospitality homes." B&Bs are often located near attractions; some are attractions in their own right. They provide a home away from home and an opportunity to meet the locals. They are usually family-owned and -operated and have four or fewer bedrooms that have been converted or restored to serve mainly foreign and domestic leisure travellers. However, they are becoming an alternative for business travellers, especially in the off-season. The washroom facilities at a B&B may be communal, although recently opened properties have them in the guest rooms. A full hot breakfast, often with fresh baking, is usually the only meal served. In some provinces, the B&B operator is allowed to serve breakfast only. Rates vary with market trends; many B&Bs are upscale and are in heritage buildings. Guests typically meet gracious hosts and interesting fellow travellers.

Country inns are larger versions of B&Bs and are found in urban as well as country settings in many countries. Typically, they are family-owned properties with 5 to 25 rooms. The property might be a converted house, a restored heritage home, a renovated train station, a barn, or even a lighthouse. They appeal to guests looking for a unique lodging experience. The washrooms may be communal. Service is personalized. Guests can usually have breakfast and dinner, and sometimes a take-away lunch. There may be a licensed upscale restaurant on the premises.

An inn usually has a common area, such as a lounge, a parlour, or a library, where guests can meet other guests and participate in social events or presentations about the facility or local area. Inns can also fill the demand for accommodations for small corporate meetings. As with B&Bs, the rates vary with the services and amenities provided. An outstanding experience can be had at the prestigious Ripplecove Inn at Ayer's Cliff in Quebec's Eastern Townships, where guests are promised "discreet Anglo-Saxon charm blended with *Québécoise joie de vivre.*"

In Spain, a *parador* is a castle or other historic building that has been converted into a hotel by the government. In Portugal, they are called *posadas*. These cater mainly to vacationers, offer full meal plans, and are reasonably priced. More luxurious castle accommodations are available in France (châteaux) and in Germany and Austria (schloss).

Capsule hotels are very popular in Japan, especially in Tokyo. They have regular-sized rooms in which there are multiple capsules the size of twin beds, minibars, and common showers. A guest can either lie or sit down; each capsule has lighting and its own door. A hotel might have from under 100 to over 600 capsules. These hotels provide cheap, convenient lodging. Typically they are located near train stations and business areas.

In *youth hostels*, several unrelated guests are accommodated in the same room. Basic services such as clean sheets, towels, and showers are provided for a modest fee. Youth hostels serve mainly university-aged travellers. For a small fee, travellers can tap into the Hostelling International reservation system to book lodgings ahead. Senior citizens can tap into a similar network of elder hostels, which are growing in popularity and availability. The YMCA and YWCA often sponsor hostels in North American cities. In summer, many universities provide dormitory lodging for university alumni and others. Universities also provide lodging, facilities, and programs for seniors through the internationally established Elderhostel program.

Private clubs are usually city clubs with services and facilities for members. Other clubs such as military clubs and university alumni and yacht clubs sometimes offer accommodations for lodging and for meetings and special events. The services and facilities provided might include

ILLUSTRATION 9–2

Country inns and B&B accommodation, such as the mid-nineteenth-century Kiely House Inn and Restaurant in Niagara-on-the-Lake, offer unique surroundings and a change from modern hotels.

SOURCE: Courtesy of Kiely House.

guest rooms, dining and meeting rooms, and access to recreation and health facilities. Prices vary based on location, the organization, membership fees, and the levels of service and facilities provided. There are generally fewer than 100 rooms. Private clubs are not as common in Canada as elsewhere.

4. Market No single hotel type meets all consumers' needs. Hotel companies have responded to this by segmenting their responses to the market. In 2008, Choice Hotels International, Marriott International, and InterContinental Hotels Group PLC (formerly Bass Hotels and Resorts and Holiday Inn) had ten, nineteen, and seven brands, respectively. Each of these companies has a website that describes the brands it is currently offering to various market segments.

Convention Hotels and Conference Centres

The meeting business has expanded over the past 60 years. Whether the meeting is called a convention, conference, congress, forum, symposium, lecture, seminar, workshop, clinic, retreat, or trade show, and whether it is large or small, certain needs must always be met. One or more of the following must be provided: meeting rooms, registration areas, food and beverage services, communication and audio-visual services, entertainment, security, lodging, travel services, and transportation. Meetings are now big business. Some lodging properties specialize in providing the required services and facilities.

Convention hotels are sometimes part of a convention complex. Alternatively, they are near a convention centre

in an urban area (or near a resort) where extensive recreation and entertainment are provided as well as the services that conventions require. Convention hotels have enough rooms (as many as 2000, or even more) to accommodate large groups of people. They have a full range of facilities and services: a variety of restaurants and banquet facilities, various sizes of meeting rooms, a business centre, audio-visual and communication services, full-service rooms, and health and fitness facilities. Toronto's InterContinental Hotel is attached to the Toronto Convention Centre and is adjacent to the CN Tower and the Rogers Centre (formerly SkyDome). Conventions, trade shows, and the like generate business for convention facilities, hotels, auditoriums, and exhibition halls. Political, civic, fraternal, religious, and social organizations all use them to hold large gatherings on a regular basis (please refer to Chapter 11).

Conference centres serve the group travel market. They can be located in a city or at a resort. Some of these centres are purpose-built and focus entirely on the meeting market; some resorts target the meetings market in the off-season (e.g., Mont Tremblant Ski Resort in the summer). Lodging may or may not be provided. If it is, there may be between 100 and 1000 guest rooms; prices can be moderate to expensive. Prices are usually flexible because of the location and the volume of business. Some conference centres concentrate on selling to groups; this cuts down on unsold meeting space and lodging. The International Association of Conference Centers (IACC) North America has established universal criteria for conference centres, and promotes awareness of the unique features of conference centres around the world. Visit the IACC website for more information (www.iacconline.org).

In recent years, universities have begun providing lodgings and meeting spaces for conferences. They can offer residences that are vacant after academic semesters, as well as other university facilities. The Banff Conference Centre is one of the largest and best-known full-time conference centres in Canada. ARAMARK Harrison Lodging (formerly Harrison Conference Centres), a conference centre management company established in 1967, manages conference centres throughout the United States and in select global markets.

Lodging and Entertainment

Lodging and entertainment have been associated with each other for a long time. In the twentieth century, advances in transportation, technology, and economic development allowed more travellers to experience gaming, ski resorts, theme parks, resorts, leisure cruising, and other forms of recreation and entertainment at destinations around the globe.

For many years, *casino hotels* were permitted only in Nevada (1931) and New Jersey (1978). According to the Las Vegas Convention & Visitors Authority website, there

ILLUSTRATION 9–3

The Coach House is part of the Manoir Hovey, an historic inn located in North Hatley, Quebec. The Inn, member of the prestigious Relais & Chateaux collection, has been awarded five stars for accommodation (1987 to 2008) and four diamonds for restaurants (1990 to 2008), among numerous other prestigious awards.

SOURCE: Image courtesy of Manoir Hovey.

are over 300 hotels with 136 000 hotel rooms and some 9.7 million square metres of meeting and exhibit space in Las Vegas, with more under construction.

In Canada, the first hotel casino was the Crystal Casino in Winnipeg's Fort Garry Hotel. It has since been removed, and the hotel has reclaimed its heritage. In 1995, the ITT Sheraton in Halifax added a casino to its hotel; in 2000, the gaming operation was transferred to a stand-alone casino next door (the Casino Nova Scotia) on the Halifax waterfront; the casino was bought by Great Canadian Casinos of B.C. in 2005. Interest in casinos and casino hotels has grown across Canada, as governments began to realize the economic benefits (which admittedly had social costs). Destinations have found it a challenge to balance the demand for gaming with the supply. According to casinocity.com, Canada has 129 casinos, at least one in each province and one in the Yukon. Canada doesn't have any destinations with the pull of Atlantic City or Las Vegas. In many communities, the citizens don't want gaming. Some people refuse to book a room or attend an event at a hotel connected with a casino.

Casino hotels are usually full-service hotels with upscale amenities, attractions, and services. Food and beverage prices and room rates are kept reasonably low to encourage patrons to spend money in the gaming facilities.

Destination resorts are a fairly recent response to mass tourism. Besides lodging, they provide full amenities, programs for adults and children, and a variety of food and beverage options. They are usually four- or five-star hotels in exotic places and/or near major attractions or sports facilities. Typically offered are swimming, boating, golfing, and/or skiing.

All-inclusive resorts have become very popular with a package including accommodations, meals (usually buffet style), soft drinks, tips/gratuities, recreational activities, entertainment, domestic (locally produced) alcoholic drinks, nonmotorized water sports. Some packages also include airfare and hotel transfers. This concept provides a 35 to 40 percent profit margin (compared with 25 percent for resort hotels) (Valhouli, 2003).

The originator (and now the largest supplier) of this concept is the French operator, Club Med, which operates over 100 resorts in 44 countries. Other operators include Sandals, Superclubs, and Couples. Some resorts are restricted for couples only, others cater to families. Certain countries have specialized in this concept: Jamaica, Cuba, Dominican Republic, and Mexico, among others.

These packages are popular because they offer a good value for money and provide a "no hassle vacation" (guests prepay for everything so they know in advance how much the total vacation will cost). This concept has created some controversy since guests do not have to leave the property and therefore they may not "experience" the local culture and do not frequent the local restaurants or retail shopping areas, so some say there is little or no cash benefit to the local economy.

Families and affluent vacationers usually purchase packages for specific resorts that cover airfare, transportation, activities, and lodging. The resorts may also serve as convention or conference facilities and attract the meeting and incentive travel market. Resort hotel construction has boomed in tropical areas as well as across Canada. At the opposite end of the scale from Intrawest's four-season pedestrian village developments at Blue Mountain (Collingwood, Ontario), Whistler (British Columbia), and Mont Tremblant Ski Resort (Quebec) are smaller resorts such as Grandview Lodge in Muskoka, just 90 minutes from Toronto, and the Aerie Resort on Vancouver Island, with its Mediterranean-style mansion.

Megaresorts are a recent trend, and casino hotels try to widen their market by attracting family vacationers as well as gamblers. The Mirage casino hotel in Las Vegas became the first of this new generation of resorts when it opened its 3000-room fantasy world in 1989. In response to the Mirage's success and consumers' apparent willingness to spend money on fun, the Luxor (now 4408 rooms), Treasure Island (2885 rooms), and MGM Grand (5044 rooms) were built. Outstanding architecture and entertainment and the fantasy ambience draw people to megaresorts. At the Mirage, guests can watch sharks swimming in a tank behind the front desk; at the MGM Grand they can see replicas of famous structures from around the world. The Las Vegas resorts are providing a megatravel experience for people who don't want to gamble, or who want to do more than gamble.

Of the top 25 largest megaresorts, 22 are located in the United States (19 in Las Vegas); the international megaresorts are located in Malaysia, Thailand, and Macau. Since

2006, the largest hotel in the world has been the 6118-room First World Hotel in Genting Highlands, Malaysia. As part of a $27 billion resort project, Dubai is building the 6500-room Asia hotel which, when open, will become the largest hotel in the world.

Urban resorts are an alternative to remote destination resorts and often attract guests from within the region or even the same city. They offer facilities and services similar to those of destination resorts, and do so inside full-service commercial or luxury hotels. Typically, these properties offer spa facilities, fitness facilities, tennis courts, and golf courses. Service levels dictate prices. An example of an urban resort is the Park Plaza and Ramada Plaza, Vancouver Airport Conference Resort. Set on beautifully landscaped grounds, it offers swimming, squash, tennis, a health club, restaurants, and lounges, 20 minutes from the downtown core and 5 minutes from Vancouver International Airport.

Time-share resorts and hotels allow people to invest in future vacations by buying shares in properties at resort destinations or in urban settings. This allows them to spend a designated amount of time annually for a decade, or forever, at their choice of destination. The segment of time purchased is worth points to be redeemed at a later date; the average share cost is around $10 000. If it is a condo-type arrangement, there are also annual condo fees. Often the points allow people to swap with other time-share owners around the world. Many time-share properties are condo-type facilities with resort amenities. This means the owner has full ownership of a unit in a complex for the amount of time purchased. Recently, hotels chains with resort amenities have begun selling time-share rights for a portion of their properties; people holding time-shares can choose when and where in the chain they would like to spend their vacation time.

Fractional ownership, which originated in 1994, is fractional ownership of a vacation home where an individual can purchase a fraction share (1/4, 1/8, 1/13) of a luxury condo or waterfront home (with resort style amenities) from a major luxury hotel operator such as Ritz Carlton, Four Seasons, Disney, or Marriott. Like a timeshare, this share purchase "can be bought as a deeded property . . . and can be rented out, shared with family and friends, sold or left to someone in a will." Purchase costs vary, but could start at US $100 000 with thousands in maintenance fees (Curry, 2003).

Theme parks are about show business and technology. By the 1990s, theme parks and complexes were being developed around the world based on the success of Disney. (For further information on Disney, please refer to Chapter 4.)

The SkyDome Hotel (now the Renaissance Toronto Downtown Hotel), opened in 1989, was the first hotel to be integrated with a major sports and entertainment complex. In Virginia, a theme park has been built adjacent to historic Williamsburg. Following this trend, many hotels connected with theme parks have developed facilities around themes. One outstanding example is the Palace of the Lost City resort, built in the Republic of Botswana in 1992. It was developed around an actual palace ruin destroyed by an earthquake. The myth of a lost city has been created amid the natural vegetation and wildlife of Africa (Lane and Dupre, 1997).

Spa facilities have existed since Roman times and were highly popular among Europe's leisure classes for centuries. Day and destination spas are now developing rapidly in North America. Modern spas—not unlike Roman spas—offer mud baths, massage, fitness programs, and attention to healthy eating. They are now available throughout the accommodation sector. Spas are found inside resorts and at hot springs and along seacoasts and are located in both urban and country settings; often golf, tennis and hiking are available in country venues. Spas offer a variety of services and treatments to enhance guest's health. They are no longer seen as a hedonistic indulgence; especially in some European countries, many doctors prescribe them. This should be good news for spa hotels and resorts such as the Prince of Wales in Niagara-on-the-Lake, Ontario; Temple Gardens Mineral Spa and Resort Hotel in Moose Jaw, Saskatchewan; and the Ancient Cedars Spa at the Wickaninnish Inn on Vancouver Island (which also markets itself as *the* place to observe ocean storms). Spa Canada's resort spas, hot springs, day spas, and spa suppliers are working together to make Canada a world-class spa destination (Watts, 2000).

Cruise ships have become more accessible to more people in recent years. The cruise industry grew dramatically in the 1990s and the 2000s. (For further information on cruises, including riverboats, ferries, etc., please refer to Chapter 8.)

Parks and Recreation Lodging

Since national, provincial, and state parks were established in North America years ago, people have been exploring them. A variety of facilities have been developed for campers, from simple clearings to full-service sites with water and shower services and interpretive programs. Campers can often reserve sites, and are charged fees related to the length of the stay and the services used. Campsites in Canada's national parks (which are found in every region) are monitored by Parks Canada personnel to ensure that campers can experience a clean and safe environment. Hut-to-hut hiking is available along the Appalachian Trail, which stretches from Canada to the state of Georgia; also, in the European Alps, there are many huts for hikers.

Campgrounds and recreational vehicle/mobile home parks tend to be located near natural or human-built attractions. Tourists have access to electricity, sewer hookups, sites to park RVs and tent trailers or pitch tents, communal showers and restrooms, laundromats, and convenience

ILLUSTRATION 9–4

The Scandinave Spa offers health and wellness at three locations: Blue Mountain (Collingwood, Ontario), Mont Tremblant (Quebec), and Whistler (B.C.). The services include Scandinavian baths, massage, yoga, sauna, and nordic spa.

SOURCE: Courtesy of Le Scandinave.

stores. Often there are also gift shops and recreational facilities for swimming, fishing, hayrides, campfires, minigolf, and so on. Franchise campgrounds like Kampgrounds of America (KOA) and tourism industry systems like Check In, Nova Scotia, provide reservation systems for travellers. Entrance fees may be charged per vehicle or per person; there is a pay-as-you-use system for optional services.

This lodging option appeals to cost-conscious tourists, nature lovers, and RV renters or owners, who, like the turtle, want to bring their lodging facilities with them. Some KOA franchisees, like the KOA in Niagara Falls, offer Kamping Kabins for tourists who don't want to bring tents or RVs. Beds and picnic tables are provided, and guests bring the rest. Beaverfoot Lodge in Golden, British Columbia, offers a covered wagon for campers to spread out their sleeping bags; you can sleep in a teepee on Slocan Lake, British Columbia, if you check into Valhalla Lodge and Tipi Retreat.

Basic cabins at resort sites are common in Europe. Wholesalers like Contiki Tours, who target the under-35 market, often use cabins for lodging group tours at their various overnight stops in Europe.

Ranches include dude, guest, working cattle, hunting, cross-country skiing, and fly fishing ranches. Usually family-owned and -operated, ranches offer simple to luxurious accommodation for vacationers who want an outdoor experience. Demand is increasing from city folk who want to get back to basics. During their stay, vacationers can involve themselves in the ranch's day-to-day operations; at luxury ranches the activities may be more recreational. Bunkhouses, with communal washroom facilities, are often provided as lodging. People tend to stay more than a few days. At dude ranches they ride horses, learn roping and branding, and enjoy the occasional cookout on a trail or at the ranch headquarters. Many working ranches offer "bed and work" options.

Check Your Product Knowledge

1. What criteria are used to classify facilities in the accommodation sector?
2. What are the newest types of lodging? Why have they evolved?

ILLUSTRATION 9–5

The Drake Hotel in Toronto is part of the wave of small boutique hotels that have become popular in upscale cities.

SOURCE: Image courtesy of Drake Hotel, copyright STIPCO photography.

ACCOMMODATION OWNERSHIP

Until the twentieth century, almost all hotels were individually owned and operated. With the development of hotel and motel chains, a number of new forms of ownership evolved, such as leases, joint ventures, partnerships, franchises, and management contracts. In the 1990s, a new form of ownership for the accommodation sector, the real estate investment trust (REIT), emerged.

Individual Ownership

About 50 percent of all lodging properties in Canada and the United States operate as individual proprietorships. Most of these—the family-owned establishments with fewer than 100 rooms—still make up the backbone of the accommodation sector. They include B&Bs, mom-and-pop motels, small hotels, and country inns.

The chief benefits of individual ownership are that the owner enjoys complete control of policies and operating procedures and can keep all profits from the property. An obvious disadvantage is that the owner also assumes full risk for the property. Also, the owner does not have access to national advertising or reservations systems and may find it difficult to acquire capital for expansion or renovations. To compete with chain and franchise properties, many individually owned properties affiliate with associations such as the American Automobile Association (AAA) and the Canadian Automobile Association (CAA), or with rating systems like Canada Select. They can also have themselves listed in their province's travel guide.

An independent property can also join a referral system such as the one operated by Best Western. Sometimes known as consortia, affiliations, or voluntary chains, referral groups involve a number of independent properties joining together after meeting a specific set of criteria. In return for a service fee—generally less than the fee to join a chain—the property receives brand recognition, access to a worldwide toll-free reservation number, global advertising, discounts on credit card fees, and purchasing advantages. To keep its membership, it must maintain the property at a standard set by the referral company.

Chain Ownership

A chain is two or more operations under the same name. When one parent company owns several properties, it is a corporate-owned chain. Canadian Pacific Hotels (now under the Fairmont Hotels & Resorts management company) and Four Seasons (predominately a management company) are examples of chains that originated in Canada and are now in the luxury segment internationally.

Management decisions for all of the properties in a chain flow from corporate headquarters, where decisions relating to changes in management, services, programs, training, and decor are centralized. For example, Marriott Hotels & Resorts, Courtyard, Residence Inn, Fairfield Inn, Ritz Carlton, and several other Marriott brands, all under Marriott International Inc., are headquartered in Washington, D.C. The following chains are headquartered in other parts of the world: Club Méditerranée (France) and Prince Hotels (Japan). Smaller regional chains have been established across Canada over the years; however, in recent years many have begun to fly internationally recognized brand flags.

Franchises

When a parent company gives an individual, or franchisee, the right to open a property in return for a set of fees laid out in a franchise agreement, the operation is a **franchise**.

Under a franchise system, the hotel owner contracts with an established chain to operate the property under

ILLUSTRATION 9–6

As of 2008, the MGM Grand in Las Vegas is the largest hotel in the Americas with over 5000 hotel rooms (the First World Resort in the Genting Highlands, Malaysia, is currently the largest hotel in the world with 6118 rooms).

SOURCE: Image courtesy of MGM Mirage.

the chain's name. The owner of the hotel, or franchisee, pays an initial development fee (a fixed amount of several thousand dollars, or an amount per room, whichever is greater), as well as a monthly franchise fee of between 2 and 6.5 percent of gross room sales (see Table 9–2). In addition, the franchisee agrees to abide by the management policies of the chain. In return, the chain (franchisor) provides assistance in staff selection and training, and in marketing, sales, and advertising. It also provides access to a central computer reservations system. Perhaps most importantly, the franchisor provides a recognizable image, the familiarity of the chain's name, and—usually—the advantages of a successful business.

Franchising, which developed during the 1950s and early 1960s, is the most common hotel operating format after individual ownership. It provides a way to expand without substantial capital investment. Kemmons Wilson of Holiday Inn was an early pioneer of franchising. He realized that his chain would never grow fast enough if it relied on direct ownership. Franchising was the most viable alternative, and within five years the company went from owning four motels to operating 100 franchises. Franchises you will recognize include Days Inn, Hampton Inn/Hilton Hotels, and Ramada Inn.

There are, however, disadvantages to franchising:

- Initial and ongoing fees must be paid.
- The franchise can suffer if the other franchisees don't meet customer expectations.
- The franchisee lacks flexibility, since policies and procedures are set at head office.
- The franchisor can buy back or cancel the agreement if the franchisee does not follow it.
- The franchisor might not provide the management assistance that the franchisee needs, or might allow other properties to operate in too small a market area.

Franchise advisory councils (FACs) have been created to foster better working relations between franchisors and franchisees. FACs provide a forum for franchisees to address issues and to solve problems with the interpretation of franchisee agreements. In this way they improve working relationships.

Management Companies

With a **management contract** agreement, there are two parties involved: the owner and the operator (possibly a chain). The operator enters into a management contract with the owner and receives a management fee based on gross revenue for operating the property. Sometimes the management company owns a percentage of the property. The owner enjoys all the benefits of having a professional management team and doesn't have to become involved in the daily operation of the property.

Through management contracts, individual properties and chains can access financing more readily. A management company may operate as a silent partner, or it may operate openly under a brand name with all the advantages that entails: access to a reservations system, well-honed operating standards, and proven marketing expertise.

A management company may manage one or more brands. Red Roof Inns has only one brand. In contrast, Fairmont Hotels & Resorts manages Princess and Fairmont as well as CP properties under the Fairmont brand. The management company provides expertise the owner may not have.

The management contract was developed in the 1950s as a means for American-based chains to expand overseas. It enabled them to open hotels in countries where laws or political conditions impeded foreign ownership. Overseas

TABLE 9–2 Franchise Report, 2008 (Selected franchises and fees in CDN$)

Franchisor	Number of Properties in Canada	Initial Fee	Advertising/ Marketing Fee	Reservation Fee	Royalty Fees	Other Fees
Best Western	179	US$48 000 per 100 units	$4150 per Month	$4490 per year	$39 238 Membership fee	$720 per month QA $4121. annual dues
Comfort Inn	141	$40 000 minimum	1.30%	1.75%	5.00%	—
Days Inn	85	$350 per room Minimum $35 000	n/a	2.30%	6.5%	—
Econo Lodge	45	$25 000 minimum	1.30%	1.75%	4.00%	—
Holiday Inn Hotels/Resorts	63	Minimum US$50 000 $500 per room	2.5%	n/a	5.0%	—
Holiday Inn Express	45	Minimum US$50 000 $500 per room	3.0%	n/a	6.0%	—
Howard Johnson	40	$350 per room Minimum $35 000	2.00%		4.00%	$700–$5000 per room Equip. & Site Costs $15 000 to $25 000 2.5% Distribution fee
Quality Inn & Suites, Hotels & Resorts	64	$35 000 minimum	1.30%	1.75%	4.00%	—
Ramada Franchise Systems	70	Minimum $36000 +1400 per room App. fee	4.50%	—	4.00%	$80 000 per room Equip. fee
Super 8 Motels	125	US $21 000	3.00%	n/a	5.00%	—
Travelodge Hotels	90	$35 000	4.25%	n/a	4.25%	—

SOURCE: *Hotelier* (January–February 2004), pp. 21–30. Reprinted by permission of Kostuch Publications.

hotel developers who wanted the managing and marketing expertise of American chains began to invest in properties and to contract American hotel companies to operate them.

Real Estate Investment Trusts (REITs)

In the 1990s, 15 real estate investment trusts (REITs) emerged in the United States. By 1997, the Canadian version of the REIT had evolved as a means of raising capital. REITs are public companies traded on a stock exchange. In 1997, REITs increased their investment in Canadian hotels from 30 to 74 percent ("Looking Back," 1999). Anyone could buy shares in a hotel REIT that buys hotel properties worldwide and participate in the growing tourism industry. REITs provide dividends for investors from the profits made on pools of hotel assets.

InnVest REIT InnVest Real Estate Investment Trust currently holds Canada's largest hotel portfolio. It has a 50 percent interest in Choice Hotels Canada (Quality Inn, Comfort Inn, Travelodge) and a total of 150 hotels and

19 606 rooms throughout the country. The primary objectives of InnVest REIT (and other REITS):

1. To provide stable and growing cash distributions to Unitholders.
2. To maximize long-term value of assets by investing in, and managing the hotel assets.
3. To pursue selective acquisitions expected to be accretive to earnings and cash flow. (InnVest, n.d.)

Check Your Product Knowledge

1. What percentage of hotels in Canada and the United States are individually owned? What are the chief benefits of individual ownership?
2. What is the difference between a franchise and a management contract?

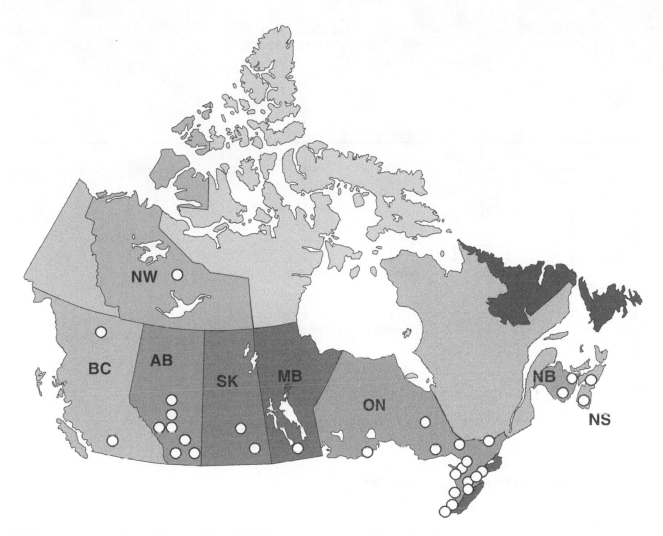

FIGURE 9–1 Location of Royal Host REIT Properties as of June 2008
SOURCE: CHIP REIT, www.chipreit.com.

ACCOMMODATION MANAGEMENT

Whatever type of lodging a guest visits, there will be a **front of the house** and a **back of the house**. The front-of-the-house staff members are the ones that have actual contact with guests: the front desk, waitstaff and bartenders, entertainers, tennis pros, and so on. The back-of-the-house staff are the ones that guests may sometimes see but usually don't need to see: housekeepers; engineers; maintenance workers; and sales, marketing, reservations, and accounting personnel. How a property's functional departments are organized depends on the size of the building and the amenities offered. Figures 9–2 and 9–3 show two organizational charts: one for a country inn, one for a downtown hotel.

Some departments, such as the front office, restaurants, recreation facilities, and parking, are referred to as *revenue centres* because they generate revenue for the property. Others, such as marketing, accounting, maintenance, and

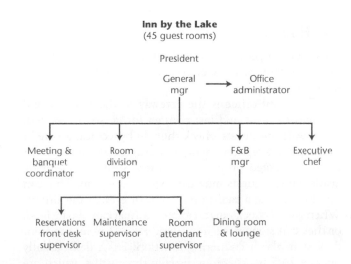

FIGURE 9–2 Country Inn Organization Chart

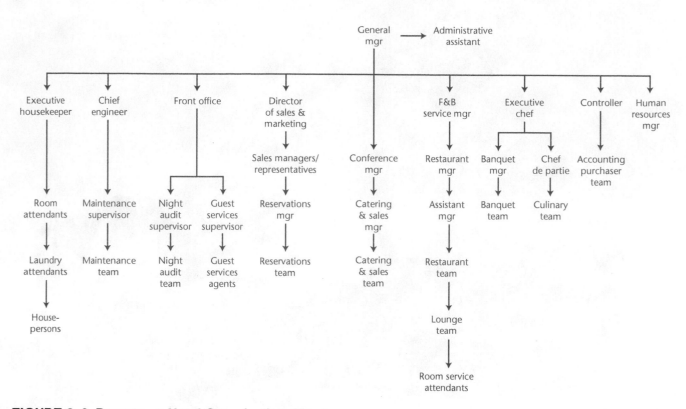

FIGURE 9–3 Downtown Hotel Organization Chart

engineering, which incur expenses, are known as **cost centres**. The goal of every lodging operation is to generate revenue and control costs while maintaining the physical assets and ensuring guest satisfaction. The key functional departments of an accommodation property are discussed in the following sections.

The Rooms Division

This division generally includes the front office, reservations, communication services, uniform/guest services, and housekeeping.

The front office is the gateway to the property and provides the first and last contact for guests. Front desk clerks welcome guests, check them in by recording a credit card number, register them, and assign them a room. At more automated properties, or those wishing to provide faster service, guests may use express check-in. This can involve swiping a card in the lobby or even at the airport. When guests check out, an express format can also be used, or they can stop at the front desk. At that point the front desk staff play a cashiering function. Front desks usually operate 24/7, so there are usually three shifts, which are supervised by a day manager and a night manager.

The **reservations** office often operates at the back of the house, but also has an important front-of-the-house function, since reservations work involves public relations and sales duties. Years ago, there were no reservations systems; guests simply arrived at a lodging place and hoped a room was available. Motels still rely on "walk-ins" for much of their business, but most rooms at other properties are now booked in advance. Travellers can make reservations themselves or through agencies. Most hotels see travel counsellors/agents as important extensions of their sales forces.

The reservations process has become more automated in the past few decades. Almost all chains now have a computerized reservation system (CRS) linking their properties worldwide. Early in 2001, Bass Hotels and Resorts (now part of the InterContinental Hotels Group) launched the world's most comprehensive (at the time) wireless service for locating hotels and reserving rooms. Guests wanting to contact the Holiday Inn, Holiday Inn Express, InterContinental, Crowne Plaza, and Staybridge Suites operations, for example, can obtain information any time of day or night from wireless devices through Air2Web, a mobile Internet platform. Maintaining its reputation as a leader in initiating reservation systems, this

ILLUSTRATION 9–7

Some hotel chains are experimenting with self-service check-in kiosks, located in the lobbies of several of their hotels, such as the Fairmont Vancouver Airport Hotel.

SOURCE: Image courtesy of Fairmont Hotels and Resorts.

company was the first to allow real-time reservation bookings online. Its e-commerce team works constantly to build alliances with travel sites such as Travelocity, the Last Minute Club, and Priceline.

Hotel reservations can also be made through airline global distribution systems (GDSs). Airlines that own hotels obviously try to promote their own properties. Even so, many of the large hotel chains also subscribe to the airline GDSs, which are especially convenient for clients making airline and hotel bookings at the same time. Another alternative is to book accommodations through a hotel representative company. A number of chains have appointed a single company to handle reservations for all properties in the chain. Yet another method is to make reservations by direct contact (i.e., by the World Wide Web, letter, telephone, fax, e-mail, telex, or cable). At many small, individually owned properties that are not linked to a reservations system, or that do not have a hotel representative, direct contact may be the only way to book a room. This is especially true for overseas properties. Reservations can also be made through a tour operator or wholesaler if the hotel accommodation is bought as part of a tour package. Whichever system is used, guests with **guaranteed reservations** expect to have a room when they arrive. Managing reservations so that supply equals demand is a challenge faced by most properties, and is central to yield management.

Communications have advanced to the point that accommodation properties require specialists to manage them. Properties may provide telecommunications, teleconferencing, videoconferencing, fax machines, voice mail, modem connections, and websites. Such systems may or may not be a source of revenue. Some properties have

established "electronic concierge" programs; others provide extensive business centres or Internet suites on executive floors as well as guest room hookups. In the early days, the installation and servicing of communication systems was completely outsourced. Today, the same amenities and services are being managed in-house, with technical assistance contracted out. Even smaller properties are expanding their communication services. Worth noting is that cellphones have cut deeply into the revenues that used to be generated from in-room calls. Information technology, in the form of "intelligent buildings," has become a vital amenity for guests. Property management systems (PMSs) enable departments to communicate better with guests and interdepartmentally. The outline of one PMS is presented in Figure 9–4.

Guest and uniformed services include the services provided by the concierge, bellstaff, lobby porters, valets, and doorstaff. People in these positions have direct contact with guests; besides performing their specific tasks, they act as salespeople and answer questions. Uniformed services are usually found at more expensive hotels and resorts.

The housekeeping department cleans guest rooms, public areas, and behind-the-scenes areas. It also coordinates laundry services and distributes linens, ironing boards, and the coffee services that are provided in most rooms. Usually, a head or executive housekeeper supervises all the room attendants, floor supervisors, and housekeepers, as well as the laundry attendants if the laundry isn't outsourced (sent off property).

This department requires pleasant, well-trained individuals who can work efficiently and independently. They must be able to interact one-on-one with the guests while respecting their privacy. Usually room attendants are

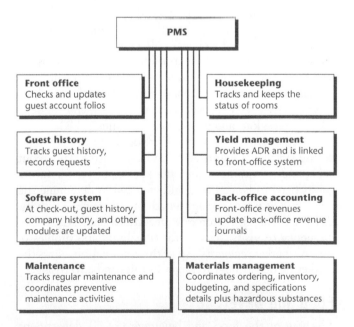

FIGURE 9–4 Example of a Property Management System

assigned a quota of rooms (often 12 to 14) to make up per shift. The workload is driven by the status of the rooms—that is, if the guests have checked out, the room is ready to be thoroughly cleaned and remade, while the room of a **stay-over guest** usually receives just bed-making and a quick clean. Separate crews clean public areas (e.g., lobby) during low-traffic times, often late at night or early morning.

Sales and Marketing

The sales and marketing department carries out four functions: sales, advertising, public relations, and market analysis. When there is more than one property, the functions are coordinated by a regional or national corporate sales office. That office may outsource some of these functions to outside firms, often called "representation companies." To learn more about these companies, visit the website of the RMR Group Inc. (www.thermrgroup.ca).

Most marketing departments have a sales force. Members of the sales team are assigned specific **target markets** (e.g., the corporate, international, association, or group market). Sales staff must understand the customer base in order to identify markets and bid effectively for their business. Remember that every employee of the property company, from manager to housekeeper, is a salesperson. All of them sell the company through their words and actions any time they are in contact with guests.

Advertising is often used to market a property or chain. Advertising can be through the mass media (television, newspaper, billboards, radio, the Internet, etc.) or through direct mail. It is essential to know which features of the accommodations package will attract specific market segments so that the advertising can be targeted. Advertising is controlled and paid for by the advertiser.

Public relations (PR) is about the generation of goodwill. Some PR is managed by the marketing department, some of it happens by chance. PR efforts are not paid for directly, and they are not necessarily controlled by the organization. Travel writers, editors, other outside media personnel, as well as sales and marketing personnel, contribute to a property's public image. Companies often send out news releases, press kits, and promotions (all forms of PR).

Market analysis is key to developing a sales and marketing strategy. Quantitative and qualitative data about occupancy, customers, and market segments for future guests need to be gathered and analyzed to determine the following: demand, average length of stay, price sensitivity, services required, customer expectations and satisfaction, frequency of visits, reasons for travelling, and profiles of specific market segments. All of this information allows the marketing department to target its sales and advertising.

Food and Beverage

The size of the food and beverage (F&B) department varies with the size and type of accommodation property. Budget hotels often operate only a breakfast bar, and that may be catered by the neighbourhood doughnut shop. Larger departments may manage food production and service in one or more food outlets; beverage outlets, from cocktail lounges to pubs; room service; the staff cafeteria; and in-house or satellite catering. A food service department typically has the following functions: planning menus for specific services, from restaurants to catered banquets; determining ingredients; purchasing, receiving, and storing food-related items; preparing and serving food products; and cleaning up. The food and beverage department has both front-of-the-house (serving areas) and back-of-the-house (kitchen) components.

The F&B department is labour-intensive; at some properties, more than half the staff members are involved directly in food preparation and service. Some services are available 24/7. Making a profit on F&B can be a challenge.

Recently, more hotels have been designing their food service outlets to compete with freestanding establishments. F&B services in hotels are now being marketed as destinations in themselves—as "eatertainment" or as "ethnic extravaganzas." Guests are encouraged to eat in-house instead of going to off-site restaurants. Many who don't have the expertise or resources to develop and support successful restaurants in-house are leasing the available space to those who do (Hendsill, "Destination Dining," 1997). Chapter 10 discusses the F&B sector in greater detail.

Other Services

Other services besides F&B may be part of an accommodation property's operations. Many resorts have facilities for golf, tennis, water sports, and skiing. Downtown hotels often have retail outlets, from convenience stores to fashion boutiques; other hotels—especially those with casinos—may have entertainment venues. Country inns may have extensive entertainment or spa services. Services like these can be departments within the property organization, or they can be independent business units under contract. These contracts take into account scope and quality of service, hours, rent, maintenance, utilities, and share of profits. If the services are managed internally (as opposed to being contracted out), support functions will be provided by other departments such as housekeeping, maintenance and engineering, human resources, marketing, accounting, and security. Also, there will be a manager assigned for the specific functions of the service.

Human Resources

The human resource (HR) function is multifaceted. In chain properties, human resource policies are often set by head office and managed locally by the human resource manager. The following human resource tasks are often carried out at a property:

- Recruiting (e.g., attending job fairs, creating recruitment page on the property website).

- Managing performance (e.g., conducting quarterly performance appraisals).
- Bargaining with unions (e.g., for scheduling workloads).
- Managing turnover (e.g., administering a service recognition program to retain employees).
- Managing diversity (e.g., arranging an English as a Second Language (ESL) program at the worksite for non-anglophone staff).

Human resources can help create a competitive advantage if employees' skills and talents and the operational environment are managed effectively, and if HR functions as a strategic partner with management. "Projecting a competitive advantage in human resources involves hiring and supporting forward thinkers, investing in training and development, and offering competitive benefits and compensation" (Lane and Dupre, 1997, p. 272).

Accounting

Accounting departments record day-to-day financial data, classify and summarize them, and report the results to other areas in the organization. There is usually a controller—either on site or at head office—who oversees the accounting for revenues and costs. Usually there is also a team that handles night audit, accounts receivable, payroll, cashiering, and purchasing. At the end of each day, a night audit is conducted to balance the books by reviewing charges posted to guest folios and by reconciling point-of-sale records and payments with cash deposits. At that time, sales revenues are classified into categories: rooms, food and beverage, and other front-of-the-house and back-of-the-house departments. Revenue may also be categorized according to method of payment (e.g., cash, cheque, credit card, in-house charge account). Many companies use a standard framework known as the Uniform System of Accounts for Hotels, which follows generally accepted accounting procedures (GAAP).

The accounting department also generates various necessary reports on a more or less fixed schedule: tax returns; shareholders' reports; financial summaries for lenders; and for managers, daily room rates, occupancy levels, and total sales from revenue activities. The managers of hotel departments then use this information when making operating decisions.

Security

The security staff is responsible for the interior and exterior of the property and for the physical safety of guests and employees. Security is now a major consideration, and security systems are becoming even more sophisticated. Owners and managers implement high-security systems as part of their **risk-management strategy**. Strong security can prevent accidents, reduce claims, and lower insurance and legal costs. Security requires specialized knowledge, as the equipment required for it (locks, keys, etc.) is now mostly computerized. Basic emergency medical and police training

is no longer enough. Smaller properties may outsource security, or personnel with other responsibilities may be designated to the security team when they are on duty.

Maintenance and Engineering

The maintenance and engineering (M&E) department, usually under the leadership of the chief engineer, is responsible for:

- Furniture, fixtures, and equipment (FFE).
- The physical plant (lighting, heating, air quality, elevators, and escalators), and the related technology.
- The building "envelope" (roof, foundation, and interior and exterior walls).
- Grounds and parking lots.

This department's staff members have little direct contact with guests. Most properties focus on preventive maintenance to prevent downtime; they also forecast and balance costs over a cycle. An M&E department, when it runs well, provides functional, aesthetic, and human benefits. Its work involves both long-range planning and immediate responses. Besides conducting routine inspections, it is often called on to carry out work orders in response to guests' requests and complaints. When the property has a property management system, M&E staff can track and schedule routine and preventive maintenance throughout their areas of responsibility; they can also "work around" the occupancy forecast when assigning personnel (in-house or outsourced). In many operations, the M&E department is heavily involved in waste, water, and energy management.

Materials Management

The purchasing function is closely aligned with accounting, and decisions about purchasing are often decentralized. That being said, materials management requires a comprehensive strategy and operating policies. The Green Partnership Program instituted in 1990 at CP Hotels (see this chapter's Profile) is an example of how materials management can be thoroughly integrated not just at one property, but throughout a chain.

In the past decade, accommodation operations around the world have realized that it is good business to have ecofriendly facilities and to promote sustainable development. Awards have been established for green hotelkeeping in collaboration with the International Hotel and Restaurant Association, American Express, and the United Nations Environment Programme. The American Hotel & Lodging Association's Engineering and Environment Committee can be called on for help in greening a property. Ecofriendly practices such as green purchasing (which considers the impact that products and services have on guests, employees, the community, and the environment) are starting to be considered. Corporate purchasing agreements to buy "green" are negotiated not only around price but also around attributes such as better efficiency, reduced toxicity, and longer useful life. Also, when a purchaser states an intention to buy green, suppliers are encouraged to seek out green alternatives. Green agreements between suppliers and purchasers address specific needs, reduce operating costs and environmental impacts, and strengthen purchasing relationships (Petruzzi, 1999).

Facility Management

Facility management (FM) integrates a property's functional departments, its architecture and engineering systems, the principles of business administration, and the needs and behaviour of guests and staff. Through careful management, an operation can transform its physical assets into a valuable resource. Physical assets are a prominent component of any facility's accommodation product (refer to Figure 9–5). In the past two decades the practice of facility management has evolved; it now addresses a broad range of tangibles and intangibles. Elements that affect the core and noncore activities of the functional departments influence the quality of the accommodation product produced.

Facility management must consider all building users and all who are affected by the management of the building. These include shareholders, employees, guests, the local community, and suppliers and partners.

Facility management is hardly a new concept, but it is more holistic and more tactical than it used to be (see Figure 9–6). This is a response to environmental

FIGURE 9–5 The Accommodation Product

SOURCE: From *MANAGING FACILITIES STANDARDS*, by Jones & Jowett. Reprinted by permission of Elsevier Science Ltd.

forces that must, it is now realized, be managed strategically. These forces include technological change (especially relating to information technology); new building, product, and communications design; and changes in human expectations and needs that have created a gap between users and technological developments—a gap that must be bridged.

It is management that translates the organizational objectives with respect to the organization's mission into plans for developing and maintaining the physical assets and services that comprise the accommodation product. It is management that assesses whether the property is meeting the demands of the markets it is in business to serve. Some of the topics that should be addressed from the comprehensive perspective of a facility management system include total quality management, productivity, yield management, rating standards, green hotel-keeping, diversity, and accessibility.

Total Quality Management

Total quality management (TQM) is a way of doing business to improve service. Four elements are involved: "attention to process, commitment to the customer, involvement of employees, and benchmarking of best practices" (Jacob, 1993, p. 66). TQM requires that all aspects of the accommodation product be considered, and it involves management by commitment rather than management by control.

TQM focuses on customer expectations to prevent problems, builds commitment to a quality workforce, and promotes open decision making (Gilbert, 1992). TQM is mainly about hands-on people management. It allows people to admit mistakes so that mistakes, not people, are corrected. Problem-solving teams are formed to find solutions to identified problems, and a seamless interface between departments is facilitated through training and communication. Departments are no longer stuck within rigid boundaries; instead, systems are devised for special projects and operational functions.

Meeting expectations and delighting customers is an ongoing process that involves consistency, quality assurance, and continuous quality improvement. Staff members play an essential role in delivering set quality standards of service. Continuous quality improvement becomes a reality only when there is team-building, peer support, and motivated staff at all levels.

Quality requires preventive rather than reactive measures. In the long run, TQM results in gains in efficiency, reduction of wasted time and materials, elimination of costs and complaints, and improved standards of service. These things offset whatever costs may be incurred in establishing and maintaining quality management techniques.

Productivity

Productivity—that is, output in relation to input—does not mean that quality has to suffer. Productivity and

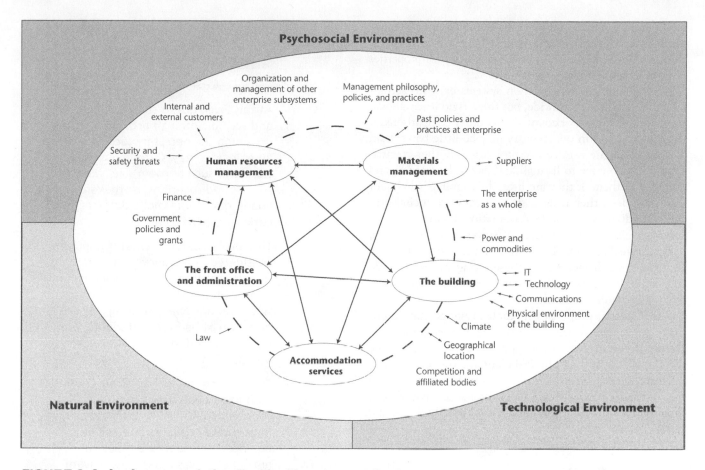

FIGURE 9–6 An Accommodation Facility Management System

SOURCES: Adapted from C. Jones and V. Paul (1993), "The System of Accommodation Management," *Accommodation Management,* and C. Jones and V. Jowett (1998), "The Concept and Scope of Facilities Management," *Managing Facilities.*

quality improvements should go hand in hand. Within an organization, improvements in productivity can be realized at four levels: corporate, systems, process, and workplace.

Productivity can be improved in one of three ways: through research that leads to new materials or processes; through the results of research and knowledge being applied to develop technology; and through procedures developed to utilize knowledge and available technology. In facility management, the challenge is to keep abreast of advances in knowledge and technology so that they can be combined effectively in the day-to-day operations of the total facility system to improve productivity.

Yield Management

Hotel location, room location, room size, length and season of stay, and availability of special services and facilities are the main factors affecting the price of a room. However, yield management, which hinges on differential pricing, is now being used in the accommodation sector to bring prices in line with actual market forces. Many hotels strike a balance between supply and demand by constantly adjusting prices. They try to match the kinds of rooms available (supply) with the kinds of customers who want those rooms (demand). Yield management differs from traditional pricing in that it relies on accurate demand forecasts for specific dates rather than seasons. It requires an information system that is constantly updated and that can track the facility's booking history for specific dates. Yield management involves two basic strategies:

1. Emphasizing the highest rates possible when demand is high. Guest service agents are encouraged to charge the maximum **rack** (or standard) **rate** if only a few rooms are available, rather than offer discounts.
2. Emphasizing room sales when demand is low by discounting room rates on weekends to attract the leisure market to a hotel where mainly business travellers stay during the week.

Rating Systems

Rating systems are established by external organizations, but the standards that properties are rated on are set and maintained internally. Whether a facility is rated voluntarily or involuntarily, maintaining acceptable standards throughout the whole operation is necessary for properties to have a competitive advantage.

Many different classification systems exist for accommodation facilities worldwide, but there is no international standard that allows for country-to-country comparisons. A five-star property in one country may be little better than "standard" in the eyes of a visitor from another country. Properties subscribe to listings, and pay to be rated by and included in them. If they are listed by Mobil, Michelin, or Canada Select, they receive stars. If they are included in the Canadian Automobile Association listing under its sister organization, the American Automobile Association, they receive diamonds. Three stars may not mean the same thing as three diamonds. All these rating systems provide independent evaluations that customers can check when making decisions about where to stay.

In Canada, properties in each province can voluntarily participate in the **Canada Select Accommodation Rating Program**. After they apply to be rated and pay the fee, the quality of their physical plant and the services they offer are assessed and full and half stars between one and five are assigned (see Table 9–3). Properties may also be rated by automobile clubs, guidebooks, travel writers, and hotel critics.

Facilities, Guests, and the Environment

How green should a facility be? There is some evidence that the higher the price segment, the lower the involvement in promoting environmental action. Properties may not want to detract from the perceived luxury of the facility by asking guests to involve themselves in towel and linen reuse or recycling programs. Yet there is evidence that ecofriendly programs like Fairmont's Green Partnership Program, the American Hotel & Lodging Association's Good Earthkeeping Program, the Hotel Association of Canada's Green Leaf Program, as well as overall attention to materials management, can be very beneficial. "The lodging industry spends almost $4 billion per year on energy," said Pedro Mandoki, AH&LA chairman and president and CEO of Plantation Resort Management. "Hotels can easily save 10 percent of that energy—amounting to $400 million every year—through opportunities that require little capital investment" (Brodsky, 2005). All that is needed is a facility management system grounded in the concept of responsible environmental management.

According to their website, Eco Hotels of the World "is a free online guide for travellers to the most eco-friendly hotels in the world . . . [Their] green-star system has been designed to get the best perspective on how 'green' a Hotel is." They have created five key indicators to rate each property: Energy, Water, Disposal, Eco-Active, and Protection. They also emphasize the need for hotels to address the following criteria prior to being rated:

TABLE 9–3 Canada Select Accommodation Rating Program (2008)

The following are the star rating descriptions in 2008:

*	At this level, guests should expect clean and well-maintained accommodations providing the necessary facilities for an enjoyable stay. Criteria includes standards such as room size, window screens and coverings, clothes storage, linens, door lock, smoke detector, and parking facilities.
**	This level equates to what is popularly considered "mid-range" accommodation. It exceeds the 1 star level in quality of mattress, bed linen, floors/window/wall coverings, and in provision of bedside and seating area lighting, additional room furniture, and parking space.
***	These properties will offer larger units with additional room furniture, coordinated furnishings, better quality mattresses and linens, and will be equipped with clock/alarm, extra amenities in washrooms, etc. Private baths for all BB rooms is a requirement for a 3 star and higher rating. Three star properties offer above average facilities and services.
****	This rating indicates exceptional quality in all areas of facilities and services offering superior quality throughout the property in areas of guestrooms, bath and common areas. The property typically provides laundry/valet service as well as many additional amenities.
*****	A 5 star property is luxurious at a world standard, offering outstanding facilities, guest service and amenities.

SOURCE: Courtesy Hotel Association of Canada.

- Dependence on the natural environment
- Ecological sustainability
- Proven contribution to conservation
- Provision of environmental training programs
- Incorporation of cultural considerations
- Provision of an economic return to the local community. (Eco Hotels of the World, n.d.)

ILLUSTRATION 9–8

From 1996 to 2003, Sandals was voted World's Best All-Inclusive Resorts by travel agents.

SOURCE: Courtesy of Sandals Resorts.

Diversity Management

Every organization must consider its policies for hiring and promoting minorities (i.e., racial and gender minorities and the physically challenged) and the socially and economically disadvantaged. Otherwise, their employees will not realize their maximum potential, and neither will the organization. Every employee must be treated as a candidate for advancement. This may involve establishing educational programs for skills development (especially for language and literacy); accommodating employees who are hearing or visually impaired, or who require barrier-free work spaces; establishing race relations policies; and monitoring the gender profile of employees to prevent "pink ghettos" or "blue ghettos" from developing in specific departments or levels of employment in the organization.

Accessibility

In the past decade, two segments of the tourism market have grown substantially: seniors and people with disabilities. Both groups require accessibility and are drawn to facilities and activities that meet their needs or are barrier-

free. Also, more employees with disabilities are being integrated into workplaces. Their needs are met when paths and corridors are easily accessible, when room layouts and furniture and equipment do not present barriers, when signage is appropriate, when there are alternative modes of communication and good information systems, and when staff are trained to be sensitive to their needs. In sum, these groups must not be doubly handicapped by a facility's built and social environment.

The Access Canada Program was initiated in Alberta and is now promoted by the Hotel Association of Canada. This is a national voluntary program that provides information and tools for adapting properties to be functionally accessible, as well as materials for fostering staff awareness and providing sensitivity training. The program has four rating levels based on criteria in four categories: service training, information services, physical access, and portable equipment/technical aids. Properties that meet the criteria can post the appropriate logo (see Figure 9–7). Fact sheets detailing information on each facility and the services offered are available for guests (Szwender, Waugh, and Campbell, 1996).

Accessibility Levels   **Level Provides Services For**

1st Level
Seniors with normal aging, limitations of hearing, vision, and agility and mild disabilities

2nd Level
People with mild hearing impairment
People with strength/agility limitations
People with mild visual impairment

3rd Level
People with mild to moderate hearing impairment
People with strength/agility limitations
People with mild to moderate visual impairment
People who are independent wheelchair users

4th Level
People with mild to severe hearing impairment
People who are deaf
People with strength/agility limitations
People with mild to severe visual impairment
People who are dependent wheelchair users

FIGURE 9–7 Accessibility Rating Levels
SOURCE: Courtesy Hotel Association of Canada.

Although each accessibility level targets a specific market and builds on the lower level, the principles of ergonomics and functional use benefit all users of a facility—guests and employees. Since 1990, when the Americans with Disabilities Act (ADA) was signed into law, American organizations hosting conferences in Canada have been likely to request that establishments meet "reasonable accommodation" standards. The four levels of the Access Canada Program meet aspects of the ADA requirements; in fact, some criteria in Level 4 of the Access Canada Program exceed the ADA requirements. Clearly, participating in the Access Canada Program expands an operation's potential to meet the demands of the American market and the needs of an expanding market here at home. Meeting such needs should be an integral part of any property's facility management system.

CHANNELS OF DISTRIBUTION

Until the advent of property-specific websites, hotels, motels, country inns, and bed-and-breakfasts depended mainly on the travel trade sector to bring in their guests (see Chapters 14, 15, and 16). Accommodation services are being tailored to meet the needs of business travellers, conventioneers, and vacationers. The lodging place is no longer just somewhere to stop en route to a destination; often it is a destination in itself.

References

Besides the information about accommodations available on the corporate lodging websites listed in Internet Connections at the end of this chapter, there are two reference websites ("Hotel and Travel Index Worldwide" and "Star Service Online") for tourism professionals and travellers that contain both objective information (such as factual descriptions of hotel facilities) and subjective comments (evaluations of individual properties in terms of service, atmosphere, etc.). In 2006, the *Official Hotel Guide* (OHG) merged with the *Hotel & Travel Index* (HTI) to create *Hotel and Travel Index Worldwide* and 2007 was the last year of their printed reference guide due to the increasing cost of printing and the rise of the Internet. Many travellers are accessing consumer-generated websites or blogs such as Trip Advisor to get unbiased opinions of guests who have actually stayed at the property being critiqued.

Several consumer guides provide subjective information about selected properties in different areas and countries. These include *Frommer's $.....-a-Day* and other guides, *Fielding's*, and *Fodor* and *Frommer's* guides. Budget travel guides include *Lonely Planet*, *The Rough Guide*, *Let's Go*, and Rick Steves' many books. Upscale travel guides include *Eyewitness Travel Guide*, *National Geographic Traveler*, and the *Michelin Green Guide*. There are even . . . *for Dummies* travel guides now. Hotels are listed and rated in guides such as *Michelin's Red Guide* series and the *Mobil Travel Guide* series.

On a regional basis, provinces and territories in Canada have guides that provide listings and descriptions

---

Check Your Product Knowledge

1. What key functions are part of accommodation management?
2. Describe two accommodation rating systems that can be used to classify Canadian hotels.
3. What factors affect the price of a room?
4. Identify five ways a hotel can be an ecofriendly operation.

Check Your Product Knowledge

1. Which references would travel counsellors draw on to identify accommodations for customers wanting a customized vacation?
2. What references are available for individuals wanting to plan a trip across Canada for themselves?

of both fixed-roof and camping accommodations. Properties pay to be listed in these guides, and for advertisements of their facilities. These guides also serve as important marketing tools for promoting regional destinations. Nova Scotia's *Doers and Dreamers Guide* features the travel trails in the province and showcases accommodations as part of Nova Scotia's tourist product. Provincial and territorial travel guides are available from tourism departments, usually by going to the pertinent tourism website.

ACCOMMODATION: CURRENT TRENDS

Self-Service Kiosks

Self-service kiosks were introduced by Starwood at the W New York–Times Square Hotel and at the Sheraton Boston Hotel. On check-in, the guest swipes his or her credit card, the room reservation is confirmed, and an electronic room key is produced—the process should take less than a minute. On check-out, the guest can request a receipt from the machine or wait for a receipt in the mail. Positive guest acceptance is leading to chainwide distribution in many chains such as Hyatt, Hilton, Marriott, Fairmont, among others.

According to consultant Kasavana (2008), IBM has more than 3000 units installed at more than 200 locations, including airports. Benefits attributable to successful self-service kiosks include speedier customer service, decrease in employment costs, and opportunities for upselling or cross selling (Amdekar and Chrestman, 2007). Hotel operators may face one or more of the following challenges when trying to reach the full potential of self-service kiosks:

1. Non-standard and insufficient information may restrict automated check-in.
2. Certain Property Management Systems may be unable to handle stayovers, late checkouts, discount coupons, room reassignments, etc.
3. Integration of the traditional key technology may be complex and expensive.
4. Inappropriate kiosk design—kiosk interface may be too complicated for guests.
5. Kiosks may require significant changes to other rooms management modules (Amdekar and Chrestman, 2007).

goconcierge.net

With the "Guest Task Calendar" feature of goconcierge, a Web-based task-tracking and database solution, concierge or bellstaff can log, track, and view tasks, guest requests, and guest preferences, and create personalized guest confirmation letters, group itineraries, and even directions to the hotel or other points of interest. Also, goconcierge has a link to OpenTable.com to make instant reservations at selected restaurants, and has a database of local attractions (Wolff, 2004).

High-Tech Hotel Amenities

Hotel amenities are going more high-tech, with plasma TVs, high-speed and wireless Internet connectivity, DVD players, cordless phones, video game consoles, and in-room fax machines. Some hotels are now offering "technology butlers" (hotel technology consultants who will come to a guest room 24/7 to assist with laptop connections and/or Internet access) (Graziani, 2004).

Many hotel chains, like Fairmont Hotels & Resorts, offer free high-speed Internet access (HSIA) to its Club and top loyalty clients, but charge regular guests a daily fee. The most common rate is $9.95 for 24 hours. Tim Aubrey, Fairmont's senior vice president of finance noted, "You only need 3.5-percent usage to pay back HSIA installation in two years. It costs us about $300 to enable a room, so I need to sell it about 16 times a year" (Wolff, 2003).

According to Lou Paladeau, Marriott's vice president, technology business development, "Wireless high-speed internet access is the next major technology initiative for the hotel industry. The number of travelers who carry laptops with wireless capabilities is expected to continue to increase as wireless technology becomes more widely available" (Marriott International Inc., 2004). The general feeling is that all major hotel chains will have to go "wireless" to meet the competition.

New Brands

PwC hotel analyst Bjorn Hanson believes "The hotel industry continues to reinvent itself to accommodate the ever-changing face of the business traveller." Young business travellers are not attracted to the traditional hotel brands; they are seeking brands that complement their lifestyles with a promise of pampering and a unique accommodation experience.

Starting in April 2004 with the opening of Intercontinental's first Hotel Indigo, Atlanta became a popular launch city for new brands which later included NYLO, Capella, Solis, and TWELVE Hotels. During the period of 2004 to early 2008, a total of 38 hotel brands have been introduced in the U.S. According to Hanson, " This is the largest number of new luxury brand hotels in a three-year period since 1982 . . . In 2008, Marriott International and boutique hotel guru Ian Schrager partnered to launch a new luxury brand named Edition," which will debut in 2010. According to a PwC study for 2004 to 2007, "Record average daily [room] rates (ADR) and the availability of financing have also helped fuel the growth of new brands in the U.S. lodging industry" (Ramos, 2007). The recent credit crunch starting in 2008 has caused a forecast of decreased construction and expansion for 2008 and 2009 in all sectors of accommodation (PKF, 2008).

Check Your Product Knowledge

1. What are the features of a goconcierge.net system?
2. What do the younger business travellers want and what has fuelled the growth of new brands?

ACCOMMODATION ISSUES

The Distribution Shift

"One of the biggest trends on the Internet has been the shift in the balance of power toward hotel chains (versus online travel agencies)" (Carroll and Sileo, 2007); this being the result of greater price consistency across channels by the large hotel chains.

According to the *PhoCusWright Consumer Travel Trends Survey, ninth edition* (2007), the percentage of online travel consumers who surf online travel agencies, but in the end reserve directly with the hotel, has increased from 31 percent in 2005 to 42 percent in 2006. In 2006, hotel-branded websites represented 55 percent of online hotel sales; online travel agencies represented 45 percent. By 2008, PhoCusWright predicts that hotel-branded websites will increase their share to 57 percent. According to Carroll and Sileo (2007), "Hotels have asserted themselves at the bargaining table, improved their Web sites, maximized search marketing strategies and offered extra value to the consumer through loyalty points and flexible cancellation policies . . . Hoteliers report that rising occupancy levels allow them to shift inventory availability to higher ADR and direct channels, where customer relationships can be enhanced. As these executives see it, brand direct bookings are an investment in the future. They cost less and represent an opportunity to create more loyal customer relationships or at least lessen the opportunity for intermediaries to create deeper relationships with their guests" (Carroll and Sileo, 2007).

CarePar

CarePar, also known as the Hotel Carbon Index, is a carbon emission measurement designed specifically for hotels. Hotels submit information that is translated into the carbon cost of using a room overnight or meeting room per half-day. Hotel management can use this data to identify areas where improved sustainable practices will result in potential savings and to promote the results of the hotel's greening practices to meet clients' requests to offset their travel emissions (CarePar, n.d.).

Check Your Product Knowledge

1. What are some major hotel chains doing to enhance distribution?
2. How can CarePar assist hotels?

CAREER OPPORTUNITIES

According to tourism industry consultants, the accommodation sector in Canada employed approximately 199 000 people in tourism-related employment (directly or indirectly, on a full-time, part-time, or seasonal basis) in 2006. The industry is projected to grow and the employment outlook should remain generally good for most accommodation occupations. In fact, some markets are experiencing a labour shortage, and employers are being encouraged to invest more in training employees and creating a positive work environment to attract and retain staff.

In smaller properties, individual workers often have multiple duties. There is a wide variety of job settings in the accommodation sector. Job titles may be the same, but the duties vary depending on the type of operation.

Traditional career progress in the accommodation sector has been from the front lines to supervisory to management to executive levels. Many of today's tourism program graduates might not start in front-line positions merely because they gained experience at the entry level while they were studying. It is encouraging to know that one's career can go from one organization to another because skills, knowledge, and attitudes are transferable.

According to its website, hCareers has been the number-one job board for restaurant and hospitality positions since 1998 (based on site traffic and the number of jobs and résumés online). The website also has two monthly newsletters—*Restaurant News* and *Ask the Experts* (which contains good interview tips). There is a "Job Detective" option that will contact you via e-mail whenever a job vacancy is posted that matches the position you requested. hCareers has formed partnerships with the Hotel Association of Canada (HAC), The National Restaurant Association (NRA), and others. The Canadian website has links to the U.S. and U.K. hCareers sites.

A DAY IN THE LIFE OF A

Front Desk Manager

I am a front desk manager at a large resort hotel. My work is often demanding, but I enjoy the challenge. I supervise a staff of dozens of employees involved in guest services, and I must deal with such daily crises as overbooked rooms and missing luggage. I am the person guests come to with their complaints, questions, and comments. If I serve guests well, they will form a good impression of my hotel and they will come back again. Despite its demands, I love my work. I like supervising people and working as part of a team with the other managers in the hotel.

I didn't start out as a front desk manager, of course. My first hotel job was waiting tables in a hotel restaurant during summer vacations from college. After graduation, I took a job as a front desk clerk. When I started out in my first hotel job, my manager told me, "Do every task to the best of your ability because managers are always looking for ambitious, capable people to promote to better jobs." She turned out to be right, because I have been promoted three times since then. Most hotels promote their managers from within.

Some hotel managers whom I know started working in hotels right after high school. They took entry-level jobs and learned the business as they progressed up the career ladder. However, many hotels prefer to hire people who took hotel and restaurant management courses at a community college or university. There are programs in hotel and restaurant management available across Canada. While in college, I took courses in accounting, hotel management, food and beverage control, business administration, law, finance, and human resources.

Of course, once I started my first hotel job, I received a lot of on-the-job training. This was very important, because some tasks you can learn only by actually performing them. I have to be able to do any of the jobs of the people I supervise—cashiers, bellstaff, reservations clerks, desk clerks, and telephone operators.

People sometimes ask me what special qualities a person needs to be a good front desk manager. I think that it is especially important that you like people and enjoy serving the public. In fact, sometimes I am as much a public relations person as I am a front desk manager. Like any employee who has contact with guests, I have to be friendly and helpful so they will carry away a good opinion of the hotel and its employees. That way, they will stay at the hotel again when they are in the area, and they will recommend the hotel to friends and colleagues.

Front desk managers must be patient, tactful, and skillful not only in dealing with guests but also in directing other employees. I want the employees I supervise to enjoy their jobs and work well with one another, because they reflect their feelings and attitudes when dealing with guests. It is also part of my job to coordinate the front desk operations with those of other departments, such as housekeeping and food services.

If I checked in guests to rooms that had not been cleaned or overbooked reservations in the hotel's restaurants, it would annoy both the guests and my co-workers.

Front desk managers must be calm and capable in the face of emergencies. They must be able to make decisions and solve problems quickly. I have to deal with many different kinds of problems every day. Some are minor, such as when one of our electronic keys fails to open a room door or the television in a room doesn't work. Others can be serious or very aggravating. Just this morning, I had to deal with a family of six whose rooms had been accidentally booked to other travellers. Since my hotel was full, I had to find them accommodations at another hotel and arrange transportation for them.

There are several advantages to my job that you won't find in many other jobs. Among them are that I get to meet people from all over the world, and I live year-round in a comfortable hotel at a beautiful, sunny beach resort. I eat in the hotel restaurant and can use its pool and other facilities whenever I am off duty. Also, my pay is comparable to other kinds of management jobs.

One disadvantage to my job is that the front desk operates 24 hours a day, so I sometimes have to work a second or third shift. Since I live in the hotel, I am on call around the clock, seven days a week. For me, though, the advantages greatly outweigh the disadvantages. I plan to stay in this field for a long time.

Summary

- The accommodation sector is an integral part of the tourism industry.
- Early lodging places developed along trade and travel routes.
- The accommodation sector grew tremendously with the expansion of the railway network.
- Luxury hotels were built in the major cities; smaller hotels appeared along the railway lines.
- The automobile and the airline industry have had an enormous impact on the tourism industry in modern times in that they have fostered the development of motels, resort hotels, convention hotels, and airport hotels.
- Market segmentation has been a major development in the past 40 years.
- Hotels market their products to specific groups of customers, including business travellers, convention groups, vacationers, weekenders, and local residents.
- Forms of hotel ownership include individual ownership, chain ownership, and franchise. Management contracts and REITs have encouraged investment and developments in the accommodation sector.
- Accommodation enterprises usually have functional departments such as the rooms division, sales and marketing, human resources, food and beverage, accounting, security, maintenance and engineering.
- Hotel location, room location, room size, length and season of stay, and availability of special services and facilities are the main factors affecting the price of a room.
- Methods for making accommodation reservations have advanced from central reservation offices to comprehensive wireless services and Web-enabled devices; new services are being offered to guests to assist them in researching and making reservations
- In hotels with self-service kiosks, a guest swipes his or her credit card, the room reservation is confirmed, and an electronic room key is produced.
- Using goconcierge.net, concierge or bellstaff can log, track, and view tasks, guest requests, and guest preferences, and create personalized guest confirmation letters, group itineraries, and even directions to the hotel or other points of interest.
- Hotel amenities are going more high-tech, with plasma TVs, high-speed and wireless Internet connectivity, DVD players, cordless phones, and in-room fax machines.
- Many hotel chains offer free high-speed Internet access (HSIA) to its Club and top loyalty clients, but charge regular guests a daily fee.
- CarePar is an actual calculation that may be utilized to certify and verify carbon values per hotel rooms.

Key Terms

Internet Connections

WORKSHEET 9–1   Choosing Facilities

Refer to the Internet Connections section and check out several websites in the accommodation sector to locate appropriate Canadian hotels, motels, or resorts for the following customers. Narrow down the possibilities to two, and then describe them in the space provided. Include location, type of accommodation, cost, facilities, services, proximity to tourist attractions, number of rooms, and any other information that would appeal to the customers' MNEs.

1. A married couple from Ontario plans to visit friends living in Yourtown. Since their friends do not have room for guests in their apartment, the couple must stay at a hotel. The couple would prefer a moderately priced, older facility.

    _____

    _____

    _____

    _____

2. A tired, overworked executive is looking forward to a two-week vacation. Since she travels a great deal for her job, the last thing she wants to do is spend her vacation travelling. A nearby resort with spa facilities sounds appealing. The executive imagines herself having a relaxing vacation and being totally rejuvenated.

    _____

    _____

    _____

    _____

3. A man from Korea must travel to your province on business. He wants a suite in an all-suite hotel, preferably an American chain hotel. The hotel must provide a full array of business services, including a fax machine. He will need a translator and he would like to be near the airport, if possible.

    _____

    _____

    _____

    _____

4. A family comprising two adults and three children (14, 11, and 7) from Washington, D.C., plans to visit your province's capital and the surrounding area in the first week in July. They would like to stay in a motel in a suburb so they don't have to pay for parking. The children want the motel to have a swimming pool and to be near a variety of fast-food outlets.

    _____

    _____

    _____

    _____

WORKSHEET 9–2 Employment in the Accommodation Sector

You are the human resource manager at a new hotel and conference centre. You have job openings in all departments. After interviewing the applicants listed below, you would like to offer each of them a job.

What department and position would be best for each applicant? What opportunities would each have for advancement at your new hotel?

1. Jane has completed the local two-year community college program and worked summers on the bellstaff of a large city hotel in another province. She has a friendly, outgoing personality and enjoys dealing with people.

_____

2. Liu, a university graduate with a tourism and hospitality management major, is very organized and has been employed for two years as a front desk supervisor at another hotel in town.

_____

3. Simone, a high school graduate, has worked summers for a fast-food chain and wants to be a chef.

_____

4. Rich has taken finance, advertising, and marketing courses in an MBA program. Past employers report he is a go-getter with excellent communication skills. He would like to work part-time until he finishes his MBA.

_____

5. Yves is a former peacekeeper with the Canadian Armed Forces who has been a security guard for a large office building. He would like to have more contact with people.

_____

6. Marita is a former travel counsellor who specialized in convention planning. She has a college degree in hotel administration and experience in public relations.

_____

7. Steve is a licensed plumber who has worked as an electrician and a carpenter. He prefers not to work with the public because he often stutters.

_____

8. Farah is a university graduate with a major in accounting who has worked summers in the administration office of a large hotel chain.

_____

9. Peter is a high-school graduate who has worked in the laundry room of a large nursing home for a year.

_____

10. Alyssa is a single mother who has raised a family for the past 18 years and now wants to work to help support her oldest child, who is starting university.

_____

Objectives

When you have completed this chapter, you should be able to:

- Discuss the role the food and beverage sector of the tourism industry plays in the Canadian economy and labour market.

- Explain how Cara is an integrated food service company.

- Differentiate between commercial and noncommercial food service operations.

- Identify milestones in the development of food and beverage service that have influenced the food service we have today.

- Distinguish among food and beverage market segments.

- Explain the influence that tourism has on the sales and profits of food service operations.

- Compare the characteristics of types and segments of food service operations.

- Discuss the factors that contribute to demand for restaurants.

- Discuss the impact of changing demographics on market demands for food service.

- Identify career opportunities in the F&B sector of the tourism industry.

- Identify career planning references and other sources of information for the food and beverage sector.

The Canadian Restaurant and Foodservice Association (CRFA) reports that the food service industry in Canada will bring in more than $55 billion annually in 2008 (CRFA, June 18, 2008). With a forecasted sales growth of only 3.3 percent over 2007 sales of $53.4 billion, and a forecasted menu inflation of 2.7 percent, the real sales growth will be only 0.6 percent. The low growth rate in 2007 was attributed to slower disposable income growth in most parts of Canada, and a 9.3 percent decrease in international visitors to Canada. The weak economy is forecasted to continue through 2008 resulting in moderate disposable income and lower employment growth, which should curb spending in the foodservice sector (CRFA, December 11, 2007).

In 2007, the food service industry in Canada received 39.4 percent of the food dollar spent by tourists, local consumers, businesses, etc. (CRFA, March 17, 2008). Demand for full-service restaurants is expected to grow, and the already tight labour market is expected to keep getting tighter (Deibert, February 2001). Industry reports indicate that food service employment rose in 2003 to 1 020 700 (about 6.6 percent of the Canadian workforce), well over the 900 000 that was originally projected for 2005. "Between now and 2015, the demand for workers in Canada will exceed supply by 800 000 people. The food-

service industry alone will require an additional 181 000 workers over the next nine years. At the same time, the number of youth aged 15 to 24—a group that accounts for nearly half of all foodservice employees—will continue to decline" (CRFA, April 23, 2008).

In Canada, the F&B sector currently accounts for more than 46 percent of tourism-related employment, and provides first-job work experience for more young people (generating one in five jobs for young Canadians) than any other industry (CTHRC, "2006 Food," 2006). According to a 2006 CRFA report, more than 44 percent of F&B employees were under 25 (CRFA, 2006). In 2006, industry statistics showed that the average food service profit margin was 4.3 percent of F&B revenue; "with an [average] annual sales volume of $573,650, the average [restaurant] operator earned an annual pre-tax profit of $24,667" (CRFA, June 18, 2008).

FOOD SERVICE IN HISTORY

The Rise of Restaurants

The Egyptians ate together in public places as early as 1700 B.C.E., and restaurants have existed since the 1500s. The modern concept of restaurants originated in Paris in

PROFILE

Success Attributed to Five Principles

Cara Operations Limited

Founded in 1883 as the Canada Railway News Company, today's Cara Operations Limited emerged in 1961. The name "Cara" came from the "C" and "R" in "Canada Railway" and is the Irish word for friend. Cara's strength lies in developing and operating around living clearly stated principles. Today Cara operates in the branded restaurant food service segment of the food service industry and is Canada's largest integrated food services organization. Its diversity provides stability across divisions, seasons, and regions. Among its divisions are chains such as Swiss Chalet, Harvey's, Kelsey's, and Montana's. Cara also operates Cara Airline Solutions and owns Milestone Restaurants. In 2007, Cara converted a Swiss Chalet into a Coza Tuscan Grill in Langley, B.C.

Cara also pioneered twinning and multibranding—that is, offering two or more concepts at the same or nearby locations. In one five-year period, its Kelsey's and Montana's chains grew at a compounded rate of more than 20 percent. Today, according to the company profile on Cara's website, its vision is to be "Canada's leading branded restaurant and airline services company."

Cara's Five Principles influence the results Cara achieves (Cara Airline Solutions, "Five Principles," n.d.). In everything Cara does, the following prin-

ciples must be applied with balance: Quality, Responsibility, Integrity, Efficiency and Independence. Also important to Cara's success are the following leadership qualities that Cara interviewers search for when recruiting potential employees: Drive, Inspiration, Anticipation, and Focus.

The company believes that its people are its sustainable competitive advantage and refers to them as "teammates." These teammates are responsible for understanding the company's principles and are expected to demonstrate them every day in their actions and interactions. By living these principles, Cara believes that its people will come to trust one another to deliver in any situation that requires judgment, confidentiality, discretion, support, performance, or results. All of this is necessary for success. Recognizing that change is constant, Cara College was developed to provide the necessary tools to enable Cara teammates to pursue their professional development, develop their leadership potential and meet future challenges facing the industry (Cara Airline Solutions, "Cara College," n.d.).

Cara says that its success is reflected in its real growth in sales and profits; in the continual improvement in the equity of its brands and businesses; in the development of its people to their full potential; and in its top rat-

ings from stakeholders, who include teammates, franchisees and operating associates, customers, clients and guests, investors, business partners, and the community at large. Cara's sales for its various divisions and strategic alliances in 2003 are presented in Table 10–1. (Since Cara is now a private company, more recent sales are not available.)

In late 1997, Cara won food contracts from VIA Rail to prepare meals for trains in the Windsor–Quebec City corridor. Meals for VIA Rail are precooked and quick-frozen in Cara's flight kitchen at Toronto's Pearson International Airport and then moved to Union Station in downtown Toronto. There they are placed on trains, reheated, and served. The program Cara implemented in the airline catering division, based on total quality management, focuses on customer expectations, problem prevention, increased commitment to quality in the workforce, and the promotion of open decision making. The program is instrumental to the company's success in catering.

Cara's sense of environmental responsibility has led to initiatives based on the 3Rs—reduce, reuse, and recycle. The company also supports the community by donating a percentage of its profits to charitable organizations and by encouraging volunteer activities among its employees.

TABLE 10–1 Cara Divisions and Strategic Alliances, 2003

Brand Profile	Annual Sales	Number of Outlets	Number of Customers
Swiss Chalet	$413 million	186	40 million+
Harvey's	$209 million	345	50 million+
Kelsey's	$207 million	111	35 million+
Montana's	$124 million	53	10 million+
Outback (sold)	$ 42 million	16	2 million+
Second Cup (sold)	$174 million	372	80 million+
Milestones	$ 69 million	22	4 million+
Airport Solutions	$221 million	10	30 million+
Summit (sold) (3 sold after 2003)	$387 million	n/a*	n/a*

*Not available

According to the Cara website, the corporate charitable focus is health promotion and education—e.g., Swiss Chalet supports Children's Miracle Network through their Festival Day Miracle program.

In a company press release on February 24, 2004, Cara announced that a "going private" transaction had been approved by the shareholders, effective February 25, 2004. The company's president and CEO, Gabe Tsampalieros, said "We are delighted with the positive outcome of the vote allowing Cara to privatize. In a very real sense this is a return to our original structure as Cara."

SOURCE: Cara Operations Limited (www.cara.com).

SOURCES: Oliver Bertin, "Cara Suffers Sharp Setback after Attacks," *The Globe and Mail*, October 30, 2001, p. B9; Cara Operations Limited, annual reports; Company profile, Cara Operations Limited website, September 7, 2008.; "Cara Sells Beaver Foods," *Atlantic Restaurant News*, November–December 2000, p. 3; S. Silcoff, "Long-Term Rise in Cara No Mistake," *Financial Post*, May 11, 2001, p. D3.

the 1760s. In the nineteenth century, restaurants that catered to residents of towns and cities, rather than to travellers, became more common in Europe, England, and North America. Expansion in the number and type of food services continued into the twentieth century. In this new century, North Americans are spending more and more on food prepared outside the home; by 2010, full-service restaurants in the United States are expected to grow by 3.2 percent annually, and quick-service restaurants by 2.1 percent. The trend in Canada is expected to be similar, as working parents don't have as much time to cook at home (Deibert, February 2001). Demand for grab-and-go meals offered by quick-service restaurants will continue to grow.

People expect a wide range of choice, excellent service, healthy and safe food, and value for the money they spend. In-house restaurants compete with freestanding restaurants. To attract local residents as well as travellers, hoteliers and entrepreneurs worldwide are developing **eatertainment** concepts (combining entertainment with dining) that are destinations in themselves. Besides restaurants and food service opportunities in the travel and accommodation sectors, there are the institutional, catering, club, and vending markets. In these, food services meet the demands of businesses, industries, schools and colleges, and health care and recreational facilities.

The Evolution of Food Service in Canada

Over the past 100 years in Canada, food service for travellers has evolved from breakfast being an event in grand hotels to doughnuts and coffee from a doughnut shop being gobbled on the run. F&B service is no longer limited to hours specified by the establishment. When travellers arrive at midnight, they don't have to go to bed hungry. There is usually a 24-hour service food outlet, or room service, or at the very least a vending machine (if you have the right coins). Travellers no longer feel compelled to pack a hamper for a trip; a predictable variety of food service options is usually available en route, with the quantity and quality of food standardized in many outlets across the country.

Since the centennial year of 1967, people who eat out in Canada have been more aware of distinctive Canadian cuisines and more interested in their history and tradition. In response, food services across Canada are now offering more choices. Training for chefs and cooks has improved, and efforts are being made to use local and regional products and to expand the cultural dimensions of tourism products and food services. The CRFA and the Canadian Culinary Federation (Fédération Culinaire Canadienne) are striving to advance the quality of food service in Canada. Culinary teams are participating in international competitions and showing that our cooks and chefs are among the world's best. They bring home the gold; in 2000, the Students Culinary Team Alberta, Culinary Team British Columbia, and Chef Chen of the Pan Pacific Hotel did just that after competing in the World Culinary Olympics in Germany.

As this book is being printed, Culinary Team Canada is preparing for the 22nd World IKA/Culinary Olympics in Erfurt, Germany, in October 2008, and Chef Daniel Wong is preparing for the famous Bocuse d'or competition in Lyon, France, in January 2009. In recent years, more attention has been paid to preparing foods that are representative of Canada's regions. For example, there is Nova Scotia's Taste of Nova Scotia, a province-wide restaurant program that "highlights Nova Scotia's finest harvests of both land and sea. Its member restaurants are committed to offering quality local food products and genuine hospitality" ("Taste," 2001). The Canadian Tourism Commission is leading an initiative to establish cuisine as integral to Canada's cultural offerings.

The Maple Restaurant in Halifax (originally established by Michael Smith, star of the TV program *Inn Chef*) features progressive Canadian cuisine, offering items such as beef, salmon, lobster, mussels, Arctic char, wild rice, potatoes, fiddleheads, locally grown fruits, cheese, and maple syrup. Tourtière, tarte au sucre, screech pie, bannock, and rappie pie are found on menus in various parts of the country. In recent years, an aboriginal peoples' cuisine has been developed through the efforts of people like chef

David Wolfman of George Brown College in Toronto, who has his own aboriginal cooking show, *Cooking with the Wolfman*.

Canada has become a multicultural country, and many of us from all walks of life are now travelling to many parts of the world. We are expanding our tastes, and we expect an array of foods and beverages both overseas and at home. All of this means that more consumers are aware of what is available from the cuisines of other cultures and are seeking out new taste experiences. Independent operators represent 63 percent of food service units, and many of them specialize in ethnic food.

Check Your Product Knowledge

1. How has food service changed through time?
2. How did the idea of the restaurant evolve?
3. How have culinary practices changed in Canada?

FOOD AND BEVERAGE OPERATIONS

Today's F&B operations fall into two major categories: commercial and noncommercial food service. Commercial food service operations include full- and limited-service restaurants, bars, social and contract catering, and eatertainment venues (see Table 10–2). All of these compete in the free market and are open to everyone. Noncommercial operations are set up in accommodation properties, retail stores, and venues such as stadiums and theatres. In these places, the primary business is something other than food service. Institutional food services usually operate under contract with an institution. They are found in schools and colleges, factories, health care facilities, military bases, and correctional centres. Employee cafeterias and executive dining rooms also fall into this category.

Also, according to Lane and Dupre (1997), there are seven main subcategories within the broader commercial/ noncommercial classification. After a brief discussion of the F&B sector and tourism, we will consider the characteristics of eight segments of food service, which will include Lane and Dupre's seven main subcategories or **segments of food service** and an additional segment—en route food services.

Tourism and Food Service

For most tourists on vacation, food and beverage costs are second to airline ticket costs. However, many restaurant

ILLUSTRATION 10–1

Culinary Team Canada takes part in the Culinary Olympics in Europe every four years and also in Culinary World Cups.

SOURCE: Courtesy of the Maritime Museum of the Atlantic, Halifax and Marvin Moore Photography.

TABLE 10–2 Food Service Classification

Commercial Food Service (Operations whose primary business is F&B)

- Limited-service restaurants—quick service, cafeterias, food courts, take-out.
- Full-service restaurants—fine dining, family and casual, restaurant–bars.
- Social and contract caterers—for transportation, institutions, recreation, special events.
- Bars—bars, taverns, pubs, cocktail lounges, nightclubs serving alcohol for immediate consumption; may have limited food service.

Noncommercial Food Service (Self-operated establishments whose primary business is not F&B)

- Accommodation food service—hotels, motels, resorts.
- Institutional food service—hospitals, residential care facilities, prisons, factories, offices.
- Retail food service—food service in department and convenience stores and other retail outlets.
- Other food service—vending machines, clubs, movie theatres, stadiums, seasonal or entertainment operations.

SOURCE: Based on definitions presented in *Canadian Restaurant and Food Services Association, 2001 Foodservice Facts,* p. 7.

managers do not know which of their customers are tourists. Residents are easier to spot. Knowing your market is important, and this includes knowing how much of that market is composed of tourists. Dining out on vacation is a necessity as well as an entertainment and a treat. Of vacationers, 53 percent eat at fast-food outlets, like McDonald's, usually for breakfast and lunch; 14 percent opt for full-service fine dining; and 32 percent choose family-style/midscale restaurants. Of residents, 69 percent choose fast-food outlets, 8 percent fine dining, and 23 per cent family-style/midscale restaurants (Polovitz Nickerson and Kerr, 2001).

Group tours are a unique tourist market segment. Providing food services for them can create demand at nonpeak times. Profit margins are usually good for this segment because the number of guests is known ahead of time and food production and labour can be planned accordingly. However, there may be drawbacks if other customers feel neglected because service is slow and facilities are crowded.

Segment 1: Food Service in Accommodation Facilities

Accommodation food services offer a variety of choices including restaurants, room service, minibars, meeting and event catering, and lounge and bar services. Such services range from casual coffee shops to discos to signature or formal dining rooms. Sometimes a central kitchen supports all of a property's food outlets; alternatively, restaurants can be managed under contract and operated as independent businesses. A location that is good for a hotel, motel, or resort property may not be as good for the in-house restaurants or lounges. F&B is a necessary part of a lodging property, but making a profit from it can be a challenge. Often hotels use themes to make their food and atmosphere attractive and memorable. The preferences of hotel guests are not always predictable, and guests may need to be coaxed into eating on-site. A hotel may consider offering an incentive for guests to dine "on the property" by giving a discount dining coupon to the guests upon check-in.

Dining room size, menus, services, prices, and design vary with the markets the establishments are targeting. Full-service hotels usually have a fine dining room for lunch and dinner as well as a quick-service option for all meals, especially breakfast. Unlike full-service hotels, mid-scale hotels will have one dining room and offer a less casual service and table setup for dinner than they do for breakfast and lunch. Budget properties may serve no meals, or only a continental breakfast that does not require an on-site kitchen. Country inns and B&Bs often offer signature foods and facilities. Inns may employ a chef; B&Bs usually provide a breakfast prepared by the owner(s). The prices charged reflect the type of food and level of service.

Room service around the clock is common in luxury hotels, and is offered at least 18 hours a day in most full-service properties. Because of the unpredictability of demand and the cost of labour in providing room service, many lower-priced hotels do not provide room service or may offer only branded fast-food delivery options. Others lease their room service to outside contractors. Room service charges make eating in the room more expensive, but many travellers find the convenience and flexibility worth the price. It can be one of the services that attract guests to a hotel property.

Minibars are commonly available in full-service and luxury hotels. Prices charged include the cost of F&B items and the cost of labour involved in providing the service. Over the years this service has evolved from an honour system for payment to computerized systems that provide accurate data about each minibar in each room. With computerized systems, tracking inventory and assigning charges is less of a hassle because charges for products removed from the minibar are automatically added to guests' bills. Many hotels in all hotel market segments are providing coffeemakers with well-known brands and gourmet blends to differentiate themselves.

Lounges and bars are found in most luxury, commercial, and midscale hotels, usually near the lobby and restaurant so that they are accessible to local patrons as well as hotel guests. Besides snacks and a range of alcoholic and nonalcoholic beverages, there often is live music during specific hours. Prices range from moderate to expensive, in keeping with the markets that patronize the establishment and the level of service provided by the hotel.

Banqueting and catering departments in hotels often cater to outside events as well as events on the property. Some hotels lease catering services from outside contractors. Whatever the source, the service provided can range from white-glove service for a banquet for several hundred people to self-serve nutrition breaks for small or large meetings. Banquets are usually priced higher than meals selected from a restaurant menu and are guaranteed through contracts, which may require clients to pay a deposit. Banquets often have a *cash bar* or an *open bar*, and hotels usually turn a profit on these.

Banquet costs for a meal are frequently lower than restaurant costs because the number to prepare for and serve is known. Banqueting is made easier with loading racks that hold 19 to 100 meals. These are cooked ahead of time and then chilled on plates on the racks. The meals are then heated on the rack at serving time. However, turnover is slower compared to a restaurant dining room. Also, bookings are sometimes cancelled; when they are, opportunities to book other events are lost and the space sits idle.

Catering services can be used to generate demand for a hotel's guest rooms, particularly at convention and resort hotels. In a major hotel, the catering department negotiates with clients prior to their events with regard to the food to be served, the services to be provided, and the setup arrangements. For its part, the banqueting department schedules the servers, sets up the room(s), and executes the event; it coordinates with the kitchen staff and stewards accordingly.

Breakfast carts and *convenience stores* are now found in many hotels. Travellers who are in a hurry or who don't like to eat alone are able to pick up juice, coffee, and pastry items in the lobby. Convenience stores, usually in hotel lobbies, have been set up to look like corner stores on the street. Some hotel chains, such as Hyatt, have launched in-house brands. The stores may offer a lunch counter as well as the food and sundries expected at a convenience store. The prices charged reflect the cost of the product and the cost of making the products easily accessible. In other words, they usually are higher.

Vending machines provide prepackaged full meals as well as snacks and beverages in many accommodation settings. Because of developments in technology, more hot and cold food items can be made available. Beverage machines sporting a brand label are commonly found in easily accessible locations in lodging properties. Vending machine items can be accessed by inserting money or debit cards.

Employee cafeterias are usually a part of the food service in large hotels. Food often is provided for employees at no

ILLUSTRATION 10–2
Restaurants like Swiss Chalet need to update their menus and physical settings from time to time.
SOURCE: Courtesy of Cara Operations Ltd.

charge or at minimal cost. The cafeteria serves freshly prepared meals and beverages throughout the day. Special arrangements are made for employees working nights. In some properties, food for employees is provided entirely through vending machines, which provide hot and cold meal items as well as snacks. The food in these machines is accessed by debit card; an amount to spend on food during a specified period of time is allocated to each employee. In some properties, both methods are available.

Cruise dining, a special type of accommodation food service, is being revolutionized. Traditional formal dining at appointed hours is being replaced by "flexible dining." Staggered seating times have been introduced, and passengers are being given the choice of dining in a main restaurant or selecting casual alternatives. "Team service" with three waitstaff instead of two is elevating service quality, and menus are being upgraded. Both full-service and indoor and outdoor all-day buffet services are being offered. Eating formats and menu options range from Italian to Asian fusion. Disney rotates people through theme restaurants during their cruises. Norwegian Cruise Line offers so many culinary experiences—including classic cruise menus—that a passenger never has to eat in the same dining room twice or eat the same style of food twice (*Cruise Travel*, 2001). Making dining such a strong feature of a cruise presents challenges, not only for food production but also for the purchasing and storage of food, as the inventory is usually brought on board at the beginning of the cruise and needs to last until the end of the cruise.

Segment 2: Stand-Alone Restaurants

Stand-alone restaurants are probably the best-known category of restaurant. There are many types of them. They range from upscale restaurants to ice-cream parlours; they may be branded or not. Customers come to the restaurant primarily to eat. This category encompasses a variety of locations, sizes, configurations, service styles, menus, and prices. To stay in business, every stand-alone restaurant has to be especially attentive to its customers, because it can't benefit from referrals through affiliations the way brand restaurants in hotels and food courts can.

Quick-service restaurants (QSR), or fast-food outlets, have developed into three market subsegments in the past 30 years: traditional, quick comfort, and double drive-through (a drive-through with two drive-in lanes). The major chains tracked by the CRFA include those serving burgers, chicken, pizza, subs, and coffee and doughnuts.

Quick *traditional* service outlets offer limited-choice menus that are standardized and inexpensive. They attract a broad customer base for their counter and drive-through services. Most of these operations are branded and operate as part of a chain or as a franchise. Since the 1930s, the hamburger has been one of the most popular fast-food items. Today, chicken, French fries, pizza, salads, low-fat sandwiches, and breakfast food items are commonly available at quick-service outlets.

The *quick-comfort* segment has developed in response to the increasing demand for traditional family meals in a fast-service format. Roast chicken, mashed potatoes, baked ham, fish and chips, vegetables, salads, breads, and desserts are now available quickly and inexpensively through restaurants (most of them chains) with take-out counters and limited seating.

Drive-through outlets provide limited service and a limited number of inexpensive menu items such as fries, burgers, and/or seafood. There is no indoor seating, but picnic tables may be provided for customer convenience in warm weather.

Cafeterias can be stand-alone operations, but most of them are found in schools, universities, and hospitals. They provide inexpensive to moderately priced hot and cold food items in a self-service format. Many have introduced a "scrambled" format that includes a variety of ethnic options and branded foods in addition to the menu of the day. Flexible seating for up to several hundred is provided. This format attracts customers who are price-conscious (such as families and seniors), who want speedy sit-down service, and who want a wide choice of food items and serving sizes. Stand-alone cafeterias are common in the southern United States; they aren't as common in Canada. The service format at Ponderosa is based on the cafeteria model. Many supermarkets provide a small cafeteria-style food service outlet in conjunction with their deli counter.

Buffet and *smorgasbord* formats are popular for Sunday brunch in many hotels and restaurants and for catered events. They can also be the format for stand-alone outlets, especially in Germanic and Scandinavian countries. They feature "all you can eat" from an extensive display of a great variety of foods, a fixed price, and sometimes family-style seating at large tables that seat many guests. Prices are usually moderate to expensive and vary with location, service, and food quality.

Diners are the traditional North American restaurants of the 1950s. Today there are refurbished originals as well as authentic reproductions. The menu includes breakfast, lunch, and dinner. Often, breakfast is served all day. Customers can have inexpensive to moderately priced meals served at the counter, at tables, or in booths. Diners are located in downtown areas, in the suburbs, and near attractions and major highways.

Theme restaurants are organized around a theme that is reflected in the facility's appearance, menu, and service format. The inspiration can come from an era in history, a real or fictional character, a type of music, a notable feature of the community, a movie, or a sport. The atmosphere thereby created is meant to be part of the attraction. Many international chains have developed theme restaurants, for example, the Hard Rock Cafe. Other examples are found in theme parks such as Disney World. Prices vary but tend to be moderate, as is appropriate for a customer mix of young adults and families.

Ethnic restaurants are often owned and operated by families of a specific cultural heritage. Their food and design reflect the family's ethnic background. However, some ethnic restaurants are operated by chains or franchisees—for example, Mandarin and Mr. Greek. Prices tend to range from inexpensive to moderate; however, some of these restaurants offer outstanding service and food at premium prices. Consumer demand for ethnic restaurants, especially Japanese (Edo) and Indian (Bombay Palace) restaurants, is rising in Canada.

Beverage service options are increasing in Canada. *Wineries* and *coffee outlets* have joined *bars*, *pubs*, *taverns*, and *microbreweries* as providers of beverage services. Starbucks, Second Cup, and Tim Hortons, as well as independent outlets, are responding to the demand for specialty coffees and regular brews.

Wineries are being developed across the country, especially in Ontario and British Columbia, and have become part of tourists' cultural experiences in a region. Some wineries have established restaurants that feature their wines; others have opened tasting facilities to foster an appreciation of Canadian wines. Ice wine has become a Canadian specialty. Both Ontario and British Columbia wines merited more space than ever before in the 2001 edition of Hugh Johnson and Jancis Robinson's *World Atlas of Wine*, and many Canadian wines are winning international awards. According to Gill (2001), food-friendly wines are being created in this country, and Canadian vineyards are developing ways to showcase them. Sumac Ridge Estate has hired a full-time chef; Gray Monk Vineyard has arranged for local restaurateurs to fire up an open grill at their vineyard; Quail's Gate Winery features wine with British Columbia salmon; Summerhill Winery has an indoor tapas bar.

ILLUSTRATION 10–3

Peller Estates, one of Canda's leading winemakers, operates wineries in the Niagara Peninsula, Ontario, and in the Okanagan Valley, B.C. Icewine is harvested "at the coldest moment of a winter's night, each frozen grape creating just one drop of Icewine."

SOURCE: Photo courtesy Peller Estates.

At other types of beverage outlets, lighter meals are offered at bars and pubs than at taverns. Microbreweries such as Maritime Beer Company in Halifax provide local and international beer listings to accompany lunch and dinner menus. Having the production plant in full view contributes to the atmosphere. In other beverage outlets, the atmosphere is often enhanced through various themes, ranging from sports (such as hockey and baseball) to ethnic or lifestyle themes (e.g., an Irish pub or a tango bar). The hours at beverage establishments are commonly from midafternoon to after midnight; prices can be anywhere between expensive and inexpensive, depending on the outlet's location, format, design, and type of service.

Upscale/luxury or haute cuisine restaurants are distinguished by their prices and their unique character. Most are independently owned and exhibit the qualities promoted by the owner, chef, or owner/chef. Usually they offer a refined, coordinated atmosphere, impeccable service, gourmet cuisine, well-trained waitstaff, and an impressive choice of wines supported by a knowledgeable wine steward or (more and more often in Canada) a certified sommelier. The menu may be ethnic or eclectic or fusion, and often it will have signature items. Prices range from expensive to "through the roof." Most of them provide dinner service only, are located in business districts and cultural centres, and require that patrons reserve

ahead and observe a dress code; examples of these are Le Baccara in the Casino du Lac-Leamy in Gatineau, Quebec, and Auberge du Pommier in Toronto.

Family restaurants, as the name implies, serve mainly families. They are located in towns and suburbs, at major highway intersections, and near tourist attractions. Many, like Red Lobster, are franchises or part of a chain and offer table service for hundreds of customers. Their menus usually offer breakfast, lunch, and dinner options. Some, like Denny's, feature breakfast 24 hours a day.

Specialty restaurants can be sit-down or counter service. They feature specific foods such as steak, chicken, fish, pizza, vegetarian options, or pancakes. Both independents and chains use this format. Prices are moderate. Chains such as KFC could be considered specialty restaurants as well as fast-food outlets. Pizza Delight could be considered an ethnic restaurant as well as a specialty restaurant. Restaurants specializing in various types of Indian and Asian food—Thai, Malaysian, Chinese, or Japanese, for example—tend to be independent.

Delicatessen menus are built around a variety of meats and cheeses, which are made up on the spot as hot or cold sandwiches, or sold sliced ready for customers to make their own. Delis used to be found solely in Jewish neighbourhoods in inner cities. Today, in our more multicultural society, there are more delis. They tend to be stand-alone; however, many supermarkets now have deli counters. Consumers from many ethnic backgrounds enjoy the convenience and variety that delis provide.

Specialty coffee outlets have burgeoned in the past few years. Chain operations such as Starbucks and Second Cup and independents such as Java Moose in Saint John,

ILLUSTRATION 10–4

The Banffshire Club at the Fairmont Banff Springs Hotel has been the recipient of several prestigious awards, including the CAA/AAA Five Diamond Award.

SOURCE: Image courtesy of Fairmont Hotels and Resorts.

New Brunswick, offer beans sold whole or ground, along with an extensive menu of coffee drinks—espressos, cappuccinos, lattes, americanos, and so on. In a few outlets, coffee is all you can buy; in most, you can buy something to eat with it, typically a doughnut but possibly also sandwiches, muffins, bagels, pastries, or cookies. Tim Hortons is the most famous doughnut chain in Canada, and a national icon. At Tim Hortons, you can also buy inexpensive lunches, such as chili and chicken stew. Chapters (owned by Indigo) has incorporated Starbucks outlets into its stores. The typical coffee bar is small and on a street where there is heavy foot traffic. But there are also drive-through coffee outlets, which often offer 24-hour service.

Ice-cream outlets can be franchised or independent and tend to flourish in warm weather. Some are strictly counter service with limited options; others offer full sit-down service with a variety of ice-cream flavours, and products such as yogurt, shakes, and specialty cakes. Dairy Queen has developed cool-weather demand by offering "Hot eats and cool treats"; COWS, established on Prince Edward Island in 1983, has complemented its ice cream with branded merchandise available at its Canadian and U.S. outlets, by mail order, or online. Patrons wearing COWS T-shirts provide free advertising for the company. Most ice-cream outlet prices are inexpensive to moderate.

Chain restaurants, like hotels, are either owned and operated by, or franchised by, international chains. They may feature any of the specific foods discussed earlier and any of the service formats except the luxury restaurant. Location, service, and the food served dictate prices and clientele and the number of outlets in the chain. A single

ILLUSTRATION 10–5

Tim Hortons, a Canadian coffee institution, is the largest coffee and baked goods chain in Canada, with over 2200 outlets.

SOURCE: Courtesy of Elke Price.

company may offer multiple brands through corporate divisions and strategic alliances. Examples include: Pepsico through its subsidiary, Tricon Global Restaurants, owns Pizza Hut, Taco Bell, and KFC; Cara, Canada's largest integrated food service company, owns Swiss Chalet, Harvey's, Kelsey's, Montana's, and Milestone's.

Segment 3: En Route Food Services

En route food services are, obviously, patronized by travellers, who may be tourists, or by local residents. These operations include coffee shops, family restaurants, and quick-service fast-food outlets. Many are affiliated with service stations or part of a chain. Some are found in food courts or hotels, while others are stand-alone. Travellers have plenty of options with these, usually at low to moderate prices. Some operations serve breakfast 24 hours a day, and most are open at least 18 hours a day. Many Wendy's–Tim Hortons combo outlets (called "twinning") have sprung up to serve a market on the move, and succeed by being visible and by providing the right type of food at the right place and time (i.e., stage) of travellers' journeys.

Many food services are provided at *terminals* for passengers on planes, trains, buses, and ferries. Food outlets at these transfer locations usually serve brand-name products and often are managed under contract. Companies realize that travellers when passing through terminals constitute a captive audience, and that travellers yearn for familiar brand names when in unfamiliar territory. The owners and operators of terminals can rent or lease to food service companies and in this way avoid having to serve food themselves.

Service areas in a facility may include vending machines, snack counters with limited seating, and restaurants, lounges, and executive-class clubs. Travellers usually have a wide range of options for what they can eat and drink at terminals. The hours at terminal venues are dictated by the ebb and flow of passengers. Meals can be either catered or prepared on-site.

Segment 4: Catering

Food services that provide **catering services** prepare food and drink for a variety of occasions and serve people both on- and off-premises. Catering services can range from providing food for a private dinner for a few people to feeding several hundred people on a transatlantic flight. Catering delivery systems have developed in response to the demands created by people attending social, leisure, recreational, and business events in both the private and public sector. Lane and Dupre (1997), and others before them, have identified a variety of types of catering delivery systems. Eight systems are presented in Table 10–3 as well as specific challenges faced by each system in the process of delivering its type of catering service.

TABLE 10–3 Catering Services

1. Accommodation catering involves preparing food (mostly off-site) for occasions at private residences, serving, and then cleaning up. Often a well-known chef provides expert skills.

2. Airline catering requires the contracted company to provide appealing meals, meet a variety of special needs, and differentiate food service for first-, business-, and economy-class travellers, all within a budget.

3. Concession companies are contracted to provide food at sports stadiums, racetracks, airports, and attractions. This is a logistical challenge. Service is often around the clock; travellers have departure schedules to meet, attendance numbers are often unknown, labour must be coordinated, and the customer mix must be taken into account. Furthermore, venues can require everything from fine dining to counter service.

4. Mobile caterers range from bicycle-driven ice-cream wagons to motorized chip wagons with preparation facilities on board. They serve in all types of weather and at various locations, such as construction and film production sites, special events, and permanent attractions. The challenge they face is to supply the required products and services where and when they are needed.

5. Off-premise caterers prepare food off-site and then deliver it to sites, which can be outdoor or indoor. Systems have to be set up for safely storing the food and for service. The challenge for these caterers is to coordinate the production and equipment aspects of operating in many places.

6. On-premise caterers rent or lease their facilities and provide a variety of food services on-premise to meet the needs of corporate and private customers. They serve small to large groups for business meetings and social events, often serving numerous groups at the same time. Many clubs and universities provide space and food services to generate revenue.

7. Special occasion caterers provide food service for mega-events, such as the Olympics and World Summits, which require strategic planning, sophisticated delivery systems, and staff and managers with the ability and experience to meet many different needs.

8. Wholesale caterers provide cooked and prepared foods to organizations that provide catering services. They don't serve food. They have to deliver fresh foods, including desserts and breads, to a variety of food services at acceptable prices that cover the cost of production, storage, and transportation.

SOURCES: Cracknell, Kaufmann, and Nobes (1983), *Practical Professional Catering*. London: Macmillan Press; Glew (1984), *Advances in Catering Technology*. London: Elsevier Applied Science Publishers; Lane and Dupre (1997), *Hospitality World!* Toronto: Van Nostrand Reinhold; Shock and Stefanelli (1992), *Hotel Catering: A Handbook for Sales and Operations*. Toronto: John Wiley and Sons Inc.; Weiss and Weiss (1987), *Catering Handbook*. Jenks, OK: J. Williams Book Company.

Segment 5: Eatertainment Concepts

Several eatertainment concepts exist today. Lettuce Entertain You and Hard Rock Cafe have led the way over the past 20 years in creating restaurants that entertain as well as serve. Many restaurants, often in sports-related markets, have added super-screen television for their patrons. Dinner theatre has been enjoying a resurgence. The shows, which are presented concurrently with dinner, can be anything from musicals (Stage West in Toronto and Calgary) to murder mysteries (Mysteriously Yours). Over the years, cabarets and other musical performances have also been presented with meals. The food itself can be entertainment. This category includes open kitchens and prepared-at-the-table menu offerings (flambées, for example). And if the wait-staff does it well, the service itself can be a form of entertainment.

Segment 6: Clubs

Clubs provide services for members and their guests. Some provide food service and nothing else. Others provide food service as a complement to other services such as lodging, meetings, or recreation activities. Country clubs, city clubs, and fraternal clubs often serve food. This can involve on-premise dining for members and/or banquet facilities for rent. Many fraternal and other organizations run meal programs for seniors, such as Wheels to Meals and Meals on Wheels.

Segment 7: Food Service in Other Establishments

Many establishments provide food services for people who are there for other reasons than to eat. Examples of such venues are shopping malls, department stores, specialty retail stores, corporate headquarters, truck stops, and convenience stores. The outlets can be any of the following:

- *Food courts* in shopping malls are fast and inexpensive, and serve both shoppers and mall employees.
- *Cafeterias* in offices and department stores are often contracted out to food service firms.
- *Chain-brand food services* such as Subway, Baskin Robbins, and McDonald's are often found at travel plazas and truck stops, and also in hospitals and other public buildings.
- *Convenience stores* often have coffee bars and prepared snacks. These are prepared off-premise by a contract food service supplier.

Segment 8: Institutional Food Service

Institutional food services are noncommercial and have a more captive audience than commercial operations. Revenue is received in lump sums through a contract agreement with a university, hospital, or other organization. Institutional food service includes service for correctional, health care, and military facilities, and for schools. It also includes corporate dining rooms and employee cafeterias. The food service can be provided in-house or contracted out to companies like ARAMARK Canada or Cara. These firms may offer brand products or produce them in-house. Some companies that provide food service also provide facility management services such as housekeeping, laundry, engineering, and security.

Check Your Product Knowledge

1. How does tourism influence food service operations?

2. What types of food service may be part of accommodation operations?

3. Why have more forms of eatertainment been implemented in recent years?

4. What makes airline catering different from other types of catering?

5. What are the differences between stand-alone food services and food services in other establishments? What examples of each category have you visited? What service formats were being used?

THE RESTAURANT FOOD SERVICE MARKET

The restaurant market is the largest segment of the food service market. In 2007, full-service restaurants in Canada held 36 percent of the food service market, and limited-

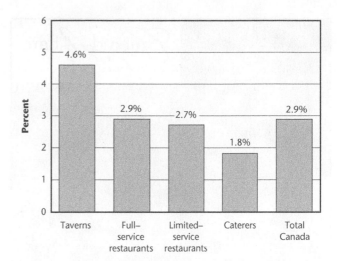

FIGURE 10–1 Food Service Annual Real Growth Forecast by Sector, 2000–04

SOURCE: Reprinted by permission from Canadian Restaurant and Food Services Associations.

service restaurants 32 percent (CRFA, "Facts about," n.d.). The restaurant market is highly competitive because it depends on customer demand. Several factors contribute to the demand for this type of food service:

- More people travel and are familiar with a variety of restaurants and types of service.
- More people eat out while travelling and at destinations.
- Two-income families have less time to prepare home-cooked meals.
- Two-income couples eat out more often, make short trips more often, and seek eating experiences at destinations.
- More people have more discretionary income.
- More people consider eating out an entertainment experience.
- Older people need or want food service because they want the company or are unable to prepare meals.

According to the CRFA, there are more than 63 000 food service establishments in Canada. Of these, 63 percent are independently owned. It is predicted that food services will continue growing. (See Figure 10–1.)

Toronto and Vancouver have started to challenge Montreal, but Quebec's gastronomic culture and passion for food keep it at the head of Canada's table. Toronto's F&B market has grown and become more cosmopolitan, and Vancouver keeps trying to steal Montreal's avant-garde thunder, but Montreal continues to stay ahead with its new offerings and its Old World style (Ferguson, 2001).

Compared with international destinations, and contrary to popular belief, restaurants in Canada are relatively inexpensive. Edmonton is the least expensive city; Montreal and Toronto, the most expensive.

ILLUSTRATION 10–6

Catered Affare is a successful fine-food catering and event planning company based in Toronto, and has won numerous industry awards.

SOURCE: Image courtesy of Catered Affare.

Check Your Product Knowledge

1. What factors contribute to the demand for food service in restaurants?
2. What is the forecast for growth in the full- and limited-service restaurant markets?
3. Why is Montreal considered the leading Canadian restaurant market?

FOOD AND BEVERAGE MANAGEMENT

When it comes to managing systems and processes, all the many categories/segments of food service have a number of things in common. Management systems are affected by the type of ownership, the operating philosophy, and the service's mission and goals. A food service venue must coordinate operations, human resources, marketing, finance, and research and development (R&D).

Ownership

Food service operations are more likely now than they have ever been to be under some form of joint ownership. There are many **forms of ownership**: partnerships, silent or limited partnerships, corporations, individual ownership, chain ownership, leasing arrangements, joint ventures, franchises, and management contracts (see Chapter 9 for more about forms of ownership). That being said, restaurants, unlike hotels, are mostly independently owned. In 2003, 63 percent of Canadian restaurants were independents. However, franchises are increasing in importance. Franchises involve less risk for entrepreneurs, as their menus, production methods, service formats, and training are more structured. Many independents fail soon after they open, and as many as 80 percent may go bankrupt eventually as more and more chains and franchises enter the marketplace. According to the CRFA, "The number of commercial foodservice bankruptcies in Canada fell 3.1% in 2007 to 683, the fewest since 1980. In the past 10 years, the number of foodservice bankruptcies has fallen by 60%, even in light of rising operating expenses and shrinking profit margins" (CRFA, February 20, 2008).

Food Service Franchising

The origin of the word "franchise" is French, meaning "free from servitude." To assist in understanding franchising, the following definitions are provided:

- A franchise is a legal agreement between the franchisor and the franchisee.
- The franchisor is the owner of a concept based on one or more of the following: an idea, a name, a process, and/or a product.
- A franchisee is a person or group that purchases a franchise, with all its rights and privileges, from a franchisor.
- Franchising, according to the International Franchise Association, is "a continuing relationship in which the franchisor provides a licensed privilege to do business, plus assistance in organizing, training, merchandising and management in return for consideration from the franchisee."
- The consideration paid by the franchisee includes an annual franchise fee, usually royalty fees, and often advertising fees (see Table 10–4) (Khan, 1999).

Oliver Bonacini Restaurants is one food service corporation that has been extremely successful in the past decade and has been able to diversify and expand its restaurant operations (see Figure 10–2).

Operating Philosophy

The philosophy of the owner and/or the operator dictates how a business is run. An operation's *ethics*, *morals*, *core values*, and *principles* are expressed in its everyday *policies*

Peter Oliver + Michael Bonacini = Oliver Bonacini (OB) Restaurants

Since 1993, Oliver and Bonacini have demonstrated how to select locations in Toronto and create concepts with moods to suit the needs of various upscale client groups. In 2001 they received *Toronto Life's* award for "Lifetime Achievement." As well, Toronto's local magazines *Where* and *Now* both voted Canoe the number-one restaurant in the city, while competitor *Eye* magazine voted Biff's number one. (This kind of competition Oliver Bonacini can handle!) The nation's leading food service industry publication, *Foodservice and Hospitality* magazine, named Oliver and Bonacini "Entrepreneurs of the Year" in 2001. Included in their unique portfolio of restaurants are the following:

Auberge du Pommier A cozy chateau with Provencal-style charm, where fireplaces blaze in winter and in the summer guests can dine al fresco under a canvas-covered terrace. From appetizers, like warm goat cheese in Niagara vine leaf, to entrées of sage-roasted pheasant breast, diners enjoy a quality fine-dining experience with expert service.

Jump Café & Bar A sprawling New York-style bistro located in Toronto's financial district that serves power brokers at lunch and brings them back for after-work drinks and dinner. Whether putting deals together or celebrating, traditional or adventuresome diners have many choices from an eclectic North American-style menu. Jump is known for its consistent, ultra-smooth service.

Canoe Restaurant & Bar With a unique location high atop the TD Bank Tower, this restaurant affords a breathtaking view of the city. The design is clean and simple, yet absolutely stylish—a brilliant reflection of this country's rich, raw environment. Chef's interpretations of regional Canadian cuisine include skin-roasted Arctic char, herb-stuffed breast of Ontario pheasant, roast Yukon caribou, Quebec foie gras—the menu is a tribute to the freshest and the finest ingredients this country has to offer. The service is inspired and the wine cellar is excellent.

BIFF'S

Biff's This charming and classic upscale French bistro feels a lot like Paris in the 1930s. Comfortable, upbeat, and handsomely accoutred, it is cleverly pitched to please both schmancy opera buffs and the more casual Sunday brunch crowd. Robust bistro cooking matches the rich warmth of the room, including braised lamb shank with white bean cassoulet, roast duck confit, and coq au vin. The authentic zinc-topped bar is a real stunner. Biff's opened to resounding critical review in 2000.

Oliver & Bonacini
cafe · grill

Oliver & Bonacini Cafe and Grill opened in March 2002 and is located in Bayview Village shopping complex in Toronto. The concept is slightly downscale from the company's usual positioning, but was intended to bring Oliver Bonacini quality, service, and sizzle to neighbourhood markets.

Oliver Bonacini is also involved in another co-venture, **Soma Chocolatemaker,** which opened in 2004 in the Distillery Historic District in downtown Toronto. **Square**, with a "Euro modern cuisine in a stylish, sophisticated dining environment," also opened in 2004 (since closed). In November 2005, OB opened a second Oliver & Bonacini Cafe and Grill in the Westin Trillium House in Collingwood at the Blue Mountain resort.

FIGURE 10–2 Example of a Diversified Food Service Corporation

SOURCE: T. Suraci (Oct. 2001) Oliver Bonacini Restaurants, Toronto, Ontario.

and *practices*. These in turn determine whether the operation succeeds.

Environmental consciousness is linked closely to the management's philosophy. If management initiates and rewards environmentally conscious practices, the employees are likely to be committed to an **ecofriendly** operation. They will "think green" when selecting products and packaging, determining portion sizes, conserving energy, and managing materials—including hazardous materials.

As in all other areas of the tourism industry, **ethical policies** should be an integral part of doing business, from employment policies to internal communications. Ethics has been defined as "knowing what ought to be done, and

ILLUSTRATION 10–7

Businesspeople and students have been frequenting local pubs for years to enjoy beer and "pub grub."
SOURCE: Stuart Clarke/Bloomberg News/Landov.

having the will to do it" (Hall, 1992, pp. 9–23). Applying a **code of ethics** helps managers and staff members to consider the impact of their decisions on others regarding everything from sanitation practices to making a profit.

Vision, Mission, Goals, and Objectives

A company may not have clearly outlined its vision nor have a formal mission statement that states why it is in business. Most operations, however, have short- and long-term goals and objectives. Table 10–5 illustrates what might be included in these.

Controls

Controls are internal processes that ensure specific tasks are carried out according to set standards. A lack of controls in the F&B sector leads to poor-quality products, thefts of cash, and misuse of food, beverages, and other supplies. Variances between forecasts and what actually happens need to be investigated. If products and services are not up to expected standards, or food costs are

higher than expected, it may mean that personnel are not producing acceptable products, that food and supplies are going out the back door, or that the menu is underpriced.

Total Quality Management and Service

In this highly competitive marketplace, F&B operations must deliver products and services that meet or exceed the expectations of patrons. The customer is the final judge. However, the process is directed by standards as well as by products and services. Whatever the type of F&B operation, maintaining standards leads to consistent delivery of quality. Such consistent delivery of quality is recognized by awards given to the top restaurants in Canada. The Banffshire Club, the signature dining room at the Banff Springs hotel, was awarded the coveted CAA/AAA Five Diamond Award in 2003—only its second year of operation, and in 2007 received its fifth consecutive award. In 2007, Le Baccara restaurant in the Casino du Lac-Leamy (Gatineau, Quebec) was awarded the AAA Five Diamond status for the eighth consecutive year. In 2007, Truffles

TABLE 10–4 Selected QSR Franchises and Their Costs and Fees ($US unless indicated otherwise)

Franchise	Franchise Started	Cdn. Units	World Units	Start-Up Capital ($)	Franchise Fee ($)	Royalty Fee
Baskin Robbins	1948	150	5 800	146K–528K	40K	5.9%
Ben & Jerry's	1981	19	359	199K–385K	9–32K	3.0%
Burger King	1961	345	11 220	520K–970K	55K	4.5%
Dairy Queen	1944	574	6 574	55K–1.3 M	30K–45K	4.5%
Domino's Pizza	1967	n/a*	6 712	120K–460K	0–25 K	5.5%
Dunkin' Donuts	1955	108	8 000	750K–1.5 M	50K	5.9%
KFC	1952	788	8 334	300K–1.2 M	41.9K	4.0%
McDonald's	1955	1 400	31 000	506K–1.6 M	45K	12.5%
Mr. Sub	1972	460	0	75–177K†	15K†	5.0%
Pizza Hut	1959	452	7 287	320K–1.2 M	41.9K	6.5%
Pizza Pizza	1978	313	0	300K†	30K†	6.0%
Quiznos Subs	1983	213	4300	235K–311K	25K	7.0%
Subway	1965	1 803	29 095	94K–225K	41.9K	8.0%
Taco Bell	1964	186	5 403	3M	45K	5.5%
Wendy's	1971	236	6 645	846K–6 M	40K	4.0%

*Not available.
†CDN$.

SOURCE: Adapted from Entrepreneur's Annual Franchise 500 (www.entrepreneur.com) and Individual Corporate websites.

restaurant in the Four Seasons Hotel Toronto was awarded the AAA five Diamond status for its fourteenth consecutive year.

To provide customers with what they want when they want it, many operations have implemented total quality management (TQM). Under TQM, the employees, who are the service providers, are treated as **internal customers,** and the people seeking service are considered **external customers**.

Servers can be encouraged to identify positive and negative aspects of the service that was provided and suggest how to improve it. TQM is a top–down, bottom–up, continuous process that focuses on error prevention, not just error detection (Gilbert, 1992; Walker, 2001).

Communication

Effective communication involves more than providing channels. It is also critical that people understand the messages they receive. When communication is poor, the entire organization suffers because operational functions such as forecasting, planning, organizing, and motivating lack the lubrication that effective communication provides. Food service managers must think carefully about how to communicate best. They need to find the right balance between "high touch" and "high tech."

TABLE 10–5 Sample Vision, Mission Statement, and Objectives for an F&B Operation

Vision	We will be the best family-service restaurant in the city.
Mission	We will be recognized in the city as the number-one restaurant for quality of food and friendly service; we will strive to improve and prosper as a business for the benefit of our customers, employees, and owners.
Short-term	We will reduce food costs by 5 percent this quarter and serve 5 percent more customers.
Objectives	• Reduce portion sizes. • Target seniors market for this month's promotion. • Introduce Monday luncheon special.
Long-term	We will reduce our turnover rate this year.
Objectives	• Begin training program for food and beverage servers for new and old employees. • Use forecasting to determine schedule requirements. • Shorten probation period to one month and provide more frequent feedback on performance.

Check Your Product Knowledge

1. What type of ownership is usually found with fast-food outlets?
2. What dictates how a business is operated?
3. Define *ethics*.
4. How do goals and objectives relate to an operation's vision and mission?
5. What is involved in TQM in food services?

TABLE 10–6 Why Culinary Tourism Is Important: Highlights from ICTA website

The Food is the Attraction

Culinary Art is the only art that speaks to all five human senses

Culinary Tourism is at the Turning Point, like where Ecotourism was 20 years ago

Culinary Tourism is the fastest growing sector in tourism in many countries

Culinary Tourism is a tool for economic and community development

Culinary Tourists are explorers—a new discovery with every meal

Culinary Tourists are not exclusive to any particular age, gender, or ethnic group

Cuisine is the only attraction that is available all year round, in any weather, at any time of day

Cuisine is experiential, offering hands-on interactive experiences

Dining is an opportunity for visitors to experience local food and people

Dining has the greatest potential to make a long lasting impact on visitors

SOURCE: International Culinary Tourism Association, www.culinarytourism.org

FOOD AND BEVERAGE TRENDS

Food service trends are influenced by the natural, psychosocial, and technological environments. Today, energy efficiency is re-emerging as a concern, and more people are sensitive to air quality and have developed food allergies. To address air quality concerns, many jurisdictions are banning smoking in public places such as restaurants and lounges. Customers of all ages and ethnicities are demanding more flavourful foods. Also, nutrition continues to be a focus, and low-carbohydrate and vegetarian options are being sought. More operators are leveraging the power of the Internet, using e-commerce to promote their businesses and to enable various customer process and relationship marketing.

According to Novo (2004), "Using the relationship marketing approach, you customize programs for individual consumer groups and the stage of the process they are going through, as opposed to some forms of database marketing where everybody would get virtually the same promotions, with perhaps a change in the offer. The stage in the customer life cycle determines the marketing approach used with the customer."

Culinary Tourism

The International Culinary Tourism Association (n.d.) defines **culinary tourism** as a "unique memorable gastronomic experience, not just four stars or better . . . and a tool for economic and community development. Culinary Tourism encompasses cooking schools, cookbook and kitchen gadget stores, culinary tours and tour leaders, culinary media and guidebooks, caterers, wineries, breweries, distilleries, food growers and manufacturers, culinary attractions and more." Culinary tourism is contrasted with agritourism, which has more rural roots. Culinary tourism depends on a place's culture, rather than its geographical features. Culinary travelers are more inclined to search and buy from a culinary travel website such as Foodtrekker which is designed for their specific target market.

Culinary tourism starting being recognized as the travel industry's most important new niche (see table 10–6), with ICTA's first International Conference on Culinary Tourism in May 2004, in Victoria, British Columbia, and the Canadian Institute of Advanced Culinary Arts' first Culinary Tourism Symposium at the School of Hospitality & Culinary Arts at George Brown College in Toronto in 2005. In April 2008, there was a New England Culinary Tourism Symposium which included a full day of in-depth, highly targeted culinary tourism marketing and development sessions, and Culinary Tourism BC hosted their first Culinary Symposium in March 2008.

Carb Craze and No Trans fat

Many restaurants have been adapting a part of their menus to appeal to diet-conscious consumers. **Low-carb diets** have been on the market for years, but the trend became increasingly more fashionable starting in 2003. Now, the buzz is "no trans fat." Trans fat, which has been linked to heart disease, was previously used in most restaurant cooking oils and store-bought margarines and spreads. Under consumer pressure, F&B businesses have been voluntarily removing them from their products and cooking processes, though the federal government has warned that it will step in with legislation if progress with trans fat removal isn't made. The city of Calgary banned restaurant cooking oils with over 2 percent of trans fats, as of January 2008.

ILLUSTRATION 10–8

Native Canadian cuisine or aboriginal cuisine has been promoted for several years by Toronto-born chef Professor David Wolfman from the Xl'xlap nation and his television cooking show called *Cooking with the Wolfman*.

SOURCE: Photo courtesy of Aboriginal Cuisine Inc. from Cooking with the Wolfman™.

BYOW and THTR

On January 24, 2005, Ontario implemented a "Bring Your Own Wine" (**BYOW**) program for restaurants on a voluntary basis, as well as "Take Home the Rest" (**THTR**). This allows customers to bring a bottle of preferred wine for dinner at a participating restaurant (or hotel/motel banquet hall) with a liquor sales licence. This is generally cheaper for the customer than ordering one from the restaurant's cellars, so restaurants are allowed to set fees, such as corkage fees, to offset lost income. Alberta, B.C., Manitoba, New Brunswick, Quebec, and Nova Scotia already have similar legislation.

The Smoke-Free Ontario Act

Since 2006, Ontario has banned smoking in any enclosed public places, which includes restaurants, bars, casinos, hotels (except in designated smoking guest rooms), and patios that are protected with a roof/awning. It is the responsibility of establishment owners/operators to ensure that no smoking occurs on their property, whether by customer or employee. There was considerable concern among restaurant and bar operators that their businesses would suffer significantly, and there was a decline in clientele for a short period of time until customers accepted the law. Many countries have similar legislation, such as the U.K., Ireland, Italy, and France.

New Canadians to Shape Foodservice Trends

With the growing population of immigrants from Asia, foodservice operators have an expanding group of potential customers whose needs should be addressed. A report by Ipsos Reid indicated that "almost three in four (73%) Chinese Canadians visit western-style fast food restaurants at least occasionally, but only fourteen percent are regular visitors. Similarly, more than one in five (22%) Chinese Canadians are frequent coffee shop customers, but a sizeable proportion of Chinese Canadians (41%) have never visited a coffee shop" (in CRFA, September 19, 2007). The challenge is to cater to not just to their cuisine, but in terms of their dining habits as well.

Restaurant Food Trends

According to Chef John Kinsella, president of the American Culinary Federation (ACF), "The trend of small plates is definitely hot, including offering tasting menus of small portions of food, wine or other alcohol beverages. The trend I see as the fastest growing going into 2008 is the alternative-source ingredients—local produce, organics, sustainable seafood, grass-fed and free-range items" (NRA, 2007).

A 2007 survey of ACF chef members also included the following hot trends: alternative red meats (buffalo, ostrich, venison); incorporation of ethnic cuisines, flavours, and ingredients; fusion ethnic cuisine; flatbreads; Asian entrée salads; Asian appetizers; Latin American cuisine; ciabatta bread; and Mediterranean cuisine; and in preparation techniques, braised items were considered the most trendy. For hot trends in beverages, the survey listed Craft beer, energy-drink cocktails, martinis/flavoured martinis, mojitos, artisan liquors, organic wine, specialty beer (seasonal, spiced, fruit, etc.), and flavoured/enhanced water (NRA, 2007).

For a more detailed perspective of selected restaurant food trends, please refer to Table 10–7.

FOOD AND BEVERAGE ISSUES

Personal Information Protection and Electronic Documents Act

On January 1, 2004, new privacy legislation from the federal government came into effect: the Personal Information Protection and Electronic Documents (PIPED) Act. According to the Privacy Commissioner of Canada's website (www.privcom.gc.ca):

> The purpose of this Part [3] is to establish, in an era in which technology increasingly facilitates the circulation and exchange of information, rules to govern the collection, use and disclosure of personal information in a manner that recognizes the right of privacy of individuals with respect to their personal information and the need of organizations to collect, use or disclose personal information for purposes that a reasonable person would consider appropriate in the circumstances.

TABLE 10–7 Restaurant Food Trends

Smaller portions and snack sizes. Are we, or have we, become a 'nation of snackers'? Are the mini burger and tapas style dishes a long term trend or a short term fad?

Caribbean Latin cuisine. Consumers tasting abilities decrease slightly with age, so more flavourful spicy foods are becoming popular with the aging population.

Healthy food choices. To satisfy consumers, more restaurants are offering organic food, locally grown food and free range meats, and using healthier cooking oils and eliminating trans fat.

Healthy spices. More spices such as cumin, tumeric, ginger, etc. are being added to food recipes for their antioxidant capabilities and their claim to potentially prevent certain chronic diseases; they also enhance food flavour and personality.

Casual environment. Consumers seem to want five star food in a more relaxed setting

Grocery stores with restaurants. Accessibility and convenience seem to be the reasons grocery stores are hiring chefs who are cooking higher quality hot food; some stores have opened full service restaurants. (Leong, January, 2008)

SOURCE: Adapted from "2008 Restaurant Food Trends," Kristie Leong, MD. Associated Content, January 2008.

This legislation affects all commercial operations, including food and beverage outlets. Food service outlets with delivery service may still keep their previous customer orders and customer credit card numbers on file for future reference, provided that they obtain consent when the order is taken and inform the customer why the information will be maintained on the company's records. Customers may give their consent in person, by phone, by mail, or by e-mail; companies should retain a copy of this consent (CRFA, February 2004).

Previously collected information is also subject to the new rules, so customers must be informed and their consent obtained. For further information, companies may request a *PIPED Act E-Kit for Businesses* from the Privacy Commissioner's website.

Check Your Product Knowledge

1. How can F&B service be improved?
2. What is culinary tourism?
3. List three reasons why culinary tourism is important.

CAREER OPPORTUNITIES

The F&B sector is one of the fastest-growing sectors and is expected to continue growing quickly. The food service industry is one of the top 10 job creators in Canada; every $1 million in food service sales creates 34.5 jobs (CRFA, 2001). The Canadian food service industry is generating $55 billion in sales. Finding people to work in food service has become a problem. With the increasing labour shortage, there are many first-time employment and career opportunities in food services.

Occupational Settings

There are a variety of occupational settings for pursuing a career in the F&B sector. Check out the Tourism Work Web (www.tourismworkweb.com), Canada's online recruiting and resource network, to see what is available.

Descriptions of food service occupations can be found on the Canadian Tourism Human Resource Council (CTHRC) website. This council has worked with industry to establish standards and certification for many occupations in the F&B sector of the tourism industry. Training and education councils (TECs) work with food service associations and the CTHRC to advance training and education opportunities. They also train workers to improve the quality of service in the F&B sector. More information is available by contacting the CTHRC or TEC in your part of the country.

Other organizations that play a role in careers/occupation in the F&B sector include:

- Canadian Culinary Federation (Fédération Culinaire Canadienne).
- Canadian Association of Foodservice Professionals.
- Canadian Restaurant and Foodservices Association.
- National Restaurant Association (U.S.).
- Canadian Sommelier Guild.
- Provincial restaurant associations.

A DAY IN THE LIFE OF A

Food and Beverage Manager

Chris, the vice president of F&B for the hotel and casino had just asked Gary if he would be interested in the F&B director position for the casino. Gary thought, *"Wow!* What an opportunity! What a challenge!"

Some questions immediately came to mind: "Do I want to change positions? Do I have the experience and ability to do a good job? Is it too soon to change my current position as the hotel's manager of restaurants and lounges?" Gary had held that position less than a year, but he had received the hotel's Leadership Award based on his efforts in opening the new restaurant. Gary knew that becoming an F&B director was the next step if he wanted to advance his career.

So he pulled up his résumé file and looked over the stages in his career since 2002. He noted that it had been longer than he thought since he'd updated it. He reviewed what he had done since coming to the hotel in 2005. All in all, he had met more than a few management challenges and had developed a pretty positive track record. He'd never regretted completing a degree after the two-year diploma program at the local community college. Mandatory work terms at The Fairmont Algonquin in St. Andrews, the Hotel Roxborough in Ottawa, and The Fairmont Banff Springs hotel had provided him with experiences across Canada in F&B services, including catering and lounge management. And the two years as F&B manager at a luxury hotel in the West Indies, right after graduating from university, had also been good experience.

Now he mused, "Where do I begin? What should I highlight?" Gary knew the new position would make him responsible for the casino's new 70-seat, fine-dining, full-service restaurant; the 24-hour buffet adjacent to the gaming floor; the banquet and catering department's 150-seat banquet facility; the 120-seat entertainment lounge; and the 24-hour beverage service for the gaming area of the casino. He would also have to work with the manager of TGI Friday's.

"What have I learned?" he asked himself. Well, as manager of restaurants and lounges in the hotel since 2007, he'd assisted in the restoration of the hotel's food service. That had been an experience! He knew he was lucky to be managing such a unique fine-dining restaurant—unusual layout, spectacular views of the harbour, open-concept show kitchen, and lots of new and return customers. Granted, the view might be the attraction initially, but Gary figured it took quality food and service to keep customers coming back. The quality of the Canadian and regional cuisine—blueberries, fresh greens, breads, and fresh seafood year round—certainly was the result of having an exceptional executive chef with a unique style. Gary and the chef were committed to delivering a menu that focused on flavour, taste, presentation, and value. "Will I have the same degree of support from the new chef at the casino restaurant?" he wondered.

Gary thought about the concept of the new restaurant, which was unique and would be a far different management challenge. First, Chris, the vice president of food and beverage, had been the F&B director when the restaurant opened. "Would he still feel it was his special project?" Gary asked himself. There was no denying that the restaurant was a special operation targeted at a niche market with sophisticated tastes. Second, having wine as an integral part of the dining experience made the restaurant the only one of its kind in the city. Gary couldn't help asking himself, "Is there really a market here for diners who want the ultimate dining experience, an opportunity to sample prestige wines, old and new, in a casino setting? Is it possible to draw dining-only clientele to the restaurant, as well as casino patrons?"

He knew the intention was for the food and ambience to be as important as the wine. There wasn't a view of the harbour, but the elaborate wine display cases, fine linen, crystal stemware, Royal Doulton china, and fireplace made it a spectacular dining room. It was a comfortable but not intimidating upscale atmosphere for dining. "Will there be enough business from the niche market we've targeted to sustain the concept?" he wondered. "What will it take to make it profitable? What menu selections will it take? Will introducing a chef's table be a good idea?" Gary knew that the new executive chef they'd hired had cooked for royalty all over the world. "Will I be able to work with the chef, and will we be able to attract patrons who are be satisfied enough to return?

"To whom does the menu appeal? Weren't casino patrons risk takers? If so, did that charac- teristic apply to eating? Is leisurely fine dining really going to be a complementary compo- nent of the casino F&B opera- tion?" He understood that the market feasibility study had indi- cated it would.

Career decisions could take you down the wrong path as easily as the right one. Gary fig- ured he would take the position if it was offered. So he started applying the finishing touches to his new résumé.

Summary

- The food and beverage industry is a major compo- nent of the tourism sector and has a significant effect on labour markets and the economy.
- The development of food services has paralleled changes in travel modes, travel opportunities, destination development, work patterns, and demographics.
- French culinary practices have influenced food service throughout the world.
- The modern concept of the restaurant originated in France in the eighteenth century. Restaurants include both greasy spoons and fine dining, and both leisurely dining and fast-food formats. They serve both tourists and local people.
- Consumers are attracted to service formats that meet their needs at specific times.
- Food service operations must adapt to the changing needs in the marketplace.
- People who eat out in Canada can experience distinctive cuisines that reflect ethnic customs and local foods.
- Restaurants in accommodation facilities do not have to be as competitive as freestanding restaurants because overnight guests have fewer choices and cannot eat at home.
- The F&B service in an accommodation property usually has several departments: room service, bars and lounges, catering operations, dining rooms, coffee shops, vending machines, and possibly a staff cafeteria.
- Modes of transportation dictate types of en route food service.
- Ethical policies should be an integral part of doing business.
- Consumers are the key to creating successful con- cepts for food service operations.
- The F&B sector is one of the fastest-growing sectors. Monitoring changes and conducting operational and market research is an ongoing part of staying competitive.

Key Terms

banqueting department p. 234
BYOW p. 245
catering services p. 237
code of ethics p. 242
controls p. 242
culinary tourism p. 244
eatertainment p. 231
ecofriendly p. 241
en route food services p. 237
ethical policies p. 241
external customers p. 243
forms of ownership p. 240
institutional food service p. 239
internal customers p. 243
low-carb diets p. 244
segments of food service p. 232
THTR p. 245

Internet Connections

Canadian Association of Foodservice Professionals (CAFP)
www.cafp.com p. 246

Canadian Culinary Federation (Fédération Culinaire Canadienne)
www.ccfcc.ca p. 232

Canadian Restaurant and Foodservice Association (CRFA)
www.crfa.ca p. 229

Canadian Tourism Human Resources Council (CTHRC)
www.cthrc.ca p. 246

Cara Operations Limited
www.cara.com p. 230

Casino du Lac-Leamy (Gatineau, Quebec) (Le Baccara Restaurant)
www.casinosduquebec.com/lacleamy/ p. 236

Cooking with the Wolfman (Aboriginal cuisine)
http://Cookingwiththewolfman.com   p. 232

Cuisine Canada
www.cuisinecanada.ca

International Culinary Tourism Association
www.culinarytourism.org   p. 244

National Restaurant Association (NRA)
www.restaurant.org   p. 246

Oliver Bonacini Restaurants
www.oliverbonacini.com   p. 240

Quail's Gate Winery
www.quailsgate.com   p. 235

Red Lobster
www.redlobster.com   p. 236

SIR Corp
www.sircorp.com

Starbucks
www.starbucks.com   p. 235

Swiss Chalet
www.swisschalet.ca   p. 230

Taste of Nova Scotia
www.tasteofnovascotia.com   p. 232

Tim Hortons
www.timhortons.com   p. 235

WORKSHEET 10–1 | Choosing a Restaurant

You are a tourism/visitor information counsellor at Yourtown's visitor information centre. Refer to a visitors' guide or the Internet for DineAid.com or a similar website for your community or region, and identify the eight food service segments you learned about in this chapter. Now make suggestions for the following customers. Describe your selections in the space provided, and explain why you believe each food service operation is suitable. Remember that as an information counsellor you are only to give information. You should not recommend one food service operation over another.

1. A retired couple from out of town has come to Yourtown to visit because the man lived there 50 years ago until he went away to university. He has never been back. The couple would like to eat at a moderately priced restaurant where they will be able to experience local food and possibly meet people from the area.

_____

_____

_____

_____

_____

_____

2. An executive is looking for a place to have dinner after being in town for a three-day conference. She will be staying at a local hotel but wants to eat at a place by herself that is within walking distance and offers an ethnic menu.

_____

_____

_____

_____

_____

_____

3. A mother and father with two children (4 and 14) are on a two-week vacation. They are passing through Yourtown and want to know where they can eat dinner at a full-service restaurant that serves local foods.

_____

_____

_____

_____

_____

_____

_____

WORKSHEET 10–2   Food and Beverage Service Segmentation

Food service is provided for a variety of reasons. Using the Internet, identify four commercial food service outlets that serve different markets. Complete the boxes by entering the information related to each of your four choices.

Name of establishment _____

Internet URL_____

Type of food service _____

Target market _____

Location _____

Price range_____

Facilities/services/menu _____

_____

_____

_____

_____

_____

_____

_____

_____

Name of establishment _____

Internet URL_____

Type of food service _____

Target market _____

Location _____

Price range_____

Facilities/services/menu _____

_____

_____

_____

_____

_____

_____

_____

_____

Name of establishment _____

Internet URL_____

Type of food service _____

Target market _____

Location _____

Price range_____

Facilities/services/menu _____

_____

_____

_____

_____

_____

_____

_____

_____

Name of establishment _____

Internet URL_____

Type of food service _____

Target market _____

Location _____

Price range_____

Facilities/services/menu _____

_____

_____

_____

_____

_____

_____

_____

_____

PART 5

Tourism Generators

Objectives

When you have completed this chapter, you should be able to:

- Explain what is included in the meetings, events, and conferences sector of the tourism industry.

- Explain why the number of meetings and conferences held every year has grown dramatically in recent decades.

- Identify the different categories of associations that hold meetings and conferences.

- Explain the needs of the association market.
- Outline the characteristics of the corporate market.
- Describe the role of the meeting/conference planner.
- Identify the channels by which the meetings/conferences product is distributed to the consumer.

Meetings, events, and conferences are treated as one sector in the Canadian tourism industry. Since the 1950s, this sector has grown to be a very important and valuable tourism generator, and involves planned cultural, political, business, and sport occasions where people meet for a specific purpose. Events range from mega-events like world's fairs for the public to an auction for charity held by a small community organization.

Meetings and conferences have become an important source of income for the travel industry. Overall, the meetings and conferences business is a multibillion-dollar-a-year industry. It is estimated that more than 100 000 meetings and more than 60 000 conferences are held in Canada annually. Meetings and conferences create a demand for the services provided by the other sectors of the tourism industry.

The meetings, events, and conferences sector has an economic impact in many areas. People are attracted to destinations for a conference, a convention, a festival, a special event, or a sporting event. If the event makes a positive impression, people are motivated to return again in the future, possibly for a longer period of time. In recent years, opportunities for professional and volunteer meeting planners have increased. Facilities have become more specialized. They are no longer simply rooms in hotels that are taken for granted—they may be buildings constructed specifically for conventions, conferences, trade shows, and special events. Services have become more sophisticated, and the service professionals who compete for and

negotiate bookings in public and private facilities are professionally educated.

EVENT MANAGEMENT

Event management covers a broad range of functional areas: planning, special-event production, sponsorship, marketing, finance, human and public relations, and project management. Events often rely on volunteers as well as on tourism and leisure/recreation professionals and event planners and managers. The events management field has expanded so much in relation to the number and variety of planned events that new business opportunities arise daily. Because of each one's uniqueness, events constitute one of the fastest-growing and most exciting forms of leisure, business, and tourist-related phenomena (Getz, 1997).

Types of Events

Whether they are planned or unplanned, events are temporary occurrences; each one has a unique ambience. The ambience is the result of the setting, program, staffing, design, and participants, as well as the event's duration. These factors are common to all events, but each event is a unique blend of them. Generally speaking, events are classified as mega-events, hallmark events, or special events.

PROFILE

We Create Experiences

Michelle Planche, CMP, Owner/President, Paradigm Events

Michelle Planche, CMP, is the owner and president of Paradigm Events, an event planning firm based in Toronto. Since 1997, she has built the company from the ground up and has embodied the true entrepreneurial spirit. "We plan more than spectacular events, we create experiences"—Paradigm's catch phrase—also applies to Planche's determination to build a career in a highly competitive industry.

Since the age of 19, Planche has put herself into positions outside her professional comfort zone in order to build confidence and event planning skills. Through university events she realized that her dream was to open an event planning firm. Shortly after she graduated from Bishops University, Paradigm Events was born. With a short client list in the early years, Planche dreamed up a way to gain prospective clients—by staging her first charity event, The Art of Fashion (an annual event, now in its tenth year of production; last year drawing an audience of over 7000). What resulted was a creative showcase that embodied "making vision a reality" and created opportunities for everyone involved in the event; several of the people who attended the event became clients. In retrospect, Planche says of the first show, "It was a great opportunity for me to showcase what I could do." Planche states, "I've always believed that opportunities don't come to you—you have to create them."

The success of The Art of Fashion events has led to many other business relationships. One was with an association director who hired Planche to coordinate an annual industry association conference in Las Vegas, Nevada. Since then, Planche has moved on to coordinate events for that association and for other organizations in locations around the world, such as New York, San Francisco, Cancun, Niagara Falls, and all across North America.

In addition to being owner of Paradigm Events, Planche also produced *Career Moves*, a television series that featured entrepreneurs across Canada and highlighted the trials and tribulations of starting your own business. Recognizing the value of networking, Planche has served as VP Membership (2002) and VP Partnership (2003) for the Canadian Society of Professional Event Planners, formerly the Independent Meeting Planners Association of Canada, and she is a member of Toronto Tourism and the Muskoka Lakes Chamber of Commerce. A sample of Planche's wide-ranging professional accomplishments:

- Organizer of the North American Automobile Annual Conference 1997–2002 in Las Vegas, Cancun, and Niagara Falls.
- Branding and advertising for Liberty Motor Company, including logo design, promotional brochures, photography, and production of a corporate video that has been distributed across North America.
- Organizer of the International Association of Young Lawyers

(AIJA) Toronto Congress in 2007, which hosted delegates from around the globe.
- Event Director of Portfolio Night World Tour, 2003–2008 which was held in 23 countries around the world in 2008.

The educational community recognized the value of Planche's knowledge, experience, and entrepreneurial flair, and she was hired as part-time faculty in the Special Events for Destination Tourism diploma program at George Brown College in Toronto. Planche has also been a guest speaker at numerous industry events.

"The satisfaction of the job is really derived from seeing a project through from start to finish," says Planche, now only in her early 30s. "You have to be able see the big picture and work well under pressure to deliver a great event to your client or audience."

Throughout the years, the industry has changed and demand has grown for greater flexibility. Paradigm Events has adapted to meet this new demand. When asked to identify some emerging trends in the event planning industry, Planche replied, "increased need for engaging the audience with unique interactive entertainment, creative culinary themeing, increased risk-management and contingency planning, shorter planning periods with more conservative budgets, and increased participation in events by the sponsors." She also believes that planners will start to develop more defined niches or specialties within the industry.

Planche has summarized her company's wide range of services on her website:

> Specializing in international corporate conferences and creative special events, Paradigm will work within your parameters, using time management, interpersonal skills and our solid supplier relationships, in order to save you time, money and frustration, while bringing your event to life. Paradigm Events also offers exclusive and unique entertainment and team building strategies for corporate functions, such as group salsa lessons, interactive comedian chefs, golf professionals and custom networking programs. Para-

digm Events has become synonymous with creativity and adding unique flair to each event. Entertainment is an essential part of enhancing your event. Whether you are looking for a live band or a magician, we can assist in finding the perfect fit . . . Through your events, we can help you increase profit, motivate your staff, improve customer loyalty, as well as raise public awareness of your enterprise.

Planche's firm is on the launching pad to growth. Her greatest challenge, she says, is to expand Paradigm Events by relinquishing control to benefit the company in the long term. Through the recruitment of talented young planners, Planche's newer challenges lie in shifting

from a role of planning and logistics to one of manager and company expansion responsibilities, a logical step for a true entrepreneur. In 2005, Paradigm opened an office in Port Carling, Muskoka, and Planche has recently purchased a new building in Toronto where the Paradigm Office will now reside.

Planche was named the winner of the 2005 Canadian Event Producer of the Year Award (and nominated again in 2006 and 2007). In March 2008, *Canadian Event Perspective Magazine* announced their nominees for the 2007 Star Awards. Paradigm Events has been nominated for the following awards: AIJA Toronto 07—Best Conference; CSNM- BEAT 07—Best Conference; Michelle Planche, CMP—Producer of the Year!

SOURCE: Michelle Planche, Owner & President Paradigm Events, biography and c.v. and July 2004: "Doing it your Way" Spring 2003, *Realm*.

Mega-Events A **mega-event**, according to the International Association of Tourism Experts, is defined in terms of its high cost, large volume of visitors, or psychology. Getting approval through the political process can create the reputation of a "must-see," as happens when an Olympic Games site is chosen—many people want to go to that location, even before and after the Games. Mega-events must also attract publicity worldwide. In brief, "mega-events, by way of their significance, are those that yield extraordinarily high levels of tourism, media coverage, prestige, or economic impact for the host community or destination" (Getz, 1997, p. 6).

Hallmark Events According to industry experts, when an event aspires to be a symbol of the quality of its organization, facility, or destination, it can qualify as a **hallmark event**. These events have been defined as "those that possess such significance, in terms of tradition, attractiveness, quality or publicity, that the event provides the host venue, community or destination with a competitive advantage" (Getz, 2007, p. 24).

Over time the event and the destination may blend together, as in the case of the Quebec Winter Carnival and

the Ottawa Tulip Festival. Definitions for hallmark and mega-events are not mutually exclusive.

Special Events These events are probably the most difficult to define because guests and organizers may not agree on an event's "specialness." Getz (1997) offers two definitions of a **special event** to address the dichotomy between guests and organizers:

1. A special event is a one-time or infrequently occurring event outside the normal program or activities of the sponsoring or organizing body.
2. To the customer or guest, a special event is an opportunity for leisure, social, or cultural experience outside the normal range of choices or beyond everyday experience.

Industry experts have suggested that special events are always planned, always arouse expectations, and always offer a reason to celebrate that motivates people to attend. The quality of specialness can be heightened by a variety of factors; those suggested by Getz are provided in Table 11–1.

ILLUSTRATION 11–1

The annual Tulip Festival in Ottawa is a display of over 3 million blossoms beautifying the nation's capital during the month of May.

SOURCE: Image courtesy of Canadian Tourism Commission.

Categories of Events

Getz suggests that there are seven **categories of events**. In Figure 11–1, the first two columns list public events and the column on the right lists private events. Some events can be private *or* public—for example, a celebration. Arts and entertainment events can be celebrations or they can stand on their own; often they are in a for-profit environment. Business/trade events can be held for a private business or an association, or they can be trade or retail initiatives. Educational and scientific events are discussed more fully later in this chapter. A political/state event can be a small, infrequent gathering or (more usually) a high-profile, high-impact one. Before turning to event tourism generally, we'll look closer at arts events. Attractions, festivals, and special events are presented in the next chapter.

TABLE 11–1 Factors That Heighten the Specialness of Events

A multiplicity of goals: Specialness is related to the diversity of goals that events successfully pursue.

Festive spirit: Specialness increases with the ability of events to create a true festive spirit. The ambience can encourage joyfulness (even revelry), freedom from routine constraints, and inversion of normal roles and functions.

Satisfying basic needs: All the basic human needs, and related leisure and travel motivations, can be satisfied in part through events. Specialness increases as the number of needs and related motives are better satisfied.

Uniqueness: Mega-events rely on a "must-see," "once-in-a-lifetime" uniqueness to attract visitors; all events, to some degree, can manage their product and promotions to create the specialness associated with a unique happening.

Quality: Poor quality will destroy the pretence of being special; high-quality events will go beyond customer expectations and generate high levels of satisfaction.

Authenticity: This is related to uniqueness, in that events based on indigenous cultural values and attributes will be inherently unique. To the tourist, specialness will be heightened by a feeling of participation in an authentic community celebration.

Tradition: Many events have become traditions, rooted in the community, and attractive to visitors because of the associated mystique. Hallmark events, which are closely associated with the host community so that event and destination images are mutually reinforcing, are traditional by nature.

Flexibility: Events can be developed with minimal infrastructure, and can be moved in space and time and adapted to changing markets and organizational needs. This makes them special products for organizations and destinations.

Hospitality: The essence of hospitality is to make every event-goer feel like an honoured guest. In destinations, the tourist is provided with community hospitality and the resident is proud to be a host. Some events and communities are recognized for the special welcome they give to visitors.

Tangibility: The event-goer can experience the "specialness" of a destination theme, and its ambient resources, through its events. This applies to culture, hospitality, and natural resources.

Theming: All elements of the event can be themed to maximize festive spirit, authenticity, tradition, interactions, and customer service. Theming adds to the feeling of specialness.

Symbolism: The use of rituals and symbols together adds to the festive atmosphere, and can also give an event special significance above and beyond its immediate purpose and theme.

Affordability: Events providing affordable leisure, educational, social, and cultural experiences will be special to large segments of the population without the means to pay for alternatives.

Convenience: Events can be special opportunities for spontaneous, unplanned leisure and social opportunities. This is of increasing importance in a hectic, work-oriented world, and especially in urban environments.

SOURCE: Reprinted with permission of Cognizant Communication Corp.

Cultural celebrations	Sport competitions	Private events
• Festivals • Carnivals • Religious events • Parades • Heritage commemorations	• Professional • Amateur **Educational and scientific** • Seminars, workshops, clinics • Congresses • Interpretive events	*Personal celebrations* • Anniversaries • Family holidays • Rites of passage *Social events* • Parties, galas • Reunions
Art/entertainment • Concerts • Other performances • Exhibits • Award ceremonies	**Recreational** • Games and sports for fun • Amusement events	
Business/trade • Fairs, markets, sales • Consumer and trade shows • Expositions • Meetings and conferences • Publicity events • Fundraiser events	**Political/state** • Inaugurations • Investitures • VIP visits • Rallies	

FIGURE 11–1 A Typology of Planned Events
SOURCE: Reprinted with permission of Cognizant Communication Corp.

Arts Events

Arts events have been part of society for generations. As a multicultural society, Canada has a diversity of artists who can draw visitors. Art events can be classified as follows:

- Visual (e.g., sculpture, painting, handicraft).
- Performing (e.g., dance, drama, music, cinema, poetry, storytelling; usually performed for an audience).
- Participatory (audience and performers interact).

Concerts, exhibits, art festivals, and stage performances are nothing new. That being said, arts events linked to tourism are a growing phenomenon in Canada. Combined with other attractions and services, arts products that appeal to both domestic and international tourists are being taken to market. As this market grows, arts events will require management that is just as specialized as any other type of event management. Thus, arts events provide an excellent opportunity for people with an interest in the arts to enter the tourism industry.

Event Tourism

Events are the reason most people travel. Even if they didn't plan to when they left home, most people attend events while they are tourists. So it is important to explore the concept of **event tourism**. Getz (1997, p. 16) suggests that event tourism can be looked at in two ways:

1. The systematic planning, development, and marketing of events as tourist attractions, catalysts for developments, image builders, and animators of attractions

and destination areas; event strategies should also cover the management of news and negative events.
2. A market segment consisting of those people who travel to attend events, or who can be motivated to attend events while away from home.

Event tourism is one way of attracting tourists with special interests to a destination. The development and promotion of events has become big business in the past decade both in Canada and abroad.

Many communities and provinces formulate event tourism strategies. For example, a World Acadian Congress was held in Halifax, Nova Scotia, in 2004, and Alberta has had the Calgary Stampede for years.

For a variety of reasons, not every event reaches its potential as an attraction or image-maker. Perhaps the organizers fail to integrate event marketing with destination planning and marketing; perhaps the event is produced and/or managed badly. It also has been noted that many destinations do not understand their own tourist potential and so do not organize events to reach that potential.

Check Your Product Knowledge

1. What functional areas are involved in event management?
2. What are two ways to look at event tourism?

THE WHAT, WHY, AND WHERE OF BUSINESS MEETINGS

Until the late 1950s, most business meetings were regional. For example, Ford Motor Company might hold a meeting in Calgary for Alberta Ford dealers, and another meeting in Sherbrooke for dealers in Quebec. National meetings were rare because long-distance travel was impractical. Trans-Canada Airlines (now Air Canada) offered some transcontinental services in the early 1950s, but most long-distance travel was still by rail or by road. Business executives could rarely afford the time to travel to meetings on the other side of the country.

The Growth of Meetings

The breakthrough for the meetings business came with advances in the transportation industry. The jet age brought major changes with it. When Trans-Canada Airlines introduced nonstop passenger jet service between Montreal and Vancouver, coast-to-coast times were cut to

ILLUSTRATION 11–2
Quebec City is the home of "Bonhomme" and the largest winter carnival in the world.
SOURCE: Corel.

five hours. Jet planes made travel to meetings faster, more convenient, and often less expensive. With the extension of domestic jet routes, many destinations became accessible for national meetings. International meetings became possible after daily flights to overseas destinations were introduced. The relatively lower airfares of recent years have also stimulated the growth of the meetings business. However, in order to compete as a corporate travel destination, Canada is going to have to become more competitive in a slowing economy.

Improvements in ground transportation have also helped the meetings market expand. State-of-the-art motorcoaches now transport delegates and businesspeople to local meetings in luxury. Car rental fleets have been expanded to accommodate even the largest of meetings crowds.

Yet another factor in the growth of the meetings market is automation in the tourism industry. Computer reservation systems (CRSs) have made it possible to coordinate meetings of 10 000 or more delegates from around the world.

More and more destinations now have the facilities to handle large business gatherings. Hub cities—those cities at the centre of an air carrier's route structure—are presenting themselves as ideal meeting sites. Hubs include mid-sized cities such as Halifax, Winnipeg, and Calgary. The 1970s and 1980s were a boom period for the building of convention centres throughout Canada and the United States. Resort locations have also become more attractive as sites for meetings, especially if they offer reduced rates in their nonpeak season.

The growing demand for meetings has generated a corresponding demand for new services, including meeting planning and destination management.

Kinds of Meetings

A "meeting" is by definition a gathering of people. More specifically, a meeting is a planned encounter between two or more people for a common purpose such as to learn something, to influence people, to be entertained, or to solve a problem. Despite the rising costs of transportation and hospitality, as well as advances in telecommunications, people gather for many reasons: for special occasions, to keep up with information or changing technology, to develop a strategic plan, and so on.

Meetings can be classified according to the number of participants, the kinds of discussions and presentations involved, the amount of audience participation, and whether the meeting is formal or informal. The type of meeting dictates the design, planning, management, and facilities required. Some meetings need to be planned 10 years in advance; others can be planned in only a few hours.

A **convention** is one type of meeting. Conventions typically involve a general group session in a large auditorium, followed by committee meetings in small breakout rooms. Most conventions are held regularly (usually annually) and meet for at least three days. Trade and technical conventions are often held in conjunction with exhibitions. Attendance varies from 100 participants to 30 000 or more.

Conferences are similar to conventions but usually deal with specific problems or developments rather than with general matters. For example, the Canadian Medical Association might call a conference to discuss a breakthrough in the treatment of a particular disease. Conferences involve a lot of member participation. Attendance varies, though it is rarely as high as at conventions.

Teleconferences and satellite conferences are two methods for holding one meeting at several locations simultaneously. Participants use advanced communications technology that enables them to see and hear participants at other locations. Teleconferencing is a way of bringing people together without the time and expense of long-distance travel. Several hotel chains, convention centres, and conference centres have introduced teleconferencing facilities in response to growing demand.

Congresses are similar to conferences. The term is commonly used in Europe to describe large international gatherings.

A *forum* involves back-and-forth discussion on a particular issue. It is usually led by panelists or presenters. Audience participation is expected and encouraged. A *symposium* is similar to a forum but tends to be more formal and to involve less audience participation. *Lectures* are even more formal. An individual expert addresses the audience, usually from a raised platform. The presentation is sometimes followed by a question-and-answer session. Attendance at forums, symposiums, and lectures varies greatly.

Seminars are informal meetings involving face-to-face discussion. Participants share their knowledge and experiences in a particular field under the supervision of a discussion leader. *Workshops* are small group sessions (usually with a maximum of 35 participants) held for a period of intense study or training. The emphasis is on exchanging ideas and demonstrating skills and techniques. *Clinics* offer drills and instruction in specific skills for small groups. For example, an airline reservations agent might attend a clinic to learn how to operate a CRS. Many people attend clinics when they want to learn a sport, such as golf or tennis. Both clinics and workshops can last for several days.

The *panel* format calls for two or more speakers and a moderator. Panellists present their views on a particular subject. The meeting is then opened for discussion among the speakers, who may also invite comments from the audience.

Institutes offer conferences, seminars, and workshops. Many of these are organized for a professional or trade group to provide professional development or training opportunities on a topic over an extended period.

Retreats are small meetings that are usually held in remote locations to foster bonding in preparation for intensive planning sessions, or simply to provide an opportunity to refocus.

At *exhibitions*, vendors display their goods and services. They are staged as part of a convention or conference. The term *exposition* is used in Europe to describe this kind of presentation.

Trade shows (or *trade fairs*) feature freestanding vendor displays. Unlike exhibitions, they are not held as part of a convention. Trade shows such as HostEx held annually in Toronto for the hospitality industry, are typically the largest type of meeting. (In March 2008, Hostex united with the Canadian Food & Beverage Show to become The CRFA Show.) Attendance at a major show lasting several days can top 500 000.

Consumer shows are exhibitions open to the public, such as home shows and boat shows. A small entry fee is usually charged. They usually draw local people and so do not contribute to occupancy rates.

ILLUSTRATION 11–3

Teleconferencing is a way of bringing people together without the time and expense of long-distance travel.

SOURCE: PhotoDisc Green/Getty Images.

Locations for Meetings

Off-site meetings Off-site meetings are those that don't take place on the premises of the sponsoring company—can be held at various locations, such as hotels,

ILLUSTRATION 11–4

Opened in July 1987, the Vancouver Trade and Convention Centre (now the Vancouver Convention & Exhibition Centre) is undergoing a huge expansion to be completed Spring 2009. It will have 52 meeting rooms, a 223 000 square foot exhibition hall, a 55 000 square foot ballroom, and will boast a "living roof": a six-acre garden with 400 000 different indigenous plants. It can cater to 6000 banquet guests or 10 000 for a reception.

SOURCE: Image courtesy of Canadian Tourism Commission.

resorts, conference centres, convention centres, civic centres, and cruise ships.

Hotels Today, meetings generate about 20 percent of all hotel revenues. Thirty-five years ago, few hotels actively solicited meetings business. In fact, many were reluctant to open their doors to convention groups, preferring to rely on individual business travellers and vacationers. What meeting rooms there were in hotels were usually small and designed for weddings, balls, and other social functions.

By the mid-1960s, hoteliers were beginning to realize that the growing meetings business could provide a valuable source of income, especially during off-peak periods. Giant showcase hotels such as the Hyatt Regency in downtown Atlanta, built in 1967, were being designed specifically to cater to the meetings market. These hotels were equipped with spacious assembly rooms and exhibition areas and a full range of audio-visual aids.

Convention hotels were also built at airports and in suburban locations. By the 1980s, almost all new commercial hotels in both the United States and Canada featured facilities for meetings. Most Canadian cities have followed the American convention facility trend and now have hotels where conventions are held.

Resorts Resorts have become more and more popular as sites for meetings. A resort's secluded, scenic location is a

prime attraction for meeting planners, as is the availability of on-site recreational facilities. The development of resorts as sites for meetings mirrors that of hotels. In the early days, resort owners had little interest in attracting group business. Convention-goers were regarded as second-class citizens, inferior to the wealthy upper classes who constituted the bulk of the resort's clientele.

However, changing social values in the post-World War II period forced resorts to review their policies. Fashionable resorts such as the Fairmont Banff Springs Hotel and The Fairmont Algonquin in St. Andrews, New Brunswick, changed with the times and added extensive conference facilities. Meetings now account for a large percentage of business at these facilities. Many older resorts have been converted to accommodate the growing meetings market; some new resorts have been built as year-round convention sites.

Conference Centres Conference centres cater almost exclusively to meetings, especially corporate meetings. For this reason, many meeting planners regard conference centres as ideal meeting locations. The emphasis is on a working environment with few outside distractions. Conference rooms are designed specifically for meetings (in contrast, in many hotels the conference space often has to double as a banquet room or ballroom). Guest rooms have work areas with plenty of lighting so that delegates can work in their rooms. A professional meetings staff is on hand to cater to the needs of delegates and planners. The Banff Centre was specifically designed and built for the meetings of both corporate and nonprofit groups.

To provide delegates with some relief from work, some conference centres have added, or arranged, packages with other operators to provide resort-type amenities, such as health facilities, tennis courts, and/or a golf course. These conference centres are not much different from resorts with meetings facilities.

Convention Centres Few hotels, resorts, or conference centres can accommodate groups of more than 1000. Larger meetings and exhibitions are held in convention centres. Convention centres differ from conference centres in other ways besides capacity. For example, they are always located in cities, and they do not have guest rooms on the premises. Also, they are usually built with public funds.

Before 1960, there were only a few sites capable of hosting large national conventions and trade shows. These included the Automotive Building on the grounds of the Canadian National Exhibition in Toronto, Maple Leaf Gardens (now unavailable as the property was sold to Loblaws in 2004), and Madison Square Garden in New York City. The first convention centres with extensive exhibit areas all on one level were opened in 1960. Since then, convention centres have been built in cities all over Canada and the United States, and more are on the way.

Canada has several major convention centres with extensive facilities, including those in Montreal (capacity 11 300), Vancouver (10 795), Edmonton (8000), and Winnipeg (7200). The Metro Toronto Convention Centre can handle groups of 40 to 40 000 with facilities including 64 meeting rooms, two ballrooms, and 600 000 square feet of exhibit space.

Many of Canada's convention centres were built in the 1970s and 1980s in a rather rare example of the public and private sectors working well together. Funding was provided by the three levels of government (federal, provincial, and municipal); the private sector offered advice and did the actual building. Some of the centres, especially the ones in Montreal and Toronto, were built to cater almost solely to the American convention market. Toronto's Sheraton Hotel, the largest of that chain's hotels, was built in the 1970s to host meetings held by American groups.

Civic Centres Civic centres have much the same function as convention centres. They are used for large regional and national conventions, exhibitions, and trade shows. They are usually located in the city's central business district. Meetings are not necessarily their main source of income, however; cultural and sporting events are also held in them. The Halifax Metro Centre (capacity 10 000) is adjacent to the World Trade and Convention Centre in Halifax (capacity 1300). Similarly, the Pengrowth Saddledome (capacity 16 700) provides extra room for the Calgary Convention Centre (capacity 2500).

Cruise Ships In the late 1960s, meeting planners looking for more exotic locations began to use cruise ships. Foreign-owned cruise ships were popular until 1976 because they offered tax advantages over American ships. In 1976, however, the U.S. government changed its tax laws and took away the advantage previously enjoyed by foreign vessels. American cruise and yacht companies were quick to step into the market, and several now have vessels fully equipped to handle small and medium-sized meetings. Cruise ships are also used for incentive travel programs (discussed later in this chapter).

Check Your Product Knowledge

1. What have been the major factors in the growth of the meetings business in the past 40 years?
2. List the kinds of locations used for off-site meetings.

THE MEETINGS MARKETPLACE

The meetings market can be divided into two basic segments: the association market and the corporate market. Each market has different characteristics and different motivations, needs, and expectations (MNEs).

The Association Meetings Market

The **association market** is the better-known and more visible segment of the meetings field. There are associations for almost every subject and interest. Of the 80 000 associations in Canada and the United States, about one-third are national or international; the remainder are regional, provincial, or local. Most associations in Canada and the United States hold an annual convention; many have several meetings a year. Besides holding conventions, associations also sponsor thousands of educational seminars and workshops. The association market can be divided into at least nine categories: trade, professional, scientific and technical, educational, veterans' and military, fraternal, ethnic and religious, charitable, and political and labour union.

Trade Associations Almost every trade has at least one national association, as well as several regional and provincial ones. Within a single trade, there may be separate associations for manufacturers, wholesalers and distributors, and retailers. Trade conventions at the national level tend to be large; in the United States, the National Restaurant Association's annual meeting in Chicago attracts more than 100 000 delegates over five days. Trade conventions are often held in conjunction with exhibits.

Professional Associations Members of professional associations can be individuals, companies, or corporations with similar business needs. Examples include the Canadian Medical Association, the Canadian Bar Association, and the Canadian Bankers' Association. All hold annual national conventions and conferences as well as regional meetings throughout the year. They use exhibits less often than do trade associations.

Scientific and Technical Associations Organizations in this category are another lucrative source of meetings business. Representative associations include the Engineering Institute of Canada and the Chemical Institute of Canada. Besides holding regularly scheduled conventions, these organizations often call special meetings when the need arises to discuss new developments. These meetings tend to be highly technical and often require sophisticated presentation equipment. Social events are typically kept to a minimum so that delegates are not distracted from the business at hand.

Educational Associations National and provincial teachers' associations are the best known of the educational

ILLUSTRATION 11–5

Trade shows bring together exhibitors who demonstrate their products to the general public.

SOURCE: Photodisc/Getty Images.

organizations, although this group also includes professional educators in a wide variety of other fields. In the travel industry, for example, the International Society of Travel and Tourism Educators and the Council on Hotel, Restaurant and Institutional Education are prominent associations. Educational meetings are often held in the summer, when schools are closed. This makes them especially attractive to downtown hotels in cities where hotel occupancy levels are at their lowest in summer. Educational conventions tend to be longer than most other kinds, commonly involving a full five days of meetings.

Veterans' and Military Associations Veterans' groups such as the Royal Canadian Legion hold annual reunions for former members of the Armed Forces. Conventions at the national level attract large numbers of attendees and are mainly social in purpose. Military organizations such as the Air Force Association have conventions for active service personnel.

Fraternal Associations There are probably more fraternal associations in Canada and the United States than any other type of association. These can be divided into three main categories: student fraternities and sororities; service groups, whose members have a common interest or purpose, such as helping the needy; and special-interest associations. All hold regular conventions. National conventions of service groups such as the Elks, the Loyal Order of Moose, and Rotary International are especially large gatherings. The emphasis is on social events, recreation, and entertainment rather than on technical, business, or professional matters. Examples of special-interest associations are the Royal Philatelic Society of Canada, the American Contract Bridge League, and the Soaring Association of Canada.

Ethnic and Religious Associations Ethnic organizations are similar in general philosophy and purposes to service groups, with a similar emphasis on comradeship. Examples are the Order of the Sons of Italy and the Canadian Association in Support of Native Peoples. Religious conventions are held both for those people whose vocation is religion (such as priests and ministers) and for the laity. The Canadian Catholic Conference is an example of the former.

Charitable Associations These include the Canadian Red Cross and the National Multiple Sclerosis Society. They exist to raise money for charitable causes and to sponsor research.

Political Associations and Labour Unions The most visible political conventions are those held by national parties, such as the Conservatives, the Liberals, and the New Democrats. These can be leadership conventions or policy conventions. Many other political meetings are held at the provincial and local levels. Labour unions such as the Canadian Auto Workers also hold national and local meetings. National meetings are usually held in large convention centres and attract thousands of delegates.

Characteristics of the Association Meetings Market

The main characteristics of the association market are as follows:

- A lot of people participate, especially at national conventions.
- Attendance is voluntary—participants often pay for their own travel and accommodation.
- A tourist attraction or resort is often chosen as the destination.
- A different destination is chosen each year.
- Meetings are held on a regular cycle, usually annually or semiannually.

- Annual meetings are planned two to five years in advance.
- They usually last between three and five days (less for smaller meetings and seminars).
- The larger conventions often include exhibitions.

The MNEs of the Association Market

Destination is a key motivator in attracting participants to an association meeting. Since attendance is voluntary, the organizers must choose a destination that appeals to the maximum number of potential attendees. Delegates often like to combine a business trip with a vacation, so the destination selected must have adequate recreational facilities and access to sightseeing and entertainment attractions. Spouses are more likely to attend if there is something for them to do while their husbands or wives are in a meeting. For these reasons, resorts are popular venues for association meetings. Some destinations are selected because they relate to the particular interests of the association. The Canadian Ski Council, for example, would probably hold its convention at a ski resort.

Delegates who regularly attend annual conventions do not want to go back to the same destination over and over. For this reason, associations usually choose a new meeting place each year. There is little point, however, in choosing an exotic, faraway location if delegates can't afford to get there (remember that most association members have to pay their own travel expenses). Ease of access is an important consideration in selecting a site, especially for regional meetings. The destination chosen will often be the one that is closest to the greatest number of members.

An association's decision makers rate availability of suitable meeting rooms as the number-one factor when choosing the meeting site. Depending on the size and scope of the meeting, a large general auditorium might be needed, as well as smaller spaces for workshops and committee meetings. The availability of exhibit space, meeting support services, and audio-visual equipment may also be crucial. Another very important consideration is the experience and efficiency of the convention centre's management.

Almost all national conventions need overnight accommodations. Hotels must be within the delegates' budgets. Ideally, an association tries to book all attendees into a single property. This isn't always possible if the convention is large. In such cases, a number of hotels in close proximity often cooperate to accommodate all the association's members. The quality of guest rooms (and suites, if necessary) is clearly an important factor in the selection of hotels. Other considerations might be the quality of food service and the efficiency of check-in and check-out procedures.

ILLUSTRATION 11–6

A ballroom set up in classroom style for a meeting at the Queen Elizabeth Hotel, Montreal's largest hotel.

SOURCE: Image courtesy of Fairmont Hotels and Resorts.

Check Your Product Knowledge

1. What are the main characteristics of the association meetings market?
2. What are the MNE's of the association meetings market?

THE CORPORATE MEETINGS MARKET

The **corporate market** is the fastest-growing segment of the meetings market. As communication becomes ever more essential in the modern business world, the need for meetings as a point of information transfer continues to increase. The corporate market generates a greater volume of meetings business than the association market, yet corporate meetings are less visible to the public, because companies generally have no need to publicize off-site meetings. The delegates are required to attend.

The corporate market in Canada and the United States is made up of tens of thousands of businesses and corporations. Meetings are held at all levels of business and industry and can be divided into six main types: sales, dealer, technical, executive/management, training, and public meetings.

The Six Main Types of Meetings

Sales Meetings Sales meetings, which can be regional or national, are the best-known kind of company meeting. They can be used as morale builders, or to introduce new products or new company policies, or to teach new sales techniques. Locations for sales meetings vary considerably.

Some are conducted at hotels with access to the company's manufacturing plant, so that salespeople can see the product in the production stage. Others are held in major market areas so that salespeople can make customer contacts between meetings. Average attendance is 60 for regional meetings, 175 for national meetings.

Dealer Meetings These are meetings between a company's sales staff and the dealers and distributors who represent the retail sales outlets. Like sales meetings, they are held to encourage sales performance. Dealer meetings are often used to introduce new products and to launch new sales and advertising campaigns. Attendance can vary from less than 20 to 2000 or more, depending on the size of the corporation and the number of retail outlets maintained.

Technical Meetings These meetings are held frequently to update engineers and other technical personnel on the latest technological developments and innovations. The seminar and workshop formats are widely used for technical meetings.

Executive/Management Meetings This category includes both executive conferences and management development seminars. The former vary greatly in attendance; the latter are usually small. As the most prestigious company personnel, executives expect the finest in accommodations and service. Deluxe hotels and conference centres, especially those in isolated resort locations, are suitable venues.

Training Meetings Training meetings form the largest and fastest-growing segment of the corporate meetings market. They are conducted for all levels of personnel, from entry level to top executives. Attendance at workshops and clinics is usually under 50 and can be as low as 10. Isolated resorts with a minimum of outside distractions are popular locations, especially in the off-season. For shorter training sessions, a location convenient to the company workplace is usually chosen.

Public Meetings Public meetings are open to nonemployees. Shareholder meetings are the most common type. They rarely last longer than a day and so require no overnight accommodations.

Characteristics of the Corporate Market

The corporate market is different from the association market in a number of respects. Its main characteristics include the following:

- There are fewer participants per meeting.
- Attendance is mandatory—travel and accommodation expenses are paid for by the corporation.
- The destination is sometimes tied to the location of a company office or factory.

- The same destination may be used year after year.
- Meetings are held as the need arises.
- The planning/booking period is significantly shorter—often less than one year's notice.
- They last a slightly shorter time—usually around three days.
- They use exhibits less.

The MNEs of the Corporate Market

An attractive destination is not as important for the corporate market as it is for the association market. Attendance at corporate meetings is mandatory, so the choice of destination has no effect on the number of people attending. **Corporate meeting planners** do not have to "sell" the destination, nor do they have to vary the meeting site to attract participants. In fact, many companies use the same hotel year after year (especially for training meetings). A hotel with a proven service record is usually guaranteed repeat business. This is a fundamental difference between the corporate and association markets.

Location is an important factor in destination selection. Sites close to the company facility are usually chosen. The more distant and inaccessible the location, the more it costs the company in travel expenses. Time spent travelling also means time away from the job for company employees, who must be paid while they are attending the meeting.

The emphasis at corporate meetings is on work, with considerably less time for leisure and social activities than is provided at association meetings. This means that privacy and a distraction-free environment are of more importance in site selection than the availability of recreational facilities and ease of access to entertainment, sightseeing, and shopping.

Corporate decision makers have similar needs to association decision makers when it comes to selecting a particular hotel or other venue for the meeting. They look for properties with adequate meeting space, enough guest rooms, and quality service. Because corporate meetings tend to have fewer participants, they can often be held in small and medium-sized hotels. Since many corporate meetings last for less than a day, not all of them require overnight accommodations.

Check Your Product Knowledge

1. List six ways in which association meetings differ from corporate meetings.
2. In what ways are the MNEs of the corporate and the association markets similar? In what ways are they different?

ROLE OF THE MEETING PLANNER

The meetings market has become larger, more sophisticated, and more specialized. There is a need today for professional decision makers who can supervise all stages of meeting preparation and presentation. Until recently, meeting planning was one of several functions performed by association and corporate executives. Now it has emerged as a specialized field.

The Meeting Planner Defined

In Canada and the United States, more than 100 000 people are involved in meeting planning. We can identify three main categories of meeting planners:

1. Association executives.
2. Corporate meeting planners.
3. Independent meeting planners and consultants.

Association Executives These meeting planners are full-time professional administrators employed by the various associations. They are responsible for the planning, coordination, execution, and promotion of annual conventions and smaller association meetings. Association executives are the key decision makers in the selection of meeting sites. Many belong to the Canadian Society of Association Executives (CSAE), based in Toronto (www.csae.com), or to the American Society of Association Executives (ASAE) (www.asaecenter.org).

An example of a hospitality association that tourism and travel industry sales and marketing executives and staff should join is the Hospitality Sales and Marketing Association International (HSMAI), which presents a comprehensive lineup of industry events and programs, educational sessions and strategy conferences as well as business-to-business forums for buyers and suppliers of hospitality, travel, and tourism. Student memberships are available at CDN$60 (www.hsmai.org).

Many smaller associations cannot afford to employ a full-time meeting planner. These groups can outsource the services—that is, engage a management company that specializes in planning association meetings.

Corporate Meeting Planners Corporate meeting planning is a relatively new and rapidly growing field. Until recently, the planning of meetings and conferences was usually up to the CEO's executive assistant, the director of sales, or the vice president of marketing. Today most large corporations and businesses have a full-time meetings department that arranges all meetings. Some companies appoint a training executive to organize group training sessions. (If a company does not have a meetings department, corporate group travel and meetings arrangements are often arranged through the in-house business travel department.)

Meeting planners have formed their own professional associations. Meeting Planners International (MPI), founded in 1972, is the most prominent of these. Its 24 000 members in 80 countries plan hundreds of thousands of meetings each year. MPI members include corporate meeting planners, association executives, and independent consultants, as well as travel and meeting service suppliers.

ILLUSTRATION 11–7

The Banff Centre in Alberta is both a school of performing arts and a management conference centre.
SOURCE: Donald Lee/Banff Centre.

MPI has local chapters in Canada. Student memberships are available for an annual fee of CDN$50.

The Association of Collegiate Conference and Events Directors–International (ACCED-I), founded in 1980, is an organization of over 1600 campus professionals who design, market, coordinate, and plan conferences and special events on the campuses of colleges and universities around the world. Student membership is US$85 (www.acced-i.org).

Independent Meeting Planners Associations and corporations that do not have in-house meetings departments often hire independent consultants on a freelance basis. The number of individuals and companies offering this service is growing rapidly. The Canadian Society of Professional Event Planners or CanSPEP (formerly the Independent Meeting Planners Association of Canada) promotes education and communication among planners in this field. Student memberships are available for an annual fee of $75, plus a one-time administration fee of $50.

The Meeting Planner's Responsibilities

Whether meeting planners work for associations, corporations, or independent consulting firms, their main objective is to run successful meetings. The fundamental responsibilities of the meeting planner include:

- Establishing meeting objectives.
- Selecting the meeting site.
- Scheduling meetings and meeting rooms.
- Negotiating rates with suppliers.
- Budgeting and controlling expenses.
- Making air and ground transportation arrangements.
- Planning audio-visual and technical details.

From this list—which could easily be extended—it is clear that meeting planners are more than just travel and accommodation organizers. They are involved from the earliest planning stages to the final execution of the meeting. The success of a meeting depends heavily on how well they perform their tasks.

The MNEs of Meeting Planning

The meeting planner must bear the employer's needs in mind when selecting destinations, choosing hotels, making travel arrangements, and so on. When negotiating with suppliers, the meeting planner must ensure that the sponsoring organization is getting the best possible deal and the best value for its money. Strong negotiating skills are a key requirement for the meeting planner.

Top priorities in selecting sites for meetings are the quality of service and the availability of meeting room facilities. Meeting planners must ensure that meeting areas are large enough, suitable for both general sessions and breakout meetings, well lit, soundproof, and so on. Each meeting that a planner organizes will have different requirements. Other important priorities are the site's accessibility, the quality of guest rooms, room rates, and the quality of food service. The availability of recreational facilities is usually of lesser importance; so is geographic location.

The Meeting Planner and the Hotel Staff

Meeting planning involves a high degree of cooperation between the meeting planner and the hotel staff. The convention service manager is usually the meeting planner's contact person in the hotel. The relationship between the two is important to the success of the meeting. Both must keep the needs of the meeting participants in mind. The meeting planner wants to secure the best possible services at the lowest possible rates. The convention service manager wants to satisfy the guests so that they will return for subsequent meetings, but must also ensure that the hotel makes a profit.

Meeting planners who use the same hotel time and time again can often negotiate favourable rates and secure other privileges, such as free function rooms. For an especially large or important meeting, the hotel may agree to host a cocktail party for delegates or offer complimentary coffee and breakfast. Using the same hotel over and over again is not always a good idea, however. Meeting planners may find that the hotel's services deteriorate over time, or that other hotels can offer better services at better prices.

Some hotel chains have set up special Event Planning Guides to assist meeting planners; Fairmont Hotels, for example, who designed an Eco-Meet Event Planning Guide. According to its website, "The Eco-Meet program helps meeting planners by providing a meeting structure that encourages maximum waste diversion and environmental awareness for conference delegates" (Fairmont Hotels & Resorts, "Eco-Meet," n.d.).

ILLUSTRATION 11–8

The uniquely structured Saddledome in Calgary is used for major meetings and conferences.

SOURCE: Image courtesy of www.viewCalgary.com.

CHANNELS OF DISTRIBUTION

Buyers do not always purchase travel products and services directly from sellers. In the meetings business, sellers use intermediaries as distribution channels when selling services to buyers. Intermediaries in the meetings field include tour operators, travel agencies, and meeting planners. Other companies that intervene between suppliers and consumers include site destination selection companies, destination management companies, convention services and facilities companies, and convention and visitors' bureaux.

Tour Operators

In many ways the business and convention product is similar to the product the vacationer buys as a holiday tour package. The product includes transportation, accommodations, activities, and events in some combination. Just as it is more convenient—and less expensive—for a vacationer to buy a package of travel products from a single source, so too is it more convenient for people attending meetings.

Tour operators are experienced in group travel arrangements. Some tour operators arrange packages for meetings and conventions, especially for the association market. Because the tour operator buys in bulk from suppliers, the package will be less expensive than if each member made arrangements individually.

Tour operators don't sell directly only to consumers. Some will place a deposit on an allotment of rooms for a large, popular trade show and package the rooms for resale through retail travel agencies and business travel departments. In doing so, the tour operator is taking a risk but is also creating the potential for increased business.

Travel Agencies

A travel agency (e.g., Carlson Wagonlit or Fraser and Hoyt) that has an ongoing relationship with a corporation or company often makes travel arrangements for meetings. Agencies are also becoming more involved in incentive travel programs. The companies they work with are often small or medium-sized firms that do not employ a full-time, in-house meeting planner. The meetings and incentive programs that the travel agencies service typically have fewer than 100 participants.

The work involved in making arrangements for meetings and incentives is more complex than for group travel. An agency usually assigns this work to its convention department or incentives department. Also, the agency may staff a service booth at the convention site to handle reconfirmations, complaints, and so on.

Meeting Planning/Incentive Travel Companies

These firms or individual consultants provide full-service planning for businesses and associations for a fee. They are involved not only with travel and accommodation arrangements but also with the promotion and marketing of the meeting or incentive program. Usually, meeting planning companies and incentive travel companies don't use travel agencies or tour operators; they deal directly with carriers, hotels, and other suppliers.

Airlines, Hotels, and Car Rental Companies

An airline is often designated the "official carrier" for a particular meeting or conference. The airline will then assist in that group's promotion and marketing efforts, and offer a discount for participants. Similarly, a hotel may be appointed as the "official hotel," and a car rental company as the "official car rental agency."

The official carrier may help clients select an appropriate meeting site, secure discounted fares, arrange hotel accommodations, and coordinate car rentals and ground transportation. They may also provide assistance with audio-visual equipment and recommendations for multimedia presentations.

Site Destination Selection Companies

Site destination selection companies suggest possible meeting sites based on corporate or association needs. Meeting planners and incentive travel planners may consult a site destination selection company several years before a meeting or incentive program is scheduled. Destination selection companies conduct FAM tours so that planners can inspect and sample hotels and meeting facilities at potential sites. One destination selection company provided a five-day FAM tour of Atlanta for corporate and association meeting planners and a seven-day tour of Thailand for corporate incentive travel planners. For a nominal registration fee, participants were provided with round-trip air transportation, lodging, ground arrangements, many meals, and special activities.

Destination Management Companies

Destination management companies (DMCs) provide on-the-scene assistance for corporations and associations holding meetings at a particular location. If, for example, a Toronto company is planning a meeting in Las Vegas, it may hire a DMC in that city to handle all the details. The

DMC arranges ground transportation, deals with restaurants, lines up local speakers, and performs many other useful services.

Convention Services and Facilities Companies

This group includes a wide variety of independent companies that provide support services that are not available at the convention site. Some of these companies design and install stages, booths, and modular exhibit systems; others are audio-visual specialists, or sound and light specialists. Still others provide temporary personnel, or actors and entertainers for industrial shows, or security staff.

Convention and Visitors' Bureaux

Not that long ago there were only around 300 **convention and visitors' bureaux (CVBs)** in Canada and the United States. Today, there more than 1000. A CVB can be a department within a city's Chamber of Commerce, or an office of a municipal government, or a completely independent organization. Centres such as Destination Winnipeg and Ottawa Visitor Information have two main functions: to promote travel to the city they represent (be it for pleasure, or business, or meetings), and to help service the conventions and trade shows that are held in the city. Their job is to sell the whole city—not only convention centres and other meeting sites, but also hotels, restaurants, stores, transportation companies, and other suppliers.

A CVB is a nonprofit organization funded by its members. Most of these are suppliers who profit when conventions are held in their city. The International Association of Convention and Visitor Bureaus represents major CVBs around the world.

Check Your Product Knowledge

1. What role do tour operators play in the distribution of the meetings product?
2. What do site destination selection companies and destination management companies do?

MEETINGS, EVENTS, AND CONFERENCES: CURRENT TRENDS

Cost Concerns

The increased costs of airline security and the rising cost of fuel should increase airfares, and this will have an immediate effect on meeting, event, and convention markets.

Sandy Vura Harwood, a certified meeting professional and a director of meetings and conventions, states, "I think that overall costs of getting to a destination will affect our functions in the future, but it's hard to predict the impact on attendance right now" (Chatfield-Taylor, 2003).

Hotel Attrition

Since 2001, the number-one concern for professional meeting planners has been **hotel attrition**. A meeting planner who signs a contract with a hotel must agree to guarantee the sale of a certain number of rooms, which is referred to as a "room block." If the actual number of delegates is less than the room block, then the meeting planner and/or the association becomes responsible for the revenue that the hotel would have made if the room block had been filled. In prior years, the hotel accepted back into inventory any unsold rooms at the cutoff date (usually 30 days before arrival) and then tried to resell those rooms. Recently hotels have been billing for these unsold rooms and the meeting planners have tried to avoid paying.

A major cause of this attrition has been the continuous increase in online travel sites where reduced rate inventory hotel rooms were being sold. Many meeting/convention delegates have been booking hotel rooms at a cheap rate usually through one of the top three online travel sites: Hotels.com, Expedia, or Travelocity (these three sites account for 75 percent of online sales of hotel rooms). In 2002, online sales of hotel rooms increased 49 percent to $6.3 billion.

To counter the outside-the-room-block reservations, in June 2002, five major hotel chains—Hilton, Hyatt, Marriott, InterContinental Hotels Group (then Six Continents), and Starwood—entered into an agreement with Pegasus Solutions and Priceline.com to launch Travelweb, an online hotel reservation service. With Travelweb, the hotel chains would be able to manage their own inventory of hotel rooms and offer any discounted rooms on Travelweb (McNulty, "Project Attrition," 2003).

As of 2008, Travelweb has one of the largest net rate inventories online and features over 13 000 hotel properties in North America, Europe, and the Caribbean (Kovaleski, 2007).

Other potential tactics to avoid attrition could include having all meeting reservations prepaid, with a large dollar amount for a cancellation penalty. Also, planners could "bundle" the hotel room rate with some fees for other activities (spa, Internet connection, etc.) to remove the financial incentive to reserve a room outside the room block (McNulty, "Project Attrition," 2003).

To avoid litigation, an attrition clause has been inserted in group contracts (which protect both parties). An attrition clause is a specific provision indicating the formula required to calculate the revenue lost if a room block is not filled. Originally attrition damages represented the amount of lost revenue, based on the number of rooms not picked up (i.e., not guaranteed). Since 2005, some hotels have been calculating the "attrition penalty" based on a "revenue minimum" or "lost revenue dollars."

"By agreeing to a revenue minimum," explains Kovaleski, "no penalty is assessed and the planner doesn't have to take the fall when it's time to pay the attrition fee." The planner knows how much the revenue shortfall will be and can convert this extra revenue into grades of standard rooms to deluxe rooms, or even suites. A similar approach may be used with food and beverage: the planner may be able to convert this revenue shortfall into more expensive wine, more appetizers, or more expensive menu items (Kovaleski, 2007).

Canada Revenue Agency: Foreign Convention and Tour Incentive Program

In 2007, the new Foreign Convention and Tour Incentive Program replaced the Visitor Rebate Program. This program provides rebates in GST for nonresidents on accommodations associated with tour packages. GST relief is also supplied to foreign sponsors and/or organizers on convention facilities and supplies when at least 75 percent of participants are nonresidents.

Canadian Chapters of MPI Environmental Policy Statement

In an effort to support environmental sustainability, the Canadian Chapters of Meeting Planners International have ratified the following policy:

> We recognize the immense potential impact our community has on our environment and will make a deliberate commitment to the power of meetings and events to support sustainability. We will establish leadership and demonstrate commitment in the area of environmentally friendly meetings in Canada by including environmental factors in every decision we make on behalf of our members, and by making the best use of resources for maximum impact and alignment with our objectives. We will educate and inform our members about our environmental actions. We are committed to building our brand and connecting our community in an environmentally sustainable way. (MPI Canada, n.d.) (See also Table 11–2.)

Check Your Product Knowledge

1. List the predicted top four technology investments by suppliers.
2. What is attrition and what is the recommendation to alleviate the concerns of both parties?

TABLE 11–2 Top Ten (Plus 1!) Things You Can Do To Green Your Event

Here are the top ten easy things you can do to make your meeting greener.

1. Offer bulk condiments for things like sugar and cream
2. Do not use disposable items like plastic or paper coffee cups or paper plates
3. Offer water in jugs. Do not offer bottled water[1] . . . but offer re-usable water bottles.
4. Offer local food choices and stay away from endangered species (such as Chilean sea bass)
5. Donate left-over food to local programs such as Food Runners
6. Ensure the accommodation offers in-room recycling of towels, sheets, plastic, paper and bottles
7. Eliminate hand-outs. Offer information on-line or burn a CD
8. Eliminate give-aways that are not edible or re-usable
9. On-line registration and confirmation for both delegates and media
10. Ensure you publicize your environmental efforts to stakeholders
11. Go carbon neutral.

[1]Bottled water is: a. Not safer than most tap water (Dasani and Aquafina are bottled tap water); b. Generates billions of tons of waste plastic a year; c. Generates transportation waste in trucking bottles around the globe (Fiji water. Evian or Pellegrino, for example).

SOURCE: From "VERTigo Plan to Meet Green," MPI Canada, www.mpiweb.org.

CAREER OPPORTUNITIES

Events often rely on volunteers as well as on tourism and leisure professionals and event planners and managers. Anyone who becomes involved in planning and managing events needs above-average skills in organization, marketing, finance, planning, project management, and human and public relations.

The tremendous growth of the meetings business in recent decades has bred a demand for specialists in several fields. Examples of meetings-related careers:

1. Event managers, who need excellent communication skills, intelligence, integrity, experience, and a positive attitude.

A DAY IN THE LIFE OF A

Meeting Planner

I'm a full-time meeting planner for a large corporation. I do just what my title implies: I plan, schedule, and supervise all the elements of the meetings the corporation holds. My goal is simple—to run a successful meeting—but my job is not. Coordinating travel, accommodations, food, and sometimes even entertainment takes a lot of doing. A good meeting planner needs to be aggressive in making deals with hotels, but sensitive in communicating needs. He or she has to be detail-oriented, yet creative. The best way to show how important these qualities are is to go through the steps I usually follow in planning a large meeting.

The first step is to choose where the meeting will take place. I have to consider a number of factors, including the nature of the event (What is its purpose?), the makeup of the attendees (Will spouses attend?), the geographical location of the site (Is it easy to get to?), and so on. I have to investigate a number of things about a hotel, from banquet facilities to the kinds of lighting available in meeting rooms. Most of all, I have to learn about the quality of service a place gives. Attendees will remember how they were treated long after they've forgotten what they had for dinner each night.

I always visit and inspect a possible site personally, even if I've booked meetings there before. Mostly, I'm concerned about the meeting facilities. Meeting rooms come in all types. I remember once when I visited a prospective site that used accordion-type flexible partitions to divide a large room into two smaller rooms. I had been told that the rooms were soundproof, but in fact they let in plenty of noise. I could just imagine a serious discussion being punctuated by bursts of laughter from a sales presentation next door.

Lighting is another important but easily overlooked aspect of a meeting's setting. Early in my career, I booked a meeting in a room with several of those wagon-wheel-type fixtures that have bare bulbs hanging from them. A lot of the people complained about the glare. After that, I paid special attention to lighting.

Once I decide on a site, I sit down with the hotel's convention service manager. I provide the service manager with as many details about the program as I can; the more he or she knows, the better. Then I make my requests for accommodations, meals, meeting rooms, equipment, and so on, and get every guarantee in writing. I'm always wary of people who say things like "Don't worry, we'll take care of everything." I need written confirmation. At the same time, I try to get every concession I can—like complimentary morning coffee and newspapers for attendees—from the hotel. Little touches like that score points with people.

During the preparation phase, I use lots of checklists. They help me keep track of which things are done and which need to be done. I also negotiate with airlines, car rental firms, and other services to ensure that attendees will get to the meeting and back comfortably.

A couple of days before the meeting, I fly to the site. Once there, I make sure everything is set up. The night before the meeting opens, I check all the equipment and run through any slides in the actual rooms where they'll be used, even if I've been assured that everything was checked "back at the office." One time, a worker had jostled a slide carousel while packing it, dislodging some slides. He put them all back, but some were upside down and out of order. My preliminary run-through saved the speaker an embarrassing moment.

During the meeting, I always assume that Murphy's Law will operate: Everything that can go wrong will go wrong. I'm on hand to figure out how to prevent disaster when emergencies arise. The hotel helps me there, too. I've returned to some hotels partly on the basis of their ability to replace a dead microphone quickly or change a meeting room at the last minute.

Even when the last attendee has gone home, my job isn't done. After the meeting, I get together with hotel representatives for a post-meeting critique. At these face-to-face meetings, I often gain valuable insights into how attendees and meeting planners can make meetings run more smoothly. After a good meeting, I have a feeling of accomplishment. I know that I've planned well, the company's business needs have been met, and people's personal and social needs have been met, too.

2. Meeting planners, who work for conference and convention facilities, associations and trade groups, educational and religious organizations, government agencies, corporations, independent companies, hotels, travel agencies, regional marketing agencies, industry associations, or United Nations affiliates.

3. Convention service managers, who work in hotels, resorts, conference centres, convention or civic centres, and on cruise ships.

4. Meetings business entrepreneurs, who run their own companies specializing in convention services and facilities, trade show management, site destination selection, and destination management.

Summary

- Generally speaking, there are three types of events: mega-events, hallmark events, and special events.
- Events are the reason why most people travel to a destination.
- Advances in the transportation industry—the advent of jet travel, in particular—have spurred the growth of the meetings market.
- Meetings can be classified as conventions, conferences, forums, seminars, workshops, exhibitions, or trade shows.
- The association market and the corporate market are the two main segments of the meetings market.
- Association meetings differ from corporate meetings in that they are held on a regular cycle, at a different destination each year, and attract a larger number of participants, who attend voluntarily.
- Meeting planners work for associations, corporations, or travel agencies, or as independent consultants.
- Tour operators package convention travel for sale to associations and corporations. Sales can be direct or through retail travel agencies.
- Site destination selection companies, destination management companies, and convention services and facilities companies provide support services for meeting planners.
- Convention and visitors' bureaux promote and service conventions for a particular destination.

Key Terms

association market   p. 262
categories of events   p. 257
conference   p. 260
convention   p. 260
convention and visitors' bureaux (CVBs)   p. 269
corporate market   p. 264
corporate meeting planners   p. 265

destination management companies (DMCs)   p. 268
event tourism   p. 258
hallmark event   p. 256
hotel attrition   p. 269
mega-event   p. 256
off-site meetings   p. 260
site destination selection companies   p. 268
special event   p. 256
teleconferences   p. 260

Internet Connections

Calgary Stampede
www.calgarystampede.com   p. 258

The Canadian Society of Professional Event Planners (CanSPEP)
www.cspep.ca   p. 255

Canadian Tulip Festival
www.tulipfestival.ca   p. 257

Carlson Wagonlit
www.carlsonwagonlit.com   p. 268

The CRFA Show
www.cfra.ca   p. 260

Destination Winnipeg
www.tourism.winnipeg.mb.ca   p. 269

Halifax Metro Centre
www.halifaxmetrocentre.com   p. 262

Halifax World Trade and Convention Centre
www.wtcchalifax.com   p. 262

Hospitality Sales & Marketing Association International
www.hsmai.org   p. 266

International Association of Convention & Visitor Bureaus
www.iacvb.org   p. 269

Las Vegas Convention and Visitors Authority
www.visitlasvegas.com   p. 268

Meeting Planners International (MPI)
www.mpiweb.org   p. 266

Metro Toronto Convention Centre
www.mtccc.com   p. 262

Ottawa Congress Centre
www.ottawacongresscentre.com

Paradigm Events
www.paradigmevents.com   p. 255

Pengrowth Saddledome in Calgary
www.pengrowthsaddledome.com   p. 262

Quebec Winter Carnival
www.carnaval.qc.ca   p. 256

WORKSHEET 11–1 **Events**

You are an independent event planner. You have been asked to help plan the Canada Day celebrations for the local Volunteer Fire Department fundraiser. First identify the type of event the department should have and the format the event is likely to follow. Then suggest an appropriate location for the event. What will you suggest to make the event special? Who will help put on the event? Who will want to attend? What cost will be involved?

_____

_____

_____

_____

_____

_____

_____

_____

_____

_____

_____

_____

_____

_____

_____

_____

_____

_____

_____

_____

_____

_____

_____

_____

_____

_____

_____

_____

_____

_____

_____

WORKSHEET 11–2   **Convention and Visitors' Bureau**

Use the Internet to locate the CVB closest to Yourtown, and obtain information and promotional materials from it. What facilities does the city offer for the following?

Small to medium-sized meetings

_____

_____

Conventions

_____

_____

Exhibitions and trade shows

_____

_____

_____

Visitors in general

_____

_____

_____

How large a convention or conference could the city accommodate?

_____

_____

_____

Are any improvements or expansions planned? If so, what are they and when will they be completed?

_____

_____

_____

Read the Yourtown newspapers. List the conventions, conferences, trade shows, and exhibitions that will be held in Yourtown in the next six months.

_____

_____

_____

List the ones that will be open to the public.

_____

_____

_____

ATTRACTIONS, FESTIVALS, AND SPECIAL EVENTS

Objectives

When you have completed this chapter, you should be able to:

- Describe the nature and functions of public museums, zoos, fairs, and festivals.
- Describe the kinds of facilities provided by the commercial recreation sector.

- Distinguish between festivals and special events.
- Identify the channels by which the attractions product is distributed to consumers.

Canada is the second-largest country in the world, which affects how we see ourselves and how visitors see us. Canadians think of their country as one of wide-open spaces, forests and lakes, and a vast Far North. Most urban Canadians are within an hour's drive of the countryside.

For better or worse, this vision of Canada affects our international tourism. Many people decide not to visit Canada because of preconceived notions that this country has only "mountains, Mounties, and moose" to offer. Overcoming tourists' present image of Canada is a marketing challenge that must be addressed. Tourists may not see Canada as an exotic or cultural destination, but our country does impress them once they are here. We do have attractions that generate tourism.

According to a study by the Canadian Tourism Commission (CTC), travellers are more likely to participate in cultural and entertainment activities than in outdoor activities. Culture and heritage are important travel motivators. One-third of all travellers to Canada engage in cultural and heritage activities as part of their trip. The CTC recognizes this, and in 2001 began a three-year program to integrate soft adventure (e.g., hiking, cycling, fishing) with cultural, artistic, and learning vacations. Canada doesn't lack world-class product to market, but it will have to develop partnerships between its cultural and tourism industries.

This chapter focuses on the attractions sector generally, and on the roles that festivals and special events play in attracting tourists, both to Canada and to destinations in the rest of the world. Attractions draw people to destinations and provide leisure, recreational, and business activities. Some

attractions are ongoing; others are special events that occur frequently or once in a lifetime.

Attractions are either natural or built by humans. Natural attractions include Niagara Falls, the Grand Canyon, the seashore, lakes, and forests. Attractions built by humans include the Great Wall of China and the CN Tower.

Special events can be core attractions. Some, like the Olympics, are mega-events. Others are smaller, one-time occurrences such as a concert or boxing match. Then there are regularly scheduled events such as the CFL's Grey Cup and the Academy Awards.

A **festival** is a specific type of event. Typically, a festival is annual, has a specific theme, and involves a public celebration. Many festivals are cultural. Some have existed for centuries, but most are much more recent.

ATTRACTIONS

Attractions can be natural, cultural, or heritage. They draw visitors and are the reasons why other tourism services exist. The more special the attraction, the more visitors it draws. A visitor attraction is a place or activity that attracts visitors, provides an enjoyable way for them to spend leisure time, has been developed and managed to realize this potential and to satisfy visitors, and provides facilities and services to serve their needs, demands, and interests. A fee may or may not be charged for admission.

There are many types of attractions. They range from "white-knuckle" thrill rides at an exhibition to a designated lookout on the Cabot Trail in Nova Scotia. Some

PROFILE

On the Cutting Edge of Agtourism

William (Bill) D. Reynolds
Co-Leader, AgTourism Initiative, Local/Domestic Expansion

Alberta Agriculture and Rural Development

As a seasoned tourism professional, Bill Reynolds is best described as a "details guy with a passionate appetite for learning, someone who is an information junkie and is always looking for the 'cutting edge.' This combination of traits has served as the basis for Bill's success in his 30-year career in federal, provincial, and municipal travel- and tourism-related government positions. "I'm a very thorough planner at heart. On many levels I plan my own career like I would any project," says Bill.

Bill's love for travel and tourism began at an early age with annual family vacations and weekend skiing, hiking, and camping excursions. Joining the Field Naturalists Society as a teenager, Bill learned to appreciate Canada's environment and the abundance of flora and fauna that our country is known for.

Majoring in ecology, Bill graduated with an undergraduate science degree with great distinction from Montreal's McGill University. His appetite for learning was not quenched, so he enrolled in Chicago's George Williams College, where he earned a Masters of Science in leisure and environmental resources administration, specializing in interpretive services and the analysis of communication strategies. Summer jobs during his university years included one as a seasonal interpretive naturalist at the Mont St. Hilaire Nature Conservation Centre (Quebec) and at Banff National Park.

Upon graduation, Bill accepted a position as nature centre programmer at the John Janzen Nature Centre (part of Edmonton Parks & Recreation). Later, a thoroughly prepared application for professional development resulted in an approved leave of absence and in a Canadian Museums Association bursary for Bill to undertake an Australasian study tour. The focus of the research was a market-oriented operational assessment of nature centres, museums, park interpretive facilities, and science centres in that region.

Bill, accompanied by his wife Marion, toured Australia, New Zealand, Indonesia, Papua New Guinea, Malaysia (including Borneo), the Philippines, Singapore, Hong Kong, and Thailand for a year. On returning to Edmonton, Bill was hired as visitor services supervisor, Capital City Recreation Park, Edmonton. When he was initially hired, he was told "to make the river valley come alive." Bill recalls that he was attracted to this position because of its potential for creativity and innovation, which fit with his reason for his career change: "You gravitate to what excites you."

After completing a project focusing on an opportunity assessment of Edmonton's river valley as a tourist destination, Bill's career path veered toward destination tourism.

Bill was then hired by Alberta Economic Development, first as heritage tourism development planner and later as tourism facility development analyst. With a thirst for more knowledge of the North American tourism field, Bill negotiated a one-year leave of absence. Bill, wife Marion and sons, Vincent and Colin, began a North American trek, with planned detours to visit a variety of tourism facilities in Canada and the United States. On returning to a new job as director, tourism product development and enhancement for Alberta Economic Development, Bill's recently acquired knowledge was utilized to assist in the development of new and improved tourist operations.

From 2002 to 2007, Bill has been leader of the Agtourism Initiative, with Alberta Agriculture, and Food. Agtourism (or agritourism) is the marriage of two of Alberta's top industries—agriculture and tourism. Alberta has divided agtourism into three sectors: ag-based attractions (heritage farms and ranches, farm recreation, and ag-industry tours), ag-based services (tour operators, retail, food and beverage, and accommodation), and ag-based events (festivals, fairs, rodeos, trade shows, and horse and livestock shows).

When asked for his opinion on the future outlook for agtourism in Alberta and the world, Bill states, "Agtourism will grow in leaps and bounds as people continue to want to revisit their agrarian roots, recharge their batteries at country getaways, reconnect with rural values, relax enjoying the country lifestyle, and relearn where their food comes from. However, delivering a service will not be enough. Creating experiences will be the name of the game. Agtourism success will hinge on fulfilling this promise, combined with some innovative 'purple cow' thinking."

In Bill's opinion, "Working together in partnerships will also be critical. In Alberta, we have been notably successful with our cluster development process. As catalysts, we connect regional operators together in a critical mass to assist with economies of scale and create a call to action. Relationships forge, cross, and word-of-mouth promotion builds, marketing consortia engage, events occur, and profit at the farm gate goes up. Growth will be in agri-edutainment centres where agricultural themed play and learning combine. As well, the focus on health and consuming fresh, locally grown food will drive attendance at regional harvest, food and wine festivals."

Bill is a firm believer in lifelong learning and has completed numerous post-degree courses and seminars. He says, "Innovation needs ideas that come from both insights and intuition. The former is stimulated by staying on top of competitive intelligence in your tourism field but also by researching outside your field for solutions to problems. Intuition comes from being receptive to events and openly listening to nature."

Bill's advice to achieve success is to find your voice, help others to find theirs, and enjoy the journey. Bill is now working in Agtourism Research, Market Expansion, Experience Development.

SOURCE: Interviews with Bill Reynolds, August 1, 2004 and April 2007 and Reynolds' curriculum vitae.

ILLUSTRATION 12–1

The "hallowed" Hockey Hall of Fame in Toronto celebrates the history and excitement of one of Canada's two national sports. Lacrosse is Canada's first official national sport.

SOURCE: Image courtesy of the Hockey Hall of Fame.

are internationally famous (Yosemite), others only locally so (Cape Split in Nova Scotia), though this can be changed. **Natural attractions**, places that are preserved or are in their "original" state, such as scenic landscapes or seascapes and national or provincial parks, include the beaches of Prince Edward Island, the Rockies, and the Northern Lights, **Constructed attractions** in Canada include Butchart Gardens in Victoria, a Niagara Peninsula winery, the Confederation Bridge between Prince Edward Island and New Brunswick, and the Museum of Civilization in Gatineau. Overall, attractions generate tourism dollars and create employment.

Events can be large-scale (the Calgary Stampede) or much smaller (the Wellesley Apple, Butter, and Cheese Festival in a town west of Kitchener, Ontario). They all serve the same purpose: to attract people to an enjoyable organized activity of short duration. Unlike attractions, events are usually temporary, but as events last longer, become more regular, and have more time and resources invested in them, the distinction between attractions and events is becoming less clear (see Chapter 11).

Museums

Museums are storehouses and display centres for objects considered worthy of preservation because of their artistic, historic, or scientific value. Almost anything—from prehistoric artefacts to antique cars to television sets—can be the subject of a museum exhibit.

Public Museums Until the seventeenth and eighteenth centuries, the pleasure of collecting and displaying works of art and curiosities of nature were reserved for the upper classes. As education spread to the middle classes, the concept of public museums took root and grew rapidly.

There are thousands of museums in Canada and the United States. Many are owned and operated by governments (federal, provincial or state, or local) and are financed mainly by tax revenues. Others are owned by nonprofit groups. Museums are supported by admission fees, private donations, government grants, and corporate contributions. Some museums are supported by universities, such as the Redpath Museum in Montreal, which is supported and operated by McGill University. Table 12–1 lists and briefly describes the major types of museums. Art museums and historical museums are the most popular.

Today's museums are centres of learning and culture, but they are also places for recreation and entertainment. An art museum may offer courses in painting and lectures on art history; it may provide trained guides to talk about the artists whose works are represented; it may provide or rent audio guides to visitors. It may also hold film festivals, concerts, and similar events to educate and entertain patrons.

Commercial Museums Most commercial museums are small and are devoted to one type of collection, such as automobiles, in the Canadian Automotive Museum in Oshawa.

Nostalgia for the golden age of the railways has resulted in many railway museums being established across the continent. The largest one in Canada is the Canadian Railway Museum at Delson, Quebec, just south of Montreal. Many of these museums offer steam train excursions.

Sometimes a museum is the result of one community's special interest or collection—for example, the town of Springhill, Nova Scotia, built the Anne Murray Centre to honour its most famous citizen.

Model Cultures and Restorations

In a **model culture** or restoration, visitors learn about the material culture (houses, vehicles, artifacts) and performing arts of a historical age or a different nation. Buildings have been constructed or restored so that they

TABLE 12–1 Major Types of Museums

Type	Characteristics	Example
Historical museums	Show collections or buildings of historical interest	Maritime Museum of the Atlantic (Halifax)
Art museums	Show collections of paintings, sculpture, or other art	National Gallery (Ottawa)
Science and technology museums	Illustrate principles, uses, and history of science	Ontario Science Centre (Toronto)
Natural history museums	Show animals, fish, and insects in their natural habitats	Provincial Museum of Alberta (Edmonton)
Encyclopedic or general museums	Exhibit a wide range of objects	Royal British Columbia Museum (Victoria)
Special-interest museums	Focus on a single subject	Hockey Hall of Fame (Toronto)
Children's museums	Specialize in exhibits that explain how things work	Manitoba Children's Museum (Winnipeg)

ILLUSTRATION 12–2

A very popular Prince Edward Island tourist attraction is the Anne of Green Gables house, home of the young Anne Shirley in the novel by Lucy Maude Montgomery.

SOURCE: Image courtesy of Canadian Tourism Commission.

resemble an actual town, village, or fort. Costumed employees serve as guides and demonstrate the arts, crafts, and daily practices of the time or culture. Kings Landing Historical Settlement north of Fredericton, New Brunswick, in the St. John river valley, re-creates New Brunswick rural life between 1820 and 1890. Fort Steele re-creates life in southeastern British Columbia at the turn of the century. Restorations in Ontario include Upper Canada Village (Morrisburg) and Sainte-Marie among the Hurons (Midland).

Heritage Sites

According to the UNESCO (United Nations Educational, Scientific and Cultural Organization) website, its list of World Heritage Sites includes many of the planet's most outstanding attractions and grandest monuments of the past (see Table 12–2 for Canadian sites and the years in which they were added to the list). For tourism promoters they act as magnets, while for the nation in which they are found they serve as icons that continue to influence current values. UNESCO's World Heritage List resulted from a global treaty that seeks to identify, recognize, and protect places that are of outstanding universal value. These places fall into two main categories: human-made sites and natural sites.

TABLE 12–2 UNESCO World Heritage Sites in Canada, 2007

Year	Site
1978	L'Anse aux Meadows National Historic Site
1978	Nahanni National Park
1979	Dinosaur Provincial Park
1981	SGaang Gwaii (Anthony Island)
1981	Head-Smashed-In Buffalo Jump
1983	Wood Buffalo National Park
1984	Canadian Rocky Mountain Parks
1985	Historic District of Quebec
1987	Gros Morne National Park
1995	Old Town Lunenburg
1999	Miguasha Park
2007	Rideau Canal
2008	Joggins Fossil Cliffs

Listed jointly with the United States:

Year	Site
1979	Kluane/Wrangell–St. Elias/Glacier Bay/Tatshenshini–Alsek
1985	Waterton Glacier International Peace Park

SOURCE: Properties inscribed on the World Heritage List, September 2004. Reprinted by permission of UNESCO.

Zoos and Aquariums

A **zoo** is a place set aside for the study and display of wild animals. **Aquariums** are special exhibits of fish and other aquatic animals, such as dolphins and seals. Zoos and aquariums are museums that collect and exhibit living creatures rather than inanimate objects. The various types of zoos and aquariums are shown in Table 12–3.

Zoos entertain and educate visitors and care for the wildlife in their charge. Zoos also serve as centres for scientific research in all areas of zoology and biology. Many zoos are involved in efforts to rescue endangered species through carefully controlled breeding programs. The Toronto Zoo has more than 5000 animals living in outdoor settings and glass-roofed pavilions.

Aquariums have a long history. The Sumerians built the first known aquariums 4500 years ago, and, in ancient China, ornamental goldfish were bred in artificial ponds. Marineland, near St. Augustine, Florida, opened an outdoor aquarium in 1938 featuring large tanks, ramps, and viewing windows. Visitors were able to observe large aquatic animals such as sharks and porpoises from both above and below the water line. Marineland proved to be so popular that many other aquariums around the country adopted the same basic design. Aquariums that specialize in saltwater animals are called **oceanariums**. Many of these feature shows by trained seals and dolphins, along with more formal exhibits and educational programs.

The Vancouver Public Aquarium, next to the Stanley Park Zoo, displays some 9000 freshwater and saltwater marine animals. Visitors can walk through a humid Amazon rain forest gallery and see displays of the underwater life of coastal British Columbia, the Canadian Arctic, and other areas of the world.

Spectator Sports

Armed with peanuts, hot dogs, and soft drinks, more than 50 million fans of professional baseball get out to the ballpark each year to root for their favourite team. The Toronto Blue Jays was the first baseball team to attract 4 million in attendance (1991–93) (this record was broken by the Colorado Rockies in 1993—4 483 350, to the Blue Jays' attendance of 4 057 947 that season).

Spectator sports are also a wonderful way to vent emotions. Along with baseball, Canadians like to watch hockey, football, lacrosse, basketball, curling, boxing, tennis, golf, and racing (car, thoroughbred, harness, and greyhound). The Olympic Games are the world's largest single spectator mega-event. Montreal hosted the 1976 Summer Games; Calgary, the 1988 Winter Games; and Vancouver–Whistler will host the 2010 Winter Games.

Spectator sports bring profits to the community as well as to the owners. As with other recreational events, people attending sporting events spend money at concession booths and for transportation and parking. Many patronize local stores and restaurants before and after the event. Fans from out of town spend money on hotels and entertainment. Amateur sporting events also bring profits. By hosting the 1988 Winter Olympics, Calgary put itself on the map as a major destination.

Because of the economic impact, cities vie with one another to host major events such as the Grey Cup and the Super Bowl. They also compete for major league franchises. To win a franchise in any sport, a city must be able to offer a first-class arena or stadium, or show that it will soon build one. The enclosed 60 000-seat BC Place Stadium in Vancouver could host a major league baseball team. These facilities are enormously expensive to build and maintain and so are designed to serve many purposes. When a facility has several uses, more events can be held, and more operating revenue is generated. The Rogers Centre, home of the Toronto Argonauts and the Blue Jays, also hosted the Vanier Cup for university football, as well as rock concerts, religious gatherings, and other events, such as one of the largest book readings ever with J.K. Rowling reading from a Harry Potter novel.

The tourism industry also profits from spectator sports. For some time, it has been building package tours around major sporting events such as the World Series, the Grey Cup, the Stanley Cup, the Kentucky Derby, and the

TABLE 12–3 Types of Zoos and Aquariums

Type	Characteristics	Examples
Municipal zoos	Animals are maintained for public display, mostly in large, natural enclosures	Metropolitan Toronto Zoo
Wild animal parks	Animals roam freely in natural settings	San Diego Wild Animal park
Children's zoos	Young people can see and touch various animals	Philadelphia Children's Zoo
Inland aquariums	Exhibits of freshwater fish and animals	John G. Shedd Aquarium (Chicago)
Oceanariums	Sharks, whales, dolphins, and other marine life are maintained in saltwater tanks	Vancouver Aquarium

SOURCE: Tourism Satellite Accounts, Canadian Tourism Commission/Statistics Canada.

Indy 500. But now a new phenomenon is appearing: When the home team goes on the road, instead of staying at home and watching on television, the fans are going on the road, too. And the most avid sports fans—those who can't wait until the baseball season opens—can now take package tours to Florida or Arizona to watch their team in spring training.

Theme Parks

As the first major theme park in the United States, Disneyland was an immediate success. It has inspired the development of many other theme parks, including Disney World (see Chapter 4).

Canada's Wonderland is a world-class, 150-hectare theme park featuring various activities such as amusement rides, lifelike cartoon characters, and aquatic shows. The world's top 25 theme parks entertain more than 186.5 million tourists each year.

The Themes Most tourist attractions have their roots in the natural or historical environment in which they are located. The **theme park** is an exception. By establishing a theme and then having all exhibits, rides, shops, and restaurants relate to it, the theme park creates its own environment.

Themes derived from history, animal life, and cartoons have been especially popular for theme parks. Some parks hold to a strong central theme. Busch Gardens in Tampa, Florida, revolves around an African theme. The three SeaWorld parks (Orlando, San Diego, and San Antonio) are devoted to marine life.

Canada has only a few theme parks. Among them are Frontierland, south of Whitehorse, Yukon; Marineland in Niagara Falls, Ontario; and Magic Mountain near Moncton, New Brunswick.

Characteristics of Theme Parks Before the family automobile became commonplace, amusement parks were built at the end of a streetcar line, as Belmont Park was in Montreal. Customers came mainly from the immediate community. Today's theme parks are located on the outskirts of major urban areas, cover vast tracts of land, and offer a wide range of recreational activities and events: roller coaster rides, theatrical performances, exhibits, tours, movies, and celebrity appearances, all of which can be entertaining and educational. People drive or fly for miles to get to these parks; having arrived, they tend to stay longer and spend more money.

Theme parks try to draw tourists from all over the country and beyond by advertising in newspapers and magazines, on television, and on the Internet. Because a visit to a theme park is now likely to be part of a vacation trip—or the destination itself—hotels, restaurants, and other entertainment facilities have sprung up around theme parks to serve the needs of tourists.

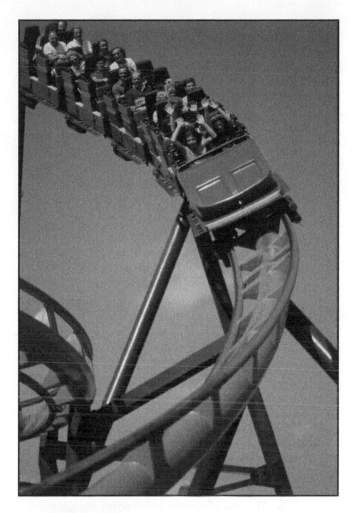

ILLUSTRATION 12–3

Local and international visitors are attracted by large commercial recreation enterprises like Paramount Canada's Wonderland.

SOURCE: Corel.

Amusement Parks, Carnivals, and Circuses

For generations, circuses, carnivals, and amusement parks were great places to spend a Saturday afternoon. In recent years these old standbys have been overshadowed by theme parks, television spectaculars, and other more trendy forms of entertainment. But circuses, carnivals, and amusement parks are still around, and are popular with young people and families.

Amusement Parks Coney Island was established in the 1880s on 10 kilometres of beach in New York City. It became the model for the gaudy amusement parks of the twentieth century. Besides a midway with rides, freak shows, cotton candy, and penny arcade, traditional amusement parks had tables and benches for family picnics. Those with waterfront settings offered beaches for swimming.

Amusement parks typically charged a low admission fee, but an additional fee for every ride or event. Theme park developers have reversed this, charging a high fee at the gate that includes all the rides and events inside.

Because of the overwhelming popularity of theme parks, the number of amusement parks has decreased considerably over the years. La Ronde, a summer amusement park on Île Ste-Hélène opposite Montreal Harbour, is one of the most popular amusement parks, with clean, modern, and safe facilities, and is now part of the Six Flags amusement park chain.

Carnivals A **carnival** is a travelling amusement park. In the late 1890s, newly developed technology allowed entire midways—rides, refreshment and souvenir stands, and shows—to be transported by train from city to city. Today's carnivals are not as elaborate as earlier carnivals. They usually travel from small town to small town and set up their rides in the parking lot of a shopping mall.

Circuses With daring and skilled performers, trained animal acts, and clowns, a circus offers audiences a wonderful spectacle. In the golden age of the circus, around 10 major circuses travelled the continent, and the arrival of the circus was the major event of the summer. The Ringling Brothers and Barnum & Bailey Circus is still a major circus; a number of small local circuses still delight children across North America. Cirque du Soleil (CDS) is the circus with a difference—there are no performing animals (animal performances have become increasingly controversial)—the performers are acrobats, gymnasts, clowns, musicians, dancers, etc. CDS, which originated in Baie Comeau, Quebec has revived the format of the circus to once again capture the title "the Greatest Show on Earth." According to the CDS website, "Since its creation in 1984, Cirque du Soleil has thrilled more than 80 million spectators in over two hundred different cities on five continents. The company currently has 8 touring shows and 7 resident shows around the world and will be adding new shows in Japan, Macao and Dubai in the near future."

Recreational Shopping

Visitors to the CN Tower usually buy a souvenir to remind them of their trip. Shopping has long been a byproduct of travelling. Three new types of facilities—megamalls, waterfront shopping complexes, and factory outlet centres—have greatly increased recreational shopping. These facilities are promoted as tourist attractions. Chartered buses and planes bring thousands of tourists to them each year.

Megamalls A **megamall** is a gigantic indoor shopping and entertainment complex—a shopper's paradise. Under one roof, shoppers can find department stores, hundreds of shops, restaurants, theatres, banks, health clubs, and art galleries. Sculptures, fountains, and tropical gardens add to the luxurious atmosphere. The West Edmonton Mall (WEM) was listed in the *Guinness Book of World Records* as the largest mall in the world until 2004—around the size of 85 football fields. The mall includes a huge wave swimming pool with a concrete beach, an ice-skating rink, an amusement park, and a reproduction of Bourbon Street in New Orleans. WEM is now listed as the fifth largest mall in the world (with 3.8 million square feet in gross leasable area), according to Forbes magazine (Riper, 2008). The South China Mall in Dongguan, China, with 7.1 million square feet in gross leasable area, is currently the world's largest mall.

ILLUSTRATION 12–4

West Edmonton Mall (Alberta) is the largest mall in North America, featuring a 2-hectare indoor waterpark (kept at about 30°C), more than 800 stores and 100 restaurants, plus nine world-class attractions.

SOURCE: Image courtesy of West Edmonton Mall Property Inc.

Waterfront Marketplaces Waterfront marketplaces are shopping and entertainment complexes built on a river or bay. The architecture of the complex gives visitors a pleasant view of the waterfront. A waterfront marketplace is usually part of an effort to restore the historic section of a city; in this capacity, it becomes the scene of civic events and festivals. The success of waterfront marketplaces in Halifax, Saint John, Toronto, and Winnipeg has stimulated similar developments elsewhere.

Factory Outlet Centres A factory outlet centre has several stores that sell name-brand merchandise at reduced prices. Megamalls and waterfront developments have been an economic boon to large cities; factory outlet centres have revitalized once-dying small towns. The zest for shopping has spilled over, so that the stores on some towns' main streets have reopened for business. One area that has become a prime location for factory outlet centres is along the border between the United States and Canada. The Niagara Factory Outlet Mall in Niagara Falls, New York, and outlets in Freeport, Maine, are popular destinations for Canadian shoppers looking for good buys. Prices for many items in these outlet stores are much lower than in Canada, even after the exchange rate is factored in.

Celebrity and Industrial Tours

Recognizing the public's fascination with the lives of famous people, the commercial recreation sector has been quick to turn the homes of celebrities into tourist attractions. For example, thousands of Japanese tourists travel from Japan to visit—even to be married at—the Anne of Green Gables house on Prince Edward Island. (In 2008, PEI celebrated the 100th anniversary of the publication of *Anne of Green Gables* with many special events.) Several provinces, as part of their museum systems, maintain a number of heritage houses that were the homes of famous Canadians, such as Bellevue House in Kingston, Ontario, once the home of Sir John A. Macdonald, the first prime minister of Canada.

Factories, processing plants, wineries, and breweries around the country have also become tourist attractions. People enjoy seeing how various products, from breakfast foods to jet planes, are made. The company often provides a guided tour through its plant, and explains its products through an exhibit or a video. Pelee Island Winery offers tours and wine tastings (for a $5.00 fee) in Kingsville, Ontario. Many companies generally do not charge admission, so industrial tours are often nonprofit ventures for the commercial sector. However, companies find these tours a very useful exercise in public relations.

Live Entertainment

Live entertainment includes symphony orchestras; stage, ballet, and opera companies; rock concerts; and nightclub shows. Live entertainment is sometimes the main attraction

for a vacation trip, such as visiting Nashville just to hear country and western music at the Grand Ole Opry or a theatre tour to see Broadway plays in New York. Regional theatres such as the Neptune Theatre in Halifax and the Stratford Festival in Ontario stage outstanding productions.

Sometimes people attend a concert or a play just to see the hall. Place des Arts in Montreal, New York City's Carnegie Hall, and Toronto's Pantages Theatre are all famous. The Charlottetown Festival's Main Stage has featured the musical *Anne of Green Gables* each summer since 1965 and brought other original Canadian musicals to the stage.

Gambling and Gaming

North Americans spend more money on gambling than on movie tickets—billions of dollars every year. Gambling (also known as gaming) has been a leisure activity for centuries. There are four types of gambling: pari-mutuel wagering, lotteries, the activities of nonprofit organizations (mainly bingos and raffles), and casino gambling. Whether it's Caesars Palace in Las Vegas or the McPhillips Street Station Casino in Winnipeg, the facilities, the dining, and the shows, as well as the gaming opportunities, are all part of the attraction.

Lotteries, bingo, and raffles are geared toward the residents of a particular area. Consequently, the tourism industry is interested mainly in casino gambling and pari-mutuel wagering. Pari-mutuel racing (in which winnings are divided in proportion to the amounts wagered) is the most popular spectator sport in the United States and draws millions of people each year.

According to the Canadian Gaming Association, the gaming industry in 2006 contributed to the economy $15 billion in direct revenue, over $2 billion in salaries, and $10 billion in current capital investment (see Table 12–4). Of that $15 billion, 57 percent ($8.6 billion) went to government programs and charities (Canadian Gaming Association, 2007).

TABLE 12–4 Economic Contribution to Canada Comparison (2006)	
Full Service Restaurants	$17.2 billion
Limited Service Restaurants	$15.4 billion
Gaming	$15.3 billion
Accommodation Services	$14.3 billion
Air Travel with Air Canada & WestJet	$11.9 billion

SOURCE: Canadian Gaming Association. (April 26, 2007). "Landmark Economic Impact Study Reveals Gaming Industry in Canada Worth $15.3 billion in Direct Spending Alone," www.canadiangaming.ca/english/press/pressrel_detail.cfm?id=15.

ILLUSTRATION 12–5

Casino Nova Scotia organizes tours for special groups such as seniors.

SOURCE: David Tonen.

Casino Gambling Casino gambling involves slot machines, keno and table games such as roulette, craps (dice), blackjack (21), baccarat, poker, and new games such as Caribbean stud poker and pai gow poker. Casinos are either freestanding or part of a large hotel/entertainment complex. They are privately owned by independent businesspeople or by corporations. In Nova Scotia, the casinos in Halifax and Sydney are a partnership between the provincial government and The Great Canadian Gaming Corporation of Richmond, B.C.

The biggest concentrations of casinos are in Macau (China); Las Vegas, Reno–Sparks, and Lake Tahoe (all in Nevada); and Atlantic City (New Jersey). Nevada's 200-plus casinos make gambling the basis for that state's most important industry—tourism. According to Net Global Indexes LLC, Macao's gross gaming revenue rose 46.6 percent in 2007 to approximately $10.4 billion, making Macau number one in gaming revenue worldwide (Las Vegas had been number one for years). Macau is now marketing itself as "the Monte Carlo of the Orient" and the "Vegas of Asia" (Macau.com, n.d.).

Slot machines bring in more money than all table games together. The first "cashless" casino opened in Australia. Its slot machines take debit cards rather than quarters, dimes, and nickels.

Pari-Mutuel Betting This is the kind of betting people do at horse races, dog races, etc. People bet on the first-, second-, and/or third-place finishers (known as win, place and show); the winners then share the total amount bet, less a percentage for the track.

More people attend thoroughbred racing than any other racing event. There are more than 100 thoroughbred tracks in Canada and the United States, many of them located in Ontario, New York, and California.

Harness racing, in which the driver sits behind the horse in a small, two-wheeled cart, is especially popular in southern Ontario, Montreal, and the Maritimes.

In Florida, betting is also legal in jai alai, a ball-and-racquet game, originating from the Basque regions in France and Spain.

Attractions Abroad

Every nation and continent has its own culture, history, climate, and natural resources, all of which determine the attractions that can be offered to leisure travellers. Nations with great natural beauty and a pleasant climate emphasize sports and recreational opportunities. The islands of the Caribbean, for example, attract vacationers with their sun, sandy beaches, and tropical waters. Countries with long

ILLUSTRATION 12–6

The Ontario Lottery and Gaming Corporation operates several racetracks in Ontario, such as the Windsor Raceway.

SOURCE: Photo by Indu Ghuman.

histories, such as Greece, concentrate on preserving, displaying, and promoting the structures and artifacts of their national heritage.

A nation's attitudes and values also do much to determine what attractions and facilities it develops and promotes. For example, Mexico and the other nations of Latin America have museums and archaeological sites that highlight their pre-Columbian past. And the conservation of wildlife and other natural resources has become a priority in most parts of the world, so national parks and nature reserves are found in many countries.

Museums around the World The history, resources, and culture of a region or a nation largely determine the kinds of museums it develops. Thus, nations such as Egypt and Israel have museums that feature antiquities. The Museum of Egyptian Antiquities in Cairo contains treasures from the tomb of King Tutankhamen; the Israel Museum in Jerusalem displays many of the Dead Sea Scrolls.

Visitors on a tour of Europe can expect to spend a great deal of time in art and history museums such as the Louvre in Paris and the Uffizi Gallery in Florence. The nations of Europe have also turned hundreds of castles and churches into museums.

The countries of Africa, Asia, and Latin America abound with anthropological and archaeological museums that celebrate their pre-colonial heritage. The museums of newer nations settled by northern Europeans, such as Canada, the United States, and Australia, are more likely to emphasize art, science, natural history, and colonial history.

Coming: The World's Biggest Attraction?

Dubailand, built on 3 billion square feet, will consist of theme parks, ecotourism projects, shopping malls, restaurants, and residential units, and when completed a minimum of 55 hotels. Dubai hopes this massive complex will attract 15 million visitors by 2015 (*Travel Weekly*, 2008).

Check Your Product Knowledge

1. What benefits are gained from attractions?
2. What are the characteristics of theme parks?

ECOTOURISM AND ATTRACTIONS

Market research has identified ecotravellers as educated and affluent (see Table 12–5). Ecotravellers are interested in natural settings; they also want opportunities to participate in educational activities that do not disturb the environment or ones that involve interaction with indigenous cultures and communities. The Travel Industry Association of America estimates there are 43 million ecotourists in the United States alone.

Demand for Canadian ecotourism is growing. Environmentally sensitive tours and projects are being developed—for example, Roots Lodge in Ucluelet, British Columbia. Also growing in popularity are experiential resorts and historical learning vacations.

TABLE 12–5 Ecotourist Profile

Profile of ecotourists in Europe

- Experienced travellers
- Higher education
- Higher income bracket
- Age: middle-age to elderly
- Opinion leaders
- Ask & tell their friends & colleagues about trip
- Are the most important source of trip information

Profile of ecotourists in the U.S.

- 35–54 years of age
- 82 percent have a college education or higher

SOURCE: Reprinted with permission.

Ecotourism Attractions

Ecotourism often involves the building of ecoresorts. These are resorts with sustainable sites whose facilities do not upset the environmental balance. Ecoresorts are attractions in themselves. They reflect the area's natural environment and indigenous culture as well as its archaeology, history, and architecture. Above all, an ecoresort looks like it belongs—an easy blend of nature, community, and culture.

Central to an ecoresort is the ecolodge—a concept promoted by the guide developed by the Ecotourism Society. An ecolodge is a facility for tourists that depends on nature, offers an educational and participatory experience, is developed and managed in an environmentally sensitive manner, and protects its operating environment.

Ecoprograms as Attractions

The Miraval Resort north of Tucson, Arizona, is a 106-room resort developed as a cost-effective and sustainable desert oasis. It features healthy lifestyle ecoprograms. Shortly after opening, Miraval was awarded the 5-Globe Ecotel certification from Hotel Valuation Services, which acknowledges environmental sensitivity in areas such as solid waste management, energy efficiency, water conservation, training, and legislative compliance. (More information on ecotourism is in Chapter 13.)

Experiential Tourism

The Learning and Enrichment Alliance defines *experiential tourism* as "a form of travel that provides the visitor with greater insights, increased understanding, and a personal connection to the people and places they visit."

There is a growing trend of tourists who want to actively engage the culture they visit, as opposed to just observing it. Experiential tourism is as one of tourism's greatest growth sectors (The International Ecotourism Society, 2008).

An experiential tourism experience is now available in the Yukon, as a result of a partnership created between Parks Canada and Holland America Westours Inc. in February 2004 that gives cruise ship passengers the

Check Your Product Knowledge

1. Why are hotel operators becoming convinced that ecofriendly facilities make sense?
2. What practices are involved in making a facility ecofriendly and environmentally sensitive?

TABLE 12–6 Themes for Attraction Events

Historical	Newfoundland's Cabot 500 in 1997, celebrating Cabot's arrival 500 years earlier
	The 400th anniversary of the founding of Quebec City in 2008
Pageantry	The 1995 Louisbourg Encampment (Cape Breton Island)
Constitutional	Opening of Parliament
Sporting	Commonwealth Games, held every four years
	Vancouver–Whistler Olympics in 2010
Cultural	Carnaval de Québec
	Highland Games
Promotional	Rendez-vous Canada
	Career Fairs

opportunity to take hiking excursions in Kluane National Park and Reserve.

EVENTS

Various possible event themes are identified in Table 12–6. An event can be used to promote an area's tourism or it can be an independent happening. Events are important to any destination's strategy since they draw more visitors to an area and can be organized to do any of the following:

- Create a strong product profile and identity.
- Entertain visitors.
- Showcase regional and national products and services in the marketplace.

Events also have both real and perceived benefits for tourism operations because they:

- Complement and extend the tourism season.
- Attract new visitors.
- Provide new products and services or improve existing products.
- Generate economic benefits.
- Create opportunities for marketing and merchandising.

Events such as the Tall Ships visit to Halifax and the Calgary Stampede add to a destination's drawing power. Events, especially festivals, are becoming more popular in the cities that hold them as a result of more professional event management and general agreement that an imaginative, well-executed event can complement other tourism investments.

Festivals

The term "festival" no longer refers only to a religious feast day or celebration. Nowadays a festival can involve merrymaking

ILLUSTRATION 12–7

Since 1962, The Shaw Festival, located in historic Niagara-on-the-Lake, in southern Ontario, has specialized in plays by George Bernard Shaw and his contemporaries, and recently in plays about the period of Shaw's lifetime. An independent study by Genovese Vanderhoof and Associates stated that "the Shaw generated $95 million in economic activity for the Niagara region and the Canadian economy in 2003."

SOURCE: Image courtesy the Shaw Festival.

and entertainment of many kinds, or it can honour people, places, and events of little or no religious significance. The terms "festival" and "special event" are often used interchangeably; however, festivals are usually held annually and are not one-time-only special events.

Since the 1980s, the federal and provincial governments have encouraged community groups to launch festivals to promote local history and special attractions. Nova Scotia uses festivals for its tourism marketing program because so many festivals are held throughout the province each year. Every festival requires organization, planning, division of responsibilities, and attention to detail, as well as human labour and economic support. Festivals offer communities benefits such as the following:

- A showcase for new ideas in art, music, drama, dance, crafts, food, and sports, as well as for competition.
- A focus on local, regional, or national culture.
- Visitors and tourism dollars that create demand for tourism products and services and, in some cases, new businesses.

ILLUSTRATION 12–8

One of the most popular spectator sports is professional car racing. From 1978 to 2008, the Formula 1 Canadian Grand Prix took place on Ile Notre Dame, Montreal. Unfortunately this race was discontinued and replaced by the Abu Dhabi Grand Prix in 2009. The Montreal track is known as Circuit Gilles Villeneuve and is still used by two annual NASCAR races.

SOURCE: © Mr Zap/Shutterstock.

ILLUSTRATION 12–9

The Olympic flag will be flown in Vancouver and Whistler during the 2010 Olympic Winter Games.

SOURCE: CP Picture Archive.

Community involvement is essential if a festival is to succeed. An effort is usually made to involve as many people from the community as possible at every stage of the operation. People are recruited for their specialties and business expertise. For instance, hotels and motels, restaurants, travel counsellors, and transportation companies may become partners and develop packages, or they may help sponsor a festival.

During a festival there are usually many short-term jobs—selling tickets, working in a concession, hosting or guiding, maintenance, security, and so on. This kind of involvement provides firsthand experience in the tourism industry. As well, volunteering to be part of the planning and development committee helps individuals gain experience, which they can then transfer to full-time positions, perhaps in the events and conferences sector.

Special Events

Some special events are large-scale, once-in-a-lifetime shows. Others evolve into annual events. Whichever is the case, the event must offer a memorable, exciting spectacle. Whether the event is small or large, every detail needs careful attention. Special-event planning involves consideration of the following five factors:

1. **Location**—with easy access, sufficient parking
2. **Signage**—well designed
3. **Customer services**—food and beverage outlets, comfort stations, information booths, and safety and security services
4. **Staff**—must be trained
5. **Schedule**—from promotion to cleanup

Event management involves organizing the event, finding and coordinating everyone involved (often volunteers), setting budgets and financial controls, developing plans for marketing and public relations, fundraising, and evaluating the success of the event.

The event marketing, public relations, and media relations team sells the event to the public and handles all communication with the public. It is also responsible for communications with media outlets such as radio and television stations and newspapers to arrange publicity.

Trade Shows

Thousands of trade shows are held annually in Canada and the United States. Vendors rent booths to display a wide variety of products, from computer hardware to boats, and often demonstrate those products to potential buyers. Some trade shows, such as auto shows and home and garden shows, are open to the general public. They attract people to a destination and create demand for a wide range of tourism services from exhibitors and consumers.

International Trade Shows International trade shows provide an ideal means for companies to test overseas markets. Representatives have the opportunity to meet potential buyers and distributors from all over the world. Buyers come to sellers in one central location, so there is no need to spend time and money on individual sales calls. Even allowing for transportation costs, international trade shows are the most cost-effective way to enter world markets. Germany is the leading host country for international trade shows.

International trade shows differ from trade shows in Canada and the United States in several ways. First and foremost, they are more heavily sales-oriented. People go to trade shows to do business, not to attend meetings. Also, attendance is considerably higher at international shows. The Hanover Fair in Germany regularly attracts as many as 500 000 attendees over an eight-day period. Individual exhibits at these shows are more elaborate than at North American trade shows. A company may have as many as 1000 employees working a single exhibit. The largest exhibitors' booths (or *stands*, as they are called in Europe) include several meeting rooms as well as display space. Another difference is the international flavour of overseas shows. Interpreters are on hand to assist visitors from all over the world.

Canada's federal and provincial governments often provide financial help so that small and medium-sized companies can exhibit their products at overseas trade fairs. The point, of course, is to help them penetrate overseas markets. These same governments also encourage foreigners to attend trade shows in Canada.

North American Trade Shows Trade shows in Canada and the United States grew up as extensions of conferences featuring trade booths. These shows generally place more emphasis on attending meetings and are not as sales-oriented as international trade shows. They are also less formal and are attended by fewer people. Even so, domestic trade shows can be an important source of business for hotels in the host city. The largest shows are held in the giant convention centres, such as the Vancouver Convention & Exhibition Centre, the Metro Toronto Convention Centre, and McCormick Place in Chicago, the largest in the Western Hemisphere. A number of convention hotels have exhibit space for smaller trade shows.

Trade shows generate more than $20 billion in expenditures in North America. There are shows for every conceivable trade, industry, and profession. Rendez-vous Canada and the International Travel Expo are examples of shows for the tourism industry. At these shows, industry suppliers set up booths to showcase their products and services, and travel agents visit the booths to gather information and make contacts.

Exhibitions

Unlike a trade show, an **exhibition** is always staged as part of a convention. The number of exhibitions held every year has increased with the growth of the meetings business as a whole. Exhibitions are used often in the association market, especially by trade, technical, scientific, and professional associations, and help attract participants to the meeting event.

Exhibits are important for associations both as a way to attract attendance and as a revenue producer. By allowing exhibitors to promote their wares at the convention, associations are able to sell exhibit space and make money to offset the expenses of staging the meeting.

Vendor displays and booths vary from simple to elaborate, although they are rarely as elaborate as at trade shows. A vendor sometimes sponsors a hospitality suite, offering free food and beverages to delegates. Exhibitors may also agree to sponsor coffee breaks and meals during the convention in exchange for recognition and, possibly, the right to display their products in the refreshment area.

Attendance at the exhibition necessarily depends on the number of people attending the convention. Exhibitions are not open to the general public. The duration of the exhibition is tied to the length of the meeting, though many are at least three days long; exhibitors dictate the minimum number of hours.

The International Exhibitors Association is the major organization in the exhibitions field.

Check Your Product Knowledge

1. What types of organizations commonly hold exhibitions?
2. What skills do event managers need?

ATTRACTION PRODUCTS

To the tourism industry, recreation is a product—something that must be created, packaged, and sold in the same way as other products. Attractions are at the core of the products that are sold. They serve as the catalyst for creating demand for accommodation and other hospitality services.

The Package Tour

To make travel more appealing and convenient, as well as less expensive, the tourism industry groups its products into packages. Package tours are discussed in detail in Chapter 15.

Some travel packages are built around specific recreational attractions. To enhance the attraction, the package generally includes transportation and accommodations. Extra features, such as meals and free baggage handling, can be included to make the package more enticing. Recreational package tours can be put together by hotels, airlines, travel agencies, wholesale operators, or the attraction itself. Packages vary greatly, depending on the options selected, the length of stay, the quality of accommodations, and the number of people participating. The following are selected examples of recreational packages:

- **Gambling junkets** "By invitation" all-expenses-paid trip (bus fare or airfare, accommodations, a supply of poker chips, tickets to nightclub shows, and a discount coupon book).
- **Theme park vacations** e.g., Walt Disney World packages (hotel transfers, accommodations, admission to Disney World, additional sightseeing, or a cruise).
- **Adventure tours** e.g., rafting tours with necessary gear, an experienced guide, transportation to and from the river, accommodations and meals.
- **Ecotourism tours** Learning vacations that blend cultural and nature-based recreational activities with ecofriendly transportation and facilities (e.g., Kw'o:kw'e:hala eco vacation retreat in the mountains in B.C.).

CHANNELS OF DISTRIBUTION

Many museums, zoos, aquariums, and other attractions have established marketing and public relations departments that advertise group discounts, annual memberships, and cooperative tie-ins. Admission and entrance fees are often included in tour packages. More public sector sites are now considering using mass distribution systems like Ticketron to sell their products.

The growth in travel and tourism has led to problems of overcrowding and congestion. To keep the crowds within bounds, public facilities must use automated reservations systems. The days of first come, first served may soon be a thing of the past at many attractions, especially our parks.

Check Your Product Knowledge

1. What does a tour package based on a recreational attraction generally include?
2. Why is the first-come, first-served system in our national parks likely to change?

CAREER OPPORTUNITIES

In 1998, the Canadian Tourism Human Resource Council (CTHRC) estimated that 120 000 people were employed in the attractions sector. The same year, more than 80 occupations were listed in the adventure/recreation sector. (The CTHRC does not maintain separate statistics for this sector any longer.)

Public and commercial recreation systems related to attractions employ more part-time and temporary workers than most components of the tourism industry. These workers are needed to handle crowds during peak seasons or one-time events. The public sector also relies on volunteer workers to help with fundraising or routine clerical work, or to serve as guides.

Attractions

In the attractions sector there are career opportunities at every level, from the front lines to the executive suite.

Parks and Ecotourism

There are occupational standards for the job of heritage interpreter, and interpreters who are qualified through training and experience can be certified nationally through CTHRC. For further career information, see the Career Opportunities section at the end of Chapter 13.

Special-Events Managers

People who work in special events need above-average organizational skills, and knowledge of and experience in marketing, finance, planning, project management, public and human relations, and exhibit services. People may work year-round for a special event (e.g., the Calgary Stampede), or they may be involved part-time (e.g., to coordinate a gala event for a convention). Often people begin as volunteers for a nonprofit organization, advance to assistant manager, and go on to planning and management positions.

More opportunities are now available for education and training in special events management. George Brown College in Toronto began offering a two-year management diploma in Special Events for Destination Tourism in 2002.

A DAY IN THE LIFE OF A

Trade Show Organizer

How does a person get into the business of putting on travel trade shows? I did it almost by accident. I was working in the advertising department of a large Toronto newspaper when a group of travel advertisers asked my paper to sponsor a travel trade show. After running a small annual trade show for the paper for a few years, I branched out on my own and started International Trade Shows, Inc. (ITS). Today, ITS stages nearly 70 mini-travel trade shows in Canada and the United States each year. The company is still a family-owned business, run by my son and me in Mississauga.

Our mini-shows are very different from a typical travel trade show. A typical show takes place in a large exhibition hall and lasts one or more days. It involves 100 or more exhibitors and attracts thousands of people. Shows like these usually feature elaborate displays, tons of literature, and plenty of wining, dining, and entertainment.

My son calls these kinds of trade shows "pipe and drape" shows, after the materials used to construct the exhibition booths. Our mini-shows are much less elaborate. Each is just three hours long—not three days—and takes place in a hotel ballroom. Each show is limited to a maximum of 30 exhibitors and 100 local travel counsellors. We believe the mini-shows are actually more efficient than the large trade shows because they cut out the "browsers" who attend the large shows without intending to buy anything.

The exhibitors who participate in our mini-shows include hundreds of hotel chains, resorts, airlines, tour operators, car rental firms, and cruise lines, as well as several government tourist bureaux. The British Tourist Authority, Club Med, Peter Pan Tours, Atlantic Tours, and Budget Rent-A-Car are among our clients.

The format of our shows for the tourism industry is simple. During the first hour, the travel counsellors visit tables placed around the edge of the ballroom and staffed by the exhibitors. The second hour is reserved for a sit-down dinner for the suppliers and counsellors. Many of the suppliers then spend the third hour speaking informally and handing out door prizes such as free trips, airline tickets, travel bags, and champagne.

We recruit our exhibitors by sending out mailers several times a year announcing the schedules for upcoming mini-shows. Once the suppliers sign up for a specific mini-show or week of shows, they provide ITS with lists of travel counsellors to invite to the shows. From each agency invited, only two people are permitted to attend. Usually they are the owners or managers of the agency.

The mini-shows serve several purposes. They enable the suppliers to reach 100 travel counsellors in just three hours. It would take each supplier several weeks to visit the same agents by travelling from office to office. Also, by limiting the numbers of participants, the suppliers and counsellors have the time and opportunity to really get to know one another.

I believe that the ITS shows are so successful because they tap a market that the large shows don't reach and that the suppliers can't cover as efficiently any other way.

Summary

- Attractions and the promise of entertainment are magnets that draw people to destinations and provide reasons for leisure and recreational activities; they are tourism generators.
- The public sector includes government-funded and -operated facilities—mainly national and provincial parks, zoos and aquariums, museums, and fairs and festivals. These are not intended to make a profit, but rather to preserve the country's natural and historic heritage.
- The commercial sector includes recreational facilities operated by private businesses. Theme parks, stadiums, resorts, shopping malls, theatres, and casinos are generally part of the commercial sector. The purpose of these facilities is to make money for their owners.
- Museums serve as repositories for valued objects, centres of learning and culture, and places of recreation and entertainment. Museums reflect the culture, history, and resources of the nations in which they are found.
- Zoos and aquariums are museums that display live animals and marine life and provide education and entertainment for visitors.
- The theme park—for example, Disney World—is an outstanding example of a commercial venture in recreation.
- Model cultures and restorations demonstrate how people of other times lived.
- Spectator sports are an example of passive recreation. They attract spectators and earn millions in profits for the commercial sector.
- Megamalls, waterfront shopping complexes, and factory outlet centres have turned shopping into an important tourist activity.

Key Terms

amusement park   p. 282
aquarium   p. 280
carnival   p. 282
constructed attraction   p. 278
event management   p. 288
exhibition   p. 289
festival   p. 275
megamall   p. 282
model culture   p. 278
natural attraction   p. 278
oceanarium   p. 280
spectator sports   p. 280
theme park   p. 281
zoo   p. 280

Internet Connections

Alberta Agriculture and Food
www.agric.gov.ab.ca   p. 276

Anne of Green Gables House
www.gov.pe.ca/greengables   p. 279

BC Place Stadium (Vancouver)
www.bcplacestadium.com   p. 280

Canada's Wonderland
www.canadaswonderland.com   p. 281

CN Tower
www.cntower.ca   p. 275

Disney Corporation
www.disney.ca/vacations

Disneyland
www.disney.ca/vacations/disneyland   p. 281

Disney World
www.disney.ca/vacations/Disneyworld   p. 281

Dubailand
www.dubailand.ae/company_history.html   p. 285

George Brown College
www.georgebrown.ca   p. 290

Kings Landing Historical Settlement (New Brunswick)
www.kingslanding.nb.ca   p. 279

Kw'o:kw'e:hala eco retreat, B.C.
http://eco-retreat.com/index.htm   p. 289

La Ronde (Montreal)
www.laronde.com   p. 282

Metro Toronto Convention Centre
www.mtccc.com   p. 289

Miraval Resort (Tucson, Arizona)
www.miravalresort.com   p. 286

Niagara Falls
www.city.niagarafalls.on.ca   p. 275

Park World
www.parkworld-online.com

Rendez-vous Canada
www.rvc.org   p. 286

Sainte-Marie among the Hurons
www.saintemarieamongthehurons.on.ca   p. 279

Rogers Centre
www.rogerscentre.com   p. 280

Stratford Festival
www.stratfordfestival.ca   p. 283

UNESCO World Heritage Sites
www.travel-images.com/unesco-canada.html   p. 279

Upper Canada Village
www.uppercanadavillage.com   p. 279

West Edmonton Mall
www.westedmontonmall.com   p. 282

WORKSHEET 12–1 Recreation and Leisure Attractions

Governments and private companies throughout the world provide opportunities for leisure and recreation. The chart below lists just a few examples. Using the Internet, travel guides, or other references, locate and describe each attraction.

Legoland Park

Location: _____

Description: _____

_____

_____

_____

_____

Serengeti Plain

Location: _____

Description: _____

_____

_____

_____

_____

_____

State Hermitage Museum, St. Petersburg

Location: _____

Description: _____

_____

_____

_____

_____

Upper Canada Village

Location: _____

Description: _____

_____

_____

_____

_____

_____

The Ginza

Location: _____

Description: _____

_____

_____

_____

_____

_____

Great Barrier Reef National Park

Location: _____

Description: _____

_____

_____

_____

_____

Trail of '98 (excursion follows the legendary Gold Rush trail)

Location: _____

Description: _____

_____

_____

_____

_____

WORKSHEET 12–2   Recreation and Leisure Attractions

Check out the Festival Seeker website (www.festivalseeker.com) and locate examples of 10 events, half from the winter season and the other half during July and August. Compare the events by considering when each occurs, its notable features, who you think would be attracted to the event, and the purpose you think the events serve.

Name of Event	Location	Month	Notable Features	Who	Purpose
1.					
2.					
3.					
4.					
5.					
6.					
7.					
8.					
9.					
10.					

Which is the best event? Why? _____

Objectives

When you have completed this chapter, you should be able to:

- Discuss the role played in adventure and outdoor recreation activities by national, provincial, and municipal parks.

- Discuss why ecoadventure products should be offered by the Canadian tourism industry.

- Describe the main areas of outdoor recreation, and the role each plays in making Canada a four-season destination.

- Identify and describe the kinds of facilities provided by the commercial sector for adventure and outdoor recreation activities.

- Give examples of how the adventure tourism and outdoor recreation sector packages and sells its products and services.

With its abundant natural resources, Canada offers many world-class opportunities for adventure tourism, outdoor recreation, and ecotourism, so these are important components of pleasure travel. As well, the baby-boom generation is demanding different experiences, and this is making the adventure tourism, outdoor recreation, and ecotourism market one of the fastest-growing sectors of the tourism industry.

In 1997, the adventure and outdoor recreation sector employed more than 71 000 Canadians—5.1 percent of tourism-related jobs in Canada (Canadian Tourism Human Resource Council, 1998). More than 80 occupations have been identified in this sector. Within seasonal limits, these activities provide people with opportunities to "work at play" in one of the most exciting areas of the tourism industry. (Separate statistics on this sector are no longer kept by CTHRC.)

PARKS

Canada's National Parks

Canada began establishing its system of national parks in 1885, when it set aside for public use roughly 2600 hectares on the north slope of Sulphur Mountain, Alberta. This area of hot springs was the beginning of what is now Banff

National Park. By 1895, five other land reserves had been set aside, all in British Columbia. These would became the following parks: Yoho, Kootenay, Glacier, Mount Revelstoke, and Waterton Lakes.

Early in the twentieth century, Canada began to develop national parks in the east. The first of these, in 1904, was St. Lawrence Islands National Park.

Today, Canada's national parks are administered by Parks Canada, which has the following mandate: "On behalf of the people of Canada, we protect and present nationally significant examples of Canada's natural and cultural heritage and foster public understanding, appreciation and enjoyment in ways that ensure their ecological and commemorative integrity for present and future generations" (Parks Canada, "About Us," n.d.).

Parks Canada ensures the integrity of 156 national historic sites, seven operating historic canals, 650 historic sites (public and private), and various heritage railway stations and federal heritage buildings. Parks Canada also directs and implements heritage tourism programs and provides visitors' services for the millions of visitors who use our national parks each year. It also coordinates the federal/provincial program for Canada's heritage river system. According to Parks Canada, "Parks Canada operates with an annual budget of approximately $600 million and 5400 employees (1600 seasonal) located in more than 460 communities across Canada."

PROFILE

Two Outdoor Recreation Services— Trans Canada Trail and Churchill Wild

"Canada has the natural and human resources to support a thriving and competitive ecotourism and adventure travel industry" (White et al., 1999).

Trans Canada Trail

The Trans Canada Trail concept was conceived by the Canada 125 Corporation in 1992 to celebrate the 125th year of Confederation. When it is complete, it will be a shared-use recreation trail—usually a three-metre wide accessible path—winding through every province and territory. It will accommodate five core activities: walking, cycling, horseback riding, cross-country skiing, and snowmobiling (where possible and desired).

The trail is being built on existing trails wherever possible, assuming they can be adapted to the shared-use principle. It will run through provincial and federal parks and Crown lands; along railway lines, both abandoned and in use; and across private lands. It will be the longest trail of its kind in the world, 18 000 kilometres, plus 3000 kilometres of water routes. About 12 000 kilometres is already usable, and should be "substantially complete" by fall 2010 (Trans Canada Trail, n.d.).

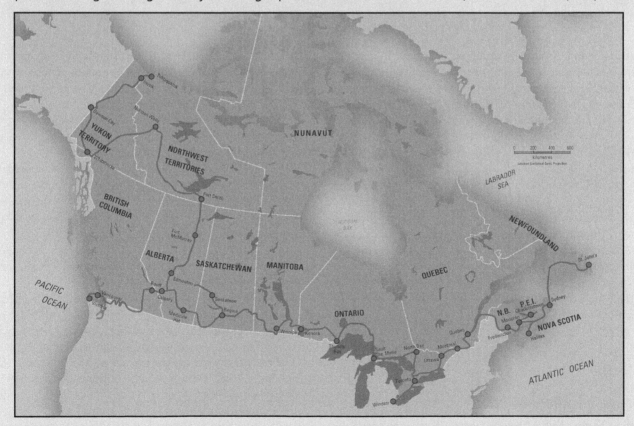

ILLUSTRATION 13–1

The Trans Canada Trail is the longest trail in the world (18 000 km) and when finished will pass through all ten provinces and three territories.

SOURCE: © Nelson.

The trail's development—planning, designing, and building—is being coordinated by the Trans Canada Trail Foundation. Trail-marker pavilions and interprovincial gateways are being constructed along the way. The name of anyone who donates $50 for development of a metre of the trail will be permanently noted in a pavilion (or the name of another person, chosen by the donor). The founding sponsors included Canada Trust, Canada Post, Chrysler Canada, and TSN (The Sports Network).

The trail will be a legacy for future generations; it will help strengthen communities, provinces, and Canada as a nation. On a more practical level, the trail will help preserve and protect the natural and built environments (railway stations are being restored, for example). It will also stimulate local economies (e.g., by providing ecotourism opportunities), provide safe and secure recreation facilities, and foster natural and historical education programs.

One of the newest initiatives is the Trans Canada Trail Discovery Program, which is supported by the Stephen R. Bronfman Foundation: The Discovery Program "will see the development and permanent installation of over 2000 interpretive panels along the route of the Trail. Each panel will feature a specific topic on flora, fauna or geography that is indigenous to a particular trail segment" (Trans Canada Trail, n.d.).

Churchill Wild

"Far away in the distant reaches of civilization, discover a new frontier in a land virtually untouched by man's restless hand . . ." So reads the Churchill Wild brochure, which advertises "ecolodge adventures on the untamed Hudson Bay coast." There are currently five exciting adventures with Churchill Wild.

"The Great Ice Bear" adventure allows guests to observe and photograph the great white polar bears from the comfort of the Polar Bear Lodge, or the guests may trek with one of the company's guides on the footpaths along the coastline in search of the ice bears.

The "Birds, Bears & Belugas" expedition involves an encounter with numerous beluga whales, where the guests have an opportunity to pet the whales from a boat, and the more daring may slip on a dry suit and swim alongside the gentle whales in the Seal River estuary.

The "Fire & Ice" excursion is beautifully described in the brochure: "Experience a winter fantasyland of sculptured snow and ice brought to life under the brilliance of the arctic sun and the dancing aurora borealis." There are also two new adventures: "Lights in the Wild" and "Wildlife of the Arctic."

Additional activities available at the three Churchill Wild resorts include dog sledding, building an igloo, cooking bannock, snowmobiling, building a tepee, learning local culture, hiking, exploring the nearby ancient Dene and Inuit hunting sites, and more. Many animals that can be observed there include wolves, moose, arctic foxes, seals, snowy owls, caribou, black bears, wolverines, and a variety of birds and wildflowers.

An authentic northern adventure viewing spectacular wildlife in a pristine wilderness with luxurious ecolodge accommodations and fabulous food in a family atmosphere will ensure an unforgettable experience at Churchill Wild.

SOURCES: Trans Canada Trail website (www.tctrail.ca), and Churchill Wild brochure and website (www.churchillwild.com); accessed July 2004.

Canadian Natural Regions

The federal government has designated 68 natural regions—39 terrestrial and 29 marine—and plans to establish a park in each region. At present, around half of Canada's regions have national parks. Parks Canada operates 42 national parks (see Table 13–1) and 158 historic sites across Canada. In cooperation with other organizations, it is responsible for more than 1100 provincial parks and many municipal parks. It conserves the characteristic features of areas, develops and maintains designated areas, preserves historic sites, and provides opportunities for visitors to enjoy adventure and/or recreation and to participate in learning vacations. In addition, "The Canadian federal government plans an aggressive expansion of the national parks system in Canada, adding 10 new national parks in the next five years, and creating five new marine conservation areas" (Munroe, 2002).

Sustainable Tourism

In May 2001, the Tourism Industry Association of Canada and Parks Canada announced they were joining forces to foster **sustainable tourism**. Working cooperatively, their mandate is to identify opportunities for sustainable tourism

TABLE 13–1 Canada's National Parks—A Sampling

Name	Setting	Classification	Activities
Gros Morne	Newfoundland, the shores of the Atlantic: flat-topped mountains and boggy plains, fjords and lakes, beaches	World Heritage Site	Hiking, backpacking, nature programs, camping, canoeing, swimming, boat tours, fishing, cross-country skiing, winter camping
Banff, Jasper, Yoho, Kootenay	The Rockies (Alberta and British Columbia)	World Heritage Site	Skiing, hiking, climbing, kayaking, rafting, riding, fishing, visiting glaciers
Wood Buffalo	Northern Alberta and the Northwest Territories: bogs, forests, streams, rivers, muskeg	Largest national park in Canada	Nature programs (buffalo sanctuary, whooping crane sanctuary), skiing, snowshoeing, canoeing
Northern Yukon	The Canadian Arctic: mountains, rivers, forests, tundra, Arctic seacoast	Wildlife habitat	Hiking and rafting, nature programs (caribou, snow geese, grizzly and polar bears, wolves, foxes, lynx)

practices and maintain and enhance the integrity of the country's national parks and historic sites.

International Role

Over the years, as a member of the World Tourism Organization, UNESCO, and the Council of Europe, Canada has worked with developing nations to establish natural and cultural habitats based on sound practices. Canada's national park system is part of a global network of more than 3500 protected areas in 130 countries. Canada is a member of the International Union for Conservation of Nature and Natural Resources.

Parks Canada is the primary agency responsible for fulfilling Canada's obligations to the United Nations Education, Scientific and Cultural Organization (UNESCO). That group holds all nations responsible for protecting places of unique natural and cultural value that are considered part of the heritage of all mankind. For example, UNESCO declared Head-Smashed-In Buffalo Jump near Fort MacLeod, Alberta, a World Heritage Site in 1981. That highly important site shows the techniques that native people used for 6000 years to stampede buffalo as a means of hunting them. It is now being preserved as a cultural component of our heritage.

Parks in the United States

The national parks system in the United States was founded in 1872, when Congress voted to preserve Yellowstone as a means of ensuring the region's spectacular natural beauty for future generations. The purpose of national parks was soon broadened to include not only the conservation of natural wonders but also the preservation of historic and cultural sites.

According to the U.S. National Park Service website, there were 272 million recreational visitors in 2006 to the 380 national parks and 544 wildlife reserves. These are

classified according to type: parks, mountains, preserves, seashores, rivers and waterways, historic parks, memorials, parkways, and recreational areas.

National Parks around the World

Parks Canada and the U.S. National Park Service have helped many other countries establish national park systems. By area, the largest systems are in the United States, Canada, and Africa. Parks vary widely in the accommodations they offer tourists, and many are open only during certain seasons of the year. In Asia, for example, parks often close during the summer monsoons.

The national parks of Africa serve mainly as game reserves. Two of the best-known wildlife sanctuaries on that continent are Kruger National Park in South Africa and Nairobi National Park in Kenya.

Provincial and Municipal Parks and Gardens

Every province has its own network of parks offering many of the same facilities as national parks. And almost every city and town has one or more public parks. Municipal swimming pools, tennis courts, and golf courses are common in urban and suburban areas.

Provincial Parks Canada has more than 1100 provincial parks. They have been created for the same reasons as national parks—to conserve wilderness areas, preserve historic sites, and provide recreation and enjoyment. Some offer uncrowded beaches (Prince Edward Island), others wooded hills (Saskatchewan), still others pristine rivers (Ontario). These parks typically offer picnic areas and trails.

Most provinces have a parks department and a forestry board, as well as a fish and game commission to regulate hunting and fishing on provincially owned lands. There may also be a historical society that oversees the province's historic sites. Some popular parks suffer from overcrowding and many now try to control the number of visitors or campers.

Municipal Parks Municipal parks offer welcome relief to city dwellers hemmed in by concrete and steel. Urban parks provide green space, typically along with picnic areas and paths for walking, jogging, and bicycling. Many parks have tennis courts, basketball courts, and other sports facilities.

Some city parks have become tourist attractions in their own right. Stanley Park in Vancouver is probably Canada's most famous urban park. Mount Royal Park dominates the Montreal cityscape. Halifax has Point Pleasant Park and the Public Gardens, a Victorian botanical-style showcase complete with swans and a bandstand.

Gardens According to Pengelly (2001), **garden tourism**, or horticultural tourism, is blossoming across Canada. Garden tours are being created to showcase horticultural gems across Canada. Quebec is promoting its gardens throughout Europe. B.C. Tourism's provincial spring blossom tour attracts Asian markets.

The B.C. Landscape & Nursery Association sees garden tourism as an outdoor recreation alternative for people who are not active in recreation sports. "Garden-and-" tours are being established that combine an interest in horticulture with interests in wine, theatre, and so on. Tours combine floral sights with visits to public and private gardens.

Parks Management and Operations

Parks, public or private, don't just happen. Once established, they have to be well managed to protect and maintain them and to provide services for users.

Park Facilities National park facilities in North America vary widely. Some large or remote parks offer hotels, cabins, and campgrounds, as well as service stations, general stores, gift shops, and restaurants. Parks in or near cities or major highways may offer just a visitors' centre and gift shop, since food and accommodations are readily available nearby.

Visitors usually have to pay a small entry fee or camping fee at each park. Seasonal passes are available for Canada's national parks, and holders may use them for admission to any national park in the country.

Campsites at the largest and most popular parks have to be reserved. Some parks belong to computer reservation systems that enable visitors to reserve accommodations or campsites by phone, by mail, or through ticket services. According to the Parks Canada "Camping Reservation Service" website, 18 of the 43 national parks had an online reservation service.

ILLUSTRATION 13–2

L'anse aux Meadows National Historic Site of Canada (in the northwestern corner of Newfoundland) is the site of the earliest known European settlement in North America and was declared a UNESCO World Heritage Site in 1978. The reconstruction consists of three Norse buildings.

SOURCE: © Parks Canada/J. Steeves/H.01.11.01.26(14).

Depending on their location and climate, national parks offer a wide variety of recreational possibilities, including hiking, swimming, boating, fishing, horseback riding, skiing, bicycling, and scuba diving.

National and provincial parks have paved roads, scenic overlooks, and sometimes shuttle bus service to take visitors from one site to another. One of the functions of the park service is **interpretation**—educating, informing, and even entertaining visitors by offering marked trails, signs, demonstrations, lectures, pictures, and so on.

Accessibility Parks Canada has set a standard for its facilities for people with disabilities and sensitized its staff about their needs. Unfortunately, in many regions, transportation, accommodation, and other hospitality services are not as accessible as they should be, and people with disabilities may be less able to get around and participate in what parks have to offer. One exception is the wilderness resort Mersey River Chalets (near Kejimkujik National Park in Nova Scotia), which is fully wheelchair-accessible and is the winner of a Tourism Award of Excellence for Accommodation 2002. Some parks have tactile exhibits, audiotapes, and Braille and large-type signs for visitors with vision impairment, as well as captioned films and slides, sign-language interpreters, and written materials for people who are hearing impaired.

Today's Park Issues Since the 1970s, park managers, naturalists, environmentalists, and legislators have been addressing the problems of pollution, vandalism, and environmental stress that have been created through increasingly heavy use. Should the parks be preserved mainly as wilderness sanctuaries? Or in response to demands for new recreational uses, should they be allowed to become public playgrounds? In an attempt to balance the two objectives, the park services are experimenting with programs that restrict the number of visitors to parks, encourage off-peak seasonal use, and promote the use of some of the less-known parks.

There are other problems: How can visitors be protected from bears? How can fish stocks be maintained? How can forest fires be prevented? How can accidents from high-risk activities such as mountaineering be reduced? And how should snowmobiles, hang gliders, and mountain bikes be dealt with?

In the national park on the north shore of Prince Edward Island, for example, the dunes have been designated a sanctuary for the piping plover, and boardwalks have been constructed to protect the dunes and their vegetation from walkers, snowmobiles, and all-terrain vehicles.

> ## Check Your Product Knowledge
>
> 1. Why did governments begin creating national parks?
> 2. What are major issues confronting parks today? How are they being addressed?

ADVENTURE TOURISM

Adventure tourism is typified by high-energy, high-risk, high-reward activities. Adventures are sought throughout the year, which extends the demand for tourism accommodation services. The perception of adventure tourism is that it takes place in unusual, exotic, wilderness settings. Unconventional transportation is often involved. Adventure, however, can be "soft" or "hard" depending on the level of physical exertion involved.

Soft adventure, such as cycling on the Trans-Canada Highway between communities in Prince Edward Island,

ILLUSTRATION 13–3
Prince Edward Island National Park is famous for its beaches.
SOURCE: Image courtesy of Canadian Tourism Commission.

is low-risk and mildly strenuous and requires minimum preparation. In contrast, **hard adventure**, such as mountain biking through the Rockies, involves greater risk, considerable physical conditioning, and extensive planning.

Whether soft or hard, adventure tourism provides an opportunity for a number of entrepreneurial activities. Adventure tourism is an ideal sector for individuals or family businesses, like Big Bear Adventures in the Yukon, that want to develop products and packages promoting the natural features of their area.

Special Needs Many operators have developed **niche markets** for seniors, people with disabilities, families with young children, and so on. People with special needs seeking soft adventure are another niche market. At the Mersey River Chalets wilderness resort in Nova Scotia, people with physical disabilities can go canoeing, follow boardwalks to view nature, and stay in a teepee.

Winter Tourism Products

Operators in many regions of Canada have made it their goal to develop Canada as a four-season destination. To that end they are developing winter products that appeal to adventure tourists. For example, hospitality facilities in northern New Brunswick, northern Ontario, and Newfoundland and Labrador are now catering to snow-mobilers. Canadian Mountain Holidays, a British Columbia company, sells packages for heli-skiing and heli-hiking in the Bugaboos. Dogsled safaris in the Yukon appeal to the German market. In the Yukon, tours to view the *aurora borealis* (Northern Lights) have been popular with Japanese tourists since the 1980s. People who visit an area for wildlife viewing travel according to nature's schedules and often create demand for food and lodging throughout the year.

It is possible that one day Atlantic Canada will be as popular as the Rockies with winter vacationers. Abandoned rail lines can be developed for cross-country skiing or snowmobiling. Country inns and B&Bs can offer escape weekends featuring beach hiking and skating on frozen marsh ponds. Prince Edward Island uses the slogan "Summer is only part of our story" to market its winter tourism products. In Nova Scotia, accommodation is available in winterized cottages, complete with fireplaces and not far from the sound of the pounding surf.

Check Your Product Knowledge

1. What are some pros and cons of developing outdoor adventure businesses?
2. What winter outdoor adventure activities are or could be available in your area?

OUTDOOR RECREATION

Outdoor recreation is an important motivator for tourism. It involves four main activities: skiing (alpine/downhill and cross-country), and more recently, snowboarding, golf, tennis, and marine activities. The latter can include everything from swimming in a resort's pool to sailing a tall ship around the world. Other outdoor recreational activities include cycling (of various kinds), wildlife viewing, hiking, mountain climbing, and horseback riding. These activities may not be the main reason for pleasure travel, but they are often the reason a specific destination is chosen.

Skiing

Downhill Skiing The British developed skiing as a sport in the 1880s. Between the 1960s and 1980s, the number of skiers in the world expanded by 10 to 15 percent annually (Beyrouti, 2001). By 1998–99, there were more than

ILLUSTRATION 13–4
Winnipeg's The Forks National Historic Site is a meeting place for the theatre, restaurants, and promenading.
SOURCE: Image courtesy of Canadian Tourism Commission.

3 million downhill skiers just in Canada, as well as 867 000 snowboarders. Snowboarding has been blamed for downhill skiing's decline in popularity since the mid-1990s, but cross-country (which doesn't require mountains) and heli-skiing have been growing in popularity.

According to the Canadian Ski Council's "2006–2007 Canadian Skier and Snowboarder Facts and Stats," 4.4 million Canadians (12 years and older) participated in one or more forms of skiing, snowboarding, or a combination of those sports. (Refer to Table 13–2.) The 2005/2006 ski season recorded 17.98 million ski area visits (down 6.3 percent from 19.18 million visits in 2005). This decrease in visits was attributed to unfavourable weather conditions in Eastern Canada and a shorter winter season in British Columbia. "Skier visits are dependent on weather and snow conditions, economic conditions, and tourism industry conditions" (Canadian Ski Council, 2007).

The U.S. National Ski Areas Association estimates that U.S. ski areas nationwide tallied 60.1 million visits for the 2007/08 season, making it the best season on record. The new record represents a 9.1 percent increase from the 55.1 million visits recorded in 2006/07, and a 2.0 percent rise from the prior record of 58.9 million visits set in 2005/06 (National Ski Areas Association, 2008).

Canadian ski areas also attract Europeans and Japanese. In 2003, the ski areas at Whistler Blackcomb resorts were ranked first among North American ski resorts by the readers of *Ski Magazine* for the fifth consecutive year, and have ranked in the top five ski resorts since that time. But will aging baby boomers keep skiing? Will domestic demand keep declining? What will it take to attract international skiers to Canada's slopes?

Today's skiers are accommodated in small ski resort villages as well as huge resort complexes. Good skiing attracts skiers and generates the demand for good hotels, restaurants, entertainment, services, and products. The ski business contributes more than $5 billion to the Canadian economy. Equipment retail sales alone exceed $2 billion annually.

Snowboarding In recent seasons, with the increase in snowboarding, resorts with "champagne powder" such as Steamboat Resort, Colorado, have been attracting snowboarders to designated areas with snowboard-only surface lifts. In Canada, 67 percent (in 2005) of snowboarders are between 12 and 24 (down from 77 percent in 2004), and a boarder averages eight days per season on the slopes. Older snowboarders, those between 35 and 49, comprise only 14 percent of the market (up from 7 percent in 2003) (Canadian Ski Council, 2007).

Heli-Skiing Heli-skiing has taken off in British Columbia, Alberta, and the Yukon. In British Columbia's Cariboos and Monashees, 10 people at a time pay as much as $12 800 per group to travel by helicopter high up onto a mountain to ski down virgin snow.

Tennis and Golf

Tennis and golf also attract tourists. Some ski resorts have expanded demand for their hospitality by adding tennis or golf facilities, or both.

Golf The number of golfers in Canada is growing by more than 10 percent a year. There are more than 2.2 million golfers in Canada, who spend more than $1 billion each year on equipment, green fees, and accessories. Golf courses are found almost everywhere in the world, and people can play the sport into their old age.

Golf Canada indicates there are more than 1800 golf courses in Canada, many of them at vacation resorts. In fact, there are golfing resorts in almost every country.

TABLE 13–2 Alpine Ski, Snowboard, and Cross-Country Ski Stats for 2004 to 2006				
(in thousands)	2004	2005	2006	Increase from '05
Exclusively Downhill	1377	1461	1643	12%
Exclusively Snowboarding	804	912	979	7%
Exclusively Cross Country	843	813	873	7%
Downhill & Snowboarding	232	224	254	
Downhill & Cross Country	338	351	423	
Snowboarding & X-Country	32	110	67	
All 3	172	181	126	
Total Downhill	2119	2036	2446	
Total Snowboarding	1240	1246	1426	
Total Cross Country	1385	1345	1489	

SOURCE: Reprinted with permission from the Canadian Ski Council.

ILLUSTRATION 13–5

The Butchart Gardens on Vancouver Island have a long history of providing education, entertainment, and wonderment for tourists.

SOURCE: Photograph © The Butchart Gardens Ltd., Courtesy of The Butchart Gardens, Victoria BC Canada.

(A 2002 estimate by Golf Research Group was over 30 000 courses worldwide in 119 countries, serving over 57 million golfers in a $60 billion industry.) These resorts offer golfers and their companions accommodations and services ranging from golf lessons to other fitness opportunities such as tennis, aerobics, and swimming. Almost every course has a pro shop that provides job opportunities for people who know the game well.

Tennis Tennis is a popular sport among vacationers. Tennis Canada claims more and more tennis camps are opening across Canada. These provide lessons and practice facilities for visitors. Whether it is affiliated with a tennis club or a resort, a tennis camp program is usually combined with hospitality services and other fitness opportunities.

Marine Activities

Water-Based Vacations Canada's coastlines, lakes, and rivers offer many forms of recreation. More businesses are catering to foreign and domestic vacationers who want a **water-based vacation**, be it swimming, sailing, waterskiing, kayaking, scuba diving—the list goes on.

Marinas Marinas rent and moor boats and, in cooperation with local businesses, provide hospitality services, entertainment, and supplies. Tourists in New Brunswick can scuba dive, watch whales, sail, and go kayaking and canoeing. The world's highest tides are in the Bay of

Fundy. A new national marine park is planned for the West Isles of the same bay. Grand Manan Island is a paddler's gem, with its Precambrian rocks, seabirds, and other sea life. Several whale-watching tours depart from St. Andrews, Grand Manan, Deer Island, and Campobello Island during the summer and early autumn. (The same pods of whales can be approached from Brier Island, Nova Scotia, across the bay.) Some tours have onboard naturalists or pre-boarding or on-board lectures.

Tour Operators The water-based tour operators in the Fundy region have established a code of ethics. Among other things, it calls on them to foster an environment of cooperation and trust, to protect the whales and other marine wildlife, and to look after their passengers' safety.

The Ottawa River is one of the top 10 whitewater rivers in North America, and boasts big rapids that are warm all summer. When Wilderness Tours opened on the Ottawa River in 1975 with a few whitewater rafts, it launched an industry. Today, outfitters on the river offer excursions to more than 60 000 participants annually (over 1 million participants since 1975). Whitewater enthusiasts can choose rafting or kayaking. Individuals and families find that "roughing it" describes only the whitewater. Many of the outfitters market cooperatively and provide an abundance of recreational experiences. They have developed destination resorts that offer biking, boat cruises, swimming pools, hot tubs, tennis, volleyball, and sometimes bungee jumping in addition to rafting.

ILLUSTRATION 13–6

The Canadian Tourism Commission has documented exemplary practices among ecotourism and adventure tourism operators.

SOURCE: Canadian Tourism Commission.

Check Your Product Knowledge

1. How does skiing contribute to the Canadian economy?
2. Why do ski resorts add tennis facilities to their operations?

FACILITATING OUTDOOR RECREATION

Outdoor recreation can take place at an exotic destination or in your own backyard. While millions of Canadians are sitting at spectator events, millions of other Canadians are actively participating in indoor or outdoor sports. This reflects the public's growing awareness of the importance of physical fitness.

Canadians' interest in traditional recreational sports such as bicycling, swimming, and hiking is as high as it ever was. At the same time, newer sports such as in-line skating, racquetball, and whitewater rafting are growing in popularity. For the even more adventurous, hang-gliding, parasailing, and bungee jumping are popular.

Outdoor recreational sports provide a good illustration of how the public and commercial sectors can overlap. Almost every city park provides tennis courts. Private businesses also operate tennis courts. The difference is that private tennis clubs—for a fee—offer more amenities, such as a clubhouse, reserved court times, saunas, locker rooms, and refreshments.

The sports people play are often a function of where they live. For instance, skiing and scuba diving can be done only in certain parts of the country. On the other hand, there are tennis courts and golf courses nearly everywhere. Many people travel so that they can experience new or different facilities. Clearly, then, facilities play an important role in tourism. This is why the public and private sectors are making major capital investments to develop them.

More children are taking up sports, and are doing so younger than they used to. This probably reflects the fact that parents are more health-conscious, more families have two incomes, and most people have more leisure time. Today's urban lifestyles are not as physically strenuous as the rural ones of our grandparents, which makes sports today even more important to health. Most children who take up a sport keep playing it well into adulthood. In making travel decisions, parents consider the availability of recreational facilities for the entire family.

Sports Facilities and Services Sporting goods stores provide all sorts of equipment—athletic shoes, cross-country skis, hunting rifles, racquets, and so on. Some businesses, called "outfitters," provide services, such as whitewater guides; others stage events for recreational enthusiasts. Each year the Boston Marathon generates enormous revenue for that city from tourist services.

Some facilities require more financial investment than others and are riskier to operate. Ski resorts are a good example. If the weather is too warm and there isn't enough snow, ski resorts can't open; if it is too cold, skiers stay at home. Operating costs are high, and in summer the expensive ski lifts stand idle. To generate off-season income, many ski resorts are developing year-round programs. For example, they are offering scenic chair-lift rides and convention facilities in the summer months. By clustering their facilities, resorts in the Laurentians north of Montreal have been able to concentrate more nightlife, restaurants, and shopping in one area. This draws more patrons than a string of isolated resorts would.

Recreational Vehicles One type of recreational facility that has grown tremendously is the private campground. Kampgrounds of America (KOA), North America's largest privately owned campground franchise, had seven facilities in 1964. Now it has several hundred.

This growth does not mean that more people are pitching tents and building bonfires. Rather, it means that recreational vehicles (RVs) are becoming more popular. Campgrounds cater to these homes on wheels by providing parking spots, electricity, running water, and sewer access. Some campgrounds have even installed swimming pools, golf courses, kennels, restaurants, and cocktail lounges.

The RV is a more recent method of travelling and is contributing to the tourism boom. However, because they take their beds and kitchens with them, RV owners do not make much use of motels and restaurants. Some convention and entertainment centres are seeking to capitalize on RV traffic by establishing nearby campsites.

The RV industry has added RV rentals to the channels of distribution used for other travel products. Thus, travellers can rent an RV at an airport or as part of a fly/drive package arranged through a travel agency. Virtual inspections of RV options are easily conducted online; this facilitates the selection process well in advance of hitting the road.

RV travel is especially enjoyable in the Northwest Territories and the Yukon. Wildlife abounds, and travel by RV assures safety and comfort. In less settled regions, services are not necessarily well positioned for stopping along major routes. The Mackenzie, Liard, and Alaska Highways also provide routes for travellers seeking unique beauty and adventure in the Land of the Midnight Sun, and RVs make it possible.

ILLUSTRATION 13–7

Adventure tourism can range from trips for Japanese tourists to view the northern lights to bird watchers chartering a cruise to view puffins on Machias Seal Island in the Bay of Fundy.

SOURCE: Courtesy of Raven Tours.

Check Your Product Knowledge

1. Who provides facilities for outdoor recreation?
2. How have RVs contributed to the tourism boom?

ECOTOURISM

Ecotourism draws on natural, social/cultural, and human-built environments. According to the former Canadian Environmental Advisory Council, ecotourism is "tourism that focuses on nature-related experiences that help people appreciate and understand our natural resources and their conservation." The world's oldest and largest ecotourism organization, The International Ecotourism Society's (TIES) previous definition was somewhat broader; it includes "culture" as well as "natural resources" and adds that ecotourism is "purposeful travel to natural areas to understand the culture and natural history of the environment, taking care not to alter the integrity of the ecosystem, while producing economic opportunities that make the conservation of natural resources beneficial to local people." Their recent definition is "Responsible travel to natural areas that conserves the environment and improves the well-being of local people" (TIES, 2006).

McIntosh and colleagues (1995) explain that ecotourism involves more than conservation. It is a form of travel that responds to a region's natural, social, and economic environments and offers an alternative to mass tourism. It requires airlines, accommodation facilities, tour operators, and outfitters to provide **environmentally sensitive** products and services, meaning that they are in tune with environmental forces in a particular setting.

Ecotourism fosters an ecosystem perspective that encourages travellers to understand the relationships among the natural, psychosocial, and human-built environments. Furthermore, it produces economic opportunities *and* conservation gains. In many ways, ecotourism provides the best of all possible worlds for tourists, destinations, and local people. The challenge is to turn the concept of ecotourism into a reality.

Ecotourists stand by the motto "Take nothing but pictures, leave nothing but footprints." In recent years, tourists and tourist service providers have become more aware of the environment. An ethic of social responsibility is being encouraged throughout the tourism industry.

Ecotourism provides outstanding experiences for tourists. It also benefits destinations by:

- Encouraging heritage and environmental preservation and enhancement. Parks and forest preserves are created or expanded. So are biosphere reserves, recreation areas, beaches, marine and underwater trails, and natural and human-built attractions.
- Providing opportunities for environmental education.
- Generating funds for purchasing and improving natural and protected areas, which attract still more ecotourists.
- Creating employment and economic benefits for local people (McIntosh et al., 1995).

Canadian Ecotourism Activities

Ecotourism has been growing steadily since the 1990s, about 20 to 34 percent per year (TIES, 2006).

Many projects across Canada have contributed to the recent development of ecotourism. Several examples to consider are the following.

Exemplary Ecotourism Practices In 1999, the CTC identified operators engaged in exemplary practices in Canada's adventure and outdoor recreation sector. It then commissioned The Economic Planning Group of Canada to prepare *On the Path to Success: Catalogue of Exemplary Practices in Adventure Travel and Ecotourism.* The hope was that the best practices highlighted in the catalogue would serve as models for the industry as a whole. The catalogue can be ordered from the Canadian Tourism Commission Distribution Centre in Ottawa.

Nine main areas of competency were considered: business management, product and delivery, customer service and relations, training and human resources development, resource protection and sustainability, social and community contribution, packaging, marketing and promotion, and product development (see Table 13–3 for examples of five of these).

Coastal Tourism Coastal tourism in British Columbia is sustainable, high end, and high tech. Tourists are able to experience once-in-a-lifetime adventures that include viewing rugged and pristine areas and learning about the region's rich cultural history. The hospitality provided is luxurious. Guides offer extensive interpretive services. All operations are environmentally sensitive. Tourists' choices on where to go specifically in the region are often based on the impact the resort/outfitter has on the environment. From Vancouver Island north to Princess Royal Island, helicopters, float planes, and specialty marine vessels are being used for ecotourism packages. Operators in this region are marrying commerce to a strong stewardship ethic. A **stewardship ethic** is the moral principle that operators manage property effectively because it will be beneficial.

Whale Watching The Bay of Fundy, between New Brunswick and Nova Scotia, is a world-class ecotourism destination. Tours for observing a variety of whales in this rich feeding ground run from June to October. Their boats have interpretive staff on board, often biologists knowledgeable about local culture and history as well as the local marine life. The local operators have developed a code of ethics to limit the impact of their activities on the whales. For example, only two boats are allowed to view any whale or pod of whales at one time (Goodwin, 2000).

In the Saguenay–St. Lawrence Marine Park in Quebec, whale watchers can either observe belugas from land-based sites, without the risk of disturbing the whales, or join one of the many water tour operators. These operators also have developed a voluntary code of ethics, and

TABLE 13–3 A Sample of Exemplary Practices in Adventure Travel and Ecoadventure

Areas of Competency Exemplary Practices

Business Management

"Our goal is to offer the best interpretive program in all the North, while becoming profitable enough to pay dividends as well as salaries to our partners."
—Bathurst Inlet Lodge

Product and Delivery

"Our company's goal is to achieve the well-known social/environmental reputation that The Body Shop has, based on our proven social environmental track record."*—Niagara Nature Tours*

Resource Protection

"We hope and try to ensure that our tours provide our passengers with an educational experience that emphasizes the need for a healthy and diverse ecosystem not only in our area of operation, but worldwide."*—Quoddy Link Marine*

Packaging

"We developed a Teacher's Course that was offered through the University of Calgary and the Arctic Institute of the North."*—Bathurst Inlet Lodge*

Marketing

"We no longer produce 'the brochure'—a static publication does no good in a dynamic market."*—Borealis Outdoor Adventures*

SOURCE: *Catalogue of Exemplary Practice in Adventure Travel and Ecotourism, 2001.* Reproduced with permission of the Minister of Public Works and Government Services Canada, 2002.

tourists are encouraged to select a company that respects that code and also offers interpretive services.

The Economics of Ecoadventure

Villemaire noted in 2000, "Ecoadventure travel is one of the fastest growing tourism markets in Canada, increasing between 10 and 15 percent a year. . . ." **Ecoadventure** is adventure travel that is sensitive to the environment and strives to protect rather than destroy it.

Demand British, French, and German tourists are increasing their demand for Canada's outdoor adventure and nature experiences and some are seeking physically challenging adventure. Others are interested in soft adventure— in viewing this country's natural and cultural environment, especially the cultures of our aboriginal peoples.

Are we prepared to respond to the demand? Will we be able to maintain the ecological integrity of our natural cultural and human-constructed environments?

Supply When buyers were surveyed by Rendez-vous Canada in 1999, they indicated that the top outdoor activities tourists wanted were whale watching, horseback riding, rafting, snowmobiling, skiing, and viewing the Northern Lights. Other popular activities were hiking, bird watching, visiting national and provincial parks, scuba diving, canoeing and camping, mountain biking, catch-and-release fly fishing, rock climbing, storm and iceberg watching, and snowshoeing. Clearly, existing and new operators can pursue growth in many directions.

Industry associations are being established across the country to foster product development and monitor service quality. Among other endeavours, these groups are establishing "leave-no-trace" policies and codes of ethics, considering ways to reduce group liability insurance premiums, and exploring risk-management programs. They are also developing joint packages and marketing initiatives, as well as accreditation programs and quality labels.

Canada has a competitive advantage in wilderness adventure experiences. To maintain that advantage, issues of sustainability will have to be addressed. This must include addressing overcapacity problems and safeguarding this country's ecological integrity and cultural integrity.

According to Parks Canada ("What Is," n.d.), for a location to have ecological integrity, the ecosystems must have their indigenous components intact (the physical elements), a biodiversity must exist in the ecosystem (landscape diversity and species diversity), and the ecosystem processes must be functional.

McElroy (n.d.) defines cultural integrity as involving "the protection, conservation, interpretation and presentation of the heritage and cultural diversity of a particular place." It also includes respect for the ways of one's own heritage and respect for the ways of other nationalities and their cultures, according to a 1999 report by the ICOMOS International Scientific Committee on Cultural Tourism.

All of these requirements call for strategic planning, careful product development and market research, and effective marketing, as well as environmentally sensitive operating practices.

Most ecoadventure operations are a few hours drive from urban centres. A popular ecoadventure tour is at the Scenic Caves site near Collingwood, which is only about one hour north of Toronto. The tour consists of a three-hour guided tour including a suspension bridge, treetop walk, zip line, and cave tour.

Less Developed Nations In less developed nations, ecotourism generates funds for fresh water, waste-treatment facilities, roads, and electricity. Tourism attracts investment.

Check Your Product Knowledge

1. How can ecotourism and ecoadventure contribute to a region's economy?
2. What is the tourist industry in Canada doing with respect to ecotourism and ecoadventure to maintain a competitive advantage in the marketplace?

ILLUSTRATION 13–8
Golf provides recreation on business trips as well as during vacation travels.
SOURCE: Corel.

ADVENTURE TOURISM: TRENDS

Geotourism

In 2003, the Travel Industry Association of America published a report, sponsored by *National Geographic Traveler*, called *Geotourism: The New Trend in Travel*; this study was the first to identify geotourists as specific psychographic groups. It was estimated that more than 56 million Americans maybe could be classified as geotourists. The study defines geotourism as "tourism that sustains or enhances the geographical character of the place being visited, including its environment culture, aesthetics, heritage, and the well-being of its residents."

According to the National Geographic Center for Sustainable Destinations, "Travel businesses do their best to use the local workforce, services, and products and supplies. When the community understands the beneficial role of geotourism, it becomes an incentive for wise destination stewardship."

Significant results from this study: 58.5 million Americans (38 percent) would be willing to pay more to a travel firm that encourages the protection and conservation of the environment (60 percent indicated 5 to 10 percent more); about 96 million Americans (61 percent) consider their travel experience to be better whenever their destination has succeeded in preserving its natural, cultural, and historic sites (Keffe, 2003).

Social Ecology

During the last few years, many national parks have had to reconsider their position on the issues of "people versus parks" and "fences and fines," since the support of the local population is usually a significant factor in the success of the management of the parks.

According to the South Africa National Parks (SANParks) website, "Social ecology is a new philosophy and approach to conservation in which ecological, cultural and socio-economic issues are recognized as critical to the management of the parks."

The SANParks corporate plan details the social ecology process, in which it will interact with the local community to foster relationships and understanding; "The process ensures that the views of the community are taken into account to the largest possible extent and are acted upon, that the parks' existence is a direct benefit and that, in turn, communities adjacent to the parks welcome the conservation effort of SANParks" (SANParks, 2003).

Adhering to the social ecology process should ensure that SANParks' 1995 vision—"National parks will be the pride and joy of all Africans"—becomes a reality. National parks in other countries could use SANParks as a model.

Geocaching: A New Adventure and Staycations

Geocaching is an interactive adventure game in which you use a global positioning system (GPS) device to find clues and rewards in caches that another person or organization has hidden, often all over the world. GPS users can utilize location coordinates found on specific websites to locate the caches. Cache protocol for cache visitors is to take an item and replace it with another item. As a minimum, a cache is usually a logbook where the visitors may write notes. Larger caches could include a buried waterproof plastic bucket containing many items such as pictures, tools, games, etc., and are usually sealed in individual plastic bags for protection (Geocaching, n.d.).

Bruce County in Ontario has included six new geocaches in their 13 adventure passport stops throughout the county, and 2008 marked the fourth Annual Explore the Bruce Adventure Passport event. Over 20 000 people have used the Adventure Passport to get out there and "Explore the Bruce" (Explore the Bruce, n.d.).

Bruce County is also promoting **staycations**—a vacation spent in one's local region—to encourage budget-minded travellers to explore locally and save on rising travel costs (*Guelph Tribune*, 2008).

New Trends in Adventure Tourism

Author Ralph Buckley (2006) in "Adventure Tourism" describes 11 Adventure Trends. Five of these trends are listed below.

- **Increased growth**—in both the low-skill and high-skill end of the adventure sector.
- **Product price pyramid**—includes a few very highly priced products and many short, low-priced, unskilled products.
- **More luxury and amenities**—such as spas.
- **Adventure events**—as destination marketing tools
- **Increased insurance costs**—due to litigation over issues of potential liability.

ADVENTURE TOURISM: ISSUES

Environmental Certification

An initiative known as "A Partnership for Effective Implementation of Tools for Monitoring Ecotourism and Sustainable Tourism" was started by four organizations—the World Tourism Organization (UNWTO), Rainforest Alliance, the International Ecotourism Society, and the Center for Ecotourism and Sustainable Development—to promote more advanced environmental and social standards for tourism.

This partnership has been developing a process to encompass all the criteria of tourism's numerous "green" certification programs and is hoping to formulate an international tourism accreditation committee to ensure that all certification systems are in conformity with the environmental and social standards set by the partnership.

Eugenio Yunis, chief of Sustainable Development at the UNWTO stated in 2004, "Certification systems and ecolabels in tourism are essential to inform consumers and to encourage more sustainable production and consumption patterns in tourism services. However, these systems must follow some universally accepted criteria in order to increase their creditability in the eyes of the tourists."

Poverty Tourism: Exploratory or Exploitive?

In contrast to touring opulent Beverly Hills, tour operators are leading guided tours through shantytowns outside Buenos Aires (Argentina), immigrant neighbourhoods in Rotterdam (Holland) and Birmingham (England), and even impoverished areas in the US such as Houston, Washington, D.C., and New York City (Vincent, 2006). There are similar **poverty tours** in Mumbai, India ($15 a day), Nairobi, Kenya ($100 per day), Johannesburg, South Africa ($117 per day), and Mazatlan, Mexico (free) (Yurchyshyn, 2008).

Critics object to the voyeurism and sensationalization of impoverished people: "This is a kind of slum tourism, a clear invasion of somebody's privacy. . . . You are treating humans like animals" (Lancaster, 2007).

On the other hand, organizers argue that poverty tours raise awareness and understanding of the realities of the poor, and "bring money into areas that don't benefit from tourism. Some companies donate as much as 80 percent of their profits, while others give less" (Yurchyshyn, 2008). Is this really an exploratory form of tourism or is this exploitation?

Check Your Product Knowledge

1. What were the significant results from the Travel Industry Association of America survey?
2. What is the controversy concerning "poverty tourism"?

CAREER OPPORTUNITIES

Public and commercial recreation systems employ more part-time and temporary workers than most components of the tourism industry. Other sources also indicate that the sector is developing, which will provide opportunities for entrepreneurs as well as regular employment service providers and the related support services. Also, there are career opportunities related to parks, adventure tourism, skiing, golf, tennis, marine recreation, and ecotourism.

Parks

Parks Canada offers various unique and challenging jobs such as park warden, interpreter, historian, archaeologist, and conservator. Details of these and many others are on Parks Canada's website. Parks Canada has more than 5400 employees (1600 seasonal) employees across Canada.

Employees may be able to become certified nationally through the Canadian Tourism Human Resource Council in the following occupations—hunting, outdoor, and freshwater angling guides; a ski resort operator; or a golf club manager. Occupational standards have also been developed for the occupations of leisure facilities manager, and marina operator.

Adventure Tourism

In the past 35 years, adventure tourism employment opportunities have increased. There are job opportunities for outfitters, guides, and instructors, and in related sectors such as transportation and hospitality services. Snowmobile occupational standards have also been developed.

Skiing

The ski and snowboard industry needs instructors and patrollers, guides, lift operators, and avalanche controllers, as well as people to work in hotels, restaurants, and the entertainment industry. There are also career opportunities with equipment suppliers and in retail. Ski area resort operation guidelines have been developed.

Golf and Tennis

Golf and tennis specialists are employed by operations that have facilities for these forms of recreation. Club management, operation of equipment and facilities, and marketing and sales all provide career opportunities related to these activities. Also, tennis or golf instructors are employed at most clubs and resorts.

Marine

There are job opportunities for marina managers, operators, and attendants; lifeguards; instructors; guides; developers; and marketers. In addition, there is a demand for people who can provide catering and on-land tourism services, as well as for equipment suppliers.

Ecotourism

People who are environmentally sensitive and flexible and who have a wide range of knowledge, skills, and interests are the most likely to succeed in ecotourism activities and related businesses.

A DAY IN THE LIFE OF A

National Park Interpreter

I just spent the summer working as a student interpreter in Banff National Park. I got to work outdoors all day, make new friends, and meet people from all over the world who came to visit the park.

An "interpreter" at a park does not work with languages but instead "interprets" the sights and sounds of the park for visitors. I gave many talks to groups of visitors about the park's history, wildlife, plant life, and geology. Some summer interns in Canada's national parks work in the visitors' centres answering questions about park attractions, giving directions, and taking reservations. Other interpreters do clerical work in the park offices. A few of us even dress up in pioneer costumes and give presentations about early settlers at the park's pioneer history centre.

During the training session, our instructors took us around the park so we could become familiar with all of its attractions and facilities. We were assigned to a specific area of the park and given roommates for the summer. Many interpreters lived in tent cabins— large, tent-sided, wooden platforms containing a wood stove for heat and cooking, cold running water, and electricity. Bath and toilet facilities were in a separate building.

Some of us worked repairing trails, picnic areas, and other facilities, or taking people hiking. My favourite assignment was to lead groups of children on junior ranger hikes. Usually I would teach the children how to spot animals and animal signs, such as tracks and nests. I liked to show the children how animals survive by adapting to their environment. At night, the interpreters took turns leading the campfire talks. I've taken geology courses in university, so I sometimes gave presentations about the special geology of Banff and the surrounding mountains.

The national parks try to choose student interpreters who have had some part-time work experience, are studying in a related field and who have had some experience in public speaking. Students learn how to manage natural resources and work with tourists. In addition, this job is a great way to get your foot in the door if you are aiming for a career in conservation management or tourism.

I made several good friends and had a lot of fun working as an intern at Banff. During our off-duty hours, we were able to hike, rock climb, canoe, ride horses, swim, and camp throughout the park.

Summary

- Ecotourism is currently one of the largest global tourism trends.
- Parks have been an integral part of North American society since the 1700s.
- Canada has more than 1100 provincial parks. Like the national parks, they were designated to conserve wilderness, preserve historic sites, and provide recreation and employment.
- Increased use of parks creates problems of pollution, vandalism, and environmental stress.
- Adventure tourism includes both "hard" and "soft" adventure.
- Outdoor recreation is a major component of tourism, as it motivates people to travel and creates demand for services at a variety of destinations.
- Golf and tennis attract tourists to destinations; ski resorts are adding golf and/or tennis facilities to create demand for accommodation and other hospitality services year-round.
- Both domestic and international tourists are participating in a variety of marine experiences, and creating a demand for other products and services at the same time.
- Water-based tour operators in the Bay of Fundy and the Saguenay–St. Lawrence Marine Park have established codes of ethics for operating in an environmentally sensitive manner.
- The growth of private campgrounds is attributed to the increased popularity of RVs, especially among European visitors.
- Ecotourism draws on natural, social and cultural, and human-built environments. The interests of people who embrace the principles of ecotourism can lie in cultural experiences, adventure activities, or nature interpretation.
- Ecoadventure is one of the fastest-growing markets in Canada.

- Geocaching is a new entertainment adventure game where individuals hide a series of items in a secret location and post the GPS coordinates on a website for adventurers to locate.
- A staycation is a vacation spent exploring one's local area.
- The annual growth in the adventure tourism and outdoor recreation sector is creating opportunities for entrepreneurial involvement and employment.

Key Terms

adventure tourism   p. 300
ecoadventure   p. 306
ecotourism   p. 305
environmentally sensitive   p. 305
garden tourism   p. 299
geocaching   p. 308
hard adventure   p. 301
heli-skiing   p. 302
interpretation   p. 299
niche market   p. 301
poverty tourism   p. 309
soft adventure   p. 300
staycations   p. 308
stewardship ethic   p. 306
sustainable tourism   p. 297
water-based vacations   p. 303

Internet Connections

Big Bear Adventures
www.planetcharters.com   p. 301

Canadian Biosphere Research Association (CBRN)
www.biosphere-research.ca

Churchill Wild
www.churchillwild.com   p. 297

ECONOMUSEUM® Network Society
www.economusees.com/iens_en.cfm

Golf Canada
www.worldgolf.com/courses/canada/index.html   p. 302

Heli-Skiing in British Columbia with Canadian Mountain Holidays (CMH)
www.canadianmountainholidays.com/heli-skiing/lodges/where-we-ski   p. 302

Kampgrounds of America (KOA)
www.koa.com   p. 304

Mersey River Chalets (Nova Scotia)
www.merseyriverchalets.ns.ca   p. 299

Mount Royal Park (Montreal)
www.lemontroyal.qc.ca   p. 299

Parks Canada
www.pc.gc.ca   p. 295

Rendez-vous Canada
www.rvc.org   p. 306

Saguenay–St. Lawrence Marine Park
www.pc.gc.ca/amnc-nmca/qc/saguenay/activ/activ1_e.asp   p. 306

Stanley Park (Vancouver, B.C.)
www.seestanleypark.com   p. 299

Tourism Industry Association of Canada (TIAC)
www.tiac-aitc.ca   p. 297

Trans Canada Trail
www.tctrail.ca   p. 296

U.S. National Park Service
www.nps.gov   p. 298

Whistler Blackcomb
www.whistlerblackcomb.com   p. 302

WORKSHEET 13-1   Yourtown Outdoor Recreation Facilities

Identify outdoor recreational facilities and services in the categories listed below found in Yourtown. Which are public? Which are commercial? What is the entrance charge? Which facilities have websites? How effective is the website visually and in terms of providing the information you were seeking?

A. Winter outdoor activities

_____

_____

_____

_____

_____

B. Parks and forests

_____

_____

_____

_____

_____

C. Water-based activities

_____

_____

_____

_____

_____

D. Golf/tennis

_____

_____

_____

_____

_____

E. Other

_____

_____

_____

_____

_____

WORKSHEET 13–2   Parks Canada

Parks Canada administers scores of separate sites. For each kind of national site listed below, locate the ones closest to Yourtown (or your province). Describe the facilities offered at the site. Information on Parks Canada is available at www.pc.gc.ca.

National park

_____

_____

National region

_____

_____

National historical park

_____

_____

National recreational area

_____

_____

National monument

_____

_____

National seashore

_____

_____

National river or riverway

_____

_____

National memorial

_____

_____

Performing arts centre

_____

_____

PART 6

Travel Trade Sector

Objectives

When you have completed this chapter, you should be able to:

- Describe some of the transformations in distribution channels brought about by e-commerce.
- Explain how travel retailers differ from retailers in other industries.
- Distinguish among the three different systems of distribution.
- Explain the difference between business-to-consumer (B2C) and business-to-business (B2B) transactions.
- List the main printed references available to travel professionals.
- Discuss how the Internet has changed the way travel professionals research and book travel products.
- Distinguish between the informational functions of a global distribution system (GDS) and its transactional functions.

- Explain the differences among electronic ticketing, booking tickets on the Internet, and ticketless travel.
- Outline the development of automated reservations systems.
- List the main vendors of global distribution systems.
- Describe the relationship between host vendors and co-hosts.
- Discuss the issue of bias.
- Differentiate the various types of e-commerce systems on the Web.
- Show how automated back-office systems can facilitate a travel agency's internal operations.
- Explain how hotel and car rental reservations systems differ from airline GDSs.

Tourism products and services are one of the success stories of **e-commerce**. The transformation from traditional marketing ("bricks") to the marketspace ("clicks") has been phenomenal. The term "marketspace" was introduced by Rayport and Sviokla (1994) to distinguish between electronic and conventional markets. In marketspace, information replaces physical goods as the content of the transaction. Face-to-face meetings are replaced by on-screen communications, and the infrastructure of marketspace consists of computers and networks instead of buildings and paper documents.

Two facts need to be recognized before discussing electronic distribution channels: First, the tourism industry and especially travel intermediaries have always been open to automation and have long been automated; and second, as recently as the mid-1990s some academics were upset

about advertising on the World Wide Web and did not want it to be there. How far we have come! The changes have been dramatic. Some examples:

- Traditional travel agencies have developed websites (e.g., Uniglobe Travel Online).
- New online travel agencies have become available, such as Expedia, Travelocity, and Orbitz.
- Internet service providers (e.g., AOL) have travel information on their home pages and provide links to travel websites where users can make bookings.
- Some global distribution systems (GDSs) have opened online travel systems (e.g., Sabre Holdings developed Travelocity).
- Firms in various tourism sectors (e.g., accommodation, transportation) have opened websites and online booking services.

PROFILE

Simplifying Travel Transactions

AgentShopper

In 2001, travel-related websites generated more revenue on the Internet than any other Internet-related industry. The owners of AgentShopper, a private software company, noticed that a small number of these websites had special log-in areas just for travel agents. It seemed that a select few suppliers recognized early that distribution costs through the Internet were much less expensive than those of the computer reservation systems (CRSs). Also, they recognized that by having these special agent-only sites, they could save even more dollars by decreasing the size of their staff in reservations departments or call centres.

A combination of experienced travel industry people and some of the most innovative programmers in the technology field founded AgentShopper. The company principals noticed that while the CRS era is far from over, the travel world is changing at such a rapid pace that the old model is unable to keep up. Thus, they developed the company as an alternative Internet GDS that will allow users to directly participate in global distribution, without the expense of CRS and segment fees.

AgentShopper is a 100 percent Web-based technology exclusive to travel agents. Its mission is to simplify the total Internet travel transaction for the retail travel industry by streamlining the business processes of an agent in a multiple Web supplier environment. The company is dedicated to helping travel agents to profit by researching

and identifying the best travel Web booking sites in the world. This means that a travel agency's list of potential revenue sources is no longer limited to local suppliers—it's now global. With over 670 websites, covering every sector of the industry, agents can now more effectively utilize the Internet to their advantage. About 250 of these sites are agent-only booking engines, many of which quote net fares or pay **commission** (a percentage of the selling price) on Web bookings only. The majority of these sites either pay an equal or higher rate of commission than those that are paid on a GDS, or are not available to book on a GDS.

Today, an average travel agency does up to 40 percent of its business on the Web. That percentage is expected to grow exponentially. A significant problem in the past has not been access to online inventory, but the lack of a means of automating the searching and booking process from many different online suppliers, without having to go to each Web page individually and filling in the search criteria over and over. This can translate into as much as two hours per day of clicking on and filling in Web page inquiries.

As more suppliers create websites to handle online bookings for both the consumer and the trade, travel professionals are being forced to abandon the old technology for newer, faster technologies. Online agencies like Expedia, Travelocity, and Orbitz are making huge gains daily. Traditional agencies are trying to

redefine their role and business model to keep pace with the change. Suppliers know that for every sale they make online, it is one less sale they have to make through a very expensive GDS. Many in the industry foresee that soon all suppliers of travel products will be on the Internet and they will be paying commissions—possibly bonus commissions—to agencies that use online technologies because the GDS channels are too expensive. They too would love to have a newer, cheaper and more efficient means of distribution.

The AgentShopper's multiple-browser technology permits an agency to control and manage the Internet sales process better than ever. The AgentShopper system is built to give its users total control of where, when, and how they search for the best fares and schedules for their clients, without many of the delays associated with Web search services, allowing agents to speed up the shopping process when researching the right product for their clients. With the system's multiple-browser capabilities, agents are not only able to search for air, hotel, and car rentals, but also cruises, tour packages, consolidators and other products simultaneously. This allows users to shop and choose from various suppliers quickly and easily. With the growing proliferation of Web-only fares in every sector of the travel industry, AgentShopper offers its users a wide array of global Web products and a unique, streamlined approach to this information.

A major feature of the AgentShopper program is automation of the process of inputting client data into information fields on Internet sites. For example, if a client wants to fly from Toronto to Montreal next week and a travel counsellor wants to check fares for the client online, the counsellor would type the client's data into the AgentShopper interface (dates, cities, etc.), pick a website from the AgentShopper list, and sit back as the program flips through the site's pages, inputting the client's data as it goes (about one page per second) until the page with the fares is presented on the screen.

In addition to airline and online travel agency sites, Agent-Shopper also features sites for consolidators, accommodations, car rentals, cruises, tour operators, and more. The program also links to the major GDSs. In 2005, the company introduced a new B2C search option for travel agency and tour operator clients.

The Association of Canadian Travel Agencies and Agent-Shopper announced a partnership agreement in November 2003. Today, more than 3000 agents use AgentShopper.

SOURCE: Adapted from information on the following websites: www.agentshopper.com, www.knowledgestorm.com, www.travelpress.com, www.travelweek.ca (September 2002), and www.acta.ca (November 5, 2003).

- Government tourism agencies have developed websites.
- Wireless application protocol (WAP) devices are allowing access to websites without a computer or a telephone line.

A long time ago, tourists booked passage directly with the company that operated the shipping line, railway, bus service, or airline, called a "carrier." Then tour operators and travel agencies developed as **intermediaries**, or links, between the carriers and the **demanders** (the travelling public and business travellers). After World War II, the travel trade sector of the tourism industry began to grow spectacularly. This growth paralleled the development of the airline industry. In the late 1990s, new options were introduced to provide consumers with even more direct contact with transportation providers. These new options included electronic ticketing, booking tickets on the Internet, and ticketless travel.

Every industry has products that it tries to sell to consumers at a profit. Most industries sell tangible products; for example, the automobile industry sells cars and trucks. The products of the tourism industry are usually intangible—for example, a flight on an airplane, a stay at a hotel, the use of a rental car, or a complete tour package.

Travel products are perishable. They must be sold within a certain time period or they become worthless: An empty seat on an airplane can never be sold once the flight has left. Also, some tourism products are seasonal—they are in great demand during certain times of the year and in low demand at others. A trip to the Prince Edward Island seashore is a seasonal product.

Like other industries, the tourism industry uses a distribution system to move its products and services from producer to consumer. Manufacturing industries typically use wholesalers and retailers as intermediaries between producers and consumers. The sales distribution system of the tourism industry also involves intermediaries, including tour operators (wholesalers) and travel agents (retailers).

An important difference between the tourism industry and other industries is the status of the retailer. A traditional retailer buys goods and services and sells them to the consumer with a price markup. In contrast, travel retailers do not buy goods and services, and often they do not mark up the price. Instead, the supplier or wholesaler pays them a commission, or a percentage of the selling price. The exception to this general rule is when travel agents use consolidators, who sell travel products to travel agencies at a net price that the agency then marks up. Travel agents may also apply a service charge when selling products such as airline tickets, on which there may be no commission. Travel retailers are most often called travel "agents" because they act as agents for the suppliers or wholesalers who are selling the product. A person who works in a travel agency serving the public is now generally called a **travel counsellor**. Another difference between the tourism industry and most other industries is that the consumer can bypass the intermediaries and purchase products directly from suppliers.

In this chapter, you will learn how the different channels of distribution used in the tourism industry are structured. You will also learn about earlier automated systems for getting travel products from suppliers to consumers. In addition, this chapter will review how e-commerce, the Internet, and websites are transforming the ways that consumers, suppliers, and intermediaries are meeting to exchange information, services, and products. The ideas in this chapter will be developed further in Chapter 16.

The examples in this chapter are mainly for the airline industry. The chapters on the surface transportation industry, the cruise and marine industry, accommodations, and tours and charters have their own sections on channels of distribution and making reservations.

CHANNELS OF DISTRIBUTION DEFINED

There are three main channels of distribution in the tourism industry. Their differences relate to level of complexity:

1. *Unilateral*, which involves no intermediaries between supplier and consumer. This is known as **business-to-consumer (B2C)**.
2. *Bilevel*, which involves one intermediary. This is known as **business-to-business (B2B)** and then business-to-consumer (B2C).
3. *Multilevel*, which involves two or more intermediaries. The emphasis is on B2B.

Retail versus Wholesale Distribution

Usually, a travel agency is thought of as a retail firm, which it is. It provides services and products to consumers from suppliers (e.g., cruise lines). In the channel, these suppliers are considered to be **wholesale distributors**, or intermediaries. These channels can be bilevel or multilevel. However, more wholesale firms are approaching consumers directly as well as through traditional retail travel agencies. It is now easier for wholesale firms to obtain direct bookings by developing active websites. Those who do this have in effect become **retail distributors** on a B2C basis.

Consumers are free to decide which channel they prefer. Whether they buy a travel product directly from the supplier or through an intermediary, identical products usually cost the same. This feature is unique to the tourism industry.

Unilateral Distribution System

The unilateral system is the simplest of the three distribution systems (see Figure 14–1). It involves the direct sale of travel products and services by a supplier to a consumer. Suppliers include airlines, railways, bus companies, cruise lines, car rental firms, hotels, resorts, and sightseeing companies. Customers can telephone the supplier to make a reservation, or go in person to the ticket or sales outlet, or visit a website. Most major suppliers in the tourism industry maintain national and regional sales offices. Some own or lease counter space at airports, hotels, convention centres, and other high-visibility locations.

In recent years, suppliers have begun to experiment with automated methods of direct distribution. Automated ticketing machines (similar to automated teller machines) have been installed at airports, railway stations, and ticket offices in major cities.

The unilateral system of distribution is ideal for simple travel arrangements, such as domestic airline reservations and hotel bookings. More complex arrangements, such as cruises and tour packages, generally require the assistance of a travel counsellor at a travel agency or some other sales intermediary.

The great advantage of the unilateral system is its simplicity. Suppliers deal directly with consumers; this minimizes the misunderstandings that can arise when a third party is involved. Many clients prefer to talk directly to the supplier, in the belief that this provides greater personal control over the transaction.

Suppliers may also make a greater net profit per unit sale if they sell directly to the traveller. Suppose someone wants to fly from Edmonton to Toronto on Air Canada. The quoted fare is $600. If the consumer buys the ticket directly from Air Canada, she will pay the airline $600. If she decides to book the flight through a travel agency, it will still cost her the same amount, but Air Canada may not receive the full $600. The reason is that suppliers often pay a commission to travel agents to compensate them for making the booking. At one time, all suppliers paid commission to travel agents. Today, however, the situation has changed. While cruise lines and tour operators still pay commission, airlines generally do not pay commission for flights booked through a GDS. Most airlines pay commission on flights booked through their website, and many airlines negotiate individual commission arrangements with various travel agencies. When Air Canada paid a 10 percent commission, the travel agency would receive $60 on a $600 sale. In other words, Air Canada would earn only $540 on the sale instead of $600. You can see why airlines like to sell directly to travellers.

In the unilateral system, the supplier has an opportunity to make additional sales. When dealing directly with the client described above, Air Canada may well convince her to book her return trip to Edmonton on Air Canada or to upgrade her seat. The growth of B2C e-commerce has resulted in more direct sales by suppliers. At first many suppliers developed websites only for informational purposes. Nowadays many have online booking features.

Bilevel Distribution System

Two main forces work against the unilateral system of distribution. First, many suppliers cannot afford to maintain

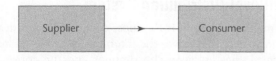

FIGURE 14–1 Unilateral Distribution System

regional sales offices and so must rely on intermediaries to get their products to consumers. Also, many tourists would rather make their travel arrangements through a retail agency than deal directly with suppliers. In some provinces, only consumers who purchase through a registered retailer are protected if they do not receive the services that they paid for.

The bilevel distribution system usually involves a travel agent as intermediary (see Figure 14–2). The agent represents the suppliers and sells their travel services to consumers. Suppliers also use business travel departments (BTDs) as distribution channels. In many large corporations, there are in-house BTDs that sell travel products and services to employees. Tour operators may also serve as intermediaries, buying travel products from various suppliers and packaging them for sale directly to consumers.

Supermarkets, department stores, and other retail outlets have begun distributing travel products, especially airline tickets. This is more convenient for travel consumers, but it may eventually take business away from travel agencies. Some Wal-Mart stores have well-known travel agencies inside. The success of **video marketing**—television cable channels showing catalogues of items on the screen—has not gone unnoticed by the tourism industry.

For the consumer, the bilevel system's greatest advantage is that most travel intermediaries can provide professional assistance and personalized advice. In the present deregulated marketplace, travellers face a baffling maze of airfares. Professional travel agents have the expertise to make sense of the airfare maze and to recommend arrangements that suit the needs and budgets of individual travellers.

Furthermore, travel intermediaries can provide travellers with information on a greater variety of travel options. Suppose a traveller wants to take his family to Walt Disney World for a week's vacation, but he isn't sure where to stay. He doesn't have a computer to look up various websites. If he has the time, patience, and money for long-distance telephone calls, he could call several hotels and motels in the area to find suitable accommodation. His other option is to call or visit a local travel agency and explain his specific needs. The travel counsellor will be able to eliminate the hotels that are beyond his budget or unsuitable for other reasons. If the family plans to fly to Disney World, the counsellor will also be able to make the necessary flight arrangements and possibly reserve a rental car for the family's use. In other words, the client can make

all of the family's travel plans in one simple step, instead of calling a host of different suppliers.

Until recently, travel retailers did not usually charge clients for their services, so the clients were not paying any extra for trips. Generally, the customer was charged only if the agency had to make overseas phone calls, or if an especially complicated itinerary was involved. This has changed, however (see Chapter 16). Until this century, airline commissions were the major source of travel agency revenues, accounting for almost two-thirds of total receipts. Since deregulation, suppliers have been free to choose how much commission they pay, and many airlines now pay no commission on fares booked through a GDS (although they often pay 9 percent on website bookings made by the travel agency). The reduction of airline commissions has prompted most travel agencies to charge fees for their services.

Travel intermediaries usually have more influence with suppliers than do individual travellers. Suppliers value retail intermediaries as an important source of volume bookings, and generally give preferential treatment to these customers. If space is limited—which it often can be during peak seasons—a traveller who books through an intermediary is more likely to get a seat on a plane or a room in a hotel than is a traveller who books independently. Suppliers cannot afford to disappoint intermediaries. You perhaps have heard of travellers who have been "bumped" from a flight or who turn up at a hotel to find that the front desk has no record of their reservation. Often, these are clients who have booked independently.

Clearly, the bilevel distribution system has a number of distinct advantages for consumers. What about the supplier? Travel intermediaries are an extension of the supplier's own sales force. Sometimes they are the supplier's sole sales force. In the latter case, the supplier has no sales overhead except for the commissions it pays to retailers. Many suppliers would rather pay commissions to travel counsellors at agencies than maintain a network of sales offices requiring full-time reservations staff. This is especially true of smaller suppliers.

Bilevel distribution systems in e-commerce combine both B2B and B2C elements. When the consumer contacts an intermediary (e.g., an online travel agency) it is B2C; when the online travel agency is in contact electronically with suppliers (e.g., tour operators), it is B2B. A term used to describe purchases by electronic means is **e-procurement**.

Multilevel Distribution System

The multilevel system is the most complex type of distribution system. It involves the intervention of two or more intermediaries between the supplier and the consumer (see Figure 14–3). The system is most commonly used for distributing tour packages. Suppliers such as airlines and

FIGURE 14–2 Bilevel Distribution System

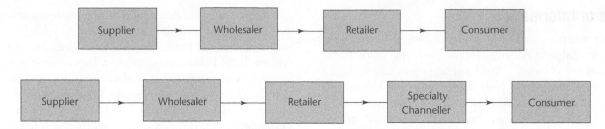

FIGURE 14–3 Multilevel Distribution Systems

hotels sell their products and services to tour operators (i.e., wholesalers). These in turn package the various components into a tour (transportation, accommodations, meals, sightseeing services, transfers). The operator then sells the tour to the consumer through a retail outlet (usually a travel agency).

An additional intermediary is sometimes involved in the planning of a tour package. This intermediary can be an incentive travel company, a meeting/convention planner, a travel club, or some other **specialty channeller**. All intervene between the retailer and the consumer.

For the consumer, the advantages of the multilevel system are similar to those of the bilevel system. An additional advantage arises from the role of the wholesaler in the distribution process. Wholesale distributors buy travel services and products in bulk from suppliers. Advance sales, and the savings that arise from bulk buying, enable suppliers to offer their services to wholesalers at substantially reduced prices.

Unlike the retailer, the wholesaler is not paid a commission by the supplier. Instead, the wholesaler makes its profit by marking up the price of the product. The markup must be high enough to cover overhead and commissions paid to travel agencies and other retailers. Even after markup, the final package is still cheaper than if the traveller had bought the various components directly from the suppliers.

The multilevel system involves the largest number of distribution intermediaries. Occasionally, one company uses several different channels of distribution to promote its services and products. This concept is known as employing **multiple channels**. For example, Air Canada may sell airline tickets through a website, by phone to an agent, in its own sales office, or through a travel agency.

Often a single member of the distribution channel sells products from other suppliers as well as its own products. For example, most of the large airlines sell hotel rooms, car rentals, and tour packages in addition to airline tickets. Similarly, American Express Travel sells airline tickets and hotel accommodations as well as escorted tours. Cruise lines sell airline tickets as well as cruises. This means that a traveller can usually buy a package of two or more products from almost any part of the distribution channel. The

emphasis in e-commerce for multilevel distribution channels is on B2B; the last link in this channel is B2C.

Check Your Product Knowledge

1. Name some of the dramatic changes that have taken place in the channels of distribution.

2. Explain the difference between B2C and B2B operations.

3. What advantages does the unilateral distribution system offer to consumers and to suppliers?

4. How will the growing use of automated ticketing machines, personal computers, and supermarkets as channels of distribution affect the role of travel agents?

5. What is the difference between the bilevel system of distribution and the multilevel system?

PRINT-BASED INFORMATION SYSTEMS

To operate successfully, the tourism industry depends on a continuous flow of information from suppliers to consumers. The information must be accurate and up to date, especially since fares and schedules can change overnight. What is this information? And how do travel retailers and consumers access it? We'll answer these two questions in this section. Almost all travel agencies now use automated information systems, but it is still important for today's travel counsellor to know about print-based information sources. That way, in the event of a computer breakdown or similar problem, a travel counsellor will still be able to obtain current information. Also, many consumers still prefer printed information, such as brochures and timetables, and counsellors must know where to find them and how to interpret them for clients. Let's take a look at how travel agencies operated before automated systems came into wide use.

Types of Information

A client wants to fly from Charlottetown, Prince Edward Island, to Calgary, Alberta. In the past, she made travel arrangements through a local agency—let's call it Alpha Travel. She had always been happy with Alpha's service and decided to use the agency again to make her reservation. Having established where she wanted to go (Calgary), where she wanted to fly from (Charlottetown), and that she needed hotel accommodations and a rental car in Calgary, the travel counsellor at Alpha Travel had to determine the following:

- Which airlines had flights from Charlottetown to Calgary.
- The seat availability on these flights.
- The fares of the different flights to Calgary.
- When the flights left Charlottetown and arrived in Calgary.
- How the flights got to Calgary—how many connecting flights were necessary.
- Where the relevant flight information could be found.
- Where the relevant information on hotel and rental car availability and rates could be found.

Alpha Travel was a nonautomated agency—that is, it did not have access to a global distribution system (GDS) or the Internet. As a result, the travel counsellor had to rely on printed reference sources and on telephone inquiries to suppliers.

Primary Printed References

A nonautomated travel agency needs a large number of printed reference works. All of these works must be updated regularly. Today, the subscription cost for many of these references is such that it is less expensive for an agency to purchase a computer and connect to the Internet than to subscribe to all the required printed references.

Airlines There are three main print sources of information on flight schedules and fares:

1. Timetables and fare sheets.
2. Airline guides.
3. Tariffs.

At one time, timetables and fare sheets were published by all major airlines and distributed to travel agencies on a regular basis. To get a comparative picture of all the available schedules from a single source, the agent had to consult the *Official Airline Guide* (OAG), published by Official Airline Guides Inc. This is available in North American and world editions and lists all scheduled flights. The North American edition is updated every two weeks; the world edition, once a month. Today, the OAG is available online. In addition, fares and timetables can be accessed through a GDS or the suppliers' websites on the Internet.

Tariffs list scheduled airfares and provide a summary of rules and regulations that apply to the flights. There are two main types of tariff. The ATPCO Tariff, issued by the Airline Tariff Publishing Company, lists American flights. International tariffs are published by individual international carriers such as Air Canada, Lufthansa, and SAS, or by consortia of foreign airlines. It is much easier to update a computer every time a fare changes than it is to reprint a tariff. As a result, printed tariffs are rarely used in the tourism industry today. As with the OAG, travel agencies can view fares and rules through a GDS or on airline websites. Companies that need access to the ATPCO can subscribe online. Canadian carriers are no longer required to file tariffs with the government; however, fares and rates must be published, with accessible records kept at the airline's offices for three years.

Ground Transportation Ground transportation includes railways, intercity buses, rental cars, and mass transit and public transportation systems. Information on schedules and fares can be found in:

1. Timetables.
2. Rail and bus guides.
3. Car rental rate sheets.

All ground transportation companies, such as VIA Rail, publish timetables, which they update as schedules change. The *Official Railway Guide* is the main source for VIA (in Canada) and Amtrak (in the United States) schedules and fares. It also contains information on commuter rail services in major North American cities. Rail services worldwide are listed in the *Thomas Cook Overseas Timetable*. *Russell's Official National Motor Coach Guide* lists domestic long-distance bus schedules. Car rental companies clearly have no need to publish timetables, but they must distribute information on rates to travel intermediaries. Car rental rate sheets issued by individual companies, such as Avis and Hertz, serve this purpose. Again, much of this information is available through a GDS or on the supplier's website. However, these printed references provide valuable and comprehensive overviews of the services offered.

Cruise Lines There are two major printed reference sources for information on cruises:

1. Brochures.
2. Official cruise guides.

Cruise lines rely heavily on retailers to distribute their products. (Travel agencies, before Internet websites and online booking, accounted for 95 percent of total cruise sales.) Individual companies supply agencies with lavish brochures detailing the season's cruise offerings, complete with sailing times, deck plans, rates, and related information. Official publications include the *Official Steamship Guide International* and the *Worldwide Cruise and Shipline*

Guide. Both contain listings of cruise schedules throughout the world. Detailed information on its member lines and ships can also be found in the *CLIA Cruise Manual*, now available in electronic form. As with other sources of information, cruise details are now available through a GDS or on the website of each cruise line.

Hotels and Resorts Information on hotel and resort rates and services is available from two types of printed sources:

1. Brochures.
2. Guides and manuals.

Hotel brochures serve roughly the same function as cruise brochures. They provide information on individual properties and they are also used as selling tools. Brochures emphasize the hotel's most attractive features in the hope that travellers will be encouraged to stay at the property. More objective sources are the various official guides and manuals. These include the *Hotel and Travel Index* and the *OAG Travel Planner Hotel and Motel Red Book*. This information is no longer available in print form. Agencies interested in these publications must now obtain them online.

Tours There are four sources of printed information on tour packages:

1. Brochures.
2. Tour manuals.
3. Catalogues.
4. Tariffs.

Most of the major tour operators, such as American Express Travel and Thomas Cook, put out glamorous brochures each season with listings of rates and itineraries. At one time a variety of tours were described in the *Consolidated Tour Manual* and the *Official Tour Directory*.

ILLUSTRATION 14–1

Tour brochures are informative marketing tools that contain attractive photographs with listings of rates and itineraries.
SOURCE: Thomson Nelson.

Today, however, most tour information is accessed from the tour company's website. In the United States and Canada, mail-order catalogues listing tour packages have been introduced. Catalogues have been used successfully in Europe for many years.

Travel agencies have access to tariffs, which quote net tour prices. The net price is the noncommissionable price that the supplier charges the retailer. The retailer then adds a markup before quoting the price to the client. Individual tour operators issue confidential tariffs. These provide listings of tours and excursions, giving net prices.

Telephone Service and the Reservations Centre

With a nonautomated reservations system, after the travel counsellor obtains the relevant information and discusses options with the client, the counsellor is ready to make the reservation. Let's return to our earlier example. The client wanted to fly from Charlottetown to Calgary. The counsellor at Alpha Travel informed her that two airlines had connecting flights to Calgary on the day she wanted to travel. She chose the 9:30 a.m. Air Canada flight because it was the most convenient time for her.

The counsellor then telephoned the Air Canada reservations centre to determine whether there was a seat available on the preferred flight. There was, so the client's name went on the **manifest**, or passenger list. If the flight had been full, her name could have been placed on the wait list. (A **wait list** is like the numbering system used in a bakery or delicatessen. As each passenger on the list is accommodated, or cancels, the others move up one place.) As an alternative to the wait list, she could have decided to fly at a later time or with a different airline.

The counsellor probably used a toll-free number to call Air Canada. Most major suppliers—especially airlines, hotel chains, and car rental companies—have a toll-free number. This number allows consumers and retailers to call the reservations centre free of charge from anywhere in the country. A supplier without a toll-free number is at a distinct disadvantage. Only a few very small suppliers don't have one.

Toll-free numbers not only help suppliers but also offer considerable savings to the travel agency. During the course of a working day, a travel counsellor in a nonautomated setting often makes more than 100 calls to suppliers. Bills for long-distance calls can quickly add up, eating into an agency's profits. When all of those calls are to toll-free numbers, they don't cost the agency a cent.

Once a reservation has been made and a fare or rate established in a nonautomated setting, some sort of document must be issued. These include standard airline documents, rail and motorcoach tickets, and vouchers or coupons to be exchanged for car rentals, package tours, cruises, and hotel accommodations. In a nonautomated agency, this process is often done manually.

The use of airline tickets for domestic travel was discontinued in Canada in 2003. Today, travel agencies issue an e-ticket (where clients are provided only with a receipt or confirmation number) for such reservations. Clients then show appropriate identification at the airline check-in desk, where they are issued with a boarding pass. The International Air Transport Association (IATA) set a deadline of June 1, 2008 for its more than 230 member airlines worldwide to end the use of paper tickets and convert entirely to e-tickets.

The Internet in a Nonautomated Travel Agency

Few travel agencies today are completely manual in their operations. Almost all have a computer system with basic business applications and access to the Internet. All of the information that was previously available in print form can now be found on the Internet, either free or by subscription. Many supplier websites allow travel counsellors to

ILLUSTRATION 14–2
Reservations centres handle calls from the public and from the travel industry.
SOURCE: PhotoDisc Blue/Getty Images.

search and book travel arrangements online, without the need to telephone the reservations department.

The Internet has also permitted travel agencies to lower their long-distance telephone costs. Using VoIP (Voice over Internet Protocol) and software developed by companies such as Skype, individuals and businesses can make local and long-distance telephone calls using a computer connected to the Internet. This reduces or eliminates the cost of the telephone call for one or both parties.

Check Your Product Knowledge

1. What type of information does an agent need before booking a flight?

2. In a nonautomated setting, where could an agent find information on (a) ground transportation, (b) hotels, and (c) tours?

3. How are toll-free numbers useful for (a) suppliers and (b) travel agents?

4. How has the Internet changed the way travel counsellors search for product information?

AUTOMATED INFORMATION SYSTEMS

Today, with the Internet, we can distinguish between traditional automated information systems and contemporary systems. When we talk about "traditional" automated systems in the tourism industry, we are referring mainly to airline computer systems. These systems have been developed to facilitate operations in two distinct areas:

- *External functions*, which relate directly to the consumer (such as reservations and ticketing).
- *Internal functions*, which relate to the efficient operation of the company itself (such as accounting and management).

In this section, we will look closely at the external functions of the computer systems.

The Global Distribution System

A **global distribution system (GDS)** can be visualized as a huge general store that stocks an almost unlimited variety of travel products and services in one central location. The owner of the store is most commonly an airline. The airline sells not only its own products but also the flights of other airlines, as well as the products of travel suppliers such as hotels, car rental companies, and tour operators. Until recently, a GDS was referred to as a **computer reservations system (CRS)**. However, the term "global

ILLUSTRATION 14–3

Travel counsellors can use a GDS to obtain information on flight schedules, fares, and availability; to make reservations; and even to print tickets and travel documents at the touch of a button.

SOURCE: Holden TPL/itstock/First Light.

distribution system" more accurately describes its function. The term "CRS" is still commonly used for the systems used by individual nonairline suppliers, such as hotels and car rental agencies.

A GDS offers both informational and transactional functions. *Informational* functions allow the travel counsellor to obtain up-to-date information on schedules, availability, and fares. In this way, the GDS replaces printed reference sources. *Transactional* functions allow the travel counsellor to print invoices and itineraries, and to book reservations. A number of travel agencies have joined the Travel Agents Computer Society, which provides information on system suppliers and vendors.

An agency's in-house computers consolidate the many steps that must be taken in making manual reservations. You will recall that a travel counsellor, working in a nonautomated setting, had to first consult printed reference sources, then call the airline to confirm availability and make the reservation. A counsellor in today's automated agency can communicate directly with the GDS through the computer keyboard. Information on routes, schedules, fares, and availability for participating airlines is displayed instantly on the screen. The counsellor can make the reservation by pushing a few keys and create a **passenger name record (PNR)** for the client. The PNR is a complete record of the client's travel plans, which can be retrieved at any time for additions, changes, or cancellations. Its equivalent in the nonautomated system was the reservations card.

A computer linked to an in-house printer can automatically print boarding passes and invoices or itineraries as soon as the flight reservation is made. Reservations for hotels, rental cars, and other services can be made at the

same time through the same GDS. All this additional information is stored on the PNR.

The obvious advantage to GDSs is the saving in time they allow. A counsellor can complete the reservation and ticketing process in a fraction of the time it used to take. This makes for increased productivity and sales.

The Airline as a Vendor

The airlines were the first organizations to develop automated reservations systems, and they have remained firmly in the lead as vendors of GDSs. As the **host vendor**, the operating airline receives revenue from three main sources:

- Participating airlines, which pay to have their schedules displayed through the GDS.
- Nonairline suppliers, such as hotels and car rental agencies, which pay to have their services displayed.
- Travel agencies that subscribe to the GDS.

Each GDS allows access only to those suppliers that have agreements with the host vendor. Information on nonparticipating suppliers must be secured by other means.

Before we consider the different systems available, we'll look briefly at how the airlines developed their own GDSs. In 1976, United, American, and TWA began installing their own competing reservations systems in travel agencies throughout the United States. These sophisticated GDSs differed from earlier systems in that they allowed access to several airlines (not just to the host airline) as well as to nonairline suppliers. Most agencies today subscribe to one or more of the major airline GDSs.

Major American GDS Vendors The original airline GDSs introduced in 1976 were Apollo (United), Sabre (American), and PARS (TWA). These were later joined by DATAS II (Delta) and System One (Eastern). In 1987, Northwest became a co-owner of PARS with TWA.

Sabre (Semi-Automated Business Research Environment) is the world's largest private real-time computer network and travel information database. It is the most popular GDS among travel agencies, with over 50 000 agency locations worldwide. The heart of the Sabre network is the Tulsa Computer Center in Tulsa, Oklahoma, which processes more than 100 million transactions a day. Using Sabre, a counsellor can check schedules and make reservations for more than 400 airlines worldwide, book rooms at about 77 000 hotel properties, and reserve vehicles from 32 car rental agencies. The system also allows counsellors to book 35 railroads including Amtrak and Eurail, 220 tour operators, 11 cruise lines, and tickets to Broadway shows. You can even charter a private jet through Sabre. Sabre is now a separate entity, having been spun off from AMR Corp., the parent firm of American Airlines.

The Sabre Holdings website has links to the Sabre Travel Network (for travel agencies, travel suppliers,

ILLUSTRATION 14–4

This Galileo International reservation system computer is connected to a network of over 100 000 terminals in 47 000 travel agencies around the world.

SOURCE: Photodisc Blue/Getty Images.

corporations, and government agencies), Sabre Airline Solutions (for airlines, airports, and government agencies) and Travelocity.com (a consumer travel service where one can book travel online).

Apollo, the operating subsidiary in the United States of Galileo International, was the major competitor of Sabre. It had similar capabilities to those of Sabre. In 1997, the three owners of Apollo (United Airlines with 77 percent, US Airways with 21 percent, and Air Canada with 2 percent) sold their shares to Galileo International for approximately CDN$1 billion. Galileo International was purchased by Cendant Corporation (now Travelport Inc.), which sold it to The Blackstone Group in 2006. Today, Galileo provides travel agencies at 49 000 locations with access to 425 airlines for schedules, fare information, and bookings. Galileo also offers access to 77 000 hotels, 21 car rental companies, and all major cruise lines.

In 1990, PARS and DATAS II joined forces to create Worldspan, a GDS vendor with 10 000 agency subscribers. This GDS was purchased by Travelport in 2007. Worldspan is the smallest GDS.

Canadian GDS Vendors The GDS for Air Canada is Galileo Canada, which has about 3000 travel agencies and 10 000 terminals. In 2001, WestJet added the Sabre system, but also retained its own in-house reservation system. Current estimates are that about 60 percent of airline bookings through a GDS in Canada are made through Sabre, compared to Galileo's 36 percent.

Foreign GDS Vendors A number of foreign airlines sell their own GDSs; other foreign airlines use American systems. The use of American systems in overseas markets has been a source of concern for foreign airlines, especially in Europe and Canada. Many European GDSs can offer more

complete local listings, but they cannot match the worldwide information listings and reservations capabilities of Sabre, Galileo, and Worldspan. The best-known international system is Amadeus (formed in 1987 by Air France, Lufthansa, Iberia, and SAS) which gives over 94 000 travel agencies access to over 500 airlines, 22 car rental companies, almost 77 000 hotels, 17 cruise lines, and other travel providers.

Co-hosts and Shared Databases An airline that does not have its own GDS can participate in one at one of four levels:

1. The least expensive level permits a display of the airline's schedules but not availability.
2. The next level permits a display of schedules and availability, but reservations cannot be confirmed instantly.
3. The third level permits the airline to provide instant confirmation of reservations.
4. The most expensive level permits the airline to provide the same information and services as those offered by the host airline.

An airline that participates at the fourth level is known as a **co-host**. Co-hosts pay part of the cost of developing the system. In return, they get to share the database, and their information is given preferential display over other carriers.

The Issue of Bias Bias has been a controversial topic in the automated travel industry ever since the first GDSs were introduced in 1976. Bias refers to the preferential display of host-carrier flight schedules on the video display over the schedules of competing airlines. For example, a travel counsellor requests flight availability from Los Angeles to Miami. The first display shows the flights of the host carrier. The agent could request to see the second, third, and fourth displays for additional flights, but studies indicate that most bookings are made from the first display. If an airline did display its own flights first, as in this example, the company would be guilty of bias.

Deregulation of the GDS

Until recently, Transport Canada regulated airline GDSs in Canada to ensure adequate competition. The regulations required Canadian airlines to be in every system, and for the GDS to be unbiased. However, in 2004, the government amended the regulations to eliminate all CRS contract terms and the sale of marketing data. The deregulation removed federal rules, such as standard pricing, and allowed for wider distribution of Web fares and more competition. These changes meant that airlines could choose which GDSs they would participate in. Thus, it was possible that travel agencies would be forced to purchase more than one GDS to ensure that they had access to all the information and reservations capability they needed.

In practice, however, the Internet has driven agencies to supplier websites and specialized multiple browser sites such as AgentShopper, rather than purchasing multiple GDSs. Several suppliers now offer higher commissions and/or lower prices through their websites than are available through a GDS. Also, a 2003 American Society of Travel Agents study found that the number of agents who bypassed the GDS and telephone in favour of booking entirely online had increased from 50 percent to 76 percent since 2001. More than 50 percent of Air Canada's bookings in Canada are now generated through the airline's dedicated travel agency website. At WestJet, about 70 percent of agent bookings are made via the Internet, compared to 14 percent through a GDS.

Teleticketing

Teleticketing, in use since 1960, is the simplest and least expensive form of automation available to travel agencies. It permits subscribers to have airline tickets printed on a machine in the agency office. Teleticketing machines are linked to the airline GDS by telephone line. When making a reservation by phone, the travel counsellor can ask for the ticketing information to be relayed directly to the in-house teleticketing machine. Unlike automated reservations systems, teleticketing allows only one-way communication—from the airline system to the agency. (GDSs allow two-way communication between the airline and the agency.)

Teleticketing machines are useful for small agencies that do not have the volume of business to warrant the expense of a GDS. Larger agencies that have subscribed to GDSs since 1976 usually keep their teleticketing machines, if they own them. Even though GDSs linked to printers have made them obsolete, they are still handy if the in-house computer breaks down.

Satellite Ticket Printer

The **satellite ticket printer (STP)** made its first appearance in 1986. STPs allow travel counsellors to deliver tickets electronically to a client's premises by a process similar to teleticketing. However, travel agencies, not airlines, run STPs. The machines have proved especially popular at locations such as industrial parks. STPs have been the fastest-growing category of travel agency location during the past decade.

Electronic Ticket Delivery Network

Another form of automation is the **electronic ticket delivery network (ETDN)**. These ticket printers enable travel agencies to make fast deliveries to travellers, especially business travellers, who need same-day or next-day tickets. ETDNs are similar to STPs but are not owned by travel agencies. In the near future, ETDN ticket printers will be found in such varied locations as hotels, shopping malls, office buildings, and supermarkets.

Automated Ticketing Machine

Automated ticketing machines (ATMs) directly connected to a GDS are another recent development. ATMs are owned and operated by individual airlines. By inserting a credit card into the ATM, a customer can gain access to flight information, make a reservation, and receive a boarding pass. ATMs are found in major airports; it is predicted that self-service machines will eventually be in supermarkets, shopping centres, hotel lobbies, and banks. We can also expect to see machines that are shared by a number of different suppliers. These will allow consumers to buy a complete travel package from a single automated location.

Check Your Product Knowledge

1. Why do travel agencies subscribe to GDSs?
2. Name the major GDS available in Canada.
3. Name the three major GDSs available in the United States.
4. What is meant by "bias"?
5. How do teleticketing machines, STPs, ETDNs, and automated ticketing machines differ?

CONTEMPORARY DEVELOPMENTS IN AUTOMATED SYSTEMS

Among the recent developments in automated systems are ticketless travel, electronic tickets, and online reservations.

Ticketless Travel The concept of ticketless travel is not new. For decades, passengers boarded buses and trains at smaller stops and purchased tickets on board. In the 1990s, several "low-cost" airlines such as WestJet went ticketless in order to save on reservation costs. An airline using a ticketless system can save as much as 10 percent of its operating costs. There are various systems, including:

- Passengers turn up at the airline gate without a reservation and, after paying for their flight, receive a boarding pass.
- Passengers telephone an airline and receive a confirmation number for a flight. When they arrive at the airport, the confirmation number is verified and a

boarding pass is issued. The boarding pass is numbered in accordance with the number of seats on the airplane.

- Passengers contact a travel agency. The travel counsellor issues only an itinerary with flight information and the confirmation number, received from the airline. The passenger goes to the airport, presents the confirmation number, and pays the fare. At that time the passenger receives the boarding pass for the flight.

Electronic Tickets In the spring of 1997, Air Canada ran several newspaper ads for "the new and amazing electronic ticket (e-ticket)." For **e-ticketing,** passengers call either the airline or a travel agency to book a flight and receive a confirmation number. The travel itinerary/receipt is then faxed or mailed to the passenger. At the airport, passengers show identification at the check-in counter or at the gate to receive a boarding pass. If the airport permits it, passengers with carry-on luggage only can go directly to the gate; passengers with check-in luggage must check in at the counter. Many airlines permit passengers to use the Internet to check-in in advance, select a seat, and print their boarding pass. In future, passengers will commonly be able to use a PDA or cellphone for these actions and will also be able to generate an electronic boarding pass.

The e-ticket is similar to some of the ticketless travel systems. In fact, Air Canada advertised this method as "hassle-free, easy-to-use, cutting-edge technology, not to mention a convenient and time-saving ticketless way to travel into the coming millennium."

There are some problems with e-tickets. One is that it is difficult to arrange interline travel (i.e., a trip requiring more than one airline) with e-tickets. The main difficulty is how to link the different reservations systems. Another problem involves passengers stranded by a storm or other

ILLUSTRATION 14–5

Many passengers today fly on an e-ticket and simply collect a boarding pass at the airport.

SOURCE: © HIRB/Index Stock Imagery.

difficulties who try to switch to another airline. Usually, the e-ticket has to be converted to paper before it can be endorsed to the new airline. The airlines and the Airlines Reporting Corporation in the United States are working on rectifying these problems. Other gaps include airlines and routes that do not operate e-ticketing, and payment for excess baggage vouchers and exchange fees. Pre-paid Ticket Advices (PTAs) and tickets on departure are also not e-ticketable. In the meantime, IATA mandated that from June 1, 2008 all its 230 member airlines would issue only e-tickets. As a consequence, Sabre launched a product that allowed agents to book flights and other transactions that were not yet e-ticketable.

Online Reservations Systems Since travellers can make reservations on the Internet, many now plan and book their flights, hotels, and rental cars from their home or office computer. Reservations must be confirmed by credit card. Because of concerns about the security of credit card information on the Internet, many companies are using "secure" systems (denoted by "https" in the address bar) for such transactions. Some consumers still prefer calling a toll-free number to give their credit card information after making their reservations online. An e-ticket is then issued for later pickup. The passenger must present the credit card used to book the reservation, and sometimes also photo identification, to pick up a boarding pass.

The Internet

The Internet is now the fastest-growing means of information transfer. Three aspects of this communications method are of particular concern to the tourism industry. The first is the Internet itself, which includes e-mail, file transfer protocol (FTP, for transferring documents), and information services such as newsgroups.

The second aspect is the World Wide Web, which serves as a repository of graphics and text. People use browser software (e.g., Mozilla Firefox or Microsoft Explorer) to access information, data, and graphical images from websites on many different topics. A uniform resource locator (URL) identifies the address (e.g., www.address.com); in Canada, the URL may be www.address.ca. A new extension (.travel) was introduced in 2007 to serve the needs of the travel industry. These companies would have a URL such as www.address.travel.

The third aspect is called an intranet. Intranets are internal networks—in effect, private websites. A company might create an intranet to make policies and procedures manuals available to employees, and employees might resort to the company's intranet to ask questions about products and services provided by the company, to verify inventory and check prices, and to learn about new products and prices. An intranet allows all of the company's employees to communicate with one another, even if their offices are in different countries.

Tourism Sales through Internet Channels

When data analyses showed that Internet sales represented only 2 percent of total Canadian retail sales in 1999, some analysts were disappointed. Although still a small percentage of total retail sales, Statistics Canada reported that B2C Internet sales in Canada had reached $12.8 billion in 2007, an increase of 61 percent from 2005. Table 14–1 shows that in 2005 travel surpassed books, magazines, and newspapers in online sales, and that the gap increased in 2007. Stock market analysts say that the large online travel sites (e.g., Expedia and Travelocity) are able to make money for several reasons: The services offered do not have to be inventoried, so warehouses aren't necessary, and distribution can be rather straightforward, in that these sites have suppliers lined up and customers at hand.

There has been tremendous growth in e-commerce in the past decade. The first websites were mainly for promotion. How can tourism suppliers and intermediaries establish a presence in the new marketspace in such a way that consumers reach out to and interact with them? Corporate websites and marketing websites are two available methods. A **corporate website** provides information about the company and its services to potential tourists. It is not designed to be directly (i.e., electronically) interactive. Such websites often feature pages called About Us, Mission, History, Investor Relations, Services and Products, and News Releases.

Marketing websites are designed to encourage consumers to purchase the company's products. Many tourism suppliers and intermediaries in the distribution channel have websites. Traditional travel agencies have gone online, and "all-clicks" travel agencies have been established. Firms in the various tourism sectors have developed a Web presence, and governments promote their cities, regions, and countries through websites. Two online services worth noting are new online travel agencies (such as Expedia, Travelocity, and Orbitz), and wireless application protocol (WAP). A brief overview of these is provided at the end of this section, and more detailed information is presented in Chapter 16.

Traditional Travel Agencies Online Most of the big travel agencies have gone online. Uniglobe.com was one of the first to set up on the Internet, in 1996. Many travel agency websites direct you to the local franchise in your community.

New Online Travel Agencies Hundreds of travel agencies have opened up online, but only around 20 have done any volume of business. Two of the high-volume agencies are Expedia and Travelocity. Travelocity is a subsidiary of Sabre, the leading GDS firm and is the world's largest online travel agency and third-largest e-commerce site. It can access 95 percent of the seats sold by over 400 airlines, 32 car rental firms, and the rooms of about 77 000 hotels. It also offers more than 5000 cruise and vacation packages. Its database provides information on a vast array of destinations.

Expedia went online in the United States in October 1996. It has localized versions in 15 countries, including

TABLE 14–1 What Canadians Bought on the Internet, 2005 and 2007

Product	2005	2007
Books, magazines, and newspapers	35.4	36.8
Travel arrangements	36.4	44.5
Computer software	20.2	19.7
Automotive products	5.6	8.2
Music (CDs, tapes, MP3s)	16.4	22.1
Clothing, jewellery, and accessories	24.8	29.5
Computer hardware	12.1	13.4
Consumer electronics	15.9	19.6
Other entertainment (e.g., tickets)	25.0	32.5
Housewares (furniture and appliances)	8.3	10.8
Videos, DVDs	13.5	13.8
Food, condiments, and beverages	3.4	4.5
Toys and games	11.7	14.6
Prescription drugs, health, beauty, vitamins	9.4	9.6
Flowers as gifts	13.2	15.9
Sports equipment	6.6	9.2

SOURCE: Adapted from Statistics Canada, CANSIM, Summary table 358-0136, extracted May 2008, http://www40.statcan.ca/l01/cst01/comm24.htm.

the United Kingdom, Germany, and Canada. Expedia focuses on providing branded travel services for leisure and small-business travellers. Through its websites, consumers can gather information on more than 450 airlines, 40 000 lodging properties, and all major rental car companies, and then book those products and services.

Orbitz Worldwide was purchased in 2004 by Cendant Corporation (now Travelport), which also owns Galileo, Worldspan, Cheap Tickets, ebookers, and HotelClub. Orbitz Worldwide enables users to examine the airfares of about 400 airlines and make bookings at about 80 000 hotels and 13 car rental companies.

Although consumer Internet bookings for travel products continue to rise, satisfaction with the service provided by large agencies such as Expedia, Travelocity, and Orbitz has levelled off or even declined. In 2008, *TravelMole* (an online travel industry newsletter) published the results of a study conducted by the American Customer Satisfaction Index (ACSI), which stated that customer satisfaction with large online agencies had fallen by 1.3 percent. At the same time, satisfaction with e-commerce in other areas had risen. There have also been several articles reporting that dealing with a live travel agent still provides the best service and lowest prices.

Internet Service Providers (ISPs) Many of the big ISPs have travel information on their home pages and provide links to travel websites where users can make bookings. One such ISP is AOL Canada. Travel is one of the topics listed on AOL's home page menu. The website of AOL Travel claims to have access to 21 000 destinations, 103 000 hotels, and 35 000 restaurants. The same home page sometimes runs block advertisements for travel links.

Firms in Various Tourism Sectors These firms are the traditional suppliers of tourism products and services. Most such firms that have websites originally developed them for promotional purposes, and then later added transactional capabilities. In some ways these websites are competing with the new online travel agencies; that being said, most firms recognize the need for multiple distribution channels. Some examples of organizations from selected sectors that have Internet websites:

- Transportation: Air Canada, Greyhound, VIA Rail
- Accommodation: Delta Hotels, Fairmont Hotels & Resorts, Sheraton Hotels
- Food and beverage: Tim Hortons, Swiss Chalet (Cara)
- Attractions: Marineland, Canada's Wonderland
- Events: Canadian Football League (Grey Cup), National Capital Commission (Winterlude)
- Adventure tourism and recreation: Trans Canada Trail
- Tourism services (retail): Tilley Endurables

Tourism Services (other than retail) This electronic distribution channel is mainly for informational and promotional purposes but usually also has a transactional component so that information and promotional materials can be transmitted or sent to the inquirer. Good examples are the websites of Canada's provinces and the American states.

Wireless Application Protocol As the name suggests, **wireless application protocol (WAP)** enables consumers to access websites without a telephone line or a computer. It allows them to use handheld devices such as cellphones, pagers, and personal digital assistants (PDAs) to access travel and tourism information on the Web. Until late 2000, WAP technology could be used only for information purposes. Now more opportunities are available to book travel and accommodation reservations using WAP. Some airlines foresee wireless check-ins becoming available.

Check Your Product Knowledge

1. What are the advantages of ticketless travel to the airlines? To passengers?
2. Should consumers still be concerned about Web security when using credit cards?
3. Why are travel and tourism products and services one of the few success stories in e-commerce?
4. Why did nontraditional firms online (e.g., Expedia and Travelocity) become the leaders in e-commerce?

OTHER USES OF AUTOMATION

So far we have focused on the uses of automation for information, reservation, and ticketing services, with specific reference to airline GDSs. In this section, you will learn how computer technology has been applied to back-office functions. You will also learn about the CRSs of nonairline suppliers, such as hotels and car rental agencies.

Back-Office Systems

Back-office systems are found behind the scenes and are concerned less with customers than with the efficient operation of the agency. They are used mainly for accounting and management purposes. Accounting functions include keeping track of receivables and payables, issuing cheques, keeping general ledgers, and preparing financial statements. Management functions include compiling reports for the agency's managers to review.

Like GDSs, automated back-office systems increase efficiency and productivity. Most of them are linked to one or more GDSs. In other words, information can be "exported" from the GDS to the accounting/management system. When a counsellor makes a reservation through a

GDS, the information is automatically relayed to the back-office system, which records the sale, notes the commission, credits the counsellor who made the sale, and compiles reports from the data supplied.

Uses of Automation by Nonairline Suppliers

Earlier in this chapter, you read that airline GDSs can display the products and services of nonairline suppliers. A travel counsellor with access to a GDS can, for example, make room reservations for most major domestic hotel chains.

Some suppliers, especially hotels and car rental agencies, have developed their own automated reservations systems. The Holidex system at Holiday Inn, introduced in 1964, was a pioneer in hotel CRSs. It has evolved into a network of 4000 properties worldwide in 100 countries, with a central computer in Memphis, Tennessee. About 40 percent of all Holiday Inn reservations are made through Holidex. Sheraton, Hilton, Westin, and Delta hotels have also installed reservations systems.

Hotel employees at the client's request access hotel reservations systems. This request can be made by phone or in person. All hotel reservations systems operate on a single level, which means that only the services of the host vendor can be booked on individual CRSs. For example, reservations for a room in a Sheraton hotel cannot be made through the Holidex reservations system, nor can a flight reservation be made using a hotel system. This is an important difference between airline GDSs and hotel CRSs. The advantage of making a hotel reservation through a hotel system is that the hotel CRS has the most up-to-date information on its room availability.

Car rental reservations systems function in much the same way as hotel systems. For example, the Avis Wizard Direct Input Reservation System can be used for booking Avis cars only.

Amtrak has its own automated reservations system, known as Arrow. Initially, Arrow was purely informational, providing travel agents with information on train schedules and fares. However, travel agencies are now allowed to print Amtrak tickets, using the same standard ticket stock they use for airline tickets. Like the hotel and car rental CRSs, Arrow is a single-level system. VIA Rail implemented a more comprehensive automated reservations system in 1997, which was updated in 2004.

Check Your Product Knowledge

1. What are automated back-office systems used for?
2. How do hotel reservations systems differ from airline GDSs?

CAREER OPPORTUNITIES

All the major suppliers of travel services employ large staffs of **reservations agents**. In this section, we look at the work of these agents in the airline industry, the accommodation industry, the car rental industry, the tour industry, and the cruise industry.

The reservations systems of most suppliers are now computerized. Job applicants are expected to have a working knowledge of computers and computer terminology. Some of the larger suppliers offer training courses for new reservations agents to familiarize them with the GDS. Keyboarding skills are necessary for reservations agents, and office experience is helpful. The ability to speak English and French (or another language) is also an asset. Some suppliers prefer to hire applicants who have had two years of college or university; for others, a high-school diploma is sufficient.

Airline Reservations Agents Airline reservations staff typically work in a call centre environment at large central offices and spend much of their time in front of video displays. They take telephone calls from travel counsellors and consumers who want to book flights. Using a computer keyboard, they check flight schedules, availability, and fares, and then reserve seats for passengers.

Hotel Reservations Agents Hotel reservations staff work in reservations centres and front offices, where they answer telephone calls from travel counsellors, airlines, and members of the public requesting room reservations. The agent checks room availability on a video display and books accommodations accordingly.

ILLUSTRATION 14–6
Hotel reservations staff members work in reservations centres and in the front offices at lodging facilities. They respond to telephone and online contacts from travel counsellors, airlines, and people seeking accommodations.
SOURCE: Courtesy of Holiday Inn on King.

A DAY IN THE LIFE OF AN

Airline Reservations Agent

If you're planning a trip that involves flying, I may be the first person you contact—I'm a reservations agent with a major airline. The telephone and the computer are the main tools of my trade. In many ways, I am the airline's "voice." I represent the airline every time I answer the phone and deal with a caller. Every caller is a potential customer, whether that person is a travel counsellor, an individual passenger, or someone from a company's travel department.

It's my job to make sure that callers become customers. Since I am the first contact many callers have with the airline, it's very important that I deal with every call professionally, efficiently, and courteously.

Besides knowing when and where we fly, I also have a host of information available about flights offered by other airlines and about rental cars, tours, and hotels and motels. Many people who call for flight information are pleasantly surprised to discover that I can also arrange for rental cars and accommodations. I can even book them sightseeing tours. Our prices for these services are very competitive, since the airline negotiates bulk discounts with rental car companies, tour operators, and hotels and motels. Individuals might pay a lot more if they dealt with the suppliers themselves. So besides representing the airline and helping callers book seats on flights, I also sell the other services we offer.

These telephone sales are an important aspect of my job.

The computer I use at work enables me to access all the information I need to help callers. All the information about our flights, fares, arrival and departure times, and other services is entered into the computer. I can find out anything I need to know at the touch of a few keys. With a typical call, I first find out where the person wants to go and when he or she wants to depart. I also need to know the length of stay at the destination so that I can check to see whether we can offer special fares. Once I have that information, I can give the cost of travelling in first, business, and economy class. I also explain any special fares. The advance-purchase excursion fares, for example, are cheaper than economy fares, but they have several restrictions, including an advance payment requirement and a no-cancellation policy.

To make a reservation, I type the caller's name, address, and phone number into the computer. This file is called the passenger name record, or PNR. I specify the flight the caller is taking, noting the flight number, departure date and time, and arrival time. I also handle seat assignments. Most passengers request an aisle or a window seat. Others also want to know what type of plane they will be flying on. On our 747s, passengers who want more room can elect to sit in the back of the plane, where the side rows contain only two seats. Others may request seats at the front of each section, where there is more legroom. If there will be any small children travelling, I make special arrangements for them. Finally, I make arrangements for other passenger requests, such as special meals or a wheelchair to and from the aircraft. It's my job to process this information properly to ensure that the passenger has the best possible flight.

Since our airline provides reservations information 24 hours a day, 7 days a week, 365 days a year, I work several different shifts. I like the flexibility that gives me, and I enjoy sometimes being off during the week when everyone else is working. Though I enjoy my job, I like being part of a large organization that offers me several different career paths. I have the opportunity to build on what I have learned as a reservations agent, or I can continue in my present position. Reservations agents can go on to become sales representatives, or senior agents who supervise shifts and help set policy for the entire department.

I like helping people plan their business trips and vacations. I am always pleased when they benefit from all of the extras the airline has to offer, such as our discount accommodations and tours. Each year, a good reservations agent helps thousands of travellers get off to the right start. That's a big responsibility, but it's an interesting and challenging way to earn a living.

Car Rental Reservations Agents Car rental reservations staff members also work over the phone with travel counsellors, airlines, and the public. They check the availability of cars at the location requested. When making a reservation, they enter the length of time the car will be rented as well as the location to which the car will be returned. (Rental cars do not have to be dropped off at the same place they were picked up.) Any relevant flight information is also recorded.

Most car rental reservations systems are centralized. For example, Avis reservations agents work at the central Avis reservations office in Tulsa, Oklahoma.

Tour Operator Reservations Agents Reservations agents employed by tour operators work in much the same way as other reservations agents. They check the availability of tours and confirm reservations over the telephone.

Cruise Line Reservations Agents Reservations agents working for cruise lines explain to clients what the cruise line offers and when its various cruises will take place. They also take reservations and handle routine inquiries. Most cruise line reservations agents work with travel agencies or counsellors, not directly with consumers.

Computer Careers

The number of jobs available for reservations agents is expected to decline as a result of automation. Fewer agents will be needed to operate the computers. At the same time, however, automation in the tourism industry has opened up many computer-related careers. CRS vendors employ people to train those who have purchased their systems. They also employ programmers, equipment installers, service professionals, and sales and marketing representatives. All of these jobs generally require some experience with travel agency operations or airline reservations systems.

Website Development E-commerce has opened up a new career: creating, maintaining, and updating tourism websites. A knowledge of how to create such websites is important, but even more important is a knowledge of the tourism industry. People employed in this field are known as "webmasters."

Summary

- The channels of distribution in the tourism industry are being transformed by e-commerce.
- The tourism industry uses three main systems of distribution to move its products from producer to consumer: unilateral, bilevel, and multilevel.

- Regardless of the system used, identical products will usually cost the consumer the same amount.
- A single member of the distribution channel can sell products from other suppliers as well as the member's own products. More wholesale distributors are becoming retail distributors in the channel.
- The unilateral system involves the direct sale of travel products and services from supplier to consumer. This is known as business-to-consumer (B2C).
- The bilevel system most often involves a travel counsellor as intermediary. Sometimes the supplier pays the counsellor a commission. This may involve both B2B and B2C.
- The multilevel system involves the involvement of two or more intermediaries, most often a tour wholesaler and a retail travel agency.
- The tourism industry depends on a continuous flow of up-to-date information from supplier to consumer.
- In a nonautomated agency, travel counsellors have access to information through printed reference sources. Reservations are made by telephone.
- A nonautomated agency may have a computer system for business applications and access to the Internet. In such agencies, travel counsellors research and make reservations through the Internet, either directly on the supplier's website or through multiple browser software such as AgentShopper.
- In an automated agency, travel counsellors have access to information through a global distribution system (GDS). Printed reference sources are used for supplementary information.
- A GDS allows travel counsellors to make reservations and to ticket electronically.
- Airlines are the principal vendors of global distributions systems.
- The major international reservations systems are Sabre, Galileo, Worldspan, and Amadeus.
- Air Canada now uses Galileo Canada, and WestJet uses Sabre.
- GDSs allow access to participating airlines and nonairline suppliers.
- Tickets can be delivered electronically to various locations by teleticketing machines, satellite ticket printers (STPs), electronic ticket delivery networks (ETDNs), and automated ticketing machines (ATMs).
- Recent developments include ticketless travel, electronic ticketing, and online reservation systems.
- Internet distribution channels have developed rapidly and have different types of intermediaries: traditional travel agencies online; new online travel agencies, including those developed by GDS firms; Internet service providers that provide links to travel sites on their home pages; firms in various tourism sectors; government promoters; and wireless application protocol (WAP).
- Automated back-office systems, marketed by CRS vendors as well as independent companies, have been developed to perform travel agency accounting and management functions.

- Back-office systems interface with one or more reservations systems.
- Many hotel chains and car rental agencies have their own automated reservations systems.

Key Terms

automated ticketing machines (ATM)   p. 327
back-office system   p. 330
bias   p. 326
business-to-business (B2B)   p. 319
business-to-consumer (B2C)   p. 319
co-host   p. 326
commission   p. 317
computer reservations system (CRS)   p. 324
corporate website   p. 329
demanders   p. 318
e-commerce   p. 316
e-procurement   p. 320
e-ticketing   p. 328
electronic ticket delivery network (ETDN)   p. 327
global distribution system (GDS)   p. 324
host vendor   p. 325
intermediaries   p. 318
manifest   p. 323
marketing website   p. 329
multiple channels   p. 321
passenger name record (PNR)   p. 325
reservations agent   p. 331
retail distributors   p. 319
satellite ticket printer (STP)   p. 327
specialty channeller   p. 321
teleticketing   p. 327
travel counsellor   p. 318
video marketing   p. 320
wait list   p. 323
wholesale distributors   p. 319
wireless application protocol (WAP)   p. 330

Internet Connections

AgentShopper
www.agentshopper.com   p. 317

Air Canada
www.aircanada.ca   p. 319

Airline Tariff Publishing Company (ATPCO)
www.atpco.net   p. 322

Amadeus
www.amadeus.com   p. 326

American Express Travel
http://travel.americanexpress.com/travel/
personal/?1   p. 321

AOL Canada
www.aol.ca   p. 330

Cruise Line International Association (CLIA)
www.cruising.org   p. 323

Expedia
www.expedia.ca   p. 316

Galileo Canada
galileo.com/galileo/en-ca/?cc=y   p. 326

Official Airline Guide
www.oag.com   p. 322

Orbitz
www.orbitz.com   p. 316

Sabre
www.sabre.com   p. 325

Sabre Travel Network
www.sabretravelnetwork.com   p. 316

Skype
www.skype.com   p. 324

Thomas Cook
www.thomascook.ca   p. 323

Travelocity
www.travelocity.ca   p. 316

TravelMole
www.travelmole.com   p. 330

Travelport
www.travelport.com   p. 326

Uniglobe.com
www.uniglobe.com   p. 316

VIA Rail (Canada)
www.viarail.ca   p. 322

Walt Disney World
www.disneyworld.com   p. 320

WestJet
www.westjet.com   p. 326

WORKSHEET 14–1 Specialty Channeller

Imagine that you work as a specialty channeller, who creates packages and tours for special-interest groups. Use brochures, tour manuals, catalogues, other printed references, and/or websites to find a package or tour for each of the following groups. In the space provided, briefly describe the package or tour and the reference(s) you used.

1. Railroad travel and history buffs

_____

_____

2. Wine connoisseurs

_____

_____

3. Bird watchers

_____

_____

4. Fans of the Toronto Maple Leafs living outside Ontario

_____

_____

5. Country music fans

_____

_____

6. People who want to see the aurora borealis (Northern Lights)

_____

_____

7. Enthusiasts of the plays of Shakespeare

_____

_____

8. Single-again people (widows/widowers/divorcees) in their 40s and 50s

_____

_____

9. Golf week special (at least one new course every day plus socializing)

_____

_____

10. North Americans, Europeans, and Asians interested in aboriginal people(s)

_____

_____

WORKSHEET 14–2 Distributing the Travel Product

As you have read, there are three main types of distribution: unilateral, bilevel, and multilevel. Read each situation below. On the line to the left, write the type of distribution system being used to bring travel products to the consumer.

_____ 1. Doris Skeleton, living in Vancouver, called a toll-free number to reserve a room at the Fairmont Royal York in Toronto.

_____ 2. Robert Anthony in Chicago called a travel agency in Edmonton that had an advertisement in a travel magazine for a Yukon tour in which a two-night stop would be made at a particular residence in a small community, with a good chance to see the aurora borealis.

_____ 3. Ed and Marie O'Hara went shopping at the biggest mall in London, Ontario, and purchased a television set at Wal-Mart and two airplane tickets to Ireland at a boutique travel agency, located in Wal-Mart.

_____ 4. Marguerite Tremblay had to fly to Winnipeg at the last minute for a business meeting. She was able to purchase a seat from an automated ticketing machine in the airport terminal.

_____ 5. After browsing through a tour catalogue of summer trips, Jane Oram decided to go on the 17-day Grand Alpine tour. Mercury Travel, a small travel agency in the mall, helped her make the arrangements.

_____ 6. Ian Mackellar of Halifax stopped in at VIA Rail's office in the Halifax railway station, next to the historic Westin Nova Scotian Hotel, to pick up tickets for his trip to Ottawa.

_____ 7. Sally Radford booked and paid for a Caribbean cruise on a cruise line website. She then booked a flight from Toronto to Miami on an airline website.

_____ 8. African Safaris, Inc., helped Troy and Amanda Burton plan their adventure trip to Kenya.

_____ 9. When Luke Chan booked a flight to San Francisco, the airline reservations agent also reserved a rental car and a hotel room for him.

_____ 10. Barbara Wolfe works for a large corporation. She makes all her travel arrangements—business and pleasure—through the company travel department.

Objectives

When you have completed this chapter, you should be able to:

- Describe the development of the package tour.
- List the components of a package tour.
- Discuss the role of the tour operator.
- Summarize the benefits of package travel.
- Distinguish among independent, hosted, and escorted tours.
- Classify tours according to destination and purpose.
- Explain why age is an important factor in defining the traveller.

- Describe the work of a tour manager.
- Explain how tours are regulated.
- Show how a package tour is put together.
- Give reasons for the popularity of charter travel.
- Distinguish between private and public charters.
- Diagram the distribution channels of the tour industry.
- List the career opportunities in the package tour industry.

The travel trade sector is composed of tour wholesalers and tour operators, covered in this chapter, and retail travel agencies, discussed in Chapter 16.

For Canadians, the **sunspot stayput tour** (i.e., round-trip charter flight, round trip from the airport to the hotel, seven nights' resort accommodation) to Florida, the Caribbean, or Mexico is the most prominent travel product in the marketplace. About 80 percent of tour operators' revenues come from sales to leisure travellers, and the vast majority is for foreign destination travel. Statistics Canada data reveal that only about 2 percent of nonbusiness trips are domestic package tours.

The tour and charter component of the travel trade sector in Canada is diverse and fragmented. Air Transat A.T. is one Canadian firm that has followed a strategy of vertical integration (owning several components in the distribution channel) to specialize in organizing, marketing, and distributing holiday travel. It has subsidiaries in the following areas: air carriers, hotel management, outbound tour operators, inbound tour operators, distribution, and travel agencies. In 2000, it started exitnow.ca (originally named "exit.ca"), a transactional website devoted to vacation travel. It has partnerships with seven tour operators and access to over 80 percent of Canadian vacation inventory.

PACKAGE TOURS: LESS AGGRAVATION, MORE SAVINGS

It's one thing to decide to go on a vacation, but quite another to organize the trip. Many people don't have the time or the inclination to plan a tour for themselves. They prefer to have somebody else make the decisions and the arrangements. For this reason among others, the package tour came into being. Package tours offer tourists pre-arranged transportation, accommodations, meals, and other vacation preparations—all at a predetermined price. They take some of the aggravation out of travel and usually provide significant cost savings as well.

More Canadians are turning to package tours. Today the package tour industry is one of the faster-growing segments of the travel industry. Until recently, major tour operators offered a limited range of domestic package tours for sale. The Canadian tourism industry is now creating a wider variety of domestic packaging alternatives for Canadians, which has led to growth in this segment. In this chapter, you learn about the many different kinds of tours, discover some reasons for their popularity, and read about the career opportunities that the package tour industry presents.

No Detail Too Minor

Tour East Holidays Canada Inc.

In the 1970s, Rita Tsang came to Canada to study at the University of Toronto and hoped later to start a business. Like many foreign students, she found that the high cost of airline tickets meant that her visits home to Hong Kong were infrequent, which led to the opportunity to start a business earlier than she expected. Recognizing the need in Toronto's Chinese community for affordable travel to Hong Kong and unable to find an inexpensive alternative to full-fare tickets, Tsang, together with her husband and sister, started a company to offer discounted tickets to that destination.

Tour East Holidays was founded in Toronto in 1976. Since then, it has grown to become Canada's largest wholesaler of travel to the Asia-Pacific region. Today, Tour East has offices across Canada, the United States, and China that annually sell over $400 million in travel products and services to more than 100 000 customers. With over 170 employees and an annual growth rate exceeding 35 percent, Tour East Holidays is one of Canada's most successful companies.

Tsang and her partners invested $50 000 and set up business originally as East Asian Travel. Initially, they purchased large blocks of seats at wholesale prices from airlines that flew to Hong Kong and other Asian destinations. They then sold these seats at a discount, concentrating initially on the Chinese and student community.

Within two years of startup, China relaxed its restrictions on foreign visitors. This presented Tsang with an opportunity to organize package tours to Beijing and other destinations in China and Asia. In 1978, the company name was changed to Tour East Holidays, with a focus on package tours. Over the years, new destinations were developed to exotic locations such as Bali and Tibet. Today, Tour East offers reduced-rate airfares, quality hotels, and customized tours to Asia and beyond.

Tour East is the only North American tour wholesaler licensed to operate in the People's Republic of China and currently sends about 10 000 Canadians there each year. Now that China is opening to outbound tourism, the company hopes to capitalize on this market and is lobbying the Chinese government to have Canada designated as a destination for Chinese residents.

Until recently, Tour East has targeted primarily a niche market of Chinese Canadians and other ethnic groups. However, it had to broaden its strategy after several negative events affected the tourism industry. Most notable were the massacre at Tiananmen Square; the terrorist attacks of September 11, 2001; and the SARS crisis. Tsang's response to these crises is indicative of her style and that of her company. After the attacks on New York, Tsang reassured staff that their jobs were safe, despite the downturn in business resulting from the attacks. Not only did she maintain faith in her staff and company, she also used the opportunity to hire talented people released by other operators. By giving them a competitive salary in their time of need, she added more loyal members to her team. The result was that business increased by 22 percent in the first six months of 2003, while other operators still struggled because of the decrease in business.

During the SARS crisis, Tour East's business dropped by more than 50 percent. Again, Tsang viewed the crisis as an opportunity. She reduced marketing and operating expenses and used a federal government program to cover employees' lost income when the company temporarily moved to a three-day week.

Tsang also began looking for new destinations to promote. She developed health and wellness packages for Canadian destinations that now account for 5 percent of sales. Packages to Brazil and Argentina were also added. Next, she increased investment in retail operations, correctly predicting that corporations would make more drastic cuts to travel than would people with family overseas. Tour East opened several retail locations and launched an e-commerce website, which has allowed the firm to reach beyond its traditional market and to cut internal operating costs. Recently the company formed a marketing alliance with Signature Vacations, one of Canada's largest tour operators. Under this agreement, Signature Vacations promotes Tour East holiday packages through its agents. This provides more exposure to potential clients. In return, Tour East designs Far East holidays that will appeal to Signature's clients.

Tsang's values are reflected in her company's products. She works long hours and chooses many of the components that make up the packages. No detail is too minor. She will investigate to ensure that a hotel will provide transfers to the airport and that meals can be changed to suit a customer's preference, and to learn whether clients can check in early or check out late.

Tour East is the largest female-controlled company in Canada but, although she works 50 hours per week, Tsang still makes time to do volunteer work. Her success and devotion to good causes have been recognized across Canada. The Chinese Canadian Business Association named her Entrepreneur of the Year in 2001. In that same year Canada's *Profit* Magazine ranked her number 2 of Canada's Top 100 Women Business Owners and *Chatelaine* magazine recognized her as one of Canada's Top 100 Business Executives. In 2004, Tsang was presented with the Order of Ontario, the province's highest personal and professional honour.

Tsang is active on many boards and volunteers her time willingly. She has helped organize such cultural events as the annual Toronto International Dragon Boat Race Festival, one of Canada's largest sporting and cultural events, of which Tour East is now the title sponsor, and supports the Royal Ontario Museum (as well as serving as a board member), the United Way, and the Heart and Stroke Foundation, among others.

Tsang is an amazing woman. She has survived the death of her husband and sister (both business partners) in the 1980s, and maintained the firm's business through world-changing crises. She has responded with discipline and invested in strategic partnerships and people. She has never wavered from her long-term goal of growth. As she says, "When times are tough, you need to think clearly and act with speed and intelligence."

SOURCES: Based on information from the Tour East Holidays website (www.toureast.com); *Chatelaine*, November 2002; *Profit*, October 2003, and www.profitguide.com, *Top 100 Women Business Owners*, 2002.

A Brief History of the Package Tour

The concept of travel is an ancient one, but package travel, which combines arrangements for transportation, accommodations, and sightseeing, is a comparatively recent development. We can trace its origins to the **grand tour**, an extended journey through continental Europe taken by the sons (and later, the daughters) of the British aristocracy during the seventeenth and eighteenth centuries.

The main purpose of the grand tour was to educate. Indeed, no education was considered complete without it. While abroad, the young noble expected to gain knowledge of the classical past, acquire antiques and works of art, learn foreign languages, and develop socially desirable skills and manners. France and Italy—the cities of Paris, Rome, and Naples in particular—were the main destinations. Some itineraries also included stays in Germany, the Low Countries (Belgium, Luxembourg, and the Netherlands), Austria, and Switzerland.

Travel through Europe by stagecoach and riverboat was dangerous and arduous, so the grand tour could last as long as three years. There were no travel agencies, tour operators, or tour escorts in those days. Individual travellers might carry letters of introduction to aristocratic European families, who would provide lodging and entertainment, but for the most part, they were on their own.

The development of railways and hotels in the nineteenth century encouraged more middle-class travellers to embark on tours of Europe. With this middle-class "invasion" came a change in the reasons for foreign travel. The emphasis moved away from education and culture toward recreation and pleasure. This was the beginning of mass tourism.

The Pioneer of the Package Tour

Thomas Cook, a Baptist missionary, invented the organized **package tour** (see the Profile in Chapter 1). In 1841, he chartered a train to carry 570 people to a temperance meeting in Leicester. This first tour featured a number of components that were to become standard for later package tours: transportation (a 64-kilometre, round-trip rail journey), meals (a picnic lunch and afternoon tea), entertainment (a band playing hymns), an event (the temperance meeting), and the services of a tour escort (Cook himself). Cook also invented the travel brochure, the passenger itinerary, and the travel voucher.

The Evolution of Tour Formats

Most business for the early travel agencies involved making travel and hotel arrangements for independent travellers. Someone planning a grand tour of Europe would consult a travel counsellor to arrange a personalized itinerary. The travel counsellor would then organize the traveller's steamship passage across the Atlantic, rail travel in Europe, accommodations, and sightseeing. Such custom-made tours—known either as **foreign independent tours (FITs)** or **domestic independent tours (DITs)**—were the norm for the vast majority of vacation travellers up until the early 1960s.

The breakthrough for the prearranged package tour arrived with the jet age in 1958. Transatlantic crossing times were cut to 7 hours (from 18 hours by propeller aircraft, or four days by ocean liner). Time savings, together with increased prosperity and cheaper airfares, brought overseas travel within reach of ordinary working Canadians. International travel was no longer exclusively for the wealthy few.

Tour operators developed a variety of packages to cater to the new class of travellers. The packages offered bargain prices, convenience, and reliability. North Americans took advantage of charters, reduced excursion fares, and all-inclusive package tours. The number of them visiting Europe rose substantially after 1958.

Package tours have become more accessible in the jet age; they also have become more flexible in terms of length. A few tour operators still offer lengthy packages, but most operators have scaled down their multination European tours to around 22 days (which is about as much vacation time as most Canadians enjoy). Tours are less leisurely than they used to be, and less time is spent at each destination. Shorter tours, featuring only two or three destinations, have also been developed.

Check Your Product Knowledge

1. What was the grand tour?
2. What role did Thomas Cook play in the history of tourism?
3. What effect did the jet airplane have on the package tour business?

THE MODERN TOUR

A package tour consists of several travel components provided by different suppliers. These are combined by the tour company and then sold to the consumer as a single product at a single price. The package tour typically includes two or more of the following components:

- One or more forms of transportation.
- Accommodations.
- Meals.
- Attractions and events (including sightseeing and admission to natural and commercial attractions, entertainment, recreation, and a variety of special events).

- Extras (including transfers and baggage handling, tips and taxes, the services of a professional tour manager and tour guides, travel bags, and discount coupons for restaurants and shops).

Package tours vary in complexity, ranging from the two-component package (e.g., air transportation and limited sightseeing, or hotel accommodations and rental car) to the multicomponent, all-inclusive package. With the popular **all-inclusive package,** the traveller pays one price that covers just about all trip expenses, including transportation, accommodations, meals, sightseeing, and so on. When a tour involves air travel to the destination or point of departure, the components are usually separated into air arrangements and land arrangements. Land arrangements include surface transportation while on the tour, accommodation, meals, sightseeing, and other activities. Some tour companies quote an all-inclusive price for both air and land arrangements. Others quote air and land rates separately. When the rates are given separately, clients can opt to buy just the land package and make their own arrangements to get to the starting point of the tour.

The Role of the Tour Operator

A **tour operator** or **tour wholesaler** contracts with hotels, transportation companies, and other suppliers to create a package tour to sell to the consumer. By buying hotel bed-nights, airline seats, and admission tickets in bulk, the tour operator can get lower rates than would be offered to an individual traveller. The savings are passed on to the consumer after allowance for business overheads, profit, and any commission to the seller.

The terms *tour operator* and *tour wholesaler* are often used interchangeably, although the former more commonly sells prepackaged tours, whereas the latter sells customized packages. Most tours are sold through a retail travel agency. Today, tour operators and wholesalers also market directly to the consumer through websites. For the purposes of this discussion, we will use the general term "tour operator" throughout.

Operative distinctions can be made among the following: tour wholesalers such as Holiday House; tour operators such as Sunquest Vacations, representing offshore destinations (e.g., Florida, the Caribbean, Mexico); and suppliers (air carriers, car rentals, and resorts). They all create flexible or modular vacation arrangements. These are featured in seasonal brochures that are distributed to consumers through travel agencies, or on company websites. Tour operators have **at-risk capacity** because of volume-based contractual obligations with suppliers; this means that tour operators must pay suppliers for the tour components whether or not consumers purchase the tour operators' packages. In contrast, travel wholesalers do not pre-purchase bulk capacity from suppliers. Though they have negotiated volume net rates with suppliers, they simply act as reservation brokers between suppliers and travel agencies/clients. Also, their clients may not be travelling as a group, as is the case for the tour operator.

There are four different categories of tour operator. The first is the independent tour operator, which can be an individual or a multinational corporation. American Express is an example of the latter. The second category is the travel agency that functions as a tour operator. Such an agency packages tours, which it sells to its clients or wholesales to other travel agencies. In-house tour operators make up the third category. These are owned and operated by air carriers, such as Air Canada Vacations. The fourth category consists of travel clubs and incentive travel companies, which do not sell their products to the public.

All tour operators take risks when they put together a package tour. They must make block reservations far in advance, with no guarantee that their tours will sell in the competitive market. Suppliers are willing to reserve their products for the tour operator if they are given a deposit. However, the percentage of the deposit that will be refunded decreases as the departure time nears.

Canadian tour operators have different types of tours for the different seasons: for example, fall foliage tours in the autumn; tours to Canadian ski destinations, as well as fun-in-the-sun tours, in the winter; country music excursions to Nashville in the spring; and ecotours in the summer.

The Popularity of Tours

Worldwide, the package tour industry is one of the fastest-growing sectors of the tourism industry. Package tours represent a small share of domestic tourism but a significant share of overseas tourism. They have become so popular because they offer a variety of practical benefits that independent travel cannot provide.

Known Costs Because all package tours are prepaid, the client can calculate the total cost of the tour in advance. This is especially true with an all-inclusive package. Accommodations, meals, sightseeing, entertainment, transfers, taxes, and often even drinks will all have been prepaid before departure. The only additional expense, therefore, is for personal items such as souvenirs and gifts.

Value Prices The single greatest attraction of the package tour is its relatively low cost. Because tour operators buy in bulk from suppliers, they can offer packages at a much lower price than the sum of the individual components bought separately. Just as an institutional-sized can of beans costs less per gram than a single-serving can, a block of hotel rooms costs less per room than a single room. Tour operators who provide a guaranteed high volume of bookings to a hotel chain can pay as little as 50 percent of the standard rack rate. Even after the markup and the standard 10 percent travel agent commission, the room is still less expensive than it would be for an individual. Volume discounts allow similar savings on other components of the package.

Guaranteed Arrangements When travellers buy a package, they are also buying peace of mind. Independent travellers may have to cope with unpleasant surprises en route, such as being bumped off a flight or finding that a hotel has no record of their reservation. A package tour takes the anxiety out of travelling, because the tour operator has made all arrangements in advance. In addition, group reservations are invariably honoured, because suppliers rely heavily on the business generated by tour operators.

Guaranteed Entrance It is often easier to get into a special event as a member of a tour than as an individual. This is because tour operators make block ticket purchases to ensure entrance to tour participants. For example, it's almost impossible to attend the Oberammergau Passion Play, staged every 10 years in Germany, unless you are part of a tour. There are even some countries that permit access to certain places only to visitors who are part of a tour group.

However, there are some areas in the world where access is reduced and/or restricted; for example, Antarctica and the Galapagos Islands. Even some whale watching in the Gulf of St. Lawrence and Bay of Fundy is rationed.

ILLUSTRATION 15–1
Tours of the great vineyards of France can be an educational as well as an enjoyable experience.
SOURCE: Corel.

Tried-and-True Sightseeing Tour operators know which attractions are worth a special trip. They know which local nightspots offer the best entertainment, and which restaurants to recommend. Unlike the individual traveller, tour members don't have to worry about winding up at a second-rate museum or at a restaurant with inedible food.

Time Savings With a package tour, the traveller doesn't have to spend time looking for accommodations, arranging transfers, or getting tickets for a show. Group travel can also save time at theatres and other attractions. Tour participants often don't have to wait in line; they can enter and exit more easily than individuals.

Product Quality Tour operators have earned a reputation for providing top-quality products. Major tour operators subscribe to the same high standards of service.

Check Your Product Knowledge

1. What are the typical components of a package tour?

2. What is meant by the term "land arrangements"?

3. What are the benefits of package tours over independent travel?

4. Why are tour operators able to offer reduced prices for tour components?

TOURS, TOURS, TOURS

Recent years have seen a rapid increase in the number and variety of tours to virtually every corner of the world. Tour operators have developed tours to fulfill the needs of an increasingly sophisticated travelling public. They cater both to the mass market and to specific segments of that market—there are tours tailored to attract young singles, families, middle-aged couples, senior citizens, and physically disabled people. Some tours are designed for people who prefer to relax on their vacation; others cater to those who want to find adventure, or to learn as they travel. There are one-day sightseeing tours, weekend escape packages, two-week special-interest tours, and one-month cultural packages. There are as many package tours as there are markets to buy them. Some examples of package tours are provided in Figure 15–1.

People can sign up for all-inclusive tours or for independent tours, for leisurely tours or fast-paced tours, for budget tours or deluxe tours. Tours are not limited to

 Algonquin Park

2-Day Weekend Getaways
JUNE 14 – JUNE 16
JULY 5 – JULY 7
JULY 12 – JULY 14
JULY 19 – JULY 21
JULY 26 – JULY 28
AUG 9 – AUG 11
AUG 23 – AUG 25
SEPT 6 – SEPT 8
SEPT 13 – SEPT 15
SEPT 20 – SEPT 22
SEPT 27 – SEPT 29
OCT 4 – OCT 6
Depart: 7 p.m.   Return: 9 p.m.

W.I.L.D. Adventure Programs
21-Day W.I.L.D. Adventure Program
JULY 7 – JULY 27

14-Day W.I.L.D. Adventure Program
AUG 19 – AUG 30

Introductory Sea Kayak Clinic
JUNE 21 – JUNE 23
JUNE 29 – JULY 1
JULY 5 – JULY 7
JULY 12 – JULY 14
AUG 3 – AUG 5
AUG 31 – SEPT 2
Depart: 7 p.m.   Return: 9 p.m.

3-Day Weekend Sea Kayaking Trips
JULY 18 – JULY 21
AUG 23 – AUG 26

7-Day Sea Kayaking Trip
AUG 3 – AUG 10
Depart: 7 p.m.   Return: 7 p.m.

Dumoine River

7-Day Canoe Trips
JULY 20 – JULY 27
AUG 10 – AUG 17
Depart: 7 p.m.   Return: 7 p.m.

Whitewater Clinics
Introductory Clinics
MAY 17 – MAY 20
JUNE 21 – JUNE 23
Depart: 7 p.m.   Return: 7 p.m.

2-Day Advanced Whitewater Clinic
MAY 24 – MAY 26
JUNE 14 – JUNE 16
Depart: 7 p.m.   Return: 9 p.m.

5-Day French River Whitewater Clinic
JULY 15 – JULY 19
Depart: 9 a.m.   Return: 7 p.m.

WHAT IS INCLUDED
Return transportation from Toronto (except Family 3-day Kayak trips, and Missisaibi River, all meals while on trip or at Base Camp, complete equipment outfitting (except sleeping bag), the services of an experienced guide, and use of Base Camp facilities. The Dumoine River and Temagami trips also include a bush flight. Sleeping bags are available for rental.
• Return transportation from Toronto (some exceptions)
• All meals, and accommodation once you arrive at our Base Camp
• Use of our private Base Camp including a wood-fired sauna at the end of your trip
• Services of professional, enthusiastic, dedicated guides
• All the necessary gear for a well-equipped and safe adventure. You need only bring your clothes and sleeping bag (but you can rent a 3-season bag from us if you wish)
• Park Permit fees
• The Dumoine River and Temagami trips also include a bush plane flight

WHAT IS NOT INCLUDED
All trips do not include personal clothing and gear (a detailed list is forwarded upon registration), sleeping bags (these can be rented from us with prior notice), hotels, restaurant meals during transportation to and from Base Camp, coverage for additional expenses due to safety delays or emergency evacuation, or travel to trip rendezvous in Toronto. All prices shown do not include the 7% Goods and Services Tax.

FIGURE 15–1 Sample Tours from Canadian Wilderness Trips
SOURCE: Courtesy Canadianwildernesstrips.com, www.canadianwildernesstrips.com.

tourists. Travellers visiting friends and relatives (VFR), for example, can purchase a package for the bargain price and then use only part of it, such as the airfare and the car. In such cases, the tour is called a "throwaway."

All tours can be categorized by the package format, by destination, or by purpose.

Basic Package Tour Formats

Deciding to book a package tour is just the beginning. The traveller then has to decide what kind of package he or she wants. Package tours come in many different formats.

All-Inclusive Tours For Canadians, all-inclusive tours are the most popular of all package tour formats. The ease of booking, variety of destinations, activities and quality available, and the security of a prepaid vacation with few additional costs, all contribute to this popularity. A standard all-inclusive package comprises return airfare, accommodation, all meals, and frequently all beverages including local alcoholic drinks, entertainment, transfers, and taxes. Many all-inclusive packages also include the fees for activities such as water sports in the single price. Consumers can choose the quality they desire, ranging from economical resorts featuring buffet meals and local beverages to deluxe properties offering a choice of à la carte restaurants and imported liquors. Mexico and the Caribbean are the most popular areas for all-inclusive package tours.

Independent The independent package tour is the least structured of all formats. It offers participants the benefits of package savings but allows them the flexibility and freedom of travelling alone. An independent package features a minimum of components. Typically, it includes hotel accommodation as well as one other land arrangement, such as round-trip transfers, use of a rental car, a daily continental breakfast, or a half-day sightseeing tour.

When booking an independent tour, participants can choose their departure and return dates. They can also choose from a variety of different-priced hotels, and extend their stay by adding a fixed extra-night rate for each additional night. A fly/drive package is a good example of an independent tour. Popular destinations for independent tours include resort areas such as Hawaii and Cancun.

Independent tours should not be confused with foreign independent tours (FITs) and domestic independent tours (DITs), which are custom-made for clients by travel agencies. FITs and DITs became less common in recent years because they were often more expensive than package tours and were more time-consuming for a travel counsellor to research and book. Today, however, many tour operator websites offer a dynamic packaging option that permits clients to customize tours to their specific MNEs and budget.

Hosted On a **hosted tour,** a host is on hand at the hotel to arrange optional excursions, answer questions, and help people plan their free time. The host is not an escort and does not accompany the group on sightseeing tours or on overland journeys. If the tour visits more than one destination, a different host will be available at each hotel on the itinerary.

Hosted tours are ideal for vacationers who wish to strike a balance between organized events and free time. Aside from scheduled sightseeing and entertainment, participants are free to arrange their time as they please. As with independent tours, they have the freedom to choose their departure date, level of accommodations, and length of stay.

Escorted The escorted tour is the most structured of all formats. It offers participants accommodation at a number of destinations, as well as meals, point-to-point transportation, and a full program of organized activities. A professional tour manager or escort accompanies the group for the duration of the tour. In recent years the number of escorted tours has risen, partly because of an increase in the number of tours to Eastern European countries. On these tours, participants need a bilingual escort to ease the language problem.

Escorted tours appeal to travellers who want their entire vacation planned in advance. For this privilege, they forgo the flexibility and independence that travellers on other tours enjoy. Participants travel as a group at all times and have limited free time to branch out on their own. They begin and end the tour according to schedule and stay in the hotels selected by the tour operator.

Special Package Formats A number of special types of package tours are not available to the general public:

- **Incentive tours** are offered by companies as a reward to employees for achieving corporate objectives, such as sales targets.
- **Convention tours** are packaged for sale to members of an association or group attending gatherings such as conventions, conferences, exhibitions, or trade shows.
- **Special-interest group tours** are arranged for clubs, societies, and organizations whose members share a common interest such as photography, bird watching, or opera.

The tour operator, the travel agency, and the company, association, or club jointly develop all three special tour formats. Tours designed mainly for business or professional travellers are discussed in more detail in Chapter 3.

Inbound Tours or Travel An **inbound tour** is one that originates in a foreign country and has Canada as its destination. The product is essentially the same as an outbound tour, but with the itinerary reversed. Inbound travel is a growing segment of the Canadian tourism industry. In recent years the number of foreign visitors to Canada has risen. Canada's attraction as a tourist destination has increased because of the value these international travellers receive. Foreign visitors are of great importance to Canada because they generate jobs and increase incomes and tax revenues.

There is a definite distinction between a Canadian (home country) outbound tour operator (e.g., many sunspot companies), which uses an offshore (inbound receptive tour) operator in the host country, and a Canadian (host country) inbound receptive tour operator (e.g., Jonview Canada and JAC Travel), which will probably use an offshore (e.g., German home country) outbound tour operator.

Tours Defined by Destination

Many tours aim to provide travellers with the general flavour of particular destinations. This is especially true of escorted tours that cover several countries in a short time. Grand tours of Europe are a prime example—some of them visit nine countries in 17 days. When tourists spend a maximum of three days in any one country, they can glimpse only the major highlights.

Area tours allow more time in each country, although there is little opportunity for any in-depth appreciation. A 15-day tour of Scandinavia, for example, might include four nights in Denmark, five in Sweden, and five in Norway, with two nights in each capital. Other popular destinations for area tours are Alpine Europe and the British Isles.

Single-country tours are more focused, and enable travellers to see and do much more than is possible on an area tour. Smaller countries, such as England, France, Italy, Germany, Spain, Israel, Japan, and New Zealand, lend themselves to this kind of tour. Some single-country tours concentrate on a particular area. There are, for example, eight- and ten-day tours of Shakespeare country, of the French château country, and of the Canadian Rockies.

Tours to one or two cities are the most focused of all packages. These are usually independent or hosted. **Two-city tours** are ideal for travellers who do not want to be tied to a single destination. Equal time is usually spent in each city, with transportation between the two included in the price of the package. The two cities can be in the same country, or in different countries. The two-country combination allows tourists to experience more than one culture.

Travellers who really want to get to know their destination might choose a **single-city tour**. This can be a four-day sightseeing tour, or a more extended visit focusing on the unique attractions of a particular destination (for example, theatre in London or New York, shopping in Hong Kong, art museums in Paris, or opera in Milan).

Tours Defined by Purpose

While the destination itself is often the strongest selling point, other tours are popular because they focus on a specific type of activity. The activity can be as strenuous as whitewater rafting or as relaxing as lying on a beach. Tour operators have developed packages to satisfy a wide variety of motivations, needs, and expectations (MNEs).

Relaxation Many people want nothing more from a vacation than the chance to relax, with plenty of sun, a sandy beach, good food, and perhaps some nightly entertainment. Such stayput resort vacations are available in many parts of the world (for example, the Caribbean, Hawaii, Mexico, and the Mediterranean). These vacations can be combined with some sports and recreation, or shopping, or limited sightseeing. But the main purpose is relaxation.

Sunspot Stayput This type of tour, introduced at the start of the chapter, is the most prominent travel product in the marketplace. The typical package tour includes a round-trip charter flight, round-trip transfers from the airport to the hotel, and seven nights' resort accommodation. Typical destinations are Florida, the Caribbean, and Mexico. This type of tour is distinct from the multifaceted itinerary or sightseeing package tour. The product is distinct; the market is distinct, with Canadian regional predilections; the operators are distinct; and their respective operations and the MNEs of their respective clients are distinct.

Traditionally, tourists in central and eastern Canada wanting to escape winter went to Florida. Now many are going to other sunspot destinations for several reasons, including the desire to see something different, and the availability of more flights, both charter and scheduled, to more destinations. Thus Atlantic Canadians, instead of going to Florida, may go to Arizona. There they may stay put at their hotel but will rent a car in order to sightsee, take in professional sports, play golf, or go shopping.

Scenic Tours for people who want to enjoy spectacular scenery while they are away from home exist in great variety. Most involve a fair amount of travelling, either by motorcoach (New England fall foliage packages, tours throughout Europe), train (trans-Canada packages, national parks of the Canadian west), or ship (Alaska's Inside Passage, Rhine River cruises). These are almost always escorted trips.

A variation is offered by Brewster Tours. Its Royal Glacier Tour program, created in conjunction with the Gray Line sightseeing program, offers half-day and full-day sightseeing tours in the Banff, Lake Louise, Jasper, and Calgary areas. This program is a perfect opportunity to create independent package tour products by adding hotel accommodation, meals, and various attractions.

Learning Every tour provides a learning experience, but here we are referring specifically to those tours taken by people travelling because of their interest in culture, history, science, or education. Some tour operators package these products under the generic term "intelligent travel." Cultural tours come in various formats. Typically, they involve a structured program of visits to museums and art galleries or attendance at theatre productions, music festivals, and so on. Individual travellers can also arrange to stay with host families, thereby gaining a greater understanding and appreciation of the cultures they experience.

Historical tours can involve participating in an archaeological dig or studying ancient civilizations. Members of a scientific tour might take part in a geological expedition or study the botany of a particular region. Historical and scientific tours usually feature guest lecturers and other experts. The distinction between historical or scientific tours and educational tours is often hazy, but the latter generally focus more on the classroom than on field study. All educational tours offer travellers personal enrichment. As a bonus, some offer the opportunity to earn college or university credits.

Religious and Ethnic The pilgrimage has been an important reason for travel since ancient times. Tour operators continue to develop packages to holy sites for members of different religions. Examples are the Shrine of Ste-Anne-de-Beaupre in Quebec, the Vatican, Jerusalem, and Mecca and Medina. Ethnic travel is a related category, covering Canadians who visit the country from which their parents or grandparents came.

Hard Adventure Travellers seeking adventure are a rapidly growing segment of the market. Tour operators such as Mountain Travel Sobek and GAP Adventure Tours offer a

ILLUSTRATION 15–2
Adventure travel is a rapidly growing tourism market segment.
SOURCE: Jess Alford/Photodisc Green/Getty Images.

staggering array of escorted packages to exotic destinations, including:

- Mountaineering in the Himalayas.
- Scuba diving.
- Dogsledding in the Canadian territories.
- Trekking in Nepal.
- African safaris.
- Horseback riding in the Rockies.
- Hot-air ballooning over Kenyan game preserves.
- Amazon jungle expeditions.
- River rafting in Alaska.

The selection is likely to grow larger as travellers continue to seek something new and exciting.

Soft Adventure This type of tour allows people to experience adventure travel without discomfort or personal risk. The degree of comfort may vary—for example, some soft adventure tours include lodge accommodation rather than camping, gourmet food instead of camp food, and walking without carrying any gear. There are also tours that involve walking from town to town, spending nights at different B&Bs.

Ecotourism Ecotourism, or nature tourism, is among the fastest-growing sectors in tourism. Tours that take vacationers to observe unusual ecological systems and endangered species in their natural habitat are becoming popular. Tourists are flocking to such diverse areas as the Amazon Basin, the Annapurna Massif of Nepal, and Graham Land in Antarctica. Ecotourists can view harp seals in Canada, white heron colonies in New Zealand, and hawk's-bill turtles on Antigua. Prince Edward Island offers a four-day, three-night seal-watching getaway tour.

Ethical Tourism Ethical behaviour is becoming important to a growing segment of the travel market. Such tourists not only seek out ecotourism options but also generally wish to ensure that the tour they purchase is "green" and follows the principles of sustainable tourism. Another concern is that as much of the cost of the vacation as possible is spent in the local community, rather than being retained by the tour company in Canada. An offshoot of this type of travel is "voluntourism," where the participants contribute to a host community by, for example, helping to build local housing.

Sports and Recreation The sports and recreation market has been strong since the early days of package tours and has diversified in recent years. For those who want an active vacation, there are golf, tennis, and ski packages, and organized biking and walking tours. Recreational travel can also mean a visit to a theme park, or a gambling package. The recreational activity can be the sole purpose for the trip, or it can be combined with other features, such as sightseeing, relaxation, or study.

Spectator sports packages feature a special sporting event as the main attraction. Examples include the Grey Cup, the Olympics, the World Series, the Super Bowl, the Kentucky Derby, the Indy 500, and the Masters golf tournament. Similar tours are also designed around other types of special events, including New Orleans' Mardi Gras, Munich's Oktoberfest, and Toronto's Caribana.

Special Interest These tours have great potential. Tour operators have packaged a wealth of different tours for groups sharing common interests. For example, there are chocolate lovers' tours of Switzerland, bird watching tours of China, culinary tours of France, and garden tours of the American south. Some enthusiasts travel with a pre-formed group, club, or organization. Others buy special-interest packages individually.

Weekend Canadians are taking shorter vacations and taking them more often. This means that cut-price weekend packages are becoming more popular. These can be family packages, sometimes with free accommodation for children; second honeymoon packages; recreational, educational, or special-interest packages; or theme weekends such as a murder mystery package. The common denominator is the "quick fix" escape from the daily routine.

Special Needs The needs of travellers in wheelchairs are different from those of more mobile travellers. Hotels and public buildings must be fitted with ramps, wide doorways, and other features that reduce architectural obstacles. Physically disabled people may require hydraulic lifts and specially equipped guest rooms. Special arrangements may be necessary for developmentally disabled people and for those whose hearing or sight is impaired. Tour operators have only recently begun to tailor packages for this potentially large market.

Defining the Traveller

Tour operators develop packages by determining where people want to go and what they want to do when they get there. Tours must be designed to fit the MNEs of different kinds of travellers. We can identify a number of basic MNEs:

- **Security** Many people do not feel confident about travelling alone, especially overseas, where the language and customs may be unfamiliar. An escorted tour, with a tour manager, offers these travellers the security that independent tours lack.
- **Companionship** Some people are perfectly happy travelling on their own; others prefer the companionship that group tours offer.
- **Status** Being first on the block to visit China or some other exotic destination can be an important motivation for travel.
- **Romance** For many vacationers, "Love Boat" cruises, Club Med singles' packages, and honeymoon packages fulfill a desire for romance.

The Traveller's Age Some tours are designed for people of all ages; others are tailored to specific age groups—students, young people, families, seniors, and so on. For

ILLUSTRATION 15–3
Ecotours that take vacationers to observe endangered species are becoming popular; for example, whale watching off the coast of Nova Scotia.
SOURCE: Corel.

example, Contiki Tours has an age limit of 35, which means a faculty member older than this age could not accompany students on a tour.

Each market has its own particular MNEs. Cost is likely to be a big consideration for students. Young people typically demand action, adventure, and entertainment, with free time to go off on their own. Families are attracted to packages designed with children's interests in mind, such as visits to amusement parks and zoos. Mature travellers tend to have more money and can afford to travel in style. If they are experienced travellers, they may be keen to explore new and exotic places. Senior citizens traditionally favour worry-free tours conducted at a leisurely pace and with plenty of scheduled activities.

Flexibility and Pacing Every tour must be flexible enough to suit the tastes of individual travellers. On a general-interest tour of the capitals of Europe, it would be unwise to schedule three consecutive nights at the opera. Meals have to be varied, too. Some group members may want to experience the exotic local cuisine at every stop. Others would flinch in horror at the sight of a plate of frogs' legs and will expect more familiar food.

Balance is the key word here. To keep everyone happy, the package must offer a variety of entertainment and a choice of meals. It must also strike a balance between scheduled activities and free time.

The pace of the tour is another consideration. Many tours stop at a different destination virtually every night. This may look appealing in the brochure, but in reality, a succession of long days on the road can be exhausting, especially for older travellers. A good tour operator will try to schedule a day without travel after a particularly long journey, or after a tiring initial flight.

ILLUSTRATION 15–4

Boots Adventure Tours offers adventure and ecotour products that provide unique ways to see the beauty of southern Georgian Bay.

SOURCE: Courtesy of Boots Adventure Tours.

Price Tour operators must offer a range of products at a range of prices. American Express, for example, has European package tours in four price categories—freelance, moderate, superior, and deluxe. Itineraries are often similar in each category, but the number of features included and the levels of accommodation vary.

Check Your Product Knowledge

1. What is the difference between a hosted tour and an escorted tour?
2. What is an area tour? Give examples of possible area tour destinations.
3. Name six tours that focus on a specific activity and explain the market segment for each.
4. Why are flexibility and pacing important on any tour?

THE INGREDIENTS OF A TOUR

To illustrate the many ingredients of a package tour, we have created an imaginary tour (see Table 15–1). This one is an escorted 12-day European package with overnight stops in five countries—England, the Netherlands, Germany, Switzerland, and France—and daytime passage through Belgium. The tour is tailored to general-interest travellers and has extensive sightseeing and some entertainment features.

The Human Element

Most tours are put together by a tour operator and then are sold through travel agencies. Our feature tour was created, let's say, by a Toronto-based tour operator and marketed to travel agencies throughout Canada. The 47 tour participants have come from cities all over the country and from a variety of backgrounds. Some tours are the idea of a member of an organization, known as a **tour organizer**, with little expertise in travel, who cooperates with a travel agency and a tour operator.

A key part of any escorted tour is the **tour manager** (also known as the **tour conductor** or **tour escort**). Our tour manager is Mary DeVries. It is her responsibility to oversee the group for the duration of the tour and to make sure everything runs smoothly. Mary has been involved in preparing the package from an early date. She has even negotiated contracts with suppliers at several destinations. Before departure she will have familiarized herself with the itinerary. She will know about interesting sights en route and will have thought about lunch stops for each of the days the group is on the road. Mary will take with her copies of all contracts and

TABLE 15–1 Sample European Tour Itinerary

London, Paris, and European Highlights

- First-class hotels throughout—all rooms with private bath or shower.
- Continental breakfast daily.
- Dinners included in Amsterdam, Frankfurt, Lucerne, and Paris.
- Round-trip airport transfers, including baggage handling.
- Touring by luxury, air-conditioned motorcoach.

- Rhine River cruise.
- London theatre reservations.
- Local entertainment.
- Sightseeing in all major cities, including admission charges and guide fees.
- Experienced tour manager.

Day 1	**DEPART CANADA.** Overnight transatlantic flight.
Day 2	**LONDON.** Arrival in the British capital, with a welcome from our tour manager, who sees us settled in our London hotel. Balance of the day free to relax, or perhaps to start exploring. Evening cocktail party gives us a chance to get acquainted.
Day 3	**LONDON.** Morning sightseeing with a professional London guide. See Buckingham Palace, Big Ben, the Houses of Parliament, and Westminster Abbey. Free afternoon for independent activities or to join an optional excursion to the Tower of London. Tonight, we have reserved seats to a London show.
Day 4	**LONDON–AMSTERDAM.** Morning drive to Dover on the south coast. By hovercraft to Calais. Motorcoach through Belgium, then on to Amsterdam, arriving in time for a Dutch dinner party at the hotel.
Day 5	**AMSTERDAM–COLOGNE.** Morning sightseeing features a visit to a diamond factory and a look at Rembrandt's masterpieces in the Rijksmuseum. After lunch, we head for the German Rhineland and overnight in the cathedral city of Cologne.
Day 6	**COLOGNE–FRANKFURT.** After a leisurely breakfast we board an excursion steamer and cruise the romantic Rhine, past castles, terraced vineyards, and medieval towns. Then by motorcoach to Frankfurt for dinner, complimentary beer, and entertainment provided by a local German band.
Day 7	**FRANKFURT–HEIDELBERG–LUCERNE.** Morning stop in Heidelberg for sightseeing in Germany's oldest university town and a tour of the castle. Then on through the Black Forest, past the thundering Rhine Falls, and into Switzerland. After the eventful day, a quiet night at our Lucerne hotel at the foot of the Swiss Alps.
Day 8	**LUCERNE.** Our morning sightseeing takes us around the city walls, over a fourteenth-century wooden bridge, and to the famous Lion Monument. This afternoon perhaps we shop for watches or cuckoo clocks, cruise the lake by paddle steamer, or take an optional cable-car ride up Mount Pilatus for stunning Alpine views. Tonight's Swiss folklore party features a fondue dinner, unlimited wine, and yodelling and alpenhorn blowing.
Day 9	**LUCERNE–PARIS.** Today's drive takes us into France and through the world-renowned vineyards of Burgundy. A photo stop at the Palace of Fontainebleau and then on to Paris.
Day 10	**PARIS.** Morning sightseeing takes in the French capital's famous landmarks: the Eiffel Tower, the Arc de Triomphe, and more. A special visit to the magnificent Notre Dame Cathedral. Balance of the day at leisure, perhaps to visit the Louvre, cruise on the Seine, or enjoy some shopping. Tonight, perhaps a gourmet dinner? Followed by a lively cabaret show?
Day 11	**PARIS.** A morning tour to Versailles, then a chance to relax before our gala farewell party at the hotel.
Day 12	**RETURN TO CANADA.** Jet back home, arriving the same day.

SOURCE: *On the Path to Success: Lessons from Canadian Adventure Travel and Eco-tourism Operators 1999.* Reproduced with permission of the Minister of Public Works and Government Services Canada, 2005.

correspondence with the various suppliers, just in case there is a problem with hotel bookings or dinner reservations.

The next stage is the tour itself. Mary will greet the tour members as they arrive at the hotel in London, allocate rooms to them, and briefly describe the scheduled itinerary. She will also discuss the itinerary with the driver to get an idea of travel times and suitable rest stops. In preparation for the next night, she may call the theatre to confirm reservations for the show, and possibly the hotel in Amsterdam where the group will stay on Day 4.

On Day 3, Mary will get everyone on the bus for the morning's sightseeing. She will not, however, lead the guided tour of London's landmarks (although she will be on the bus). This will be up to the professional **tour guide**, who has an in-depth knowledge of the city's attractions. There will be a different tour guide in each city. That night, Mary will accompany the group to the theatre.

The first real travelling begins on Day 4 with the trip to Amsterdam. Mary must make sure that all the baggage gets loaded onto the bus and later onto the hovercraft. She will try to break up the day with rest stops and, of course, lunch. When they finally arrive at the hotel, Mary will go inside to register while the group waits on the bus.

That is the nature of the tour manager's job. Other days will be similar: She will answer a constant barrage of questions, give advice on how best to spend free time, deal with complaints, help find medical care as necessary, and deal with any visa or documentation problems. The tour manager needs a limitless supply of patience, energy, and good humour.

Transportation

Tours include at least one mode of transportation, and many combine several different modes. Our feature tour involves travel by air (not included in the package price), motorcoach, hovercraft, and cruise ship, as well as airport–hotel transfers in London and Paris. Those opting for the Mount Pilatus excursion on Day 8 will also experience travel by cable car.

In recent years, there has been strong growth in the transportation component of Canadian domestic and international package tours. This is most evident in the marine mode, as reflected in increases in vessel callings and passengers at the ports of Halifax and Vancouver (see Chapter 8). There is also a growing interest in tours along Canada's coasts, rivers, and lakes. The motorcoach industry in North America has survived a long decline in scheduled intercity service because of an offsetting long-term increase in tours and charter service (see Chapter 7). The railways and specialized tour operators continue to diversify their offerings of train trips and tours. VIA Rail and its partners offer more than 50 train travel packages. The airlines have had package tours for decades and were instrumental in the growth of the cruise industry through fly/cruise packages.

Meal Plans

The number of meals included is a key factor in determining the overall price of a tour. If economy is uppermost in the tour operator's mind, a limited number of meals will be provided—probably just a daily continental breakfast consisting of juice, rolls, and tea or coffee. Meal plans are a factor in the selection of accommodation. Factors considered include meals as well as service and rooms. Rating systems were discussed in Chapter 9.

If the operator, through the hotels selected, provides no meals at all, the package is known as a **European plan (EP)**. At the opposite end of the scale, an **American plan (AP)** includes three full meals a day. A **modified American plan (MAP)** involves two meals a day (usually breakfast and dinner). Other combinations are also possible—our featured tour includes a daily continental breakfast, dinner on only four nights, and no lunches.

Deluxe tours tend to offer diners greater choice at each meal. **À la carte** means that you can choose from the complete menu regardless of price. **Table d'hôte**, on the other hand, limits you to a set meal (usually three courses) at a fixed price. A **dine-around plan** gives you the option of eating at any of a variety of restaurants. Tour members are issued vouchers and coupons, which they can use at participating restaurants.

There are obvious advantages to buying an American plan package (prepayment, guaranteed reservations); there are also drawbacks. You may grow tired of the hotel meals and wish you could eat in a local restaurant once in a while. You are free to do so, of course, but there are no refunds for missed prepaid meals.

Accommodations

Our tour group of 47 consists of eighteen couples, a family of four, a family of three, and four single people. Almost all tours are based on **double occupancy**—that is, on two people sharing a room. Accommodations for the eighteen couples are straightforward enough—each couple will occupy either a twin with bath (TWB) or a double with bath (DWB). The former has two twin (single) beds, and the latter has one larger double bed.

The family of four will either reserve two separate rooms or perhaps share the same room (a **quad**). Similarly, the family of three may share a **triple** room. Quads and triples are not necessarily larger than twins and doubles. A common practice is for hotels to add cots or rollaway beds to a regular room to make a triple or a quad. Under this arrangement, children are sometimes allowed to stay for free. Most tour operators offer a slight price reduction for triple or quad

ILLUSTRATION 15–5

Hotels will often accommodate families by adding cots to a room and allowing children to stay for free.

SOURCE: Image courtesy of Fairmont Hotels and Resorts.

occupants. Many hotels in North America have two double beds in most rooms to accommodate families of four.

People on their own have to pay extra if they want a room to themselves. A **single supplement** can sometimes add as much as 50 percent to the package price. A hotel may have a few smaller rooms for individual guests, with one bed and bath or shower (SWB), but most singles have to occupy a regular double room. Some tour operators get around the single supplement by matching individuals and allowing them to share a room. Not everyone wants to share a room with a stranger, however. Many prefer to pay the supplement for the sake of privacy.

The Itinerary

Our tour is considered relatively fast paced, in that participants will stop at several cities in a short space of time. The configuration is 2-1-1-1-2-3 (10 nights spent in six cities). A more leisurely tour might have three nights at each destination.

Even though the tour includes several cities, there are only three full days of travelling (Days 4, 6, and 9). Few tour operators schedule more than 10 hours or 560 kilometres of travel on any given day. Even fewer have consecutive days of almost nonstop travelling. Our tour strikes a good balance between scheduled activities and free time. There is no day when participants are free from dawn to dusk; Days 2, 3, 8, 10, and 11 offer free afternoons; Days 5, 7, and 9 have quiet evenings. Days 4 and 6 are the only two filled with scheduled activities.

Another consideration in fixing the itinerary is the location of the hotel. A central location is preferable, especially on our tour, which has overnight stays in major cities. Participants do not want to have to travel a long distance into the city centre when they have free time to spend.

Check Your Product Knowledge

1. What is the difference between a tour manager and a tour guide?
2. Define each of the following: (a) European plan, (b) American plan, (c) modified American plan.
3. Give three considerations involved in planning an itinerary.

SELF-REGULATION AND ETHICS

In Canada, tours and charters and their components are regulated by different jurisdictions and departments. The federal Canadian Transportation Agency regulates air and rail travel; the public utilities boards or agencies of the provinces regulate motorcoach travel. The provinces

TRAVEL INDUSTRY COUNCIL OF ONTARIO

ILLUSTRATION 15–6
The Travel Industry Council of Ontario's Consumer Awareness Campaign advises: "Always look for the TICO sign when you book your travel time."
SOURCE: Image courtesy of the Travel Industry Council of Ontario.

license tour operators. For example, Sunquest Vacations is a tour operator licensed in Ontario, British Columbia, and Quebec. Provincial departments of consumer affairs protect the interests of consumers in most provinces. The Travel Industry Council of Ontario (TICO) was formed in 1997 and assumed responsibility from the Ministry of Consumer and Corporate Relations to administer the Travel Industry Act in that province.

The Association of Canadian Travel Agencies (ACTA), profiled in Chapter 16, has a two-part code of ethics. The first part relates to dealings between ACTA members and the public, and the second part to dealings between ACTA members.

In the United States, two trade organizations—the United States Tour Operators Association (USTOA) and the National Tour Association (NTA)—set standards for the tour industry. Recent years have seen a greater emphasis on education in the tour industry. For example, the NTA has established the Certified Tour Professional (CTP) program. In Canada, all sunspot stayput tour operators belong to the Canadian Association of Tour Operators (CATO).

The International Air Transport Association

The International Air Transport Association (IATA) plays a key role in the regulation of tours outside the United States and Canada. Its requirements include the following:

- The tour must include air transportation on the flights of an IATA member (although the airfare can be quoted separately).
- Accommodation must be included for the duration of the tour.
- At least one additional feature must be included (e.g., sightseeing, entertainment, transfers).
- The tour price must be not less than 20 percent of the airfare (if departure is from the United States).
- The tour brochure must meet IATA standards.

These requirements are specifically for overseas tours; however, many domestic tour operators choose to follow the same guidelines.

Once a tour has been approved, it is registered with an identifying number (**IT number**). American Express's "French Impressions" tour, for example, might appear in the brochure with the IT number IT8AF1AE549. Here's a translation of that number:

IT	Inclusive tour.
8	2008 (the year the tour was approved).
AF	Air France, the carrier.
1	Area 1 (the Western Hemisphere)—the area in which the tour will be sold.
AE549	The identifying number chosen by the tour operator (American Express).

The Performance Bond

The tour operator is a speculator and risk taker. Individual suppliers—hotels, motorcoach companies, and sightseeing companies—insist on a deposit from the tour operator before reserving the product. The client and travel agency need protection in case the tour operator goes into default or out of business. A **performance bond**—a special type of insurance policy that guarantees payment to all parties owed any money—offers protection to the clients, their travel agencies, and all suppliers in the event that the operator experiences financial difficulties. The tour operator pays a premium and posts a bond. Performance bonds are sometimes worth millions of dollars.

In Canada, the provinces of British Columbia, Ontario, and Quebec require all tour operators to be registered. These provinces have similar provisions for registration, maintenance of trust accounts, payment into a compensation fund, and detailed financial requirements.

Statement of Conditions

All tour operators are required to include in their brochures a statement of terms and conditions. This appears at the back of the tour brochure, usually in fine print. Typically, it includes information such as:

- What is and is not included in the package.
- Reservations procedures.
- Deposit and payment schedule.
- Travel and health documents required (passports, visas, vaccinations).
- Cancellation and refund policy.
- Status of fares, rates, and itinerary (all may be subject to change).
- The tour operator's limited responsibility and liability.

In this age of many lawsuits, it is essential for travel counsellors to make sure their clients understand the statement of conditions.

The Travel Industry Council of Ontario

As of June 1997, the travel industry in Ontario became self-managing through the Travel Industry Council of Ontario (TICO), which administers the Travel Industry Act. This Act governs some 3000 travel wholesalers and retailers. These wholesalers and retailers finance TICO. According to its mission statement, TICO's goal is "to promote a fair and informed marketplace where consumers can be confident in their travel purchases." TICO works with the following principal stakeholder groups:

- Consumers—to increase their awareness of their rights and responsibilities.
- Restaurants and industry associations—to harness their knowledge and commitment to ethical and open communication.
- Government—has delegated responsibility and holds TICO accountable for administering the Travel Industry Act.

TICO also administers the industry-financed compensation fund. This fund is used to cover the cost of travel services not delivered as a result of the bankruptcy or insolvency of a registered agency or travel wholesaler. This fund's benefits are available only to travellers who have booked with TICO-registered agencies. There are a number of restrictions on what the fund covers, such as no compensation for poor-quality service. As part of a revision of the Act, in 2008 TICO introduced minimum education standards for anyone selling travel in Ontario. The Act requires all travel sellers in Ontario to pass a test based on the Ontario Travel Industry Act, 2002 by July 1, 2009. The Canadian Institute of Travel Counsellors (CITC) administers the test on behalf of TICO. A similar test is planned for supervisors and managers.

Chapter 16 discusses changes to the Act and their potential impact on travel agencies. For information on TICO's planned future programs, visit its website at www.tico.on.ca.

Check Your Product Knowledge

1. In Canada, how are tours and charters regulated?
2. What is an IT number?
3. List the items that would appear in a tour brochure's statement of conditions.
4. Analyze and discuss who participates in and who benefits from TICO.

THE TOUR AS A PRODUCT

A package tour is the end result of the work of many different people. Putting together a tour product involves a close working relationship among the following groups:

- Suppliers (hotels, restaurants, airlines, cruise ships, bus companies, sightseeing companies, attractions, resorts).

- Public sector organizations (provincial and local tourism agencies, convention bureaux).
- Tour operators.
- Travel agencies.

The suppliers are the producers of the various components of the tour product. Suppliers usually sell to intermediaries rather than to consumers. Contact between suppliers and prospective tour clients takes the form of group presentations, public speeches, and public trade shows.

Sales offices for most suppliers are organized and structured in much the same way as airline sales offices—that is, by city, region, and nation. Locally owned or franchised suppliers, however, seldom have the need for a nationwide sales force.

Public sector organizations (PSOs) promote group travel to particular cities or provinces. PSOs include provincial departments of tourism, local and municipal tourism councils, and convention and visitors' bureaus, all of which market their destinations to tour operators. Popular marketing approaches include direct mail and catchy slogans such as "Beautiful British Columbia," "Halifax Likes Company," and "I Love New York."

Tour operators consolidate the services of suppliers into a marketable package tour. This package is then sold either directly or indirectly to consumers. Travel agencies are the final link in the chain—they actually sell the package tours to consumers. They are the outlet for the suppliers' and tour operators' products, and are compensated for their services through commissions, usually starting at 10 percent. Generally, when a travel agency receives commission, the client does not have to pay a fee for the travel agency's services.

Packaging the Components

The work involved in producing a package tour can be divided into four main stages: operations, costing, brochure production, and promotions.

Operations The operations stage begins with planning. Market research tells the tour operator which tours will sell. Tours can also be created in response to an offer from a supplier. Once the tour destination, approximate dates, and length of tour have been determined, the next stage is to negotiate with the suppliers of transportation and ground services. A detailed itinerary is developed.

Costing The package must be offered to consumers at an attractive price that still allows markup for promotional costs, business overhead, commissions, and profit. Costs can be fixed or variable. Fixed costs must be paid regardless of the number of tour participants. If a tour operator books hotel rooms or bus seats in blocks, the cost will be the same whether 15 or 25 people take the tour. Variable costs are charged on the basis of the number of people on the tour. If hotel rooms are not block-booked, the tour operator pays the supplier only for the rooms that are used.

ILLUSTRATION 15–7

A tour manager or director is responsible for the day-to-day operation of an escorted tour.

SOURCE: Tim Hall/Photodisc Red/Getty Images.

Tour operators can vary the cost of a package by omitting or including various features—for example, by limiting the number of meals included, by choosing first-class rather than deluxe hotels, and by scheduling more free time and fewer organized activities.

Brochure Production The next stage is the production of a brochure for distribution to travel agents and potential clients. The brochure typically contains general information on the tour operator, listings of all available tours featuring what is included, detailed daily itineraries, prices, and maps, and a statement of conditions.

Promotions The final stage is the promotion of the tour. This includes advertisements aimed at tourism industry professionals in trade publications such as the NTA's monthly *Courier*, *Travel Weekly*, *Travelweek Bulletin*, and *Travel Courier*, and at potential consumers. Trade advertisements tend to be more informative, while consumer advertisements stress the glamour of particular tours. Tour operators also use direct mailings as well as group sales presentations to retailers who might be interested in selling their tours. Familiarization (FAM) tours, offered to travel agencies either free or at a discount, are another common promotional technique.

References

A number of publications listing both domestic and overseas tours are available to the trade. The *Consolidated Tour Manual* (CTM) catalogues tours to destinations in various countries. Gray Line Corporation publishes the *Official Sightseeing Sales and Tour Guide* annually. This guide lists net rates for sightseeing, transfers, limousine rental, and even shore excursions. The *Official Tour Directory* covers tours to destinations around the world. It also provides an alphabetical listing of tour operators.

Individuals can look up tours and charters on websites, either directly or using a search engine.

CHARTERS

A **charter** is a travel arrangement whereby transportation equipment is leased or rented at a net price. The company or individual that charters the airplane, bus, ship, or train is the charterer. Tour operators handle the bulk of charter business, but travel agencies, individuals, and groups can also act as charterers. Charters offer a number of advantages and disadvantages, both for charterers and for travellers. First, the advantages:

- The price can be as low as 40 percent of the regular fare, if fully sold out.
- The operator can make a higher per-passenger profit when the charter is fully occupied or sold out.
- Charters can offer greater convenience than scheduled transportation—for example, direct flights without stopping.
- Charters give a group or an organization a sense of exclusiveness. Group members will refer to the charter vehicle as "our plane" or "our bus."
- Charters can often be customized to meet the MNEs of the passengers.

The disadvantages:

- Pricing is based on the assumption that the flight will sell out. If it does not, the cost per seat can be high.
- The operator can lose money if the number of seats sold doesn't cover costs.
- Charter flights have a worse on-time record than scheduled flights and are also subject to cancellation.
- A charter ticket is nontransferable if a traveller misses the flight.
- Charter operators can consolidate two or more flights if their charters are not selling well. This can cause last-minute changes in departure times, airports, and itineraries.
- The charterer may add a last-minute surcharge. An increase in fuel costs, for example, can lead to a sudden fare hike. Charterers are allowed by law to increase fares by as much as 10 percent up to 10 days

before departure. In Ontario, the maximum surcharge permitted by tour operators for charters or package tours is 7 percent. If the price increases by more than 7 percent, clients can legally cancel without penalty.

The charter operator, like a tour operator, is a speculator and risk taker. When arranging a charter with a carrier, the operator must sign a contract and pay a deposit. The cost of the deposit is passed on to the sales intermediaries, or passengers, or both.

Different Types of Charters

Charters can be private or public. **Private charters** are not for sale to the general public. Some private charters, known as **single-entity charters**, are paid for in full by a single source. IBM might charter an Air Canada 767 and fly 250 of its top salespeople and their spouses to Barbados for an incentive holiday. As a rule, the passengers do not pay for their own tickets: The company that arranges the charter provides these, along with any accommodations.

Other private charters are sold through organizations, such as clubs, and are called **affinity charters**, indicating some sort of voluntary membership or "affinity" to an organization.

Either a travel agency or a tour or charter operator sells **public charters** to the general public. There are no restrictions in terms of membership in an organization. The public charter may include either one-way or round-trip transportation only, or be part of a package known as a "charter tour."

Chartering Different Modes of Transportation

Most people think of charters as involving a plane or a bus. However, it is also possible to charter a train, a single passenger car, or a ship. Vessels that are available for charter, such as windjammers, riverboats, and yachts, tend to be small.

It is less complicated to charter a school bus than a cruise ship or a 767, but regardless of size and price, all charters require some sort of contractual agreement.

Many charter flights take place on board scheduled carriers; others are provided by all-charter airlines known as supplemental carriers, which usually do not have scheduled services.

Airline deregulation in the United States had a significant effect on the charter market there. Scheduled airlines now compete in price with the supplemental carriers and offer equally attractive packages with fewer restrictions and less risk. Several supplemental carriers chose to become scheduled carriers after deregulation. Deregulation of the American motorcoach industry made it easier for bus companies in that country to obtain tour broker's licenses. This has led to a large increase in the number of charter companies.

ILLUSTRATION 15–8

Price and availability are two criteria for choosing a charter carrier.

SOURCE: Photo by Indu Ghuman.

Canada's airlines were given greater pricing freedom in the 1980s. Charter airlines such as Air Transat emerged around that time. In the 1990s and especially after the Open Skies agreement, the major regular scheduled airlines reduced their charter services to destinations in the southern United States and replaced them with regular scheduled services. The former mainly charter carriers increased their regularly scheduled services. Air Transat and Skyservice offered domestic packages through their tour operator subsidiaries and intermediaries.

International air charter travel patterns are fairly stable: transatlantic in the summer, southern destinations in the winter.

Pricing

Charterers determine their product prices by dividing the total price quoted by the carrier, plus any markup, by the number of seats, berths, or cabins. Most private charters are not marked up, since they require no commissions to sales intermediaries. As an example, a school charters a 40-seat bus for a trip to the circus. The bus company charges $200 for the bus. If all seats are sold, the price per passenger will be $5 ($200/40).

Important Charter Terms and Concepts

You will understand better how charters work if you remember the following:

- When the carrier provides the crew, this cost is included in the quote.
- If the driver of a motorcoach has to wait for three hours while the group tours an attraction or attends a show, an hourly wait charge is figured into the price.
- Most charters base their price on cost per kilometre, or cost per hour, or a combination of these. This means a one-way charter can cost as much as a round-trip charter, because the operator has to get the vehicle

home (unless the operator practises back-to-back scheduling, whereby the vehicle returns with a full load).

- When planning multiple charters, operators try to establish a pattern. They might organize, for example, one flight per week, May 15–August 31, Toronto–Rome, as well as one flight per week, May 15–August 31, Montreal–Rome. Patterns make consolidation much easier; for example, if the May 30 departures from Toronto and Montreal are both undersold, the operator can stop the Toronto flight in Montreal and proceed to Rome with all passengers in a single plane.
- Consolidation can also involve consolidating dates. A Friday departure and a Sunday departure, for example, can be consolidated into a single Saturday departure.

References

Charters are never listed in the *Official Airline Guide* or other travel schedules. The best source of charter information is *JAX FAX Travel Marketing Magazine*, a monthly directory of air tours. Other sources include charter operators' programs and brochures, and websites.

Check Your Product Knowledge

1. List three advantages and three disadvantages of travelling by charter flight.
2. What is the difference between a scheduled carrier and a supplemental carrier?
3. How are charters priced?
4. What is meant by the term "back-to-back scheduling"?

CHANNELS OF DISTRIBUTION

All products, including package tours, must be moved from producer to consumer. The tour industry has its own distribution system, with wide variations, combinations, and interactions. Here we review three types of distribution channels—one direct and two indirect.

With the unilateral or one-stage, direct-sale system, an individual or group buys the tour product directly from the producer or supplier of tour services. This cuts out all sales intermediaries. An example would be a client who buys an air tour through an airline reservations centre.

The bilevel or two-stage distribution system involves a single sales intermediary—usually a tour operator who packages the various supplier services into a single tour product. Some travel agencies also buy directly from suppliers, as do incentive travel companies, travel clubs, convention planners, and corporate travel offices.

The multilevel or three-stage system involves the intervention of a second sales intermediary between the tour operator and the consumer. The additional intermediary is usually a retail travel counsellor, who is paid a commission for handling the tour operator's products.

Tour operators try to avail themselves of every channel of distribution. Retail travel agents, who are remunerated by commission when they make a sale, have been efficient and cost-effective distributors for tour operators. In the past, tour operators—especially the sunspot stayput—would not risk alienating travel agencies by soliciting clients directly. Today, as a result of electronic distribution, this situation has changed.

Outbound sunspot stayput and scenic/sightseeing tour operators have particular requirements in developing a channel. They need inbound receptive tour operators in every destination where they intend to offer products. Supplier requirements include air carrier to destination, accommodation at destination, and transfers and ground service while at/in the destination. A receptive tour operator provides the latter.

Development of a Distribution Channel

Canadian tour operators marketing to a local or regional market may wish to expand to reach potential clients in national, North American, or overseas markets. But how do they go about doing this? In looking at the structure of the travel trade channel, we see potential tourists, domestic and foreign travel agents, outbound and inbound tour operators, inbound receptive operators, and other members such as group leaders, airlines, wholesalers and brokers, travel clubs, and destination marketing organizations.

Table 15–2 compares the strengths and weaknesses of channel members that an adventure travel operator may select in order to extend its market reach.

Even though an adventure travel operator has to discount its product to pay for the services of member(s) within the channel, the additional business should be profitable. The operator's costs may even be reduced if members within the channel assume the costs of developing the package and marketing it.

The Tour Organizer

A tour that is promoted and sold to a specific group or within a local market often involves a tour organizer, who may be a member of the group or a media celebrity who shares an interest with the group. The tour organizer is compensated with a free trip if enough people (15 is usually the minimum) are on the tour.

Local and Nationwide Tours

The terms "local tour" and "nationwide tour" refer to the marketplace in which the tour is promoted, not to the destination. An example of a **local tour** is a high-school spring trip to Ottawa; such a tour would be marketed only to local high school students. Local tours are often joint efforts involving a tour organizer, a local travel agency, a tour operator, and a transportation rep.

Nationwide tours are promoted and sold from coast to coast in Canada and the United States. You can buy the same American Express, Tauck, or other big-name tour in any travel agency in the United States and Canada.

TABLE 15–2 Strengths and Weaknesses of Travel Trade Networks

Channel Members	Strengths	Weaknesses
Travel Agents	• They have established presence in their local market. • Convenience for customers inquiring and booking, and for additional travel arrangements required.	• Most are order takers—you have to create the demand for the product.
Tour Operators	• The tour operators' name and participation in the program provide quality assurance to travel agents and consumers. • Their established market presence guarantees some sales. • They handle all the sales administration.	• They require net rates at a substantial discount from regular prices. • You lose control of some of your inventory.
Receptive Operators	• They can assemble packages at your destination more readily. • They have established clientele (i.e., other tour operators who may buy the product).	• Commissions and discounts are substantial—you have to support up to three levels of intermediaries.
Group Leaders	• They have a customer base readily available. • They can handle a lot of the sales administration for the suppliers. • The cost of doing business with them is reasonable.	• Tour operators consider sales direct to group leaders as an end run, bypassing them. • The time and costs involved in dealing with group leaders on one-off packages can be onerous.

SOURCE: *On the Path to Success: Lessons from Canadian Adventure Travel and Eco-tourism Operators 1999.* Reproduced with permission of the Minister of Public Works and Government Services Canada, 2005.

CAREER OPPORTUNITIES

The tour industry is expanding rapidly and offers a wide variety of career opportunities at the entry level, as well as good prospects for advancement. Many people are attracted to the tour sector by the promise of unlimited free travel to glamorous destinations. In reality, few travel.

Careers are available in four main areas: tour operator office, tour management, tour sales and promotion, and entrepreneurship.

The Tour Operator as Employer

A tour operator's office employs a number of clerical workers and supervisors. Some positions are described below.

Reservationist The main duties of a reservationist are to handle incoming calls and computer bookings from travel counsellors who are interested in booking the operator's tours. This is the most common entry-level position in many tour operators. Individuals learn the company's product line, organization, and culture. After six months to one year in the position, reservationists can then apply for a transfer or promotion within the company.

Operations Clerk Clerks process information from the reservationists to prepare passenger lists, rooming lists, and updates on the status of tour availability. Other duties include typing confirmations and mailing them to travel counsellors, and preparing passenger tour documents.

Reservations Supervisor Supervisors are in charge of all reservations staff and procedures. They are also responsible for interviewing, hiring, and training new reservationists. Group bookings and major accounts will usually be handled by the supervisor rather than by a less experienced reservationist.

Operations Supervisor This person is responsible for all operational staff and procedures. Other positions include group coordinator (who handles special-interest groups booked by travel agencies), accountant, and costing specialist.

Tour Management

A tour manager or director is responsible for the day-to-day—even minute-by-minute—operation of an escorted tour. This is a pivotal position: The reputation of a tour operator can hinge on how successfully the tour manager does his or her job.

A tour manager must have strong skills in negotiating, finance, accounting, and planning, as well as limitless patience and energy. Knowledge of at least one foreign language is essential for a tour manager who hopes to conduct tours overseas. Opportunities for managers of European tours are extremely limited, since tour operators like to employ native Europeans.

Certification by the NTA program is an excellent qualification for a tour manager. So is membership in the International Association of Tour Managers. Tour management is not only a career in itself, but also an entry-level step toward managing an entire tour operator company. There are plenty of opportunities for part-time tour managers, tour guides (who work at local sites and attractions), and tour organizers.

In Canada there are about 7000 tour guides. Most are women (63 percent), young (61 percent under 25), part-time (92 percent), and well educated (19 percent have a university degree). Native people are well represented.

Tour Sales and Promotion

The sales representative is the most visible employee in any sales and promotion department. This position involves calling on travel agents and making presentations to various groups. Other positions within the promotional department include publicist, writer, and graphic artist.

Entrepreneurship

Since deregulation, tour operators, transportation companies, and charter operators have entered the market in a flood. Most people need experience working in the tour industry before they go into business for themselves.

Specific Opportunities

Other opportunities for employment include:

- Sunspot stayput tour operators need product managers (who negotiate space and rates with destination suppliers).
- Sunspot stayput tours require destination representatives at each specific destination and airport representatives at the gateway airports.
- Escorted scenic/sightseeing tour operators require tour managers (tour escorts).
- Incentive travel houses require trip directors.
- Hosted tours require a host hired by receptive (inbound, local, or ground) tour operators.
- Receptive tour operators require tour guides.

A DAY IN THE LIFE OF A

Tour Manager

If you have ever taken a tour, you probably already have a good idea of what a tour manager does. I am the person who shepherds the tour group from place to place and makes sure all aspects of the tour run smoothly. I take care of hotel reservations, arrange for meals and transportation, obtain tickets for local attractions, and so on. This allows the members of the group to simply relax and enjoy their vacation.

The first day of the tour, I greet the members of my tour group, make sure they have all of their luggage, and brief them on the schedule for the day. Then we set off to our first destination. Most of the travellers in my tour groups are retired people, and we usually travel by bus. When we arrive at our hotel, I check in for my group and get everyone room assignments. Later, at dinner, I will tell everyone about the next day's schedule.

A lot of people have misconceptions about what tour managers do. Some people think I'm some kind of drill sergeant who bosses people around and tries to fill every minute of the day with organized activities. Nothing could be further from the truth. My job is to take care of the paperwork and headaches involved in travelling so that people can concentrate on doing the fun things they want to do.

It is true that I do organize group activities, because the group expects it and because it is cheaper for people to visit local attractions at a group rate. However, the members of my tour always have the option of joining in the activity, doing something else, or simply relaxing. In addition, on my tours, I always leave plenty of free time in the schedule for people to go off and do things on their own.

Some people think tour managers are experts on the history of the tour area. This is not necessarily true. Many tour managers lead tours of the same routes over and over again and do become knowledgeable about the local area. In some cases, however, the tour company provides a sightseeing guide, in addition to the tour manager, to inform the tour members about the history of the area. Sightseeing guides specialize in one specific region, museum, park, or building.

My main job is to act as the liaison between my tour group and the hotels, restaurants, and attractions that my group visits. I make all the reservations, pay the bills and tips, and stand ready to solve any and all problems that may arise during the course of a tour. I must always be resourceful and calm in the face of a crisis, because no tour ever goes completely smoothly. On a recent tour, our bus broke down. I had to arrange for another bus to pick us up, and then I had to keep the tour members occupied while we waited.

My job requires tact, organizational skills, and leadership ability. Knowledge of more than one language is a major advantage, because so many foreign tourists have started visiting our country in recent years. Some tour managers lead tour groups on wilderness and adventure tours. They may lead tourists on hikes through the foothills of the Himalayas, on whitewater rafting trips down the Ottawa River, or on horseback tours of the Rocky Mountains. These managers need strength and stamina as well as all the other attributes of a good tour manager. Some tour managers specialize in archaeology, art history, fine dining, or wine appreciation. These managers need special training in those fields.

When my tour company hired me, it put me through an intensive training course. Then it sent me out in the field with an experienced tour manager. That's how I learned my job. Being a tour manager is not a high-paying job, but it gives me the opportunity to travel and stay at nice resorts for free. Many tour managers work only part-time, with long gaps between tours. Some are freelance, and keep busy by working for several tour operators instead of just one company.

I like being a tour manager because I like people and I like to travel. I think the nicest thing about my job is that I start out with a group of strangers and I help them become a group of friends who are sharing the fun and adventure of a trip together. When that happens, I know I have done my job well.

SOURCE: Tim Hall/Photodisc Red/Getty Images.

Summary

- The tour has evolved from the grand tour, through the custom-made tour, into the package tour.
- A package tour is a combination of two or more travel components put together by a tour operator and sold to the consumer as a single product at a single price.
- Package tours have become increasingly popular because they offer travellers known costs, bargain prices, and guaranteed arrangements—they are the most worry-free form of travel.
- Tours can be categorized by format, destination, and purpose.
- All-inclusive, independent, hosted, and escorted are the four basic package tour formats.
- Tour operators develop packages to fit the MNEs of different kinds of travellers.
- Flexibility, pacing, and different price ranges are important considerations in developing tours.
- A tour manager accompanies a group for the duration of an escorted tour, making sure all the tour ingredients come together as planned.
- Since deregulation, the United States Tour Operators Association (USTOA) and the National Tour Association (NTA) have set financial and ethical standards for the tour industry.
- All overseas tours are required to conform to International Air Transport Association (IATA) regulations.
- The production of the tour product requires a close working relationship among suppliers, public sector organizations, tour operators, and travel agents.
- Operations, costing, brochure production, and promotions are the four main stages in the preparation of a package tour.
- Charters, which can be private or public, offer travellers considerable savings on transportation costs.
- The tour product is channelled from producer to consumers by one of three distribution systems.
- Tours can also be categorized as local or nationwide, depending on the area in which the tour is promoted.

Key Terms

Internet Connections

Gray Line Canada
www.grayline.ca   p. 344

International Air Transport Association (IATA)
www.iata.org   p. 350

International Association of Tour Managers
www.iatm.co.uk/backinf.htm   p. 356

JAC Travel
www.jaconline.com   p. 344

Jonview Canada (Receptive Tour Operator)
www.jonview.com   p. 344

Mountain Travel Sobek
www.mtsobek.com   p. 345

National Tour Association
www.ntaonline.com   p. 350

Sunquest Vacations
www.sunquest.ca   p. 340

Tauck
www.tauck.com   p. 355

Tour East Holidays
www.toureast.com   p. 338

Travel Industry Council of Ontario (TICO)
www.tico.on.ca   p. 350

WORKSHEET 15–1   Inbound Tourism

You are a receptive tour operator. Your job is to package and promote tours for upper-class Mexican visitors to Canada. A major part of your job is to negotiate contracts with suppliers of transportation, hospitality, and tourism. Besides basic services, you expect your suppliers to furnish special services and amenities for your Mexican customers. What could each of the following tour components do to help your tour groups feel welcome in this country? (For example, hotels along the tour route might agree to make Mexican newspapers available for guests.)

Airlines

_____

_____

_____

_____

Hotels/motels

_____

_____

_____

_____

Restaurants

_____

_____

_____

_____

Stores

_____

_____

_____

_____

Tourist attractions

_____

_____

_____

_____

WORKSHEET 15–2 Terms and Conditions

Visit websites and/or obtain brochures for two tours that are currently available. Compare the terms and conditions.

	Tour 1	Tour 2
Name of tour		
Apparent/perceived market target(s) for tour		
MNEs of market target(s)		
What is and is not included		
Reservations procedures		
Deposit and payment schedule		
Travel and health documents required		
Cancellation and refund policy		
Status of fares, rates, and itinerary		
Tour operator's limited responsibility and liability		

Objectives

When you have completed this chapter, you should be able to:

- Identify recent developments affecting traditional travel agencies.
- Explain how a travel agency is similar to, and different from, a traditional retail store.
- Discuss how travel agencies are compensated.
- Describe the relationship among the travel agency, the customer, and the supplier.
- Understand the important role travel counsellors play in addition to making travel arrangements and selling travel products.
- List several types of travel agencies.
- Define the differences among types of online (e-commerce) travel agencies.

- Explain how airline regulatory reform, the competitive market decision, and automation have affected travel agencies.
- Describe the trend toward consolidation of travel agencies.
- List the steps involved in opening a retail travel agency.
- Describe how a travel agency functions.
- Identify other travel and tourism distributors.
- Name the main professional associations for travel counsellors.
- Discuss the future of traditional travel agencies.

Sally Ayers, a self-employed management consultant based in Ottawa, is also her own travel counsellor. She watches a number of travel shows on television and regularly scans various travel websites, both for entertainment and for planning purposes. However, Sally is reluctant to give credit card information over the Internet. She recently planned the itinerary and made all the arrangements for a trip to Ireland for herself, her husband, and another couple. Sally borrowed books on Ireland from the public library and read about places to visit. She also picked up a travel video at her local video store. Months before their departure, she checked out the websites of B&Bs. She sent e-mails to those that interested her, requesting accommodation. To buy round-trip air tickets from Montreal to Dublin on an international carrier, she drove from her home in the suburbs to a downtown airline office. To buy tickets for a connecting flight to Montreal, she phoned a Canadian carrier and decided to use ticketless travel. And by dialling a toll-free phone number from her home, she was able to reserve a rental car for ground transportation while in Ireland.

Sally is an exceptional traveller. Most travellers have neither the time nor the know-how to make their own

travel arrangements. They're also not interested in sorting through complicated schedules and fares. And they don't want to worry about everything connecting smoothly. Instead, they depend on travel and tourism distributors—travel agencies, business travel departments (BTDs), and travel clubs—to take care of all the arrangements.

In Canada, travel agencies are grouped under the travel trade sector, along with wholesale tour operators. This sector is the smallest of the five tourism-related employment sectors in Canada, with about 33 000 employees in 2003—only 2 percent of total tourism-related employment. However, since all employees in this sector are classified as entirely employed in tourism, they comprise about 6 percent of direct tourism employment. There are an estimated 5000 travel agencies in Canada, according to the Association of Canadian Travel Agencies (ACTA). About 2600 retail travel firms belong to ACTA. That is more than 40 percent of all Canadian travel agencies; however, ACTA members account for an estimated 75 percent of the travel agency sales in Canada.

The revenues from travel agency services (commissions and fees on sales of travel products and services) amounted to almost $1.6 billion in 2005, according to the

PROFILE

Focal Point for the Retail Travel Services Industry

Association of Canadian Travel Agencies

The Association of Canadian Travel Agencies (ACTA), founded in 1977 as the Alliance of Canadian Travel Associations, represents the travel industry in Canada. Seven provincial associations (now known as Regional Councils for ACTA Atlantic, ACTA Quebec, ACTA Ontario, ACTA Manitoba/Nunavut, ACTA Saskatchewan, ACTA Alberta, and ACTA British Columbia/Yukon) formed the alliance.

ACTA has more than 3000 members in two categories: retail (travel agencies) and allied/supplier (travel service and marketing service suppliers such as airlines, tour operators, hotels, tourist boards, cruise lines, railways, car rental companies, and computer reservations system [CRS] vendors).

ACTA's mission is to serve as the focal point for the retail travel services industry, where ideas and resources are pooled into initiatives designed to create and maintain a healthy business and legislative environment in which the retail travel industry will thrive.

Each of the seven regional councils works with a network of volunteers and professionals, and undertakes a broad range of projects significant to its own members. For example, ACTA Ontario made a submission to the provincial government in 2000 on proposed changes to the Travel Industry Act. Similarly, ACTA National participated in the public hearings regarding deregulation of the global distribution system (GDS) in 2004. ACTA has also lobbied against the elimination of paper tickets and for clear, all-in pricing by airlines. ACTA National is overseen by a board of directors, which is composed of the seven regional council chairs and one representative each from the Canadian Institute of Travel Counsellors and consortium and franchise travel agencies. ACTA's president and CEO manage the Ottawa secretariat and the seven regional offices. The national board works together to respond to both regional and national issues.

ACTA maintains a continuous dialogue within the industry (e.g., with the Tourism Industry Association of Canada and the Air Transportation Association of Canada). It also represents its members in front of government bodies on issues of concern and relevance to all ACTA members. These government bodies include Transport Canada, Foreign Affairs Canada, the Canadian Transportation Agency, the Canadian Tourism Commission, the Canada Border Services Agency, the Canada Revenue Agency, and Finance Canada. ACTA expresses its members' views on key issues such as consumer and trade protection, air transportation taxes, tariffs, customs, Canadian tourism, regulation of tour operators and travel agencies, and regulation of supplier organizations such as airlines.

ACTA contributes to international dialogue in the travel industry through alliances with relevant associations in other countries, and through its alliance with the Universal Federation of Travel Agents' Associations. In 2001, ACTA worked with other organizations to promote the concept of "dot-travel" as the top-level domain name in e-commerce websites for the travel and tourism industry.

To help provide the public with the highest-quality travel services, and to promote the most efficient and amicable dealings with other members, every ACTA member has accepted a two-part code of ethics. The first part applies to relations between ACTA members and the public; the second applies to relations among ACTA members.

ACTA sponsors national and provincial education courses and seminars. In addition, ACTA members can participate in group health and insurance plans, and in a business insurance plan. This is a desirable feature, as many members are categorized as small businesses.

In 1997, ACTA formally changed its name to the Association of Canadian Travel Agents, and then in 2001 to the Association of Canadian Travel Agencies, to reflect the nature of most of its members more accurately.

National Tourism Indicators of Statistics Canada. This was an increase of 6.1 percent over 2004. Domestic sales dominated; sales to foreigners (an "export"—for example, an American using a Canadian travel agency to purchase airline tickets) were minimal. As a commodity, spending on travel agency services ranked fifth in the travel industry after transportation, food and beverage, accommodation, and recreation and entertainment.

What will be the form and functions of travel agencies in the future? Today, they are being affected by a number of changes in the environment, including:

- A dramatic rise in online competition (see Chapter 14).
- A reduction in commissions on products sold, especially airline tickets.
- A change in consumer perspectives. Some consumers are more knowledgeable and want to "do it themselves," which means bypassing travel agencies; other consumers perceive tourism products and services as "commodities" and go directly to suppliers.

Even with all these changes, it is interesting that a travel agency, Flight Centre, has been named by *The Globe and Mail's Report on Business Magazine* as one of the top four employers in Canada each year since 2001.

THE TRAVEL AGENCY AS AN INTERMEDIARY

In all channels of distribution there is usually an intermediary, or link, between suppliers and customers. One type of intermediary is the retail store. Hardware stores, supermarkets, clothing boutiques, drugstores, and other retail outlets provide convenient places for consumers to buy a variety of products. Retail stores are also convenient for suppliers. Without them, suppliers would have to set up their own outlets or send sales representatives all over the country.

A travel agency acts much like a retail store in that it provides suppliers with a link to the public. In this case, the suppliers are airlines, cruise lines, bus companies, railways, hotels and motels, car rental agencies, tourist boards, and tour wholesalers and tour operators. The customers include vacation and leisure travellers, business travellers, and travellers visiting friends and relatives (VFRs). The travel agency is the retail link between suppliers and customers in the distribution channel. The channels are both bilateral and multilateral (see Chapter 14).

Note that the travel agency is not the only distributor between suppliers and customers. Most suppliers usually have at least two channels to customers—one through travel agencies, and the other direct (unilateral). Also, some travel agencies—especially the agency chains—act as wholesalers to other (usually smaller) travel agencies.

Travel agencies are the most important of all travel intermediaries. Retail travel agencies reserve more airline seats, cruise berths, hotel rooms, and package tours than any other intermediary. Percentages will fall as more consumers buy direct from suppliers and increasingly through websites.

Compensation

Like other retail stores, travel agencies are in business to make money. However, travel agencies do not earn their money the same way as most other retail outlets.

Most retailers buy goods for certain prices from suppliers and then sell these goods for higher prices to customers. Retailers need to stock their stores with inventory. For example, the owner of a hardware store buys nuts and bolts, tools, wood, and other merchandise from manufacturers or wholesale dealers. The owner buys these products in bulk and so gets them for reduced rates. Before selling them to the public, the owner marks up the items' prices. The customer pays for the item at its retail price, and the difference between the wholesale price and the retail price—the markup—is the owner's compensation.

Travel agencies do not "stock" products in this manner. Rather, for the time and money the agency spends promoting and selling the supplier's products, the supplier compensates the agency in the form of commissions and overrides (a bonus for selling in greater volume). Customers pay no more for travel products at a travel agency than they would by going to the supplier directly. In fact, travel counsellors can often save clients money by comparing different products to determine the best value. And travel counsellors offer advice on destinations, routing, transportation, accommodation, and sightseeing.

For a long time, travel agencies received more than half their compensation from the sale of airline products and services, but this has been dropping (see Table 16–1). Because the airlines have such a tremendous influence on travel agencies, much of this chapter focuses on the relationship between airlines and travel agencies.

TABLE 16–1 Travel Agency Revenue by Source, 2004

Source of Revenue	(%)
Tour package	25.0
Cruise package	7.0
Transportation fares	42.0
Accommodation	4.2
Auto rentals	2.5
Insurance products	5.0
Other sources	3.5
Service fees	11.0

SOURCE: *Canadian Tourism Commission, Canadian Travel Arrangement Services Survey,* Year 2004 report, 2006. Reproduced with the permission of the Minister of Public Works and Government Services Canada, 2006.

The Canadian Tourism Commission's *Canadian Travel Arrangement Services Survey* report for 2004 reveals the following:

- Canadian travel agencies received about 75 percent of their revenues from commissions on the sale of transportation, which were mostly airline tickets (42.0 percent) and tour packages (25.0 percent).
- Service fees contributed 11.0 percent, but this had tripled from 2001.

In addition, about half (59 percent) of travel agency revenues in 2004 came from leisure travel. Business travel accounted for 37 percent, while government and foreign sales accounted for the remainder.

Commissions A commission is the percentage of the total sale price that is paid to an agency. If an agency (or counsellor) sells a cruise ticket for $1000 and the cruise line has agreed to pay a commission of 10 percent, the agency (or counsellor) receives a commission of $100 ($1000 × 0.10 = $100). At 10 percent commission, $1 million in sales will result in $100 000 in commissions, from which operating expenses and corporate taxes must be paid. Since profit margins in the travel industry can be quite low, managers and owners must watch finances carefully.

The standard commissions paid by selected tourism suppliers—mainly those in the transportation sector—to travel agencies in Canada are shown in Table 16–2. In the past, most commissions were around 10 percent of the ticket purchase price. The impact on revenues of the change in airline commissions has been quite dramatic. Airline commission has been virtually eliminated, except for bookings through airline websites and special arrange-

ments negotiated between an airline and agencies that sell in volume. This is one reason why some travel agencies have changed their focus—for example, to emphasize the cruise industry.

Tours pay big commissions. Tour operators and tour wholesalers create distinct products, which are then retailed (in Canada) mainly by travel agencies. Recently, more tour operators and wholesalers have been promoting direct sales by developing transactional websites. Between 2000 and 2004, for example, travel agency revenue from the sale of tour packages dropped from 32 percent of income to 25 percent. For travel agencies, already hit hard by the airline industry's commission caps, this poses yet another threat to bottom lines. Given these pressures, most if not all travel agencies have imposed service charges, especially for airline ticket sales, to reflect what they do for customers.

Why would a travel agency deal with a supplier that does not pay a commission? Perhaps to satisfy a client who wants to stay at a particular hotel. The agency may expect to make money on other components of the client's trip, or may apply a service fee to compensate for the effort and expense involved in making the reservation.

Overrides Suppliers also compensate travel agencies through overrides. An **override** is a bonus or extra commission for selling in greater volume. Say, for example, that a cruise line pays a travel agency a commission of 10 percent on the sale of every cruise package. After the agency sells $10 000 worth of cruises, the cruise line then pays an additional 1 percent commission—a total of 11 percent—for every cruise sold after that. That extra 1 percent is the override.

TABLE 16–2 Comparison of Travel Agency Commissions for Selected Components, 1995 and 2008

	1995[1]	2008[2]	
Transportation			
Air:			
Domestic	8.25%	0%	Airlines generally do not pay commission
Transborder	10%	0%	on reservations through a GDS; however,
Within U.S.	10%	0%	some airlines make special agreements with
International	11%	0%	volume producers.
Online websites	n/a	0–9%	
Car rental	10%	10%	
Cruise	10% plus	10–16%	
Rail	—	5%	
Accommodation			
Hotel	—	10%	Some do not pay commission
Tours and charters			
Tour components	10%	Usually 10%	
Tour packages	11–22%	10–15%	

SOURCES: [1]1995: *Passport,* 2nd U.S. ed., 1993; and *Passport,* 1st Cdn. ed., 1995.
[2]2008: Prepared from material in authors' possession and various website articles.

Some suppliers offer overrides on a graduated scale up to 15 percent. Following is an example of a graduated scale:

Sales	Override
$10 000–14 999	1%
$15 000–24 999	2%
$25 000–34 999	3%
$35 000–44 999	4%
$45 000+	5%

Overrides are sometimes retroactive once the agency has reached a certain total. For example, when an agency has reached a sales total of $45 000, the supplier may pay a 15 percent commission for all previous sales. Some overrides in Canada are a matter of individual negotiation between the supplier and the agent. Most Canadian suppliers that pay overrides do so on larger sales volumes than are shown in the above example.

Rebates To attract and maintain customers, some travel agencies share a portion of their commissions and overrides with their clients. This takes the form of **rebates**, or money back on the price of the ticket. Rebates for airline tickets are commonly given to corporations. In fact, some corporations demand a certain percentage of an agency's commissions before they will contract to do business with it. Some rebates in Canada are arrived at by individual negotiation between the carrier and the agent.

Service Charges Service charges are common in the United States; they were less common in Canada until recently. To cover their expenses, travel agencies may charge customers for certain services. This is largely because of airline deregulation—with the onslaught of low airfares, travel agencies are earning less in commissions.

Some agencies now charge for preparing a lengthy and involved itinerary, making noncommissionable hotel reservations, obtaining visas, sending telegrams, and making long-distance telephone calls. Because it is time-consuming to undo arrangements, agencies may also charge for trip cancellations. A consulting fee may be charged if the travel counsellor spends an hour talking to a customer about a trip and the customer doesn't book. Fees can be waived in certain circumstances. For instance, clients booking a round-the-world cruise would probably not be charged for long-distance calls made in connection with their trip.

Service charges in Canada generally range between $35 and $75. Agencies that charge service fees should state this clearly to customers before starting any transactions. In Ontario, the disclosure of a service charge is a legal requirement. Many people, however, feel that charging fees violates the service nature of the travel agency industry.

Consolidators and Net Prices As the number of suppliers paying commission has fallen, travel agencies have turned to other sources of income. Many introduced service fees as described above. Today, however, many agencies use the services of consolidators or other companies that sell travel products at net prices (i.e., without any markup). Consolidators are sales companies that offer various types of travel services (such as hotel reservations, flights, or car rentals) to travel agencies. These companies purchase large volumes of product from suppliers and then resell it to travel agencies. They do not usually sell directly to the public. Consolidators tend to specialize in one type of supplier (e.g., airlines) or in particular destinations or regions. Generally, consolidators focus on international destinations and long-haul travel. Travel agencies purchase the travel products from a consolidator at a net price and then add their own markup before selling to the consumer.

Relationships

Travel agencies have relationships both with suppliers and with clients. They have **agreements**, written or implied, to sell the products of their suppliers. They are expected to represent suppliers honourably and faithfully and to avoid dishonest practices. At the same time, agencies depend on suppliers to deliver products and services as promised. Once a trip has started, travel counsellors have no control over supplier errors, although clients tend to blame the agency or counsellor when things go wrong. Agencies need to select carefully the suppliers with whom they will do business. A written or implied agreement between a travel agency and a supplier is known as a **preferred supplier agreement**.

Travel agencies also act on behalf of their clients. Travel counsellors have an obligation to provide competent travel planning for clients who are spending money on travel products, which—unlike most other consumer goods—cannot be returned if the buyer is not pleased. Clients expect travel counsellors to represent suppliers' products truthfully. They also expect counsellors to be knowledgeable about transportation and accommodation and to offer them the most complete and up-to-date information about destinations. Clients would certainly want to know, for example, if there was serious political unrest at their planned destination. Travel counsellors must be meticulous in seeing to the details of a client's trip. Inserting the wrong departure time on a client's itinerary or forgetting to inform the client about visa requirements could ruin a trip and make the agency liable for damages.

Relationships among travel agencies, suppliers, and customers are very complex. As an intermediary, the travel agency must relate well to both suppliers and customers. This often means walking a fine line.

Agency and Supplier Relationships An automobile dealership generally sells the products of only one manufacturer—perhaps Chrysler, Ford, or Nissan. A travel agency, in contrast, generally represents many suppliers. The fact that a travel agent can show customers a variety of products and help them select the best for their needs has long been one of the strongest arguments for purchasing through a travel agency.

However, certain circumstances may prevent an agency from maintaining a neutral role as a general supplier of travel products. To obtain lucrative overrides, an agency may use one airline (a preferred supplier) for most of its business, even though this may not be in the best interest of the customer. Some suppliers offer other incentives, such as yearly bonuses and free travel, to persuade travel agencies to promote their products. Also, an agency that leases the global distribution system (GDS) of a certain carrier tends to favour that carrier.

Agency and Customer Relationships Travel counsellors relate to their clients in three ways: as counsellors who advise clients on trip planning and provide information about destinations; as sales representatives who interest customers in new products and services; and finally, as clerks who make reservations and input itineraries.

Most travel counsellors find that advising clients is the most rewarding aspect of their profession. It presents a challenge and allows them to be creative. That is why many of them feel that the term "agent" no longer gives the full picture of what they do. Instead, they prefer to call themselves "travel consultants" or "travel counsellors."

TYPES OF TRAVEL AGENCIES

A look in the *Yellow Pages* or an Internet search for any size of city will yield several pages or many websites for travel agencies. To meet the various needs of consumers, different types of travel agencies offer a variety of travel products and services. There are two main types of travel agencies: general and specialized. First, we will discuss traditional travel agencies, then online travel agencies.

General Agencies

Most travel agencies in Canada and the United States offer general services. These agencies are like travel "department stores" in that they offer a wide variety of products and services to suit a wide range of customers. These full-service agencies handle all types of travel—airplane, rail, bus, cruise, rental car—and all types of accommodation. They book all sorts of tours, from sightseeing trips through Europe's capitals to 12-day rafting trips on the Tatshenshini River in northwestern British Columbia. Customers can find products to fit almost any budget.

There are some differences between full-service agencies in Canada and those in the United States. Business travel, which offers lower commissions, is less common in Canada, so revenue from that source is lower for both reasons. On the other hand, more package tours and charters are sold in Canada, and commissions are generally higher.

Owners of full-service travel agencies believe that offering diverse products and services results in steadier income. Brisk business in one area can offset slow business in another area. So counsellors must know something about every aspect of travel, and this is a challenge.

ILLUSTRATION 16–1
A travel agent performs the roles of both travel counsellor and sales representative.
SOURCE: Thomson Nelson.

Check Your Product Knowledge

1. Identify a number of pressures affecting traditional travel agencies.
2. Which suppliers have had the most influence on travel agency operations?
3. Name two ways that suppliers compensate travel agencies. How are these methods different from those used in most other areas of retailing?
4. What are rebates? Why do suppliers and agencies offer them?
5. What is the dealership concept of retailing? In what way is the retail travel agency different?
6. What advantages does a travel agency gain by dealing with a consolidator rather than an airline?

Larger travel agencies are usually divided into departments, such as corporate and leisure (formerly classified as commercial and vacation). These departments can be further divided into international and domestic. Travel counsellors with specialized knowledge staff each department.

Corporate Agencies

A **corporate** (commercial) **travel agency** specializes in the business travel requirements of firms and corporations. Because destinations are determined by the nature of the business, agents do less counselling with business travellers. The emphasis is on making arrangements quickly and efficiently. Commercial travel agencies tend to enjoy consistent year-round business, free from the seasonal or economic fluctuations that are part of vacation and leisure travel. Some commercial agencies branch into leisure travel for their business clients.

Major Canadian corporate agencies include American Express, Carlson Wagonlit Travel, and the Hogg Robinson Group (HRG). HRG is the parent company of Business Travel International (BTI), the world's largest organization of travel management companies. The company, which started up in Toronto in the 1980s as Rider Travel, has become one of the three largest business travel firms in Canada.

More corporate agencies are providing travel management services for clients. Before, corporations would receive advice and purchase tickets from an agency. They would keep track of employee travel and entertainment expenses themselves. Now, with corporate downsizing and the development of specialized software for travel agencies to track these expenses, more firms are outsourcing this function to travel agencies.

Vacation and Leisure Agencies

A vacation and leisure agency generally has a more relaxed atmosphere, and its front-line workers do more counselling. This type of agency may sell nationally advertised tours or it may organize its own tours. Vacation and leisure agencies also design foreign and domestic tours for individual clients. Called "foreign independent tours" (FITs) or "domestic independent tours" (DITs), these arrangements may cost more, but they meet travellers' personal expectations better. Vacation and leisure agencies may also assist VFR travellers, although travellers driving to familiar locations usually don't require the services of a travel agency.

All-Cruise Agencies

Some agencies, with names like "Ship Shop" or "Cruise Holidays," specialize in vacation cruises. Since only about 7 percent of travellers have ever taken a cruise, tremendous potential for business exists in this area. Also, since cruises represent a complete vacation package (transportation, accommodations, meals, sightseeing), commissions are calculated on the full amount of sale, which means the compensation can be quite high. Through workshops and mailings, the National Association of Cruise Only Agents helps agencies promote its sector.

Specialty Agencies

Some agencies run a full-service business but also have a branch or division that concentrates on one form of travel or on services to a special group of travellers. These agencies are usually located in metropolitan areas, where there is greater market segmentation. Agencies also tend to specialize when there are many agencies competing in one location. Some specialty agencies reflect the talents and interests of the owner and staff. The following types of specialty agencies are worth noting.

Adventure Adventure travel is a fast-growing segment of the travel market. Adventure travel agencies specialize in package trips to exotic and difficult-to-reach destinations. Such trips often involve much physical activity. Examples are rafting on Chile's Bio-Bio River, camping on Easter Island, and cross-country skiing in the Arctic.

Ecotourism As ecotourism developed (see Chapter 13), some travel agencies began catering to this segment of the market. Some agencies see this as a subset of adventure travel and feature "adventure travel and ecotourism"; others use the term "ecoadventure." This can be confusing, because in some cases "adventure travel" is required to arrive at the "ecotourism" site or destination. In this specialized field, the ecotourist is often quite knowledgeable. Such travellers can often be reached most easily through websites. For example, B.C. Ecotours offers marine tours from Delta, British Columbia.

Seniors Many people say that their dream for retirement is to travel more. Agencies that concentrate on seniors' travel help make those dreams come true. Escorted tours for seniors are another fast-growing segment of the travel market. In planning such tours, agencies recognize that many seniors have special needs. For example, travellers whose hearing is weakening appreciate a guide who speaks clearly and loudly. For travellers who tend to tire easily, no long walks or flights of stairs should be necessary for viewing attractions.

Senior Tours Canada specializes in tours for age 50-plus travellers. It has seven offices.

Singles Singles can take advantage of tours and cruises arranged exclusively for them. Some agencies provide matching services to help singles find travel companions. Many tour operators, such as Friendship Travel, Solo Vacations, and O Solo Mio Singles Tours, specialize in singles travel and sell their tours through travel agencies.

ILLUSTRATION 16–2

Many agencies now specialize to attract a particular target market.

SOURCE: Image courtesy of CruiseShipCenters Canada Inc.

Ethnic Ethnic travel agencies are found in cities with large ethnic communities. They arrange individual or group travel to the parent country—for example, to Greece, Italy, Poland, Israel, or Japan. Rex Travel Agency in Toronto features holidays to Greece. Several Vancouver travel agencies specialize in travel to China.

Physically Disabled At present, only a few travel companies offer tours specifically designed for people with physical disabilities. The companies that do exist have organized trips in North America and abroad for quadriplegics, for people who are visually or hearing impaired, and for people with emphysema, muscular dystrophy, multiple sclerosis, or renal failure. Other types of travel agencies are willing to adapt travel plans to the needs and abilities of the physically disabled if they are told specifically what is needed.

Student More than 40 years ago, Canadian students established a national student travel bureau. This was the beginning of Travel CUTS (Voyages Campus in Quebec). Travel CUTS is the travel company of the Canadian Federation of Students, Canada's national student organization, and is affiliated with the International Student Travel Confederation. As Canada's only national student travel bureau, Travel CUTS provides unique, student-oriented products and services to more than 200 000 students each year. It develops and promotes student discount cards, student tour packages, travel insurance, and student fares on airlines and trains in Canada and abroad.

Travel CUTS has more than 50 offices on campuses across Canada, and a total of more than 60 retail shops under a variety of names. These outlets specialize in serving Canadian students and have developed an expertise in language courses and work programs in foreign countries. The company has also created a specialized tour operator called the Adventure Travel Company.

Youth standby fares are available exclusively through Travel CUTS. Flights are available one way or return, are valid up to one year, and are at prices below regular

standby tickets. The International Student Identity Card (ISIC) is also available through Travel CUTS.

THE ONLINE TRAVEL AGENCY

Traditional travel agencies are facing increasing competition from traditional travel agencies that have gone online, new online travel agencies, wireless application protocol (WAP), and suppliers going direct to consumers. One firm, Uniglobe.com, estimated in 2000 that there were more than 100 000 travel companies on the Internet, but only about 20 real full-service travel websites. Following is an overview of some of these e-companies: Orbitz, Expedia, Priceline, Travelocity, Uniglobe, and itravel2000.

Orbitz Worldwide This firm was founded by five airlines (American, Continental, Delta, Northwest, and United) to develop a website for direct sales to consumers. The company operates Orbitz, as well as several other online travel businesses, including Cheap Tickets which it purchased in 2003, ebookers, and HotelClub. It is one of the world's largest hotel franchisers, and is one of the world's largest car rental operators.

Expedia This firm, a subsidiary of Microsoft, started in 1996 and has become a leading provider of branded online travel services for leisure and small-business travellers. It employs more than 7000 people worldwide and has acquired Hotels.com and TripAdvisor among other travel companies. It has several key elements in its strategy for the 2000s:

- **Continue to increase brand awareness** Through advertising, for example.
- **Expand merchant business activity** This involves acquiring inventory at discounted wholesale prices from preferred suppliers and then determining retail prices.
- **Enhance its technology platform** This involves improving its software features, developing the best fare-search technologies, and eliminating downtime at websites.
- **Expand internationally** Expedia already has localized websites in Canada, the United Kingdom, and Germany.
- **Continue diversifying revenue sources** Expedia plans to expand its travel service offerings beyond airline, hotel, and car rentals to include more complex travel products and destinations.

Priceline This firm opened on the Internet in 1998. In its first three years, it sold more than 7.5 million airline tickets, 2.5 million hotel room nights, and 2.5 million rental car days. It pioneered a new type of e-commerce known as a "demand collection system." Priceline's approach is different. Consumers tell Priceline what they are willing to pay for the product. Then Priceline communicates this to participating sellers or to its private databases. A match is made. Consumers have to be somewhat flexible with respect to brands and times (e.g., name of airline, time of flight).

Travelocity This firm started as the Internet arm of Sabre, a GDS company that itself was a subsidiary of AMR, the holding company for American Airlines. In the early 2000s, it was the leading online travel website and the third-largest e-commerce site. It can access 95 percent of the seats sold by airlines, more than 49 000 hotels, more than 50 car rental firms, and more than 5000 cruise and vacation packages. In addition, its database provides information on a vast array of destinations.

Uniglobe Uniglobe.com started in 1996 as the Internet arm of Uniglobe Travel. It changed its original strategy in 2001, no longer acting as a wholesaler to other travel agencies, but rather concentrating on the retail cruise segment and retail air, car, and hotel sales. It now has over 750 travel agencies in 40 countries.

itravel2000 Although set up as a travel agency in 1994, itravel2000 was designed to meet the needs of online

ILLUSTRATION 16–3
Although there are thousands of travel companies on the Internet, very few are full-service websites.
SOURCE: Corbis/Magma.

consumers and it opened its website in 1996. Since then, the company has become one of Canada's largest online travel companies with annual sales of $300 million in 2007.

It is predicted that online travel agencies will continue growing, as more consumers become familiar with online purchasing. But which firms will share in this growth? Many firms have lost money, but they regard these losses as investments for a profitable future. There will probably be more consolidations to achieve economies of scale. There will also be increased competition from suppliers such as airlines, either directly or through consortia. Already there is some evidence of more rapid growth at airline websites relative to online travel agencies. Some online travel agencies will increase their advertising to attract and retain customers, even though this will increase costs.

The environment for online travel agencies is a very dynamic and exciting one. Perhaps new technologies will alter their growth patterns. Sabre Holdings Corporation of Dallas has introduced a new suite of e-products and e-services, named Sabre eVoya, designed to allow travel agencies and their clients to connect in a wireless world.

The Canadian online travel industry is growing, as evidenced by the following Statistics Canada information:

- Total Internet spending in Canada grew from $417 million in 1999 to $7.9 billion in 2005.
- 7.9 million households in Canada (61 percent) were connected to the Internet in 2005.
- 36 percent of Canadians purchased travel online in 2005; roughly half that percentage did so in 2000. Even more (37 percent) browsed travel services and arrangements online.

Individual travel agencies have developed their own websites to tap this potential market and to expand their potential client bases beyond their local geographical areas.

Some consumers using Web search engines become overwhelmed and frustrated. TripAdvisor (www.tripadvisor.com) is a website designed to alleviate this situation.

THE GROWTH OF TRAVEL AGENCIES

As you learned in Chapter 1, the agency of Thomas Cook and Son dominated the early travel industry. Cook conducted tours to Europe and later to the United States and Canada. His agency represented various transportation companies, including several steamship lines. In 2007, Thomas Cook merged with the MyTravel Group to form the Thomas Cook Group. Today, the global Thomas Cook AG group has 800 company-owned and franchised travel agencies worldwide.

The idea of organized travel assistance spread to Canada and the United States. By the end of the nineteenth century, many agencies were in operation, including the American Express Company, an offshoot of the famous Wells Fargo Company. Travel agencies at this time specialized in selling steamship tickets and grand tours to the wealthy.

Where there were no agencies, suppliers found other ways to sell their products. Steamship companies sent agents on horseback to small towns across Canada and the United States. These agents sold steamship tickets to people who wanted to bring their relatives from Europe to North America. In the 1920s, railway companies compensated hotel porters for getting train tickets for hotel guests. Early airlines also sold tickets through hotel porters, giving them a 5 percent commission.

Airlines soon realized that travel agencies offered a more efficient way of distributing airplane tickets. In particular, they saw the potential of travel agencies for selling pleasure travel on the popular DC-3s. At the beginning of World War II, there were more than 1000 agencies in the United States and Canada. When public acceptance of air transportation increased after the war, the commercial airlines continued to grow, and so did the number of travel agencies.

The Effects of Jet Travel

In the tourism industry, 1958 is considered to be the dawn of the modern age of travel. The flight of the first transatlantic passenger jet ushered in an era of pleasure travel for millions of people. Between 1965 and 1988, the number of passengers on Canadian scheduled carriers increased 414 percent, from 7 million to 36 million; after this it levelled off and did not start increasing again until the mid-1990s. However, air travel is now hampered by congestion at runways and terminals and by a downturn in the economy. The growth in travel in the second half of the twentieth century was matched by the growth in the number of travel agencies. In 1958, there were about 3000 agencies in Canada and the United States. Today, even though the number of agencies in the United States has declined each year from 1997 to 2004, there are more than 5000 in Canada and about 21 000 in the United States.

In 1958, before most people had taken their first jet flight (or any airplane flight, for that matter), travel agencies were quite different from most travel agencies today. The travel agency of the 1950s was usually a part-time business with a staff of one or two people. Often it was located in the back office of the local bus depot or in a café. Office furnishings were basic and there were no computer terminals blinking information. Selling bus and railway tickets was often the main business. If a customer wanted to travel to a faraway place, the agent wrote letters to make reservations.

The Travel Agency Today

Of the more than 26 000 travel agencies in Canada and the United States today, about half are located in attractive offices in metropolitan areas. Two-thirds have revenues of less than $2 million a year. Women own most agencies, and more women than men work in agencies.

In the late 1950s, travel agencies were concerned mainly with pleasure travel; today, business travel accounts for a large percentage of a general agency's bookings. Modern travel agencies offer products that were not dreamed of 40 years ago. At the same time, travellers are more sophisticated and are demanding more services. The environment in today's agencies is likely to be fast-paced and hectic. Before, business was done in person and over the telephone. Now, in addition, business is done by fax and e-mail and by referral from websites to local agencies. Counsellors receive and send information instantaneously, using sophisticated technology. The work is complex and intense, and made even more so by airline deregulation and competitive marketing by both travel agencies and suppliers.

Deregulation Airline deregulation has led to an increase in the number of airlines. This, in turn, has resulted in a multitude of new routes, schedules, and airfares, all of which are constantly changing. For flights between any

ILLUSTRATION 16–4

WestJet was founded in 1996 by four Calgary entrepreneurs who saw an opportunity to provide low-fare air travel across western Canada. Today, WestJet flies across Canada and to the United States, with charter services available to Mexico and the Caribbean.

SOURCE: Photo courtesy of WestJet.

two cities, several price alternatives are often available, depending on the airline, day, and various restrictions. As airlines scramble for passengers, price wars often break out. A highly competitive climate has developed, with offers of rebates and discounts.

Deregulation had an instantaneous effect on travel agencies. In the regulated environment before deregulation, routes and airfares followed orderly, predictable patterns. Travel counsellors could practically memorize the information they needed. After deregulation, the system became confusing and difficult to handle. And, as noted earlier, lower airfares and negotiable commissions decreased travel agencies' revenues. Many agencies must now deal in volume sales (i.e., sell large quantities of product at reduced prices) to counteract low revenues.

Most travel counsellors believe that deregulation has made their job even more important. Customers are baffled by the lists of complex airfares and routes, and need travel counsellors to help them through the maze. Suppliers, too, depend on travel agencies to sort things out for customers.

Automation Almost all travel agencies now have GDSs, which are needed to keep up with the rapid changes in airfares and schedules. Automation has also become necessary for gathering and managing information. Travel counsellors need to be familiar with GDSs such as Galileo (Air Canada) and Sabre (WestJet). In 2004, Transport Canada deregulated GDS conditions. Today, for example, a GDS need not include all of the data on its competitors' fares and schedules. This may result in travel agencies

having to purchase more than one GDS to ensure they have access to all fares for clients. More likely, however, is that deregulation of the GDS system will drive agencies to supplier websites. This has already occurred with respect to airline commission: Agencies booking through an airline website can earn a commission not available through the GDS.

Consolidation of Agencies

Travel agencies can be categorized by size—specifically, the amount of business they do each year:

- **Small** $1 million or less (the International Air Transport Association has a different financial standard for accreditation for agencies with annual sales of less than $2 million).
- **Midsized** $1 million to $1.99 million.
- **Large** $2 million to $4.99 million.
- **Very large** $5 million and over.

Most travel agencies are small. However, a handful of mega-agencies have a disproportionate share of the business. Only 1 percent of Canadian travel agencies are mega-agencies, but the top 20 agencies in Canada accounted for 21 percent of total revenue generated by the industry in 2001. Mega-agencies grew (and continue to grow) by taking over medium-sized and large agencies or by squeezing them out of business.

Impact of Globalization Globalization has had an impact on the travel business. Travel agencies in various countries are associating with one another to meet the needs of multinational firms. These firms want to channel their business through one agency. In 1993, Thomas Cook purchased Marlin Travel, then Canada's largest travel agency. This allowed Thomas Cook to expand in Canada. Marlin, for its part, is expanding globally—something it could not have done by itself. Thomas Cook and MyTravel merged in 2007 to form the Thomas Cook Group. In 1997, Carlson Travel of Minnesota and Wagon-Lit Travel of Paris merged to form Carlson Wagonlit Travel. This network has more than 3000 locations in 141 countries.

The presence in Canada of agency chains such as Carlson Wagonlit, Thomas Cook/Marlin Travel, and Sears Travel should be noted. These organizations are corporations in their own right. Some of them are franchise or "associate" operations (e.g., the Thomas Cook/Marlin Travel brand).

Mega-Agencies One mega-agency is the Canadian Automobile Association, which has about 130 locations across Canada. Others are the Flight Centre, Carlson Wagonlit Travel, Thomas Cook Travel, and American Express. Some are interested mainly in multimillion-dollar corporate accounts.

ILLUSTRATION 16–5
Agency consolidation means fewer agencies but better career prospects for counsellors.
SOURCE: Photo by Indu Ghuman.

Mega-agencies with offices in many cities—and perhaps several offices in a single city—function as the supermarkets and giant discount houses of travel. Because they are so large, they can purchase travel products in bulk. The more volume they do, the more easily they can offer rebates, which cost-conscious corporations earnestly seek. Mega-agencies can offer many services, such as monitoring frequent flyer programs and compiling travel and entertainment expenses. These services are often beyond the capability of smaller agencies.

Consortia To compete against the mega-agencies, some independent travel agencies have formed consortia. A **consortium** is a group formed to achieve a goal that is beyond the resources of any one member. Travel agencies pay a fee to become members of a consortium. Membership rules may also specify that the agency must have a certain gross income or a certain level of automation. Not all independent agencies are able to join a consortium.

Consortia exist for both leisure and business travel. They can be regional or national. Ensemble Travel (formerly GIANTS) is Canada's largest group of travel agencies, with over 1000 members in large and small communities in Canada and the USA. Other consortia are Advantage Travel, a member of the Worldwide Independent Network with 259 agencies in Canada, and Vacation.com (which has over 8000 agencies in Canada and the United States).

Independent agencies benefit greatly from the bargaining power of consortia, which can obtain bulk discounts for their members. They also provide forums for information exchange.

Consortia do have some drawbacks, however. With the help of a consortium, some independent agencies become so successful that they become mega-agencies themselves. If an agency—especially a strong one—leaves the consortium, the entire organization is weakened. Consortia also tend to raid one another's ranks for members.

TABLE 16–3 Comparison of Some Travel Agencies

Organization	Number of Members	Location
Advantage Travel T-Comm Inc.	5000 as part of WIN (250 in Canada)	Worldwide
Canadian Automobile Ass'n (CAA)	Over 1100 locations (145 travel agencies in Canada)	U.S. and Canada
Carlson Wagonlit Travel	3000 locations (200 in Canada)	153 countries
Ensemble Travel	2000 companies; 1600 locations (1000 in Canada and the USA)	U.S. and Canada
Flight Centre	1000 locations (110 in Canada)	Worldwide
Thomas Cook (Marlin Canada)	3600 agencies (200+ in Canada)	International
Travel Distribution Resource Group (TDRG)	114 companies; 2000 locations	International
Sears Canada Travel (acquired tripeze.com)	106 locations	All provinces except PEI
Travel CUTS	50 locations	Canada
Uniglobe	More than 750 locations (135 in Canada)	Worldwide
Vacation.com	Over 8000 locations (700+ in Canada)	U.S. and Canada

SOURCE: *ASTA Agency Management*, American Society of Travel Agents; company websites.

A variation of the travel consortium is the **cooperative**. In a cooperative, independent agencies band together temporarily to achieve a goal. Usually, they have a joint interest in promoting a product or an event.

Franchises To combat mega-agencies and consortia, an independent agency can join a nationwide franchise group such as Uniglobe. An agency that joins such a group retains its individual ownership. But in contrast to the agencies in a consortium, it also adopts a company name and image. Franchises deal mainly with leisure and vacation travel.

To join a franchise group, an agency pays an initial fee and agrees to pay an annual percentage of its gross earnings. In return, it acquires bulk-buying power, advertising support, training programs in business development, and brand-name recognition. Agencies can convert to franchises, or they can start out in business as franchises.

Small Agencies Small agencies are the corner grocery stores or the modest boutiques of the travel industry. Some employ only two or three people and have little automation.

Large and medium-sized agencies are in constant danger of being gobbled up; small agencies can often survive if they find the right market. For example, they might specialize in organizing FITs, arranging travel for small commercial firms (such as law offices), or arranging ethnic travel or travel for seniors. Locating in a small town or city may also be a key to success if less competition exists.

Small agencies can offer personalized service and more thorough trip counselling. When clients return from a trip, small agencies are more likely to call them and ask how things went. Agents will often write letters expressing regret if a trip is cancelled or if something goes awry. Says one small-agency employee, "If you make yourself valuable enough on a personal level, customers will not be looking around for discounts." Table 16–3 shows the sizes and locations of several travel agencies.

Check Your Product Knowledge

1. What has been the most important influence on the growth of travel agencies?
2. What effect did airline deregulation have on travel agencies?
3. What new channels of distribution challenge travel agencies?
4. Why has automation become necessary for most travel agencies?
5. What has been the effect of mega-agencies on the travel agency sector?

OPENING A TRAVEL AGENCY

Compared with other retail businesses, the travel agency industry is still highly accessible to entrepreneurs. Of the more than 26 000 travel agencies in Canada and the United States, more than half started up after 1980. Many people become travel agency owners as a second career after retirement or as a career change in midlife. The owner must have qualified employees working at the agency.

Suppose you want to enter the retail travel business. Assuming you don't want to purchase a franchise or an existing agency, how would you go about opening your own full-service travel agency? How would you get airlines, cruise lines, and other suppliers to furnish you with tickets and pay you commissions?

An entrepreneur wanting to open a travel agency should become familiar with conference appointments, conference requirements, and provincial requirements.

Conference Appointments

To open officially, a travel agency must be appointed, or approved, by industry conferences. In this context, a conference is not a meeting but a regulatory body that formulates standards for acceptance, reviews and appoints new agencies, and disciplines existing agencies when necessary.

Air Transport Association of Canada The Air Transportation Association of Canada (ATAC) represents commercial aviation in Canada. All the major scheduled and chartered carriers and regional airlines, and many smaller operators, belong to ATAC. ATAC members account for more than 97 percent of commercial aviation revenues earned in Canada.

The ATAC Traffic Conference, a separate branch of ATAC, oversees all matters dealing with interline standards, ticketing, and passenger and baggage processing. It also oversees the Canadian Travel Agency program, which sets the rules that govern domestic and transborder air transportation sales. In 1986, ATAC contracted with the IATA to operate the Canadian program.

Major Conferences The major conferences in Canada are:

- Air Transport Association of Canada (ATAC).
- International Air Transport Association (IATA), headquartered in Montreal—for selling air tickets; the International Airline Travel Agency Network is a subsidiary of IATA that serves as a link between retail travel agencies and IATA.
- Cruise Lines International Association (CLIA)—for selling cruises.
- VIA Rail, Inc.—for selling domestic rail tickets; VIA is also the Canadian agent for Amtrak.

Each conference comprises companies that sell transportation. IATA, for example, comprises more than 230 airlines in over 120 countries. These companies, of course, want the people selling their products to be competent and honest, and the **conference appointment system** is a way of ensuring this. An agency that receives a conference

ILLUSTRATION 16–6
Travel counsellors sell dreams.
SOURCE: Courtesy of Travel Alberta International.

appointment has the right to sell the products of all the conference's members and to receive commissions from them.

Conference Requirements Each conference establishes requirements, or standards, that an agency must meet in order to be approved. Although an agency needs the approval of all conferences, it should concentrate on meeting the airline conference requirements first, because the sale of air tickets forms a major part of any agency's business. Having satisfied the airline conference, the agency is likely to satisfy the other conferences.

IATA provides an accreditation kit for new applicants who want to become approved passenger sales agents. IATA publishes the *Travel Agent's Handbook*, which states in detail the rules and regulations for setting up a travel agency, as well as for many other procedures involved in selling air transportation. These rules and regulations are modified from time to time. Anyone who is planning a career as a travel counsellor or who is considering opening a travel agency should read this handbook.

ATAC and IATA issued a joint handbook in 1994. To reduce confusion and work toward an international standard, the Canadian air carriers incorporated into the Canadian requirements almost all IATA resolutions dealing with travel agency rules. Some of the requirements for opening an agency are:

- **Open for business** To apply for IATA and ATAC accreditation, a travel agency must already be open and operating. You might wonder how the agency can sell tickets before it's even been approved. While waiting for approval, it can obtain tickets from the airlines on a cash basis. Once the agency has been accredited, it can apply to receive any commissions retroactively to the date of application.

- **Experience** At least two people must be employed full-time at the agency for which the application is made: a management person and a ticketing agent, both of whom must meet conference standards. Both of these people also must have experience in their respective fields.

- **Location** The agency must be accessible to the public and clearly identified as a travel agency by a sign that is visible from the street. (Exceptions are sometimes made for agencies that organize inclusive tours.) The agency must be in a location separate from any other travel agency or air carrier, and it must be open for regular business. Also, the location should be such that proper security can be maintained at all times. No unauthorized person should have access to the agency's documents and equipment. An ideal location is a downtown store with a good display area that can be seen by pedestrians and by people in cars, as is a store in a high-traffic urban or suburban mall.

- **Finances** Careful attention to financial requirements and procedures is essential for anyone wishing to gain and keep IATA accreditation. Current financial statements, prepared in accordance with generally accepted accounting principles and reviewed by an independent accountant, must be submitted on an ongoing basis. Minimum standards for accreditation include $25 000 of working capital and a tangible net worth of $35 000. The *Travel Agent's Handbook* gives precise details about these financial requirements.

- **Promotion** The agency must be actively involved in the promotion of travel. It is encouraged to promote and sell domestic, transborder, and international air transportation in a competitive and efficient manner that is in the interests of consumers and the industry. It can do this by advertising its products and services in newspaper, television, and radio ads, and through brochures, flyers, direct mail, and the Internet.

Procedure for Appointment A travel agency that desires accreditation from IATA (for international flights) and ATAC (for domestic and transborder flights) makes application to IATA/ATAC. Included with this application must be very detailed documentation about the agent and the place where the agency is located. On receiving the application, IATA notifies its member agencies and arranges for an inspection of the agency and its staff.

Once approved, the newly accredited agency becomes linked up with the Billing and Settlement Plan (by which payments are sent to the airlines for tickets sold), which has been developed over the past several decades. This centralized reporting and remitting system benefits both carriers and agents, as it standardizes and automates travel documents, thereby streamlining services and payments. Details of this plan are available in the *BSP Manual for Agents*, published by IATA.

Once accepted, the accredited agency must, of course, maintain IATA standards at all times.

Provincial Requirements Some Canadian provinces—for example, Ontario, British Columbia, and Quebec—require travel agencies to register with the provincial registrar. In Ontario, travel agencies must follow the rules and regulations stated by the Ontario registrar under the Ontario Travel Industry Act, 2002. The Ontario Act includes a travel protection section, which requires travel agencies and tour operators to maintain a trust account and pay into a compensation fund to protect the travelling public if a travel agency goes out of business. The Ontario government has granted the travel industry in that province a degree of self-regulation, which mandates the Travel Industry Council of Ontario to administer the Act.

The Travel Industry Act of Ontario (TIA) came up for revision in 2000. ACTA Ontario was quite concerned about the need to provide support to travel agencies in case of the failure of an end supplier. This proved to be prescient. The failure of the airline Canada 3000, following the September 11, 2001 attacks, had a profound influence on the changes made to the Act. At that time, end suppliers such as airlines and cruise lines, were not covered by the Act's compensation fund. Travel agencies were responsible. Canada 3000's collapse would have required travel agencies, therefore, to compensate clients who had booked and paid for flights with the airline but who did not receive them. This would have caused serious hardship, even insolvency, for many travel agencies.

In late November 2001, Ontario announced changes to the Travel Industry Act, effective January 2, 2002. Travellers could now access the Travel Industry Compensation Fund directly; individual limits for the failure of an end supplier airline or cruise line were raised to $5000 from $3500 per event for each individual. The fund limit was set at $5 million per major event. The revised Ontario Travel Industry Act, 2002, was enacted in 2005. In addition to protecting consumers from the failure of an end supplier airline or cruise line, the Act introduced minimum education standards for everyone in Ontario who sells travel services. The legislation specifies that by July 1, 2009, all such sellers (including those selling through a website based in Ontario) must pass a test on the Act. A more advanced test for supervisors and managers will be introduced at a later date. However, anyone registered with TICO as a supervisor or manager as of July 1, 2009 will be exempt from this advanced test. The online test is administered by the Canadian Institute of Travel Counsellors (CITC) on behalf of TICO.

Check Your Product Knowledge

1. What are the four major conferences?
2. Why must an agency receive conference appointments?
3. What are the main requirements for receiving accreditation by a conference?
4. List the procedures for obtaining conference approval.

HOW A TRAVEL AGENCY FUNCTIONS

When customers enter most retail stores, they expect to see the merchandise on display. Before purchasing an item, they want to look it over and learn something about it. They'll try on a new suit or coat to see how it looks and fits. They'll ask the salesperson to demonstrate how to operate a washing machine or a microwave oven. And they would never buy a car without first taking it for a test drive. If after purchase, the product turns out to be defective or otherwise unsuitable, customers can return it to the store or receive some sort of adjustment to their account.

What's For Sale?

The products sold by a retail travel agency are quite different. Although some are tangible, most are intangible.

The Travel Product Travel agencies sell products such as a trip on an airplane, a stay in a hotel room, or a cruise on a ship. None of these products can be displayed in the retail agency. Nor can they be inspected or tried out before they're purchased. Once customers buy these products, they have them for only a short time. If travel products prove unsatisfactory, they can't be returned—although suppliers and agencies may compensate dissatisfied customers in some way.

Why would anyone buy a product that can't be seen or touched and that doesn't come with a warranty? The reason is that when it sells travel products, the industry doesn't emphasize the technical features of an airplane or the dimensions of a hotel room. Instead, it is promoting the psychological benefits of its products.

Travel counsellors sell dreams to vacation and leisure travellers. A travel ad might show a beautifully tanned young couple dancing in a moonlit tropical garden. The ad is suggesting that by purchasing certain travel products,

travellers can experience glamour, romance, relaxation, pleasure, and excitement. The vacation, long after it is over, will continue to exist as a wonderful memory.

To business travellers, travel counsellors sell time-savings, convenience, and prestige. A travel ad might show a flight attendant serving a gourmet meal to a distinguished-looking executive, or a chauffeur placing a business traveller's luggage into a limousine. Such ads tell travellers how important they are. By purchasing certain travel products, they will receive the efficient, prompt service they require.

Related Products To make a major purchase more enjoyable, customers often buy accessories or optional items. Travel agencies sell products that make trips safer, easier, and more pleasant. These products include traveller's cheques, passport photos, luggage, sportswear, and travel books.

A related product that has become a significant source of revenue for agencies is travel insurance. Different types of insurance are available, which can be sold separately or in a package:

- Flight insurance.
- Accident and health insurance.
- Insurance for baggage and personal possessions.
- Trip cancellation or interruption insurance.
- Bad weather insurance.

Even though travel insurance seems to emphasize what can go wrong on a trip, it is offered to clients as a means of adding to their peace of mind. Some major suppliers of travel insurance products in Canada are RBC Insurance, Mutual of Omaha, and Blue Cross Canada. Out-of-province and out-of-country medical insurance became more important in the 1990s, as several provinces cut back on their out-of-province coverage.

A product that is being combined with travel insurance is travel assistance. Travel assistance not only covers the costs of emergencies during travel but also provides personal counselling and assistance. For example, say that a husband and wife are travelling in Mexico. The husband, who has a history of heart trouble, becomes seriously ill. The wife calls the 24-hour assistance hotline and receives directions to the nearest hospital. The assistance-insurance company also pays the required on-the-spot hospital admission costs and all hospital and doctor bills. In addition, it consults with the man's doctors in Canada regarding his treatment.

The Staff

In a retail travel agency, the number of employees depends on the size of the agency. So does the work those employees do. A mega-agency is often organized like a corporation, with separate departments for sales, personnel, accounting, public relations, and word processing. A small agency may simply have an owner–manager and a handful of travel counsellors and outside sales representatives.

ILLUSTRATION 16–7

Travel insurance is vital in case of an out-of-country emergency.

SOURCE: © John Burke/Index Stock Imagery.

Manager By assigning duties and work schedules, the manager directs the work of the other employees. He or she trains new employees or trains current employees in new procedures. The manager is responsible for developing new products, improving the agency's efficiency, and overseeing financial transactions. He or she must also plan the agency's future.

Travel Agents As mentioned earlier, travel agents function as clerks, sales representatives, and counsellors—whichever role is appropriate at the time. As clerks, travel agents use automated systems to secure airline reservations, lease cars, and reserve hotel rooms for customers. As sales representatives, travel agents interest customers in various destinations and types of travel. As counsellors, travel agents help clients get in touch with their dreams, which are usually only partly formed when they come into the agency. Most clients need help in deciding which travel arrangements best suit their values and lifestyle.

Outside Sales Representatives A travel agency often has agreements with outside sales representatives, whose work involves arousing people's interest in travelling. They might show slides or movies at a meeting of a social or special-interest group, or arrange meetings with business managers. Wherever they are—in the produce section of the supermarket or on the telephone with their friends—outside sales representatives seek to direct business toward the agency with which they have contracted.

Many outside sales representatives work on commission. If people they introduce to the agency actually make a booking, they get between 25 and 50 percent of the commission, depending on how much work they've done for the sale. For example, if the commission on a product is $20, the representative might get $5. All transactions must go through the travel agency office, and transactions must be made under the name of the travel agency, not that of the sales representative.

Outside sales representatives are often homemakers, retirees, or other people who want to work part-time. Aggressive representatives who work full-time, however, can sometimes develop a large clientele, who are often more loyal to them than to any agency.

In recent years, some larger agencies such as Sears Travel and some newer companies such as TPI, have developed the business of home-based travel counsellors. These individuals are supplied with a computer and other office equipment, and are connected to the agency via the Internet. This arrangement allows the counsellors to work and develop their business from home but still offer the reservations and other services available at a bricks and mortar agency.

Money Matters

Travel agencies handle large sums of money. As trustee of both the customer's payments and the supplier's funds, the agency must keep accurate records of monies received and disbursed.

Sending Payment to the Airlines How do agencies forward money to the airlines from the sale of tickets? Does each agency send each airline a payment—say, twice a month? That's the way it used to be done, and the amount of record keeping, reporting, and auditing was staggering for both the agencies and the airlines.

In Canada, as mentioned earlier, payments (as well as record keeping and standard traffic documents) have been simplified for both travel agents and carriers by the development of IATA's **Billing and Settlement Plan (BSP) Canada**. The first BSP was developed in Japan in 1971; there are now plans in 160 countries and territories around the world.

Streamlined methods for payment have reduced both paperwork and the time spent on that paperwork. Much of this system is now automated so that agencies report sales electronically to their designated clearinghouse (a firm that collects payments from various businesses). Payments are made to a clearing bank (which collects payments from various clearinghouses), which then settles the agency's accounts with the designated airline. Therefore, payment goes from customer to travel agency to clearinghouse to clearing bank to airline.

IATA advertises the **IATA Travel Settlement Service (ITSS)** as an electronic billing and settlement system for today's digital marketplace. ITSS allows a client to simply bill and settle accounts online and set its own settlement calendar.

Sending Payment to Other Suppliers Since most agencies generally sell fewer products for cruise lines, railway companies, tour operators, and other suppliers, they issue cheques directly to them. Before doing so, they must be sure that the client has paid in full. Agencies deduct their commissions before sending payment to the suppliers. A cover letter explains what the cheque is for and how payment was calculated. For clients who pay by credit card, the agency must remit the full amount to the supplier and then invoice the supplier for the commission owing.

The agent gives the client the appropriate tickets and vouchers. **Vouchers** are coupons and documents that can be exchanged for travel products such as hotel accommodations or sightseeing tours.

Check Your Product Knowledge

1. What is the difference between products sold by retail travel agencies and those sold by other retail stores?
2. What are some related products sold by travel agencies?
3. Name staff positions held by employees in a typical small agency.
4. What is the function of an outside sales representative?
5. What is the Billing and Settlement Plan Canada?

OTHER TRAVEL AND TOURISM DISTRIBUTORS

Instead of using travel agencies, some travellers go to other established intermediaries to obtain travel products and to receive help with trip arrangements. These channels of distribution include business travel departments and travel clubs.

Business Travel Departments

Some business travellers are able to use the services of their company's business travel department. As you learned in Chapter 3, some companies employ their own staff to make travel arrangements for the company's employees. Since BTDs are not open to the public, and since BTD employees are paid by the company, BTDs are not accredited. Nor do they receive commissions on the sale of airline tickets. Instead, BTDs operate as freelancers. They negotiate with the airlines for the right to sell their products and to receive discounts and rebates.

A variation of the BTD is the in-plant agency. An in-plant agency is a retail travel agency that is located on the premises of a corporation and does business mainly with that corporation. The classification of in-plant agencies is currently a subject of hot debate in the travel agency industry. A major advantage to having an in-plant agency is convenience, because face-to-face meetings can be held to determine client needs. At one time, when airline commissions were in the 8 to 11 percent range, these commissions were split with the corporation. Today, with lower commissions and e-ticketing, many travel agencies do not feel it worthwhile to have an in-plant agency. Similarly, many corporations are concerned about the cost of business travel. Therefore some are reducing travel; others are looking at online booking through other channels.

Another variation is the out-plant agency. An out-plant agency is an accredited, full-service travel agency located near a corporation's premises. The corporation has its own BTD to handle most travel arrangements, but it depends on the out-plant agency to issue documents. The out-plant agency splits airline commissions with the BTD.

Travel Club As you know by now, travel products are extremely perishable. A seat on the Air Canada 2 p.m. flight from Calgary to Toronto on March 23, 2008, exists only for that moment. If it isn't sold, the airline receives absolutely no income from it. Because of the perishability of travel products, travel suppliers, like other retail suppliers, are making use of marketing techniques such as clearance sales.

The **travel club** is the travel industry's version of a clearance sale. Travel clubs specialize in the sale of unsold travel products to vacation and leisure travellers. These products are usually cruises and international flights to Europe. To take advantage of bargain prices (anywhere from 20 to 60 percent off), travellers must belong to the club. They join by paying a nominal annual fee—usually about $50.

There are two main types of travel clubs. One type deals almost exclusively with last-minute bookings. The other is more like a tour operator—it publishes a catalogue of tours and distributes it to all members. Some travel clubs even operate their own aircraft and offer private charter packages that range from weekend gambling junkets to trips around the world.

Here is how travel clubs generally work. At some point before the departure date, suppliers discount unsold inventory. To avoid offending travellers who have paid the full price, suppliers advertise their clearance sales only through travel clubs. Club members find out the latest information on departures by calling a special hotline. They must keep all information they hear confidential. A member who wishes to purchase a sale item can use a credit card number to complete the transaction over the telephone. The travel club then receives the commission for the sale.

Although travellers can save a lot of money by joining a travel club, the selections on offer may be quite limited and may not meet their personal MNEs. Members must also have very flexible schedules so that they can leave for a trip on short notice. One Canadian travel club is the Last Minute Club, which advertises a toll-free number across Canada. The Last Minute Club negotiates special rates with Canada's leading travel companies, buying their unsold inventory of airplane seats, package holidays, and cruises at up to 50 percent off (and sometimes even more). Its website informs the public that both members and nonmembers are welcome to visit the site, but only members can actually book a trip.

To promote membership, some travel clubs offer their members additional bargains, such as discounts on car rentals and rebates on tour and hotel bookings. Some clubs have frequent traveller plans. For instance, after purchasing $3000 in air travel, a member might be entitled to a free week aboard a cruise ship.

Check Your Product Knowledge

1. How is a business travel department different from a commercial travel agency?
2. What is the purpose of travel clubs?

TRAVEL ASSOCIATIONS

The major Canadian travel association is the Association of Canadian Travel Agencies (ACTA), founded in 1977 (see this chapter's Profile). It has more than 3000 members representing retail agencies and allied members in the tourism industry. Some 2400 travel agencies belong to ACTA. Two of the association's main purposes are to promote the goals of the travel industry and to improve travelling standards for the public.

The major association in the United States is the American Society of Travel Agents (ASTA), which includes members worldwide. It was founded in 1931. One of its goals is to protect the public from fraud. ASTA also promotes and advances the interests of the travel agency industry, and provides a forum where travel counsellors can speak out on issues that concern them. With over 20 000 members in 170 countries, ASTA is the world's largest professional association of travel counsellors and agencies. ASTA's membership also includes airline, steamship, railway, and bus companies, as well as car rental firms, hotels, government tourist offices, and other travel-related organizations.

ASTA provides many services to its members. For example, it publishes a newsletter and magazine and sponsors workshops and seminars. In these ways, ASTA keeps its members informed on current happenings in the industry and helps them develop new skills.

Another professional association for travel counsellors is the Association of Retail Travel Agents (ARTA). With around 3500 members, ARTA is smaller than ASTA or ACTA. Unlike the other two organizations, ARTA does not allow travel industry suppliers to be members. ARTA's purposes are similar to ASTA's, although ARTA emphasizes improving the working relationship between the airlines and travel agencies. ARTA was founded in 1963.

ILLUSTRATION 16–8

As well as representing their membership, associations provide training opportunities.

SOURCE: John A. Rizzo/Photodisc Green/Getty Images.

The Canadian Institute of Travel Counsellors (CITC) is the professional association for individuals in the Canadian travel industry. (ACTA, ASTA, and ARTA are corporate associations, in that membership is for the agency rather than the individual.) The CITC was formed in 1968 and currently has over 3000 members. The CITC's main goals are education and professionalism. As such, the CITC offers training seminars and publications, and promotes the professional designations CTC (certified travel counsellor) and CTM (certified travel manager). The CITC monitors training standards for travel counsellors in Canada with the Canadian Tourism Human Resource Council (CTHRC) and educators in colleges and private schools across the country. The CITC also administers a travel insurance test in British Columbia and the TICO minimum education standards test in Ontario.

ISSUES AND THE FUTURE OF TRADITIONAL TRAVEL AGENCIES

The opening question in this chapter was: What will be the form and functions of travel agencies in the future? Traditional firms are facing several pressures. To reiterate: More experienced tourists perceive travel products as "commodities" and are seeking the lowest cost (money saved on basic travel and accommodation can be spent on something else); airlines are reducing or eliminating commissions; alternative distribution channels are growing, for example, online and wireless technology; more suppliers are approaching consumers directly; and corporations are becoming increasingly concerned about travel costs.

Many traditional travel agencies will survive—but they need to thrive, not just survive. More suppliers are going direct, but they view this as a dual distribution or multiple distribution strategy. They will still need travel agencies. Travel agencies that are members of national or international chains will receive guidance from head office on making adjustments. Many of these chains have already gone online. It is the smaller, owner-operated agencies that may have the most difficulty adjusting. All traditional travel agencies will need to know their target markets and satisfy the MNEs of different market segments through specialized product and service offerings. Some companies may become **boutique travel agencies**; others may relocate to stores or malls where pedestrian traffic is heavy. The key will be to build customer loyalty by providing value-added products or services that provide sustainable competitive advantages. Perhaps the most difficult issue will be service fees. Clients will likely become used to paying "airport improvement fees," but will probably need some time to adjust to a fee-for-service approach.

The major growth period for travel agencies ended around 1980, when transportation deregulation resulted in true airline competition and price competition. It is predicted that the demand for travel services will increase. The front end of the baby boom, born in 1946, will be 65 in 2011. Many baby boomers will retire before then. Even though the proportion of the population using travel agencies is expected to decline from 70 percent in 2001 to 60 percent in 2010, that 60 percent will be a much larger market target. There is a golden opportunity on the horizon for travel agencies. Will they make the necessary adjustments?

Check Your Product Knowledge

1. Name two professional associations for travel agencies.
2. What are the main purposes of professional associations?
3. (a) What form do you think travel agencies will take in the future?

   (b) What functions will they perform in the future? Will they be different from the past?

CAREER OPPORTUNITIES

The importance of postsecondary education and specific training for the travel industry needs to be emphasized. Most if not all travel professionals require at least one year of postsecondary training in travel counselling before an employer will consider hiring them. This is a profession where the employee must be an "expert" in a number of fields.

The career path for travel counsellors depends on the size of the agency. In a small or medium-sized agency, a person might start out as a counsellor, then specialize in a certain type of travel or destination, and then advance to manager. Many managers go on to become owners. In a large or mega-agency, there are more levels of management and thus more opportunities for advancement. Larger agencies or chains tend to operate call centres and these also provide career opportunities. Customer Service Representatives (CSRs) or reservationists can progress to call centre supervisor and manager.

New opportunities have opened up in the field of e-commerce. Suppliers and online travel agencies require knowledgeable people to prepare and update websites and to answer questions at call centres.

People with training and experience as travel counsellors can work in places other than retail travel agencies. They can own a travel club, or work for a business travel department, automobile club, or government tourism office. Travel agency experience is also excellent preparation for work with an airline, cruise line, or other transportation company.

A DAY IN THE LIFE OF A

Travel Counsellor

In my work as a travel counsellor, service is top priority. I do a lot of different tasks, but they're all aimed at serving the customer well. I do this by developing a relationship with my clients and by researching to find travel products that will best meet their needs. If I am successful, then my clients will be satisfied (and will return to purchase other travel products) and I will earn more commission by selling more. Although my main job is to sell travel products that meet my clients needs, often I'm also a counsellor and information provider. I answer the many questions that travellers have. People who are making their first trip abroad, for example, often rely on me to advise them about obtaining passports, getting required immunizations, and figuring out exchange rates. I have to have the latest information to serve my customers well. I'm also an intermediary—between clients and airlines, clients and hotels, clients and resorts. The most detailed part of my job comes as I arrange for flights or room reservations or make out itineraries—double-checking facts is important to ensure a smooth trip.

I'm also, at times, a "friend in need." I remember one incident a few years ago when a honeymoon couple lost their voucher for their prepaid accommodations. The hotel in Puerto Rico refused to let them register unless they paid or came up with the voucher. The couple was frantic by the time they called me. I got on the telephone with the manager and convinced her to locate the copy of the voucher that had been mailed to the hotel and have the couple

sign that. A very relieved couple enjoyed the island that day. Efforts like this are part of good service.

The most crucial skill for a travel counsellor, however, is the ability to size up a client quickly and to translate that client's ideas into tangible plans. If clients don't really know what they want, I ask a few questions to get started. Different kinds of people have different needs. Suppose a retired couple walks into my office. I discover through conversation that they want to relax in a warm climate and that they like to be waited on. Money is not an issue. I suggest a cruise on one of the lines that specializes in slow-paced, luxurious trips. They've never been on a cruise before, but they love the idea.

Perhaps an engaged couple comes in to plan a honeymoon. They want some seclusion, but also the possibility of evening entertainment. They're very athletic, and they want to be able to enjoy the outdoors during the trip. And their budget is limited. My suggestion? A hotel in Bermuda that has separate beachfront cottages. The island has plenty of nightlife and lots of opportunities for activity—swimming, hiking, tennis, and so on. And the complete package is value for the money.

The next clients to walk in may be a couple with young children. They want a place the whole family can enjoy. My suggestions to them include Prince Edward Island, with its beaches, family farm vacations, and theatre featuring *Anne of Green Gables*; Disneyland or Walt Disney World; and some of the "club" package

vacations that provide activities for both adults and children. Their needs are totally different from those of another typical client—the business traveller, who wants the right flight at the right time and a hotel that is convenient to business contacts. To serve each of these clients well, I have to discover and translate their unique needs.

Other skills are important, too. Travel counsellors need good math skills, keyboarding ability, a good command of English, a knowledge of geography, and an awareness of what's going on in the world. (I don't want to send someone to an island that is about to experience an armed revolution!) In addition, I need to be able to locate information about schedules and prices quickly, and to be able to react fast in an emergency such as an airline strike or a resort shutdown.

Being a travel counsellor has some disadvantages. I deal with the public all the time, and some people can be demanding and difficult to please. Business is affected by the season—with overtime one month and layoffs the next—and by the economy. On the other hand, my job allows me to take free or inexpensive trips, and since I love to travel, that's very important. The flip side of putting up with demanding people is being able to serve appreciative ones well. I encourage clients to come back and tell me how their trip went. It's satisfying to know I did a good job, and I get to relive their trips with them. It's a way of travelling without leaving my desk, while learning how best to serve my future clients.

Summary

- The travel agency is the main intermediary in the travel industry's channels of distribution. In many respects, a travel agency is like a retail store, linking suppliers to the public.
- The airlines have had the most influence on the growth and development of agencies.
- The traditional travel agency is being affected by airlines lowering or eliminating commissions, by better-educated consumers perceiving some travel products as "commodities," by the development of e-commerce, and by more suppliers approaching consumers directly, often through websites.
- Travel agencies have traditionally been compensated through commissions and overrides. To attract and maintain customers, agencies grant rebates.
- More travel agencies are introducing service fees to compensate for the reduction or elimination of commissions.
- Besides making arrangements for trips and selling travel products, counsellors provide information about destinations and legal documents. Counselling clients as to the products best suited to their MNEs is the service that distinguishes the travel agency from other intermediaries.
- Different types of travel agencies exist to meet the needs of various segments of the travel market. These segments include commercial, vacation and leisure, all-cruise, and specialty.
- Online travel agencies have developed since the mid-1990s, and are among the few successful industries on the Internet.
- There are now more than 5000 travel agencies in Canada. Many agencies are operated as small businesses.
- Airline regulatory reform has made the travel agency industry more complex in Canada. Automation has become a necessity for sorting out a multitude of fares and schedules.
- There is a trend toward combining smaller, independent agencies to create larger, more powerful agencies—mega-agencies. Consortia, cooperatives, and franchises have developed in response to this trend.
- To sell suppliers' products and obtain commissions, an agency must receive conference appointments. Accreditation by the airline conference is the most important. The conference has specific requirements regarding the location, finances, and management of agencies.
- Most of the products sold by travel agencies can't be seen, touched, tested before purchase, or returned. Agencies sell experiences, which yield psychological benefits. As in other retail stores, employees are needed to sell the products.
- Agencies send payment to airlines through the Billing and Settlement Plan (BSP) Canada.
- Business travel departments and travel clubs are other distributors of travel products.
- The Association of Canadian Travel Agencies, the American Society of Travel Agents, and the Association of Retail Travel Agents promote the travel industry and uphold the professional standards of their members.

Key Terms

agreement   p. 367
Billing and Settlement Plan (BSP) Canada   p. 379
boutique travel agency   p. 382
conference appointment system   p. 376
consortium   p. 374
cooperative   p. 375
corporate travel agency   p. 369
IATA Travel Settlement Service (ITSS)   p. 380
override   p. 366
preferred supplier agreement   p. 367
rebate   p. 367
service charge   p. 367
travel club   p. 380
voucher   p. 380
youth standby fares   p. 370

Internet Connections

Advantage Travel
www.accessadvantagetravel.com   p. 374

Adventure Travel Company
www.atcadventure.com   p. 370

Air Transport Association of Canada (ATAC)
www.atac.ca   p. 376

American Society of Travel Agents (ASTA)
www.astanet.com   p. 381

Association of Canadian Travel Agencies (ACTA)
www.acta.ca   p. 363

Association of Retail Travel Agents (ARTA)
www.artaonline.com   p. 381

Blue Cross Canada
www.bluecross.ca   p. 378

Canadian Institute of Travel Counsellors (CITC)
www.citc.ca   p. 364

Canadian Tourism Human Resource Council
www.cthrc.ca   p. 382

Carlson Wagonlit Travel
www.carlsonwagonlit.com/en/   p. 369

Cruise Lines International Association (CLIA)
www.cruising.org   p. 376

Ensemble Travel
www.ensembletravel.com   p. 374

Flight Centre
www.flightcentre.ca   p. 365

Hogg Robinson Group (HRG)
www.hrgworldwide.com   p. 369

International Air Transport Association (IATA)
www.iata.org   p. 373

Last Minute Club
www.lastminuteclub.ca   p. 381

Mutual of Omaha
www.mutualofomaha.com   p. 378

RBC Insurance
www.rbcinsurance.ca   p. 378

Singles Tours and Cruises (p. 369)
Friendship Travel
www.friendshiptravel.com

Solo Vacations
www.solovacations.com

O Solo Mio Singles Tours
www.osolomio.com

Travel CUTS
www.travelcuts.com   p. 370

Travel Industry Council of Ontario (TICO)
www.tico.on.ca   p. 377

TripAdvisor
www.tripadvisor.com   p. 371

Vacation.com
www.vacation.com   p. 374

WORKSHEET 16-1   Travel Agencies, Near and Distant

Compare six travel agencies from two categories: traditional ("bricks") located in Yourtown or in the closest town or city that supports a large number of agencies, and online ("clicks"). Select at least two in each category. Briefly describe each as best you can; do not be concerned if you do not have complete information. Include whether the agency is accredited or awaiting accreditation by a conference; its size; whether it is completely independent or a member of a consortium, cooperative, or franchise; the type of product it sells (e.g., general, commercial, vacation and leisure, all-cruise, specialty); what computer reservation system(s) it uses (if available); and any special services it offers or special marketing methods it employs. For the online agencies, consider ease of website navigation as well.

1. _____
_____
_____

2. _____
_____
_____

3. _____
_____
_____

4. _____
_____
_____

5. _____
_____
_____

6. _____
_____
_____

Do you think there are travel needs in Yourtown that are not being met by existing travel agencies? If you do, what are they, and how would you meet these needs?

_____
_____
_____
_____
_____
_____

WORKSHEET 16–2 Conference Appointments

You have learned in general about the standards a travel agency must meet to receive conference approvals. You have also learned in general about the procedures for receiving conference accreditation. Choose one of these major conferences: International Air Transport Association, Cruise Lines International Association, or VIA Rail. Research the conference's requirements and procedures for accreditation. Write your findings in the spaces below.

Name of conference

_____

Requirements for appointment

_____
_____
_____
_____
_____
_____
_____
_____
_____
_____
_____

Procedure for appointment

_____
_____
_____
_____
_____
_____
_____
_____
_____
_____
_____
_____
_____

PART 7

Research, Training, and the Future

RESEARCH, TRAINING, AND FUTURE PORTS OF CALL

Objectives

When you have completed this chapter, you should be able to:

- Recognize the role of research in the tourism industry.
- Identify human resource challenges, issues, and concerns.
- Understand the role of education and training in professional development and in producing quality tourism products and services.
- Explain the role of occupational standards and certification in developing a competent workforce and enhancing careers in the tourism industry.

- Understand the challenges and opportunities faced by the eight sectors of the tourism industry and by you as a tourism professional.
- Discuss some of the world problems that affect the tourism industry.
- Identify future issues in each of the eight sectors of the tourism industry.

Information is essential to making wise and timely decisions. Researchers, statisticians, analysts, and information technology specialists gather and analyze data for the tourism industry to use in decision making. The more the tourism industry grows, the more information and research it needs.

All areas of the tourism industry require competent workers. In this regard, tourism educators and trainers develop and deliver essential programs for the industry. As tourism grows, the need for training and education will grow with it.

In this chapter, we discuss research, education, and training, and the roles these play in the world's tourism industry; and to complete this text, we will present an overview of the future outlook of the tourism industry.

TOURISM RESEARCH

Tourism research involves collecting and analyzing data from primary and secondary sources. McIntosh and colleagues (1995) state that research is the systematic, impartial designing and conducting of investigations to solve problems. They emphasize that research does not make

decisions but does reduce risks in decision making and does help decision makers operate more effectively.

How Research Is Used

Knowing when to use research is important. It can be used to:

- Track the performance of the industry.
- Measure economic impacts.
- Identify the different types of tourists, what they want and like, and how they can be reached.
- Address specific operational problems or business issues.

Research can also be used to:

- Delineate significant problems.
- Keep in touch with the market (facts about trends can be interpreted to develop policies).
- Develop new profit sources (from new markets, new products).
- Aid sales promotion (by determining consumer attitudes and preferences).
- Reduce waste (by eliminating inefficiencies).
- Create goodwill.

PROFILE

Medical Tourism: An Emerging Global Trend

What Is Medical Tourism?

Medical tourism is the practice of travelling to another country in order to receive healthcare treatment (medical, dental, or cosmetic); it is quickly becoming a worldwide multi-billion dollar industry (Medical Tourism, January 3, 2008). In the 1990s, medical tourism generally consisted of cosmetic, plastic, or elective surgery. Recently, the most popular medical procedures are joint replacements, fertility work, cancer treatments, and dental and cosmetic surgeries; patients are even travelling "out of country" for life-saving operations such as heart surgery (Healism, n.d.). A recent McKinsey study found that Canadians represent 6 percent of medical travellers, and 60 percent of these patients travel to the U.S. for cardiovascular, neurosurgical, and cancer treatments (Prashad, 2008). However, the U.S. isn't the only place to go, and Americans themselves also travel out of country to receive treatment: "India is considered the leading country promoting medical tourism—and now it is moving into a new area of 'medical outsourcing,' where subcontractors provide services to the overburdened medical care systems in western countries" (Medical Tourism, January 3, 2008).

Benefits of Medical Tourism

Why should patients travel out of country for certain medical treatments?

- Significant potential savings since many medical destinations offer treatments at a very low cost.
- Reduced waiting time from months or years to the time it takes to plan and get to medical destination.
- May receive better and more personal care at a foreign hospital that specializes in medical tourism.

- A relaxing recovery in an exotic destination city or resort.
- Possible insurance reimbursement for medical costs (depends on many factors).
- Affordable and convenient travel to medical destinations. (Medical Tourism Guide, "12 Reasons," 2007)

Medical Travel Packages

Patients may plan their own medical vacation, but most patients are using the services of travel agencies specializing in medical tourism marketing (or medical tourism companies) where these agencies/companies build medical travel packages (combining the cost of medical treatment with airfare, hotel or resort post-operative accommodation, travel insurance, meals, airport transfers or car rentals, etc.) that are, depending on the location and procedure, 10 to 50 percent of the cost of domestic healthcare in the U.S. (Miles, n.d.; Healism, n.d.).

Example of Medical Cost and Potential Savings for a Hip Replacement

Destination	United States	India	Costa Rica
Cost of medical care	$40 000	$5 400	$6 600
Cost to arrange care	n/a	$800	$1 000
Cost of travel	n/a	$2 700	$1 200
Cost at destination	n/a	$1 100	$1 050
Total cost	$40 000	$10 000	$9 850

SOURCE: "Financial Savings in Medical Tourism," Michael D. Horowitz, MD, MBA. *Medical Tourism*, December 2007.

Medical Travel Destinations

Author Jeff Schult ("Beauty from Afar: A Medical Tourist's Guide to Affordable and Quality Cosmetic Care Outside the US") states that medical travellers select their medical destination after considering the following factors: cost, closeness (travel distance), and culture (how similar to their own) (in McGinn, 2008). Quality of staff and facilities should also be considered (Healthbase, 2008).

The following is a list of selected countries promoting medical tourism: Argentina, Belgium, Bolivia, Brazil, Brunei, Colombia, Costa Rica, Cuba, Estonia, Hong Kong, Hungary, India, Jamaica, Jordan, Lithuania, Malaysia, Mexico, New Zealand, Panama, Philippines, Saudi Arabia, Singapore, South Africa, South Korea, Thailand, Tunisia, and UAE (Medical Tourism, 2008; Hutchinson, 2005; Miles, n.d.; Prasad, 2008).

Potential Risks of Medical Tourism

1. Many countries promoting medical tourism may not regulate medical professional licensing and certification as required by countries such as Canada, the U.S., and European countries.
2. The low cost of medical treatments in many countries is partially due to the non-existence of expensive malpractice insurance. If a problem occurs resulting from medical treatment, the patient may have little recourse against the facility or staff and may incur considerable expenses to rectify the medical problem.
3. Patients who travel home by air too soon after surgery may incur serious (and even fatal) complications and side effects such as blood clots and pulmonary embolisms.
4. Patients must ensure that they receive sufficient postoperative care locally as they may be vulnerable to infection from local diseases.
5. Patients must "vacation" in moderation after medical treatment: avoid excessive drinking and sun exposure, and rest sufficiently to avoid scarring and infection (Medical Tourism Guide, "Risks," 2007).

The Future of Medical Tourism

More and more countries are entering the medical tourism destination market. Estimates predict that the medical tourism industry will become a $40 billion industry by 2010. A McKinsey study predicts that medical travellers will total 500 000 to 700 000 patients over the next 10 to 15 years; other experts estimate that there will be over 1 million patients (Prashad, 2008). Reports from India estimate that medical tourism is growing at 30 percent per annum and the country is expecting medical tourism revenue to reach $2.2 billion per year by 2012 (Medical Tourism, 2008).

Authors DeMicco and Cetron in a 2005 interview made the following forecast: "By 2015, the health of the vast Baby Boom generation will have begun its slow, final decline, and, with more than 220 million Boomers in the United States, Canada, Europe, Australia and New Zealand, this represents a significant market for inexpensive, high-quality medical care . . . Medical tourism will be particularly attractive in the United States, where an estimated 43 million people are without health insurance and 120 million without dental coverage" (in Hutchinson, 2005).

Who Is Involved?

Individuals and small groups, as well as large organizations, conduct and/or use tourism research. Every sector of the tourism industry and every operator are—or should be—doing research. Below we offer a brief overview of such efforts.

Government Provincial tourism offices can do any or all of the following: conduct their own research, use Canadian Tourism Commission (CTC) and Statistics Canada data, or hire consultants.

Educational Institutions Some universities have established research centres and conduct research on a contract basis for private operators and governments.

Consultants Tourism businesses can hire consultants—people who conduct research on a fee basis—to do research for them. KPMG and PricewaterhouseCoopers (PwC) are multinational consulting firms that specialize in tourism development and management. The Canadian Tourism Research Institute (CTRI) is a not-for-profit organization within the Conference Board of Canada that concentrates entirely on tourism research. For a fee, it will conduct

ILLUSTRATION 17–1

The Research Committee of the Canadian Tourism Commission worked with Statistics Canada and the World Tourism Organization to introduce the Tourism Satellite Account program to analyze the economic importance of tourism.

SOURCE: Canadian Tourism Commission.

customized research for organizations and provide advice and expertise in planning, designing, conducting, and interpreting research studies and applying the results.

Associations, Boards, and Councils Professional, trade, and industry associations (or boards or councils) also conduct research—or their members do. Such groups often provide ongoing statistical bulletins for their members, and publish peer-reviewed journals and/or proceedings from conferences. Examples of publications:

- World Travel & Tourism Council (WTTC): WTTC report, *Travel and Tourism: The World's Largest Industry* (1993).
- Pacific Asia Travel Association (PATA): *PATA Annual Statistical Report*.
- Council on Hotel, Restaurant & Institutional Education (CHRIE): *Hospitality Research Journal*.
- Travel and Tourism Research Association (TTRA): *Journal of Travel Research*
- International Federation for IT and Travel & Tourism (IFITT): *Information Technology and Tourism Journal*.
- Canadian Tourism Research Institute (CTRI): *Travel Markets Outlook*; *Travel Exclusive Newsletter*.
- Tourism Industry Association of Canada (TIAC): *TIAC Bulletin*.

Accommodation This sector conducts research on topics such as management practices, human resources, marketing, customer satisfaction, information technology, and e-commerce.

Food and Beverage Food franchises and chain operations were among the first tourism firms to conduct extensive research. Obviously, the results from one franchise or chain outlet can be applied to the next ones opened. All food and beverage (F&B) operations need market research to improve products and services by identifying their customers and learning what they want. Also, research identifies industry trends and is necessary to evaluate operational practices.

Attractions Theme parks rely heavily on research. The Disney Corporation was a pioneer in this. Firms conduct feasibility studies before they build attractions, and conduct research into management after they are operating.

The Research Process

Identifying a research question or problem is at the heart of good research. The following nine-step process has produced good results for both small and large research projects:

1. Identify the problem.
2. Conduct a situation analysis (identify natural, social, economic, and technological factors).
3. Conduct an informal investigation (by talking with key people such as customers and suppliers).
4. Develop a research design (establish what information is needed).
5. Collect the data (secondary data and/or primary data via surveys, observations, case studies, critical incident analyses, and/or experiments).
6. Tabulate (primary and secondary data analyzed—results can be quantitative or qualitative).
7. Interpret (conclusions are drawn; recommendations made).
8. Write a report.
9. Follow up.

Research provides profiles of industries, sectors, and/or enterprises. It also measures tourism's impact on the economy. It helps manage change and development in the public and private sectors. It helps identify trends, and it helps organizations respond in a manner that keeps them competitive. Tourism managers must understand just how heavily their industry relies on huge amounts of information.

Check Your Product Knowledge

1. Who uses research?
2. What steps are usually included in the research process?

EDUCATION AND TRAINING

As you are probably aware, there are four main levels of jobs in the tourism industry:

- Level I:　　Entry-level and front-line jobs.
- Level II:　　Supervisory jobs.
- Level III:　　Management jobs.
- Level IV:　　Executive jobs.

To advance up a career ladder in the tourism industry (or any industry), a person must build up experience, skills, education, and training. Employees in small businesses must be able to perform a variety of functions; in larger businesses their jobs may be more specific. However, with industry restructuring, the workplace "map" is changing. Employers stress that people need to get the best possible education, including a postsecondary education, and need to be willing to learn and to take advantage of as much training as possible. They should also know how to use computers and speak more than one language. The need for cross-training and multiple skills is increasing. Cross-cultural training and language training are both beneficial for careers in tourism.

Some people with no formal training have advanced in the tourism industry by working their way up from the very bottom; but doing so without a formal education is less likely today than it once was. The industry is changing and becoming more complex. No one in the industry at any level can afford to stop learning, both formally and informally.

There are a variety of ways to be educated and trained for a career in the tourism industry, including two-year and four-year programs, short courses, and on the job. Once employed in the tourism industry, individuals can achieve national recognition and become certified in a variety of occupations through professional certification programs offered, for example, through the Canadian Tourism Human Resource Council (CTHRC). An excellent guide to tourism careers, education, and training is the CTHRC publication *The Student's Travel Map: A Guide to Tourism Careers, Education and Training*, which is available free of charge online at http://www.tourismhrc.com/student-travel-map.php (located on the Nova Scotia Tourism Human Resource Council's website; the publication cannot be located on the CTHRC website). It is one of the most comprehensive sources available for tourism career information for Canadians and provides:

- An overview of the tourism industry.
- Testimonials from tourism professionals.
- Occupational profiles from the five tourism industries, from front line to executive level.
- Education and training references relating to tourism programs in Canada.
- Resource section listing career development and job search websites.

Programs are offered in various ways: on the job, through distance education via television or the Internet, and at seminars and workshops, as well as in classrooms. Access to education and training is possible throughout Canada at community colleges, universities, and private colleges, and through corporate programs.

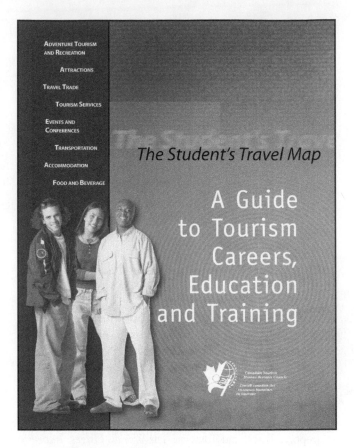

ILLUSTRATION 17–2

The Student's Travel Map is one of many tools provided by the Canadian Tourism Human Resource Council for people interested in tourism as a career.

SOURCE: Canadian Tourism Human Resource Council.

Occupational Standards and Certification

The CTHRC works to develop human resource programs to support a globally competitive and sustainable Canadian tourism industry. In consultation with industry, the CTHRC has already developed **occupational standards** for more than 50 occupations. The standards describe the knowledge, skills, and attitudes required for competence in occupations such as bartender, front desk agent, and outdoor guide. By reading the standards, people learn what a job entails. Certification programs are based on occupational standards and can serve as a helpful reference as an individual works toward certification. Employers also benefit from standards. Developing training for employees and assessing employee performance are two examples of how employers use standards.

Certification makes a person more hireable and increases his or her chances of promotion. It also indicates that the individual is serious about the job and the industry. To become certified, people must go through several steps. After completing the required training programs, they must have supervised work experience and then have their job skills rated by a trained evaluator. Finally, they must pass an exam about the job that tests their knowledge and attitudes that have been shaped by training, self-study, and experience. Certification helps make tourism a viable and fulfilling career choice and enhances the public's image of careers in tourism. Certificates based on the occupational standards awarded by CTHRC are recognized nationally by the various sectors of the tourism industry.

More information about standards and certification is available from the CTHRC, **tourism education councils** (TECs) in the provinces and territories (contact the CTHRC or go to its website for more information), and from professional associations such as the Canadian Institute of Travel Counsellors, the Association of Canadian Travel Agencies, the Institute of Certified Travel Agents, Meeting Planners International Society, the American Hotel and Lodging Association, the Canadian Restaurant and Foodservices Association, and the Canadian Hotel Association. Canada Employment Centres can also provide information.

Formal Education

Formal education can be acquired through a single course or through a more intensive specialized program at a trade school, college, or university. Universities offer four-year degrees and master's degrees in fields related to tourism. Some specialize in hospitality or hotel management, others in tourism development, recreation, resort management, and so on. Secondary schools, trade schools, technical colleges, community colleges, private colleges, and some universities offer one- to three-year diploma and certificate programs. For a listing of some colleges and universities in Canada, the United States, Australia, and Europe that have well-known hospitality, tourism, and culinary management programs, go to the Hospitality Careers Online (hCareers) website at www.hcareers.ca.

Anyone who wants to go into tourism management will find that employers expect and often require formal education. Besides having specialized knowledge and skills in tourism operations, managers must understand the components of business administration: economics, accounting, finance, management, marketing, human relations, ethics, and law. The CTHRC says that future managers and owners also need to understand international marketing and distribution channels, as well as international law, finance, and business practices.

Tourism as an academic discipline is relatively new. Because it is such a complex and dynamic field, there are various ideas about what should be included in an academic education. North American programs combine a management-oriented approach with industry training. British programs are similar to North American ones.

French programs tend to emphasize techniques and professionalism. Swiss programs, noted for their success, strive to adapt to industry needs. They develop management competencies through practical experiences; they also insist on competency in more than one language.

Most programs in Europe are still based on centuries-old traditions of apprenticeship. Apprenticeships have also been used in hospitality education in North America. However, the newer programs, especially at community colleges and universities, follow a theoretical management model, and combine classroom instruction with practical experience both on and off campus. In most of these programs, students must complete several hundred hours of practicum or cooperative education work terms. Opportunities in Canada for formal education in tourism and hospitality have increased in the past decade. Individuals who wish to pursue a formal education in tourism need to determine which programs best suit their career aspirations, wherever in the world those programs are offered.

According to John Walker, the dynamic Dean of the Centre for Hospitality & Culinary Arts at Toronto's George Brown College, "the Hospitality and Culinary industry is the world's largest growing, job creating profession." Our tourism industry is about action and adventure; and the flexibility and choice available allows for career movement between the industry's many sectors, which is attractive to both students and employers (*Accolade*, 2008).

On-the-Job Training

Many employers offer on-the-job training or in-service training in customer service, communications, safety standards, and other topics related to their operations. Through these private programs, individuals can increase their knowledge and skills and advance within their workplaces and the industry. Sometimes this training is offered by in-house trainers; other times, the firm sponsors individuals to attend training sessions offered by industry associations or provincial education councils.

Apprenticeship training is very much alive in the tourism industry, especially in the food and beverage sector. Cooks and chefs are often trained on the job by qualified chefs, or they work under another chef for an extensive time period after completing initial training at a community or technical college. Advance certification is also possible.

Canadian Tourism Human Resource Council

The Canadian Tourism Human Resource Council (CTHRC) was established in 1993, with the mandate to advance the status of tourism as a career. The vision of the CTHRC is to set a direction for human resource development throughout the Canadian tourism industry, to coordinate human resource development activities, to promote the use of good management practices for human resources, and to create a strong training culture in the industry.

The CTHRC is based in Ottawa. It works closely with governments, business, and labour, with education and training communities across Canada, and with provincial and territorial tourism education councils that deliver programs (refer to the CTHRC website, www.cthrc.ca, where you will find an up-to-date listing of publications and career planning tools).

Education/Certification Programs

The goal of the Education Standards Division of the Canadian Institute of Travel Counsellors (CITC) is to ensure that its members meet professional standards. Originally, the Association of Canadian Travel Agencies (ACTA) and CITC established a program known as ACCESS (the ACTA and CITC Canadian Educational Standards System) for this purpose, but in 2003, CITC bought out ACTA's interests in this program. Certification of travel counsellors in Canada is conducted through the Educational Standards Division of the CITC.

The International Air Transportation Association/ United Federation of Travel Agents' Association (IATA/ UFTAA) runs travel agents' professional training programs worldwide. For further information, go to www .radiobhuvan.com/IHCTM/IATA.htm.

Specialized Schooling Courses in travel agency operation and the travel sector are offered in private schools and public institutions across Canada. Mega-agencies and franchises provide similar training. Advanced training is offered through the Canadian Institute of Travel Counsellors, as discussed in the previous section. Once travel counsellors have successfully completed a national knowledge examination, gained 1000 hours of relevant work experience, and had their skills assessed on the job, they can apply for membership in the CITC, which confers the right to use the designation **certified travel counsellor (CTC)**. A travel counsellor can join the CTC as an associate member while still completing certification requirements.

Counsellors continue their professional development by attending industry seminars, product launches, and the like. Experienced travel counsellors can take an advanced program through the CITC and earn the **certified travel manager (CTM)** designation. The CITC also offers a variety of professional development programs to help travel counsellors learn new skills and procedures.

The CITC is working with the CTHRC to develop a new program for national certification based on the skills, knowledge, and attitudes identified by the industry as necessary in a professional travel counsellor. Membership in the CITC signifies that a counsellor has professional status.

Council on Hotel, Restaurant & Institutional Education

Many schools affiliated with the Council on Hotel, Restaurant & Institutional Education (CHRIE) have student groups known as Hosteur Societies. Twice a year, CHRIE publishes an electronic magazine called *Hosteur* for future hospitality and tourism professionals. Its articles help students make the transition to graduate programs or study-abroad programs in all varieties of travel-related businesses. For member colleges and universities, *Hosteur* is available as an e-zine on the CHRIE website.

Check Your Product Knowledge

1. How can people become certified nationally in an occupation?
2. What areas of knowledge are managers expected to have today?

THE FUTURE

The tourism industry caters to the needs and wants of the travelling public. It is unique among businesses in that it markets experiences as well as products and services. For the tourism industry to thrive, all eight of its sectors (or five industries) will have to work together. The outlook for the tourism industry is generally good. Tourism operators will be able to write their own tickets provided they have a vision, adapt to society's demographics, are technology smart, reduce costs and increase services, and form alliances and affiliations.

It is difficult to predict exactly what the future holds for the industry. In the remainder of this final chapter we discuss some trends, issues, and possible developments— future ports of call you may visit during your career. This discussion should help you understand the challenges and opportunities faced by the industry and by you as a tourism professional.

Continued Growth of Travel and Tourism

The international tourism industry is the world's fastest-growing industry. According to the World Tourism Organization (UNWTO), the number of international arrivals has increased 6.5 percent annually from 1950 to 2007. There are no signs that tourism growth will slow down in the twenty-first century. The potential for job creation in the next 10 years is vast. Quarterly statistics on travel and tourism published by the Canadian Tourism Commission (CTC) indicate that employment in tourism is outpacing the economy as a whole.

Will the growth in tourism continue? With its recovery after the terrorists attacks in September 2001, the outbreak of SARS and "mad cow disease" in 2003, the tourism industry has shown in its tenacity and its determination to continue growing. "In 2006, tourism spending in Canada reached $66.9 billion and tourism's share of the economy-wide GDP was 2.1%. It also provided employment for 10.1% of the Canadian labour force in 2006" (CTHRC, "Total Tourism," 2006). The CTHRC (n.d.) forecasts that there will be 290 690 new jobs in tourism between 2006 and 2015. According to a WTTC forecast (March 6, 2008), the tourism sector should experience an average annual growth rate of 4.4 percent for the period 2009 to 2018, resulting in 297 million jobs and a 10.5 percent global GDP by 2018. Over the next 20 years, some analysts have forecast worldwide tourism growing at an annual rate of 7 to 14 percent. Also worldwide tourism receipts are predicted to reach $8 trillion in 2008 and increase to $15 trillion by 2018 (Eturbonews, March 7, 2008).

Many countries with emerging markets and developing economies have become emerging tourist destinations, and have experienced double the growth rate of destination countries with established high income levels. With the removal of barriers to trade and tourism in the 1990s, the popular destinations in the future will probably include China, the former Soviet Union, and the countries of Eastern Europe, as well as India and Brazil (Heyer, 2008). Because of its culture and history, Europe will always be a traditional destination for outbound North Americans. However, as these travellers become more experienced, they will also become more adventurous and look for more variety. The Pacific Rim—Hong Kong, Thailand, Singapore, and Japan—is already enjoying tremendous growth in tourism, and this trend is likely to continue. Improved infrastructures and control of costs will make mass travel to these areas possible.

More trouble may lie ahead, however. A potential global recession in 2008 has caused concern that the 25-year growth in world GDP will not continue and international tourism will be affected. However, the UNWTO believes that past experience has shown that the tourism sector has proven resilient (UNWTO, January 29, 2008).

Vacation and Leisure Travel Outlook

The conditions that gave momentum to the growth of vacation and leisure travel are expected to continue, including:

- Increased discretionary incomes.
- More leisure time.
- Higher educational levels and the desire for nonmaterial experiences.

ILLUSTRATION 17–3

The UNWTO supports industry development by making available publications that educate members of the tourism industry.

SOURCE: World Trade Organization.

In *Boom, Bust and Echo 2000*, David Foote and Daniel Stoffman (1998) credit Sam Blyth of Blyth and Co., a Toronto travel agency, for suggesting that the following trends explain the travel market:

- People are retiring younger.
- People have more money (fun money for luxuries like travel).
- Older people are healthier.

As well, travel promotions and new travel products stimulate interest in tourism. For example, the CTC is working on a national strategy to showcase Canada's cultural diversity, the goal being to counterbalance the predominant image of Canada as simply a nature destination. According to Aboriginal Tourism Canada (ATC), "Aboriginal tourism in Canada is finding its niche. Aboriginal tourism is defined as 'any business that is owned and operated in part or whole by the First Nations (North American Indian), the Inuit (Eskimo) and the Métis nations who form the First Peoples of Canada and offering a full spectrum of tourism products and services, traditional and contemporary, that include adventure tourism, attractions, events and conferences, accommodation, transportation, food and beverage, travel trade, and tourism services.' The Aboriginal Tourism Canada website advertises the Significant 29 which are 29 significant Aboriginal tourism sites which embody their traditions, heritage and culture" (Aboriginal Tourism Canada, n.d.).

A burgeoning market for aboriginal culture is expected to provide up to 40 000 jobs in Canada. From an economic or "yield" perspective, inbound markets—especially the American inbound market—represent the most lucrative target for aboriginal communities. Such tourism products will have to respect the culture, which is not "for sale." More new businesses and tourism organizations like the ATC are on the horizon, and mainstream tour operators such as Brewster and Jonview are expected to add aboriginal programs to their itineraries.

The demand for cultural tourism is growing at least in part because of an aging population that wants enriched experiences through individualized and custom-built vacation packages. Canada will be a player in the world market for cultural experiences if it continues to build partnerships between the cultural and heritage product and the travel trade sector.

New Travel Trends

Jennifer Jasper (of the California Travel & Tourism Commission) identified the following travel trends:

- Shorter vacations.
- More multi-generational travel (e.g., grandparents with grandchildren).
- More local travel (i.e., domestic tourism/within the U.S.).
- Singles travel.
- "Babymoons" (parents taking a last-opportunity trip before baby arrival). (in Eturbonews, January 7, 2008)

Business Travel Outlook

Business travellers will continue to travel to meetings and conventions as well as for sales, operations, management, and consulting purposes. More than half of business travellers today are women. All business travellers will be more independent and will rely more on technology to make bookings and to stay in touch with the home office while on the road. Business travellers will be staying a little longer on the road to do more for less cost. This will further increase the demand for support services on the road, especially in hotel guest rooms. The number of employees taking business trips will probably increase as a result of globalization.

An American Express (Amex) study expects corporations to take full advantage of e-commerce and e-booking tools. However, there may well be opportunities for travel agencies—Amex included—to provide travel management services geared specifically to mid-sized companies. These agencies could provide access to corporate rates for air tickets, hotels, and car rentals; personalized service delivered by small teams of travel counsellors; the option of outsourcing expense management services; and access to online interactive booking facilities. Other companies and individuals will turn to centres such as Travelocity's Business Travel Center to access resources, travel news, and business planning and reservation tools.

According to the Amex *Business Travel Monitor*, international airfares and hotel rates were increasing and corporate travel policies were becoming more rigid; fewer companies were using first-class travel, and many were using less expensive airport hotels instead of going downtown. When prices are high, companies pull back on first-class travel and resort more to negotiated discounts and cheaper, nonrefundable, leisure-type airfares. When an economy weakens, business travel reacts accordingly. Companies use lower leisure fares whenever possible and negotiate corporate discounts with preferred carriers. Also, if fuel costs continue to rise, car rental agencies will raise their surcharges and car rental costs will increase.

Travel for meetings and conventions will increase in the coming decade as people recognize the need to communicate more with others in their fields and to keep their skills and knowledge up to date. The tourism industry will continue to develop new marketing techniques to meet the needs of business travellers. The business market wants trips to be as free from hassle as possible: Amenities must function, products must meet women's expectations as well as men's, and facilities must be provided to let travellers get their work done away from their offices.

The trend toward combining pleasure experiences and business travel will continue, especially among travellers who are not frequent business travellers. International travellers are likely to continue folding leisure time into their business trips and taking their spouses or families along.

According to the American Express annual Global Business Travel Forecast (October 2007), corporate eco-initiatives will evolve into "Responsible Business Travel," which Amex predicts will include the following:

> Companies are expected to increase the focus on responsible business travel practices related to the environment and the safety and security of travelers.
>
> Companies are expected to increasingly focus on understanding and measuring a trip's "carbon footprint."
>
> Although carbon offsetting remains popular, we [Amex] think that this is likely to prove to be a short-term solution that will be combined with policy and program management strategies.

ILLUSTRATION 17–4

As the population of Canada continues to grow and the proportion of retired people increases, more people will be visiting friends and relatives.

SOURCE: PhotoDisc/Getty Images.

Outlook for Travel to Visit Friends and Relatives

Canada began as a nation of immigrants, and Canadians continue to migrate. To find or maintain employment or to change their lifestyles, people move from the country to the city, from the city to the country, from city to city, or from one coast to another. Today's families are also likely to have members scattered throughout the country, and most people have friends who have moved to different regions. As Canada's population continues to grow and more and more people retire, more people will be visiting friends and relatives. Visiting friends and relatives is already the main reason for travel and will likely continue to be.

Check Your Product Knowledge

1. What is needed to foster growth in tourism in the future?
2. What conditions give momentum to growth in vacation and leisure travel?

INCREASED INDUSTRY RECOGNITION

At the Organisation for Economic Co-operation and Development (OECD) 2001 seminar in Berlin, presenters pointed to the size and growth of tourism and discussed how important tourism is to national economies. They also emphasized that more attention would need to be paid to creating and promoting sustainable tourism networks; accessing capital markets; accumulating human capital with respect to innovation, product development, and cross-border activities; and—most important—securing and developing communication technologies as they relate to tourism.

Sustainable Tourism

Tourism can foster sustainable development. Culture, society, and the natural environment are the foundations for sustained tourism development. More countries and regions are working to ensure that *all* tourism products and services are sustainable—not just niche markets such as ecotourism and cultural tourism. This requires specific actions in education, training, and culture. Means have to be found to protect natural areas and preserve and manage fragile archaeological areas. Also, laws must be passed to soften the potential impact of tourism projects, especially regarding land use.

Access to Capital

The shortage of financing for upgrading and renewing tourism facilities is a growing problem. New forms of financing are being found that reflect the relatively high risks and small returns associated with SMEs (small and medium-sized enterprises). SMEs can often reduce their operating costs through better management, careful planning, and alternative sources of financing (e.g., government/industry partnerships). Countries need to develop policies that will make the tourism industry more attractive to entrepreneurs.

Human Capital

A country's **human capital** strongly affects its competitive position in the global tourism marketplace. Education and training are essential for maintaining the quality of the tourism product, for supporting productivity, for improving conditions of the labour movement, and for attracting people to tourism as an occupation.

Professionalism A professional is a person who has mastered a specific body of knowledge and who possesses certain skills not generally possessed by those outside the profession. After people have completed an approved curriculum at an accredited institution, the government licenses them to practise their profession. They may be required to demonstrate knowledge of their field by passing difficult examinations. To maintain their status, they must keep up to date with the latest developments in their field and constantly refine their skills. Professionals are also expected to maintain high ethical standards. Years of experience add to their professional stature.

At the present time, most workers in the tourism industry don't need to be licensed. That being said, professional behaviour is expected throughout the tourism industry. Increasing competition, the complexity of the industry, and the increasing demand for quality services and products mean that future tourism personnel will need to be better educated and trained. To inspire the public's confidence, the tourism industry must continue to develop tourism professionals. The CTHRC, industry associations, and private and public postsecondary programs focus on the attitudes, knowledge, and skill competencies required for tourism careers.

More and more operations have come to realize that training builds professionalism and requires appropriate investment. Effective training programs pay for themselves; this is why the CTHRC and the various training and education councils are helping to develop them. Staff gain respect for themselves and for their work, and gain an extra level of professionalism. Increased professional certification will lead to the development of human capital.

Tourism Partnerships More and more tourism operators now acknowledge that tourism's eight sectors (or five industries) are closely intertwined (see Figure 17–1). Partnerships among tourism businesses have been very beneficial. More of them are expected as destinations are promoted (i.e., instead of single attractions or facilities), and as marketing strategies are developed around nature and cultural/heritage tourism.

The following is an example of a successful partnership that can serve as a model for the future. In Italy, the CTC partners with local tour operators to increase awareness about Canada. The Canada Specialist Program has been initiated to educate travel agents. Also, each year Italian tour operators and Canadian destination marketing officers take the Canada Roadshow to five Italian cities to educate travel agents about Canada. Canada's popularity with Italian leisure travellers has increased in the past 20 years; more pleasure travellers than VFR tourists are expected to visit Canada in the future.

Information Systems

Information technology (IT) is changing the tourism industry. Knowledge today is power. In the future, firms will succeed by knowing their customers and using that knowledge well. According to Olsen and Connolly (2000), IT has had three main impacts:

1. Travel consumers no longer display much product loyalty.
2. Consumers expect firms to provide "experiences."

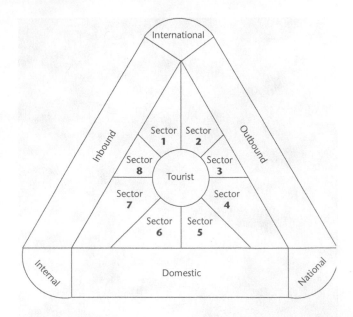

Sector 1 — Food and Beverage
restaurants
catering
food contractors
taverns, bars, clubs

Sector 2 — Accommodation
resorts
hotels
motels
hostels
campgrounds
cruise ships

Sector 3 — Transportation
automobiles
buses
cruises/marine
airlines
railways

Sector 4 — Travel Trade
tour wholesalers
tour operators
travel agents

Sector 5 — Tourism Services
departments of tourism
Canadian Tourism Commission
industry associations
boards of trade
retail services
convention centres
academic institutions

Sector 6 — Adventure Tourism and Recreation
skiing
marine activities
golf and tennis
outdoor adventures
ecotours

Sector 7 — Meetings, Events, and Conferences
trade shows
conventions
conferences
seminars
congresses

Sector 8 — Attractions
zoos
festivals
museums
amusement parks
casinos
natural attractions

FIGURE 17–1 Tourism Components

3. Employees of tourism enterprises have evolved into stakeholders who add product value.

In the past, the tourism industry was affected by "hard" changes such as the advent of jet travel and the building of interstate and interprovincial highways. The newer changes are being driven by "soft" developments, including the following:

- **Connected computers** The Internet allows consumers real-time direct access to product offerings, rates, availability, and product features.

- **Real time** Customers now insist on being able to make transactions quickly.
- **Regulating cyberspace** E-commerce and the Web will become more regulated.
- **Data warehousing and data mining** Operators will learn how to apply these to determine the value of customers, monitor relationships with them, develop more sharply focused relationship marketing strategies, and provide customized services.
- **Segments of one** It will be possible to collect and synthesize information and use the resulting knowledge to provide high levels of personal service.
- **Archaic technology** A multimedia approach to customer transactions will become commonplace.
- **IT for executives** Executives will become well versed in the capabilities, potential, and limitations of IT.
- **Cost of technology** Financing could include leasing hardware; paying according to use and occupancy; requiring guests to pay a "technology" tax.

Olsen and Connolly's report indicates that these forces will show themselves in some of the following ways:

- Marketers will find it a challenge to keep customers from moving to the next website.
- By evolving into gatekeepers for guest experiences, companies will be able to create custom experiences to meet individual needs. This may become an additional role for travel agents. It will not be easy to match needs with opportunities. Perfecting the matching process will redefine the tourism business.
- Employees at all organizational levels will be value-creating stakeholders. They will require the conceptual skills to serve as consultants for customers. They will have to be knowledgeable about their company's products and services.
- Employees will serve on creative-response teams that develop solutions for customers' overall experience needs, timed to the customers' schedules.
- Employees will also require advanced social skills in such things as conflict resolution, communications, and personality identification.

New technologies are challenging the industry to critically rethink core competencies, service delivery methods, and customer/employee interactions. Olsen and Connolly emphasize that assets and capital will no longer produce a competitive advantage. Intellect will be required if companies constantly have to reinvent themselves to create value and provide the ultimate in individualized service.

WORLD ISSUES

Although the future of the tourism industry seems bright, things can happen to set it back. The September 11, 2001, terrorist attacks in the United States provide an obvious although apparently temporary example. A few pessimists believe that congested and unsafe airways, hijackings and bombings, strikes, and overcrowded and polluted destinations may return travel to its original meaning of "travail"—that is, dangerous and hard work. Some of these problems can be addressed; others will probably always be with us. All of them will play a role in the growth of tourism.

Overcrowding and Pollution

A Canadian couple from Calgary recently returned from a trip to Yellowstone National Park in Wyoming with their children. Both adults had visited the park before as children and were surprised at the changes in the park, both physical and managerial. Forty years earlier, tourists had been allowed to park their cars close to the geysers and hot springs. They could toss coins for good luck into Morning Glory Pool. From the safety of their cars, they could feed candy and ice cream to the bears along the road.

Today, Yellowstone operates under a strict management program. Car traffic has been diverted from the geysers and hot springs. Visitors must now walk along a boardwalk—sometimes for more than half a mile—to view many of the attractions. There are many more park rangers. Besides teaching tourists about the wonders of Yellowstone, the rangers manage and protect its resources. For instance, the park service now confines bears to the backcountry, where they will not serve as entertainment for tourists.

These regulatory measures became necessary because overcrowding, with all its accompanying abuses, was threatening to destroy Yellowstone's beauty. For example, several of the geysers had been plugged up by garbage. Coins and litter had discoloured Morning Glory Pool.

This story illustrates the dangers that overcrowding and pollution present to many popular attractions and destinations, both natural and those built by humans. When these problems are not addressed, attractions begin to lose their appeal and visitors stay away. Canada was one of the first countries to rein in development inside and around parks. Parks Canada is especially concerned about Canada's Rocky Mountain parks—Banff, Jasper, Kootenay, and Yoho—and the sand dunes in the national parks on Prince Edward Island. It has established an ecosystem-based approach to park management, the main purpose of which is to preserve the wilderness character and ecological integrity of this country's parks.

Check Your Product Knowledge

1. What four areas will need to have more attention paid to them in the future?
2. What changes are related to IT?

An important task for the tourism industry in the years ahead will be to manage attractions carefully. Requiring reservations, limiting the number of visitors, and charging user fees will be some of the techniques employed. A few countries, having decided that the environmental and social damage generated by tourism is not worth the economic benefits, may even develop anti-tourist policies or restrict the number of visitors they allow to enter.

Availability of Oil

Oil is the lifeblood of the tourism industry. Without it, there would be no travel and facilities would be rather chilly or have to charge higher rates to pay for a fuel in short supply. An increase in oil prices means an increase in the cost of travel products, transportation, and hospitality services; if travel products become too expensive, consumers won't buy them. They'll stay home.

All of this means that oil prices are an ever-present concern to the industry. When Syrian and Egyptian forces invaded Israel in 1973, disrupting oil shipments in the Persian Gulf, a worldwide energy crisis was set off. This seriously curtailed airline and automobile travel. Again in 1979, when Iranian terrorists seized the U.S. embassy in Tehran, the United States cut off oil imports, and another oil crisis resulted.

Oil prices dropped sharply in the early 1980s and then remained stable for several years. But as tensions in the Middle East increased again, prices began to edge up once more. The Persian Gulf, an essential transit point, was mined and the passage of tankers through it was interrupted a number of times. In the summer of 1990, Iraq invaded Kuwait, cutting off a major oil supplier. This act, and the ensuing Gulf War in early 1991, sent oil prices soaring once again.

After 2000, the price of gasoline and heating fuel increased dramatically because of reduced availability of OPEC oil and the production imbalances arising from tightened environmental standards. Even so, North Americans continued travelling, according to the Travel Industry Association of America. Only 5 percent of the people polled indicated that fuel prices were a reason to curtail travel. In March 2008, economist Diane Francis predicted, "Oil will march toward $150 a barrel and other commodity prices will continue to increase, as investors race toward holding real things instead of currencies" (Francis, 2008). Then on June 23, 2008, the *Globe and Mail* printed that the oil price had risen to US$137.04 a barrel (Berman, 2008).

With rising costs, PATA issued a news warning: "Global economies will be at risk if airlines are forced to dramatically reduce their operations and close important routes due to record high fuel costs." This warning was a response to the news that major airlines had been announcing route reductions and employee layoffs. It was also predicted by the Hawaii Visitors and Convention Bureau that destinations such as Hawaii could suffer a 25 percent reduction in scheduled flight service (PATA News, 2008).

Although as of November 2008, fuel prices dropped to around US$65 a barrel, some smaller airlines, including Zoom Airlines, didn't make it through the summer.

Energy supplies will continue to vary. When the supply becomes restricted again, the tourism industry can expect the following developments:

- Fewer people will travel.
- Package tours will become more popular (as opposed to independent travel).
- People will travel closer to home.
- Operations will be motivated to adjust their management practices to reduce their fuel bills.

Political Instability

June 1985 was to have been the beginning of the season for global tourism. Instead, it was the beginning of the season for global terrorism. According to one report, there were more than 800 international terrorist incidents in 1985. Because of continued unrest in the Mediterranean region, 1986 was a disastrous summer for European travel. Millions of North Americans decided to stay home or go elsewhere, rather than risk being victims of terrorist attacks. The Persian Gulf War in the early 1990s had a similar effect on travel. Travel was affected again after the terrorist attacks on New York City and Washington in September 2001.

Terrorism and warfare are still major deterrents to travel and tourism. Although a traveller's chances of being on a hijacked plane are very slim, many people have become more wary of travelling since the September 2001 incidents. In response, international airports are improving their security measures. Books such as *Everything You Need to Know Before You're Hijacked* (by Douglas McKinnon, former chair of the Civil Aeronautics Board) advise travellers on how to minimize the risk of being victimized by terrorists. A survey by Yesawich, Pepperdine, and Brown found that after the September 11 attacks, more than half of leisure and business travellers expected to take fewer international trips (*Tourism*, November 2001).

Fluctuating Currency Rates

Currency rates have a big impact on tourism by shifting demand and altering travel patterns. Rates can make or break a destination. When the exchange rate is favourable at a destination, travellers go there; when their money buys less, tourists tend to stay away. The Canadian dollar has fluctuated greatly relative to the U.S. dollar since the early 1990s, between a high of $1.10 (November 2007) and a low of $0.64 (early 2000s). The currency rate influences cross-border shopping, overseas travel, and the number of snowbirds who travel to the southern United States.

ILLUSTRATION 17–5

Terrorism, once again, had a severe impact on travel and the tourism industry after the attack of September 11, 2001, on the World Trade Center in New York City.
SOURCE: Corel.

In recent years, the value of the U.S. dollar has been weak in Japan and in most of Western Europe. The Canadian dollar, relative to other currencies, tends to move in the same direction as the U.S. dollar. Table 17–1 shows the exchange rate for the Canadian dollar with major currencies on a particular day.

Even if the dollar remains weak against many foreign currencies, many Canadians will continue to travel abroad. They'll compensate for having less buying power by shortening their trips, choosing lower-cost accommodations, taking package tours with guaranteed prices, and seeking the lowest possible airfares. They'll also switch to destinations where the dollar will buy more—possibly Greece, Brazil, Australia, and Cuba. Some American operators along the U.S.–Canada border offer services at par to encourage Canadians to travel from Canada.

Prior to late 2007, a devalued Canadian dollar made outbound travel to some destinations less appealing, but it also pulled in more visitors from abroad, especially from the United States, because these people could buy more Canadian dollars with their currency. It made travel in Canada a real bargain.

TABLE 17–1 Canadian Dollar Compared to Major Currencies as of March 20, 2008 (Bank of Canada) (Based on nominal exchange values)

Major Currencies	CDN$ per unit	US$ per unit
U.S. dollar	1.0269	0.9738
Australian dollar	0.9200	1.0870
Brazil real	0.5901	1.6946
Chinese renminbi	0.1456	6.8681
EU Euro	1.5830	0.6317
Hong Kong dollar	0.13203	7.5739
Japanese yen	0.01039	96.2464
Mexican peso	0.09576	10.4418
Russian rouble	0.04313	23.1857
Swiss franc	1.0162	0.9843
U.K. (British) pound	2.0356	0.4913

SOURCE: Bank of Canada, March 20, 2008.

Sexual Exploitation of Children

Sexual tourism, especially when it involves children, is detestable and must be eliminated. The UNWTO has initiated several programs to eradicate it through its Child Prostitution and Tourism Task Force. Countries such as Thailand, the Dominican Republic, Ghana, and the Seychelles, as well as representatives from the European Union, International Air Transport Association, and Pacific Asia Travel Association, have pledged to step up

ILLUSTRATION 17–6

The World Tourism Organization has established a program to fight child prostitution.

SOURCE: World Tourism Organization.

their efforts to combat the exploitation of children. The UNWTO has established a code of conduct for tour operators, strengthened media awareness, and developed a comprehensive website. It also plans to raise awareness of the problem among communities and tourism administrations in countries where child sexual exploitation is a particular problem.

Disease and Poverty

Travellers avoid going to areas where they might become seriously ill. For example, in 2003, the SARS outbreak in Toronto deterred most tourists from coming to the city or even to Canada. For about three months in the summer, daily tourism losses reached about $30 million; the overall tourism loss to Toronto was estimated at $500 million, and thousands of hotel and food service workers became unemployed (Smith Travel Research, 2004).

Tourists also avoid areas where poverty is widespread. They want to be able to enjoy themselves, and seeing impoverished people living in shacks on garbage tips is too distressing for most tourists. This is why some resorts in the Caribbean and other places are built in secluded areas.

In this regard, Africa is suffering from an especially poor image. Only about 2 percent of North Americans travelling abroad visit the continent. Years of television viewing—especially news coverage of drought, famine, and civil war in Ethiopia—have reinforced the idea that Africa is a land of disease, poverty, and strife. Unfortunately, political conflicts have prevented tourism development, especially in Sudan and the Great Lakes region in central Africa. While it's certainly true that parts of Africa have these problems, the continent is home to 53 different countries and a wide variety of cultures, traditions, scenery, and wildlife. Many African countries are working at creating a new image. In 2000, for example, Angola celebrated World Tourism Day with a new promotion campaign (With Tourism, a Clean Angola) aimed at strengthening national identity, peace, integration, and international cooperation.

Continued Airline Reregulation and Deregulation

Each time there is a midair collision or an airline goes bankrupt, a certain segment of the population cries out for reregulation—that is, a return to regulated competition. Indeed, there are signs that deregulation may not be achieving what was intended. Three areas in particular concern both advocates and opponents of reform and deregulation:

1. **Level of service and safety in the airline industry** In an attempt to cut costs, airlines may reduce service or take shortcuts that compromise safety.
2. **Trend toward concentration** Just a few large carriers could end up controlling all of the business.
3. **Inequitable spread of savings among travellers** Airlines may charge higher fares on routes where they have less competition and use the profits to subsidize discounted fares on intensely competitive routes.

Airline deregulation has achieved lower airfares and improved operating efficiency, and will continue for the immediate future. However, if abuses caused by the pressures of competition become too great and steps aren't taken to correct them, there will probably be a swing back toward government regulation.

Governments abroad are beginning to deregulate airlines and other travel components. (Actually, the word "privatize" would be more accurate, because overseas foreign governments not only regulate but also own travel enterprises. Governments privatize industries when they transfer control or ownership of them from public to private hands.) For example, in 1987, the British government sold British Airways to private investors. By that year, the airline had become a severe drain on the public treasury.

Climate Change and the Carbon Footprint

According to the UNWTO's "Climate Change and Tourism: Responding to Global Challenges" report, "The nature and intensity of climate change impacts will differ for tourism destinations around the world"; with developing countries being the most vulnerable to the impacts of climate change. The impacts of climate change may also affect other economic and financial sectors (such as agriculture and local tourism suppliers), and their climate change strategies, or lack of, may have implications for the travel and tourism sectors, an adverse effect on the global economy, and a possible security risk in some countries (UNWTO, 2007).

Influential international organizations are trying to encourage governments and tourism operators to develop conservation strategies to promote sustainability. In June 2008, the Secretary-General of World Meteorological Organization, Michel Jarraud, renewed his request for "governments and the industry to strengthen climate-tourism partnerships and to incorporate climate factors in tourism policies, development and management plans, so as to ensure a sustainable future for the sector" (ehotelier, June 2008). The Executive Director of UNEP, Achim Steiner, advised, "Tourism can assist in combating poverty in developing countries, in reducing its own carbon footprint and make a contribution to the conservation of natural and nature-based resources" (ehotelier, June 2008).

Check Your Product Knowledge

1. What are some factors that discourage or curtail travel and tourism?
2. What can be done about overcrowding and pollution at tourist attractions?

BEYOND 2008

The potential for the tourism industry looks bright as the population ages, family structures change, technology advances, markets shift, demand develops, products and services are made available, and more attention is paid to human resource development. Natural, social, economic, and technological factors will continue to influence all sectors of the industry.

Future of the Transportation Sector

Air There will be greater emphasis on cooperation among airlines in different regions, countries, and continents, resulting in strategic alliances that create "around the world" seamless air travel. New low-cost carriers will continue to emerge, seeking particular market niches; most of these will not survive. The airlines are replacing their aging fleets with new, more fuel-efficient planes. Bombardier will continue to succeed in the international marketplace with its short-haul jets. Infrastructure requirements for airport terminals and runway expansion will be considerable. More airports in Canada will levy "departure fees" to pay for these improvements. Security will continue to be a constant concern.

Passenger traffic will continue to expand in the first two decades of the twentieth-first century. Transport Canada predicts the following average annual growth rates in 2009: within Canada, 2.8 percent; to the United States, 4.3 percent; to the North Atlantic, 4.4 percent; to South America and the Caribbean, 4.9 percent; and to the Pacific, 8.8 percent. Vancouver's airport will benefit as the gateway between North America and Asia, even with an anticipated economic slowdown in certain countries in Asia.

For the two-year period 2002–03, the number of airport self-service kiosks increased from 1500 to 3000. The advantages of these kiosks are reduced check-in time and a saving for airlines of millions in labour costs. Continental Airline domestic passengers with e-tickets are able to use the airline's 779 kiosks in 130 U.S. airports; about 60 percent of all Continental passengers are using this technology. Passengers can use the kiosk not only to check in, but also to change their seat assignment, upgrade their tickets, and print receipts.

A new common-use check-in system, called Speedcheck, will have passport readers for international flights. Assuming the Speedcheck system is successful, most large airports will want one (Jones, 2004).

According to the IATA annual Corporate Air Travel Survey (November 2007), "Air travelers not only embrace new technology, but are keen for more high-tech travel options and are demanding 'opportunities to take more control of their travel experience.'" The results of the IATA survey are summarized in Table 17–2.

TABLE 17–2 Results of November 2007 IATA Air Travellers Survey

Overall preferences of IATA survey respondents:
89% prefer electronic tickets to paper tickets
56% have used Internet check-in
69% have used self-service kiosks instead of check-in desks
54% favored more self-service options

Self service features that IATA survey respondents plan to use most often in future:
75% online booking
69% online reservation changes
60% e-mail notification service
58% printing boarding pass at home
53% common-use self-service check-in kiosks, or kiosks serving multiple airlines
41% re-routing of missed or cancelled flights
33% remote baggage drop-off service
28% post-arrival assistance

NEW self-service options *wanted* online:
82% ability to select or change seats
55% change reservations
49% update frequent flyer information
45% purchase or request upgrades

NEW self-service options *wanted* at the departure gate:
62% obtain last-minute upgrades
46% make last-minute changes to seating
27% get transfer information
21% updated frequent flyer information
19% check-in additional baggage

SOURCE: IATA Annual Corporate Air Travel Survey (November 2007).

Airlines are also looking at updating their fleets to more efficient airplanes, and airplane manufacturers are responding to this need. Airbus' new 525-seat A380–800, for example, "is designed to have 10–15% more range, lower fuel burn and emissions, and less noise," which will minimize its effect on the environment as well as reduce operating costs per seat 15–20 percent compared to the 747-400 (Airliners.net., n.d.).

Surface There will be slow growth in intercity rail transport in North America.

Growth will take place in the nontraditional areas of rail passenger transport. More excursion lines, including dinner trains, will be established. More "land cruise" operations similar to the Rocky Mountaineer and the Bras d'Or will start up. Environmental concerns, including overcrowding and pollution, will lead to increased rail service to major attractions like national parks. An example is the Grand Canyon Railway.

On October 11, 2007, the Minister of Transport, Infrastructure and Communities, Lawrence Cannon, stated "Canada's New [Conservative] Government is acting to provide faster, cleaner, more frequent and reliable passenger rail service across Canada" by allocating "funding of $691.9 million over the next 5 years . . . to revitalize inter-city passenger rail services in Canada," which should improve both domestic and international tourism (VIA Rail, 2007).

The motorcoach industry has a mixed future. Regular intercity service will continue to stagnate or decline; tours and charters will experience growth as baby boomers age and the number of retirees increases. The highway infrastructure in Canada needs to be rebuilt and expanded. Much of this will be financed through toll charges, even though at the present time less than 10 percent of gasoline taxes collected is spent on our highway system.

Congestion in cities will continue to increase. It is difficult to persuade commuting drivers to switch to mass transit, especially with the growth of "edge cities," that is, suburbs that have grown substantially. Out-of-city tourists, many of whom cannot afford higher-priced downtown hotels, will stay overnight in the suburbs and commute to downtown destinations. There will be attempts to link airports with downtown areas through express commuter rail services.

Cruise and Marine The fastest growing tourism sector, the cruise industry has experienced more than 2100 percent growth since 1970 (CLIA, February 2008). CLIA provides the following figures:

The number of cruise passengers:

- 1970   500 000 (estimated)
- 1995   5 000 000
- 2003   10 000 000
- 2006   12 000 000
- 2007   12 500 000 (estimated)

The number of new passenger ships:

- 1980–1989   nearly 40 new ships
- 1990–1999   nearly 80 new ships
- 2000–2007   88 ships
- 2008–2012   35 new ships (currently being constructed)

The next generation of ships have two major advantages over the older ships in the fleet: a cost advantage and the ability to offer an increased choice of onboard experiences such as dining (more healthy and/or vegetarian dishes), entertainment, and recreation (such as luxury spas) (CLIA, "As Consumers," January 16, 2008). Other new amenities include Internet capabilities, climbing walls, and surfing pools. Cruises have also developed a variety of options for passengers in terms of ports of call, embarkation ports, duration, and intermodal packages.

The cruise industry will continue growing at an average of 10 percent per year, the recent economic downturn should not affect the cruise industry since cruising is still perceived as offering a good "value for money" experience (Eturbonews, March 12 2008).

Marketing in the cruise industry in the next decade will concentrate on two major targets: empty-nesters/baby boomers and young families with children. Several cruise lines, including Princess, Carnival, Celebrity, and Royal Caribbean, are revising their on-board programs with children in mind; this is to compete with the Disney Cruise Line, the first to become "kid-friendly." It is anticipated that cruise lines will continue consolidating.

Future of the Accommodation Sector

The forces facing the accommodation sector include continued consolidation, changes in distribution systems, greater diversity, and convergence with entertainment. Hotels will need to offer wireless fidelity (WiFi) services since it is predicted that more than 80 percent of all corporate laptops will be WiFi-ready (Haley, 2003).

Lifestyle Accommodation The Pricewaterhouse Coopers (PwC) 2005 European Hotel Lifestyle survey identified the following characteristics of the "new consumer": wants to be seen as unique; tries to fulfill his/her self-actualization need; and "invests time and money in individualised pursuits." Hoteliers responded by designing "lifestyle" properties to fulfill the customization and personalization wants of this new consumer (PwC, 2005). David Pepper, Senior VP Choice Hotels, believes brand "lifestyles" are "a reflection of a person's life through products and the items they consume" (Haussman, 2006).

How popular are these lifestyle hotels? Lifestyle/ boutique properties comprised almost 70 percent of European hotels (20 out of 29 hotels) of the Condé Nast's Hot List 2005 (PwC, 2005). Who stays at these lifestyle hotels? The PwC study revealed the following age demographic of lifestyle guests:

Ages		
	16–24	6%
	25–34	23%
	35–45	39%
	45–54	25%
	55+	7%

However, as the global economy faces a downturn, hoteliers will have to balance cost-conscious guests and providing desired amenities.

Hotel Management Leadership Style Hotel managers may not stand a chance unless they change their leadership styles. They are going to have to do things smarter and better. This will involve strengthening their human capital and managing diversity—in relation to both employees and guests. It will involve better facility design and security practices. Employees will need to be empowered and equipped with the best tools, whether on the technology side, the administrative side, or the support side.

Some attributes for business success in the accommodation sector in the era ahead are presented in Table 17–3. Greger and Peterson (2000) created this list of 22 attributes based on experience and interviews with industry leaders. The authors recommend attributes to retain, to acquire, and to leave behind. Furthermore, they point out that companies can lead with their hearts, nurture their souls, and still make money.

Future of the Food and Beverage Sector

An operation's success will depend on management understanding and responding to an ever-changing marketplace.

Market Factors The needs and wants of market segments will continue to change. Generally, promotions, products, and services, especially menus, will be more customized. Diet awareness will continue to be a concern, and people will expect choices while travelling and at their destinations. They will be willing to experiment with new foods while demanding access to familiar items. Expectations will continue to rise with respect to food service concepts, quality of service, decor, and other facets of the eating experience. As consumer loyalties change, facility and product life cycles will be shorter. More marketing will be done through the Internet, and more and more consumers will consult promotions and descriptions online. More reservations and take-out orders will be placed on the Internet.

Economic Factors Competition will continue to intensify. Some food service operations will grow at the expense of others. Food producers will increase the pressure on food service operations by improving the quality, variety, and distribution of prepared foods in supermarkets. Consumers' standards will rise. Independent food service operations will compete with more and more brand-name operations.

TABLE 17–3 Attributes for Business Success

Attributes to Retain

1. Vision, passion, and the ability to communicate those to others
2. Core values, including integrity
3. Attentiveness to culture
4. Compassion and approachability
5. Personal touch and involvement (answering complaint letters, making property visits)
6. Being an example
7. High energy and a committed work ethic

Attributes to Revive or Acquire

8. Listening, listening, and more listening
9. Youthful curiosity and enthusiasm
10. Imagination and creativity
11. Sense of humour
12. Global business perspective
13. Understanding and effective use of technology
14. Orchestrating acquisitions, consolidations, and cultural integration
15. Ability to deal with labour shortfalls and more discerning employee talent
16. Being of service to employees—thinking and behaving as an "us"
17. Celebrating with the team

Attributes to Leave Behind

18. An inflated ego and any notion of omnipotence (greatness)
19. The idea that technology and the Internet are fads
20. Policies and procedures that don't work anymore
21. References to employees as "them"
22. Complacency and predisposition

Social Factors Social values, priorities, and problems influence food service operations. Workers' expectations and attitudes are changing. Fewer individuals are satisfied with jobs that offer no career possibilities. Operators will be expected to provide opportunities for economically, socially, and physically disadvantaged workers. Other societal issues in the F&B sector are pollution, energy use, security, the use of nonbiodegradable packaging, and the commercialization of historic areas and parklands.

Technological Factors Food production, presentation, and distribution will continue to change. Operators will have to adapt to new products and processes. Food products will be available throughout the year and around the world. The food distribution industry and equipment manufacturers will be more aware of food service needs. Operators will have closer contact through the Internet. Online connections with distributors will make purchasing more effective and efficient. Menu engineering and pricing will be enhanced by automated programs and technologies, and information on fluctuations of supply and price will be more accessible. Facilities of the future will be more likely to incorporate technical innovations that maximize resources. Marketing technologies will become more exact, and operators will have access to information that allows better strategic planning. Advances in technology will need to be supported by education and training that allow both managers and employees to use the technology productively.

Educational Factors According to Adrian Caravello, the Food & Beverage Management Program Co-ordinator, at George Brown College, a Professional Advisory Committee (PAC) from the Food & Beverage industry indicated the need for more specialized education and training to meet the emerging needs of the F&B industry. Thus, the Centre for Hospitality and Culinary Arts (CHCA) at George Brown College developed five exciting new programs (see Table 17–4).

Future of the Meetings, Events, and Conferences Sector

Face-to-face meetings are a multibillion-dollar business involving major cities as well as smaller ones. In spite of advances in teleconferencing, face-to-face meetings will continue in the future, generating demand not only for convention centres but also for hotels, restaurants, and other tourism services. In fact, many resorts are adding facilities for capturing the conference market. Demand for meeting planners with professional credentials is expected to increase.

Role of Convention and Visitors' Bureaux Convention and visitors' bureaux (CVBs) will be major players in the meetings, conventions, and expositions market.

TABLE 17–4 New Education Options

George Brown College (www.georgebrown.ca)
- Advanced Wines and Beverage Management Program (1-year Postgraduate)
- Hospitality Management—Catering Program (2-year Diploma program)
- Nutritional Cuisine Program (2-year Diploma program)
- Food Concept Management (1-year Certificate program)
- Culinary Tourism Management (1-year Postgraduate)

Centennial College (www.centennialcollege.ca)
- Kitchen Management (2-semester Certificate program)
- Hospitality Management: Food & Beverage Catering (4-semester Diploma program)

Niagara College (www.niagaracollege.ca)
- Wine Business Management (2-semesters Certificate program)

SOURCE: School of Hospitality & Tourism Management, George Brown College www.georgebrown.ca/hospitalityandtourism/programs.aspx; www.centennialcollege.ca; www.niagaracollege.ca.

Besides representing a location's various tourism sectors, as they have in the past, CVBs will be involved in selling on the Internet. To be competitive, CVBs will have to ensure that the information on their websites is comprehensive, up to date, and linked to individual properties and other organizations in the area. This will require collaboration between the conference sector and service providers, and a commitment by everyone to selling the destination, not just individual services. FAM trips will be replaced by "virtual visits" to destinations via websites.

Americans with Disabilities Act The Americans with Disabilities Act, signed into law in 1990, will continue to affect the meeting and conference business in Canada as well as the United States. American meeting planners and attendees cross the border expecting to find American standards of accessibility in place. This means that people arranging conferences in Canada for American-based groups will most likely request "reasonable accommodation" according to the U.S. Act. Canadian facilities that can meet the third or fourth level of the Access Canada program, promoted by the Hotel Association of Canada, will be attractive options for American conference planners. These establishments will also be able to expand their markets to include Canadians with disabilities—both groups and individuals.

Theme Meetings Theme meetings—meetings with programs based on themes that provide memorable experiences and that enhance team-building—will grow in popularity for both large and small groups. Resorts with conference facilities are well positioned to offer such meetings. Creative meeting planners will be able to develop packages for less sophisticated facilities if they draw on the cultural and recreational opportunities in their areas and offer learning opportunities (existing or created) for specific occasions.

Family Services Meeting planners will be required to create programs not only for spouses but also for children. Programs will need to be more than baby-sitting services—attendees will expect their children to learn something. This will require qualified personnel to plan and deliver programs, as well as food services dedicated to children. Resorts with conference facilities and all-inclusive services will be in an excellent position to meet this demand. These facilities will be well placed to develop packages for families that combine conference and vacation features.

Meeting Trends Benchmark Hospitality International, an independent hospitality management company based in Texas, annually formulates a list of top meeting trends, as seen in Table 17–5.

Future of the Attractions Sector

Attractions are relatively permanent features that constitute the reasons to visit a destination. They will continue to provide activities for tourists visiting an area or city. However, the demand for certain types of attractions is expected to change.

Attractions Development The growth in international tourism, the increased demand for authentic tourism experiences, increased leisure time, and an older, affluent, well-educated population will drive the demand for attractions. Major developments will appear in emerging destinations such as Japan, Australia, Korea, and some South American countries. Economic prosperity, combined with better international transportation systems, will encourage tourists to travel to attractions throughout Europe. Appropriately themed and scaled developments will feed off one another and will encourage new tourist traffic. Florida's Disney World and neighbouring attractions provide models for future developments around the world. Natural constraints to development will be pushed back by advances in technology. Society will control development by encour-

TABLE 17–5 Top Meeting Trends
1. "Green" meetings are being requested; environmental concerns are popular.
2. Keep up with advanced technology (such as 360-degree cams in conference rooms to patch in global participants).
3. Participants' use of laptops for "note-taking or facilitator-directed research."
4. It is estimated that "More than 80% of RFPs, proposals and contracts are now delivered and returned online."
5. Meeting break snacks should be "healthy, low fat and low cal."
6. Team-building is viewed as a significant "learning through doing" exercise.
7. Less meetings, but more participants per meeting.
8. Stay "current"; "Listen in on pertinent blogs and popular social networking sites."
9. "Experience all that a destination has to offer. Destination recreation!"
10. "Interactive Event Websites"; eliminate handouts.

SOURCE: Benchmark Hospitality www.benchmarkhospitality.com.

aging and regulating sustainable development. Some operators will develop facilities and activities in response to an aging population; others will target specific market niches.

New Venues Fresh types of attractions will emerge; authentic attractions will have strong appeal. Traditional zoos and aquariums will not be as popular, and parks and protected areas will grow in importance. The demand for experience-based leisure will continue to encourage hands-on participation in fantasy simulation. More live performances will be expected; high-quality performances and film/video presentations will be necessary to meet market demand. High-quality staff will be an important component of any tourism enterprise.

City developments that combine retail with attractions, such as the West Edmonton Mall, will continue growing in popularity. Destinations will continue to partner with local cultural venues to attract tourists. For example, Niagara-on-the-Lake and the Shaw Festival in combination draw more than 300 000 visitors a year to the theatre productions and other hospitality/entertainment services the town offers.

Mega-Attractions According to Walsh-Heron and Stevens (1990), there is room for only a handful of mega-attractions such as the Disney theme parks. Large-scale national attractions are expected to increase in number, as are regional attractions. All attractions will be measured by the quality of the experience they provide, whether they are replicas or real attractions. The success of attractions, whatever their scale, will depend on the quality of the experience and the quality of the service. Attractions in North America will continue to compete with Disney products. Disney has set a standard for the mega-attraction sector and will continue to be a major provider of entertainment for the leisure market. The most exciting major attraction that will open by 2015 is the three Legends theme parks, part of the huge Dubailand project.

Future of the Adventure Tourism and Recreation Sector

The adventure tourism and recreation sector will continue to offer tourists memorable activities. Canada will continue to attract visitors to its outdoors for both "hard" and "soft" adventure as well as for learning vacation programs. The sector is growing, and companies will continue providing opportunities for employees to grow with them. Summer activities will continue to be the most important, but demands for fall, winter, and spring activities are expected to grow. To develop products that satisfy them and meet their expectations, it will be necessary to understand the "new" tourists.

The Challenges of Parks Canada Sustainability is vital for our parks in order for them to survive. "Because parks have been so accessible and enjoyable for Canadians, and so desirable to the tourist trade, the very qualities that make them special are threatened by overuse" (Kingsmill, "Resorts and Parks," 2001).

Parks Canada explains its responsibility:

Canadians are blessed with many truly remarkable heritage areas. The difficulties that the Agency faces in ensuring that these areas are put under a protection regime are very real: more than 20 per cent of pre-1940's built heritage has already been lost forever; increasing the number of parks in unrepresented natural regions requires a large and growing resource investment and extremely complex negotiations; and the development of national marine conservation areas poses its own set of complications. . . .

Once a building is demolished, it is gone forever; once wilderness disappears, it cannot be replicated; once marine ecosystems are impaired, they are difficult or impossible to restore. Parks Canada will strive to meet these challenges and work with Canadians to increase the number of protected Canadian heritage areas. Targets have been revised

to reflect the limits imposed by available funding and are now more realistic given the evolving complexity of the establishment environment. (Parks Canada, 2007)

The New Tourist According to industry experts, new tourists want to be individuals and to be in control. New tourists are attracted to **learning-type products** that add value to life. They will be seeking adventure travel and aboriginal and other cultural and heritage tourism products. New tourists are more spontaneous and unpredictable and are prepared to buy hybrid products (such as first-class accommodation with outdoor adventure, or economy accommodation and first-class air travel). They seek products with spiritual or educational value and/or those that test them physically. Many such products involve national parks such as Alberta's Waterton Lakes, Quebec's La Mauricie, and Cape Spear in Newfoundland.

Learning-type products will require more collaboration among travel suppliers. Transportation, accommodation, dining, and program activities will be combined so that each contributes to the total image and experience sold. Operators will be expected to collaborate in offering flexible pricing and options for a variety of tourism products and services. A demand for more customized and targeted holidays is predicted.

Future Products Growth tourism products, designed with the new tourist in mind, will include ecology cruises and guided hiking tours. The quality of service will be important. Many products that will be in demand have yet to be developed. **Authentic tourism** will become important as the demand declines for zoos, aquariums, and attractions built by humans. Experiences in real situations will appeal more to tourists of the future. Wine festivals in the fall, rail tours at Christmas, and "snow experiences" such as sugaring off and sleigh rides are expected to be future product possibilities. Demand for companies offering products that add spiritual, psychological, or physical value to tourists' travel experiences is expected to increase.

Future of the Travel Trade Sector

The two major components of the travel trade sector are travel agencies and tour operators. Travel agencies will have to adjust to new technologies. The trend toward a few large operators and a greater number of small ones satisfying niche markets will continue.

Travel Agencies The traditional North American travel agency faces major threats and challenges. Among these are new channels of distribution, capped commissions, consolidated agencies, more demanding customers, and the need to become information consultants rather than order takers. New channels of distribution such as e-ticketing and the Internet enable consumers and suppliers to bypass traditional travel agencies. So, to attract and retain clients, agencies will need to offer enhanced services. In an interview with Raini Hamdi of TTG Asia, Peter Gowers (CEO of IHG Asia Pacific) stated, "travel agents must play a part in finding out how travellers [are] changing and feedback this to chains in order for the market to grow effectively" (Hamdi, 2008).

Suppliers will try to reduce their distribution costs by capping commissions one way or another. Or they will approach tourists directly either online or through in-house sales agents.

The future is likely to see consolidation, resulting in fewer but stronger agencies. Independent agencies, unless they are highly specialized, will affiliate themselves with national and international chains to gain access to the information and services that are provided by the chain system and demanded by clients.

Tourists will ask more of travel agencies and travel counsellors. The aging baby boomer with discretionary income will probably be a demanding client who wants more information from the travel counsellor and more services from the agency. This presents both a challenge and an opportunity. Those counsellors and agencies that make the adjustment to becoming information consultants will survive the transition the travel business is going through. The proportion of travel booked through agents is expected to fall from 70 percent in 2001 to 60 percent in 2010. Since the tourism pie is growing, that is 60 percent of a larger pie. A survey by Ipsos-Reid indicated that most people research their trips on the Web and then book offline. This means travel counsellors will spend less time passing out brochures and providing basic information.

Tour Operators The Canadian tour industry will continue to be dominated by large operators such as Air Transat Holidays, Signature Vacations, and Sunquest Vacations. The trend toward vertical and horizontal integration will continue. Air Transat Holidays is a subsidiary of Transat A.T. Inc. (vertical integration), which owns Air Transat, and in the mid-1990s took over Canadian Holidays (horizontal integration).

Smaller tour operators will have to focus on niche markets such as adventure tourism, or else merge with other tour operators to achieve economies of scale.

There will also be alliances formed between tour operators and suppliers, such as hotels and resorts. In addition, Canadian suppliers will try to achieve a greater number of links with tour operators in the United States to bring more American tourists to Canada year-round.

ILLUSTRATION 17–7

The tourism industry is on the route to sustainability.

SOURCE: Point Pelee National Park.

Future of the Tourism Services Sector

Three major components of the tourism services sector support the tourist industry and help it grow: information services, both governmental and private; education and training; and promotion and sales. Governments, industry associations, educational institutions, and marketing and research organizations will all need to work together for the good of the tourism industry.

Information Services The tourism services sector assists tourists by providing information on travel and on associations and businesses involved in tourism products globally. In the future, more information services will be like TraveLinx, which offers one-stop planning, reservations, and literature services. Businesses will pay annual membership fees to be listed with these information systems because it makes it easier to find them.

With its website, the Canadian Tourism Commission has the potential to lead the tourism industry in the use of Internet technology. The Canadian Tourism Exchange, which is the CTC website for businesses that promote tourism in Canada, will evolve into an important gateway for those who want to travel to any part of Canada or do business in the country. The CTC has also established the Work Web, on which employers can list job openings. In the future, people across Canada looking for employment will be able to indicate they are available and search for jobs.

Research Since the advent of IT systems, research is not just something done by consultants and academics in ivory towers. Data gathering and analysis play a role in daily decisions in private and public operations at the local and global levels. More people are involved in research. Through course work in tourism and hospitality management, more students are exposed to research theory and practices. More in-house research will be utilized, even conducted, in more business operations, and not just in large corporations.

The CTC's Research Group has set out specific objectives for itself: to work with the UNWTO and the OECD to establish common statistical standards; to improve the coordination and integration of information from all national research partners; to implement planned changes in the International Travel Survey; and to develop a university-based research and industry training network. The entire industry will benefit if it meets these objectives.

Education and Training The passing years have seen a variety of philosophies about education and training. French schools have emphasized techniques and professionalism; the Americans have developed a management-oriented approach. Education and training opportunities will continue to expand. In Canada, a learning system is evolving that will embrace a core of skill and knowledge competencies common across postsecondary programs. Partnerships between colleges and the tourism industry,

and partnerships among postsecondary institutions, are likely to increase. This will facilitate students' passage from high school to two-year programs to four-year programs.

These alliances will be complemented by technologies that will provide access to education from anywhere in the world. Postsecondary institutions will need to be able to modify their curriculums quickly to develop appropriate technical, professional, and managerial competencies. Peter Armstrong of Rocky Mountaineer Vacations said he believes that superior training and orientation programs will be the competitive advantage of the future. His company's efforts are paying off as they are maintaining an 80 percent return rate of seasonal staff.

Provincial and territorial tourism education councils, the CTHRC, and industry associations, as well as the education community, will need to work together to provide leadership and respond to regional and global needs. However, more support from industry will be necessary to provide the resources required for education and training, and to provide opportunities for top-quality on-the-job training.

Promotion and Sales Moving forward as a Crown corporation, the CTC is continuing to promote Canada as a destination and encouraging the development of travel products that fall within its vision and mission. Its meetings across the country with tourism development professionals will facilitate sharing plans and information. The result of efforts to date has been better cooperation in product development and marketing.

As a result of stronger promotion and sales efforts in Italy, more Italian visitors are visiting the Maritimes and eastern and western Canada. This is in spite of competition from the United States and from resorts in the Caribbean and Thailand for long-haul Italian travellers. The CTC's Canada Specialist Program, offered around the world, educates travel counsellors in other countries about Canada so that they can sell Canada more effectively.

The CTC has succeeded in enticing more American tourists to Canada. It will continue this work—and encourage more Canadians to vacation at home.

Travel Blogs Blogs (originally Weblogs) began to appear around the year 2000 and now there are millions of blogs where anyone with Internet access can share their impressions, photos, experiences, etc. with the online world. Travellers who enjoyed keeping travel journals or diaries, and/or created travelogues were the original candidates to write their opinions and recommendations concerning travel destinations (and their accommodations, restaurants, attractions) in an online travel journal, which has become known as a **travel blog**. Going to the about.com website and searching for "travel blogs" yielded over 77 000 sites (June 22, 2008).

The first annual travel and tourism blogs conference, organized by Krems Research (Austria) and the

Charles Darwin University (Australia) in July 2007 aimed to bring experts on travel blogs together for the "analysis of the content of tourism blogs and forums, the understanding of the process of information exchange and the development of industry strategies for handling these virtual communities."

According to a Krems Research press release, "Blogs are a valuable basis for decision-making concerning travel preparation for other travellers and can be used for market research and product development in tourism by professionals" (Krems Research, 2007).

Retail Sales Retailers who want to sell to tourists often seek products with a Canadian regional or national connection. The CTC has launched a merchandising program that licenses manufacturers to create products that are noticeably Canadian. In the future, retailers will have access to goods marketed under the CTC's Maple Leaf logo that are high in quality and have a distinctively Canadian character. Several manufacturers have already signed agreements, and more are expected. Retailers will have access to a wide range of products: clothing, food products, one-of-a-kind art objects, souvenir items, and so on.

Check Your Product Knowledge

1. How will changes in the transportation sector affect tourism in your region?
2. What leisure products and services need to be available in order to meet the MNEs of the "new" tourist?

CAREER OPPORTUNITIES

There are many career opportunities related to research, education, and training in tourism. Both the public and the private sector require people with this kind of expertise. For example, governments need them, but so do consulting and market research firms, as well as secondary schools, colleges, and universities.

At the national level, the Canadian Tourism Commission and the Canadian Tourism Research Institute employ researchers, statisticians, and analysts to study tourism trends, markets, and issues. Provincial tourism ministries (or related departments) conduct similar research.

Tourism industry associations employ researchers, educators, and trainers to arrange and promote education and networking events, to conduct research, and to inform the public and their own members about issues and trends. Some of these associations are listed below:

- Tourism Industry Association of Canada (TIAC).
- Canadian Restaurant and Foodservices Association (CRFA).
- Association of Canadian Travel Agencies (ACTA).
- Hotel Association of Canada (HAC).
- Provincial and territorial tourism education councils.
- Provincial and territorial tourism industry associations, such as the Tourism Industry Association of Nova Scotia (TIANS) and the Tourism Industry Association of Prince Edward Island (TIAPEI).
- Convention and visitors' bureaux.

The CTHRC employs trainers and programmers who work with the tourism education councils and on national initiatives related to human resource development.

There are numerous opportunities for tourism educators to teach in schools, colleges, and universities across Canada.

There are career opportunities in market research with destination marketing organizations such as the Calgary Visitors' and Convention Bureau, Tourism Halifax, and the Tourism Industry Association of Winnipeg, and with advertising and public relations firms that work in the tourism industry.

Careers are also available with research and consulting firms, which come in all sizes and usually work on a contract basis. Some of these firms specialize in tourism. Typically, they are asked to determine how a given industry or operation is performing and how it could be improved, or to figure out what tourists want and how the industry or operation can supply the services markets demand.

CONCLUSION

The world is changing, and so is the tourism industry. Technological, social, and geopolitical changes will make future tourism markets—and consumers—different from how they are today.

As the world becomes smaller, tourism professionals will have an excellent opportunity to help the world's peoples get to know one another. As tourism increases, the industry will become even more intertwined with the economic health of nations. Countries will be less likely to engage in conflict if it means risking economic benefits. Thus, the tourism industry can play an important part in establishing political stability.

To succeed as a tourism professional, you need to be open to change and flexible in dealing with it. You also need the knowledge and skills to manage change. The tourism industry can be the finest school for learning about yourself and others. If you enjoy change and growth, you will find a career in the tourism industry—in whatever sector—rewarding.

We hope this book is your passport to a career as a tourism professional.

A DAY IN THE LIFE OF A

Festivals and Events Provincial Coordinator: Margot Rumley

"Festivals and events are noted for culturally connecting people. The festivals and events industry is also connecting nationally to support the industry and this has potentially huge benefits for . . ." Margot Rumley reviews the article she wrote on festivals and events. It just arrived in the May 2001 issue of CTC's monthly publication, *Communiqué*. The article includes information about the Nova Scotia Festivals & Events study tours to industry conferences. These began in 1994 to the then International Festivals Association Convention in Minneapolis. Since then, Margot has coordinated and facilitated Nova Scotia study tours to the International Festivals & Events Association conventions in Montreal (1997) and Phoenix (1999), and the Festivals & Events Ontario Conference, Ottawa (2001). Study tour participants are now required to compile session reports and handouts so others back home can access and use the information in their organizations.

As the festivals and events provincial coordinator with the Tourism Industry Association of Nova Scotia (TIANS), Margot has been successful in securing the partnership of the Nova Scotia Department of Tourism and Culture, Atlantic Canada Opportunities Agency, and the participating festivals and events to facilitate groups of seven or more festivals and events organizers to attend national and international festivals and events conferences. This "grass-roots" approach to

professional and product development is a well-received activity but it takes a great deal of time and effort. Having seen the rewards first-hand with those who have participated, Margot is always enthusiastic about facilitating another group and is excited when other Nova Scotian delegates not officially included in a study tour join the group. The study tour process has proven to be an excellent way to get the most from a conference.

Participants are selected from festivals and events organizations throughout Nova Scotia. They are expected to work as a team to cover the conference, take notes, gather handouts, build networks, apply new skills, and spread the information among their regional communities when they return. Tour participants also attend study tour group meetings prior to, during, and following the conference. Margot believes there is consensus that participants improve their communications and networking skills and bring back ideas that they are able to implement in their own events. Plus, it is evident that more organizations are now implementing better business practices in managing their events. And network building, probably the greatest gift from the tours, continues among festivals and events players even after they return home to Nova Scotia.

Despite knowing there are over 700 festivals and events annually to influence and assist, Margot has seen the impact this

activity has had on the festivals and events industry. The work of the study tour participants is reaching into the communities and to the delegates of the Annual TIANS Tourism Conference & Trade Show's festivals and events program.

Reviewing previous participants' follow-through correspondence confirms the value of the study tour program: participants all maintain their study tour helped them learn about new trends in tourism, provided ideas to incorporate into their events, and opened doors. The benefits of sessions on topics like sponsorship, site design, liability, safety measures, financial management, the Internet, volunteer recruitment, and a myriad of other event-related issues have proven important to their organizational activities back in Nova Scotia.

The results of the 1998/99 TIANS Survey of Festivals & Events—126 festivals and events reported attendance of 970 000 people and volunteers totalling 11 000 annually—provide, from a tourism perspective and as a community economic generator, convincing evidence of the significant role the festivals and events industry has. The study tour outcomes make a major contribution to better business practices supporting communities.

As Margot works through each proposal, budget, and coordination of all aspects of the study tour, she is enthusiastic about rekindling networking with friends she has made at earlier conferences. Each study tour experience helps to keep her informed about the needs and trends in Nova Scotia's festivals and events industry. Over the years, the experience has definitely assisted her in working with the provincial Festivals & Events Committee and in consultations with industry organizers.

SOURCE: Based on conversations with Margot Rumley and the TIANS Study Tour Reports: IFEA Convention Montréal 1997 and Phoenix 1999, FEO Conference Ottawa 2001. *Communiqué*, May 2001.

Summary

- Tourism research involves collecting and analyzing data from secondary and primary sources.
- Research can help track performance, measure economic impact, and profile customers.
- The CTHRC Student's Travel Map is a good resource for career planning, as it lists programs, describes occupations in the eight sectors, and lists references.
- Occupational standards exist for at least 50 occupations in the tourism industry; they describe the knowledge, skills, and attitudes required to be competent in those occupations.
- Occupational certification makes a person more employable, increases his or her chances of promotion, and indicates that the person is serious about a career in the tourism industry.
- Provincial and territorial TECs coordinate certification programs for secondary school students and for people employed in various sectors of the industry.
- All three types of travellers—vacation and leisure travellers, business travellers, and travellers visiting friends and relatives—are likely to travel more in the years ahead.
- Airline deregulation and reform have been major influences in the tourism industry for the last decade and are likely to continue in this role.
- Technological advances, mainly in communications and material sciences, will have a significant impact on the tourism industry.
- Pollution, overcrowding, disease, poverty, political instability, and fluctuating currency rates and oil prices can all have a negative impact on tourism.
- People are living longer and retiring earlier, so the senior citizens' market will become more important.
- Being "technology smart" will be mandatory.
- Governments around the world are recognizing the importance of tourism by creating tourism agencies and ministries and establishing tourism policies.
- The Canadian Tourism Commission was established in 1995 to work in partnership with the tourism industry and provincial, federal, and territorial governments to market Canada as a four-season destination.

Key Terms

authentic tourism   p. 410
certification   p. 394
certified travel counsellor (CTC)   p. 396
certified travel manager (CTM)   p. 396
human capital   p. 399
learning-type product   p. 410
occupational standards   p. 394
tourism education councils (TECs)   p. 395
travel blogs   p. 412

Internet Connections

Aboriginal Tourism Canada (ATC)
www.aboriginaltourism.ca   p. 397

American Hotel & Lodging Association (AH&LA)
www.ahla.com   p. 395

Association of Canadian Travel Agencies (ACTA)
www.acta.ca   p. 395

Canadian Institute of Travel Counsellors (CITC)
www.citc.ca   p. 395

Canadian Tourism Commission (CTC)
www.corporate.canada.travel   p. 392

Canadian Tourism Human Resource Council (CTHRC)
www.cthrc.ca   p. 394

Canadian Tourism Research Institute (CTRI)
www.conferenceboard.ca/ctri   p. 392

Council on Hotel, Restaurant & Institutional Education (CHRIE)
www.chrie.org   p. 393

Disney Corporation
www.disney.com   p. 393

Hospitality Careers Online (hCareers)
www.hcareers.ca   p. 395

Hotel Association of Canada (HAC)
www.hotelassociation.ca   p. 408

Hosteur e-zine
www.chrie.org/i4a/pages/index.cfm?pageid=339   p. 396

International Air Transport Association/United Federation of Travel Agents' Association (IATA/UFTAA travel agent training courses)
www.radiobhuvan.com/IHCTM/IATA.htm   p. 396

Organisation for Economic Co-operation and Development (OECD)
www.oecd.org   p. 399

Statistics Canada
www.statcan.gc.ca   p. 392

Tourism Industry Association of Canada (TIAC)
www.tiac-aitc.ca   p. 393

Travel & Leisure Awards 2007
www.travelandleisure.com/slideshows/global-vision -awards-2007

World Travel & Tourism Council (WTTC)
www.wttc.org   p. 393

World Tourism Organization (UNWTO)
www.unwto.org   p. 396

WORKSHEET 17–1   The Tourism Industry Past and Future

Choose an aspect of the tourism industry that you might like to work in. How has that part of the industry changed in the past 10 years?

_____

_____

_____

_____

_____

_____

_____

How do you think it will change over the next 10 years?

_____

_____

_____

_____

_____

_____

_____

Are there any ways that you prefer the industry as it was in the past compared with what it may be in the future? If so, explain. If not, why not?

_____

_____

_____

_____

_____

_____

_____

WORKSHEET 17–2   The Future of Travel

Below are several trends that are expected to be important for the tourism industry. For each one, suggest what the Canadian tourism industry should do in response.

1. Increasing attention given to civil rights for physically and mentally disabled Canadians.

_____

_____

2. Increased Economic Union activity in Europe.

_____

_____

3. More single-parent families in Canada.

_____

_____

4. Greater demand for energy conservation and environmental safeguards.

_____

_____

5. Continued terrorism globally.

_____

_____

6. An increase in the number of North Americans over 65 who want to travel.

_____

_____

7. Continued advances in information technology.

_____

_____

8. More overseas travellers to Canada.

_____

_____

9. A continued increase in outbound tourism from Canada.

_____

_____

10. Your choice of a current trend noted through checking websites for one or more of the tourism industry sectors.

_____

_____

adventure tourism Tourism that provides opportunities for physical exertion through hard and soft activities (see *hard adventure* and *soft adventure*). It may, but not always, embrace ecotourism practices (see *ecotourism*).

advertising Any paid form of nonpersonal communication about an organization, product, service, or idea by an identified sponsor.

affinity charter Private charter sold through an organization to which the traveller belongs.

agreement A written or implied statement accepting certain conditions, such as regulatory commercial air services between countries.

à la carte A meal choice from a complete menu, regardless of price.

all-inclusive package A vacation package for which the traveller pays one price that covers almost all trip expenses, including transportation, accommodations, meals, and sightseeing.

all-suite hotel A type of hotel offering units that include a living room, kitchen, and bedroom.

American plan (AP) A hotel rate that includes the room and a continental or full breakfast, lunch, and dinner.

amusement park A park that provides entertainment such as rides, shows, and food and beverage services as a commercial enterprise.

aquarium A facility that has various types of fish and sea animals displayed in tanks and may provide opportunities to observe performances of trained animals.

area tour A tour that spends a limited amount of time in several countries.

association market The meeting and conference market comprised of professional and fraternal associations that hold local, regional, national, and international meetings on a regular basis (e.g., weekly to annually).

at-risk capacity This situation develops when tour operators sign contracts with suppliers for a specified amount of product; they need to sell the full supply to tourists or risk losing money.

authentic tourism Tourism products designed for the "new" tourist, offering real experiences of a cultural, educational, or spiritual nature. "New" tourists are attracted to learning-type products that add value to life.

automated ticketing machine (ATM) A self-service machine that provides customers with flight information, reservations, tickets, and boarding passes.

back-office system A computer information management system used for behind-the-scenes business operations.

back of the house The support areas behind the scenes in lodging facilities, including materials management, housekeeping, laundry, engineering, purchasing, receiving, storage, and food service preparation areas, in a lodging facility or elsewhere.

banqueting The catering process provided by hotel catering departments for meals served to groups.

berths Sleeping accommodations that are either double beds, twin beds, or bunk bed arrangements on trains or ships.

bias The preferential display on a global distribution system (GDS) of host carrier flight schedules.

Billing and Settlement Plan (BSP) Canada A streamlined and automated method of payment by travel agencies to airlines, developed by the IATA.

boutique travel agency An agency that develops customer relationship management with its clientele, develops knowledge of clients, and provides specialized service.

brand Any word, "device" (design, sound, shape, or colour), or combination of these, used to distinguish a seller's goods or services from those of the seller's competitors.

BritRail pass A pass used for train travel in Great Britain.

business centres Facilities developed to support business communications, utilized by business travellers who are away from home base or businesses that require services not available on site.

business class A level of service that provides additional comfort and convenience greater than an airline's basic level of service; targeted at individuals travelling for work purposes.

business to business (B2B) Transactions between one business and another.

business to consumer (B2C) Transactions between a business and a consumer.

business travel department (BTD) The department in a corporation that handles travel arrangements for the corporation's employees.

business travellers Persons who take trips to a place or places outside their home communities for any purpose other than commuting to and from work.

BYOW On January 24, 2005, Ontario implemented a "Bring Your Own Wine" (BYOW) program for restaurants on a volunteer basis, as well as "Take Home the Rest" (*THTR*). This allows customers to bring a bottle of preferred wine for dinner at a participating restaurant (or hotel/motel banquet hall) with a liquor sales licence.

Canada Select Accommodations Rating Program A program, in which properties voluntarily participate, that rates the quality of the physical facilities and services offered.

CANPASS Similar to NEXUS, the Canada Border Services Agency (CBSA) has implemented the CANPASS Air program for those pre-approved, low-risk travellers who will only need to have a camera recognize the iris of their eye as proof of identity to clear Canadian customs and immigration when arriving at participating Canadian international airports.

Canrailpass A VIA Rail fare that allows unlimited travel throughout Canada for a fixed period of time.

CarePar Also known as the Hotel Carbon Index, CarePar is a carbon emission measurement designed specifically for hotels. Hotels submit information that is translated into the carbon cost of using a room overnight or meeting room per half-day.

cargo terminal A separate building at an airport for freight, mail, and packages.

carnival An event with amusements such as entertainment, a parade, or competitions in celebration of an event, person, or date.

carrying capacity The maximum number of people who can use a tourism destination with only "acceptable alteration" to the physical environment and with only "acceptable decline" in the quality of experience gained by subsequent visitors.

categories of events The seven types of planned, public events that are found in most communities: cultural celebrations, art and entertainment, business/trade, sport competitions, educational and scientific, recreational, and political/state. Some private events also fit into some of these categories.

catering services The services required to feed people at special events, ranging from a dinner party for two to a picnic for thousands. These services can take place on-premise or off-premise, on the ground, in the air, or on the sea. Catering involves planning and preparing the food, setting up the tables and required serving implements, serving the guests, and cleaning up.

certification A process that involves a trained evaluation of skills and the passing of an exam that tests the individual's knowledge of and attitude toward the job.

certified travel counsellor (CTC) Professional designation conferred by the Canadian Institute of Travel Counsellors on completion of training and examination requirements.

certified travel manager (CTM) Professional designation conferred by the Canadian Institute of Travel Counsellors on completion of training and examination requirements.

charter (1) To hire an airplane, bus, or ship for group travel, usually at lower rates than regularly scheduled transportation. **(2)** The purchase of the use of transportation equipment at a cut price.

charter airline An airline that offers charter flights and other non-scheduled flights. Also called a *supplemental airline*.

charter tour A tour taken by a club, organization, or other pre-formed group.

circle trip A type of round-trip journey in which the return journey differs from the outbound journey in terms of routing or class of service.

city package tour A motorcoach tour to a single city destination that may include accommodation, meals, and sightseeing.

code of ethics Standards based on moral principles and values that identify the conduct that is expected of professionals in respect to integrity, competence, conformity to standards of practice, loyalty, fairness, concern for negative impact, and confidentiality.

code-sharing agreement An agreement between a major airline and a small regional airline, under which the small airline flies under the larger company's code.

co-host A company that does not own its global distribution system (GDS) but instead shares a database with a host vendor.

commission The percentage of a selling price paid to a retailer by a supplier.

common carrier A privately owned air carrier that offers public transportation of passengers, cargo, and mail.

compact car An average-sized car.

computer reservations system (CRS) A computer system that provides information on availability and fares or rates. These systems are limited to one supplier (for example, Holiday Inn's Holidex system) as opposed to a global distribution system (GDS), which gives access to suppliers from different sectors. It permits reservations agents to make reservations and produce tickets or vouchers.

concierge A hotel employee who handles restaurant and tour reservations, travel arrangements, and other details for hotel guests.

conference Similar to a *convention* (see below) but usually deals with specific problems or developments rather than with general matters.

conference appointment system A system whereby regulation bodies formulate standards for acceptance of new travel agencies and to discipline existing agencies.

conference centre A facility that caters to group gatherings and provides support services for meetings and recreation; has guest rooms and often is in a remote or resort-type setting.

configuration An airplane seating arrangement; a food service space plan.

consortium A group of independent firms that band together to pool financial and company resources.

constructed attraction An attraction that is man-made, such as a Niagara winery and the Confederation Bridge.

controls Processes that establish standards of performance, measure current performance against expected performance, and respond to variances—specifically of the financial dealings of an organization.

control tower A tower from which air traffic controllers direct planes in the air and on the ground.

convention A meeting involving a general group session followed by committee meetings in breakout rooms.

convention and visitors' bureau An organization that promotes travel to the city it represents and assists in servicing conventions and trade shows held in the city.

convention centre A facility that caters to large groups, meetings, and trade shows, usually in the downtown area of major cities.

convention tour A tour for members of an association or group attending such events as conventions, trade shows, or conferences.

cooperative A group of independent travel agencies formed temporarily out of a joint interest in promoting a product or event.

corporate market The market segment composed of top-level management from both business and non-profit operations.

corporate meeting planners Meeting planners who specialize in meetings for upper-level corporate management, as opposed to association, scientific, or incentive meetings.

corporate rebate An arrangement whereby money is returned to a company based on the volume of business it conducts with another company.

corporate travel agency A travel agency, or out-plant office, that specializes in making arrangements for corporate and government accounts.

corporate website A website designated to accommodate interactive communication initiated by a company's employees, investors, suppliers, and customers.

cost centre Departments within an operation, such as marketing, accounting, maintenance, or housekeeping, that incur expenses as they provide support services to enhance the operation and ensure customer satisfaction.

couchette A sleeping bunk in a second-class train compartment.

cruise/rail package A tour package that combines travel by rail and cruise ship.

customs The government regulation of goods entering and leaving a country.

decline stage To fall in value, quality, or quantity; the fourth and last stage of the product or service life cycle, when sales and profitability decline.

deluxe car A large luxury car, usually equipped with many amenities.

demanders Business and leisure tourists that need and want specific products/services from suppliers (e.g., air transportation, spa resorts, entertainment).

demographics Statistics and facts, such as age, gender, marital status, occupation, and income, that describe a human population.

Dependable A personality type that travels close to home, needs consistency and reliability in their travel products, and doesn't want to experiment with accommodation, food, or entertainment.

deregulation Removal of government control over the operation of an industry.

destination management companies A company that provides on-the-scene meeting assistance for corporations and associations.

destination visitors Visitors who travel a long distance to visit a destination as opposed to local residents and regional visitors.

dine-around plan A plan that permits tourists to dine at a variety of restaurants using vouchers and coupons.

direct or through service A flight with one or more stops en route where the passenger remains aboard the same plane.

discounted airfare A less expensive airfare that includes certain restrictions, such as advance-purchase requirements, minimum/maximum length of stay, nonrefundable cancellation penalties, etc. Same as *excursion airfare, promotional airfare, and restricted airfare.*

discretionary income Available income in excess of basic expenses such as mortgage payments, food, clothing, and education.

discretionary travel Travel undertaken voluntarily or by choice.

documentation Government-issued papers used to identify travellers.

domestic independent tour (DIT) A custom-made tour of a part of Canada planned exclusively for a client by a travel agent.

domestic tourism Residents of a country visiting, at least overnight, places farther than 80 kilometres from their usual environment for purposes other than remuneration.

domestic travel Travel by residents of a country in that country.

double occupancy Hotel accommodations for two people who share a room.

drop-off charge A fee charged for dropping a rental car at a location different from the one where it was picked up.

duty A tax paid on items purchased abroad.

eatertainment The integration of entertainment into the food and beverage service format.

ecoadventure Adventure travel that is sensitive to the environment and strives to protect rather than destroy it.

ecofriendly Being sensitive to the environment and taking action to protect it.

e-commerce Business transactions done electronically through websites and the Internet (both B2C and B2B).

ecotourism A type of tourism in which vacationers travel to unusual places to observe ecological systems and endangered species in their natural habitat.

electronic ticket delivery network (ETDN) A ticket printer that is similar to a *satellite ticket printer* but owned by an outside vendor rather than a travel agent.

embarkation The boarding of passengers onto a ship, plane, train, etc.

en route food services Food service operations patronized by travellers; include coffee shops, family restaurants, and quick-service, fast-food outlets. They may be chains or stand-alone facilities.

environmentally sensitive Being in tune with environmental forces in a particular setting.

e-procurement The purchase of tourism products/services by electronic means.

escorted tour An organized tour led by a professional tour manager.

ethical policies Policies based on moral principles and values that determine behaviour in doing business.

e-ticketing The process that produces an electronic or "paperless" ticket.

Eurailpass A pass that allows unlimited train travel throughout certain European countries.

European plan (EP) A hotel rate that includes the room only and no meals.

event management The responsibility for organizing the event, coordinating everyone involved, setting budgets and financial controls, developing plans for marketing and public relations, fundraising, and evaluating the success of the event.

event tourism A major component of special-interest tourism and a significant ingredient of destination and place marketing strategies when an event plays a tourism role.

excursion airfare A less expensive airfare that includes certain restrictions, such as advance-purchase requirements, minimum/maximum length of stay, nonrefundable cancellation penalties, etc. Same as *discounted airfare, promotional airfare,* and *restricted airfare.*

exhibition A display of goods and services staged as part of a convention or conference.

external customers Local patrons and tourists.

FAM trip A familiarization trip for travel professionals to inspect hotels and restaurants, sample attractions, and experience local culture.

festival The term "festival" no longer refers only to a religious feast day or celebration. Nowadays, a festival can involve merrymaking and entertainment of many kinds, or it can honour people, places, and events of little or no religious significance.

fixed-base operator (FBO) A company that rents space at an airport and provides a particular service.

flag carrier A national airline representing an individual nation.

flag of convenience A flag flown by a ship of one nation that is registered under the flag of another nation.

fly/cruise package A vacation package that includes air transportation to the port of embarkation and the cruise itself.

fly/drive package A vacation package that includes air transportation and rental car use.

foreign flag A term for any carrier registered in a nation other than Canada.

foreign independent tour (FIT) An international tour planned exclusively for a client by a travel agent.

forms of ownership Food and beverage operations and hotels may be operated through partnerships, corporations, chain ownership, leasing arrangements, as joint ventures, franchises, and management contracts.

franchise A contract between a company owner and an established chain under which the owner pays a fee to operate the company under the chain name.

frequent flyer program A program that awards travellers free travel, discounts, and upgrades for flying a certain number of miles on a single airline.

frequent stay program A program that awards travellers discounts, special rates, and upgrades for frequently staying at a lodging facility; a form of customer retention.

front of the house The staff members who deal directly with the guests, such as the front desk, waitstaff and bartenders, and entertainers.

garden tourism Tourism based on horticulture in public and private spaces.

gateway airport An airport that serves international flights.

geocaching Geocaching is an interactive adventure game in which you use a global positioning system (GPS) device to find clues and rewards in caches that another person or organization has hidden, often all over the world.

global distribution system (GDS) A computer reservations system that permits access to a wide range of travel products and services for reservations and information purposes.

grand tour An extended journey through continental Europe by sons and daughters of the aristocracy during the seventeenth and eighteenth centuries.

gross registered tonnage (GRT) A number representing the amount of enclosed space on a ship.

growth stage The period of expansion in the life cycle development of a destination or distribution of a product/service.

guaranteed reservation A reservation that has been secured by paying in advance or providing a credit card number as a deposit to hold a room; if the hotel is overbooked, a room in another hotel is guaranteed, at the same rate.

guest and uniformed services Services provided directly for guests and indirectly through back-of-the-house employees.

hallmark events Major one-time or recurring events of limited duration developed primarily to enhance the awareness, appeal, and profitability of a destination.

hangar A place where airplanes are stored and repaired.

hard adventure Hard adventures often have very basic facilities, a higher risk factor, and greater physical challenge. Hard adventure providers cater less to the needs of the vacationer, expecting a higher degree of knowledge and experience of the particular adventure from the vacationer.

heli-skiing Skiers are transported by helicopter to otherwise inaccessible slopes for downhill skiing.

hosted tour A tour whose members are assisted by a host who arranges optional excursions and answers questions.

host vendor An airline or other organization that owns and operates a global distribution system.

hotel attrition When meeting/convention delegates book hotel rooms themselves instead of going through a meeting/convention planner who has booked a block of rooms, the planner might be left with a number of rooms that are not used. The meeting planner and/or the association becomes responsible for all the revenue that the hotel would have made if the room block had been filled.

hub-and-spoke route A flight pattern in which a major airport is the centre point, or hub, for arrivals from and departures to smaller airports that surround it. The smaller airports are considered the rim; the connecting flights are the spokes.

hub-buster strategy A strategy where hub cities are bypassed in favour of providing direct service to a destination.

human capital Skills and knowledge available as a resource for operation and development of an organization.

IATA Travel Settlement Service (ITSS) An electronic billing and settlement system for airplane tickets in today's digital marketplace, originated by the International Air Transport Association.

inbound tour A tour that originates in a foreign country and has Canada as its destination.

inbound tourism Vacation and leisure travel to Canada.

incentive tour A tour offered by companies to employees as a reward for achieving a corporate goal.

incentive travel Marketing and management tool used to motivate people by offering travel rewards for achieving a specific goal; may include a training session or meeting at the travel destination.

inception stage The beginning of a process of the product or retail life cycle.

independent package tour A tour that visits several cities or places of interest on regular scheduled buses.

indirect spending Money that is spent initially by a tourist and then respent within the destination.

infrastructure The basic facilities of a site, such as local roads, sewage system, electricity, and water supply.

inside cabin A ship's cabin that has no access to natural light and faces a central passageway.

inside sales Sales efforts conducted within the employer's office.

institutional food service A non-commercial food service found in hospitals, residential care facilities, schools, prisons, factories and offices; operated in establishments whose primary business is not food and beverage.

intangible service/product A term used to describe a product that is experienced rather than seen or touched, such as an airplane flight, a family reunion, or an ocean view.

interline connection A flight during which the passenger changes both airplanes and airlines.

interlining The use of one standard type of airline ticket that is recognized and honoured by all scheduled airlines.

intermediaries Sellers of travel products (such as travel agencies) who act as a link between a travel supplier and a buyer.

intermodal ticketing A ticketing system where the passenger buys one ticket for through travel using at least two different modes of travel; for example, a plane and a bus, or a plane and a cruise ship.

intermodal tours Tours that include more than one form of transportation.

internal customers Employees in the front and back of the house who do the work of production and service.

internal tourism Domestic and inbound tourism combined.

international tourism Inbound and outbound tourism combined.

interpretation The process of educating visitors to national parks and other recreation facilities through the use of marked trails, signs, and people who explain various aspects of the venue, etc.

itinerary A planned route for a trip.

IT number A registration number that is assigned to a tour package.

kilometre cap A car rental plan that allows clients a certain number of free kilometres each day and charges an extra fee for each additional kilometre driven.

land/cruise package A vacation package that includes cruise and hotel accommodations at or near the port of embarkation.

leakage The amount of income that flows out of a local economy to purchase outside resources needed to generate that income.

learning-type product Attractions and experiences that add value to life, such as adventure travel, aboriginal travel, and cultural tourism.

legacy carrier An airline that existed prior to deregulation in Canada and the U.S. Legacy carriers tend to be unionized, have a large bureaucratic structure, and often have a large number of older, less fuel-efficient aircraft in their fleet.

light rail transit (LRT) A modern form of mass transit, usually several transit cars travelling together on a dedicated separate rail right of way from suburb to city.

lighter A small boat that carries cruise passengers between ship and shore. Also called a *tender*.

linear route A flight pattern in which an airplane flies to its destination in one direction, then turns around and repeats the flight in the opposite direction.

liner An ocean-going passenger vessel that sails a fixed route on a fixed schedule.

loading apron A parking area at an airport terminal where the airplane is fuelled, loaded, and boarded.

local residents People residing near a particular place as opposed to regional and destination visitors.

local tour A tour that is marketed to a local group or organization.

loss/damage waiver (LDW) An option offered by car rental firms that relieves clients of their liability for an initial amount of damage to a rental car; it also provides coverage for loss of the use of the rental car should an accident occur.

low-carb diets Low-carb diets have been on the market for years, but the trend became increasingly more fashionable starting in 2003. Low-carb diets restrict the amount of carbohydrates and concentrate on sources of protein and fat. Two of the best known low-carb diets are the Atkins diet and the Zone diet.

magrodome A sliding roof on a cruise ship that is used to cover a deck area in bad weather.

management contract An agreement under which one company owns a property and pays a management fee to a chain to operate the property.

manifest A passenger list.

marketing website An interactive website designed to sell products/services to consumers (compared to a promotional website that simply promotes products/services).

market segmentation The concept of dividing a market into different parts.

mass transit The movement of people in large metropolitan areas, usually via buses, subways, and trolleys.

maturity stage The third stage of the product or retail life cycle in which market share levels off and profitability declines.

mega-agency A large travel agency with branch offices in many cities; primarily interested in multimillion-dollar corporate accounts.

mega-event Large events with respect to volume of visitors, cost, psychology, or prestige.

megamall A vast indoor shopping and entertainment complex consisting of hundreds of shops and restaurants.

megaship A cruise ship that can serve as many as 2500 passengers at a time. Such cruises are not of long duration.

model culture A facility in which the houses, artifacts, and way of life of another age or nation are displayed.

modified American plan (MAP) A hotel rate that includes the room and continental breakfast or full breakfast and dinner.

monorail An elevated urban transit system that runs on one rail.

multiple channels The use of several channels of distribution by a supplier, rather than only one channel.

nationalize To bring an industry under the control of the federal government.

national tourism Internal and outbound tourism combined.

national tourism organizations (NTOs) Organizations that national governments use to promote their countries as tourist destinations.

nationwide tour A tour that is promoted and sold to people throughout a nation.

natural attractions Places that are preserved or are in their "original" state, such as scenic landscapes or seascapes and national or provincial parks.

neutral units of construction A fictitious currency unit used to simplify calculations for international fares based on different currencies.

new entrant carrier Any one of the airlines that came into business after the deregulation of the airlines.

NEXUS To enhance security and simplify border crossings for low-risk, pre-approved travellers, the United States Customs and Border Protection (CBP) has created a NEXUS card, which can be used to enter the United States and Canada.

niche market A small market segment with specialized needs, such as people who are physically challenged or families with young children, to which some tourism operators cater.

nondiscounted airfare A more expensive fare that allows a passenger to board any plane going to his or her destination that has an available seat. Same as *normal airfare* and *unrestricted airfare*.

nondiscretionary travel Travel undertaken out of necessity, such as business travel.

normal airfare A more expensive fare that allows a passenger to board any plane going to his or her destination that has an available seat. Same as *nondiscounted airfare* and *unrestricted airfare*.

no-show A person who makes a reservation but fails to use it.

nostalgia tourists These are tourists who want to return to memorable places, such as a honeymoon location.

occupational standards Descriptions of the knowledge, skills, and attitudes required for a person to be competent in a certain occupation.

oceanarium A type of aquarium that features saltwater animals.

off-site meeting A meeting held at a location other than the sponsoring company's premises.

on-demand public transportation Those transportation services, such as taxis and limousines, that don't have regular schedules; passengers arrange individually for service.

one-way trip A journey that begins in one city and ends in another.

open-jaw trip An air journey interrupted by surface travel, or a flight that has a return destination other than the originating city.

Open Skies agreement A trade agreement between two countries (e.g., Canada–United States) to promote air transportation between them. These agreements set liberal ground rules for international aviation markets and minimize government intervention. Provisions apply to passenger, all-cargo, and combination air transportation, and encompass both scheduled and charter services.

outbound tourism Residents of a country visiting places outside that country.

outside cabin A ship cabin that has a porthole or window and a view of the ocean.

outside sales Sales efforts that involve personal calls by the sales staff to prospective clients.

overbook To sell more seats or rooms than are available.

override A financial incentive paid by a supplier to a retailer to encourage high-volume sales.

package tour Several travel components provided by different suppliers are combined and sold to the consumer as a single product at a single price.

passenger name record (PNR) A record of a passenger's travel arrangements that is stored in a global distribution system (GDS).

passenger-to-crew ratio The number of passengers aboard a cruise ship divided by the number of crew.

passport A document issued by a government that enables people to enter a foreign country and to return to their own country.

pedestrian village An assemblage of facilities in a format that encourages walking to services, such as Intrawest has done at ski slopes.

per diem A term meaning "by the day" used to indicate the amount of money budgeted each day for travel expenses.

performance bond A special type of insurance policy that guarantees payment to all parties owed money.

personal accident insurance (PAI) Insurance offered by car rental firms that provides coverage in the case of bodily injury to the client.

point-to-point service Transporting passengers from one destination to another.

port tax Tax paid by passengers on embarkation at any port during a cruise.

poverty tourism Tour operators are leading guided "poverty" tours through shantytowns outside Buenos Aires (Argentina), immigrant neighbourhoods in Rotterdam (Holland), and Birmingham (England), and even impoverished areas in the U.S. such as Washington, D.C., and New York City; the tour operators claim that such tours raise awareness and understanding of the realities of the poor.

preferred supplier agreement A written or implied agreement between a travel agency and a particular supplier favouring usage of that supplier.

pressurization Artificial increase of air pressure in a jet cabin so that the air pressure is almost equivalent to the air pressure at ground level.

primary items Transportation and the components of other tourism sectors that are sold by travel agents.

primary research Market research in which product and service suppliers study consumers' responses to surveys, questionnaires, and interviews.

private charter A charter that is not for sale to the general public.

product life cycle theory A standard marketing concept that identifies four stages in the life cycle of a product: introduction (inception), growth, maturity, and decline.

promotion Advancing an idea, service, or business through advertising, personal selling, sales promotion, and public relations.

promotional airfare A less expensive airfare that includes certain restrictions, such as advance-purchase requirements, minimum/maximum length of stay, nonrefundable cancellation penalties, etc. Same as *discounted airfare, excursion airfare,* and *restricted airfare.*

provincial and territorial tourism organizations (PTTOs) Organizations that provincial and territorial governments use to promote their areas as tourist destinations.

psychographics Relates the activities, interests, and opinions of travellers to their life stage.

public charter A charter that is open for sale to the general public, either through a travel agency or by a tour or charter operator.

public transportation Organized passenger service available to the general public within a small geographic area.

pure incentive An incentive travel program designed strictly for pleasure.

quad A hotel room that is shared by four people.

quasi-public promoters Private promotional organizations that receive government funding, such as regional tourism organizations and convention and visitors' bureaux (CVBs).

rack rate The standard (maximum) day rate for a hotel room.

rebate Cash returned to a purchaser after a purchase has been made.

receptive operator A travel professional who specializes in arranging tours for visitors from other countries.

referral group Consortia, affiliations, or voluntary chains, also called "referral groups," are groups of independent hotels that have joined together in associations based on specific criteria for membership.

regional visitors Visitors from within four hours' drive of a destination.

repositioning cruise A cruise organized to transfer a ship from one cruising area to another between seasons.

reservations Spaces booked for a function or guest rooms at a facility in advance of a specific date.

reservations agent The person who responds to requests from travellers and coordinates the bookings and rates for an operation; the function may occur in-house using a computer reservations system (CRS) or a global distribution system (GDS).

restricted airfare A less expensive airfare that includes certain restrictions, such as advance-purchase requirements, minimum/maximum length of stay, nonrefundable cancellation penalties, etc. Same as *discounted airfare*, *excursion airfare*, and *promotional airfare*.

retailer distributor A member of the distribution channel selling products/services to consumers, either a traditional retail store (travel agency) or a wholesaler.

retail sales to tourists Products and services sold directly to consumers.

risk management strategy A method of considering the safety and security of guests and employees, as well as of personal and real property.

round trip A journey that begins in one city, goes to another city, and ends in the originating city.

runway A strip of land on which airplanes land and from which they take off.

Safety of Life at Sea (SOLAS) Convention The convention that sets safety standards for cruise ships.

sales incentive An incentive travel program that combines a vacation with scheduled business meetings.

satellite ticket printer (STP) A machine that allows travel agents to deliver tickets electronically to a client's premises.

scheduled airline An airline that offers regular flights that are scheduled to depart and arrive at certain times.

secondary items Travel components such as medical insurance and trip cancellation insurance.

secondary research Market research based on information that has been collected and processed.

segments of food service Authors Lane and Dupre divided Food & Beverage Operations into seven main subcategories within the broader commercial/non-commercial classification.

service charge Charges to customers made by travel agencies to cover their expenses.

single-city tour An in-depth tour of an individual city that offers travellers the opportunity to experience that city's culture.

single-country tour A tour of a single country that gives travellers an in-depth view of that country.

single-entity charter A private charter that is paid in full by a single source.

single supplement Hotel accommodation for a single person in a private room.

site destination selection company A company that investigates and suggests potential meeting sites to suit corporate or association needs.

soft adventure Soft adventures have a lower level of risk, greater comfort in accommodations, and are less physically rigorous. Soft adventure providers also offer specialized services for the physically challenged, young children, or the elderly, and generally cater to the needs of the vacationer.

special event A large-scale, once-in-a-lifetime show.

special-interest group tour A tour for clubs, societies, and organizations whose members share a common interest.

specialty channeller An intermediary, such as an incentive travel company, a meeting/convention planner, or a travel club, that organizes specific kinds of tour packages.

spectator sports Sports viewed by an audience.

sponsor Agencies, companies, or individuals who provide money, services, or other support to events and organizations in return for specific benefits.

stabilizers A feature on a ship that minimizes the effects of the ship's side-to-side roll.

standard car A full-sized car.

staycation A vacation spent in one's local region—to encourage budget-minded travellers to explore locally and save on rising travel costs.

stay-over guests Guests who spend more than one night at an accommodation facility and need their rooms scheduled for a daily makeup.

steerage The lowest class of accommodations on board a passenger ship.

stewardship ethic The moral principle that one manages property effectively because it will be beneficial to all concerned.

stopover An interruption to a trip lasting 12 or more hours.

strategic alliances Airlines based in various countries offering seamless worldwide air travel together through service agreements.

subcompact car A very small car.

subway A rail transportation system that provides local rapid-transit passenger service either wholly or partially underground.

sunspot stayput tour The most prominent tour product purchased by Canadians. Typically it includes return airfare to a southern destination and one week of resort accommodation.

superstructure All the buildings and structures, such as hotels, restaurants, shops, and convention centres, that are built at a tourist destination.

supplemental airline An airline that offers charter flights and other non-scheduled flights. Also called a *charter airline*.

sustainable tourism Tourism that impacts the environment positively and embraces "green management practices"; meets the needs of existing tourists and host regions while protecting and enhancing opportunities for the future; an issue for tourists from the local to the international level.

table d'hôte A set three (or more)-course meal offered at a fixed price.

tangible service/product A service or product that can be held, touched, or seen.

target market One or more specific groups of potential consumers toward which an organization directs its marketing program.

taxiway A lane where airplanes travel from the apron to the runway or from the runway to the hangar.

teleconferencing A way of holding a meeting at several locations simultaneously using advanced communications technology that enables participants to see and hear each other.

teleticketing The issuing of airline tickets by a machine linked to an airline computer reservations system.

tender A small boat that carries cruise passengers between ship and shore. Also known as a *lighter*.

terminal building The heart of the airport complex; it includes ticket counters, boarding gates, waiting areas, baggage pick-up; briefing room for pilots; and airport manager's office.

theme park A park with hundreds of acres developed to replicate a setting or be an artistic interpretation of a theme that provides entertainment and recreation; requires hundreds of employees to run the operation.

THTR On January 24, 2005, Ontario implemented a "Bring Your Own Wine" (*BYOW*) program for restaurants on a volunteer basis, as well as "Take Home the Rest" (THTR). This allows customers to bring a bottle of preferred wine for dinner at a participating restaurant (or hotel/motel banquet hall) with a liquor sales licence. Customers may take any wine left in the bottle home with them.

total quality management (TQM) A process designed to focus on customer expectations, prevent problems, build commitment to quality in the workforce, and promote open decision making.

tour conductor/tour escort A person who oversees an escorted tour to make sure everything runs smoothly. Also called a *tour manager*.

tour guide The leader of a guided tour who possesses in-depth knowledge of an area's attractions.

tour manager A person who oversees an escorted tour to make sure everything runs smoothly. Also called a *tour conductor* or *tour escort*.

tour operator A company that contracts with hotels, transportation companies, and other suppliers to create a tour package and then sells that package directly to the consumer.

tour organizer A person who may have little travel expertise and who works with a travel agency and tour operator to organize a specialized tour.

tour wholesaler A company that contracts with hotels, transportation companies, and other suppliers to create a tour package and then sells that package to the consumer through a retail travel agency.

tourism The set of activities of a person travelling to a place outside his or her usual environment for at least one night and for less than 12 months, and whose main purpose of travel is for leisure rather than business purposes.

tourism destination components Natural resources, infrastructure, superstructure, transportation systems, and the hospitality of the hosts are the necessary components of tourism destinations.

tourism education councils (TECs) A network of groups organized in each province under the Canadian Tourism Human Resource Council to coordinate training for human resource development.

tourism multiplier A formula used to determine the total income generated from money spent by tourists.

tourism services Services such as research, education, training, marketing, and retail that support and promote tourism.

train à grande vitesse (TGV) The high-speed train in France. It has a cruising speed of 260 kilometres per hour and is one of the fastest trains in Europe.

transfer Any change in transportation in the course of a journey.

travel agent A front-line worker who provides services to individuals and groups regarding travel destinations, transportation, accommodation, and costs; makes reservations and sells tickets, packaged tours, and insurance; promotes particular tour packages and other travel services; and provides tips regarding attractions, foreign currency, customs, languages, and travel safety. A travel agent may specialize in product areas such as cruises, group travel, or adventure travel. Also known as a *travel counsellor*.

travel blog Travellers who enjoyed keeping travel journals or diaries, and/or created travelogues were the original candidates to write their opinions and recommendations concerning travel destinations (and their accommodations, restaurants, attractions) in an online travel journal, which has become known as a travel blog.

travel clubs Clubs that offer unsold travel products to members.

travel counsellor A front-line worker who provides services to individuals and groups regarding travel destinations, transportation, accommodation, and costs; makes reservations and sells tickets, packaged tours, and insurance; promotes particular tour packages and other travel services; and provides tips regarding attractions, foreign currency, customs, languages, and travel safety. A travel counsellor may specialize in product areas such as cruises, group travel, or adventure travel. Also known as a *travel agent*.

travel management services Services offered by a corporate travel agency to help a client control and monitor its business travel costs.

travel policy The guidelines established by an organization to coordinate travel by employees and to control costs.

triple A hotel room that is shared by three people.

trolley A streetcar that runs on electricity.

two-city tour A tour of two cities, either in the same country or in different countries.

unlimited kilometres plan A car rental plan that allows clients to drive a rental car as far as they want for a flat fee within the allotted rental period.

unrestricted airfare A more expensive fare that allows a passenger to board any plane going to his or her destination that has an available seat. Same as *nondiscounted airfare* and *normal airfare*.

Venturer A personality type that seeks adventure, variety, and excitement in travel.

video marketing The use of cable television to promote and sell products and services.

Virtual Concierge Internet service providing information about services for travellers, and a link between a guest and an area; available through websites and accessed via computer in a hotel room or lobby, or at home before a trip.

voucher A coupon or document exchanged for tourism products such as accommodation, transportation, gratuities, etc.

wait list A list of passengers waiting for a vacancy on a fully booked airline flight.

water-based vacations Features outdoor recreation involving lakes, rivers, and oceans, such as swimming, sailing, canoeing, scuba diving, and fishing.

wholesale distributor Suppliers in the channel of distribution providing products/services to other suppliers or retail distributors such as travel agencies.

WHTI In response to growing security concerns, the U.S. government has created the Western Hemisphere Travel Initiative (WHTI), which requires a valid passport or other WHTI-approved document (in lieu of a driver's licence and birth certificate) to enter the United States.

wireless application protocol (WAP) Enables consumers to access websites without a computer or telephone lines.

yield management The use of pricing and inventory controls, based on historical data tracked through managing electronic information systems, to maximize profit by gauging rates in response to demand for products/services offered.

youth standby fares Fares available through Travel CUTS for young people who are willing to wait for available seats rather than pay full fare to fly on a specific flight.

zoo A zoological garden; confined area where animals are kept for exhibit.

Aboriginal Tourism Canada. (n.d.). "Significant 29," accessed June 2008 at www.aboriginaltourism.ca/significant.php.

Access Canada: A Barrier-free Standards and Rating Program Operator's Manual. (1996). Toronto: Hotel Association of Canada.

Accolade newsletter. (April 2008). Interview with John Walker, www.georgebrown.ca/chefschool/accolade/accolade_Apr_08.aspx.

Adair, Daryl (March 2002). "Biosphere Reserve Champions Ecotourism Ideals," Tourism, Vol. 6, Issue 2, p. 8.

———. (Nov. 2001). "Success Story: Developing Winter Tourism in the North," Communiqué, Vol. 5, Issue 9, p. 12.

———. (Oct. 2001). "Rail Tour Adventure along the Atlantic," Communiqué, Vol. 5, Issue 8, p. 6.

Advertising Age (June 27, 1997). "Intermercials, Sponsorships Will Emerge as New Online Ad Models," p. 24.

Aerospace Technology. (Aug. 2008). "Airbus A380 Superjumbo Twin-Deck, Twin-Aisle Airliner," www.aerospace-technology.com/projects/a380.

Airbus. (Aug. 2008). "Aircraft Families: A380 Family," www.airbus.com/en/aircraftfamilies/a380/economics.html.

Airbus A380. (Aug. 2008). Economics. "The Solution to Growing Air Travel," www.airbus.com/en/aircraftfamilies/a380/economics.html.

Air Canada Annual Report. (2001). Montreal: Air Canada.

Airliners.net. (n.d.). "Aircraft Data," accessed Nov. 20, 2008 at www.airliners.net/aircraft-data/stats.main?id-29.

Aitken, Susan. (Aug. 1, 2004). "Return to the Cradle of Acadia," Toronto Star.

Albrecht, Karl, and Zemke, Ron. (1985). Service America! New York: Warner Books.

Aliant Pioneer Volunteers. (May 2008). www.aliant.ca/english/about/community_brochures/north_NB/index.shtml.

Allemang, John. (Jan. 5, 2001). "The Wine Queen Cometh to Canada," The Globe and Mail, p. L5.

Allentuck, Andrew (March 9, 2000). "Sick of Airports? Rail May Be the Ticket," The Globe and Mail, www.globeandmail.com/travel/rail.

Amdekar, Jay, and Chrestman, Criss. (June 1, 2007). "Kiosk CheckIn for the Hospitality Industry—Challenges and the Way Forward," Hospitality Upgrade, Summer 2007, pp. 160–62.

American Express. (Oct. 23, 2007). 2008 Global Business Travel Forecast. New York: American Express Company.

———. (2003). 2003 International Business Traveller Poll. Toronto: Amex Canada Inc.

———. (2001). Survey of Business Travel Management 2000–2001. Toronto: Amex Canada Inc.

———. (1998). Survey of Business Travel Management 1997–1998. Toronto: Amex Canada Inc.

Anne of Green Gables 100th Anniversary. (May 2008). www.anne2008.com.

Arial, Tracey. (Jan.–Feb. 2000). "The Four-season Challenge," Communiqué, Vol. 4, Issue 1, p. 3.

Arsenault, Nancy. (March 2000). "Year-round 'Ed-ventures,'" Communiqué, Vol. 4, Issue 2, p. 3.

Association of Collegiate Conference and Events Directors–International (ACCED-I). (n.d.). Accessed Nov. 20, 2008 at www.acced-i.org/imis_web/StaticContent/1/AboutACCED.htm.

Atlantic Restaurant News. (Oct. 2001). "Nature Centre Restaurant Adopts Green Kitchen, Menu," Vol. 3, No. 5, p. 13.

———. (Oct. 2001). "Together Computers and Cooks Make Beautiful Food," Vol. 3, No. 5, pp. 26–29.

———. (Nov.–Dec. 2000). "Changes in Foodservice at Sea result in Smooth Sailing," Vol. 2, No. 6, p. 11.

ATPCO Passenger Tariff Set. (n.d.). Washington, D.C.: Airline Publishing Company.

Avery, Patrick. (Jan. 28, 2008). "Make Sure Hotel Check-in Kiosks Do the Right Thing," Self Service World, www.selfserviceworld.com/article_19198_279_40.php.

Axler, B. (1987). Food Service: A Managerial Approach. Toronto: John Wiley & Sons, Inc.

Axworthy, Hon. Lloyd. (May 1984). The New Canadian Air Policy. Ottawa: Department of Transport.

Babineau, Guy. (June 28, 2001). "Boutique Staying Power," National Post, p. E4.

Baird, Bonnie. (Jan.–Feb. 2002). "TAMS: Casino Gaming in Canada," Tourism, Vol. 6, Issue 1, p. 9.

Balint, S. (July/Aug. 1997). "Keeping the 'Eco' in Ecotourism," The Bluenose Tribune (Halifax).

Banffshire Club Restaurant. Fairmont Banff Springs Hotel. (Nov. 17, 2006). Banff, Alberta, http://travel.canoe.ca/Travel/TipsTrends/Tips/2006/11/17/2392197.html.

Bank of Canada. (March 20, 2008). Exchange Rates, www.bankofcanada.ca.en/rates/exchform.html.

Bartender Occupational Standards. (1993). Ottawa: Tourism Standards Consortium (Western Canada) and Canadian Tourism Human Resource Council.

Bateson, John E.G., and Hoffman, K. Douglas. (1999). Managing Services Marketing. Toronto: The Dryden Press, Harcourt Brace College Publishers.

Baum, Thomas, and Mudambi, Ram (1999). *Economic Management Methods for Tourism and Hospitality Research*. Toronto: John Wiley & Sons, p. xii.

BBC News. (June 4, 2008). "Size Is All for Syrian Restaurant," http://news.bbc.co.uk/2/hi/middle_east/7435424.stm.

Beldon, Tom. (April 21, 2002). *AMEX Business Travel Monitor* cited in "Air-travel Spending Likely to Fall in 2002," *The Philadelphia Inquirer*.

Belford, Terrance. (March 27, 2001). "New Concept Opens Doors to Business Travellers," *National Post*, pp. E1, E3.

———. (March 27, 2001). "No Room at the Inn," *National Post*, pp. E1, E2.

Benchmark Hospitality. (n.d.). "Top 10 Meeting Trends for 2008," www.hotelnewsresource.com/article31652-Top____ Meeting_Trends_for_____.html.

Bennett, Peter D. (1995). *Dictionary of Marketing Terms*, 2nd ed. Lincolnwood, IL: NTC Publishing Group, p. 166.

Berkowitz, Eric N., Crane, Frederick G., Kerin, Roger A., Hartley, Steven W., and Rudelius, William (2000). *Marketing*, 4th Cdn. ed. Toronto: Irwin McGraw-Hill.

Berman, David. (June 23, 2008). "At Noon: Financial Woes," *The Globe and Mail*, www.theglobeandmail.com/servlet/story/RTGAM.20080623.WBmarkets20080623121151/WBStory/WBmarkets.

Berry, Leonard A., Parasuraman, A., and Zeithaml, Valerie A. (1994). "Diagnosing Service Quality in America," *Academy of Management Executives*, Vol. 8, No. 2, pp. 32–52.

Bertin, Oliver. (Dec. 5, 2001). "Comfort Foods Making a Comeback," *The Globe and Mail*, p. B3.

———. (Oct. 30, 2001). "Cara Suffers Sharp Setback after Attacks," *The Globe and Mail*, p. B9.

———. (Oct. 16, 2001). "Cooling Economy Takes Toll on Food-service Industry," *The Globe and Mail*, p. B8.

Berton, P., and Berton, J. (1966). *The Centennial Food Guide: A Century of Good Eating*. Toronto: The Canadian Centennial Publishing Co. Ltd.

Beyrouti, Monique. (Winter 2001). "Canada's Competitiveness in the US Travel Market," *Travel-log*, Vol. 20, No. 1, pp. 1–8.

Bitner, Mary J. (April 1992). "Servicescapes: The impact of Physical Surroundings on Customers and Employees," *Journal of Marketing*, Vol. 56, No. 2, p. 650.

Bogardus, Charlotte. (Aug. 2000). "Why CRM Systems Can Make Marketing More Effective," *Restaurant Hospitality*, Vol. LXXXIV, No. 7, p. 90.

Bowman, Margaret E., and Eagles, Paul E. (March 2002). "Tourism Spending in Parks: The Algonquin Park example," *Tourism*, Vol. 6, Issue 2, p. 15.

Brayley, R.E. (1991). "Recreation and Tourism: Partners in the Community," *Recreation Canada*, 49(4), pp. 19–22.

Bricker, Jon. (June 13, 2001). "Left in the Cold by an Arctic Cruise," *National Post*, p. A3.

Brodsky, Stuart. (April 18, 2005). "AH&LA Program Aims to Help Bottom Line, Environment," *Hotel & Motel Management*, www.hotelmotel.com/hotelmotel/Columns/AHLA-program-aims-to-help-bottom-line-environment/ArticleStandard/Article/detail/156592?searchString=Brodsky,%20Stuart%20%202005%20Brodsky,%20Stuart%202005.

Brotherton, Bob. (1999). *The Handbook of Contemporary Hospitality Management Research*. Toronto: John Wiley & Sons Ltd.

Bucher, Charles A., Shivers, Jay S., and Bucher, Richard D. (1984). *Recreation For Today's Society*. Toronto: Prentice-Hall Canada Inc.

Buckley, Ralph. (Sept. 21, 2007). "Adventure Tourism Trends," Quebec Tourism Intelligence Network, http://tourismintelligence.ca/2007/09/21/adventure-tourism-trends. From *Adventure Tourism*, Oxford: CABI, 2006.

Budget 2007. (March 19, 2007). Department of Finance Canada, accessed Nov. 20, 2008 at www.budget.gc.ca/2007/bp/bpa5ae.html#sales.

Buhasz, Laszlo. (March 6, 2002). "Women Travellers Seek Security, Privacy," *The Globe and Mail*, www.globeandmail.com/travel/seeksecurity.

———. (Nov. 2001). "Victoria: Canada's New Winter Hotspot," *Tourism*, Vol. 5, Issue 9, p. 10.

Cajic, Natalie. (Dec. 2001). "Canadian Cuisine—Food as Sexy and Exotic as Any," *Atlantic Restaurant News*, Vol. 3, No. 6, p. 2.

———. (Feb. 2001). "Canadians Demanding More Flavour," *Atlantic Restaurant News*, Vol. 3, No. 1, pp. 8, 9, 11.

Calvert, C. (1987). *Having Tea: Recipes and Table Settings*. London: Sidgwick and Jackson.

Campbell, Mark. (March 1999). "Industry Grapples with Vision, Mission," *Communiqué*, Vol. 4, Issue 2, p. 3.

Canada 3000. (2000). *Annual Report (2000)*. Toronto: Canada 3000.

Canada Revenue Agency. (June 26, 2008). Foreign Convention and Tour Incentive Program, www.cra-arc.gc.ca/agency/budget/2007/foreign-e.html.

The Canadian Encyclopedia, Vols. I, II, III (1985). Edmonton: Hurtig Publishers.

Canadian Foodservices Association. (n.d.). *Operations Survey*. Toronto: Canadian Foodservices Association.

Canadian Gaming Association. (April 26, 2007). "Landmark Economic Impact Study Reveals Gaming Industry in Canada

Worth $15.3 billion in Direct Spending Alone," www .canadiangaming.ca/english/press/pressrel_detail.cfm?id=15.

Canadian Press. (Feb. 26, 2004). "Canadian 'Travel Deficit' Reaches 10-year High."

Canadian Restaurant and Foodservices Association (CRFA). (n.d.). "Facts about Foodservice: Economic Impact of Canada's Foodservice Industry," accessed Oct. 30, 2008 at www.crfa.ca/ research/statistics/factsandstats.asp#units

———. (June 18, 2008). "Foodservice Margins Inch up to 4.3%," www.crfa.ca/research/2008/foodservice_profitability_improves.asp.

———. (April 23, 2008). "Labour Shortage Solutions," www.crfa.ca/research/resources/labourshortagesolutions.asp.

———. (March 17, 2008). "Foodservice Market Share Shrinks in 2007," www.crfa.ca/research/2008/foodservice_market_share_ shrinks_in_2007.asp.

———. (Feb. 20, 2008). "Foodservice Bankruptcies at 27-year Low," www.crfa.ca/research/2008/foodservice_bankruptcies_at_ 27-year_low.asp.

———. (2008). 2008 Foodservice Operations Report, Statistics Canada (2008), www.crfa.ca.

———. (2008). "CRFA 2008 Foodservice Forecast: Part 2," http://crfa.ca/research/2008/crfas_2008_foodservice_forecast_ part_2.asp.

———. (Dec. 11, 2007). "CRFA Unveils 2008 Foodservice Forecast," www.crfa.ca/research/2007/crfa_unveils_2008_ foodservice_forecast.asp.

———. (Sept. 25, 2007). "CRFA Launches New Foodservice Industry Event," www.crfa.ca/aboutcrfa/newsroom/2007/crfa_ launches_new_foodservice_industry_event.asp.

———. (Sept. 19, 2007). "New Canadians to Shape Foodservice Trends," www.crfa.ca/research/2007/new_canadians_to_shape_ foodservice_trends.asp.

———. (June 2006). "Help Wanted: The Foodservice Industry Labour Shortage and Canada's Foreign Worker Program," www.crfa.ca/research/reports/pdf/labourshortage.pdf.

———. (Oct. 8, 2004). Press release: "Foodservice Sales to Grow 4.7% in 2005."

———. (March 25, 2004). Press release: "Tourists Give Canada the Cold Shoulder."

———. (Feb. 5, 2004). Press release: "Foodservice Sales Poised for Recovery."

———. (Feb. 5, 2004). Press release: "Privacy Legislation and the Foodservice Industry."

———. (2001). Foodservice Facts 2001. Toronto: Canadian Restaurant and Foodservices Association.

———. (2000). Foodservice Facts 2000. Toronto: Canadian Restaurant and Foodservices Association.

Canadian Ski Council. (Sept. 2007). "2006–2007 Canadian Skier and Snowboarder Facts and Stats." Prepared by the Print Measurement Bureau.

Canadian Society of Professional Meeting Planners or CanSPEP (formerly Independent Meeting Planners Association of Canada). (n.d.). "Membership Categories," www.cspep.ca/ Membership/categories.htm.

Canadian Tourism Commission (CTC). (n.d.). "About the CTC," accessed Nov. 19, 2008 at www.corporate.canada.travel/ en/ca/about_ctc/index.html.

———. (2007). 2007 Annual Report. Ottawa: Canadian Tourism Commission.

———. (2006). "Tourism Snapshot. Year in Review. 2006 Facts & Figures Key Highlights," www.corporate.canada.travel.

———. (2001). Annual Report 2001. Ottawa: Canadian Tourism Commission.

———. (2001). "Tourism Satellite Accounts: Credible Numbers for Good Business Decisions." Ottawa: Canadian Tourism Commission; Statistics Canada.

———. (2000). Annual Report 2000. Ottawa: Canadian Tourism Commission.

———. (March 1999). On the Path to Success: Lessons from Canadian Adventure Travel and Ecotourism Operators. The Economic Planning Group. Ottawa: Canadian Tourism Commission.

———. (1999). Annual Report 1999. Ottawa: Canadian Tourism Commission.

Canadian Tourism Human Resource Council (CTHRC). (n.d.). "Labour Market Information," accessed Oct. 31, 2008 at www.cthrc.ca/en/research_publications/labour_market_ information.aspx.

———. (2006). "2006 Food & Beverage Services: Total Tourism Sector Employment in Canada," www.cthrc.ca/en/research_ publications/labour_market_information/TTSE-2008-Food-Beverage-en.ashx.

———. (2006). "Total Tourism Sector Employment in Canada: 2006 Update," prepared by Jennifer Wright, jaiTec solutions, www.cthrc.ca/en/research_publications/labour_market_ information.aspx.

———. (2001). Career Planning Guide. Ottawa: Canadian Tourism Human Resource Council.

———. (1998). "The Workforce Series," Ottawa: Canadian Tourism Human Resource Council.

Canadian Travel Experience Network. (Feb. 2001). "Emerging Trends in the Tourism Market and Their Impact on Tourism Development," newsletter, www.letacanada.com.

Capital Ex (and Klondike Days). (June 2008). www.westerntour .com/Edmonton/Kdays.htm.

Cara Airline Solutions. (n.d.). "Our Five Principles," accessed Aug. 2008 at http://working.canada.com/profiles/cara/profile.html#principles.

————. (n.d.). "Cara College," accessed Sept. 2008 at http://working.canada.com/profiles/cara/profile.html#college.

Cara Operations Limited. (n.d.). "Cara Company Profile," Cara Operations Limited website, accessed Sept. 2008 at www.cara.com.

CarePar. (n.d.). Home page, accessed Nov. 3, 2008 at www.carepar.com/index.html.

Carlzon, J. (1987). *Moments of Truth*. New York: Balligen.

Carmichael, Matt. (July–Aug. 1999). "Canadian Cuisine—An Authentic Cultural Resource," *Communiqué*, Vol. 3, Issue 6, pp. 9, 12.

Caro, Margaret Rose. (July 2000). "Nutrition Nirvana," *Lodging F&B*, pp. 21–24.

Carroll, William, and Sileo, Lorraine. (Spring 2007). "Chains Gain Ground Online—Hotels Have Much to Celebrate," *Hospitality Upgrade*, www.hospitalityupgrade.com/_magazine/magazine_Detail.asp?ID=86.

Casino City. (n.d.). "Canadian Casinos and Gambling in Canada," accessed June 2008 at www.casinocity.com/ca/provinces.html.

CBC News. (July, 7, 2005). "38 Dead, 700 Injured in London Blasts," cbcnews.ca.

————. (Nov. 12, 2004). "Da Vinci Code "Tourist Letdowns,'" www.cbsnews.com/stories/2004/11/01/earlyshow/living/travel/main652625.shtml.

Centennial College. (n.d.). Programs. New Programs '08/'09. School of Hospitality, Tourism & Culture. "Hospitality Operations—Kitchen Management" and "Hospitality Operations—Food and Beverage (Catering)," accessed Nov. 20, 2008 at www.centennialcollege.ca

Central Intelligence Agency (CIA). (2004). "The World Factbook. Cayman Islands: Economy," www.cia.gov/library/publications/the-world-factbook/geos/cj.html.

Chaisson, Diane. (Oct. 2001). "The ABCs of Starting a Franchise—Move Cautiously," *Atlantic Restaurant News*, Vol. 5, No. 5, p. 2.

Chatfield-Taylor, Cathy. (June 1, 2003). "Air Travel Tactics," *Primedia Business Magazine*, www.meetingsnet.com.

Chatto, James. (April 2001). "And the Winners Are . . . " (*Toronto Life* Restaurant Awards), *Toronto Life*, pp. 96–101.

Chavich, Cinda. (Nov. 5, 2001). "Serving up Solace," *The Globe and Mail*, p. L5.

Cheek, Neil, and Burch, William. (1976). *The Social Organization of Leisure in Human Society*. New York: Harper and Row Publishers, Inc., p. 224.

CHIP REIT. (June 2008). www.chiphospitality.com/former_unitholders.html.

Cirque du Soleil (CDS). (n.d.). "CDS at a Glance," accessed May 2008 at www.cirquedusoleil.com/world/en/cn/about/cds.asp.

Clark, Andrea. (May 2000). "Atlantic Canada Ports Cashing In," *Communiqué*, Vol. 4, Issue 4, p. 22.

Cruise Lines International Association (CLIA). (Feb. 2008). "Profile of the U.S. Cruise Industry," *Cruise Industry Source Book*, www.cruising.org/press/sourcebook2008/index.cfm.

————. (Jan. 16, 2008). "2008 Cruise Trends: The Inside Story, From Those Who Know Best," www.cruising.org/cruisenews/news.cfm?NID=333

————. (Jan. 16, 2008). "As Consumers Respond Strongly to Innovation, Diversity of Cruise Experiences, Industry Anticipates Record Year," www.cruising.org/cruisenews/news.cfm?NID=332.

————. (2008). *CLIA Cruise Manual*. (Annual). New York: Cruise Lines International Association.

Club Med. (Sept. 5, 2008). Home page, www.clubmed.com.

CNN. (May 19, 2003). "Bombs Kill at least 20 in Downtown Casablanca," http://edition.cnn.com/2003/WORLD/africa/05/16/morocco.blasts/index.html.

Collins, V.R. (Feb. 1996). "What Is De Ster's Discovery?" *Onboard Services*, pp. 30–31.

Communiqué. (Oct 2001). "Corporate America Staying Home," Vol. 5, Issue 8.

————. (Oct. 2001). "Untapped Potential: Cultural and Outdoor Experiences and the U.S. Market," Vol. 5, Issue 8, p. 11.

————. (Sept. 2001). "E-commerce and the Travel Trade," Vol. 5, Issue 9, p. 13.

————. (Sept. 2001). "Gourmet Dining Introduced at Convention Centres," Vol. 5, Issue 9, p. 7.

————. (Sept. 2001). "MC & IT Feature: Canada's Arctic," Vol. 5, Issue 9, p. 5.

————. (Summer 2001). "Aboriginal Tourism Finding its Niche," Vol. 5, Issue 6, p. 5.

————. (Summer 2001). "Marketing Down Under: *Today Show* Project Exceeds Expectations," Vol. 5, Issue 6, p. 12.

————. (Summer 2001). "Measuring the Economic Impact of Museum Exhibits," Vol. 5, Issue 6, p. 11.

————. (April 2001). "Agencies, Operators, Generate over $11 billion," Vol. 5, Issue 3, p. 22.

————. (April 2001). "What about Tourism and Airlines, anyway?" Vol. 5, Issue 3, p. 10.

————. (Jan.–Feb. 2001). "New Structure at the Top for CTC," Vol. 5, Issue 1, p. 19.

————. (Jan.–Feb. 2001). "Probing the Industry 2001/2001 Research Goals," Vol. 5, Issue 1, p. 20.

————. (Dec. 2000). "Creating a Cultural Tourism Product," Vol. 4, Issue 11, p. 12.

————. (Dec. 2000). "Cultural World Heritage Sites in Canada," Vol. 4, Issue 11, p. 10.

————. (Dec. 2000). "SMEs Account for 99% of Canada's Tourism Industry," Vol. 4, Issue 11, p. 1.

————. (Nov. 2000). "Big Creatures, Big Business," Vol. 4, Issue 10, p. 18.

————. (Nov. 2000). "Canadian Cities Light up for Christmas," Vol. 4, Issue 10, p. 3.

————. (Sept. 2000). "Financing Solutions for Small Tourism Businesses," Vol. 4, Issue 9, p. 15.

————. (Sept. 2000). "Open Forums Confirm ACTA's Direction," Vol. 4, Issue 9, p. 12.

————. (Sept. 2000). "Rivalry Yields to Cooperation for Competitive Advantage," Vol. 4, Issue 9, p. 8.

————. (July–Aug. 2000). "Touring Niagara's Wineries by Bicycle," Vol. 4, Issue 6, p. 12.

————. (June 2000). "Economic Effect of the Cruise Industry in Canada," Vol. 4, Issue 4, p. 17.

————. (Jan.–Feb. 2000). "Investment There, for Some," Vol. 4, Issue 1, pp. 3–4.

————. (Dec. 1999). "In conversation with Nancy Greene Raine," Vol. 3, Issue 10, pp. 6–7.

————. (Oct. 1999). "Overview of Canada's Travel Agencies and Tour Operators," Vol. 3, Issue 8, p. 8.

————. (May 1998). "Package Travel an Untapped Market?" Vol. 2, Issue 5, p. 8.

————. (Nov. 1997). "New Licensee for Merchandising Program," Vol. 1, Issue 11, p. 5.

————. (Sept. 1997). "An Ad Agency First: Competitors as Partners!" Vol. 1, Issue 9, p. 5.

Condé Nast Traveller. (n.d.). "Readers Awards 2007," accessed Nov. 1, 2008 at www.cntraveller.co.uk/ReadersAwards/2007/Countries/.

Conference Board of Canada. (1997). "Trends and Forecasts for the Canadian Business Travel Industry 1997." Paper prepared for American Express Corporate Services. Toronto: Amex Canada Inc.

Constantineau, Bruce. (June 3, 2008). "B.C. Wants to be Canada's Culinary Capital," Vancouver Sun, www.canada.com/vancouversun/news/travel/story.html?id=487ac800-11c1-4631-b654-d9ba912e8bb6.

Conway, L. K., ed. (1991). The Professional Chef, 5th ed. Hyde Park, NY: Culinary Institute of America, p. 5.

Cook, Lou. (Oct. 1999). "Profitability and Environmentalism Go Hand in Hand," Lodging, Vol. 25, No. 2, pp. 67–70.

Corbeil, Patruce. (March 2002). "Whales Online Produces Real Ecotourists," Tourism, Vol. 6, Issue 3, p. 7.

Cote, Raymond. (April 2004). Hospitality Industry News.

Cotts, David G., and Lee, Michael. (1992). The Facility Management Handbook. New York: AMOCOM, a Division of American Management Association.

Couture, Maurice. (April 2001). "Is Canada Organized for Adventure?" Communiqué, Vol. 5, Issue 3, p. 3.

————. (July–Aug. 2000). "All Aboard . . . Tour Packages and Tourism Products 'Engineered' to Please," Communiqué, Vol. 4, Issue 6, pp. 1, 3, 4.

Coyle, John J., Bardi, Edward J., and Novak, Robert A. (2000). Transportation. New York: West Publishing Company.

Cracknell, H.L., Kaufmann, R.J., and Nobis, G. (1983). Practical Professional Catering. London: Macmillan Press.

Cree Village Eco Lodge. (June 2008). Home page, www.creevillage.com.

Cronin Jr., J. Joseph, and Taylor, Steven A. (July 1992). "Measuring Service Quality: A Reexamination and Extension," Journal of Marketing, Vol. 56, pp. 60–63.

Cruickshank, Ian. (June 28, 2001). "Hotels Help Relieve Road-warrior Guilt," National Post, p. E2.

Cruise Travel. (Feb. 2001; June 2001). Vol. 22, No. 4; No. 6.

Curry, Pat. (Dec. 11, 2003). "Fractional Ownership: Get a Piece of a Vacation Home," www.bankrate.com/brm/news/real-estate/20031211a1.asp.

Darson, Laurie. (April 30, 2008). "New Hotel Brands Target Next-Gen Business Travelers," www.management.travel/news.php?cid=hotels-new-brands.Apr-08.30.

Dattani, Kristin. (Oct. 2000). "A Consistent Vision Creates the Finest Ski Resorts," Communiqué, Vol. 4, Issue 9, p. 6.

Davidoff, Philip G., Davidoff, Doris L., and Eure, J. Douglas. (1995). Tourism Geography, 2nd ed. Toronto: Prentice-Hall Canada Inc.

Davidson, Hilary. (2001). Frommer's Toronto. Foster City, CA: IDG Books Worldwide, Inc.

Davos Declaration. (Oct. 3, 2007). "Climate Change and Tourism responding to Global Challenges," Second International Conference on Climate Change and Tourism.

Deibert, Mike. (April 2002). "QSR Chains in Hot Competition for Sites," Atlantic Restaurant News, Vol. 4, No. 2, p. 1.

————. (Dec. 2001). "Energy Conservation a Theme at NAFEM," Atlantic Restaurant News, Vol. 3, No. 6, pp. 8, 10.

————. (April 2001). "Foodservice Looks to a Wireless World," Atlantic Restaurant News, Vol. 3, No. 2, p. 9.

————. (Feb. 2001). "Canadians Becoming More like Americans when Eating Out," *Atlantic Restaurant News*, Vol. 3, No. 1, p. 4.

————. (Dec. 2000). "Dot-com Companies Flourish at Canada's Largest Trade Show," *Atlantic Restaurant News*, Vol. 2, No. 6, p. 10.

Delta Hotels. (Oct. 2, 2007). "Delta Hotels Acquired by British Columbia Investment Management Corporation," Press release, www.deltahotels.com/en/about/press_view.html?id=209.

————. (2001). "The Delta Hotels Story," accessed May 9, 2001 at www.deltahotels.com/companyinformation.

Deneault, Mylene. (July–Aug. 2000). "Local Culture and Food Enhance Country Touring," *Communiqué*, Vol. 4, Issue 6, p. 6.

Destination Marketing Fee/Fund (DMF). (May 2008). Hotel Association of Canada. News & Resources FAQs, www.hotelassociation.ca/site/news/faq.htm.

Devereaux J. (Nov. 12, 1996). "Second Cup Gets New Coffee Deal with Air Canada," *Toronto Star*, p. D3.

Dixon, Guy. (Feb. 4, 2001). "Canadian Pacific's $18-billion Breakup," *The Globe and Mail Report on Business*, pp. B1, B9.

Doucett, Virginia. (Dec. 2000). "The Aboriginal Tourism Challenge: Managing for Growth," *Communiqué*, Vol. 4, Issue 11, p. 1.

Dubailand. (Feb. 2008). "Dubailand Highlights: Facts & Figures," www.dubailand.ae/facts_figures.html.

————. (Feb. 2008). "Dubailand Strategy & Objectives," www.dubailand.ae/strategy_objectives.html.

Earle, Teresa. (Nov. 2000). "Major Events, Major Sponsors, Major Growing Pains," *Communiqué*, Vol. 4, Issue 10, p. 15.

Eco Hotels of the World. (n.d.). Home page, accessed May 2008, www.ecohotelsoftheworld.com/homepage.html.

The Ecolodge Sourcebook for Planners and Developers. (n.d.). Bennington, VT: Ecotourism Society.

The Economic Planning Group. (March 1999). *On the Path to Success: Lessons from Canadian Adventure Travel and Ecotourism Operators*. Ottawa: Canadian Tourism Commission.

————. (1999). *On the Path to Success: Catalogue of Exemplary Practices in Adventure Travel and Ecotourism*, http://destinet.ewindows.eu.org.

————. (1996). *A Guide to Starting and Operating an Accommodation Business in Nova Scotia*. Halifax: Tourism Nova Scotia, a Division of the Economic Renewal Agency.

Edmunds, Lavinia. (Feb. 2000). "Stars and Diamonds: How Many Do You Really Need?" *Lodging F&B*, pp. 18–24.

Edzerza, Allen. (March 2002). "A New Frontier for Sustainable Tourism?" *Tourism*, Vol. 6, Issue 2, p. 12.

ehotelier. (June 13, 2008). "Encouraging Tourism Innovation for Climate Neutrality," http://ehotelier.com/browse/news_more.php?id=D13847_0_11_0_M.

El Baroudi, Gail. (Dec. 4, 2001). "Future Cloudy for Hotel REITs?" *Property Report, The Globe and Mail*, p. B18.

Elliott, Statia. (Oct. 2001). "Manitoba: Savouring the Landscape and the Dinner Table," *Communiqué*, Vol. 5, Issue 8, p. 7.

Emerit. (May 2008). "Tourism Sector Adopts New Categorization As a Result Of NAFTA," www.emerit.ca.

enRoute. (Feb. 1997). "Go West, Go West: The Best Ski Resorts of the Rockies and Beyond," pp. 29–38.

Entrepreneur. (Jan. 2004). "25th Annual Franchise 500," www.entrepreneur.com.

Environmental Management for Hotels: The Industry Guide to Best Practice. (1996). Oxford: Butterworth Heinemann, an International Hotels Environment Initiative.

Ettorre, Barbara. (March 1997). "The Bottom Line on Customer Loyalty," a conversation with Fredrick E. Reichheld in *Management Review*, Vol. 86, No. 3, pp. 16–18.

Eturbonews.com. (March 18, 2008). "Travel Industry Sees Boom in Multi-country Bookings," www.eturbonews.com/1763/travel-industry-sees-boom-multi-country-booki.

————. (March 12, 2008). "Cruise Sector Will Survive Economic Slump," www.eturbonews.com/1680/cruise-sector-will-survive-economic-slump.

————. (March 7, 2008). "Continued Growth Signalled for Travel & Tourism Industry," www.eturbonews.com/1604/continued-growth-signalled-travel-tourism-ind.

————. (Jan. 7, 2008). "2008: Where We'll Go, and what We'll Do when We Get There," www.eturbonews.com/681/2008-where-well-go-and-what-well-do-when-we-get-there.

————. (Jan. 2, 2008). "Tourists Answer the Call of Nostalgia," www.eturbonews.com/583/tourists-answer-call-nostalgia.

————. (Dec. 13, 2007). "Air Travelers Prefer Automated and Online Services," www.eturbonews.com/344/air-travelers-prefer-automated-and-online-services.

Explore the Bruce. (n.d.). "4th Annual Adventure Passport. Outdoor Activities. Geocaching," accessed May 2008 at www.explorethebruce.com/passport/geocache.cfm.

Fair and Safe Play: Risk Management. (1996). Halifax: Nova Scotia Sport and Recreation Commission.

Fairmont Hotels & Resorts. (n.d.). "Eco-Meet: Green Meeting and Conference Planning," accessed Nov. 19, 2008 at www.fairmont.com/EN_FA/AboutFairmont/environment/ProgramsandInitiatives/EcoMeetEnvironment.htm.

————. (n.d.). "Our Philosophy," accessed Nov. 19, 2008 at www.fairmont.com/EN_FA/AboutFairmont/OurPhilosophy/.

Faulk, S., and Hofman, S. (Winter 1997). "Shopping the World for Your Hospitality Education," *Hosteur*, Vol. 6, No. 2.

Ferguson, Jeremy. (May 19, 2001). "French Toast," *The Globe and Mail*, pp. T1, T4.

Finch, Bytron J., and Luebbe, Richard L. (1995). *Operations Management: Competing in a Changing Environment*. Philadelphia: Saunders College/Holt Rinehart and Winston.

Fishbein, M., and Ajzen, I. (1975). *Belief, Attitude, Intention and Behaviour: An Introduction to Theory and Research*. Reading, MA: Addison-Wesley Publishing Co.

Fitzsimmons, James A., and Fitzsimmons, Mona J. (1994). *Service Management for Competitive Advantage*. Toronto: McGraw-Hill Inc.

Foodtrekker. (May 2008). "International Culinary Tourism," www.culinarytourism.org/foodtrekker.

Foote, D. (Oct. 22, 1996). "Boom, Bust and Echo." Address given at the Tourism Industry Association of Canada, 1996 National Conference on Tourism, Jasper.

Foote, David K., and Stoffman, Daniel. (1998). *Boom, Bust and Echo 2000*. Toronto: Macfarlane Walter & Ross.

Ford's Deck Plan Guide (2002). Northbridge, CA: Ford's Travel Guides. Updated semiannually.

Ford's International Cruise Guide. (2002). Northridge, CA: Ford's Travel Guides. Updated semiannually.

Four Seasons Hotels & Resorts. (Feb. 2008). "About Us," www.fourseasons.com/about_us/.

Francis, Diane. (March 17, 2008). "Wall Street: Casino Meltdown," *Financial Post*.

French, H. (1996). "Canadian Tourism Research Institute Travel Outlook." *Proceedings*, Tourism Industry Association of Canada, Annual Conference, Jasper. Ottawa: Tourism Industry Association of Canada.

The Future Foundation. (May 2008). "Humanity 3000: Think Globally—Act Locally," http://futurefoundation.org/programs/hum_sem8.htm.

Future Watch 2008. (Feb. 2008). www.mpi.org/CMS/Uploaded files/Mortar?FutureWatch2008 Report.

Garth's Profile of Ships. (1996). Omaha, NE: Cruising with Garth.

Geocaching. (n.d.). "Frequently Asked Questions about Geocaching," accessed May 2008 at www.geocaching.com/faq.

George Brown College. (May 2008). School of Hospitality & Tourism Management, www.georgebrown.ca/hospitalityandtourism/programs.aspx.

Getz, Donald. (2007). *Event Studies: Theory, Research and Policy for Planned Events*. Oxford: Butterworth-Heinemann.

———. (1997). *Event Management and Event Tourism*. New York: Cognizant Communications Corporation, pp. 250–53.

Gilbert, John. (1992). *How to Eat an Elephant: A Slice-by-Slice Guide to Total Quality Management*. Merseyside, UK: Tudor Business Publishing Limited.

Gill, Alexandra. (Oct. 20, 2001). "Napa North," *The Globe and Mail*, p. L5 Gillette, Bill. (Dec. 1999). "Franchising in Balance," *Lodging*, Vol. 25, No. 4, pp. 54–57.

Ginzberg, Eli, and Vojta, George J. (March 1981). "The Service Sector of the U.S. Economy," *Scientific American*, Vol. 244, No. 3, pp. 31–39.

Glew, G. (1984). *Advances in Catering Technology*. London: Elsevier Applied Science Publishers.

"Globetrotter: Canada—From Vancouver to Halifax." (April 2001). *The Globe and Mail, Report on Business Magazine*, Vol. 17, No. 10, pp. 135–48.

Glynn, Tony. (Nov. 2001). "Impacts: Lessons from the Past," *Tourism*, Vol. 5, Issue 9, p. 6.

goconcierge. (May 2008). Home page, www.goconcierge.net.

Goodwin, Tom. (May 2000). "Bay of Fundy: 'Thar She Blows . . . !'" *Communiqué*, Vol. 4, Issue 4, p. 21.

Grand Manan Island Times. (June 1997). "Bay of Fundy Water-based Tour Operators Code of Ethics," p. 24.

Grant, Anthony, with Minh Tu Nguyen and Rachel Slaff. (Oct. 10, 2007). "World's Biggest Hotels," *Forbes Traveler*.

Gray, W.S., and Liquori, S.C. (1987). *Hotel and Motel Management and Operations*. Scarborough, ON: Prentice Hall.

Graziani, Jane. (March 8, 2004). "Trend-Setting Hotels Lure Guests with Amenities, Service, Says AAA," Business Wire, www.str-online.com.

Great Canadian Casinos. (May 2008). "Recent Development Trends," *Hotelier*.

Green, C. (Sept. 23, 1994). "Variety Is the Spice of Life for Airlines Eager to Please Hungry Passengers," *Financial Post*, p. B6.

Green, Carolyn. (June 28, 2001). "Plugged-in Flyers Jump the Queue," *National Post*, p. E1.

Green, Jeff. (April 2002). "Mile One Stadium Is about Food," *Atlantic Restaurant News*, Vol. 4, No. 2, p. 16.

Greening, Deb. (April 2002). "Exotic Is—Winter in Canada," *Tourism*, Vol. 6, Issue 3, p. 11.

Greger, Kenneth R., and Peterson, John S. (Feb. 2000). "Leadership Profiles for the New Millennium," *The Cornell Hotel and Restaurant Administration Quarterly*, Vol. 41, No. 1, pp. 16–29.

Guelph Tribune. (June 17, 2008). "Bruce County Promotes 'Staycations'—The Hottest New Form of Travel," p. 10.

Haley, Mark. (July 2003). "WiFi: Crossing the Chasm." *Lodging Hospitality*, p. 47.

Hall, S.J. (1992). "The Emergence of Ethics in Quality," *Ethics in Hospitality Management*. East Lansing, Michigan: Educational Institute of the Hotel and Motel Association, pp. 9–23.

Hamdi, Raini. (June 9, 2008). "Chains Compete for Changing Travelers," *TTG Asia*, www.ttgasia.com/index.php?option= com_content&task=view&id=14204&Itemid=26.

Hartlling, Neil. (Jan.–Feb. 2000). "Sustainable Tourism Means 'Long Term' Returns," *Communiqué*, Vol. 4, Issue 1, p. 13.

Haussman, Glenn. (Sept. 22, 2006). "Lifestyle Hotels Enter Limelight," Hotel Interactive, www.hotelinteractive.com/article .aspx?articleID=6277.

hCareers. (n.d.). Home page, accessed Nov. 20, 2008 at www .hcareers.ca.

Healism. (n.d.). "What Is Medical Tourism?" accessed Sept. 2, 2008 at www.healism.com/Medical_Tourism/Overview/What_is_ Medical_Tourism?/.

Healthbase. (Sept. 7, 2008). "Medical Tourism Guide," www .healthbase.com.

HEDNA's Lisbon Conference. (May 1, 2008). "Technology, Customer Expectations, Environmental Issues Will Drive Near-term Decision Making For Electronic Distribution," www .hospitalitynet.org/news/4035736.search?query=pwc+study+ documents+24+new+hotel+brand+launches+in+2005+and+2006.

Hendsill, C. (March 1997). "Building a Promising PMS," *Hotels*, Vol. 31, No. 3, pp. 83–84.

———. (March 1997). "Destination Dining," *Hotels*, Vol. 31, No. 3, pp. 76–80.

———. (March 1996). "Dining on the High Seas," *Hotels*, Vol. 30, No. 3, pp. 61–66.

Henkoff, R. (June 27, 1994). "Service Is Everybody's Business," *Fortune Magazine* 129, pp. 48–60.

Heyer, Hazel. (June 5, 2008). "Darker Days ahead for Travel Trade, Experts Claim," eturbonews, www.eturbonews.com/2891/ darker-days-ahead-travel-trade-experts-claim.

Hookey, D. (May–June 1997). "Driving the Trail of '98," *Canadian Maturity*, pp. 41–45.

Horowitz, Michael D. (Dec. 2007). "Financial Savings in Medical Tourism," *Medical Tourism*.

Hospitality Sales and Marketing Association International (HSMAI). (May 2008). "Membership," www.hsmai.org/about/ membership.cfm.

Hospitality Through the Ages. Corning, NY: Corning Glass Works Foodservice Products, pp. 8–74.

Hosteur. (Winter 1997). "Industry Talks: A Conversation with Horst Schulze," Vol. 6, No. 2.

"Hotel and Travel Index.com Worldwide." (n.d.). New Concepts Travel Marketing, accessed Nov. 20, 2008 at www .newconcepts.ca/ohgi.htm.

Hotel Association of Canada. (2008). Canada Select Accommodation Rating Program: Follow the Stars to Quality Accommodations. Brochure. www.hotelassociation.ca/site/ programs/canada_select.htm; www.canadaselect.com.

Hughes, Brad. (Sept. 2000). "Winnipeg's Urban Cuisine Tempts Travellers," *Communiqué*, Vol. 4, Issue 9, pp. 6–7.

Hutchinson, Becca. (July 25, 2005). "Medical Tourism Growing Worldwide," interview with Frederick DeMicco and Marvin Cetron. *Udaily* (University of Delaware), www.udel.edu/PR/ UDaily/2005/mar/tourism072505.html.

IATA/ATAC *Travel Agent's Handbook*. (2002). Montreal: International Air Transport Association.

INNVest REIT. (n.d.). "Corporate Profile," accessed June 2008 at www.innvestreit.com/profile.asp.

International Air Transport Association (IATA).(June 2, 2008). "Fuel Crisis a Catalyst for Change," Press release, www.iata .org/pressroom/pr/2008-06-02-02.

———. (Nov. 2007). *Corporate Air Travel Survey (CATS)*. Geneva: IATA.

International Culinary Tourism Association (ICTA). (n.d.). "Introduction to Culinary Tourism," accessed May 2008 at www.culinarytourism.org/?page=intro.

The International Ecotourism Society (TIES). (Sept. 2006). "TIES Fact Sheet: Ecotourism in the U.S.," www.ecotourism.org/ webmodules/webarticlesnet/templates/eco_template.aspx? articleid=15&zoneid=2.

———. (Sept. 2006). "TIES Fact Sheet: Global Ecotourism," www.ecotourism.org/webmodules/webarticlesnet/templates/eco_ template.aspx?articleid=15&zoneid=2.

International Hotel Association. (1995). "Into the Next Millennium." A white paper on the global hospitality industry. Paris: International Hotel and Restaurant Association.

International Scientific Committee on Cultural Tourism (ICOMOS). (1999). "International Cultural Tourism Charter: Managing Tourism at Places of Heritage Significance," www.icomos.org/tourism/charter.html.

International Speakers. (May 2008). "Jan Carlzon," www .internationalspeakers.com/speakers/ISBB-553AKW/Jan_Carlzon/.

Intrawest. (n.d.). "About Us," accessed Nov. 19, 2008 at www .intrawest.com/about-us/index.htm.

———. (n.d.). "Investor Relations," accessed Nov. 19, 2008 at www.intrawest.com/about-us/investors/index.htm

———. (1997–2001). "Company Profile," Vancouver: Intrawest Corporation, accessed Aug. 1998, May 2002 at www.intrawest .com/ about/overview/index.html.

"Intrawest Announces Leadership Change." (Nov. 2006). www.newswire.ca/en/releases/archive/November2006/02/c7730 .html.

Iris, Susan. (March 2001). "Moving Forward CTC U.S. Sales Force," *Communiqué*, Vol. 5, Issue 2, p. 5.

Isherwood, Colleen. (Nov.–Dec. 2000). "The Good News about Saving Energy," *Atlantic Restaurant News*, Vol. 2, No. 6, p. 6.

———. (Fall 1999). "Hotels Report Major Savings through Energy Efficiency," *Atlantic Restaurant News*, Vol. 1, No. 3, p. 4.

Jacob, Rahul. (Oct. 18, 1993). "TQM More than a Dying Fad," *Fortune* 128, p. 66.

JAXFAX Travel Marketing (n.d.). Darien, CT: Jet Airtransport Exchange.

Jepson, T. (1997). *Fodor's Exploring Canada*. Toronto: Fodor's Travel Publications.

Johne, Marjo. (June 28, 2001). "Take Me with You," *National Post*, p. E1.

Johnson, Gary K., and Dumas, Roland A. (Nov. 1992). "How to Improve Quality if You're not in Manufacturing," *Training*, Vol. 29, No. 11, p. 36.

Johnson, Hugh, and Robinson, Jancis. (2001). *The World Atlas of Wine*, 4th ed. Grand Rapids, MI: Zondervan Publishing House.

Jones, C., and Jowett, V. (1998). *Managing Facilities*. Oxford: Butterworth-Heiemann.

Jones, C., and Paul, V. (1993). *Accommodation Management: A Systems Approach:* "The Accommodation Project" (Chapter 1), "The Front Office Dimension" (Chapter 6), and "Quality and Productivity" (Chapter 7). London: B.T. Basford Limited.

Jones, David. (Feb. 4, 2004). "'Self-Service Check-in," *International Herald Tribune*, p. 22.

Judas, Walt. (April 2002). "Vancouver a City of Summer Festivals," *Tourism*: Vol. 6, Issue 3, p. 8.

Kaplan, Max. (1975) *Theory and Policy*. Toronto: John Wiley and Sons, Inc.

Karafil, Brad. (Oct. 2000). "Canada on Top for Helicopter and Snowcat Skiing," *Communiqué*, Vol. 4, Issue 9, p. 4.

Kasavana, Michael. (March 12, 2008). "The Convergence of Self-service Technology," *Hospitality Upgrade* (Spring 2008), www.hospitalityupgrade.com/_magazine/magazine_Detail.asp?ID=278.

Katz, Helena. (Jan.–Feb. 2001). "CTC 'Puts on the Crown,'" *Communiqué*, Vol. 5, Issue 1, pp. 1, 3.

Kazemi, Zahra. (2007). "Study of the Effective Factors for Attracting Medical Tourists to Iran." Master's Thesis. University of Isfahan, Iran.

Keffe, Cathy. (Oct. 8, 2003). "New Survey Shows Americans Willing to Pay Higher Costs for Travel Services that Protect and Preserve the Environment," Travel Industry Association of America, www.tia.org/press/releases.

Kelly, Deidre. (Oct. 13, 2001). "The Sip that Civilizes," *The Globe and Mail*, p. L5.

Kelly, John R. (1982). *Leisure*. Toronto: Prentice-Hall Canada Inc.

Khan, Mahmood A. (1999). *Restaurant Franchising*, 2nd edition. New York: John Wiley & Sons, Inc., pp. 2–4.

Kingsmill, Peter. (Summer 2001). "Changing Ownership Patterns," *Communiqué*, Vol. 5, Issue 6, p. 7.

———. (Summer 2001). "Expanding the Experience," *Communiqué*, Vol. 5, Issue 6, p. 6.

———. (Summer 2001). "Resorts and Parks: Priorities in Conflict?" *Communiqué*, Vol. 5, Issue 6, p. 7.

———. (Summer 2001). "Resorts: The Archetypical Vacation Destination," *Communiqué*, Vol. 5, Issue 6, p. 2.

———. (Nov. 2001). "Snowmobiling: A Product in Evolution," *Tourism*, Vol. 5, Issue 9, p. 9.

———. (Oct. 1999). "The Eco-tourism Product Club," *Communiqué*, Vol. 3, Issue 8, p. 19.

Kingston, B. (July 4, 1994). "Airline Kosher Fare Approaches 'Haute Cuisine,'" *Financial Post*, p. S12.

Klinkenberg, Marty. (Jan. 27, 2001). "Canadian Grapes meet Big Apple," *The Globe and Mail*, p. R16.

Kloos, Geoff. (July–Aug. 2000). "Trails System Gives New Life to Rail Travel," *Communiqué*, Vol. 4, Issue 6, p. 9.

Knutson, B., Stevens, P., Wullaert, C., Patton, M., and Yokoyama, F. (1991). "LODGSERV: A Service Quality Index for the Lodging Industry," *Hospitality Research Journal*, Vol. 14, No. 2, pp. 277–84.

Kooy, Racelle. (Dec. 2000). "Aboriginal Arts and Crafts Fulfill Tourists' Quest for Authenticity," *Communiqué*, Vol. 4, Issue 11, p. 4.

———. (Jan.–Feb. 2002). "From Slahal to Slots: Aboriginal Casinos across Canada," *Tourism*, Vol. 6, Issue 1, p. 8.

Kostuch, M.J. (1975). "Canadian Menu Manual," *Foodservice and Hospitality Magazine*. Toronto: Canadian Restaurant Association.

Kovaleski, Dave. (June 1, 2007). "The New Attrition," http://meetingsnet.com/associationmeetings/trends/meetings_new_attrition/index.html.

Krems Research. (July 13, 2007). "Analysis of Blogs for Strategy Development in Tourism," Press release, www.kremsresearch.at/en/presse_blogsconference.php.

Kurtti, Jeff. (1996). *Since the World Began: Walt Disney World the First 25 Years*. New York: A Roundtable Press Book by Hyperion.

Lancaster, John. (March 2007). "'Next Stop, Squalor': Is Poverty Tourism 'Poorism,' They Call It Exploration or Exploitation?" *Smithsonian* magazine, www.smithsonianmag.com/people-places/squalor.html?c=y&page=1.

Lane, H.E., and van Hartsevelt, M. (1983). *Essentials of Hospitality Administration*. Reston, Virginia: Reston Publishing Company, Inc.

Lane, Harold E., and Dupre, Denise. (1997). *Hospitality World!* Toronto: Van Nostrand Reinhold.

Laplante, Roger. (Nov. 2000). "Japan Consumer Study 2000: Key Findings Released," *Communiqué*, Vol. 4, Issue 10, pp. 21–22.

Las Vegas Convention and Visitors Authority (LVCVA). (n.d.). "About Us, "accessed June 2008 at www.lvcva.com/about/index.jsp.

Lavecchia, Gina. (Aug. 2000). "Next Generation Take-out," *Restaurant Hospitality*, Vol. LXXXIV, No. 8, p. 50.

Layton, Ann. (July 2001). "Environmentally Responsible Hotel Practices." Speech made at the International CHRIE Conference, Toronto.

Le Baccara Restaurant. (June 2008). Casino du Lac Lemy Casinos du Quebec, www.casinosduquebec.com/lacleamy/fr/restaurants-bars.

Legacy REIT. (June 2008). Home page, www.legacyhotels.ca.

Legends Dubailand. (Nov. 5, 2006). "Legends Dubai, Hosts Children Events at Its Headquarters," Press release, www.legendsdubai.ae/press/0019.htm.

Leidl, David, and Wiseman, Les. (Sept.–Oct. 1999). "A Brief History of Cuisine during the Past Millennium," *Hospitality Today*, Vol. 2, No. 5, pp. 4–16.

Leong, Kristiie. (Jan 21, 2008). "2008 Restaurant Food Trends," Associated Content, www.associatedcontent.com/article/542771/2008_restaurant_food_trends.html.

Levitt, Theodore. (May–June 1981). "Marketing Intangible Products and Product Intangibles," *Harvard Business Review*, Vol. 59, No. 3, pp. 94–102.

Lewison, Dale M. (1995). *Retailing*, 4th ed. Toronto: Macmillan.

Living Legends, Dubailand. (June 22, 2008). "The Legend," www.livinglegendsdubai.com/thelegend.html.

Lodging. (Dec. 1999). "Best Western's Direct Democracy: Inviting Chaos or Control," Vol. 25, No. 4, p.58.

———. (Oct. 1999). "Management Diversity: Special Report," Vol. 25, No. 2, pp. 16–17, 22.

"Looking Back." (May–June 1999). Top ten developments; top ten new hotels; top ten mergers; ten memorable hotel closings; top ten movers and shakers; top ten dining rooms, *Hotelier*, Vol. 11, No. 3, pp. 23–34.

Lorenzini, B. (Oct. 21, 1992). "The Secure Restaurant," *Restaurants and Institutions*, Vol. 102, No. 25, pp. 84–102.

Lovelock, Christopher H. (Summer 1983). "Classifying Services to Gain Strategic Marketing Insights," *Journal of Marketing*, 47, pp. 9–20.

Lynch, Allan. (May–June 2000). "Eat, Drink and Be Profitable," *Hotelier*, Vol. 12, No. 3, pp. 47–49.

———. (May–June 1999). "Greening the Bottom Line," *Hotelier*, Vol. 11, No. 3, p. 7.

Lynds, Corinne. (Jan./Feb. 2003). "Technology: The Roundtable," *Hotelier*, p. 40.

Macau.com. (n.d.). "Your Official Insider," accessed June 2008 at www.macau.com/index.php?option=com_content&task=view&id=19&Itemid=82.

MacDonald, Heather, and Denault, Mylene. (June 2001). *National Tourism & Cuisine Forum: Recipes for Success: Proceedings and Final Report*. Ottawa: Canadian Tourism Commission.

MacLean, Janet R., Peterson, James A., and Martin, W. Donald. (1985). *Recreation and Leisure: The Changing Scene*, 4th ed. New York: Macmillan Publishing Company.

Maher, Stephen. (Dec. 30, 2001). "The Best of 2001," *The Sunday Herald*, p. B4.

Maister, D.W. (1984). "The Psychology of Waiting in Line," *Harvard Business School Note* 9-684-064 (rev. May 1984), pp. 2–3.

Marriott International Inc. (April 1, 2004). "Marriott Offers more than 1,200 Hotels with WiFi High-Speed Internet Access," *PR Newswire*, www.str-online.com.

Marris, T. (1987). "The Role and Impact of Mega-events and Attractions on Regional and National Tourism Development: Resolutions of the 37th Congress of the AIEST, Calgary," *Revue de Tourisme*, No. 4, pp. 3–12.

Marron, Kevin. (March 9, 2000). "Friend or Foe to Frequent Fliers?" *The Globe and Mail*, http://businesstravel.about.com/index.htm.

———. (March 9, 2000). "Travel Agents Worry They Won't Pass Go in New Monopoly," *The Globe and Mail*, http://businesstravel.about.com/index.htm.

Matthews, Carol. (Jan./Feb. 2001). "Mix, Mingle and Learn," *Saltscapes*, Vol. 2, No. 1, p. 61.

Mazankowski, Hon. Donald. (1985). *Freedom to Move*. White paper on transportation regulatory reform in Canada. Ottawa: Ministry of Transport.

McArthur, Douglas. (March 21, 2001). "Female Guests Still Puzzle Hotels," *The Globe and Mail*, www.globeandmail.com/travel/womentravellers.

McCormick Place. (May 2008). "Facilities," www.mccormickplace.com/facilities/facilities_01.html.

McCormick, Rosemary. (May 2008). "Tourism 101: Basic Information for Selling to Tourists," Shop America Alliance, www.uscht.com.

McDougall, Laurie. (Dec. 1999). "Seniors a Market to Watch," *Communiqué*, Vol. 3, Issue 10, p. 5.

McElroy, Victoria. (n.d.). "Sacred Integrity: The Need for Cultural Integrity in the New Age," www.geocities.com/Athens/8991/need.htm.

McGinn, Dave. (Jan. 21, 2008). "Sun, Sand and Surgery," *The Globe and Mail*.

McIntosh, Robert W., Goeldner, Charles R., and Ritchie, Brent J.R. (1995). *Tourism Principles, Practices, Philosophies*. Toronto: John Wiley & Sons, Inc.

McKinnon Clinton, Dan. (1986). *Everything You Need to Know Before You're Hijacked*. San Diego, CA: Location FSL Library, House of Hits Inc.

McNulty, Mary Ann. (Sept. 2003). "Project Attrition," The Convention Industry Council, www.conventionindustry.org.

———. (Sept. 2003). "Pandora's Box," *Convene* 42, www.pcma.org/resources/convene/archives.

Medical Tourism. (Jan. 3, 2008). "A Worldwide Market," http://marketing2tourism.wordpress.com/208/01/02/medical-tourism-supplement.

Medical Tourism Guide. (2007). "12 Reasons Medical Tourism Is So Popular," www.medicaltourismguide.org/12reasons/.

———. (2007). "Risks of Medical Tourism," www.medicaltourismguide.org/risks/.

Meetings and Incentive Travel. (Feb. 2000). "The Corporate Planner Survey 2000: Meetings and Incentive Trends," Vol. 28, No. 7, pp. 22–37.

Meeting Planners International. (2004). "Future Watch 2004," www.mpiweb.org.

Meeting Planners International (MPI) Canada. (n.d.). "VERTigo Plan to Meet Green," accessed Nov. 19, 2008 at www.mpiweb.org/CMS/mpiweb/mpicontent.aspx?id=159&printview=1.

Meis, Scott. (Aug. 2004). "Research Viewpoint: Is the Tourism Sector Solidly on the Road to Recovery?" *Tourism*, Vol. 1, Issue 7.

———. (Dec. 1999). "WTO Endorses Tourism Measurement System," *Communiqué*, Vol. 3, Issue 10, p. 4.

Meis, Scott, and Naylor, Rick. (1996). "Canadian Tourism Commission." *Proceedings of the 1996 National Conference on Tourism*.

Mellander, Tricia. (Nov. 2000). "Northern Lights Are Canada's Natural Fireworks Attraction," *Communiqué*, Vol. 4, Issue 10, p. 7.

Metro Toronto Convention Centre. (May 2008). Home page, www.mtccc.com.

Michaelides, Stephen. (Sept. 2000). "Strange Bedfellows," *Restaurant Hospitality*, Vol. LXXIV, No. 9, pp. 54–66.

Mieczkowski, Z.T. (1981). "Some Notes on the Geography of Tourism: A Comment," *Canadian Geographer*, 25, pp. 186–91.

Miles, Taylor. (n.d.). "Medical Tourism Marketing, the Newest Trend in Marketing Travel," accessed Aug. 2008 at www.content4reprint.com/business/advertising/medical-tourism-marketing-the-newest-trend-in-marketing-travel.htm.

Milliman, Ronald E. (Summer 1982). "Using Background Music to Affect the Behaviour of Supermarket Shoppers," *Journal of Marketing*, Vol. 56, No. 3, pp. 86–91.

Mohan, Marilyn, Gislason, G., and McGowan, B. (1998). *Towards Related Employment: An Update*. Ottawa: Canadian Tourism Human Resource Council.

Mowat, Bob. (Nov. 2000). "New Entrants Flock to Canada's Airline Industry," *Communiqué*, Vol. 4, Issue 10, p. 12.

———. (June 2000). "Strategy Ratchets up Competition in a Wireless World," *Communiqué*, Vol. 4, Issue 5, p. 15.

———. (April 2000). "The Gloves Are off as Industry Becomes Multi-channel," *Communiqué*, Vol. 4, Issue 3, p. 11.

Mulroney, Catherine. (March 9, 2000). "Flying Takes Increasingly Big Bite of Travel Budget," *The Globe and Mail*, www.globeandmail.com/travel/travel budget.

Munroe, Susan. (Oct. 5, 2002). "New National Parks for Canada," http://canadaonline.about.com/od/parksincanada/a/newwparks.htm.

Mwakugu, Noel. (Nov. 28, 2003). "Kenya Mourns a Year after the Attack," BBC News, http://news.bbc.co.ik/1/hi/world/africa/3243042.stm.

National Geographic Center for Sustainable Destinations. (n.d.). "About Geotourism," accessed Nov. 29, 2008 at www.nationalgeographic.com/travel/sustainable/about_geotourism.html.

National Restaurant Association (NRA). (Nov. 29, 2007). "Small Is Big on Restaurant Menus and Craft Beer Tops Beverage Trend, National Restaurant Association Research Finds," www.restaurant.org.

National Ski Areas Association (NSAA). (June 2008). "National Skier Visits Top 60 Million," www.nsaa.org/nsaa/home/.

Net Global Indexes LLC. (June 2008). www.gaming.netglobalindexes.com.

New Brunswick Outdoor Adventure Guide. (1997). 1997 ed. Fredericton: New Brunswick Department of Economic Development and Culture, pp. 1–31.

"New Partnership Raises Environmental and Social Standards in Tourism Industry." (Feb. 12, 2004). The International Ecotourism Society, www.ecotourism.org.

Niagara College. (n.d.). "Wine Business Management," accessed Nov. 20, 2008 at www.niagaracollege.ca/programs/wbm_0275/.

Niagara's Seasons: Niagara Visitors Guide 2000–2001. (2001). Thorold, ON: Niagara Economic & Tourism Corporation.

Nicholls, Matt. (Feb. 2000). "Faces in the Crowd: Just Who Is Responsible for Planning these Programs Anyway?" *Meetings and Incentive Travel*, Vol. 28, No. 7, p. 5.

Northstar Travel Media. (June 2008). "History," www.northstartravelmedia.com/about.aspx?id=his.

Nova Scotia Complete Guide for Doers and Dreamers. (2002). 2002 ed. Halifax: Nova Scotia Department of Tourism and Culture.

Nova Scotia Tourism Human Resource Council. (n.d.). "Student Travel Map," accessed Nov. 20, 2008 at www.tourismhrc.com/student-travel-map.php.

Novo, Jim. (2004). *Drilling Down*, 3rd ed. Booklocker.com (www.booklocker.com).

OAG Travel Planners Hotel and Motel Red Book. (2002). European, North American, and Pacific Asia editions. Oak Brook, IL: Official Airline Guides Inc.

Octeau, Lucie. (Dec. 2001). "Healthy Potential for Health Tourism," *Tourism*: Vol. 5, Issue 10, p. 17.

Office of the Privacy Commissioner of Canada. (April 13, 2000). Privacy Legislation. PIPEDA. The Official version of the Act, Bill C-6. Protection of Privacy Sector. 48-49 Elizabeth ll. Chapter 5. Part 1. Purpose. "Protection of Personal Information in the Private Sector," www2.parl.gc.ca/HousePublications/Publication.aspx?pub=bill&doc=C-6&parl=36&ses=2&language=E&File=35.

Official Airline Guide, North American Edition. Oak Brook, IL: Official Airline Guides.

Official Airline Guide, Worldwide Edition. Oak Brook, IL: Official Airline Guides.

Official Railway Guide, North American Edition. New York: Thompson Transport Press. Bimonthly.

Official Sightseeing Sales and Tour Guide. Dallas: Gray Line Worldwide.

Official Steamship Guide International. New Canaan, CT: Transport Guides Inc.

Official Tour Directory. New York: Thomas Publishing.

Oliver Bonacini Restaurants. (Feb. 2008). "Our Company," www.oliverbonacini.com/company_profile.html.

Olsen, M. (1995). "Into the Next Millennium." A white paper on the global hospitality industry. Paris: The International Hotel Association.

Olsen, Michael D., and Connolly, Daniel J. (Feb. 2000). "Experienced-based Travel: How Technology Is Changing the Hospitality Industry," *The Cornell Hotel and Restaurant Administration Quarterly*, Vol. 41, No. 1, pp. 30–40.

Ontario's Finest Spas. (May 2008). "About Us," www.ontariosfinestspas.com/spas_about_us.html.

The Ontario Restaurant Hotel Motel Association (ORHMA). (June 2008). BYOB. "Bring Your Own Wine and Take Home The Rest," www.orhma.com/gr/new_gr/bev_alc.asp#wine.

———. (May 2008). "Smoke Free Ontario Act," www.orhma.com/gr/new_gr/smoke_free.asp.

Ontario Tourism Investment Communique. (Winter 2008). Ontario Ministry of Tourism: Toronto Fast Facts, http://ontariotourisminvestment.com/en/toronto/fast-facts.

Otte, S. (Oct.–Nov.1996). "Software Makes Jobs Easier for Caterers," *Onboard Services*, p. 5.

Page, Jean Guy. (March 2001). "Snow Sports Seek Sustainability," *Communiqué*, Vol. 5, Issue 3, p. 11.

Paradigm Events. (June 2008). Home page, www.paradigmevents.com.

Parasuraman, A., Berry, Leonard A., and Zeithmal, Valerie A. (Winter 1991). "Refinement and Reassessment of the SERVQUAL Scale," *Journal of Retailing*, Vol. 67, pp. 420–50.

Parasuraman A., Zeithaml, V.A., and Berry, L. (Aug. 1986). "SERVQUAL: A Multiple-item Scale for Measuring Customer Perceptions of Service Quality." Cambridge, MA: Marketing Science Institute, Working Paper Report No. 86-108.

———. (1985). "A Conceptual Model of Service Quality and its Implications for Future Research," *Journal of Marketing*, Vol. 49, pp. 41–50.

Parks Canada. (n.d.). "About Us," accessed Feb. 17, 2008 at www.pc.gc.ca/agen/index_e.asp.

———. (n.d.). "Campground Reservation Service," accessed Feb. 17, 2008 at www.pc.gc.ca/voyage-travel/reserve/index_E.asp.

———. (n.d.). "National Historic Sites of Canada" accessed Feb. 17, 2008 at www.parkscanada.pch.gc.ca/apps/lhn-nhs/lst_e.asp.

———. (n.d.). "National Parks of Canada" accessed Feb. 17, 2008 at www.parkscanada.pch.gc.ca/progs/np-pn/index_E.asp.

———. (n.d.)."What Is Ecological Integrity?" accessed March 15, 2004 at www.parkscanada.pch.gc.ca/progs/np-pa/eco-integ/index_E.asp.

———. (2007). *Departmental Performance Report 2006–2007 Challenges and Opportunities Affecting Performance. Establish Heritage Places*, www.tbs-sct.gc.ca/dpr-rmr/2006-2007/inst/cap/cap01-eng.asp.

PATA News. (June 5, 2008). "Fuel Price Rises Put Global Prosperity at Risk," www.pata.org/patasite/index.php?id=1303.

Pearce, Douglas. (1989). *Tourism Development*, 2nd ed. Toronto: John Wiley and Sons Inc.

Pengelly, Heather (Jan.–Feb. 2001). "Want To Be a Product Club . . . Are You Ready?" *Communiqué*, Vol. 5, Issue 1, p. 16.

Petruzzi, Mark T. (Oct. 1999). "Green Purchasing in Hotels," *Lodging*, Vol. 25, No. 2, p. 71.

Phillips, Lynn. (June 2000). "Coast to Coast Gardens," *Communiqué*, Vol. 4, Issue 5, p. 6.

———. (June 2000). "Fish Lure the Tourist at Canada's Aquariums," *Communiqué*, Vol. 4, Issue 5, p. 5.

PhoCusWright. (May 2007). *PhoCusWright Consumer Travel Trends Survey, 9th ed.* Sherman, CT: Author.

PKF. (March 10, 2008). "PKF Hospitality Research Lowers its 2008 Forecast for a Key Hotel Industry Metric, RevPAR, from Up 4.5% to Up a Below-average 3.0%," www.hotel-online.com/News/PR2008_1st/Mar08_PKFOutlook.html.

Plaine, Martha. (April 2001). "Learning in the Wilds of Canada," *Communiqué*, Vol. 5, Issue 3, p. 5.

———. (March 2001). "Selling Canada to U.S. Meeting Planners," *Communiqué*, Vol. 5, Issue 2, p. 9.

———. (March 2001). "Sophisticated Travellers Seek Learning Vacations," *Communiqué*, Vol. 5, Issue 2, p. 9.

———. (Dec. 2000). "Spiritual Tourism: A New Spin on an Old Tradition," *Communiqué*, Vol. 4, Issue 11, p. 14.

———. (Sept. 2000). "The Naserati Canada 10,000 challenge," *Communiqué*, Vol. 4, Issue 9, pp. 18–19.

———. (June 2000). "Getting Out of the Box Attractions Going after M&IT Market," *Communiqué*, Vol. 4, Issue 5, p. 16.

———. (June 2000). "National Parks as Feature Attractions: Balancing Tourism and Ecological Integrity," *Communiqué*, Vol. 4, Issue 5, pp. 1, 3, 4.

Plog, Stanley C. (1991). *Leisure Travel: Making It a Growth Market Again.* Toronto: John Wiley and Sons, Inc.

Polovitz Nickerson, N. (1996). *Foundations of Tourism*, Scarborough: Prentice Hall.

Polovitz Nickerson, Norma, and Kerr, Paula. (2001). *Snapshots*, 2nd Cdn. ed. Toronto: Prentice-Hall Inc.

Prashad, Sharda. (Aug. 18, 2008). "The World Is Your Hospital," *Canadian Business.*

Pratson, Frederick. (1995). *Guide to Eastern Canada*, 5th ed. Edited by Helga Loverseed. Old Saybrook, Connecticut: The Globe Pequot Press.

Premier Spas of Ontario. (June 2008). Home page, www.premierspasofontario.ca.

Pricewaterhouse Coopers (PwC). (Sept. 12, 2005). "European Lifestyle Hotel Survey," www.pwc.com/uk.

———. (Sept. 12, 2005). "The Secret of Lifestyle Hotels' Popularity Is Simple: They Are in Tune with the Needs of the New, Complex Consumer," Hospitality Directions. Europe Edition, www.pwc.com/uk.

Prokosh, K. (Aug. 24, 1991). "Airlines Introduce New Menus," *Winnipeg Free Press*, p. 54.

Quek, Patrick. (Oct. 1999). "Beds, Breakfasts, and Bucks," *Lodging*, Vol. 25, No. 2, pp. 29–30.

Ramos, Rachel Tobin. (Nov. 23, 2007). "Atlanta the New Birthplace of the Hot Hotel," *Atlanta Business Chronicle*,

http://atlanta.bizjournals.com/atlanta/stories/2007/11/26/newscolumn3.html.

Rayport, Jeffrey F., and Sviokla, John J. (1994). "Managing in the Marketspace," *Harvard Business Review*, Nov.–Dec., pp. 141–50.

Reader's Digest Canada Coast to Coast. (1998). Montreal: The Reader's Digest Association (Canada) Ltd.

Redekop, David. (July 1997). *Travel Forecast 2000: Twenty-one Questions for the 21st Century.* Ottawa: Canadian Tourism Research Institute for the Conference Board of Canada.

Renzetti, Elizabeth. (Jan. 27, 2001). "A Room, Please—To Go," *The Globe and Mail*, p. R5.

Reuters. (Feb. 20, 2004). "Report Highlights World Travel Risks," http://edition.cnn.com/2004/TRAVEL/02/20/biz.trav.travel.risk.reut.

"The Revitalization of VIA Rail." (2000). *Transport Action 2000*. Ottawa: Transport Canada, Vol. 22, Nos. 5/6, pp. 1–2.

Riper, Tom Van. (Jan. 18, 2008). "World's 10 Largest Shopping Malls," Forbes.com, www.forbes.com/2007/01/09/malls-worlds-largest-biz-cx_tvr_0109malls_slide_9.html?thisSpeed=15000.

"ROB Magazine's (3rd) Annual Ranking of Canada's Top Employers by Hewitt Associates." (Jan. 2002). *The Globe and Mail Report on Business Magazine*, Vol. 18, No. 7, pp. 41–52.

Robbins, Mike. (Oct. 1999). "Ecotourism a Missed Opportunity," *Communiqué*, Vol. 3, Issue 8, p. 20.

"Room with a Tyke's-Eye View." (June 1997). *Chatelaine*, p. 26.

Rouleau, Danielle. (May–June 1999). "Blue Skies," *Hotelier Special Report*, p. 7.

Royal Airlines Annual Report. (1999). Toronto: Royal Airlines.

Royal Host REIT. (June 2008). "Corporate Profile," www.royalhost.com/corporate/index.aspx.

Ruiz, Rebecca. (Jan. 17, 2008). "World's Most Dangerous Destinations," *Forbes*, www.forbes.com/travel/2008/01/16/travel-world-dangerous-forbeslife-cx_rr_0117travel.html.

Rumley, Margot. (May 2001). "Nova Scotia Supporting Study Tours," *Communiqué*, Vol. 5, Issue 4, p. 6.

———. (June 2000). "Nova Scotia Builds Professionalism among Festivals and Events through Teamwork," *Communiqué*, Vol. 4, Issue 5, p. 5.

Runzheimer Guide to Daily Travel Prices. (1996). Rochester, WI: Runzheimer International.

Russell's Official Canada Bus Guide. Cedar Rapids, IA: Russell's Guides Inc.

Russell's Official Motorcoach Guide. Cedar rapids, IA: Russell's Guides Inc.

Saltzman, Toby. (Feb. 2000). "Meetings that Move . . . ," *Meetings and Incentive Travel*, Vol. 28, No. 7, pp. 38–46.

Savard, Jolyne. (July–Aug. 2000). "Bill C-26 to Enable Collective Negotiation," *Communiqué*, Vol. 4, Issue 6, p. 10.

Scenic Caves Nature Adventures. (June 2008). "Ecoadventure Tour," www.sceniccaves.com/cms/summer.cfm?dsp=Main& Issue ID=9.

Schneider, Benjamin. (Autumn 1980). "The Service Organization Climate Is Crucial," *Organizational Dynamics*, pp. 52–65.

Scoviak-Lerner, M. (March 1996). "Ecofriendly Retreat in the Arizona Desert," *Hotels*, Vol. 30, No. 3, pp. 43–44.

Seaforth, Carolyn. (Oct. 2000). "Hard Work Pays off with Travel Rewards," in Wintrob, Suzanne (Oct. 10, 2000), special to *The Globe and Mail*, www.globeandmail.com/travel/travelrewards.

Searle, Mark S., and Brayley, Russell E. (1993). *Leisure Services in Canada: An Introduction*. State College, PA: Venture Publishing, Inc.

Sessoms, Douglas, H. (Nov. 1975). "Our Body of Knowledge: Myth or Reality?" *Parks and Recreation*, Vol. 10, No. 11, p. 30.

SFGate. (March 12, 2004). "Nearly 200 Dead in Madrid—Basques Suspected," *San Francisco Chronicle*, www.sfgate.com/cgi-bin/article.cgi?f=/c/a/2004/03/12/SPAIN.TMP.

Shaw, Duff. (Oct. 2000). "Hard Work Pays off with Travel Rewards," in Wintrob, Suzanne (Oct. 10, 2000), special to *The Globe and Mail*, www.globeandmail.com/travel/travel rewards.

Shaw, S. (1990). "Where Has All the Leisure Gone? The Distribution and Redistribution of Leisure." In B. Smale (ed.), *Proceedings from the Sixth Canadian Congress on Leisure Research*. Waterloo, ON: University of Waterloo Press, pp. 1–5.

Shock, Patti J., and Stefanelli, John M. (1992). *Hotel Catering: A Handbook for Sales and Operations*. Toronto: John Wiley and Sons Inc.

Shundich, S. (March 1997). "Champions of Green Housekeeping," *Hotels*, Vol. 31, No. 3, pp. 49–58.

———. (March 1997). "Green Hotelkeeping Information Available Worldwide," *Hotels*, Vol. 31, No. 3, p. 58.

———. (March 1996). "Ecoresorts: Dollars, Sense, and the Environment," *Hotels*, Vol. 30, No. 3, p. 58.

Silcoff, S. (May 11, 2001). "Long-term Rise in Cara no Mistake," *Financial Post*, p. D3.

Skerry, John H. (1972). *The Laws of Innkeepers*. Ithaca, NY: Cornell University Press, pp. 2–8.

Smith, Stephen. (1995). *Tourism Analysis: A Handbook*, 2nd ed. Essex, England: Longman Group Limited.

Smith Travel Research. (Jan. 4, 2004). "Toronto Hotels to Help Counter SARS Scare," www.smithtravelresearch.com.

Smithsonian Study Tours. (Jan. 10, 2002). "Cuisines of Quebec," Smithsonian Study Tours website, www.smithsonianstudytours.com/sst/uscan/tours/082801/quebec.htm.

Solomon, Michael R. (1988). "Packaging the Service Provider." In Christopher H. Lovelock, ed., *Managing Services Marketing, Operations, and Human Resources*. Toronto: Prentice-Hall, pp. 318–24.

Sommers, Montrose S., and Barnes, James G. (2001). *Fundamentals of Marketing*, 9th Cdn. ed. Toronto: McGraw-Hill Ryerson.

South African National Parks (SANParks). (2003). "A New Look at Conservation," www.parks-sa.co.za.

———. (2003). "Social Ecology—An Idea whose Time Has Come," www.parks-sa.co.za.

Spangenburg, Eric R., Cowley, Ayn E., and Henderson, Pamela W. (April 1986). "Improving the Store Environment: Do Olfactory Cues Affect Evaluations and Behaviors?" *Journal of Marketing*, Vol. 60, pp. 67–80.

Springer, M. (Feb. 1996). "Unusual Design Defines Lufthansa's Tableware," *Onboard Services*, pp. 23–24.

Stalker, Ian (March 2001). "Celebrating Spring across Canada," *Communiqué*, Vol. 5, Issue 2, p. 7.

———. (Sept. 2000). "Snowboarders Welcomed at Banff," *Communiqué*, Vol. 4, Issue 9, p. 11.

———. (July–Aug. 2000). "Selling Clients on the Trans Canada Trail," *Communiqué*, Vol. 4, Issue 6, pp. 9–10.

———. (March 2000). "Ski Destinations Look to Golf Market," *Communiqué*, Vol. 4, Issue 2, p. 9.

Stanwick, Bill. (Dec. 13, 1999). In "Growth in Canadian Business Travel to Be Fueled by Mid-sized Companies." News releases on Amex Canada website, http://home3.americanexpress.com/canada/aboutamex/newreleases.html or contact Audrey Adams White, Toronto: Amex Canada Inc.

The Star Awards. (May 2008). The 11th Annual Canadian Events Industry Awards 2008 Nominees, www.canadianspecialevents.com/ceia/ceia_nom_win.html.

Statistics Canada. (April 21, 2008). "Tourism Satellite Account: Human Resource Module," *The Daily*, www.statcan.gc.ca/Daily/English/080421/d080421c.htm.

———. (March 27, 2008). "National Tourism Indicators," *The Daily*, www.statcan.gc.ca/Daily/English/080327/d080327a.htm.

———. (Feb. 28, 2008). "International Travel Account," *The Daily*, www.statcan.gc.ca/Daily/English/080228/d080228b.htm.

———. (2007). *Exchange Rates, 2003 to 2007*, www40.statcan.gc.ca/l01/cst01/econ07.htm.

Stemming, Brian. (Jan./Feb. 2003). "Lunch to Go," *Hotelier*, p. 20.

Stevens, Blair. (June 1999). "Canada Shows Leadership at the UN Sustainable Development Meeting," *Communiqué*, Vol. 3, Issue 5, p. 16.

The Student's Travel Map: A Guide to Tourism Courses, Education and Training. (2002). Ottawa: The Canadian Tourism Human Resource Council.

Suddaby, Charles. (June 2000). "Capital Expenditures a Moving Target," *Communiqué*, Vol. 4, Issue 5, pp. 17–18.

Summary and Recommendations from Seminar "Tourism Policy and Economic Growth," Berlin, Germany. (March 6–7, 2001). Paris, France: Organization for Economic Co-Operation and Development in partnership with Canadian Tourism Commission, the federal Ministry of Economics and Technology of Germany, the Secretariat of State for Tourism of Mexico, and the State Secretariat for Economic Affairs of Switzerland.

Suraci, T. (Oct. 2001). Personal correspondence with Director of Marketing. Toronto: Oliver Bonacini Head Office.

Sweeny, Dermot. (May–June 1999). In "Shifting designs" by Andre LaRivere, *Hotelier*, Vol. 11, No. 3, pp. 39–43.

Szwender, G., Waugh, D., and Campbell, B. (1996). *Access Canada: A Barrier-Free Standards and Rating Program, Operator's Manual.* Toronto: Hotel Association of Canada.

"Taste of Nova Scotia Member Restaurants 2001." (2001). Truro, NS: Taste of Nova Scotia Society.

Taylor Parets, Robyn. (Dec. 1999). "Radisson's Shift to Management Is a Shot across the Bow of Under-performing Franchisees," *Lodging*, Vol. 25, No. 4, pp. 61–64.

Taylor, Rod. (Nov. 2000). "Dogsledding: An Industry Perspective," *Communiqué*, Vol. 4, Issue 10, pp. 4–5.

TEA/ERA Theme Park Attendance Report 2006. (April 2007). Published with April 2007 issue of *Park World*, www .connectingindustry.com/pdfs/TEA-ERA.attendance06.

Theberge, Sylvie. (April 2002). "Event Certification: Quality on Tap," *Tourism*, Vol. 6, Issue 3, p. 9.

Thomas Cook Continental Timetable. Peterborough, UK: Thomas Cook Ltd. Published monthly, seasonally.

Thomas Cook Group plc. (n.d.). "About Us," accessed May 2008 at www.thomascookgroup.com/AniteNextPage.asp?p= TCGABOUTUS&s=882730399.

———. (n.d.). "Welcome to the Thomas Cook Group PLC Corporate Website," accessed May 2008, at www.thomascookgroup .com/AniteNextPage.asp?p=TCGHOME&s=882730399.

Thomas Cook Overseas Timetable. Peterborough, UK: Thomas Cook Ltd. Published bimonthly.

"Toronto Hotels to Help Counter SARS Scare." (Jan. 4, 2004). *Milwaukee Journal Sentinel.* p. 6H, www.str-online.com.

Tourism. (July 2004). "First Quarter Tourism Spending up," Vol. 1, Issue 6.

———. (June 2004). "A Monthly Guide to Travel and Tourism Data," Vol. 1, Issue 5.

———. (May 2004). "The Outlook for Summer: It Depends on Who's Talking," Vol. 1, Issue 4.

———. (May 2002). "Golf Industry Shoots for U.S. Market," Vol. 6, Issue 4, p. 11.

———. (April 2002). "New Partners in Tourism Promotion," Vol. 6, Issue 3, p. 13.

———. (April 2002). "Northern Festivals Celebrate Living Heritage," Vol. 6, Issue 3, p. 8.

———. (April 2002). "Parks Canada and TIAC Sign Historic Accord," Vol. 6, Issue 3, p. 12.

———. (April 2002). "The 'Promised Land' for festivals," Vol. 6, Issue 3, p. 6

———. (Jan.–Feb. 2002). "Ontario Casinos Gateways to Tourism," Vol. 6, Issue 1, p. 7.

———. (Jan.–Feb. 2002). "Weak Economy Hinders Tourism Recovery," Vol. 6, Issue 1, p. 5.

———. (Dec. 2001). "Sport Tourism Means Good Business!" Vol. 5, Issue 10, p. 14.

———. (Dec. 2001). "Tobin Launches Travel Canada Marketing Campaign," Vol. 5, Issue 10, p. 4.

———. (Nov. 2001). "Tourism Economy Falling into Recession before September 11," Vol. 5, Issue 9, p. 6.

———. (Nov. 2001). "Future Shock: Tourism in the Wake of September 11," Vol. 5, Issue 9, p. 6.

Tourism Industry Association of Canada (TIAC). (Feb. 2008). "Labour/Human Resources," www.tiac-aitc.ca/english/ labourandHR.asp

Tourism Industry Association of Nova Scotia Education and Training Department. (1996). *It's Good Business: Responsible Beverage Service Program.* Halifax: Tourism Association of Nova Scotia.

———. (1993). *Food and Beverage Server Occupational Standards.* Halifax and Ottawa: Tourism Industry Association of Nova Scotia and Canadian Tourism Human Resource Council.

Tourism Intelligence Bulletin. (Jan. 2008). "Tourism Travel Trends Tempered by Mounting Economic Concerns."

Tourism Is Your Business: Marketing Management. (1986). Ottawa: Tourism Canada, Ministry of Supply and Services Canada.

Trans Canada Trail. (n.d.). "FAQ," accessed Feb. 2008 at www.tctrail.ca/faq.php.

Transat A.T. Inc. (2000). *Annual Report 2000.* Montreal: Transat A.T. Inc.

Transport Canada. (Oct. 11, 2007). News release, "Canada's New Government Revitalizes Inter-city Passenger Rail Services in Canada."

————. (2002). *Transportation in Canada 2002 Annual Report.* Ottawa: Transport Canada.

————. (2001). *Transportation in Canada 2001 Annual Report.* Ottawa: Transport Canada.

————. (2000). *Transportation in Canada 2000 Annual Report.* Ottawa: Transport Canada.

Travel & Leisure. (n.d.). "Global Vision Awards 2007," accessed Nov. 20, 2008 at www.travelandleisure.com/slideshows/global-vision-awards-2007.

Travel Canada. (Feb. 2001). Victoria, BC: Travel Canada.

Travel Industry Association (TIA). (Sept. 2003). *Geotourism: The New Trend in Travel.* Washington: Travel Industry Association.

Travel to Wellness Canada. (May 2008). Home page, www .traveltowellnesscanada.com.

Travelweek Bulletin. (Sept. 2002). Toronto: Concepts Travel Media Ltd. Published weekly.

Travel Weekly. (March 12, 2008). "Dubai: Agent Reporter Future Attractions," www.travelweekly.co.uk/Articles/2008/03/12/26322/dubai-agent-reporter-future-attractions.html.

————. (2002). Richmond BC: New Concepts. Published weekly.

TripAdvisor. (Aug. 31, 2008). "Fact Sheets," www.tripadvisor .com/PressCenter-c4-Fact_Sheet.html.

"Trip to the Mersey River Chalets." (1996). *South West Nova Scotia Vacation Guide,* Halifax: Southshore Tourism Association/ N.S. Tourism.

Truffles restaurant. (May 2008). Four Seasons Toronto, www .fourseasons.com/toronto/dining/truffles.html.

United Nations. (June 2008). UN Millennium Development Goals, www.un.org/millenniumgoals/index.html.

United Nations Educational, Scientific and Cultural Organization (UNESCO). (n.d.). "World Heritage List," accessed Sept. 1, 2008 at http://whc.unesco.org/en/list.

United States National Park Service. (n.d.). "FAQs," accessed Feb. 2008 at www.nps.gov/faqs.htm

USA Today. (May 2006). "Dubai Plans to Build World's Largest Hotel."

Vales, Guy. (April 2001). "Technology and 'Customer Relationship Management,'" *Communiqué,* Vol. 5, Issue 3, p. 20.

————. (March 2001). "Here Comes the On-line Consumer," *Communiqué,* Vol. 5, Issue 2, p. 12.

Valhouli, Christina. (Oct. 16, 2003). "Best All-Inclusive Resorts," *Forbes,* www.forbes.com/2003/10/16/cx_cv_1016feat.html.

Vegas Today and Tomorrow. (April 20, 2008). "The 25 Largest Hotels in the World," www.vegastodayandtomorrow.com/ largesthotels.htm.

Verschuren, Frank. (March 2000). "Golf Booming, Offers Tourism Benefits," *Communiqué,* Vol. 4, Issue 2, pp. 7, 8, 12.

VIA Destinations Canada. (June–July 2001). Vol. 1, No. 1.

VIA Rail. (Oct. 11, 2007). "Canada's New Government Revitalizes Inter-city Passenger Rail Services in Canada," www.viarail.ca/cgi-bin/AffichageWebComm?Commande=select&langue=en&IDX= 2&pk_webcomm=986

VIA Rail Annual Report. (1988–2003). Montreal: VIA Rail Canada.

VIA Rail Business News. (May 2008). "The Canadian Named One of the World's top 25 Trains," www.viarail.ca/en_index .html?tab=nouv.

Villela, J.A. (1975). *The Hospitality Industry: The World of Food Services,* 2nd ed. Toronto: McGraw-Hill.

Villemaire, Andre. (April 2000). "Adventure Travel, Ecotourism on Path to Success," *Communiqué,* Vol. 4, Issue 3, pp. 3–4.

Vincent, Isabel. (April 24, 2006). "Poverty Tourism: Take a Walk on the Wild Side," *Macleans,* www.macleans.ca/article.jsp? content=20060424_125530_125530&source=srch.

Wagner-Chazalon, Andrew. (Dec. 1999). "Creative Partnerships Emphasized at Cultural Heritage Conference," *Communiqué,* Vol. 3, Issue 10, p. 18.

Walker, J.R. (2001). *Introduction to Hospitality,* 3rd ed. Toronto: Prentice-Hall Canada Inc.

Walsh-Heron, J., and Stevens, T. (1990). *The Management of Visitor Attractions and Events.* Toronto: Prentice-Hall Canada Inc.

Walter, Michele. (April 2001). "Dashboard Dining Latest Convenience for Customer," *Atlantic Restaurant News,* Vol. 3, No. 2, p. 15.

Ward, Debra. (Jan.–Feb. 2002). "Canada's Airline Industry: Post-September 11 Snapshot," *Tourism,* Vol. 6, Issue 1, p. 13.

Watkins, Ed. (Jan. 2004). "Job One: Get Control of Distribution," *Lodging Hospitality.*

Watson, Julie V. (Dec. 2001). "Food Links Hospitality and Tourism to Create Edible Experiences," *Atlantic Restaurant News,* Vol. 3, No. 6, p. 1.

————. (Aug.–Sept. 2001). "Chef Michael Really Cooks," *Atlantic Business Magazine,* Vol. 12, No. 4, pp. 29–30.

Watts, Brenda. (Nov. 2000). "The Spa Canada Story," *Communiqué,* Vol. 4, Issue 10, pp. 8–10.

Weiss, Edith, and Weiss, Hal. (1987). *Catering Handbook.* Jenks, OK: J. Williams Book Company.

Weiss, Margot. (Oct. 30, 2006). "Emerging Luxury Destinations," *Forbes Traveller,* www.forbestraveler.com/adventure/new-luxury -destinations-story.html.

Welcome to New Brunswick. (2001). Fredericton: New Brunswick Department of Economic Development, Tourism and Culture.

Wescott, Kathryn. (Nov. 30, 2002). "Tourism in an Uncertain World," BBC News, http://news.bbc.co.uk/1/hi/world/Africa/2527205.stm.

WestJet. (2000–3). *Annual Report* (2000–2003). Calgary: WestJet.

"What Canadians Bought on the Web, 1999." (Jan. 28, 2000). From Ernst & Young, 1999. Canada Internet Retailing Buying Survey, Sept. 1999. *The Globe and Mail*, p. E5.

White, Fred. (April 2001). "Product Diversity and Affordability Make Us the Adventure Capital of the World," *Communiqué*, Vol. 5, Issue 3, p. 13.

White, Pam, & Associates. (March 1999). *Catalogue of Exemplary Practices in Adventure Travel and Ecotourism*. Ottawa: Canadian Tourism Commission.

Wilderness Tours. (Feb. 2008). "About Us," www.wildernesstours.com/about.php.

Williams, Randy. (March 2000). "Travel Agents Represent Consumers, Not Airlines," *Communiqué*, Vol. 4, Issue 2, p. 11.

Wintrob, Suzanne. (Oct. 10, 2000). "Hard Work Pays off with Travel Rewards," Special to *The Globe and Mail*, www.globeandmail.com/travel/rewards.

Wolff, Carlo. (Feb. 2004). "Go.Concierge Raises Fairmont's Digital Profile," *Technology Today*.

———. (Feb. 2003). "Jumping on the Bandwidth Bandwagon," *Lodging Hospitality*.

World Tourism Organization (UNWTO). (n.d.). "About UNWTO," accessed Nov. 19, 2008 at www.world-tourism.org/aboutwto/index.php.

———. (Sept. 27, 2008). "Tourism Highlights," 2008 edition, http://unwto.org/facts/eng/highlights.htm.

———. (June 4, 2008). "World Environment Day Encouraging Tourism Innovation for Climate Neutrality," www.unwto.org

———. (Jan. 29, 2008). "World Tourism Exceeds Expectations in 2007—Arrivals Grow From 800 Million to 900 Million in Two Years," UNWTO World Tourism Barometer, Vol. 6, No. 1, pp. 1–3.

———. (Oct. 2007). "The Way Forward to Adaptation and Mitigation in Tourism," in *Climate Change and Tourism Responding to Global Challenges*, Advanced Summary, www.unwto.org/media/news/en/pdf/davos_rep_advan_summ_26_09.pdf.

———. (2006). "Voluntary Initiatives for Sustainable Tourism."

———. (June 25, 2004). "Tourism's on the Rise Again," www.world-tourism.org/newsroom/Releases/2004/June/un.htm.

———. (Feb. 16, 2004). "WTO Global Campaign Stresses Importance of Tourism," News release, www.world-tourism.org/newsroom/Releases/2004/February/campaign.htm.

———. (Feb. 11, 2004). "United Nations Secretary-General Congratulates WTO," News release, www.world-tourism.org/newsroom/Releases/2004/February/un.htm.

———. (Jan. 27, 2004). "Global Troubles Took Full Toll on Tourism in 2003; Growth to Return in 2004," www.world-tourism.org/newsroom/Releases/2004/janvier/un.htm.

———. (May 2002). "International Year of Ecotourism," www.world-tourism.org/newsroom/Releases/morereleases/May 2002/EcotourismSummit.htm.

———. (2001). Conference proceedings: *Sport and Tourism: 1st World Conference*. Madrid: World Tourism Organization.

———. (2001). *Global Code of Ethics*. Madrid: World Tourism Organization, www.world-tourism.org/code_ethics/eng.html.

———. (2001). *Public-Private Sector Cooperation: Enhancing Tourism Competitiveness*. Madrid: World Tourism Organization.

———. (2001). *Tourism: 2020 Vision*. Madrid: World Tourism Organization.

———. (2000). *Tourism Market Trends*. Madrid: World Tourism Organization.

WTO News:

"Americas Ecotourism Seminar Attracts more than 500," 3rd quarter, 2001: 13.

"Technology Added to 2002–2003 Activities," 3rd quarter, 2001: 9.

"Thailand Hosts WTO Meeting on Child Sex Tourism," 3rd quarter, 2001: 15.

"The Tourism Power of Mega-events," 3rd quarter 2001: 12.

"1 Mil for Fight against Sexual Exploitation of Children," 1st quarter, 2001: 1.

"Demand for Cultural Tourism Requires Better Management," 1st quarter, 2001: 2.

"Sport & Tourism: Shaping Global Culture," 1st quarter, 2001: 11.

"Tourism Booms in Millennium Year," 1st quarter, 2001: 1

"Tourism Statistics Come of Age," 1st quarter, 2001: 12.

World Travel and Tourism Council (WTTC). (n.d.). "Tourism Satellite Accounting: World—Key Facts at a Glance," accessed Nov. 20, 2008 at www.wttc.org/eng/Tourism_Research/Tourism_Satellite_Accounting/.

———. (March 6, 2008). "Continued Growth Signalled for Travel and Tourism Industry," Press release, www.wttc.org/eng/Tourism_News/Press_Releases/Press_Releases_2008/Continued_growth_signalled_for_Travel_and_Tourism_Industry/.

Yarr, Kevin. (Feb. 2002). "Chefs Find Growing Opportunities as Personal Chefs," *Atlantic Restaurant News*, Vol. 4, No. 1, p. 25.

"Year 2000 Travel Trends Survey." (Nov. 1999). A survey conducted by American Express at the Association of Travel Executives Global Conference in Spain. Toronto: Amex Canada Inc.

Yoshino, Kimi. Napa Valley Register. (July 5, 2004). "Cities See Tourism Increases after Being Featured in a Film," *Los Angeles Times*, www.napavalleyregister.com/articles/2006/07/05/business/stories_from_ap/iq_3494784.txt.

Yovich, Daniel. (April 22, 2004). "Carnival Cruise Lines Throws Carbs Overboard," www.meetingplace.com/dailynews.

Yurchyshyn, Anya. (Feb 4, 2008). "Poverty Tourism: A Dose of Reality," *Budget Travel*, www.msnbc.com.

Zorilla, Jose. (Dec. 2000). "Authenticity in Aboriginal Tourism: The Community's Choice," *Communiqué*, Vol. 4, Issue 11, p. 5.